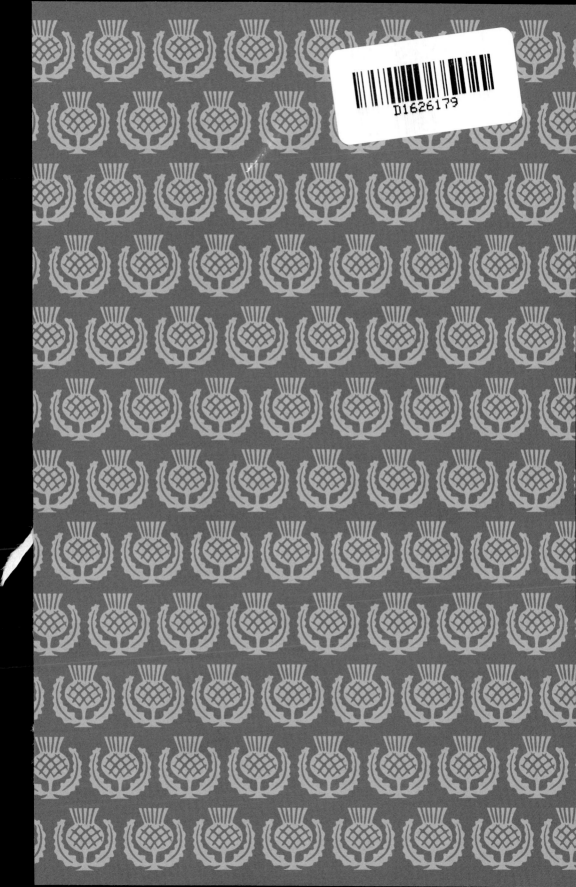

A HIGHER WORLD

A HIGHER WORLD
Scotland 1707–1815

Michael Fry

BIRLINN

First published in 2014 by
Birlinn Limited
West Newington House
10 Newington Road
Edinburgh
EH9 1QS

www.birlinn.co.uk

ISBN: 978 1 78027 233 7

The publishers acknowledge investment from Creative Scotland towards the
publication of this volume

British Library Cataloguing-in-Publication Data
A catalogue record for this book is available from the British Library

Typeset by Initial Typesetting Services, Edinburgh
Printed and bound by Gutenberg Press, Malta

Contents

Part IV Politics

Part V Culture

List of Illustrations

Highland Cattle with a Collie, by Joseph Adam and Joseph Denovan Adam.

The water wheel at Preston Mill.

New Lanark.

The Shore at Leith with the Martello Tower of 1807.

Dr Webster's sermon, by John Kay.

Cromarty east kirk, 'unquestionably one of the finest eighteenth century parish churches in Scotland'.

Duncan Forbes of Culloden, after Jeremiah Davidson.

Robert McQueen, Lord Braxfield.

Engraving of a weaver's cottage from Thomas Pennant, *A Tour of Scotland*, 1772.

Flora MacDonald, by Allan Ramsay.

Lady Nairne.

A Highland Wedding at Blair Atholl, by David Allan.

The Old Pretender, by Louis Gabriel Blanchet.

The Young Pretender, by Louis Gabriel Blanchet.

An Incident in the Rebellion of 1745, British School, eighteenth century.

John Campbell, 2nd Duke of Argyll, by William Aikman.

Inveraray Castle.

Henry Dundas, Viscount Melville, by Sir Thomas Lawrence.

The Dunmore Pineapple.

Old College, Edinburgh.

Statue of Allan Ramsay, senior, Princes Street Gardens.

Statue of Robert Fergusson, Canongate Kirk, Edinburgh.

Robert Burns.

David Hume, by Allan Ramsay.

Adam Smith, by John Kay.

Foreword

The structure of this book follows the pattern of its previous companion volume, *A New Race of Men, Scotland 1815–1914*. A century of the nation's history is treated synchronically as well as diachronically. The topics in it are set out in parallel before they move on at their own pace, in the present work from the dismaying aftermath of the Union of 1707 towards the comrade-ship-in-arms of the Scots and of the English (latterly of the Irish too) in the wars unleashed by the French Revolution – not the first, but certainly the greatest of the conflicts in which the peoples of the United Kingdom had been engaged together, and the one that did most to seal their mutual bonds.

For Scots this progress from shaky independence to an uncontested, and even privileged, position inside the United Kingdom still had its pains and penalties as well as its pleasures and profits. It did prove painful to those who had died to regain the lost freedom of their country on the battlefield or the scaffold. As for the penalties, Scotland could not really resist changes that England felt determined to impose, though at least these proved rare. But without doubt it was a pleasure to the mass of the Scots people to see their age-old struggle for subsistence at last bearing more abundant fruit. And Scottish enterprise, historically never lacking though often misdirected, finally generated profits on a huge scale.

This is the general background to the variety of particular events and processes, and of personal destinies bound up with them, that unfold in this book. But I hope it will become clear how they fit into the general pattern of Scottish history that I have sought to delineate in this and in previous publications. The historiography of the last half-century in Scotland has preferred a socio-economic approach rather different from my own. In my view it distorts the nature of the nation by concentrating on what within it has assimilated most closely to the norms of the United Kingdom. By contrast, that which remains different has been far less adequately treated. Here, as before, I correct this bias by paying equal attention to political and to cultural history.

Any good historian will try to pick out continuities yet remain sceptical of them. In the case of Scotland his task is especially fraught but especially important. We are, after all, dealing here with a nation of which the historical continuity has been broken, most obviously in 1707 but also at other times. Some historians argue there is only a tenuous relationship between the Scotland of today and the older Scotland. It had its glories but it has simply vanished, and even where it does live on in the consciousness of modern Scots it may do so only in the form of delusory myths. So, in particular, the Scottish nationalism of the present day can owe little to the Scottish nationalism of the past. The present book and its companion take a different view.

My aim has been to trace what we can of that older Scotland through the three centuries since it ostensibly vanished, to see if this time round, again faced with momentous change, we might be able to link our future back to our past in a more satisfactory manner. For the eighteenth century this is not, it turns out, too hard a task. The Treaty of Union deliberately maintained what contemporaries identified as the pillars of Scottish society: religion, law and education. In the course of the century they all flourished, and the security of the Union if anything allowed them to become more different from their English counterparts. The religion adapted its Calvinism to Enlightenment, while the law developed a Roman response to modernity and the educational system attained the highest international standards while maintaining its native virtues. Those national institutions are still with us today, if indeed showing the wear and tear of three centuries.

With hindsight this enlightened phase of the Union appears positive not so much because it made Scotland more like England as because it allowed the genius of the Scots to flourish in fresh forms. That is what we see by the turn of the nineteenth century, though it had only come about by a process of trial and error. In the early days of the Union, there was an aspiration among certain progressive Scots to turn their country into North Britain. Not the least of the obstacles they encountered was the reluctance in England to redefine it as South Britain. The rest of the Scots equally found the aspiration distasteful so that in time, being probably impossible anyway, it died. Aided by the rising romantic spirit of a new age, overlaying the more strenuous classicism of the previous one, Scotland settled down to be Scotland, forever – or at least for a long time ahead – just what it was: untidy, precarious, provisional, yet for all its faults and failures unmistakably itself and not any other country, so capable of great achievement too. That is the story of this book.

Edinburgh, April 2014

Prologue: 'My wedding day'

Edinburgh was in no mood for celebration on 1 May 1707, when the Union of Scotland and England formally took effect. Only a couple of official gestures in any manner marked the momentous event. During the morning the bells of the high kirk, St Giles, rang out the tune, 'Why should I be sad on my wedding day?'[1] Later a salute of guns boomed from the ramparts of the Castle. That was about it.

The response was perhaps bound to be subdued because so many of the great and good in the Scottish capital had hurried south to be on the spot for the consummation of the Union under the approving eye of a monarch now of one Great Britain, Queen Anne. During this exodus Daniel Defoe, a spy in Edinburgh for the English government, reported to his controller: 'The great men are posting to London for places and honours, every man full of his own merit and afraid of everyone near him: I never saw so much trick, sham, pride, jealousy and cutting of friends' throats as there is among noblemen.' Noting how the contagion spread down the social scale too, Defoe concluded: 'In short money will do anything here.'[2] Many patriotic Scots would have agreed.

Others found a personal way of celebrating. One who did so was James, the elder son of James Douglas, second Duke of Queensberry, the queen's commissioner in Scotland since 1702 and, as such, one of the architects of the Union. The duke had gone to London too, leaving the young man at home in Queensberry House, the *hôtel particulier* built after the Parisian style which was the family's residence in the Canongate (and today a portal to the Scottish Parliament). He had good reason for sequestering his heir apparent, though in fact the lad would never be permitted to succeed to the title. This was because he suffered from gigantism and had grown up into a homicidal maniac kept under lock and key at all times. Somehow, in his father's absence, he managed to escape. He caught and killed a kitchen-boy, then roasted him on a spit. The deed was discovered as he sat down to his horrid repast. Scots said it was a judgment on the duke for his part in ending the independence of his country.

Amid the sullen stillness of the Scottish capital, its people paid more heed to news of whales beached at Kirkcaldy across the Firth of Forth. A pod of the species known in Scotland as the ca'ing whale (elsewhere as the pilot whale), each about 25 feet long, had arrived 'roaring, plunging and threshing one upon another, to the great terror of all who heard the same'. Even today whales penetrate the firth, apparently because they have taken a wrong turning: in despair of finding a way out to the open sea again, they kill themselves by swimming onto dry land. A contemporary account said: 'Thirty-five of them were run ashore upon the sands of Kirkcaldy, where they made yet a more dreadful roaring and tossing when they found themselves aground, insomuch that the earth trembled.' Fifers muttered that this, too, was an ill omen of the Union.[3]

The air seemed full of foreboding in more distant parts of the country as well. Many Presbyterian parishes declared 1 May to be a day of fasting and humiliation. From another point of view, up in the Highlands, the greatest Gaelic poet of the age, Iain Lom, lamented the blow now struck to the cause of the Jacobites hoping to restore to the throne of Scotland the deposed legitimate line of the royal House of Stewart. It is hard to date exactly his poem, *Òran an Aghaidh an Aonaidh*, 'Song against the Union'. But, assuming he had finished composing it by 1 May, he would surely have been singing it round Roybridge in Inverness-shire, where his chief, MacDonald of Keppoch, held state in a dismal old castle. For the bard the whole business of the Union had been a sorry betrayal. To him Queensberry's motives were merely mercenary, *mar fhear-stràice cur thairis*, 'like a measurer raking off the surplus from the bushel'. Another typical example of the Scottish political class could be found in the corrupt pseudo-Jacobite, Thomas Hay, Viscount Dupplin: *Dh'eirich rosgal ad chridhe 'n uair chual' thu tighinn an t-òr ud*, 'turbulence rose in your heart when you heard that gold coming.' As for James, Duke of Hamilton, supposed to have been leader of the opposition to the Union in the Scottish Parliament, he was just *dùbailt*, duplicitous. Still, nothing better could be expected of all these Lowlanders. Iain Lom reserved his bitterest venom for another great Highland chief, renegade Jacobite and head of Clan Mackenzie, William, Earl of Seaforth: *Is dearbh gu leaghainn an t-òr dhuit, a staigh air faochaig do chlaighinn gus an cas e do bhòtainn*, 'truly I would melt gold for you, and inject it into the shell of your skull till it would reach your boots.' The bard consoled himself that a national revolt must be imminent against this collective noble treachery.[4]

In contrast, 1 May turned out a day of rejoicing for London. The official Scottish delegation that had gone south to take part in the jollity was led by the last two joint Secretaries of State in the government of Scotland, Hugh Campbell, Earl of Loudoun, and John Erskine, Earl of Mar. Another member of it was Sir John Clerk of Penicuik, one of the commissioners who had negotiated the Treaty of Union. He found the English not just welcoming but overjoyed to see him and his colleagues. They were lionised at Berwick, Newcastle, Durham and further stages on the road south. Especially Queensberry, dubbed the Union Duke and soon to be Duke of Dover in the peerage of Great Britain, 'was complimented and feasted wherever he went, and when he came within twenty miles of London the whole city turned out to greet him'.[5] On 16 April he made a public entry into the English capital with 46 coaches and hundreds of horsemen.

Loudoun, before he set out for the big day on 1 May from his lodgings in Whitehall, posted a letter he had written the night before to the Revd John Stirling, principal of the University of Glasgow. Loudoun was reporting back Queen Anne's response to a loyal address from the Church of Scotland, recently voted by its General Assembly. He had in person handed over the address 'which Her Majesty received very graciously and ordered me to renew to you the assurances of the continuation of Her Majesty's protection and favour. I am very glad to know by the accounts I have from you and others that there appeared in the proceedings of the assembly so much moderation and calmness.'[6] This had been quite a relief, for militant Presbyterians might have made a great deal of trouble for the Union.

Clerk would recall of 1 May: 'That day was solemnised by Her Majesty and those who had been members of both Houses of Parliament with the greatest splendour. A very numerous procession accompanied the queen to the cathedral church of St Paul, at least 300 or 400 coaches.' Her Lord High Treasurer, Sidney Godolphin, reported the scene to her chief military commander, John Churchill, Duke of Marlborough, who, called away by the War of the Spanish Succession, was on campaign in the Low Countries: 'The streets were fuller of people than I have seen them upon any occasion of that kind.' The Bishop of Oxford, the Revd William Talbot, gave the sermon on a text of Psalm 133, 'Behold how pleasant it is, for brethren to dwell together in unity.' Prayers of thanksgiving followed and 'a fine piece of music closed the solemnity'. Clerk discovered 'real joy and satisfaction in the citizens of London, for they were terribly apprehensive of confusions from Scotland in case the Union had not taken place. That whole day was spent in feasting, ringing of bells and illuminations.'[7]

Which view of the Union was going to prevail in the new United Kingdom, Scotland's glumness and gloom or England's relief and rejoicing?

Part I

ECONOMY

1

Agriculture:
'To do useful things'

We cannot be sure what the Highland brigand, Rob Roy MacGregor, was up to on the day of the Union, 1 May 1707, but probably he had his thoughts on something quite different from matters of state. He was about that time generally preoccupied with the affairs of an orphaned nephew – to whom he proved, whatever his other failings, a faithful tutor and guardian. The nephew was a MacGregor too, but the name had been officially proscribed for a century and it was better for the youngster not to use it, at least in any transaction with the English-speaking authorities. To Gaels this mattered little, for they seldom bothered with surnames anyway: what would be the point in a clan where everybody had the same surname? They called one another rather by given names and epithets: Rob Roy was *Raibeart Ruadh* (red-haired) and his nephew was *Griogar Ghlun Dubh* (with a black birthmark on his knee).[1] Now this youth, who in a more tranquil age might have been known as Gregor MacGregor, turned for all public purposes into James Graham of Glengyle.

The feudal toponym came from a small estate at the head of Loch Katrine in the Trossachs. Rob Roy, acting on James's behalf, had secured the feu in 1703 from the Duke of Montrose, and Montrose was chief of the Grahams. As a compliment to the feudal superior, or perhaps as an appeal for his protection and patronage, the lad assumed his surname. He was then set up in what security Highland life of the time might offer. Under the Scottish feudal system he could not be outright owner of Glengyle anyway, but his rights to it amounted to much the same thing. He could bequeath it to his descendants, and meanwhile it made him a desirable match for some lucky lass.[2]

It so happened Rob Roy had just the right girl in mind: Mary, daughter of John Hamilton of Bardowie, laird of a castle near the present-day Milngavie.[3] Her brother was Montrose's factor in the barony of Buchanan, which included Glengyle. The happy couple would be wed in November 1707. Rob Roy was by then getting a home ready for them, built in the Lowland style of stone and mortar rather than as the normal Highland rickle of rocks and turf. The house still stands today. The whole arrangement was clannish in inspiration, then, intended to join by blood what had hitherto been united by mere interest. It did not preclude other connections, however. Rob Roy had also entered into amicable relations with the Campbells of Glenorchy, Earls of Breadalbane, a cadet branch of the mighty Campbells of Argyll occupying territory north of the Trossachs. In fact, in his legal dealings in the English language, Rob Roy called himself Robert Campbell. His mother had been of that name but anyway he wanted and needed to identify with those powerful kinsmen. He wrote to Breadalbane:

> I long to see your lordship, and I presume to tell your lordship that I have come of your lordship's family and shall keep my dependency suitable to the samine of which I told your lordship, when I parted with your lordship last and what I sayed to your lordship or ever promised shall be keeped while I live. My nephew is to see your lordship, whom I hope will be capable to serve your lordship and will do it tho I were in my grave he is a young man so my lord give him your advice he is bigging his house and I hope your lordship will give him a precept for the four trees your lordship promised him the last time I was there.[4]

The letter was clearly addressed to a person of higher rank. Rob Roy and his nephew did not belong to the top level of Highland society, but to a second level that came to be known as tacksmen (a tack was a lease, more or less, in Scots law).[5] Its members combined the practical functions of laird and businessman, or military officer when the clan went to war. Many such people turned out as improvident as their chiefs but Rob Roy was one who exploited every opportunity to advance his fortune and standing, by means also of his fund of native wit and homespun philosophy or else, should occasion demand, by resort to cold steel. Like his forebears, his main economic activity lay in trading and raiding cattle, the principal form of Highland wealth. If he got the chance, he would blackmail potential victims of his raids and make them pay for protection from him. An alternative would be to provide them with general protection against all raiders, of whom there were many, and in this his product looked attractive – premiums tolerable, record of recovering stolen goods impressive. He was on the one hand an entrepreneur, on the other hand a bandit, and he switched roles as it suited.

Rob Roy's commercial acumen told him indiscriminate raiding would be foolish. It had to be kept down to a level that never attracted too much attention, so he needed to be careful where he did raid. It would, for example, have been stupid of him to annoy all the big landowners in the region. In fact, he left Montrose and Breadalbane alone, at least for now. Such aristocrats could then be enlisted as his patrons, though we may wonder why they should have bothered with a man who was, from their point of view, a nobody. Yet they always sought to extend their influence, and he had at least some say among the proscribed MacGregors. These no longer possessed any territory of their own but were scattered over the lands of other chieftains. While despised, they could, if shown some favour, be deterred from raiding their lordships' properties and turned instead on those of a near neighbour and rival, the noble House of Atholl, recently raised to ducal rank. Indeed Rob Roy himself took with relish to raiding the lands of Atholl, knowing that in case of pursuit he could retire in safety to Breadalbane.[6]

One of the oldest works of Gaelic literature, dating from the first century of the Christian era, is *Táin Bó Cúailnge*, The Cattle-Raid of Cooley,[7] and it might be said that not much had changed in the Highlands since. Yet Rob Roy's ventures were also just starting to connect to the emergence of modern capitalism. A recent point of growth in the Scottish economy had been the export of cattle on the hoof to England. It was already under way by the time of the Restoration of the Stewarts in 1660. In 1680 the government in Edinburgh set up a commission to consider how the traffic might be expanded; meanwhile, graziers in Yorkshire complained of being ruined by cheap Scottish imports. But the plain fact was that conditions in much of Scotland allowed more cattle to be raised there than were ever going to be eaten by the natives while, at the other end of Great Britain, stood a huge city called London, which could never feed itself. The result was a flourishing trade between the two extremities of the island.

In 1707 opponents of the Union argued that this trade, while important, did not enrich Scots as it should because it had already been taken over by English middlemen. After the long drove from the north, the herds of black

Highland cattle, always small and hardy but now lean and weary, would be sold to graziers who fattened them up on their own lush pastures ready to be turned into the finest English roast beef. Scottish patriots argued for fattening the beasts at home, then exporting them as barrelled beef not only to England but also to any other country with a taste for the succulent flesh; profits could also be made from the hides. This was in fact how Ireland exploited its cattle, so the plan was not unworkable. Still, in the prelude to the Union it became hard to propagate the notion that Scots might turn into successful economic innovators on their own account, even in the agriculture from which nine out of ten of them lived.[8]

In any event traffic in cattle on the hoof continued to flourish after 1707, and the price of the beasts would quadruple over the eighteenth century. There proved to be particular benefits for Highlanders, who had been so hostile to the Union. Even in the wake of the first Jacobite rebellion, drovers were exempted from the Disarming Act (1716) because they might need to defend themselves on their long journey south. The government in London was interested not so much in groaning boards for gourmets as in savoury scran for soldiers and sailors now making the new United Kingdom's power global. General William Wolfe's redcoats at Quebec and Admiral Horatio Nelson's tars at Trafalgar would all be kept going on salt beef originally from the Highlands. Here, to sceptical Scots, was at least one benefit of the Union.[9]

Commerce in cattle was yet not in itself significant enough to bring about much basic change in Highland society. This society remained through the first half of the eighteenth century traditional, feudal and armed. Rob Roy was typical of it, even in the impudence with which he at length swindled the Duke of Montrose, who in revenge got him jailed; it took a royal pardon to stop him being transported to the West Indies where, now aged over 50, he could not have lasted long. Within such a social order raiding was regarded as normal, if not sportive. As late as 1742 a veteran Jacobite, William Mackintosh of Borlum, noted how it still went on in western Inverness-shire, Perthshire, Stirlingshire and northern Argyll.[10] Only defeat of a second rebellion in 1745 put a stop to it, at the hands of the standing military garrisons and their patrols that afterwards treated the region as conquered territory. In any case, raiding had never halted droving because raiders and drovers might be the same people. Even as they went about armed to the teeth they promoted not just disorder but also some degree of order – for instance, when they policed the great trysts or fairs at Crieff, held for every kind of bovine business under the patronage of the Jacobite Dukes of Perth. Another result was to keep English middlemen out of the Highlands and leave everything to the enterprising Gael. Again, the military sinews of Highland society were maintained in decent trim at little expense, ready for recruitment before long into the British army. There existed in the complex of socio-economic phenomena not only a past but also a future. All this, at least in part, Scotland owed to its black cattle.

An original reason for the abundance of black cattle in the Highlands had lain in the fact that they offered the easiest way for lairds to collect their rents, in a society where money seldom appeared. But with export to England the beasts could generate cash, and cash would revolutionise the pastoral regions of Scotland in all sorts of ways, good and bad.[11] In general, and in the Highlands particularly, profits from the cattle never before the middle of the century accrued on such a scale as to alter anything basic. But in one corner of the country it was already possible to discern the sort of development that might follow once they did.

Until the late seventeenth century Galloway, at the south-western tip of Scotland, had been an unenclosed countryside of traditional subsistence farming. Within it there was a contrast between the people of the low country living in an economy of cattle, barley and oats, and the 'moor men' scattered among smaller settlements, herding sheep and cultivating plots of rye. In this timeless Scotland there suddenly appeared an economic pioneer in the person of David Dunbar, who owned an estate at Baldoon just outside Wigtown in the low country. Instead of allowing his cattle to wander at will across any untilled soil, he began to graze them over land he had enclosed, and on a large scale. He formed a park of 4 square miles capable of holding 1,000 beasts, some his own, others brought in. He sold to drovers or himself sent to England about double that number every year. He made a fortune: he was created a baronet and his son married into the noble House of Hamilton. By the turn of the eighteenth century, Galloway was showing Scotland a way forward.[12]

In part it was just a matter of recognising the opportunities for profit in the English market. Galloway had good natural endowments in abundant grazing for cattle and in proximity not just to England but also to Ireland, whence herds might be replenished on the cheap if need be. Lairds of Galloway, unlike those of the Highlands, could send their beasts off knowing these would arrive in England still in good shape. But they also took the initiative in preserving their comparative advantages. In the old Scots Parliament they had lobbied for the fixing and maintenance of traditional drove roads across their hills and moors. The final step was then to consolidate and enclose grazing land with a view to raising and fattening stock on a commercial scale. It all amounted in essence to the exploitation of lower costs, yet it was done with such aplomb as to impress Daniel Defoe when in 1724 he published his *Tour through the Whole Island of Great Britain*. In Scotland he was looking for elusive signs of the Union's blessings, so he felt delighted to find it had become 'no uncommon thing for a Galloway nobleman to send 400 sheep and 4000 head of black cattle to England in a year, and sometimes much more'.[13]

What local lairds had not reckoned with was the consequent social upheaval. The Levellers who appeared in Galloway as Defoe brought out his book mounted the fiercest rural protest in Scotland before the disturbances among Highland crofters of the 1880s. They were smaller farmers or tenants threatened with eviction. Bands of them roamed the region breaking down the dykes of enclosed parks and fields where cattle destined for southern markets grazed. From 1723 to 1725 virtual rebellion raged, involving gangs of up to 2,000 men often led by tenants under notice. The gentry crushed them, not hesitating to call on troops if need be, and the courts reinforced the repression. Despite sympathy from some ministers of the Church of Scotland, from some merchant incorporations in the burghs and even from a few radical lairds, the Levellers failed in their purpose of halting enclosure.[14]

Here and in other pastoral regions of Scotland, the interests of the beasts would finally triumph over the interests of the people. At the peaks of prosperity, at least 30,000 head of cattle crossed the border each year. In this century of intensifying rivalry among the great powers, wars were always good for the bovine business because they created huge demand for salt beef for the troops. In 1786 the average price of beasts crossing from Skye to the mainland was £2 to £3. In 1794, after the outbreak of war with France, it went up to £4. Towards the end of the struggle against Napoleon in 1814, prices peaked at £18 a head. But then they halved by 1830. An era came to an end, and over large areas production of beef then yielded to production of mutton.[15]

The saga of Highland cattle shows up flaws in an older version of Scottish agricultural history. This postulated stagnation or even decline up to the eighteenth century, which then gave way to rapid transformation, in other words, to agricultural revolution. From the example of cattle alone we can see how the processes of change were more complex, protracted and diverse than such a simple story allows. There had already been innovations in the seventeenth century, and some aspects of farming progress would remain far from complete or universal even in the nineteenth century. This was not revolution, but evolution.[16]

It was the same story in arable agriculture. Anyway we should not draw too sharp a distinction with pastoral agriculture, at least in the early stages of the evolution. In the past, crops had been grown almost everywhere in Scotland, even in Highland glens. There the extent of arable land was of course small and the reward of working it meagre. Yet during times when most people lived off cereals they needed to produce enough to meet local needs without relying on imports of grain from the more fertile Lowlands, where the crop sometimes failed. Yet even those regions of Scotland most favourable to cereals had to hold some land in pasture for grazing. Manure was required to keep the soil fertile and the cattle fed on grass, since turnips and clover were not yet introduced to Scotland. Obviously a limit then existed to the acreage that could be sown for human consumption. This complex of forces conspired to keep agricultural productivity low.[17]

Another hindrance to greater productivity was that the normal farm housed several tenants (four, six, eight, sometimes more) working together and sharing out the land. The shares were mixed up together in the system of runrig. It had arisen because of a need to divide the ground with strict regard to its quality as well as its quantity, so that each man got some of the good and some of the bad. In consequence, individual holdings consisted of scattered strips and blocks. This in itself caused waste because they were demarcated with ridges made visible by the weeds growing on them. It could anyway be hard enough to plough with teams of oxen requiring a wide circumference to turn at the head of the furrow. Beside all that, the land often proved impossible to drain properly in Scotland's cool, wet climate. And again, apart from this infield, an outfield had to be preserved to graze cattle. Few could hope for more than bare subsistence from the backbreaking toil imposed by such constraints.[18]

Still, the problems never deterred the Society of Improvers in the Knowledge of Agriculture that was formed in Edinburgh in 1723.[19] In fact, it gave a lead in the establishment of such patriotic improving societies, which were soon to spring up all over Europe. The founding of the society in Scotland, however, perhaps amounted to an admission that the Union was failing to deliver the promised economic growth. Scots had realised development would not somehow come of itself but needed to be a deliberate object of their exertions.[20] According to the society's own history, the Duke of Atholl started it up together with 'other persons of great distinction [who] consulted together, formed the plan and began the work'.[21]

The society soon had 300 members, most of them landowners or lawyers. Its first publication, in 1724, asserted that the Union favoured improvement not because it released English largesse but because it narrowed the scope of Scottish politics. The country's affairs were now managed by 'a few hands', which meant the 'main body' of Scottish gentry could reside at home and devote itself to agriculture and industry.[22] Yet society would not thrive unless 'all that were capable to do anything were provided with a proper and profitable employ; so that all hands might be at work, no drones in the hive, and none have the least excuse to eat the bread of idleness, so inconsistent with innocence, as well as the prosperity of the nation'. The tenants actually tilling the soil could not be overlooked, then: the publication was couched in a 'familiar style, such as the country farmers might easily understand'.[23] The society encouraged them to form their own local branches. It issued a steady stream of treatises, often on how to adopt into Scottish agriculture the best practice elsewhere: enclosure, plantation of trees, letting fields lie fallow and so on. It would be no exaggeration to say these topics soon gripped the civic leaders of Scotland. Not only anglophile unionists got involved. The Jacobite Mackintosh of Borlum was still imprisoned in Edinburgh Castle when he wrote two tracts for the society, belying the idea that he and fellow rebels were backward-looking champions of an archaic order of things. Improvement became more than a rural interest too. In 1733, Patrick Lindsay, Lord Provost of Edinburgh, published a book, with the brief title of *The Interest of Scotland*, launching an all-out attack on the older agriculture and its central features of runrig and common grazing.[24]

Deeds followed words. John Cockburn of Ormiston, 'father of Scottish husbandry', led the way to improvement on his estate 8 miles east of Edinburgh. An apostle of the Union, he was an MP at Westminster from 1707 to 1741, so acquiring first-hand acquaintance with advanced agricultural techniques in the south-east of England. After succeeding to his estate in 1734, he reconstructed Ormiston as a model village (most of it is still there) with feus on easy terms for householders willing to build to set standards; it also had a brewery and distillery for the other basic needs of Scotsmen. He aimed to make his estate and its people at least self-sufficient, then capable of generating a surplus. He advocated and practised enclosure, using embankments and hedges to bound his fields. He planted trees and sowed grass, clover, turnips, potatoes. He swept away runrig and divided the land into farms for single tenants, each with its own steading, field and pasture. He promoted cultivation of flax, encouraged spinning and weaving and laid out a bleach-field, so that there could be textile production too. The members of the active peasantry created by these means came together every month in a local agricultural society to assess their experiences and propose further improvements. Yet by 1749 Cockburn went bankrupt. He had inherited debts and his heavy expenses made them worse. In the end something needed to give: it was his solvency. Still, otherwise Cockburn set an excellent example. Following it, luckier landowners prospered so far that they could commemorate themselves in splendid mansions on their estates. Some – Hopetoun, Penicuik, Yester – were among the most palatial in Europe.[25]

The estate of Penicuik in Midlothian showed what effective management could do in the face of the most formidable demands of improvement. It belonged to the Clerks, originally merchants in Edinburgh who rose in wealth and influence right through the seventeenth century until Sir John Clerk, second baronet, was appointed a commissioner for the Union. When he came into his inheritance in 1722 it was still little more than bare upland waste, with a house standing on a chilly spot 700 feet above sea level. But he had money to spend not subject to the vagaries of other landed incomes. He held one of the few senior official posts left in Scotland, as a baron of exchequer. And he began to develop the coal-seams beneath his ground, though this in itself turned out 'an expensive and laborious work'. He took greater pride in his agricultural achievements, and made sure to insert a list of them in an appendix when he came to write up his memoirs: trees planted and fields enclosed along the River Esk, ponds stocked with carp and tench, 'a great square loch on the north-east side of Penicuik House', bridges and avenues, gardens and nurseries, hedges and ditches, new farms formed from the previous outfield, an extension of the kirk for the incoming tenants, a townhouse for the people of Penicuik. 'In all my projects I have studied either to do useful things, or such as would ornament my country as well as my estate,' Sir John recorded. From choice he never sought glittering prizes in London but stayed at home to attend to the detail of managing his estate. Yet astonishingly, in all the useful things he did do, he employed no more than seven or eight men.[26]

The workforce employed by George Dundas of Dundas at his estate above South Queensferry was even tinier. He had a gardener for his nurseries and, after first hiring unreliable casual labourers, he decided he would make faster progress if he took on two men full-time to perform all the tasks of planting, ditching, hedging and dyking; when it was necessary at the busiest seasons, he could still bring in extra hands. The key to development in this form was application of limited resources over lengthy periods – in Clerk's case for 30 years, in Dundas's case for 40. The latter only ever spent a fraction of his income from the estate on its improvement, and some of that was offset by sale of seeds and plants from the nurseries. A small landowner at the same time showed how much could be achieved with modest expenditure over a long enough timescale: an important example in a poor country as yet far from overcoming its basic economic problems. The improvements he carried out in person were largely confined to the mains and policies, but at length he made a start on enclosure of the entire estate, a riskier venture because rents could not rise till he completed it. Overall, though, the contrast between Dundas and Cockburn is instructive. Dundas worked on a cautious scale within the established frameworks of his time and his achievements were narrower than Cockburn's. Yet Cockburn overreached himself and, going bankrupt, was forced to sell out to Dundas's neighbour, the Earl of Hopetoun. Dundas, however, could pass on to his son an estate of enhanced value.[27]

While the Lothians were the most fertile region in Scotland, improvement spread well beyond. Sir Archibald Grant of Monymusk ruled his estate in Aberdeenshire from 1716 to 1778. Till 1734 he was, though already interested in agricultural innovation, often away in Edinburgh and London, where he too served as an MP. He returned to Monymusk burdened with debt due to rash speculations. Now he threw all his energies into making his property profitable. In the north-east of Scotland that meant more radical changes to the landscape than any required further south. Grant became a great planter of trees in this bare, windswept corner of the country. Land he wished to enclose as fields first needed to be cleared of masses of boulders and rocks lying where retreating glaciers had dropped them at the end of the last ice age. The two aspects of husbandry complemented each other because the stones made excellent material for dykes; if there were still too many of them, they could be stored in a 'consumption dyke', the biggest of which, on the nearby estate of Kingswells, remains there to this day, 500 yards long, 30 feet wide and 6 feet high.[28] On his new fields Sir Archibald altered the previous pattern of cultivation too. At first, like other progressive landlords, he urged his tenants to let their land lie fallow every so often. At the same time, he was introducing fresh crops – turnips, clover, rye grass – that cleansed the soil or put goodness back into it. He worked his way round to a system of rotation where such crops alternated with cereals; then he no longer had to let ground lie fallow. This was an innovation of great importance, and the financial results proved excellent: the rental of Monymusk tripled between 1733 and 1769. For tenants, the utility of having a resident landlord was tempered by his ruthlessness in exploiting his baron's court or his power of eviction to enforce his regime. But it helped them all that they were only 20 miles from Aberdeen with its market for produce and opportunity for seaborne export.[29]

There were, of course, also less successful efforts at improvement. On the grand scale it always proved expensive and liable to run into open or tacit opposition from the tenants. Where markets remained less accessible than round Edinburgh or Aberdeen, the increase in income a landlord might expect from his expenditures could remain slow or elusive. Even so, the shift from the concept of a countryside supporting subsistence to one expected to produce a profit proved in the long run decisive. If it worked, it was for the landlords an unequivocal good, though for their people more problematic.[30]

In the new system there was just no room for workers with as low a level of productivity as the old system had fostered. The superfluous peasants began to shift out of the former landscapes (a movement for which the not too accurate term of Lowland clearances has been coined).[31] It did suit the interest of landowners that large numbers should do something other than they had done before, which often meant their living somewhere other than they had lived before, and there was always the simple expedient of refusing to renew leases when they came to term. In fact, the lower ranks of rural society moved not only under pressure but also voluntarily out of the scattered fermtouns, some into planned villages built by their landlords, others away altogether into the growing towns and cities or to another part of the country or indeed the world – then with the chance of improving their standard of living that they would not have found if they had stayed where they were. For example, in the parish of Temple in Midlothian, which included the estate of the Dundases of Arniston, Scotland's political managers, the population dropped by one-third in the late eighteenth century, though the family never exerted the coercion it could have done.[32]

Protest would anyway have been misplaced when improvement was clearly propelling Scotland onto a higher economic plane. A demonstration of the benefits came in the ill years round 1740, which to long-lived contemporaries must at first have recalled the terrible failures of harvests and the famine of the 1690s. In 1739 there was again, in Scotland and in much of Western Europe, a poor harvest. After a bitter winter, with the ground lying frozen till April and frosts persisting till July, an even worse harvest followed in 1740. The dearth was not relieved before a good harvest in 1741, but meanwhile food riots broke out together with epidemics of typhus and measles among the weakened population. In a country like Scotland, near the northern limits of cultivation, the pattern was familiar. In the past it had brought crises of subsistence that at their worst killed thousands and caused economic disaster from which only long, slow, painful recovery was possible.[33]

In the Lowlands, at least, famine did not now ensue, nor any other dire sequel. Immediate problems of supply found an answer in more efficient import and distribution of grain than ever before. In the longer term the troubles were fairly easily redressed because higher prosperity and a better balance of payments had made the economy more resilient, so that years of debility no longer followed every crisis. Scots could afford to pay for food they did not produce themselves. This stopped short-term difficulties turning into long-term difficulties and destructive setbacks to development.[34]

Indeed the agricultural revolution in Scotland would change the country's husbandry from one of the most archaic to one of the most modern and productive in Europe. Again, however, we need at once to differentiate the picture, especially in the Highlands. This region was always going to be pastoral rather than arable, except in odd corners such as the Black Isle. Because of its remoteness, geology and climate it would also find improvement harder. As already remarked, the business of Highland cattle, though big business by the standards of the time, was still not big enough to effect any basic change in the way of life. Such change would come, however, through sheep. This might have seemed improbable to Rob Roy, who would have thought it demeaning to rustle sheep – 'the Highlander thinks it less shameful to steal a hundred cattle than one single sheep; for a sheep-stealer is infamous even among them.'[35]

But, with the emergence of capitalist agriculture, demand from wider Scottish and British markets focused attention on the comparative advantages of any particular region. In the cities of the United Kingdom, a new population of industrial workers could no longer provide for their own food and clothing but bought their necessities from markets, which in turn got their supplies from the efforts of agricultural workers in the countryside. At this division of labour, meat and wool turned into commodities to be produced as efficiently as possible. There needed to be more intense use of the factors of production, above all land, with its withdrawal if necessary from less efficient uses – such as the subsistence agriculture of peasant farmers, including the Highlanders.[36]

It was not just a theoretical matter but implied many changes on the ground. Sheep-rearing needed first a new kind of big farm. For sheep there was no existing infrastructure of drove roads and trysts, so both marketing and transport had to be set up from scratch. Only units carrying over 2,000 animals gave an ample enough return to justify the investment and trouble. Often the changes also required new men, Lowlanders and Englishmen, but the awakening spirit of enterprise that carried some Gaels to America also took others into improvement of their local agriculture. Sheep-farms flourished round the southern end of the Great Glen, for example, whence wool could easily be transported by sea to textile mills in the Lowlands. Lochaber especially generated fresh fortunes in sheep, among the Camerons of Corrychoillie, Invercaddle and Kildermorie, or Donald MacDonald of Tulloch and Alexander MacDonald of Glencoe (yes, the successor to the chief whose clansmen had been massacred, along with himself, in 1692). They were all Gaels but capitalist farmers, too, on a novel pattern. Not only the shepherds but the sheep changed as well. Highland sheep of Rob Roy's era had been small, skinny and shaggy, almost like puppies, yielding little meat or wool. With commercial production, they needed to be replaced by the Blackface and then the Cheviot breeds. These Highland sheep entered into competition with the Highland cattle. They also entered into competition with the Highland people.[37]

From the competition the Highland people were not always the total and catastrophic losers. They could hang on to arable ground if it was already productive enough, and if it had some link to urban and industrial development, or at least the prospect of one. That was what happened in the southern Highlands, especially the mainland and islands of the Campbells' empire. It helped, of course, that the Dukes of Argyll did not want their tenants to go. The most conscientious and benevolent of them, John, the fifth duke, inherited his estate in 1770. During his reign, which lasted till 1806, he saw the population rise by 20 per cent, by even more on the islands, to his delight. He was hostile to emigration, reluctant to evict and determined to stimulate enough industry to provide a living for his people. He ruled his realm through chamberlains, and to the one in charge of Mull he wrote: 'You must get the tacksmen of farms to accommodate poor people upon their different farms with cott-houses and yards free of rent where that is necessary.'[38] He believed a thriving peasantry to be testimony to his own wealth and power, a source not just of revenue but also of prestige because the sons could be recruited into Highland regiments. The Campbells felt proud enough to commission a pictorial record of their achievements (by one of Edinburgh's leading artists, Alexander Nasmyth), and here the images, of Inveraray and Loch Fyne from the old military road, are of harmony between man and nature in the craggy but improved landscape. In the end, though, the Campbells failed to halt the drift of population away to the Lowlands, though it did take another century for that to set in decisively.

As for the sheep, it was possible for the new breeds to be absorbed into the existing agricultural structures so long as these had been modernised before the flocks arrived. That happened in a few places, but for the rest there was a fatal lag. Then the destruction of runrig for the sake of the sheep entailed also the destruction of the traditional Highland society. Sutherland is usually taken as the great scene of this tragedy but the size of the ruling family's estate made it an atypical example. Their delusion that all could be subjected to a master plan rested on the limitless money they had from their huge properties and investments in England. But no others among the surviving dynasties of Highland chiefs could say the same, and most had dropped by the early nineteenth century into deep financial trouble. The lucky ones were those in the east and south of the region, areas being assimilated to the Lowland economy. The destruction of the traditional Highland society turned out in either case the same.[39]

This result could by no means be foreseen, however, at the start of the process of improvement. The first clash it provoked came in 1792, remembered in Gaelic oral tradition as *Bliadhna nan Caorach*, 'the year of the sheep'. That summer the anxious peasants of Easter Ross got together to organise a drove of all the sheep introduced by the landlords, and to move them across the boundary of the River Beauly into Inverness-shire. The drove was broken up by three companies of the Black Watch from Fort George under the direction of the civil power in the person of Sheriff Donald MacLeod of Geanies. He was a Gael himself, and his general reaction proved interesting. He did not hesitate to enforce the law against the drovers, even though they tried to play on the understanding they felt he must have for their plight. He was respected in the county as a model improver, one who took account of the people's interests as well as his own. On his estate, by the shores of the Moray Firth, he mounted an ambitious plan to convert moor into arable land by 'inclosing, mixing the different soils by trenching, and laying on lime', all of which also gave employment to locals. As a result, during the Highland crisis of subsistence in 1783, the starving had come down here from the mountains to be fed: 'But for those supplies, disorder and rapine would have prevailed, and the poor, rendered desperate by famine like so many hungry wolves, would have broken loose and laid hands on whatever they could find.' What a contrast from the previous famine! Then, in 1741, 'many were found dead on the highways and in the fields; and others, though long fasting, expired as soon as they tasted food'.[40]

Sheriff MacLeod deserved well of the people of Ross, then, and in 1792 the drovers let him know they would exempt him from their action and leave his sheep alone. Yet they got him wrong. He refused to support them in any way against lawful authority. He later wrote: 'The spirit of violence was carried so far as to set the civil power at defiance; the laws were trampled upon; there appeared to be no safety for property; and the gentlemen of the country seemed to be subjected to the power and control of an unruly and ungovernable mob.' He insisted that, contrary to some modish opinion, sheep-farming benefited everybody. Though it had been introduced to Ross 15 years earlier, there was 'not as yet one single family been obliged to emigrate on account of sheep'. To be sure, 'some families have been obliged to change their situations, and move from one farm to another.' They might dislike being shifted around, but they could hardly claim a right to live forever in one place, and their reaction was not 'a good reason why a proprietor should preclude himself from letting to a more enterprising and active occupant'. Highland lairds ought to 'have the same liberty of improving or managing their properties as seems to them the most conducive to their interest' – even if depopulation followed, which MacLeod anyway thought unlikely. He assured the people of Ross that 'introducing a source of wealth and staple of manufacture hitherto unknown amongst them [would] increase their numbers and their happiness'.[41]

Here were the thoughts of a humane, liberal, progressive landlord optimistic about the prospects both for improvement and for the people affected

by it, because confident that an expanding economy could absorb the displaced population. He represented the type of those sure they were leading
Scotland to a better future. After the chiefs, the most influential Highlanders
by now were gentlemen with an enlightened education, as MacLeod had
had in studying law at the University of Edinburgh and imbibing the values of improving Lowlanders. Application of their values brought spectacular results and made their region's economy one of the most dynamic in
Europe. That, too, had involved displacement of the population. Yet there
was no unrest to speak of. The economy absorbed people into new activities without much pain. It would not have been unreasonable of Sheriff
MacLeod to suppose that, given similar vigour and purpose, spectacular
results might be achieved in the Highlands too. Of course, the terrain and
climate made this harder: a new rural economy here would, for example, still
have more stock than grain, in contrast to the Lowlands. But the policies
could be adjusted and the commitments of men such as MacLeod, rooted in
this soil, might win the same popular assent to a process of benefit to all in
the end.[42]

So MacLeod saw no good reason for resistance. Individual occupancy had,
after all, never been assured in the old Highlands either. Clansmen might have
believed in a hereditary right to occupy some holding on their chiefs' territory,
but that could not have amounted to a right to a specific plot because no such
guarantee had been feasible in an unstable society. Clans often lost territory
to their foes, through blunder, delusion or misdeed. Mobility was nothing
new in the Gàidhealtachd. What MacLeod and his like might hope for was to
make it a force for good, not ill. Then Highland and Lowland lairds would be
espousing identical aims, public-spirited and indeed patriotic.[43]

A possible consequence might have been for the social structure in the
Highlands to move closer to that of the rural Lowlands. Out of a new
agriculture, driven by markets, a class of independent farmers could have
arisen alongside a class of labourers without land who lived by working for
them. In much of the Highlands to the east of the Great Glen, together
with the Black Isle, this was more or less what did happen, though farms
remained smaller and farmers poorer than in the Lowlands. In the north
and west things were different. Individual plots survived, but constantly
diminishing in size as ever larger numbers of tenants squeezed onto them.
In such a conservative society, to be landless was to drop out of it. So people
divided their parcels of land again and again, often to let their children stay,
marry and have a family of their own. In the Highlands the old peasantry in

communal settlements had not evaporated. It just turned into a new peasantry on smallholdings, or rather groups of such holdings, with a residual element of common grazings on the hills behind. This is the definition of crofts, as they came to be known. While one class, the tacksmen, vanished from the Gàidhealtachd, another emerged, much more numerous and precarious. The intricacy of the old Highland society polarised into uniformity on two tiers, landlords and crofters, with greater risk of a straight conflict of interest.[44]

In the end the novel structure did not make its members better off on either tier: for once, Scottish improvers failed to improve. There followed instead something like what happened in Ireland or other peripheral parts of Europe where rewards from development never offset the penalties of a rapid rise in population. In poor years it came, with bad crops or low prices for cattle, close to the margin of survival. The Highland population did not, to be sure, rise as fast as the Lowland population, because part of the natural increase continued to be creamed off by migration. People on the fringes of the region drifted into the booming economy of central Scotland. So the population grew fastest on the furthest parts. According to the unofficial census carried out by Dr Alexander Webster in 1755, the Inner and Outer Hebrides contained 19,000 people. By the census of 1801 they contained 30,000 people, an increase of 60 per cent.[45]

Certain historians have taken to labelling the late eighteenth century in the Highlands as the 'first phase of clearance',[46] in uneasy awareness of its scant resemblance to what would happen in the nineteenth century. The question arises whether it can be called 'clearance' at all. The term was never used at the time, so it is impossible to say what contemporaries might have meant by it. Nowadays it is bandied about so sloppily that some blameless souls take it as a synonym for genocide. If 'clearance' should be assumed to mean the disappearance of a population from its habitat, then in the Highlands of 1800 there was not a single county, not a single island, not a single parish, not a single estate that was cleared. On the contrary, the population continued its rapid increase. Amid the pressure on resources a good many Highlanders were bound to 'change their situations', in Sheriff MacLeod's apt phrase. Landlords, deploying ample legal powers, did often direct the movement. Their main resort to coercion, however, came in seeking to stop emigrants, not without success. Absence of depopulation, with use of coercion rather to promote the opposite result, vindicates a denial that in this era any Highland clearances took place.

In the Lowlands the changes produced by improvement had run ahead of those in the Highlands, but at first were just as patchy and gradual. Right till 1750 many peasants still lived in fermtouns. From then on the pace of rationalisation and specialisation speeded up in response to urban demand for food and raw materials. The Lowland countryside had inherited from the past a social structure on three levels: a small class of landowners at the top, in the middle the tenant farmers and their families working most of the land, and at the bottom the cotters or labourers who might pay in kind for a small plot of their own but usually toiled for other people. Even in the old Scots Parliament the landlords had been strengthening their hand – for example, by an Act for the Division of Commonties (1695) – and widening their power to reorganise and consolidate lands lying in runrig. They continued to do so right through the eighteenth century, with their lawyers (who were often their relations) strengthening aspects of absolute ownership actually alien to the prevailing feudal system: the most notable package of reforms came under the abolition of heritable jurisdictions in 1747.[47]

At the end of the century Sir John Sinclair of Ulbster in Caithness made himself the intellectual leader – if a tedious and pedantic one – of agronomy, the science of what makes farming work (at least for the ruling class). He reckoned there were 8,000 landlords in Scotland, of whom about 400 had large properties worth at least £2500 and about 1,000 possessed middling estates worth between £600 and £2,500.[48] Inside this body of proprietors several things were going on at once. One appeared in a certain tendency to still greater concentration of ownership. With it came an uneven but persistent upward trend in agricultural prices, partly due to the general growth in a prospering society's demand for food and raw materials: exports of grain died away while imports of grain grew common, though again the changes were seldom sudden or wholesale. Meanwhile, landlords demanded higher rents, something initially often connected with an urge to underwrite a more lavish lifestyle rather than with any systematic investment in improvement as such.

One way tenants could meet such demands on them was by finding extra sources of income; for example, many agricultural households took up weaving, in which the women and children of a fermtoun could lend a useful hand. The more enterprising tenants had otherwise been finding means to enlarge their holdings and assume a dominant position at least within the shared farm.[49] The logical consequence was merger of the strips and plots, with individual leases and enclosure as the sequels. Once the common grazing also got divided up, the fermtouns really lost their point.[50] In other words, farms with multiple tenants were consolidated into one unit with a single tenant.

Probably the bulk of Scotland's better land got enclosed in this way during the second half of the eighteenth century, the changes being in the end implemented so radically as to erase almost all trace of the traditional arrangements.[51] In early maps of Scotland we see patches of improvement on a generally unimproved terrain, but gradually their area spread till they pretty well covered the Lowlands.[52] By the time of Sinclair's *Old Statistical Account*, published in instalments from 1791 to 1799, everyone was clear what improved farming meant, and this set the standard against which most of his contributors measured the condition of their own parishes.

The picture was a diverse one. Though many farms retained mixed agriculture, it could readily become more specialised. On ground more suitable for arable purposes, rotation of crops now became possible, as it scarcely could have been in the regime of runrig. On ground more suitable for pastoral purposes, superior grasses for the beasts would be sown so that the business of capitalist breeding and sale might begin. A bleak and treeless agricultural landscape, with human settlement scattered scrubbily across it, gave way to the orderly modern version with a nuclear farm, spick and span steadings, neat fields, trimmed hedges and tidy copses.[53]

While the new type of tenanted farm had a structure that looked fairly similar everywhere, it did vary in size from one region to another. It was for the feudal superior and proprietor on each estate to determine the degree of variation. After the middle of the eighteenth century, the long-term tendency towards larger holdings quickened into a more positive drive, because the benefits of big farms in terms of productivity were now clearly coming to outweigh the difficulties of surmounting the social hindrances to their formation.[54] In these circumstances the ambitious tenant could also carve out a niche, typically aiming at a farm of at least 100 acres, or even a multiple of that in favourable regions, so creating an agricultural enterprise with its own team of full-time workers. The new type of tenant farmer was little constrained in directing his labours except by the terms of his lease or feu. The fermtoun's community of peasants turned into a place of work where the employer faced the employees with no mediation[55]. The unequal distribution of power minimised conflict, but the reckoning came in rural depopulation. Superior in this structure as the farmer was to his workers, he had a place within the hierarchy of his own kind too, set by the scale on which he operated – and the difference between the greater and the lesser farmers also widened. The main beneficiaries of the change were those at the top of the tree, but at the bottom stood tenants, or even owners, struggling to make an independent livelihood, perhaps with only 40 marginal acres on a cold upland edge. Most farms, of course, lay somewhere in between.[56]

The working unit now consisted of a compact block of ground under individual control, without any form of common land attached. On mixed farms, rotational crops covered nearly all the farmland and the grazing animals were fitted into the rotation. Buildings – farmhouse, steading and cottages – usually arose within the boundaries of the farm and housed the entire full-time workforce with their families.[57] The optimal course for the owner or tenant was to shape this group to be just big enough to perform the necessary tasks in the kinds of agriculture suited to his farm, its tradition, soil, climate and potential markets. He turned steadily more intolerant of any waste of space in the shape of smallholdings, especially as he needed a workforce completely under his control through the whole day and over the cycle of seasons, a workforce indeed further disciplined in terms of employment by being subject to hire for six months or a year.[58] At the base of the pyramid, the class of cotters who had earlier formed such a large part of the rural population faded away. They became in effect landless labourers with, in most regions, little chance of ever acquiring a place of their own.[59] Whatever the scale of farming, a growing gulf was evident in relations between the farmer and his workers and in their different patterns of social behaviour. So improvement turned out not merely a technical, agricultural matter: it brought deep changes in the wider economy, in Scottish society and even in politics.

The south-east of Scotland – Berwickshire, Roxburghshire and especially East Lothian – led the transformation. Here small farms steadily merged into big farms, with most people reduced to employees of big farmers. The minister of Ayton in Berwickshire, a parish where the Border hills came down to the coastal plain, caught the changes of the age in midflight. In the *Old Statistical Account* he wrote that the lands

some years ago were all runrig ... They are now divided, have convenient farmhouses and are highly improved ... The greatest part of the lands in this parish is inclosed with hedges. Fences of this kind are recommended both by their beauty and utility. The rise of rent seems to have operated here as a spur to exertion and improvement in agriculture. The farms have rather decreased in number. Some of them, though but few, extend to 500 or 600 acres.[60]

Elsewhere in Scotland small farms held their place better. Fife, Perthshire and Angus had many big farms too, but more balanced by smaller ones. The minister of Ceres in Fife described how in his parish the biggest was of 400 acres but the least of only 20: 'these, owing to the rise of the value of land, and improvements in agriculture, although feued out at the full rent, are now become of greater value to the feuars than to the superior'.[61]

The north-east of Scotland had a larger number of small farms, so offering at least a little hope that the agricultural worker might be able to better himself by acquiring one in time.[62] There was a ladder he might climb from small to big holdings, if with the greatest number available at the lowest rung, just on the margin of independent farming. Here, even so, hired hands continued to outnumber independent farmers by almost three to one. This region also saw the emergence of what were in effect crofts, though they would never be included in the crofting legislation of the late nineteenth century.[63] On them agricultural tasks had to be combined with other ways of making a living, but at least this might start an intending farmer off. The number of crofts grew till they became as numerous as the independent farms, because the foothills of the Grampian Mountains, unusually, had at the end of the eighteenth century a reserve of cultivable land waiting to be brought under the plough. Lairds, to secure the clearance and improvement of such land, placed settlers on the bare hillsides and moorlands. 'The size of farms is difficult to average,' said the minister of Alford, 'as they differ prodigiously from one another, not only in the whole extent, but also in the quantity of the different soils of land that make up a farm in that country.' The transition from runrig had not yet been fully accomplished: the farms 'are in general still under the old divisions, with very irregular marches, as when antiquated notions of convenience, and no idea of inclosing, or regular fields, were in view'.[64]

Meanwhile in the western Lowlands the farming, while modernised in technique, was consolidated within holdings much on the old scale, and the family farm of 50 to 150 acres continued to prevail.[65] The minister of Beith in Ayrshire thought he knew why:

There are in this parish 105 heritors, besides a considerable number of smaller proprietors in the village. This circumstance is supposed to have much influence upon the cultivation, and of consequence upon the produce and rent of lands. The small landholders generally reside upon their own property; and improvements made by any of them, in the cultivation of their lands, and management of their farms, are more readily adopted by the rest, than those introduced by persons who have large estates, or carry on farming upon a more extensive scale, because they are evidently more within their reach. The lands in this parish are almost all arable, and were generally enclosed many years ago.[66]

Altogether, in the Lowlands as in the Highlands, agricultural improvement remained under the control of the landowners. The rural economy was labour-intensive by later standards, but also exploitative. The exploitation came more through the market than at the hands of the landowners themselves, who even yet could not really screw up their demands on tenants of mostly limited resources. But the proprietors had to get a higher income from somewhere for the conspicuous consumption they aspired to, now that they had a position to keep up not just in remote and ramshackle Scotland but in the United Kingdom – the level on which they came to measure their prestige. This ideally entailed life in a gracious country house with social seasons spent elsewhere, even occasionally in London, more often in Edinburgh or at least in the county town, with the attendant expenses for hospitality, carriages, clothes and servants.[67]

By 1814, after 20 years of heavy investment by landlords in their estates, it was reckoned that the land-rent of Scotland had increased by a steady £100,000 to £200,000 a year. Scots landlords obtained their higher returns not from rack-renting but from step-changes when the leases fell in and were renewed by public roup. Yet this could not have happened unless prospective tenants felt sure of expanding their output and getting good prices for their produce. Agriculture always suffered from the fact that the best growing seasons might bring lower prices for the crop, because of the excess of supply over demand. The countervailing factor in contemporary Scotland was the rapid increase in population, beginning in the second half of the eighteenth century and continuing well into the nineteenth. The first official census of the United Kingdom in 1801 recorded the population of Scotland at 1,608,000, compared with 1,265,000 in Dr Alexander Webster's census of 1755.[68]

Scottish agriculture, which had probably reached its climatic limits of expansion under the old ways by the middle of the eighteenth century, afterwards passed through a momentous transition to more intensive farming sustained by increasing commercialisation and higher levels of investment. To add political to the economic terms, the mechanisms of the market transmitted the benefits of high protective barriers and soaring public expenditure to individual landlords. So prosperous were these landlords that they proved willing to invest in social capital for its indirect effect on their rental income, for example, in turnpike roads and model villages.[69]

Scotland at the Union was a backward nation by European standards. The improvers took the first forward steps but national penury made them slow: there was a desperate shortage of capital and the Union had as yet raised hardly anybody's income. During the eighteenth century this changed and the leadership of Scotland changed too. In line with that, the aristocratic Society of Improvers gave way to a broader movement incorporating the rural middle class, successful farmers and clergymen who recorded and applauded their efforts, together with others who diffused information through local reports, magazines and societies. The outlook stimulated in this way, bringing together social analysis, structural reform and technological advance, spread a more general awareness of their opportunities among the nation of Scots. In particular, it became both profitable and fashionable for landowners to make the most of their superior position, not by entrenching themselves in privilege but by placing themselves at the forefront of progress.

2

Industry: 'Very great profits'

On 13 November 1716, a party of a dozen men climbed up the Silver Glen, which rises steeply into the Ochil Hills just to the east of the village of Alva in Clackmannanshire. Half were gentlemen, the rest labourers with picks and shovels. At their head strode Charles Maitland, Earl of Lauderdale, who had fought against the Jacobites at the Battle of Sheriffmuir exactly a year before, but since settled himself into a civil sinecure as captain-general of the Scottish mint. John Haldane of Gleneagles was a second staunch supporter of the Hanoverian succession and had suffered for his pains, during the late rebellion, a raid by the rebels on his house and estate north of the Ochils. Then there was William Drummond, Lauderdale's working deputy at the mint – though not working that hard because the mint no longer produced any coins, and would never produce any more before its abolition in 1817. With them was Dr Justus Brandshagen, present on the express orders of King George I, who had previously employed him as a mining expert in the Electorate of Hanover. And then there was James Hamilton, also some kind of early geologist but, more to the point, the man who had revealed the secrets of the Silver Glen to the British government.[1]

The most important member of the party, however, was Sir John Erskine of Alva, the local laird whose estate included the glen: in fact his residence, Alva House, stood right at the foot of it. And Sir John was a Jacobite, only just returned from exile in France – a brief exile compared to what some of his fellows would be forced to endure. Before the rebellion he had been making a name for himself as one of the nation's most progressive landowners. He invested in enclosures and plantations. He introduced red clover to Scotland, a most useful plant good not only as fodder for cattle but also for fixing nutritious nitrogen in the soil. Another of his interests lay in mining for metal, a promising venture because the Ochils were composed of igneous rock where aeons ago the great heat forming them had tended to separate out the minerals within the original molten mass. Probably there were always odd, casual finds here of interesting nuggets. But Sir John took the trouble to call on the only kind of experts then known to him, men working the pits at Leadhills in Dumfriesshire, and asked them to prospect for possible profitable traces of metal. By December 1714 they had 'found great variety of ores, some rich in silver, some copper'.[2]

In July 1715, Hamilton was invited by Erskine to come and investigate the mine that the lads from Leadhills had dug: 'in some weeks' work, the vein appeared more promising but this happened a very little only before he left his own house,' Hamilton later reported. In fact, this expert managed in eight days to extract 433 ounces of silver. He handed it over to Sir John, who took it and promptly vanished: the Jacobite standard had just been raised on the Braes of Mar in Aberdeenshire. He presumably set out straight for the north, but must almost at once have been ordered by the leader of the rebellion, his kinsman, John Erskine, Earl of Mar, to go over to Europe and organise shipments of arms. By the time of Sheriffmuir he was already in France. His mission would take up all his time and energy till the collapse of the rising in February 1716. Still, Lady Erskine, left at home, was a resourceful woman and in the absence of her husband she kept four miners busy in the Silver Glen under Hamilton's supervision. Over the winter they dug out as much ore as they could. The best of it was melted down for its silver, and the rest, about 40 tons, was buried in barrels near the house. Then Lady Erskine closed the mine and had it filled up with rocks and earth. But the family's situation was by this stage alarming. She tried desperately to find ways of sending her husband money. He was stuck in Lübeck on the Baltic Sea, hoping to take ship to Sweden and seek help from King Charles XII.[3]

It was Hamilton who almost by accident came to the rescue. Having nothing more to do at Alva, he carried some of the ore to London. He went to the lord mayor, Sir Charles Peers, to tell him about the mine, and a sample of the ore was sent for assay to Sir Isaac Newton, no less, who found it 'exceeding rich' with 7.5 per cent of silver. The Erskines were quick to exploit the unexpected turn of events. They could appeal to an old Scots law, dating back to 1592, which stated that a tenth of the produce of any mine of gold or silver was the king's share.[4] On the strength of this, Sir John now made it known that, if he were to receive a pardon, he would feel able to reveal the mine's secrets. He might then resume his mining, at the price – cheap in the circumstances – of handing over 10 per cent of the revenue to the crown. Since the government in London was otherwise intent on hunting down fugitive Jacobites, Sir John's proposal had actually to go up for approval to the Cabinet. There the king's ministers swallowed his bait, though only on the condition (presumably imposed by George I) that Dr Brandshagen should travel across from Hanover to inspect the site at Alva.

That was how the party came to be mounting the Silver Glen on a winter's morning in November 1716. Erskine had got a safe conduct home and stood by with his Hanoverian minders while the workmen reopened the mine. They extracted further samples of ore, on which Brandshagen was to report to the king: 'I found it of an extraordinary nature, such as to my knowledge none like have ever been seen in Europe.' At Alva the hard labour was not yet finished, however. Hamilton pointed out the spot where he said the barrels of previously excavated ore lay buried. When the workmen dug down, they found nothing. Erskine helpfully intervened to say his servants had told him some barrels were reburied in the garden. The workmen dug down again and found six barrels, but all were filled just with stones. The Hanoverian officials began to suspect they were being codded. They interrogated the workmen, who were evasive. It seemed the rest of the ore had been removed during Sir John's absence, though nobody knew where.[5]

The officials retreated empty-handed, therefore, and Erskine doubtless saw them off with a beaming smile and a cheery wave. A couple of years later he duly received a royal licence to work his mines, so long as he gave the crown its tenth of the proceeds; this share amounted in the end to £20. Yet he had loads of money from somewhere, for he continued with a lavish programme of improvements to his estate. He enclosed the carse in front of his house, and on the hill behind he created a plantation of native and exotic trees. He imported the 'English husbandry', even though 'he had little partiality for the personal manners of that people'. He developed coal-mines and even built a canal by which the coal could be transported down the valley of the River Devon to the Firth of Forth. Some time later he had a conversation with a neighbour: 'When I first formed my scheme of policy for this place, I was drawing such sums out of the mine that I could not help looking upon the Elector of Hanover as a small man.'[6]

The episode was not only amusing but also instructive. It demonstrated an attitude to wealth that the course of the eighteenth century would transform.

At the beginning the Scots and every other people in Europe regarded precious metals as representing some sort of absolute value: the more of them that any citizen or nation could accumulate, the richer that citizen or nation became. By the end of the century the idea had been exploded. In *The Wealth of Nations* (1776), Adam Smith devoted a long 'Digression on Silver' to showing how this was a commodity which, while useful as a medium of exchange, a standard of measurement or a store of value, itself suffered fluctuations in its purchasing power.[7] When, for example, the British government advanced a bounty on the export of wheat, the value of silver fell in real terms. And look at the fate of Spain since it had imported so much silver from America: it was once a rich country but now a poor one. What enriched a nation or its citizens was not the amount of precious metal they hoarded but the uses to which they put these and indeed all the resources at their disposal. If they invested their capital at a profit, they would grow rich. If not, they would stay poor.

The Scots then began to understand how to make themselves rich, and set about doing so. Agriculture remained for the time being by far the most important sector of their economy, and its improvement was what did most to increase their riches. All the same, industry promised much for the future if only means could be found to make it flourish. Just as in the case of agriculture, however, the Union offered no magic wands to wave for industry either, something that became clear within a couple of decades. For agriculture a private initiative led to the foundation of the Society of Improvers in 1723, while for industry a public initiative seemed necessary. In 1727 the Board of Commissioners and Trustees for Improving Fisheries and Manufactures in Scotland was appointed; a judge, Andrew Fletcher, Lord Milton, became the leading figure in it.[8]

Before and after the Union, textile manufacture, especially of linen, was the only kind of industry the Scots had much of. Nobody could pretend the products were sophisticated, but not every customer bought the finest linen and Scotland enjoyed reasonable success in selling its coarser wares south of the border; in 1705, when the English had sought to frighten the Scots into the Union, they threatened to ban these exports. After 1707 the tables were turned: the Scottish market opened to English products and then at the top end of it the locally produced material scarcely stood comparison with the best imported stuff.[9] As the merchants of Edinburgh ruefully remarked in 1710, 'it may well be remembered that the great inducement made use of to engage Scotland in this Union was the prospect of improving and vending our linen in manufactories by a direct exportation as well to the west of

Germania as to the West Indies.'[10] Now the commercial liberalisation seemed to have brought hardly any benefits, certainly not the economic boom glibly predicted by unionists. Still, the idea of protectionism came readily to the contemporary mind, far more readily than free trade ever did. Surely, then, it had to be the responsibility of the authorities of the new United Kingdom to assuage Scotland's plight. If with no great alacrity, these authorities agreed they should devise some arrangement for improving the range and quality of Scottish textiles. It was the board of trustees that got the job.

Working with only a meagre budget, the board of trustees had to make a lot of things change if the Scots were to sell more of their linen to the English or to anybody else. As a matter of fact it did make things change, or at least helped to, something seen most strikingly in the figures for output. The board's practice was to stamp consignments of cloth in approval of their quality and readiness for sale. During the first year of operation in 1729, the officials stamped 2.2 million yards of cloth. By the next year the volume had already reached 3.7 million yards. By 1770, it doubled to 7.6 million yards and, by 1780, it nearly doubled again to 13.4 million yards – and all this excluding the quantities of linen never sold but consumed in the manufacturing households. The value of output over the period sextupled.[11]

Linen was produced from flax, a plant the Scots had cultivated for centuries.[12] It therefore formed part of the as yet generally unimproved system of agriculture. The women of the fermtouns span or wove the linen when they had nothing better to do in the fields, and they seldom found any great interest in putting a high finish on the cloth. This was just a small part of their daily toil, aimed at best at a local market and often only meant to clothe the family, so they had little need to worry about quality. Some of the board of trustees' plans to deal with this sort of situation were simple: for instance, they offered prizes for improved standards of flax, yarn and cloth. In 1783 the poet Robert Burns won £3 for a sample of the seed he produced from the field of flax he grew on his farm of Lochlea at Tarbolton in Ayrshire (though this did not persuade him to settle down to agricultural life).[13] The board also had a policy of bringing in foreign craftsmen, Dutch weavers or French fashioners of cambric, to demonstrate their superior skills and technical know-how to doltish Scots. Then the more efficient Dutch looms were distributed to capable craftsmen who might use them to set an example to others. The replacement of the Scottish muckle wheel by the Saxon wheel (of the type that appears as a prop in the Grimms' fairy tales) did greatly speed up production. But then the problem was getting enough spun flax to keep the weavers busy, and the mechanical spinning of linen did not reach Scotland till much later.[14]

Meanwhile, the board of trustees was also sending industrial spies abroad. One had the mission of finding out about the difficult processes of scutching and heckling flax; by scutching the woody straw round the fibres of the plant was removed, and by heckling the fibres were split and straightened ready to spin. The enterprising spook not only found out about these activities, but once he was home again also invented a scutching machine to run on water-power and set it up at Bonnington Mills by the Water of Leith. Before the end of the century more than 300 textile mills were constructed in Scotland.[15] The processing of the flax then took place right round the country, from Caithness to Dumfriesshire. There was yarn to be purchased by Lowland buyers even in the more accessible Highland glens. In 1787 capital from merchants in Dundee financed the first mechanically powered mill at Brigton in Angus. But the greatest expansion took place in the west of Scotland, where output trebled in the course of the century.

There were strenuous efforts to improve the quality of the product too. The board of trustees commissioned research from Francis Home, professor of materia medica at the University of Edinburgh, who demonstrated that sulphuric acid, or vitriol as it was then called, would be the best bleaching agent for linen.[16] Because the board had only limited resources, it tended over time to concentrate them on investment at the stage of finishing the linen, something unavoidably capital-intensive. Especially costly was the creation of bleach-fields, which required several acres of good, flat land with plentiful supplies of pure water and a lot of heavy water-powered machinery.

So a problem of finance existed too. In 1745 a dedicated kind of credit was made available with the establishment by royal charter of the British Linen Company (which at length turned into the British Linen Bank and survived in some form till 1999). The initial purpose of this company was not to conduct banking business in the conventional sense but rather to provide credit to spinners and weavers. Still, it had enough flexibility in the terms of its charter to develop its supplementary and in the end alternative role as a bank.[17] As a matter of fact, it turned away with some relief from the vagaries of financing manufacture.

But on the whole Scotland dealt successfully with the various requirements for improving its production of textiles, so successfully as to bring about not just industrial but also social and even cultural change. The manufacture of linen became much more than a domestic and part-time occupation. Always labour-intensive, it first usually flourished in the countryside where the most surplus workers were to be found. It could, for example, draw on those tenants needing means to meet their landlords' demands for higher rents or being released from agriculture altogether. In 1767 a Jacobite exile, Sir James Steuart, published his *Inquiry into the Principles of Political Economy,* in which he noted that the preparing and spinning of linen were processes that let the humble cotter put almost every member of his household to work. In *The Wealth of Nations,* Smith agreed (though on most points always dissenting from Steuart) that it was the families of cotters who carried on most of the spinning.[18]

In social terms, spinning was seen primarily as a job for women, usually a part-time one combined with others, domestic and agricultural. Weaving preserved itself as a mainly male occupation, and full-time too. It was concentrated in Fife, Angus and Perthshire on the east coast, in Lanarkshire and Renfrewshire in the west. The earliest sign of the groupings of looms under one roof on a scale worthy of the name of factory might be discerned in small ports such as Arbroath, Dundee and Montrose, where sales overseas always formed a valuable part of the local manufacturers' business.[19] The expansion even reached the prosperous county town of Perth, which was not in the event to enjoy much of an industrial future. But at the end of the eighteenth century it had 1,500 looms on the go, probably with at least the same number again in the surrounding villages: the fast-flowing waters of the Rivers Tay and Almond were the reason for this local spread, together with the carses where bleach-fields could be laid out.

Poor people could readily take up the trade because its tools were cheap, with looms and spinning wheels costing just a few pounds. Preparation of the flax did not need much equipment anyway, though large volumes of water had to be on hand together with the labour to steep and ret the raw flax, so breaking up its structure: this process gave off a foul stench. The hecklers then took over, breaking the woody fragments of the retted flax to extract the fibre and comb it out – a skilled job, but again one for which the simplest tools sufficed. This was another trade that Burns tried but did not stick at. According to his brother Gilbert, he 'wrought at the business of a flax-dresser in Irvine for six months, but abandoned it at that period, as neither agreeing with his health nor inclination'.[20]

It was through cheap labour, at least short of the finishing process, that Scottish linens became competitive in external markets. Probably they still did not at first contribute all that much to the balance of payments. While a good deal of raw flax, of superior quality, was imported from the Baltic region, helping to improve both the supply and the standard of the Scottish production, exports could only be developed in the first instance by protective tariffs and bounties. The temporary withdrawal in 1753 of one type of bounty sharply depressed the trade, which bounced straight back once the bounty was restored; so demand could not have been much of a factor.[21] A lot of the output always got retained for domestic consumption in Scotland, but over time profitable markets emerged in London, from which most of the linen was re-exported, or else, for cargoes shipped directly from Glasgow, in the colonies of North America and the West Indies.

The merchants who went on to make fortunes in this traffic had often started out as master weavers of linen, men such as David Dale, Archibald Buchanan, Adam and James Monteith. They were also to be midwives for the successor trade to the manufacture of linen, the manufacture of cotton. Even with the help of the board of trustees, it was in the end Scots that needed to liberate native enterprise. In linen, they had brought about the only early, sustained and significant growth to be found in the economy of the eighteenth century.[22] The growth remained quite slow even so, yet it did carry on through the later and more dramatic expansion of cotton. There is a tendency to forget linen's importance to the economy especially of the west of Scotland because it slumped at the end of the Napoleonic Wars in 1815, after a large transfer of capital and labour into cotton. But, till a couple of decades before, there had been nothing to rival it.

While Scottish industrial expansion might have got an initial push from the British state, that stimulus was before long no longer needed. Industrial revolution took flight out of the commercial experience and proficiency of the nation's own new class of textile tycoons.[23] When the opportunities in cotton came along, the capital and knowledge they had acquired from linen made them natural pioneers in a new line of business.[24] It was again in the west of Scotland that certain of them, often in partnership with merchants such as Dale, converted to cotton. The simple reason lay in the better commercial prospects. Every country in northern Europe might grow its own flax but not every one of them could import raw cotton from colonies in other

continents or send the finished product out again. Especially along the River
Clyde oceanic trade had developed, offering at its Scottish end fresh fields of
investment for new mercantile fortunes. It also attracted paternalist landowners extending the agenda of improvement and looking for ways to employ the
surplus labour displaced by that.

Of course these old and new leaders of Scottish society also made money,
in some cases a great deal of money. And for this ample reward they needed
no huge down-payment.[25] To begin with, cotton required little more than linen
had done in terms of skills, technology and fixed investment: for example, the
bleach-fields laid out and the dye works set up for linen could serve also for
cotton.[26] It is often assumed that the actual shift from the one to the other
resulted from the outbreak of the American War of Independence in 1776,
when Glasgow at once lost its transatlantic trade in tobacco. But its merchants
had already accumulated enough capital both to withstand the shock and to
develop fresh interests. They soon replaced tobacco from Virginia with cotton from the West Indies, and it was a natural step for other entrepreneurs
in the city then to start processing the cotton. In fact, this manufacture had
already started up out of the manufacture of fine linen and silk. Merchants
importing cotton wool began about 1770 to supply the weavers in Glasgow
and Paisley who made fustian for men's clothing from a mixture of cotton
yarn and linen yarn. To go over from production in both to production in
one or the other, or vice versa, was evidently no problem. The American war
if anything helped, for it tended to raise wages and demand at a time when
cotton was in real terms becoming cheaper, flax more expensive and silk more
expensive still. Another reason Glasgow's merchants took to the change was
that West Indian planters tied supplies of such lucrative commodities as sugar
and rum to a willingness to take more cotton. Between 1775 and 1812 imports
of it into the Clyde increased 80 times over.[27]

Cotton brought about bigger changes than linen on the Scottish industrial
and urban scene, in particular by creating early on quite large complexes of
factories for mass production. During an initial boom from 1788 to 1792
landowners and farmers also took part in setting up these mills, though often
their role was that of sleeping partners willing to lease rights over land and
water to industrialists. The Earl of Bute acted in just this way at Rothesay on
the Isle of Bute, the Duke of Atholl at Stanley in Perthshire. The hanging
judge Lord Braxfield, who feued the site of New Lanark to Dale, showed

no further interest in the factory once he had fulfilled his legal function. On the other hand there were merchants, especially West Indian merchants, who got more closely involved. James Finlay & Co., the largest manufacturer of cotton in Scotland after 1801, counted many merchants among its shareholders, while Robert Owen, Dale's son-in-law and successor, counted more. Big technological advances for cotton had already been achieved in England with the spinning jenny and the mule. When this last innovation was linked to the steam engine perfected by James Watt, maker of instruments to the University of Glasgow, the factories freed themselves from the need to be close to a river or burn for the sake of the water-power. They could then arise on a much larger scale anywhere in the cities and towns. By 1812 Sir John Sinclair estimated that the textile industry employed more than 150,000 Scots, many still working from home but with a growing number toiling in 120 mills. The mechanisation of spinning and weaving concentrated in these complexes came, more than anything else, to symbolise the industrial revolution.[28]

Much of this took place close to the older communities of individual textile workers, yet it was a world away from their small-scale production of more specialised wares, often in their own homes. True, they had been able to double their output after the flying shuttle came into general use in Scotland during the 1770s. By 1795 Scotland had 39,000 weavers producing cotton on handlooms, most full-time, supported by 13,000 women and girls who helped them with the fiddly tasks of dressing the loom and setting it up for work. What these family businesses could not do was keep up with the abundance of cheap yarns generated by mechanisation. From that point of view the weaver became a bottleneck in the process of production (though at least that meant he got well paid). Yet, even in its finer variations, weaving was quite an easy trade to master.[29]

In the final years of the eighteenth century individual handloom weaving saw its golden age. Demand for the products was high, the workforce enterprising and prosperous, though these qualities remained subdued somewhat by one inherited circumstance. In the west of Scotland textiles looked back on a long history, and most royal burghs had a weavers' incorporation; the one in Glasgow boasted a charter dating from 1528. Membership of it was restricted to the privileged group that had served a formal apprenticeship, often gained through some link of blood or obligation with the existing members. Less well-connected families just wanting to earn a living from textiles needed to fan out beyond the old boundaries of the burgh into Anderston, Calton, Gorbals or other nearby communities, where the privileges of its crafts did not apply. Part-suburb and part-village, these places were largely peopled by weavers living in characteristic cottages usually of one storey, certainly of no more than two, helped in their labour again by their relations. They had a slow and tedious job, but one which left them ample time to think and talk to friends, neighbours or workmates who might drop by their workshops. The thinking and talking were often supplemented by reading in the evening. John Galt's novel, *Annals of the Parish* (1821), set in the Ayrshire of the preceding decades, depicts a typical scene at the time of the French Revolution with local weavers clubbing together to subscribe to a newspaper from which they took turns to read aloud to one another. A school of poets at Paisley, led by Robert Tannahill and Alexander Wilson, sprang from the same ranks. They were men of independent mind and their politics tended to be radical.[30]

Yet the golden age was brief: the weavers soon faced a technological turning point that was transformed into an economic and social crisis too. The introduction of the power loom, first used successfully at Catrine in Ayrshire in 1807 and soon afterwards at the other establishments of James Finlay & Co., was a direct challenge to the methods of the individual weavers. From that point their position steadily worsened. Partly this followed on from the previous excessive influx of labour into their trade, something bound to depress wages. Partly it was owed to the catastrophic failure of an ill-judged strike in 1812, by weavers hoping to enforce obsolete regulations that would restrict entry and enforce a minimum scale of prices. But the basic reason lay in the dynamic new methods represented by the power looms. By 1813 the number of them at work in Scotland was 1,400 and rising rapidly. They would spell doom to the independent weaver, if not finally for another couple of decades. He would suffer a lot of misery meanwhile.[31]

Huge mills for cotton were being built: New Lanark had opened in 1785, Deanston in Perthshire in the same year and Catrine in Ayrshire in 1787 as the precursors of many more. They stood in stark contrast to what had gone on before in the cosy provincial world of Scottish industry. Their sheer size impressed: New Lanark more than quadrupled its number of employees from 400 in 1791 to 1,700 in 1820. Their demand for labour often exceeded what the immediate neighbourhood could supply, especially in the more remote areas where the rationale for a big mill was the availability not of workers but of water for energy. By the time steam-power became available, it was often too costly to move to a more populous place. The mills might take pauper children from local parishes, as Owen did at New Lanark, but this expedient did not in fact turn out to be much favoured in Scotland, so that migrants from the Highlands and then from Ireland filled the gap: all, yet again, momentous developments.[32]

Even so, it might at this stage have been hard to foretell the congestion and squalor taken today as the social markers of the industrial revolution. At the outset, conditions proved to be more varied than that. In the huge mills a new way of life was there for all to see, but not necessarily in itself a degraded way of life. The housing, though different from what people had been used to, represented an advance on earlier standards. At Catrine, for example, the stone-built, two-storeyed, slated homes for the workers were better than any in the nearby farming villages. In yet sharper contrast, some attempt followed to organise social services. A church, schoolhouse, gardens and even pasture for cows adorned the village. It also had policemen, though mainly seeing to the security of the mill and the owners' other property: the gates at both ends of the main street were locked every night. Such detail warns us against assuming the industrial revolution always brought woe to the people. The wretchedness at home, and at work the reactions to it suppressed by harsh discipline – these things were more often linked with the smaller operations than with the ambitious experiments for a new social and economic order in a revolutionary age, of which New Lanark reminds us still.[33]

In the industry of Lowland Scotland linen kept the lead in the eighteenth century and cotton was king for a good part of the nineteenth, but from the conquest of the Highlands by sheep a third raw material also became widely available. Scottish woollens followed the common path of mechanisation and relocation. Adam Smith tells us the Union had ruined their production at an earlier period, 'by which it was excluded from the great market of Europe, and confined to the narrow one of Great Britain'.[34] Wool had been central to the local economy in some older towns such as Stirling, Haddington and Musselburgh, but now fell away to nothing. Only Aberdeen remained the centre of a traditional regional industry sustained by export and employing thousands of workers. A fresh expansion came rather at the opposite end of Scotland in the Border towns. On the surrounding pastures and hills they had abundant supplies of wool that improved in quality as Cheviot sheep replaced Blackface sheep. And in the basin of the River Tweed they disposed of ample supplies of water for power, scouring and dyeing. The population was not dense but the restructuring of agriculture allowed an urban workforce to form. Its productivity would be raised by the use of steam-power, despite its distance from the coal-mines and poor communications with them.

Finally, we might count papermaking as part of the Scottish textile industry: it was no longer so by the time it approached its end in the late twentieth century but it had been so in the eighteenth century, when production of paper usually started off from rags. The earliest factory was set up in 1675 at Dalry on the Water of Leith, sponsored by the Scottish state. It enjoyed only a shaky start and its output reached no more than 150 tons by 1761, after which it multiplied its sales steadily to markets in Europe and America. For the purposes of papermaking Scotland did not always possess resources superior to those of other countries, and it seems to have been the enterprise and acumen of owners such as the Cowans of Penicuik that made the difference. They experimented with all manner of materials and processes. The rags first often imported from Russia to be used as the substrate for paper were replaced in the nineteenth century by esparto grass. But already by 1780 this had become a vigorous industry capable of looking after itself, though also highly concentrated. Edinburgh, with its commerce, banking, legal practice, university, publishing and bourgeois domestic demand for paper, was much the best market in Scotland. As a result, the paper excised in Edinburgh and Haddington accounted for two-thirds of the total for Scotland in the last third of the century.[35]

Mechanisation proved not to be the only big technical achievement of the Scottish textile industries. Just as impressive, and as pregnant for future economic development, was the progress in chemical treatments to enhance the final product, that is to say, to bleach and to dye the fabrics. Here too, the board of trustees offered help. But there was a role for other public bodies as well, notably the Scottish universities in their precocious study of chemistry. In Edinburgh and Glasgow, William Cullen's chemical researches formed an extension of his medical researches. Joseph Black also lived and worked in both cities; in the one he helped to finance James Watt's development of steam-power and in the other he discovered carbon dioxide. James Hutton is best known as the 'father of geology', yet he owed his learned leisure to a partnership in a chemical works producing industrial alkali in the shape of sal ammoniac, formed from the soot gathered by the tronmen, or chimney-sweeps, of Edinburgh. The invention of the modern science of chemistry was the most practically useful part of the Scottish Enlightenment, and it would become still more important during the nineteenth century.[36] In everyday terms, it meant there was no shortage of men with enough scientific experience to set up and run factories making profitable use of advances in chemical knowledge.

Bleaching was one prerequisite for production of a higher standard of textiles. Originally it had been carried out with organic substances. Oil and dirt in the raw material needed to be removed by a mild alkali, extracted from the ash of wood or of seaweed – the infamous kelp, harvested in dreadful conditions from the western seas by pitiable Gaels. Then an acid was required, most often sour milk, to get rid of earthy stains that prevented even dyeing. The knell sounded for the old processes when in 1749 Scotland's first modern chemical factory opened at Prestonpans in East Lothian. It made vitriol, which could do in five hours what sour milk did in five days. Set up as a partnership of two Englishmen, John Roebuck and Samuel Garbett, the factory stood on land belonging to a local merchant, William Cadell. By the end of the century it was the biggest acid works in Britain, exporting to Europe too, and had attracted further investment from Henry Glassford, heir to one of Glasgow's mercantile fortunes. The techniques of chemical bleaching spread fast, not least because it eliminated the need for the bleach-fields that took up so much land. Then, in Aberdeen, a manufacturer of cotton started importing chlorine for bleach but this, whether as gas or liquor, was hard to handle. A further big step forward came in 1799 when Charles Tennant from Alloway in Ayrshire, Burns's friend 'wabster Charlie', patented the production of a dry bleaching powder. He fathered an industrial dynasty and set up what was to grow into the enormous St Rollox chemical works at Springburn on the northern side of Glasgow. A by-product of the production of bleaching powder was sodium sulphate, which, in reaction with potassium carbonate, could be used to produce alkali on a large scale. This was what happened at St Rollox after 1815: it sealed the economic doom of the Highlanders harvesting kelp.[37]

As for dyes, an original purple range for wool and silk became available in the form of cudbear, a curious term derived from the Christian name of its inventor, Cuthbert Gordon, a merchant at Leith. It was a vegetable dye extracted from marine lichen by a process involving its maceration in ammonia. Gordon and his partners had started a not too successful plant to manufacture it that was taken over by George Macintosh, a Highlander who had made a lot of money from a tannery in Glasgow. He moved the whole outfit from Leith to Dennistoun where behind a 10-foot wall he built himself a chemical plant with a workforce of fellow Gaels, preferably monoglots for reasons of security. Next he tackled the challenge of producing the prized Adrianople or turkey red colour in cotton. In 1785, in partnership with David Dale, he opened at Barrowfield the first works in Britain capable of producing this dye. Known locally as 'Dale's Red', it had a long and successful run. The works were sold in 1805 to Henry Monteith of Carstairs, another of Glasgow's textile tycoons, who now used it to make gaudy bandanas all the rage among the city's fashionistas. Meanwhile, George Macintosh's son Charles had actually invented the bleaching powder that Tennant managed to patent. Charles Macintosh remained a great chemical entrepreneur in his own right. He exploited a huge expansion in demand for alum, which had a wide range of industrial uses, to set up a works for it at Hurlet near Paisley, the biggest in Britain; it was still not big enough to meet the demand and he built a second one at Lennoxtown. He would at length achieve immortality with his invention of the raincoat; in its misspelled fashion, as mackintosh, it commemorates him.[38]

Evidently it was above all a spirit of enterprise that brought these advances in the technique of textile manufacture by which Scotland's industrial revolution started to move forward. But there was no single locus for the spirit of enterprise; at the very least, lairds, merchants and the state all had some hand in the progress. Improving lairds were perhaps the most crucial because they brought the others together. If their personal contribution remained sometimes indirect, they were never going to veto developments likely to generate cash. Their monetary pressure on their tenants had the useful effect of turning these to rustic manufacture as well. The British state was perhaps the least of the partners because, as so often in a free market, its interventions could turn out to be a misguided and counterproductive waste of the taxpayers' money. Still, the board of trustees did give a push to the improved output of linen, and the English Navigation Acts now benefited the Scots by allowing them untrammelled access to America.

But none of the public policy actually caused Scotland to industrialise. That process was far more complex. The nation inherited from its artisan history many trades with low costs and overheads. In the eighteenth century they found themselves able to compete in emerging markets created by economic and political changes. This, according to the new science of political economy, was what comparative advantage consisted in. The germ of that idea appears in *The Wealth of Nations*: 'If a foreign country can supply us with a commodity cheaper than we ourselves can make it, better buy it of them with some part of the produce of our own industry, employed in a way in which we have some advantage.' The Scots were already starting to exploit the idea, even if by speculative enterprise more than by research and calculation.[39]

Also basic to success was the supply of energy, which lucky Scots had in abundance because of their resources of coal. It was not at first obvious how important these would prove. For centuries they had been exploited for domestic use and export, but they found their main local industrial outlet in the production of salt from the evaporation of seawater in huge pans, heated by fires from underneath. The steam engine would drastically change the pattern and level of demand. And apart from the use of coal as fuel, its derivatives, such as coke and liquid ammonia, became products in their own right. In 1781 Lord Dundonald extracted tar from coal, for the protection of ships and roofs, in his kilns at Culross on the Firth of Forth. He showed that coal gas could be used for lighting, but he went bankrupt before he had a chance to develop its applications in the home, the factory and the street. That development is instead usually credited to the engineer William Murdoch. Scots began to light their workshops with gas, while both Edinburgh and Glasgow had public gas lighting in advance of any English city outside London.[40]

So Scotland, as its modern economy began to take shape, did not face the problem other nations faced of high costs for the transport of fuel. Edinburgh and Glasgow, and several provincial towns, lay close to coalfields. But there was much work to be done on the development of mining. This industry, too, had suffered a setback at the Union, in the shape of competition from the pits on Tyneside and increasingly from those in the English Midlands. As late as 1760, most mines in Scotland were single shafts, no more than holes in the ground, worked by a landlord or tacksman. Apart from those round the large burghs, most lay on or near tidal water and were linked to salt-works (as at Prestonpans). Horses operated what machinery was installed for draining or winding, and even the primitive steam engines of the time found only a modest role in these small businesses.[41]

Scottish mining methods remained in fact essentially medieval, and did not advance much before the landowners responded, in the second half of the

eighteenth century, to a steady rise in the price of coal. The higher demand
might still be agricultural rather than industrial. Large quantities of coal were
needed to burn lime in kilns and reduce it to fertiliser, as recommended by
the Society of Improvers; fortunately, deposits of coal and limestone often
occurred close together in Scotland. Lime also had applications in construction for the expanding burghs, which then burned yet more coal in their
grates. That was how Edinburgh earned the nickname of Auld Reekie.[42]

People complained of the rise in prices, though it was general in the British
economy by 1800. For coal in particular, they blamed landowners on account
of their expensive investments. But, apart from the wealthy merchants in the
west of Scotland, landowners were about the only group capable of making
expensive investments. The formerly Jacobite Erskines took the lead, and even
in his Continental exile the Earl of Mar had sent suggestions for an ambitious
water-powered system of drainage in mines that he hoped to exploit on his
estates as soon as he got back to them (he never did). The loyal Earls of Elgin
also pioneered many developments on their lands near Dunfermline, where in
the 1760s they built at the coastal village of Charlestown a great bank of lime-
kilns burning coal from their own mines. The pit at Sheriffhall in Midlothian,
owned and operated by the Duke of Buccleuch, lay close to the market of
Edinburgh, though even this did not always guarantee profits for it.[43]

In any event, the whole aim of the investment was to make manufacture
more efficient and less expensive. The escalation in the real price of coal had
not been a matter of the inputs into the production, as even Adam Smith
seemed to be suggesting,[44] but of a mismatch between supply and demand.
Increasing population plus accelerating urbanisation plus incipient industrialisation made the market for coal buoyant. Edinburgh and Leith, for example,
simply outgrew the scale of output possible from Midlothian, where many
pits relied on horses for power and on women for heaving from coalface to
pithead. The capital of Scotland had to start bringing its coal, at far greater
cost, by sea from Fife or England.

Indeed the origins of another great coming revolution, in transport, could in
part be traced back to the need for this sort of freighting. In Clackmannanshire
the Erskines of Mar opened a wagon-way at Alloa in 1768, extended it in
1771 and in 1785 clad its wooden rails in iron plates. In the west of Scotland
several of the wagon-ways built in Ayrshire from 1770 to 1815 were designed
to link inland mines to ports such as Irvine, which, in addition to coastal

shipments, sent quantities of coal to Ireland. By 1791 Sir John Henderson of Fordell in Fife had a wagon-way on which horses pulled trucks of coal from his mine to the shore of the Firth of Forth. The Earl of Elgin created a wagon-way at Charlestown, the Earl of Wemyss at Methil. Increases in output and sales repaid the investments. Another new era was apparently heralded when the Monkland Canal opened in 1790, designed to bring over 12 miles into Glasgow the coal dug in the parishes of Old and New Monkland (now Airdrie). In this the richest mineral area in Lanarkshire, the canal, started in 1770, completed only in 1792 and paying no dividend till 1807, at length proved highly profitable. Others did not, and steam-powered locomotives on iron railways would come to perform the job of transport in bulk at longer distances that the canals had never really been equal to.[45]

Labour rather than technology was a more convincing culprit for the rise in the price of coal. This may seem surprising in view of the fact that miners in Scotland were serfs, bound for their lifetimes to serve the coalmasters on whose land they grew up; their sons, soon after birth, would be pledged to the same fate. It was often a harsh one. Discipline might be maintained by corporal punishment, and men absconding from their servitude were liable to be arrested and hauled back. When this happened to one of Sir John Clerk's colliers at Loanhead, the poor man also had the lesson knocked into him by the laird in person: 'I provoked him to beat me severely,' the victim testified, 'which I acknowledge I deserved.' The coalmaster of the Hillhead colliery in the Monklands struck one of his miners for quitting his work too soon, even though he had come up only because 'his candle was done'. A boy at Prestongrange in East Lothian recalled of his employer that if 'we did not do his bidding we were placed by the necks in iron collars, called juggs, and fastened to the wall or made to go the rown. The latter I recall well, the men's hands were tied in face of the horse at the gin, and made run backwards all day.'[46]

This degradation was not a relic of the Middle Ages but a product of modern times. Scots miners had only become serfs in the seventeenth century, long after the feudal system vanished from the country except as a branch of the law of property. What the old Scottish Parliament had had in mind when it reduced these men to hereditary servitude was the need for stability among a workforce of notorious instability. The skills the miners required might then more readily be passed on from generation to generation. But it could cost the coalmaster if his men turned militant, since there was little chance of replacing them by blacklegs.[47]

The consequences were meanwhile further complicated by the fact that in the later eighteenth century some new industrial enterprises employed their own miners, free ones, to dig the coal they required for their operations. Such was the Carron Company, producing iron near Falkirk. It first tried to meet its need by introducing English miners, who offered the added attraction of being more industrious and sober than the Scots, and by recruiting pauper children as apprentices. At the same time, the new enterprises still made offers the Scottish miners could not refuse, even if these then risked being apprehended and sent back to their original masters by the sheriff. The old owners of mines and serfs waxed furious at such underhand tactics from upstart rivals. Dundonald complained that 'the very great profits they now make on the manufacture of iron, exclusive of an extensive consumption and handsome profit on their coal and minerals, enables them at present to give or rather to promise . . . such wages to colliers . . . as coal-owners cannot afford to give'.[48] But it was in the end simply the demand for coal created by industrialisation that spelled doom to Scottish serfdom and the archaic attitude towards labour underlying it. The claim was made that 'the ironworks and foundries of Carron and Clyde consume as many coals as all the inhabitants of Edinburgh'.[49] Indeed, the national market for coal that began to form favoured pits willing to modernise and compete in their labour as in their technology.

Even so, only in 1775 did Henry Dundas as Lord Advocate set in motion the process to abolish the scandal of Scottish serfdom and the bottlenecks it created in the market for labour. Wages in the mines had doubled since the turn of the eighteenth century, but they doubled again by the turn of the nineteenth century. The reason was the continuing shortage of hands in a labour-intensive industry, for the miners' emancipation did not become complete till 1799 and meanwhile their job still carried a social stigma. All the same, so far from being servile, they never hesitated to exploit their strong bargaining position in the small matter of the money they were paid. After full emancipation was achieved it yet made little impact on mining wages for a decade or two, when a flow of cheap Highland and above all Irish labour solved the crisis of recruitment and at the same time strengthened the hand of the employers.[50]

With capital investment in textiles, and with abundant fuel to drive the new industrial machinery, it was also possible for Scottish iron to move onto a new level of output. Iron had been made in Scotland since at least the time of King James VI whose Scottish Minister, Sir George Hay, began in 1607 to produce it at Letterewe on Loch Maree in Wester Ross. From a later perspective, it may seem bizarre that this should have emerged as a Highland industry, but so it did. Another furnace stood at Poolewe, at the foot of the huge glen where Hay built his. When Ewen Cameron of Lochiel marched off to join Bluidy Claverhouse's rebellion in 1689, he left behind at his estate of Achnacarry on Loch Arkaig in Inverness-shire a blast furnace that made and sold good iron; it was destroyed in the subsequent warfare. About 1727 other furnaces started up at Invergarry and at Glenkinglass by Loch Etive in Argyll. They did not last long, but a further successor survives today as a museum at Bonawe, also by Loch Etive.[51]

Bonawe, in its time the biggest blast furnace in Britain, was opened in 1753 by a Cumbrian ironmaster. The attraction for him and for the earlier entrepreneurs lay in the forests of Argyll. They yielded an ample supply of charcoal, the fuel that ironworks used before coal became more widely available. To power the machinery there was also enough and to spare of running water, while the ore could readily be imported by sea from England. Unlike the previous efforts this one at Bonawe proved successful, and stayed in business till 1876. In its heyday it produced 700 tons of pig iron a year, mostly for export, and employed 600 people to chop down and process the local trees. They were Gaels working only in the summer, while the elite of the workforce consisted of the 20 or so incomers from Cumbria who operated the furnace itself. These had most to do in the winter when they toiled non-stop; they spent the summer repairing and renewing the buildings and machinery. During the Napoleonic Wars the furnace produced cannonballs. The workforce was the first in Britain to erect a monument to Admiral Horatio Nelson after his heroic death at the Battle of Trafalgar in 1805.[52]

From this sort of operation the industry had moved up a gear in 1759, with the establishment of the Carron ironworks on the river of the same name in southern Stirlingshire. The entrepreneurs here were the two Englishmen, Roebuck and Garbett, who had helped to found the factory for vitriol at Prestonpans. Carron proved to be a yet more revolutionary development, for a while the biggest ironworks in Europe. It was a pioneer not only in its use of native ore but also in its smelting with coke, a process invented half a century before but otherwise yet to be adopted in Scotland. Here in the Lowlands it would be cheaper than using charcoal.[53]

Carron produced 1,500 tons of iron in its first year, and soon the operation mounted on such a scale that the founders could more or less completely integrate their business, from mining to smelting to forging. The site by the banks of the river was chosen for the supply of water to drive the machinery, but as the premises extended it became inadequate. While, in Glasgow, James Watt was still working on his improvements to the steam engine, he entered into partnership with Roebuck and they took out a joint patent for a condenser. It was used in the large steam engine they built at Carron, not to power the works directly but to pump water that had passed over the waterwheels back into a reservoir, so allowing it to be reused. Otherwise, too, Carron remained in a Scottish context quite exceptional, and encountered constant difficulties both technological and financial for which there had been no previous experience. It used its own pig to produce consumer goods, and it did well so long as it stuck to the simpler lines: grates, stoves, pots, pans. With more advanced work, notably with fine casting and ordnance for the armed forces, problems came thick and fast. Technological leadership was not always an advantage when false starts in the process of production were at once translated into loss of cash-flow and of profit. Luckily the Carron Company managed to obtain a royal charter in 1773 which also granted it limited liability, something again exceptional in Scotland.[54]

The company at last reached firmer ground in 1788 when it inaugurated its most famous product, the carronade. This was a short quick-firing gun of limited range but heavy calibre for mounting in merchant ships. It had the purpose of deterring pirates, and brilliantly succeeded in doing so. The buccaneer had to come in close for his prey and like any predator he could not afford to be severely mauled for the sake of a single kill. The carronade then found even more deadly use in the close naval combats of the Napoleonic Wars. Carron remained the leading enterprise in its field, for dependent or rival concerns were slow to appear. It did supply Scottish markets, but always sold much of its production outside Scotland. Heavy capitalisation and advanced organisation, with a good deal of wear and tear on the nerves of the proprietors, enabled it to survive and in the long run to thrive.[55]

Carron was ahead of its time, which meant the Scottish economy was not quite ready for it. In fact, no more similar ironworks would be set up for a quarter of a century. The second appeared at Wilsontown in Lanarkshire in 1779, soon followed by four others in the same county: the Clyde, the Omoa or Cleland, the Calder and the Shotts. They followed the example of Carron as vertically integrated enterprises with their own coal-mines. Later, near the border of Ayrshire and Lanarkshire, works arose at Muirkirk and

Glenbuck, on bleak moorlands remote from urban, let alone industrial, activity but endowed with minerals such as limestone, ironstone and coal. Clackmannanshire then got the Devon ironworks and Fife the Balgonie or Markinch works. The vagaries of the market subjected them all to irregular cycles of development and stagnation. The swings from boom to bust grew less extreme and erratic as Scotland's industrial growth, urban expansion and agricultural development continued. Domestic demand then arose in great variety, making room not only for big ironworks but also for smaller operations and indeed independent craftsmen. While in this industry the supply of capital remained a problem, the inputs of labour and technology could be met without intolerable strains. And after the United Kingdom entered a long period of European peace in 1815, the strains could be eased by the exploitation of foreign markets.[56]

In this sector, as in others, the essential requirement for Scottish success lay in keeping costs down. It proved relatively easy given the nation's endowment of resources. Of special help were the many local conjunctions of the raw material and the fuel to work it, that is to say, of ironstone and coal lying close together in the ground. In 1801 the metallurgist David Mushet discovered round Coatbridge richer and cheaper fields of the blackband ironstone than those already used to some extent by the ironworks of Calder and Clyde. At first the find led to little saving, because the advantages of the raw material could not be fully exploited so long as it was still smelted from inputs of cold air into the small furnaces then common. The problem would be solved by the relatively simple expedient of using the hot blast, as patented at Wilsontown by James Neilson in 1828, which then made Scottish iron highly profitable. The hot blast and the blackband ironstone would right through the Victorian era provide respectively the technical and the geological bases for the low costs of processing in Scotland. They also meant that output remained basic. Carron made specialised finished products, but even its success in overcoming its difficulties did not encourage later Scottish manufacturers to follow the example. They preferred to produce pig, without processing the iron further.[57]

The social transformations that had followed the rise of Scottish textiles accelerated into the era of these heavy industries. Scotland made the crucial transformation from an underdeveloped to a developing industrial society. Some signs of what was coming might have been apparent before 1707, but there is little doubt that access to English markets and especially to overseas trade in the Empire did much to stimulate growth north of the border. Out of it the modern configuration of the country began to appear. In the eighteenth century the supply of water determined the location of the mills, while in the nineteenth century the use of steam-power and consequent large consumption of coal shifted industry to the coalfields and to the large towns already sited, or soon growing, beside them. New ways of life took shape as Scotland turned from an agricultural and rural into an industrial and urban nation, at least in the Lowlands. Industry's intrusions into the hinterland proved both transient and in many cases regrettable. This was and remains a stunningly beautiful country, yet there are scars on its face of deep and irreversible environmental degradation. In 1707 it had needed some kind of economic revolution to rise from backwardness and failure, a revolution necessarily to be based on investments for which at that point it just had no money. Only in the nineteenth century did it finally overcome these problems to become not only an industrial nation but also a leading one: a lapse of time that makes it quite hard to maintain all this was a direct result of the Union.

3

Trade: 'To supply all their want'

On 4 November 1719, the principal Jacobite agent in Scotland, George Lockhart of Carnwath, received a foreign guest in the home he maintained near Edinburgh, at Dryden by Loanhead in Midlothian. The young visitor was a Swede, Henric Kalmeter, doubtless especially welcome because the Swedish government remained a supporter of the apparently lost cause of the Old Pretender, King James VIII of Scotland by his followers' reckoning. The reason lay in that government's hostility to the Elector of Hanover, also known as King George I of Great Britain, with whom it was embroiled in various German territorial disputes. Since the failure of the Jacobites in the rebellion of 1715, Sweden had continued to help them despite the outrage and threats of war this policy provoked in London.

Still, the business on hand at Dryden was economic rather than political, though it did not lack for a whiff of skulduggery. Kalmeter was an industrial spy on a mission to find out for his government what major developments, especially metallurgical ones, had taken place in other countries. Sweden supplied most of Europe's iron and wanted to keep things that way, so needed to know the secrets of potential rivals. The youthful spook was an employee of the Bergkollegium in Stockholm, the public authority that ran the mining industry, and he wrote up a record of his investigations – sometimes in Swedish but also, presumably for practice, sometimes in English.[1]

Lockhart had a reputation as a genial host, and readily responded to the young man's request to view 'the engine he has had installed in his coal works . . . to draw up water by using the smoke of warmed water, or more correctly, by making a vacuum'. This would have been an early model of the Newcomen engine, only invented by Thomas Newcomen in 1712, of which a mere two or three examples in Scotland are known; the reference by Kalmeter is the sole one we have to Lockhart's. It was in essence a prototype of the steam engines that would give Scotland and Britain a global lead after James Watt of Glasgow found how to simplify them and render them economically viable. By contrast, the Newcomen engine was so inefficient in its consumption of fuel that it could really only be used in or near mines, where the supply and cost of coal were no problem. At Dryden, in the middle of Midlothian's coal-field, Lockhart found himself in that happy position. Whatever else might be said of Jacobites, they were not trapped in the commercial thinking of the past.[2] On the contrary, Lockhart belonged to a progressive elite in his county already exploiting the natural resources to make itself one of the wealthiest groups in Scotland. The Dukes of Buccleuch, the Marquesses of Lothian, the Earls of Rosebery, the Dundases of Arniston, the Wauchopes of Niddrie and the Hopes of Craighall would use the fortunes they earned from the pits to project themselves into British prominence too.[3]

The young Swede's cover for his espionage was a visit to his uncle in Edinburgh, a teacher of the violin long resident there. Kalmeter came over to spend two years with him, blending into the background while he carried out his duties. The city did not appear to him at all prosperous, and he soon came to the conclusion that the Union of 1707 was to blame: 'This decreasing of trade hath made that there is a vast number of poor people whose *gagnepain* is nothing but to sell ale and other liquors, whereof an incredible deal is drunk, the toun being filled with all sorts of tradesmen whose multitude is hinder-some to themselves.'[4] From Edinburgh he travelled the Lowlands in quest of industrial intelligence. He figured out, for example, that

> the best coal is found in the province of Fife around Wemyss and the harbour they call the Methil, which as it lies close to the sea, enables them not only to transport the coals with little expense to the saltworks and there to make use of the smallest (which could not be sold in the country), but also to ship out a good deal to Holland, for which purpose the Dutch doggers put in here in large numbers. This coal is also reckoned to be as good as the English, if not better, since it is not so heavily impregnated with sulphur and therefore not thought so harmful to the chest.[5]

Along his way Kalmeter noted how many progressive landowners were plant-ing trees, and wondered 'whether this planting might not be so improved that in time they will not only be able to provide some supply of fuel, but also of the timber and boards which they now obtain mainly from Sweden and Norway', especially as 'in many places there are enough barren marches and hills which could be utilised in this way'. He anticipated the Forestry Commission by two centuries. Still, on thinking things over, he decided Swedes need not lose any sleep: 'It would be another matter to plant enough to supply all their want of fuel and materials, particularly as the old woods will very soon be felled, and when they have been destroyed the young wood will not be fully grown, since this generally takes a long time here and the trees will be thirty or more years before they come even to a very ordinary size.'[6]

Kalmeter also dropped in on Sir John Erskine at Alva, who as a Jacobite rebel had gained a brief acquaintance with Sweden when he sought help there during his European misadventure. The visitor for his part had taken the trouble to find out about the estate. He wanted to hear from Sir John on the subject of 'that silvermine which recently caused so great a stir in Scotland on account of its richness'. He later wrote how, since the crown possessed rights in such mines, the Erskines 'found it expedient to work so quietly that no-one heard anything in particular about it and they smelted the best of the ore as well as they could at home in the house, in great pots or crucibles with lead, also refining it: this I heard from an Edinburgh goldsmith who said he had witnessed one such smelting when they obtained 600 or 700 ounces of silver'.[7]

On the strength of the discoveries at Alva, further prospecting for precious metals still went on round the country. But, Kalmeter thought, 'though these new attempts prove there must be metals hidden in certain places, little can be expected from them, considering the ignorance of the people in such matters, the scarcity of money in Scotland, and of fortune among people who wish to be enterprising in this way, as well as the small encouragement that the English government gives for improving Scotland'. By and large there was, then, little for Swedes to worry about: 'Seeing that the trade with Sweden and the Baltic has now become more secure and free, and that in England copper works are coming more and more into operation, they must find it too inconvenient to develop such works in Scotland, especially as consumption within the country is nothing, and manufactories are unknown.'[8]

Kalmeter finished his report by writing out a summary of what Scotland exported to Sweden: fish and salt, corn or malt, 'some coarse Musselburgh and other stuffs' and 'tobacco sometimes from Glasgow but not in any quantity'. In addition, 'some Scottish linen is also regularly smuggled in, it is forbidden to export wool from Scotland, but some nevertheless goes to Sweden, generally in peacetime through Norway'. Coming from Sweden to Scotland was a narrower though on the whole more advanced range of exports: iron, copper sheet, brass wire, tar and pitch, wooden boards.[9]

Before long there was another report on Scotland. Daniel Defoe, an Englishman who, as a spy for his government in Edinburgh, had played a small part in the successful conclusion of the Union, also wrote about the new order of things when he came back two decades later to see how the treaty had worked out. He was a propagandist by profession, yet his picture proved to be something less than rosy: it was 'to me the wonder of all the towns of North Britain, especially being so near England, that it has all the invitations to trade that nature can give them, but they take no notice of it'. At least the Glaswegians were an exception: 'the Union has answered its end to them more than to any other part of Scotland, for their trade is new formed by it.' And, in one of his liveliest scenes, Defoe depicted the market in the West Bow of Edinburgh, a street on which the city's merchants, who held the privilege for all its imports and exports, set out their wares for sale. This market 'is generally full of wholesale traders and those very considerable dealers in iron, pitch, tar, oil, hemp, flax, linseed, painters colours, dyes, drugs and woods and such like heavy goods, and supplied country shopkeepers, as our wholesale dealers in England do: and here I may say, is a visible face of trade, most of them have also warehouses in Leith, where they lay up the heavier goods, as they have occasion'.[10]

Though Defoe evidently liked what he saw in the West Bow, he was in fact putting his finger on one of the big problems of Scottish trade, the statutory monopoly over it of the merchants' incorporations in the royal burghs. To take the example of Edinburgh, the urban economy had here remained organised in basically the same way ever since the city received its charter from David I, King of Scots, 600 years before, and to this the Union made no difference at all. It was the incorporated merchants, and only they, that could legally sell imported goods in the West Bow, or anywhere else in the city, or at its port of Leith, where they landed and warehoused cargoes till ready to bring them up into town. As for the goods that Edinburgh itself manufactured, they had officially to be the productions of the chartered trades, of which 14 existed ranging from bakers to wrights. Entry either to the merchants' or to the tradesmen's ranks was strictly regulated: an aspirant needed to begin his career as an apprentice and learn his skills at the feet of an experienced and qualified burgess. The incorporations stood constantly on guard against breaches of their monopolies and spent a great deal of energy and time on suppressing any they discovered. The volumes of the proceedings of the Convention of Royal Burghs, and of the various town councils, underline the conservatism of their members: complaints of poverty go on and on, but the answer is always the preservation or restoration of privilege.[11]

Yet the monopolists were nowadays more often failing to get their way. The merchant class had never been a popular one. The Scottish nobility often regarded it with contempt and, though this was an order of men who by tradition took pride first and foremost in their martial accomplishments, they were starting to show an interest in economic matters too; they had no other way, inside the United Kingdom, to stop themselves slipping into insignificance. Some landowners encouraged trade at a local level by erecting burghs of barony, with the right to hold markets. This activity could put them at odds with the 66 royal burghs, supposedly independent under their own charters from the crown. But many were inconsiderable places, and some – New Galloway in Kirkcudbrightshire or Kilrenny in Fife – barely counted as urban. In fact, their councils often stood in awe of the local landed proprietors, who might in practice control them in economic and political terms. The merchants and tradesmen of the burghs had also, at the other end of the social scale, to worry about the 'unfree' townspeople, ordinary folk not skilled or rich enough to belong to an incorporation. They needed to make their living as best they could, perhaps just hewing wood and drawing water, though many also sought to better themselves. This might lead them towards a trade and into trouble with the sentinels of monopoly. Scotland did not, then, enjoy a system of free enterprise. And its economic elites often stood accused, with justice, of a stodgy caution that hampered the whole nation's progress.[12]

Small wonder Kalmeter and Defoe could conclude there had been since 1707 no decisive change for the better, in fact little change of any kind, and, if there had been a change, then perhaps one for the worse. In consequence the big problem for Scotland remained two decades later the same as before 1707. Consumption was bound to remain meagre and stagnant in such a small, poor and fragmented economy. The only way to raise output at home lay in winning more foreign markets. Unless output was encouraged by sales abroad, there could be little chance of capital accumulation. Unless capital could be accumulated, there was no hope of emulating England or Holland in any other respect. Before 1707, foreign trade offered the sole improving prospect for this otherwise sclerotic economy.[13]

Scotland imported certain necessities and some luxuries too.[14] To pay for these it needed foreign markets for its own produce, yet there was little sign of any expansion of trade into new fields beyond the traditional types of traffic. True, the backwardness might have been as much due to restrictions at home and abroad as to any inborn failure of the Scots to respond to their opportunities. On the foundation of Port Glasgow in 1668, at the behest of the fathers of the city it was named after, the purpose had been to provide for ocean-going ships to come into the River Clyde and unload their goods here, ready to be carried further up by barges. The reason for the initiative was that so many ships had started arriving from America. There was no objective reason for that traffic to dry up in the following decades; but, since it did, English prohibition rather than Scottish lethargy seems the more likely culprit. In the same period, after all, Scotland mounted the stupendous national effort of founding its own American colony at Darien in 1699–1702. The real reason for its catastrophic failure was perhaps not desperate incompetence so much as excessive ambition: the hope of, in one fell swoop, setting up a global emporium where all goods could be exchanged among all nations. It had turned out a disaster just the same, but then so did many other optimistic European expeditions in the early imperialist era.[15] After Darien, in any event, Scotland was back to depressing normality. The only long-term improvement in sight had come through the better relationship, lukewarm and unreliable as it remained, with England since the Union of Crowns in 1603. By 1707 there had been no open warfare between the two neighbour nations for half a century, and this allowed the trade in cattle, for example, to flourish.

Yet older markets in Europe retained some importance as well. The trade between Scotland and Holland had been going on since the Middle Ages. Dutch ships came to Scotland and Scots enjoyed the privilege of a trading staple at Veere in Zeeland, where they could freely unload and display their goods. Even so, this medieval arrangement was now largely overtaken because Scottish merchants preferred to do business in the much bigger port of Rotterdam, where by 1643 there had been enough of them to found a Presbyterian kirk. Before the Union the English looked askance at such cosiness among Calvinists. Sir Josiah Child, director of the East India Company, complained that 'the trades of Scotland and Ireland, two of our own kingdoms [!], the Dutch have bereaved us of, and in effect wholly engrossed to themselves.' The Scots sold raw materials to the Dutch, especially coal, and got back manufactures of all kinds. Scottish merchants also hired Dutch ships. The agreement between the two nations over Veere was renewed in 1697, but it became supererogatory after the Union because the English Navigation Acts, imposing governmental control of trade, now applied to Scotland. Basic Scottish commodities such as wool and hides could, in this mercantilist system, no longer be freely sent abroad. As a result, trade between Scotland and Holland languished, even though the Scots were clearly useful trading partners to a country that had, for example, no coal-mines of its own.[16] Altogether the Union represented a big adjustment in the zones of commercial influence round the North Sea – and to the disadvantage of the Dutch in their inveterate rivalry with the English.[17] It was England that had won the battle of minds, if not of hearts.

The Auld Alliance between Scotland and France was politically dead and economically in decline too, though remnants of former Scots trading privileges survived. The traffic was the usual one of raw materials in exchange for luxuries, and something the Union failed to do was quench the Scots' taste for French wine. Barrels of claret from Bordeaux were still landed on the Wine Quay at Leith and rolled up the streets to the merchants' cellars behind the waterfront. As a rule only the elite of Scottish society could afford this tipple but all classes might partake of it on special occasions, such as Hogmanay. It was also a tradition that at times of national festivity – admittedly rare of late – the wellheads in the High Street of Edinburgh should run with wine rather than with water. After the Union, claret attracted official British disapproval. The government in London structured its customs duties so as to favour port from England's oldest ally, Portugal. To avoid these restrictions a lot of the claret was smuggled into Scotland.[18]

Further trades went on between Scotland and all the northern European nations. To Germany and Scandinavia, to Poland and the Baltic provinces, Scots sent coal, salt, hides and fish in exchange for timber, grain, flax and iron. There were also exports of cheap and cheerful consumer goods hawked through these countries by Scottish pedlars. Finally Scotland had the Irish market, of somewhat uncertain value. It, too, took coal and cheap manufactures, but its returning foodstuffs seemed a threat to Scots farmers. Its live cattle suffered a ban from the 1660s, its beef in 1703 and its butter in 1705.[19]

Even the few exceptions, the victuals admitted for the provisioning of ships and for re-export, brought petitions from Scots landowners in 1712 against 'the common calamity arising from that universal evil'.[20]

Altogether, none of these foreign markets was undergoing much change or development: Scotland traded in them what it had always traded in them. And the aim of British official policy after 1707 lay in limiting such traffic by direct prohibition and by heavy duties. The regulations were enforced at a local level through HM Customs, bringing the imperious presence of the United Kingdom into even quite small harbours that had scarcely known of a Scottish state while it still existed. The commercial system controlled from Westminster stretched from the home nations to the Americas and the Orient. It was meant to be so far as possible self-contained, and geared above all to enriching itself: a zero-sum game indeed. According to modern conceptions the prospectus sounds bizarre and some details were just crazy, such as the simultaneous exclusion of Ireland and inclusion of Scotland.[21]

Anyway, the Scots shifting onto the inside of this system in 1707 still faced the same question as they had faced from the outside: what new trades they might be able to build up. Progress was far from assured. Scotland could have conceivably faced the opposite possibility of descending into utter economic dependence on its bigger neighbour – this was just what would happen to Ireland when, after 1780, it was finally admitted to the system too. To avoid such a fate, Scots had to exploit their new opportunities while reducing the risks to their old British and European trades. In the event, they both expanded traditional exports such as cattle or linen and successfully entered the promising colonial commerce in tobacco or other exotic goods. Yet this second part of the strategy was never straightforward. The English Navigation Acts primarily imposed restriction and prohibition, and they offered few jackpots in return. Scots all the same found theirs.[22]

New commerce emerged above all for the west of Scotland: within half a century it was clearly outperforming the east. The Scottish economy can at this stage conveniently be considered in these two halves. There was not, as a matter of fact, much communication between them, as passable roads across country barely existed and navigation round the bleak, stormy northern shores was perilous; the opening of the Forth–Clyde Canal did not come till

1790. The consequences of this primitive division were not all bad. Because of the problem of transport, the west could hardly compete with the east in producing anything but the most expensive linens, reliant as these were on European raw material and markets – which would in part explain the later readiness of western merchants and manufacturers to switch to cotton for trade and production. Similarly, the difficulty and expense of transporting Baltic iron into this region might well have stimulated the search for ways to use local ore.[23] The merchants of the west did finally break through to the east once the profits to be earned there made it worth their while – when, in the midst of war, the Emperor Napoleon in 1807 imposed the Continental System, a blockade round Europe against British exports. The higher profits therefore came with higher risk: but Glasgow by now had the men, the goods and the money too. A leading merchant house, James Finlay & Co., set up a depot on the island of Heligoland in the North Sea, which was held by the Royal Navy. From there cargoes could be run into Hamburg or smaller ports along the River Elbe, all supposedly under Napoleon's military occupation. Disaffected officers of the German customs just let everything through, and any enemy soldiers snooping about could be bribed. Local middlemen then often flogged Scottish textiles on to French commissaries who bought them to be turned into uniforms for *La Grande Armée*.[24]

That Glasgow had come so far in a century of the Union was extraordinary. Straight after 1707 it could scarcely have been suspected. At that point the local merchants, with few domestic products to offer on global markets, were not yet rich enough to pay for more imports to be consumed in their own region. What they could do, with far greater security than before, was act as dealers in colonial wares, buying them in and selling them on to final customers resident outside the British mercantilist system. Because the system required everything grown in the colonies to be landed in the United Kingdom before being sent anywhere else, Scotland, and Glasgow in particular, could find a niche in it as a 'warehouse economy', to employ the useful term recently coined.[25] Regardless of the ultimate wisdom of the policy, which would become the subject of relentless attacks by Glasgow's own professor, Adam Smith, it could at least free the city's merchants from the local limitations of their business and allow them to start accumulating capital.

The first problem those merchants faced was how to muscle in on traffic necessary to sustain a warehouse economy. Scottish trading voyages had crossed the Atlantic Ocean as early as the 1630s, and later an illegal commerce went on with the English colonies. Here lay a thread that could be picked up again.[26] Some preliminary investment was necessary. Glasgow built a quay at the Broomielaw, and carried out improvements at Port Glasgow. Then there was the expense of acquiring ocean-going ships, a risky investment if the volume of trade should fall short of its potential. But Defoe was already on record saying: 'As the Union opened the door to the Scots into our American colonies, the Glasgow merchants presently embraced the opportunity . . . for they now send near fifty sail of ships every year to Virginia, and other English colonies in America.'[27]

The only competition the mercantilist system allowed was among British ports, as to which could win the lion's share of the colonial goods to be landed. It was in competition with Bristol, London and others that Glasgow came out on top, not least because it enjoyed some natural advantages. It lay nearer to America on the Great Circle than any other part of Western Europe. Its ships could cross, through northerly seas seldom plagued by privateers, two or three weeks faster than any from the English Channel, adding up to a gain of a month or six weeks on a round trip – possibly enough to allow two trips in a good season rather than just one. The benefits further multiplied in quicker commercial information, lower oncosts for transport, freight and insurance, economies of scale and the chance to minimise or spread the risks of a traffic that remained to some extent speculative.[28] Glaswegians still had to pay duties on the imports, though their actual price fell as more and more ground in the American colonies was brought under cultivation. At the same time, the great increase in oceanic traffic cut the real cost of shipping too. And then when the merchants re-exported to European destinations, they could draw back the duty they had paid. The final price to them of their commodities was therefore low, yet capable of yielding fat profits.[29]

But this was far from the whole story. While the legal trade has been well covered in Scotland's dominant socio-economic historiography, the standard works cannot be fully accurate just because they rely so heavily on public records, that is, on statistics derived from the efforts of the always harassed, persistently overworked and often ineffectual customs. In fact, these statistics are doomed to inaccuracy since they can take no account of smuggling, which was huge. The old Scottish customs had been notoriously inefficient even before the Union; after the Union, it became a national sport to evade the new British customs.[30]

We glimpse reasons for this in the case of wool, for example, in its raw state always a valuable export from Scotland. After the Restoration of 1660, there were efforts to initiate the manufacture of fine woollen goods too. The state subsidised factories and paid foreign craftsmen to come over and show the natives how to make products of higher quality. Competitive conditions remained difficult, however, and it did not take long for the companies to start lobbying in favour of bans on the export of wool and the import of cloth. The idea was to deny raw material to foreign rivals while preserving the Scottish market for its own output. The landowners successfully resisted the attempt to interfere with their foreign sales, but the manufacturers won no more than exemption from duties on their exports. The net result was a secure domestic market for coarse woollens, before 1707 and afterwards. Otherwise, the Union upset the previous equilibrium among the interested parties. England imposed a stricter system of regulation because woollens had been its main source of foreign earnings since the Middle Ages. This system was the one to prevail now in the United Kingdom. The export of wool came under total prohibition. And since England produced cheaper and better products in fine wool than Scotland, Scottish manufacturers of them were driven out of business.[31] To add insult to injury, a sharp fall in the price of Scottish wool followed. All Scots involved in the business felt incensed.

Under the mercantilist system the lost Scottish output could only be replaced by imports from England, or so the conventional thinking said. Yet Scots had not yet completely severed their older trading links and, when they knew that cheaper goods were to be had, smuggling might well pay off. Paper offers an innocuous example – it was made on only a small scale in Scotland, where seven factories existed in comparison to more than 200 in England. Before 1707 Scots bought any extra supplies they needed from overseas, but now this traffic was officially banned. In fact, the new board of customs in Edinburgh fumed that quantities of French paper were still being smuggled into Scotland from Holland despite the state of war between Britain and France.[32]

The protectionism of the United Kingdom did not therefore immediately cut across the older trading links, for all the wheedling collaborators that it had among the merchants of Edinburgh:

Whereas the scandalous and destructive practise of running goods particularly brandy and tea and several other foreign commoditys, by the retail whereof freemen burgesses who keep shops chiefly subsist, withdraws those who deal in it from applying themselves as becomes to the improvement of trade and manufacturers in which their industry might be of service to the publick as also that a considerable share of the foreign trade is thereby ingrossed by unfree traders, and the retail of merchant ware, in stead of being carried on by freemen burgesses in their shops subject to the review and controul of the magistrates cloath'd with authority as to their sufficiency and true value, is in a great measure fallen into the hands of mein persons of no reputation who clandistinely convey the same to private houses and impose on the buyers by exacting rate for insufficient wares.[33]

Yet generally the line always remained thin in this era between legal and illegal seafaring, between normal business and smuggling or even buccaneering. A merchant (at least, anywhere other than in Edinburgh) might live off legal commerce if and when he could, but turn without qualms to illegality when he could not. Duncan Forbes of Culloden, Lord Advocate from 1725 to 1737, feared his countrymen saw the Union simply as a licence for this illicit traffic: 'In place of pursuing fair trade, they universally, with the exception of Glasgow, Aberdeen and one or two places more, took to smuggling; their small stocks they invested in goods that bore high duties, and, under the favour of running those securely on our wide and ill-guarded coasts, they flattered themselves they should soon grow rich, profiting at least of the high duty, which by running they were to save.'[34] He would have known all about this himself, being a regular consumer of the smuggled goods purveyed by a merchant handy for Culloden, the otherwise eminently respectable Bailie John Steuart of Inverness.[35]

Adam Smith took a look at the problem in *The Wealth of Nations* (1776) and found nothing much to get upset about – though this was before he became a commissioner of customs himself. His colleagues often wondered about the efficiency of their officers out in the sticks, yet it should have been plain enough that complex regulation produced quite as much dishonesty and disaffection among the lieges as revenue and respect for the government. To Smith, smuggling remained so common as to signal something deeper at work than mere individual delinquency. On the contrary, he could even see in it the beneficent operation of his invisible, here nominally criminal, hand.

When the smuggler exercised his individual freedom to supply others with what they wanted in defiance of unnatural restrictions, Scottish theories of moral sentiment might surreptitiously approve.[36]

Smuggling also served to vent political frustration. Bans imposed by the English Navigation Acts were bad enough, though they just prompted traders to hide forbidden goods inside bundles of flax or consignments of scrap iron. Far worse was the structure of bonds, rebates and incentives intended overall to impose differential levels of taxation on domestic and foreign trade, which in practice caused a vast diversion of commercial energy into creative and intricate frauds. For example, a drawback refunded the duty paid on the import of a commodity when it was later re-exported. Foreign salt used to cure fish sent for export offered a good example. Scotland made salt from the evaporation of seawater, but not of high enough quality for the curing of fish; in that business, foreign salt had to be imported and the curer received a drawback when he exported his finished product. This foreign salt was a valuable commodity, then, stored in bonded warehouses from which it could only be released against security for the payment of duty within six months. Scotland's sturdy fishing communities greatly objected to such jiggery-pokery. They might send off their cargoes of salted fish to qualify for the drawback, but then the ships would sail about and land their loads at some quiet cove up the coast ready to be sold at bargain prices and higher profits. Everybody knew what went on yet the means to prevent it were simply lacking. Indeed the sheer elaboration of the law invited the fraud.[37]

If the customs did appeal to the majesty of the British state, with recourse to law or in the last resort to armed force, it was likely to cause more trouble than it could ever be worth. It goaded rather than cowed offenders at a local level. The proof lay in the riots against the customs endemic in Lowland Scotland all through the first half of the eighteenth century. They showed not just a criminal but often also a patriotic dimension, indulged by the Scots gentry (not all of them Jacobites) manning the local apparatus of the British state. These just looked on as that state lost revenue, while its hired servants suffered insult and injury from mobs with stones, clubs, staves, pitchforks, even firearms. The mobs were most active along the south-western and the north-eastern coasts, in areas where the strongest opposition to the Union had seethed before 1707.[38]

At their height these mobs could only be deterred by a military presence, though fortunately the soldiers seldom opened fire. At Perth in 1722, when the units usually stationed in the town were withdrawn for the general election of that year, the officers of the customs felt scared enough to plead that 'we will certainly be mobbed, and our warehouse broke open'. In the same year in Dumfriesshire, a seizure by the customs of a shipment of brandy had 'raised the whole country about . . . who came with stones, clubs and firearms and violently deforced' its officers.[39] At Montrose in 1728, after the customs captured big consignments of brandy not just once but twice, the locals took revenge. Early one morning a mob armed with clubs and other weapons beat senseless the two soldiers guarding the king's warehouse, broke it open and liberated the contents. The collector went to the provost to request a warrant for a general search of the town, which was refused. In his capacity as a justice of the peace he issued a warrant to his own officers to look for the missing goods. The provost then sent people to obstruct the search, soon aided by another large and violent mob. The collector told his superiors in Edinburgh that, faced with the hostility of everybody in Montrose, there was little he could do. Perhaps in the end it would just be better to let them get on with it. In 1734, 'the back wall of one of the king's warehouses was cut through and 60 ankers of brandy seized by the excise officers and lodged there carried off, and though the guard were lodged under the custom-house stair and a sentry walking betwixt the two doors, yet they pretend to have heard no noise nor know nothing of it'.[40]

Smugglers found exotic new commodities arriving in Europe from distant continents especially attractive, what with duties on them high and consumption of them booming. Typical was tea.[41] It came from China and, as several European nations had by now engaged in oriental trade, there was no shortage of smuggling routes into Scotland. The smugglers often brought their cargoes to the Isle of Man and ran them in overnight to the tranquil estuaries of Dumfriesshire and Galloway, whence they were openly delivered inland. The Lords of Man were the Dukes of Atholl, and they did not mind a bit. By threatening to use their taint of Jacobitism against them, the British government forced them to give up the lordship in 1765. It then suppressed the illicit traffic.

One route to the Isle of Man had come by way of the Austrian Netherlands, what is now Belgium, a territory enjoying its new economic freedom after the lifting of two centuries of oppressive Spanish rule in 1713. A sign of that came in the prompt organisation of trade to India from Ostend. The first voyage set out in 1720 with an exiled Jacobite, Alexander Hume, as supercargo, that is, representative of the ship's owners, who established a factory at Bankibazar by the River Hooghly in Bengal. On the advice of another Scot, John Crawford, a shady character doubling as a British spy, the Emperor Charles VI established the Ostend Company in 1723, having founded an East India Company for Austria itself in 1719. But the Ostend Company was a bit too strategically placed for business, licit and illicit, round the North Sea. The monopolist East India Companies of England and Holland viewed it with deep suspicion and by 1731 their governments persuaded their ally the emperor that for the sake of continuing good relations it had better be wound up.[42]

Nothing daunted, the smuggling Jacobites moved on from Ostend to a warmer welcome at Gothenburg in Sweden. In 1731 they joined in founding a Swedish East India Company with the same illicit purposes. It prospered so much that at its peak in the 1770s it was illegally importing into Scotland every year over a million pounds in weight of tea. Colin Campbell had served as supercargo on the first ship the company sent to Canton in China. In fact, a majority of those involved were Scots, led by a wealthy merchant, William Chambers.[43] His son, also William, voyaged to China as a teenage trader to finance his real ambition, a grand tour of the monuments of Italy and France. He returned in 1748, went on his grand tour and made his way back to Britain where he became the greatest architect of his generation, building mainly in London but also in Scotland: the Dundas House in St Andrew's Square, Edinburgh, Duddingston House to the east of the city and then the Dunmore Pineapple in Stirlingshire. Just as Chambers left China, fresh recruits to the Scots fraternity were arriving there, hotfoot from the Battle of Culloden. From one Jacobite family in Dumfriesshire, the Herries of Halldykes, William fled to Ostend while his brother Charles, who had kept himself clean, got to London and opened a business that struck subversive deals under the noses of the Hanoverian authorities. The pair did well enough out of smuggling from the Orient to buy the family's passage back to political respectability in the next generation. During the 1760s, William and George Keith Elphinstone travelled to Canton with capital from their great-uncle, the Earl Marischal, exiled in Prussia since 1745.[44]

If at home there were already Scots who might die for a cup of tea, probably more were gasping for tobacco. This demand, too, was satisfied both legally and illegally. Some tobacco was smuggled into Scotland as tea was smuggled, just to avoid the duty, again often through the Isle of Man into the hidden havens of the Solway Firth. A case occurred at Ruthwell in Dumfriesshire in 1777, at a time when the American Revolution had disrupted normal traffic. A tide-waiter, the lowest form of life in the customs, found tracks leading from the shore to the house of a notorious smuggler. He went to fetch a sheriff officer and they returned to discover inside the house a big stash of tobacco. At that moment a crowd of women appeared, armed with clubs and pitchforks, to seize the contraband and carry it off. Some were later arrested and tried, but the crown could not persuade enough witnesses to give evidence against them. Simple smuggling of this sort flourished to such an extent that at Dumfries, which also had a legal trade in tobacco, the merchants conducting it were driven out of business. From here there was also an illicit traffic to Ireland, where at that point tobacco could still not be legally landed from America.[45]

Of course, since the Union a legal traffic in tobacco, now allowed under the English Navigation Acts, had been going on more generally from Virginia to Scotland, most often to Glasgow. Virginia was the original English colony in the New World, and its population remained overwhelmingly English in character. The Scots, arriving later, had to fit in where they could, often as factors on the estates or traders on the rivers. It was easier for them to find a niche in the back country, as this got opened up, than in the established settlements of the Tidewater region. In any event, a great many Scots regarded themselves as temporary residents meaning to go home again once they had made their pile from trade.[46]

However transient, the links with Virginia would transform the economy of Glasgow and its region. This traffic, too, resorted on occasion to illegality. With judicious bribes the shippers would arrange for cargoes to be under-weighed on arrival, while complaisant tide-waiters in charge of the scales turned away and gazed out on the quiet waters of the Firth of Clyde. Later the cargoes would be over-weighed when shipped off to Europe, as the time came to apply for the drawback. Or else, the shippers might claim part of their cargoes had been ruined by penetration of seawater into the hold on the long voyage across the Atlantic Ocean. After a while they would still demand a drawback for re-export of the supposedly damaged cargo. Illegal tobacco was hopelessly mixed up with legal tobacco, to an extent impossible to investigate or ascertain. There is one estimate that, for a couple of decades after the Union, at least half of the tobacco was smuggled inwards.[47] It was smuggled onwards too: duty also got charged on coastwise transport of tobacco from Scotland to England, yet only a fraction of it seems ever to have been paid.

Tired of the mess, the British government abolished the Scottish board of customs in 1723, after its 16 years of failure, and instead set up in Edinburgh a sub-committee of the central board in London. For good measure it fired all the Scottish officers and replaced them with Englishmen.[48] A period of lower prices and stricter surveillance apparently eliminated several weaker trading firms in Glasgow, but in the longer term the essential process of capital accumulation continued.[49]

The initial stages even of the legal trade to Glasgow are obscure because of a loss of records, but by chance one full account of a voyage in 1729 has survived and shows a rate of return of 33 per cent.[50] The earliest available port books, for 1743–44, reveal the traffic in full swing. Legal imports of tobacco that year reached 8 million pounds in weight, 40 times more than in the 1680s. Doubtless this period was when Glaswegians acquired their addiction to the deadly weed, which they have never lost and which today helps to make them the unhealthiest population in Western Europe. But the tobacco imported into the Clyde was not intended primarily for their consumption. As a matter of fact 90 per cent of what did get recorded went on to the far bigger markets on the Continent. A surge of demand from France allowed huge deals to be clinched for delivery in bulk to its royal monopoly in tobacco. In 1743–44, Glasgow sent 25 ships with tobacco to French ports, almost two-thirds of the re-exports, while another quarter of them went to Holland and the rest mainly to Germany and Italy. By 1771 legal imports of tobacco had shot up to 47 million pounds, at which point they represented more than half of total Scottish imports and of total British traffic in tobacco. The men running this trade, the tobacco lords, were the richest men not only in Glasgow but in the whole of Scotland too, the first ever to have made fortunes from international commerce. The decades of its prodigious expansion only came to an end in the American War of Independence. The security afforded by the Union had made Scotland the biggest trader in tobacco in Europe – and at England's expense. To that extent, the Scots continued to play their own game after 1707, even while supposedly subject to a British trading regime.[51]

None of this might have been, beyond a few jobs in warehousing and shipping, of any wider benefit to most Glaswegians. To reap one, they had in the first instance to respond to the need for goods in the cargoes returning to Virginia in exchange for the tobacco. Apart from all else, the mercantilist system forbade the colonists to manufacture anything for themselves. In 1742–43 33 ships from the Clyde carried back a wide range of quite simple items that Americans lacked: clothes and cloth, shoes and saddles, glass and furniture, candles, canvas and rope, ironmongery, sickles and spades. Here was an obvious stimulus to industrial development in Scotland, which could be met through local investment by the mercantile elite.[52] It is true that the imports of tobacco and other goods from the Americas far exceeded in value the domestic exports of manufactures, but earnings from the re-exports covered the deficit. John Gibson, an early historian of the city, still lamented that in his time, the 1770s, 'manufactures, the only certain means of diffusing wealth over a whole people, were almost unknown; and commerce which, without manufactures, tends to the enriching of only a few, was carried on to a very trifling extent'.[53] He was being too pessimistic, however. What Glasgow now had was a capital surplus to deploy, which it did in fact deploy in industrial investment on a scale never seen before.[54]

The American Revolution should have been a catastrophe, seeing how these arrangements suited everybody somehow or other. Trade in tobacco, having just reached a peak, was totally disrupted. Imports collapsed from 46 million pounds in 1775 to 300,000 pounds in 1777. The effects bit deeply into all Glasgow's commercial and financial services, and some merchants went to the wall. But war did offer its own opportunities for speculative gain. New markets and investments were found. The Scots returned to America after 1783 and to an extent took up where they had left off, if under a different commercial regime: imports of tobacco rose back to about 10 million pounds by 1790. From Glasgow three years later a retired tobacco lord, Robert Donald, wrote the sort of letter he might have written to any Scottish politician but addressed it to an old acquaintance from Virginia by the name of George Washington, 'to solicit your notices of the bearer . . . my nephew, who I believe intends removing to your city of Washington, where under your patronage I flatter myself he may push his way in your rising states'.[55]

The readiness to welcome the Scots back suggests the Americans had found selling them tobacco just as beneficial too. Still, unprotected now from foreign competition and dogged by outstanding debts, the trade never attained its old vigour. Here, as in other spheres, Scots and Americans were going their separate ways. Some rancour remained, not only over the recent past. A political commentator, John Knox, observed: 'Thus vanished, after a short possession, all the exclusive commercial privileges relative to that country [America], for which the Scots had annihilated their Parliament and their African and Indian Company [at Darien], and subjected themselves to excises, taxes, duties and commercial restrictions unknown before the year 1707.'[56]

The tobacco lords had all the same exploited this window of opportunity with outstanding success. A close-knit group, often intermarried, they kept the business in their own hands by pooling resources in formal partnerships. Retained profits allowed steady growth, even across generations: much of the necessary capital accumulation came in inheritance, and half the traders in tobacco were sons of traders in tobacco. They merited the epithet of lords when they bought landed estates round their city and set themselves up in the sort of social status that contemporary society most respected. Their quest for it might seem to have been the reverse of dynamic and to have confirmed the existing order of things. But infusion of new blood among old lairds released land locked up in entail and other feudal archaisms. The incomers were too canny to overlook the potential earnings from investment in an estate, especially if it had natural resources that could go into the manufacture of outward cargoes. In countless individual ways they improved their region's productive capacity, though to be sure as just one element in a complex of forces.[57] Glaswegians had invented a kind of commercial behaviour unique in the world yet well suited to their own circumstances. It was a short cut to prosperity for an economy with otherwise not much going for it. Gibson wrote: 'We may from this era date the prosperity of the city of Glasgow.'[58]

The achievement was important on a national Scottish scale too. Between 1730 and 1760 the nation's trade tripled, probably matching or surpassing any rate of growth achieved during previous decades, if not centuries. True, manufacturing remained relatively weak – the domestic economy neither exported that much, nor was it heavily reliant on imports. Yet in its own small way it underwent a commercial revolution. And since its peculiar trading pattern was conditioned by the structure of the domestic economy as well by the English Navigation Acts, it represented a commercial revolution different from England's. Altogether we can say that Scots merchants had made good use of the commercial opportunities afforded by the Union.[59]

After American independence in 1783, the question was whether Scotland's trading success since the Union could continue. For other colonies the mercantilist system remained in place. The most important lay in the West Indies, trafficking above all in sugar and cotton. Down the Clyde, the sugar supplied the basis for a new industry at Greenock. More significant in the long run was the general effect on the west of Scotland's textile industries, as entrepreneurs switched from linen to the cotton that proved so well suited to large-scale mechanised production in a rainy climate. Since this transition depended entirely on the import of raw materials, it soon drew Glasgow's merchants back to the plantations of the southern United States as well. In fact, these extended connections were better for Scotland than the trade in tobacco by itself had been, and not only on grounds of health. In the next stage of development cotton and sugar closely connected mercantile with industrial enterprise, in clusters that would enrich the region for a century ahead.[60]

Scots also acquired property in the West Indies, rather unevenly spread. Absentee ownership of the plantations remained common, and it was often the attorneys, managers and overseers that actually ran the plantations. They worked hard not only to satisfy their employers but also to enrich themselves as fast as possible and get home again. So their existence was often a race against time, before tropical disease might claim them. Robert Burns briefly contemplated a move to the West Indies, but given his state of health it was lucky the Kilmarnock edition (1786) of his poems came out first and persuaded him to pursue a poet's career instead. Zachary Macaulay, son of the minister of Inveraray, emigrated in 1784 as a lad of 16 and ever afterwards rued the memory of himself 'in a field of canes, amidst perhaps a hundred of the sable race, cursing and bawling [with] the noise of the whip resounding on their shoulders'. The experience in fact sickened him and he returned to become one of Britain's leading advocates for the abolition of the slave trade.[61]

Before the Union the Scots had been innocent of the slave trade, not possessing any successful colonies in the New World. After 1707 their participation in it did not quickly take off, open though they were in principle to all imperial opportunities. One finally arose about 1750 with the collapse of the Royal African Company, based in London, which had ineffectually pretended to a British monopoly on the shipment to America of the hapless blacks. A free-for-all now followed to take over this traffic, and among the successful interlopers was a Scottish consortium under two senior partners, Sir Alexander Grant of Dalvey, one of Jamaica's landowners with 2,000 acres, 700 slaves and property of £70,000, and Richard Oswald, hailing from Caithness by way of a commercial training in Glasgow and Virginia. In 1748 they bought a disused, ruined fort on Bance Island, near the present Freetown in Sierra Leone. They restored it to working order, and added a golf course. They set it up just at the right time. With a steady rise in the consumption of sugar in Europe, the economy of plantations was being rapidly expanded in the Americas, and the demand for labour with it.[62]

The circumstances favoured innovation in the slave trade, and these Scots responded. Till now, European slavers had often culled their human wares by the direct, brutal means of raiding along the African coast and simply seizing innocent blacks. Grant, Oswald & Co. introduced a system that at least had the merit of being more commercial. Its agents stayed put at their well-defended fort, or at outposts up the rivers nearby, and waited for local chiefs to bring down slaves, often captives taken in war. These were then bartered for goods shipped from Europe, America and India. Leaving the traffic in indigenous hands, the Scots asked no questions about its methods. They contented themselves with providing middlemen's jobs for their relations or friends, and business for their clients. Though newcomers to the slave trade, they found a way of thriving without official privilege or aid against the competition of established English rivals.[63] By the 1760s, slaving voyages were setting out direct from Scotland, from Montrose and especially from Greenock, where the connection with sugar clearly counted.[64]

After 1783 Canada was the other transatlantic territory left inside the British mercantile system. It had acquired a Scottish population in 1763, right after the conquest from France, when demobbed Highland soldiers were granted lands for settlement. Joining them later came Scots refugees from the 13 rebellious colonies wishing to stay under British rule.[65] Commerce then quickened through the merchants of Glasgow, Greenock and Leith who established Canadian agencies. This was a country less developed than the United States but it had natural products, such as timber, useful for a maritime empire, and above all furs, which could be sold anywhere in the civilised world. The latter trade, in particular, was taken over by Scots. One reason Canada filled up with settlers so slowly, compared to its southern neighbour, was that these Scots wanted to keep it empty, and did not scruple to terrorise unwanted incomers. Their commerce could indeed only continue as long as the country remained empty, since tilled land yielded no furs.[66]

At the centre of these mercantile interests stood a group of related, originally Jacobite, families from the Great Glen. The instrument of their dominance was the North West Company, actually a kind of syndicate. Several existing partnerships formed it in Montreal in 1779, with an initial accord among them for one year only. This proved successful enough to be renewed annually, and from 1784 for five years at a time. Its driving force was Simon MacTavish, known as 'the Marquis'. He had arrived as a youngster in New

York, at length set up on his own at Albany and moved to Montreal as the War of American Independence loomed.[67]

The partners of the North West Company pushed ever deeper into the interior, because in order to expand it had to explore. They hoped that their efforts, which might be tied to extensions of British sovereignty, would win support and concessions from the government in London. The company's pioneer in the west was Alexander Mackenzie from Stornoway. His first journey, in 1788, followed the river that now bears his name, 12th longest in the world, to its mouth in the Arctic Sea. He covered 3,000 miles in three months, travelling up to 16 hours a day. The company at once turned his discoveries to account by establishing a chain of outposts from the Great Slave Lake down to the delta of the Mackenzie. In 1798 it already had more than 250 men working in this basin, where the Indians became dependent on trade goods. But Mackenzie aimed above all to seek a practicable commercial communication between the Atlantic and Pacific Oceans: the old dream of a short cut to the Orient. For this the river was unsuitable. So in 1793 he set off on another expedition to look for an overland route through the Rocky Mountains. It demanded great physical exertion and the skill to overcome constant perils. Mackenzie was a tower of strength, meeting every test with restraint and courage, cheering his men on when they reached the brink of exhaustion and despair, finally bringing them all safe home. Yet his journals reveal an obsessive, highly strung character given to black depressions. He did find a westward route, though one again impossible for normal traffic. Still, he had made the first crossing of America north of Mexico. His published chronicle of it immortalised him and brought him a knighthood from King George III.[68]

With men like this in its ranks, the North West Company flourished up to the renewal of war with the United States in 1812 and beyond. It had riches enough to underwrite the next year a military expedition to the furthest American outpost, John Jacob Astor's trading station of Astoria at the mouth of the Columbia River on the Pacific Ocean. This was captured by a combination of British and Canadian forces, the first under John McDonald, McGillivray's brother-in-law, the second under John George McTavish, his cousin. From Fort George, as they renamed it, they now commanded the main outlet from the interior of the continent on this western coast. They could perhaps even control the Spanish, Russian and other traffic starting to pass along it. Their hopes were kept alive by the terms of the peace in 1814, which let them lease the fort for another ten years (though in the end it would be relinquished to the obdurate Americans). This coup could be taken as the climacteric of the North West Company. It now controlled an enormous trading empire harvesting furs from the Indian tribes, through which its own agents might travel by canoe all over North America with never more than a day's portage.[69]

So much for the west; the way to the east had remained in 1707 apparently still barred to Scots. This was because the English East India Company enjoyed a monopoly on all direct trade home and till now had been actively hostile to Scottish interests, for instance over Darien. After the Union this history did not long deter the Scots. They had by the treaty won as much right as any other Briton to get on the company's payroll. That the United Kingdom should bear such tangible results was anyway a concern of the first Prime Minister of Great Britain, Sir Robert Walpole. He put a fair share of Indian appointments the Scots' way. Given their clannishness, it soon became better than a fair share. By 1750, they took up one in three of the posts in the Orient, and later perhaps more. Henry Dundas, the Scot who as President of the Board of Control from 1793 presided over the Indian administration in London, might even out of political prudence have cut the number somewhat. As in Virginia and the West Indies, these men were transients who went out because they had to but meant to return and set up independently at home. In India they could make huge fortunes, and faster than in the New World, giving rise to an entire class of *nouveaux riches*, the nabobs. John Johnstone of Westerhall brought back £300,000 that he used to buy three estates and build up a political interest in the south-west of Scotland. Even this did not compare with the acumen of John Farquhar. In his unrivalled parsimony, he contracted with his Indian servant to feed him on 2 annas a day. Worth £1.5 million at his return, he offered any Scottish university £100,000 to endow a chair of atheism, but found no taker.[70]

Such men, while employed by the East India Company, made their real money by taking part, on the side, in the so-called country trade. This was the traffic within India or between the subcontinent and third countries, none of it covered by the English Navigation Acts. By the end of the eighteenth century 14 Scottish houses (as against 10 English) had engaged in it. Some did in fact flout the law and trade illegally to Britain too. More often they happily worked with the company's Continental rivals, the chartered trading organisations of other European countries, dealing through their own compatriots at Rouen, Ostend, Gothenburg and Copenhagen. Of great value here were the old Jacobite connections. Dundas at the Board of Control, so far from discountenancing such operations, was a free trader by conviction who also whittled away from within at the privileges of the East India Company. But he had to leave the decisive step to his son Robert, who at length succeeded him at the board and became the author of the legislation that in 1813 abolished the company's monopoly on British trade with the subcontinent. Merchants in Glasgow at once set out to traffic directly with Bengal.[71]

As for China, Henry Dundas sought to enlist the country traders in a triangular traffic. Britain usually paid for imports from India with gold or more especially silver, and he wanted to displace the precious metals with exports of manufactures. The textiles that India also produced might then, instead of undercutting British production, be sent to China to pay for the tea that also cost the United Kingdom so much of its reserves of gold and silver. He would not only solve the biggest problem in the balance of payments but also turn his country into the pivot of quickening exchanges between east and west.[72]

Yet it was to be opium, the perfect export – imperishable, easily carried, in great demand – that really set the triangular trade going. By 1800 traffic in it had grown so fast that the Manchu government imposed a ban. The East India Company, for the sake of good relations, stopped its shipments. That just drove them into the hands of the private merchants, who made far more of them than the company ever had. Production and sales of opium accelerated till this became probably the largest commerce of the time in any single commodity. The flood of cheap drugs was to undermine the ancient Chinese Empire. It sapped the ethos of an industrious and obedient race. It corrupted the machinery of government. Above all, it unleashed economic forces from the West, in a ferment that would stop short only of destroying the country's independence. These forces took even more fearsome shape after the reform of the East India Company's charter in 1813. Among other things, it allowed two young Scots who arrived in China in 1819, William Jardine from Lochmaben in Dumfriesshire and James Matheson from Lairg in Sutherland, to set up their own business, Jardine Matheson. Before the end of the century it became the greatest single European enterprise in Asia.[73]

The Scots' home market remained diminutive on this global measure, so that many of them continued to seek their fortunes abroad. In an expanding network of imperial commerce, it was no huge leap for trading profits to be pursued on routes far from the mother country, on routes that indeed never touched its shores. The Scots otherwise operated at first in the interstices of the English Navigation Acts, as smugglers, as warehousemen, as marginal traders lacking the direct support of a state – more like, say, the wandering Jews or Armenians than like other European nations in the prevailing mercantilist system. In their liberated ingenuity and initiative the Scots might have carried on this way, except that their efforts did also contribute to the might of the British Empire as it was to emerge at the end of the Napoleonic Wars, by then the only colonial power of any importance. The first, lost empire in America had been mercantilist, originally with English people on one side of the Atlantic and English people on the other side exchanging goods between themselves. The second empire, now in process of formation and destined to last a further half-century, was a commercial rather than a colonising empire with economic power and trading activity much more dispersed. It would be built on profitable outposts for the exploitation of resources that remained in the hands of alien peoples, the commodities feeding industry and consumption at home on a scale never before imagined: Darien at last.

Part II

SOCIETY

4

Rank: 'This most sacred property'

The longer a Scottish funeral goes on, the more it may change from a solemn into a cheery occasion, and a case in point was one that took place at Forfar on 9 March 1728. A local laird, Patrick Carnegie of Lour, that day buried a beloved daughter. Before he left for the kirk he offered lunch to some of the other mourners who were close to him, his brother, James Carnegie of Finhaven, Charles Lyon, Earl of Strathmore, John Lyon of Brigton and several others. The amount of drink they consumed at the table left them with a thirst for more of it after they had sat dry through the service and seen the girl to her grave. They went out on a bender. Finhaven got into the worst state of all while Brigton was not quite so bad, but in him the alcohol kindled some latent streak of aggression towards this friend and neighbour. After a while they all decided to go and pay their respects to Finhaven's sister and Brigton's sister-in-law, the widowed Margaret Lyon of Auchterhouse. Her hospitality did not stop Brigton turning even more belligerent, mocking Finhaven for problems he had with family and money. In the middle of his diatribes he reached out to grab Finhaven by the throat and, when Lady Auchterhouse sought to intervene, he swore at her too. The time had come for them all to leave. In the street Brigton persisted in his provocation, not just verbally but also physically. He pushed Finhaven into 'a deep and dirty kennel', or gutter. That was the last straw: blood would have to be drawn. Finhaven, covered in muck, unsheathed his sword and lunged at Brigton. Strathmore tried to step in but, as they grappled, he was the one that got run through the chest, suffering a wound from which he died two days later. So ended a Scottish night out, changed back from cheeriness into drunken rage and violence.[1]

Finhaven faced a charge of murder, for which he went on trial in Edinburgh in August. Since neither the accused nor the witnesses could remember much of the night in question, it seemed the jury was bound to come to a verdict of guilty on the simple grounds that a deadly blow had been struck and Finhaven had struck it. At the time there was no precedent in Scots law for taking into account such mitigating circumstances as the intention of the accused or his state of mind when he committed his crime. But Finhaven had been lucky to engage as his counsel Robert Dundas of Arniston, a former Lord Advocate, or chief prosecutor for the crown. Dundas told the jury it should consider a point of law as well as a point of fact, 'that the only object for their deliberation, was whether they could conscientiously say that Carnegie had committed murder, or whether his guilt was not diminished or annihilated by the circumstances of the case'. And Dundas's point evidently struck home, for the jury returned a verdict of not guilty and so introduced a new principle into Scots law.[2]

The affair also had a certain political piquancy about it because, while Dundas was the sternest of Whigs, the accused and the others involved in the affair were Jacobites. Jacobitism remained widespread among the lairds of Angus, as of all the counties north of the Firth of Forth, despite the fact that it had been since 1715 a fairly hopeless cause. The cause just remained ingrained at that level of local society and, given its hierarchical structure, no less so at its lower levels, among the ordinary farming folk who were the landowners' tenants. Often the Jacobite movement is remembered as in essence a Highland one, yet several clans were consistently loyal to the House of Hanover. If we want to see the Jacobites as a true popular movement, it is to the north-east of Scotland we need to look.[3]

This regional strength of Jacobitism could be defined in other ways, notably in its far greater support among Episcopalians than among Presbyterians. Analysis in terms of class, however, does not much help in understanding it. It was not just a feudal relic, for the landowners formed at this stage the most progressive class in Scotland. As we saw in the last chapter, one of the most progressive, George Lockhart of Carnwath, found no contradiction between pioneering steam-power and giving his allegiance to the exiled royal House of Stewart. In Angus, too, the Ogilvies, Earls of Airlie, who were forfeited after 1745, figured among the earliest improving landlords, and so did the successors to the unfortunate Earl of Strathmore killed by Carnegie of Finhaven.[4] These people would have referred not to their class but to their rank in society, a product of their birth and their abilities. It left them in no doubt they should take a lead among brother Scots, whether in rebellion or in improvement.

Just as Jacobites are hard for us to place in our conventional categories of social science, so their fellows found them difficult to define in contemporary terms. The error they made in 1715 was not always held against them, at least if that might lead to permanent fracture among the people in charge of Scotland: the need to stick together often seemed more important than any opinions individuals might hold or indeed actions they might take. To be sure, some consequences of rash rebellion would have to be swallowed. Common soldiers in the Jacobite cause could be hanged or held in jails with death-rates of epidemic proportions or, if they survived, be transported to the West Indies where the tropical climate was likely to make short work of them. An aristocrat or gentleman had greater hope of staying alive, and then wider considerations came into play. Even if he were to end up being executed, should this fate affect his family and its property? The government in London thought so, at least in the worst cases, but many Scots, including loyal Hanoverians, disagreed.[5]

In those worst cases the law saw in the culprits a failing again connected with rank: corruption of the blood. It demanded not just their own death but also the forfeiture of their heirs. Yet Scots at large knew the rebels could have been almost accidental Jacobites. (Sir Walter Scott was to bring out this point in his novel *Waverley* a century later.) The very leader of the rising, John Erskine, Earl of Mar, had till shortly before it nothing about him that would have stopped him becoming a conformist if hardly devoted Hanoverian Whig. Himself one of the authors of the Union of 1707, as a Secretary of State in the Scottish government that negotiated it, he afterwards served as a representative peer in the House of Lords. Still, in 1713 the English Tories managed to coax him into the government they were then forming. It turned out to be a bad move on his part. While, at the Hanoverian succession the next year, he assured King George I of his loyalty, he was, along with all his colleagues, dismissed from the royal service. Since Mar had never been a strong partisan of any kind – Bobbing John was his nickname – he understandably felt aggrieved at this arbitrary treatment. Seeing no way back into favour or security for his status and property, he resorted to the expedient of rebellion. Desperate as it was, it must still have been a matter of calculation rather than of conviction.[6]

Mar was not alone in such equivocation. The family of the Dukes of Atholl, chiefs of Clan Murray, split down the middle as between Jacobites and Hanoverians, each supplying a line of succession to the title; rebellion would occasionally allow the Jacobite branch to occupy Blair Atholl till the Hanoverian branch reclaimed the ancestral pile. Despite the reputation of Clan Campbell as a pillar of the Hanoverian state, the cadet line of the Earl of Breadalbane joined the rising in 1715 even while his kinsman, the Duke of Argyll, led the government's forces. As for Lord Lovat, the most extreme example of caprice and faithlessness, nobody could tell which way he would jump. While Scots noblemen might misjudge the odds on one side or the other, self-preservation remained their priority, political allegiance secondary. This was not always admirable, but it did help them to understand their peers who went astray and, if they could find it within themselves, to offer discreet help with the awkward consequences.[7]

That was what happened after the rising of 1715. Though the Jacobite army in Scotland never surrendered it left plenty of prisoners in the government's hands, most to be held in the castles of Edinburgh or Stirling. The mercenary Swiss or Dutch guards who escorted them there saw no need to treat them gently. The crowds that gathered to watch them trudge past called out words of encouragement and offered little gifts that might be of use to them. It was a sign Scots would never tolerate the brutality now being shown to Jacobite captives in England. The government understood this and even began to fear that Scottish juries might refuse to convict the prisoners. Many who had submitted before the end of the fighting, or who were deemed to be of no importance, were released. That still left dozens in Edinburgh Castle. The government insisted they should be tried, so in batches they were marched away again, this time south over the English border to Carlisle. Only the peers, Lords Rollo, Stormont and Strathallan, remained exempt. The Marquess of Huntly, heir to the Duke of Gordon, was sent off on the grounds of his actually being a commoner with a mere courtesy title, but soon got hauled back and then released in exchange for a pledge to use his influence in reconciling the north-east of Scotland to the House of Hanover. Politically, the trials at Carlisle proved to be a mistake. By sending men out of the country to be prosecuted the government violated the independence of the Scottish legal system supposedly guaranteed by the Treaty of Union. A surge of patriotic indignation united all shades of opinion in Scotland.[8]

There were Scots Jacobite prisoners already in England, however, because part of the Pretender's forces had crossed the border to fight – and be defeated – in the decisive Battle of Preston. From Lancashire the captives of higher rank ended up in custody in London. One was William Mackintosh of Borlum, held in the prison of Newgate but not intending to stay. While in the yard at exercise with a dozen or so of his fellows, they rushed the turn-keys, knocked them down, burst out and vanished into the teeming streets of the English capital. Mackintosh at length got himself smuggled to France, but felt committed enough to his cause to return for the abortive rising of 1719, when he was recaptured and slammed up in Edinburgh Castle; here he passed his time writing his works on agricultural improvement. Meanwhile the noblemen among the prisoners from Preston were held in the Tower of London. William Maxwell, Earl of Nithsdale, as a Roman Catholic unlikely to get out alive, saved himself on the eve of his execution by the old trick of bringing in a woman with a hooded cloak to change places with him. He escaped in her clothes, made his way at length to Rome and lived there in penniless bliss with his wife till 1744.[9] George Seton, Earl of Winton, had in his youth taken time out in Europe, where at one stage he slummed it as a blacksmith's apprentice in Flanders. He knew how to file through metal and turned this skill to account after tools were smuggled to him in the Tower; he cut his way through the bars on the window of his cell and escaped. In the end, the sole Scots peer beheaded for high treason was William Gordon, Viscount of Kenmure, who turned out merely unlucky. He observed on the scaffold that he had been so confident of reprieve that he never bothered to order the suit of mourning customary for the victim on such occasions. He was too prominent to be let off but not well connected enough for anybody to trouble with a pardon for him.

Still, many leading rebels got clean away, and all the government could do then was deprive them of their property. For this purpose it appointed a Commission of Forfeited Estates. The commission soon became hopelessly bogged down in legal niceties, being led into the labyrinth by its intended vic-tims' brother Scots, some of whom had come out in the rebellion and some not. The first thing to be done in any particular case was ascertain the accused landowner's title to his estate. If the commission's surveyor-general, Patrick Strachan of Glenkindy, thought that would be easy, he soon learned better when at Dysart in Fife he went knocking at the door of Henry, Lord Sinclair, to ask about the property of his elder son John, Master of Sinclair, now in exile. Strachan was told first that his lordship felt ill, so could not receive him in person, then that back in 1712 the Master's property had anyway been passed on to the younger son, James (who thereby gained the means for a distinguished career as a British general, MP and diplomat). Full documentation could be provided if Strachan wished, but he would be wasting his time. He departed in bafflement.[10]

If Strachan had got past the first stage of his inquiry here, he would have gone on to ask about the rental of the estate together with the location and value of movable property belonging to the forfeited Master. Against all these assets, however, he was legally obliged to set the claims of legitimate creditors owed money by the estate at the time of the forfeiture. Indebtedness was endemic in the Scottish landed class, so creditors turned up in great numbers before the Commission of Forfeited Estates. Most of their claims might even have been genuine. The cumulative effect of them was often that the estate, in its net value, had little left to confiscate, or else, if claims were to be rejected, the government would make more foes than friends – which was not the object of its Scottish policy. We cannot say the retribution wrought on the leadership of the rebels quite failed, but certainly their families and fellows closed ranks to keep the retribution at a minimum.[11]

The situation after 1745 differed because the pool of support on which this rebellion drew was smaller, which did not hinder its greater military success. The course of events caused as much surprise north as south of the border. Several of the clans and families out in 1715 had declined to renew their Jacobite commitment this time round or else limited themselves to token gestures. Lands were still confiscated afterwards, in a swathe of estates from Stirling to Inverness with others in the west and north of Scotland, 13 in all. Administered by commissioners, they were meant to become models of development in backward regions and accumulate profits that might be applied to public works. Then disaffection would be tackled at root, and the natives civilised by inculcation of hard-working, law-abiding, Presbyterian values from the Lowlands. Yet the commissioners seemed on the contrary affected by Highland indolence. Their sluggish bureaucracy did little better than all the other absentee landlords who let estates run down and lose money. The public investment in them was, according to the judge, Lord Kames, 'no better than water spilt on the ground'.[12]

Nobody really knew what to do till a new course was suggested by the fate of the lands of Lovat. Simon Fraser, their chieftain *de jure,* had reluctantly been out in 1745. After his father's execution he received a pardon on account of his youth and inexperience, but without getting back his property. Later, he raised a regiment in the British army that fought with great courage at the capture of Quebec in 1759, where he himself was wounded. In 1774 he petitioned successfully for restoration of the estates, though he was displeased to find that their debts came with them. On the strength of that the Lord Advocate, Henry Dundas, started lobbying for a general restoration. He persuaded the Treasury that this was the best way to be rid of an unwanted burden.[13] In 1783 he himself became a commissioner of forfeited estates, in effect with a brief to wind the old policy up.

In 1784 Dundas introduced a bill to disannex the forfeited estates from the crown. He reminded MPs that after 1745 the Highlands had been 'put under a kind of proscription and thereby disqualified from serving the state in any capacity'. He recalled how William Pitt the Elder, Prime Minister in the Seven Years' War, had ended this state of affairs by raising Highland regiments with the words: 'I am above all local prejudices and care not whether a man had been rocked in a cradle on this or on the other side of the Tweed. I sought only for merit, and I found it in the mountains of the north.' Dundas called on the house to be guided now by the same generous sentiments. Dispossessed families had been atoning for the crimes of their ancestors – 'and there is not one of those families in which some one person has not since spilt his blood in his country's cause'. But Dundas again stipulated that, if the estates were to be restored, then so too should be the debts as they stood when the government took over. Otherwise the heirs would be getting them back in better condition, and a premium would have been placed on rebellion. By this, according to the most eminent Gael of the time, the philosopher Adam Ferguson, 'the affection of all Highlanders was gained to the state and the king'.[14]

Dundas urged as political manager of Scotland that its ruling class should put its divisions behind it so as to extract the maximum benefit from the Union for itself and the country. It was an argument applying as much to the Jacobites as to the more liberal Whigs at odds with his regime. He reconciled men at both ends of the spectrum, and those few who still resisted him did so more likely on personal than on ideological grounds. It was the split in the parliamentary opposition over Britain's declaration of war on France in 1793 that allowed him to rope in most of its remaining supporters in Scotland, leaving behind only a tiny faction of the obdurate. With that he at last terminated the rowdy history of the Scottish nobility and remodelled it as a force for loyal, conservative unionism.[15]

If this had still been an independent country, its inveterate factiousness would doubtless have ruled out any such pattern of political action as Dundas's. But the fact of the Union did make a difference to him and the sort of career he was able to pursue. The peerage of Scotland had still formed in 1707 a feudal aristocracy, a *noblesse de l'épée*, based for the most part in inherited estates that it had built up and defended by main force if need be, though also by accommodation with the monarchy, amicable or chary, and by various legal devices. Rank was what mattered here, fortune rather less, since few of these peers had much money. It was why they showed themselves anxious once inside the Union to get promotion from the Scottish to the new British peerage, which in principle carried automatic membership of the House of Lords, while a mere Scots peer had to seek election to it. Many of the bluebloods did well enough out of the Union to remain – unlike the Irish peerage – rooted in their country and proud of it. For that, however, they still needed to seek favour in London.[16]

A step down stood the heritors or landowners, at their upper end forming a group not much different from the lesser peers. But the Union that opened opportunities for the highest rank closed many for this second one by drastically pruning the number of public offices available in Scotland. National affairs were of no great interest or importance to these lairds, however. What mattered was their own localities, where they ruled the roost. As heritors, they supervised the revenue and influenced through their patronage of the Church what welfare was afforded in poor relief and in the parochial schools. As justices, they fixed wages and otherwise adjudicated between masters and servants, built roads and maintained bridges or ferries. As barons, they sat in judgment in the barony courts till these were abolished in 1747. The inaugural professor of Scots law at the University of Edinburgh, Alexander Bayne, used to put a pointed question to their sons who filled his classes: 'What more agreeable personage can one form to himself, than that of a country gentleman, living decently and frugally on his fortune, and composing all the differences within his sphere of activity, giving the law to the whole neighbourhood, and they gratefully submitting to it?'[17]

But the lairds were always under an economic compulsion. At the end of the eighteenth century, as at the beginning, a mere 8,000 people owned Scotland. It was a self-consciously static society, yet not entirely immobile.

Its Jacobite families genteelly withered. Its younger sons needed in any event to make their own way in the world. Meanwhile, rich merchants, lawyers and manufacturers, or people returned from earning a fortune in the Empire, could pay the entrance fee with purchase of an estate. If only for the sake of higher rents, all this made the lairds into great agricultural improvers. Every one of the most famous, such as Cockburn of Ormiston or Grant of Monymusk, was below the rank of peer. That also roused their eagerness for the remaining salaried public positions, of which the main source was the law. Lawyers had once enjoyed a low social status but after the Union, with the feudal aristocracy subdued, something of a *noblesse de robe* came into existence. To the fore were the Dundases of Arniston, with Henry Dundas created Viscount Melville in 1802. After a couple of generations of political, colonial and diplomatic service, the Elliots of Minto also achieved noble status as Earls of Minto. By now the House of Lords, till the middle of the eighteenth century an overwhelmingly English assembly, was starting to represent all parts of the United Kingdom as Scots and then Irishmen took seats there. Acres ceased to be the main measure of a man's fitness for a peerage, and in the nineteenth century most new titles went to active servants of the British state, among whom Scots figured prominently.[18]

Next down in rank came the burgesses of Scotland, the full citizens of the royal burghs. In reality, they were in many such burghs never as powerful as the surrounding noblemen and lairds who imposed on them or sought to. After the Union even Edinburgh always looked for a patron to act for it at the new centre of political power in London. The effective priority of the councillors here, as of many other Scots, was to find a place on the chains of dependence by means of which the governors of Hanoverian Britain ruled it. In 1715 the capital's MP, Sir George Warrender, summarised the task when he told the town council 'to shun extremes and to consider the need we have of favour'. The councillors did indeed pursue a course of studied sycophancy, especially towards the House of Argyll soon dominating Scottish politics. In the event this won the city no favour at all.[19]

Burgesses were of two kinds: merchants and tradesmen. The merchants imported the supplies needed for production or consumption and then sold outside the burghs the goods that the tradesmen had meanwhile fashioned inside them. The merchants normally organised themselves in a single guild, while the tradesmen had to be members of the incorporation for their particular calling – in Edinburgh, which with 13 incorporations housed the biggest number of them, they ranged from bakers to wrights. Of the two kinds of burgess, the merchants everywhere held the upper hand. The magistrates of the burghs, usually merchants, reserved the right to fix the prices the tradesmen could put on their goods and services. These nursed the special grievance that they were not allowed to charge a higher rate even in times of dearth or shortage. As, in the course of economic progress, the supply of goods and services grew more extensive and elaborate, so, if anything, did the rules. The system was never meant to leave any room for competition.[20]

Right through the eighteenth century, indeed, the magistrates continued to impose commercial regulation in the most trivial detail.[21] The burgh of Perth, for instance, tried to maintain a distinction between privileged shoemakers producing finished goods and unprivileged cobblers merely repairing them.[22] In 1743 the procurator fiscal of Edinburgh prosecuted two 'unfree' traders, that is to say, vendors of goods who were not burgesses. The report of the case concluded: 'The court having considered the complaint . . . they find it proven that the defenders have sold by retail within the city of Edinburgh a parcel of lemons albeit the said John Ferguson is no a guildbrother and the said John Blyth is neither burgess nor guildbrother thereof.' In time some wider considerations did impinge, though seldom of an economic sort. When in 1755 two journeymen wrights from outside the royalty were found to 'have wrought at the bench set up in the garret lybelled', one protested that 'he served his Majestie in the Edinburgh Regiment [against the Jacobites] in the years 1745 and 1746, and so was entitled to equal privileges with the freemen'. After he showed proof of his service, he was allowed to carry on. But, except in such special cases, pettifogging interference persisted. One municipal officer, John Hutton, was employed to make minute inspection of the markets. He reported for 21 July 1793: 'This morning seized a quantity of unripe gooseberries – summoned the owners before Bailie Carfrae, acquitted on a promise to be cautious in the disposal.' In fact, it was Hutton that got called aside by the bailie, to be told 'at this critical time, when so many eyes are upon the magistrates, rather to pass over some things, viz. summoning shopkeepers'.[23] With war against revolutionary France under way, the authorities now felt not wholly confident of the people and sought to avoid casual provocations.

At the turn of the eighteenth century the merchants of Edinburgh remained the richest and most influential in Scotland, though no longer to the extent they once had been. The Union caught them in the middle of a long-term effort to reorganise themselves, probably more a sign of insecurity than of strength. The burgh's charter guaranteed their dominance yet this had started to become shaky, or so they feared. Since 1583 they had been obliged to admit successful tradesmen to their ranks, men running businesses rather than actually working with their hands. But by 1681 the wealthier merchants decided they had had enough of this. They formed a Merchant Company with a royal charter providing for surveillance of its members, evidently meant in practice to retrieve and safeguard a more exclusive and patrician privilege than was otherwise now available. Self-interest shone through the flowery formulations of the charter. It declared that a trading company had become a necessity, in particular for merchants dealing in cloth who paid more customs and taxes than others, because this company would be useful 'for enabling them to prosecute the design of manufactories'. It all looks like an attempt to foster what would today be called vertically integrated enterprises, with the owners controlling everything from the purchase of the raw material to the sale of the finished fabric. The tradesmen of Edinburgh, not exactly free market-eers themselves, objected that 'a society on the lines proposed, destructive of other people's liberties, is against all reason and without a parallel. The governors of such a company would be masters of the town.'[24] In the event the stratagem failed and over time the Merchant Company turned into an innocuous charitable body, for running schools especially.

The merchants' political control always grated, however, with the more numerous tradesmen whose own representatives were kept in subordination. In Edinburgh the merchants even decided, by a range of manipulative procedures, which particular tradesmen might get on to the council. Under the municipal constitutions, or setts, it was each lot of councillors – and not any wider electorate – that chose its successors. This tended to create permanent, petty oligarchies formed in large part of cronies and crawlers. They made themselves objects of resentment not only to the tradesmen but even to men of independent mind among the merchants who, carrying on the private business of the burgh, earned its income and then got taxed though they had no effective say in its government.[25]

Yet these distinctions of rank were starting to break down, and in some respects the two kinds of burgess no longer looked so different. In Edinburgh, in order to pursue any form of economic activity a burgess needed to live within the royalty, that is, in the Old Town, and to pay municipal taxes. The real difference was not between merchants and tradesmen resident in the royalty, but between both groups and their rivals resident beyond the royalty. Poorer townspeople – shopkeepers and manual workers – lived in the suburbs lining the walls from the outside, Calton and Canongate, Portsburgh and Potterrow. By law they could not do any business or work on the inside, though then they were never subjected to the rules of the incorporations either. Sometimes they formed incorporations of their own, voluntary ones lacking statutory privilege and hard put to enforce their rules. To neutralise this competition, the incorporations inside the city might then relax their normal standards of entry. A Lord Provost, Sir Patrick Lindsay, in his improving tract, *The Interest of Scotland* (1733), reported that 'the weavers are indeed exceeding easy upon this head, they are in use to admit any good tradesman to the freedom of their incorporation upon terms that are easy and reasonable'. Otherwise he inveighed against the power of the incorporations, 'which these many ages have served no other purpose than to render themselves idle, poor and miserable, and to keep the town to which they belong from increasing either in wealth or inhabitants'.[26] But in Edinburgh, at least, this order of things was within a generation to be profoundly transformed, when the building of the New Town gave shape to modern social distinctions in place of medieval ones. The publisher William Creech noted how 'in 1763 people of quality and fashion lived in houses which, in 1793, were inhabited by tradesmen or by people in humble or ordinary life. The Lord Justice Tinwald's house was possessed by a French teacher – Lord President Craigie's by a rouping wife or saleswoman of old furniture.'[27]

The older pattern had had its own complexities. Within each trade, too, a ranking existed. At the top were the masters, the time-served, qualified members of the incorporations who, to get in, had besides satisfied their fellow masters with their standards of work. In Edinburgh and Glasgow the richest were 'guild brethren' who enjoyed equal standing with the merchants. The incorporations commonly made provision for the incapacity of their members, or for the care of widows and orphans. It was only among the masters (though not always among them) that men of local ambition could come forward with the capacity and skill to address the affairs of the burgh.[28]

Below them were the journeymen, who had finished their apprenticeships but not yet qualified as masters (some never did for financial or other reasons). They might work regularly for a particular master, or might become in effect self-employed. Then they had good reason to form associations of their own, for mutual protection against personal misfortune and hard times, or in an effort to keep up wages. This has been interpreted as the display of a distinct economic and social mentality, of an element in the formation of a class, though it only copied at a lower level the practice of the masters. The journeymen were anyway not so tied down to their position as their workmates above and beneath them: they often originated outside the burgh because it was accepted custom for them to go 'tramping' for a few years to widen their experience before returning to their hometown and entering their mastership.[29]

At the bottom stood the apprentices, subject to strict discipline if often rebelling. For entry to a trade there was a bias, sometimes a formal requirement, in favour of sons or relations of existing tradesmen. Lindsay felt concern about problems this created for the many youngsters moving from country to town in an era of rising migration. Those from a peasant background with useful skills or aptitudes found it hard to get work. He singled out aspiring tailors, gardeners and joiners as three groups being forced to leave Scotland because they could not set themselves up in the burghs. Not that life there was easy either. In 1748 officials in Glasgow received a petition from 30 young hammermen or metalworkers

> that it is a great hardship on them to work from six in the morning to eight at night considering the hardness of their work and that they have no more time allowed them through the day than the time they take their meat when other journeymen in some other trades have an hour at breakfast and as much at dinner and give over work at six and they by their being confined to work to eight they have not time to go to school and should they be allowed to give over work at seven they would not only have time to go to school but would do their work through the rest of the day with more cheerfulness and spirit and therefore craving the trade to allow them to give over work at seven.

Their superiors retorted

> well knowing that the servants and apprentices have been used past memory of any living to work from six in the morning to eight at night and being well informed that servants at Edinburgh and elsewhere work from five in the morning to eight at night and considering that shortening the time of the servants work must

of necessity raise prices and having just reason to fear that their servants instead of employing their hours at night for acquiring useful learning would squander the same away in vaguing on the streets or in tippling and drinking and might give offence or unfit themselves for business the ensuing day. . . .

The letter went on in the same vein, but the apprentices would already have caught the drift: the answer was no.[30] Small wonder Adam Smith believed the laws governing apprenticeships to be a violation of 'this most sacred property which every man has in his own labour'.[31]

Outworn civic distinctions were turning into fig leaves for newer tensions. In big burghs the status of burgess gradually became a mark of social distinction rather than a necessary qualification for a tradesman. In 1768 the richest Scot of the time, Sir Lawrence Dundas, was elected MP for Edinburgh. A son of the city of humble origins, he had started his career selling drapery in the High Street, but ended it with a monopoly on supplies to the British army in the Seven Years' War. With this by local standards impressive background he made an impact when he started donating lavishly to the Merchant Company's charities, and he won support from tradesmen's incorporations too. The merchants disingenuously said 'it is more agreeable to our happy constitution that a member be chosen by the free voice of the electors than in consequence of solicitations or other more unwarrantable means.'[32]

Yet Sir Lawrence was also an arrogant, overbearing fellow who soon made himself unpopular. In 1774, when he sought re-election, he faced more resistance, though he bought it off. He still could not rest on his laurels, for a more formidable opposition to him arose as a vehicle for the ambitions of his remote kinsman, Henry Dundas, who would turn out to be the most consummate Scottish politician of the age. In their battles for control of the city, Sir Lawrence presented himself as the merchants' champion, while Henry ostensibly took the side of the trades. But the money on the one side remained evenly matched with the ruthless guile on the other: the battles only came to an end with Sir Lawrence's death in 1781.[33]

Then a different story unfolded. Henry Dundas put the tradesmen back in their place as pawns in his municipal manoeuvres, while in reality he turned the city over to the people who supported and financed him, lawyer-lairds from the Lothians and above all bankers. He stemmed himself from the first group, from an old landed line that trained up its offspring in the law; the Faculty of Advocates was replete with such bright youngsters from all the leading families of Scotland, ready to defend their interests in the courts. These lawyer-lairds were a product of the Union. After 1707, as noblemen decamped to seek favour in London, somebody had to stay behind to man the national institutions guaranteed by the treaty: Church, university and law. The law turned out of prime importance. With a line drawn under faction and feud, Scots now had to settle their differences through legal channels. And the aristocrats trying their luck in London needed managers of their estates at home. Edinburgh's clever, diligent solicitors stood ready. The other branch of the legal profession proved still more useful to a peerage with too many sons. Younger ones might be put to the law as advocates. By the middle of the eighteenth century, the Faculty of Advocates doubled in size to about 200 members. Of these, a third came from titled families, far in excess of their proportion in the population as a whole.[34] There emerged a landed and legal class for which practice at the bar and interest in a country estate were normal.

The second group of Dundas's supporters were *nouveaux riches* whose yearnings for social status he could help to satisfy as he rose in public life: the 'mushrooms', in the contemporary colloquialism, so called because they grew up fast out of excrement. They might buy themselves into the landed class, but anyway had a role among agricultural improvers by servicing their investments. The bankers were in effect another product of the Union. While the financial needs of the nation had been modest till 1707 and for some time afterwards, still Edinburgh became the headquarters of two banks surviving (more or less) to the present, the Bank of Scotland founded in 1695 and the Royal Bank of Scotland founded in 1727. Small though the system was, it managed to benefit humanity by inventing the overdraft. The most important thing about it was to give Scotland a banking system separate from England's.[35]

Henry Dundas's coalition of old gentry and new plutocracy simply shoved aside the merchants and tradesmen, built in with the institutional bricks of the burgh though they might be. The community of moneyed men was already established enough for him to make use of it in his political takeover of Edinburgh. When Sir Lawrence Dundas died still in harness as MP in 1781, Henry decided the city should be brought under the patronage of his neighbour and ally in Midlothian, the Duke of Buccleuch. There needed to be a system 'on which government can rely', and the common run of merchants and tradesmen 'must not be permitted to govern the town by a knot of themselves without the interposition of some such patron'.[36] This was a sort of local revolution, putting landowners and lawyers financed by bankers firmly in charge. In token of that, Sir Lawrence's successor as MP was to be James Hunter Blair, originally a partner in Coutts Bank when it still had close connections with Edinburgh; in a subsequent term as Lord Provost he began the work of rebuilding the university and had the South Bridge constructed. Over the following decades similar figures followed on as municipal leaders: Sir James Stirling of Larbert, a long-standing director of the Bank of Scotland; Sir William Fettes, who would leave the money to found the college named after him; and Sir John Marjoribanks, partner in the private bank of Sir William Forbes, scion of a Jacobite family and probably the wealthiest of them all. These and their friends at the bar, with the formidable financial and legal power they jointly mustered, made modern Edinburgh what in one of its primary aspects it still is, a city of lawyers and bankers. Here, then, an entire new order in Scottish society, the professions, had emerged in strength. Under their regime the classical embellishment of Edinburgh went on but its cronyism if anything grew worse.

The social evolution on the opposite side of the country turned out somewhat different. In Glasgow urban disputes had up to the Union gone on much like Edinburgh's, only a little behindhand. In 1605 there was an accommodation between the established merchants and the aspirant craftsmen, all now supposed to enjoy a similar status. They still remained institutionally separate, the former in their Merchant House led by the dean of guild, the latter in their Trades House under an elected deacon convener. A subsequent royal letter of 1607 defined the composition of the council, which would be formally ratified in a sett of 1711.[37] Apart from recording the precise mechanism for electing civic officers, the sett fixed the number of ordinary councillors at 13 merchants and 12 tradesmen, and specified that the provost had to be a merchant. This was generous to the tradesmen by comparison with other Scots burghs, but stopped short of giving them equality with the merchants. While the sett was amended from time to time, the merchants always kept their edge.

The town council of Glasgow, in contrast to that of Edinburgh, remained under the control of this middle rank of native sons. The formally inferior status of the tradesmen became a bone of contention here too, especially as their majority in the whole body of burgesses continued to increase. In the seventeenth century more than a third of all burgesses had been merchants, but by the time of the municipal reform of 1833 the proportion fell to less than a fifth.[38] The crafts expanded because of a booming economy, though also by relaxing their rules for entry. In 1732 the Trades House ruled it 'reasonable that any freeman weaver take what journeymen he thinks fit without distinction of town or country for what wages the master and he can agree'. And no more than in Edinburgh were the merchants or tradesmen in Glasgow by now mutually exclusive categories. The beginnings of modern industry, as opposed to the mere practice of a medieval craft, made Glasgow's tradesmen prosperous, quite as prosperous as the lesser merchants.[39] Within this latter rank an economic gradation appeared, as some contented themselves with local business while others took the much higher risks, while also reaping the much higher rewards, of overseas rather than domestic commerce. And not all of them bothered with the inherited municipal structures: some just went ahead and grew their business without applying to anybody or belonging to anything.[40]

The leaders of Glasgow were then distinguished not by rank but by wealth beyond the dreams of avarice. After the tobacco lords turned into the kings of cotton, the city's already vast riches waxed fabulous through blockade-busting in Napoleonic Europe. While merchant princes had long had the town council at their beck and call, now they almost spurned it for new structures of their own. It was anyway an imperfect vehicle for their political ambitions, because under the Treaty of Union they had to share a single seat at Westminster with their insignificant rivals at Dumbarton, Renfrew and Rutherglen, all these town councils being in theory equal. And it would have been quite hopeless to expect Glasgow's council to cope with the control and direction of an integrated regional economy amid its growing engagement in international trade. Instead the merchants preferred to work through their chamber of commerce, the first in Britain, founded in 1793 by a Lord Provost, Patrick Colquhoun, 'to watch over and take charge of matters relating to their common commercial interests and be the organ of all communications with His Majesty's government, or with the legislature, on matters connected with the trade of the district'.[41] The mercantile plutocrats stayed in charge of the city right through the huge economic and political changes of the nineteenth century.

Aberdeen, a good deal smaller than Edinburgh or Glasgow, remained a more typical burgh. In 1695 only 192 merchants there were paying tax, by 1748 only

247. Trade and population had risen, so perhaps wealth was being concentrated in fewer hands. Just 47 merchants made profits of over £1,000 Scots, while in 1771 the town's most valuable trade, in stockings, lay in the hands of only 22 trading houses. A merchant clique led by the brothers Hadden stayed in charge of the city till the municipal reform of 1833. It carried on some traffic overseas but its ordinary business tended to be with the hinterland of Aberdeenshire, so that here agricultural improvement and urban prosperity fed primarily off each other.[42]

In this narrower and more old-fashioned society the tradesmen, so far from rivalling the merchants, needed to exert themselves to defend what advantage they did enjoy. Those in New Aberdeen, which was the royal burgh, had to fend off competition from unprivileged rivals in Old Aberdeen, at that time a couple of miles away over open country. Pressure also came from an unexpected quarter. The quines, the women of Aberdeen, were a spirited sisterhood, who did not like their clothes run up for them by men. After their repeated protests, a henpecked tailors' incorporation at last agreed women might make mantles or petticoats 'but on no consideration were they to import or deal in stays and other articles of female attire'. To win this limited privilege they still had to join the incorporation, though only as an inferior sort of associate member. Even on these stingy terms, the tailors of Aberdeen were the sole tradesmen in Scotland admitting women to their craft.[43]

In Dundee, the trades were more vigorous in proposing improvements for a burgh growing faster than its local rival Perth. A minister, the Revd Robert Small, went so far as to call the trades 'the representatives of the people'.[44] The town flourished by manufacturing, finishing and marketing the coarse linen that came from its hinterland. To support industrial expansion, the council exempted the linen brought into Dundee from the payment of petty customs. According to Lindsay, 'numbers of country weavers, who used to carry their cloth for sale to the towns that lie nearest to them do now bring their cloth to Dundee, although it lies at a much great distance from them.' In the second half of the eighteenth century, linen provided 'the daily subsistence of the greater number of its inhabitants', and the business continued to prosper.[45] This was presumably why the magistrates allowed the master weavers to employ as many unfree weavers as they pleased. With Dundee on its way to becoming the regional centre for textiles, it still proved impossible to stop the municipality falling under the petty merchant tyranny of Alexander Riddoch, who served eight terms as Lord Provost between 1788 and 1818 and relegated the trades to political impotence.

Developments in smaller burghs followed various patterns. Often they had to resist attempts at control by neighbouring noblemen. In 1722 the people of Cupar Fife took to the streets to demonstrate their hostility to designs on the burgh by the Earl of Rothes. At Dumfries in 1759 there were similar demonstrations against the clique the Duke of Queensberry had inserted into the town council. Meanwhile, the Earl of Eglinton took over Irvine, but the citizens of Ayr successfully opposed a coup by the Earl of Bute. Yet in many burghs the resistance to the landed class failed, or could not even be mounted in the first place. The town councils of Anstruther Easter and Wester were under the thumb of the local Anstruther family, while the council of Haddington answered to the bidding of the Dalrymples of Hailes and so on: there was simply nothing to be done about it.[46]

At least this did not tell the entire urban story. The 1,200 burgesses of Edinburgh were at the end of the eighteenth century just a small minority of its 50,000 inhabitants. In Glasgow, while the numbers joining the tradesmen's incorporations had rapidly risen, there were only 3,500 of them by the time of the municipal reform of 1833, in a city then with a population of 200,000. Even if we double these tallies to take account of journeymen, or triple them for apprentices, and add something more for families of the tradesmen, we are still dealing with a good deal less than half of all townspeople. As for the rest, the unfree, it has been reckoned that, about 1750, they amounted to at least 60 per cent of the population in Aberdeen (and Aberdeen, as we have seen, was a typical sort of burgh). They had no economic privileges apart from an entitlement, if natives of the place, to poor relief, assuming any was paid out. Those arriving from the countryside, in an era of rising migration, had not even that.[47]

From the surviving documentation we learn little of these lower levels of society. That makes it meagre fare for the dominant post-Marxist school of Scottish historians in their characteristic quest for the origins of proletarian consciousness. Most of the unfree men in the royal burghs were presumably unskilled or semi-skilled manual workers. The women would have been dependants unless able to take up the limited urban opportunities available to their sex – which did grow, however, as industrialisation got under way. Regular work became available, if only in the form of long hours of repetitive drudgery in unhealthy factories under strict supervision. If this was the formation of a proletariat, no wonder so many felt reluctant to join it, at least while they had hope of earning some other kind of living in greater self-respect.

The early millworkers came in general from among the poorest people, even the destitute, especially women and children or Highland migrants or, before long, the still less demanding Irish. They represented a new workforce, in other words, the deployment of fresh factors of production, rather than what one Scottish academic historian, with the elegance of diction typical of his kind, calls 'proletarianisation' of the existing workforce.[48]

Disputes recurred in different sectors, but it was the weavers that stood in the van of Scottish development and did most to break down the inherited structures. In the burghs they were tradesmen in the normal manner, but less secure communities of them grew up round the country wherever the requisite resources were available. Most of them operated as individuals or in small units. In time their function turned more intermediate, once the bigger manufacturers began to build up business and contract work out to them. In the west of Scotland these manufacturers often sought to manipulate their suppliers, something quite possible given the range of raw materials and variety of products. In response the weavers might, in the term of the time, combine – that is, come together to protect their interests in some embryonic form of trade union.[49] Inside the burghs there was less need of this because the incorporations could often rely on a table of prices fixed by the magistrates. Outside the burghs – for example, in Glasgow's ring of grimy suburbs from Anderston round to Bridgeton and to Gorbals – combination must have seemed a more plausible option, though it seldom brought much benefit.

Frictions grew in the west of Scotland especially. In 1767 a group of militant weavers mounted a campaign of intimidation against others willing to work at the manufacturers' prices. The rebels cut webs from their errant fellows' looms and dragged them through the streets, 'showing them as a disgrace to the other workmen, whom they called out to see them; and beat them to excess'.[50] The trouble at length died down, yet worse was to follow in 1787 when manufacturers sought to reduce the money they were paying for muslin. Weavers from Camlachie bent on a ritual burning of webs marched along the Gallowgate towards the city. At the boundary the magistrates stood ready to read the Riot Act, but the weavers threw stones at them. Troops were summoned from barracks nearby; the weavers stoned them too. The soldiers opened fire, killing half a dozen of the protesters and wounding many more. This might look like the beginning of class conflict, though it had no sequel for three decades.

Given the infrequency of such clashes, modish Scottish historians have been obliged to search rather oddly for evidence of social stress within the trades, that is, in trouble between the masters and their journeymen or apprentices as industrialisation increased the inequalities. One scholar concedes that 'there was no way that the tensions of the workplace and of work relationships would always be avoided. But the formalisation of this tension in organisational form comes in the eighteenth century with a widening of the gap between master and man.'[51] Yet his subsequent analysis tends to elide the fact that the modern capitalist organisation of industry now just about appearing was something quite different from the traditional structure of the trades. In the one, nothing could bridge the gap between the possessing class and its wage-slaves. In the other, it had been possible, indeed normal, for apprentices and journeymen to advance and become masters in their own right, though some never did for one reason or another. Not only were the masters and their men bound within a single trade with its own strong traditions and indeed camaraderie, but the trades as a group also stood nearer the top end than the bottom end of the social scale: at any rate all their members ranked above the mean of urban society. What is more, we are often dealing here not just with a single trade but also with a single household, because many apprentices and servants lived with and under the close scrutiny of their masters while the journeymen wrought right alongside them. To regard this as even an incipient class system is surely straining the concept and the evidence for it beyond what they will bear. The three ranks of craftsmen were much more likely to be loyal workmates and regular drinking companions than to be in training for internecine class war. Whatever their differences, they readily joined together in both the defence and the celebration of their own monopolies and privileges.[52] But the real world was overtaking them.

That said, economic advance did differentially affect master, journeyman and apprentice. The numbers of journeymen rose because technological advance brought more expensive looms or other equipment, so it took longer to set up as a master. This was, for example, what accounted for the large proportion of journeymen among the weavers in the boomtown of Paisley, most producing superior fabrics for the high end of the market. Though many were designated as journeymen, they remained so in name only and in fact worked as free and independent tradesmen.[53] Elsewhere, when the incorporations relaxed or even gave up efforts to control entry to the trades, they rendered it less necessary for the journeymen to aspire to the rank of master.

Those who trained formally as apprentices underwent the opposite process. Their numbers fell because the increasing cost of indentures put youngsters off. Weaving was never so skilled that lads learning the rudiments could not quite quickly launch themselves on an independent working career, without being bound to a master for years on end. Others entered the trade through their families' connections and so hardly needed to sign on for formal instruction. Whereas the number of journeymen rose, the number of apprentices fell. With rapid increases overall in the number of weavers (especially of cotton, a sector where apprenticeship was never common), the old structure crumbled. Even while the industry expanded, wages could fall because of the loss of protective solidarity and of the consequent emergence of competition in a more flexible workforce. Where protest resulted, it was primarily of a conservative nature, resisting change in a usually vain defence against the new sort of instability that the traditional system had sought to exclude.[54]

Since nobody had any idea how to cope with the economic cycles emerging in industrial society, they waxed all the more extreme. But what they did besides, after throwing thousands out of work, was favour the survival of the fittest, in other words, of the more efficient and advanced parts of the textile sector that would produce, in the longer term, expansion and diversification all over again. This did not for every individual caught up in the process lead inevitably to 'proletarianisation', because it could also pay a premium to hard work and adaptability. By the early nineteenth century the aristocracy of the Scottish handloom weaving force consisted of adult males in the prime of life, highly skilled and active in their trades. These qualities had become more important determinants of wages and status than any traditional rank inside the incorporations. For example, a journeyman weaver at Galashiels or Dunfermline earned more than a master weaver of cotton in Glasgow, and a journeyman weaving shawls at Paisley was paid more than a master weaver at Airdrie who wrought ginghams.[55] Besides, what did most to dismantle the old structure was the development of large-scale enterprises employing hundreds of people. They needed no masters, journeymen or apprentices for employment that was routine, mechanical and repetitive. It was not personal skill but technological advance that wove on the machines the mass-produced textiles ready to be sold on straight to their final consumers. Here too, however, we need to be careful about analysis in terms of class.

In 1806, one commentator in Paisley drew a sharp distinction between the independent, educated weavers and the wretched, illiterate hands in the factories:

The cotton spinning trade now established in this part of the country is highly valuable, on account of such numbers of poor children and women as are employed in its various operations, but it appears to have no tendency to improve the morals of the country. The numbers collected in large cotton mills, from families immersed in ignorance and vice, spread the contagion among such as have been more regularly educated, and profligate conduct is the natural result.[56]

This was a disreputable underclass, different from the respectable working class Paisley had already bred. Now skilled weavers, schooled, sober and decent, feared a fall into the pit of unskilled ignorance, intemperance and immorality. They refused to be dragged under, even if they could find nothing else. In their spirit of independence, they felt superior to the pitiable creatures forced into hours of soul-destroying grind at power looms, helpless women and children or hapless migrants from the Highlands and Ireland. In other words, the progress of industrialisation, from crafts to factories, weakened and divided the working class. If anything, it ran counter to the Marxist theory of class formation. Besides, Scotland was during the Victorian era to find its own ways of maintaining easy relations among the social classes.

According to the theory, a capitalist system is required for social classes to develop, yet by the end of the eighteenth century no free Scottish market in prices or wages had so far developed: why else should Adam Smith have argued so vehemently against the existing rigidities? The originally medieval system of regulation only broke down for good in the middle of the nineteenth century. Meanwhile its paternalism continued to make the *ancien régime*, if not always popular, at least acceptable. The first stages of the industrial revolution made little difference to the power of the landed class in Scotland, which often itself invested in manufacture. Unlike in Ireland, there was here no discontented bourgeoisie either. And for almost everybody, at least in the Lowlands, living standards rose enough to ease the early pains and strains of industrialisation. The existing order of things therefore continued to enjoy a legitimacy that carried it fairly unscathed through an era that may have been revolutionary, but only elsewhere. All Scots had before them that spectacle, first in America, then in France, and there were individuals in Scotland who got excited about it all. But it left the great majority cold. Such trouble as did occur at this stage came in Edinburgh, the centre of political authority, and scarcely spread to Glasgow, the economic crucible of the future.[57]

So it is no surprise to find that thinkers of the Scottish Enlightenment, men not incapable of analysing society in original ways, never resorted to analysis in terms of class.[58] For Frances Hutcheson, Adam Smith and John Millar, all at various times academics in Glasgow, civil society was primarily a network of relations between husbands and wives, parents and children, masters and servants, the whole bound together by obligations of natural justice and by whatever rights had become embodied in positive law.[59] Economic considerations put in an appearance in the matter of individual contract, but otherwise the household rather than the market was the implied frame of reference. That is precisely the case in the seminal work by Millar, *Observations concerning the Distinctions of Ranks in Society* (1773).

Millar's book stands in the mainstream of the Scottish Enlightenment, in the sense of using conjectural history to develop its subject 'by real experiments, not by abstracted metaphysical theories'; the overall purpose is one in which 'the general laws of our constitution are laid open . . . and history is rendered subservient to moral philosophy and jurisprudence'.[60] More especially, Millar asks how different types of social authority arise and change, together with the rights attaching to them or affected by them. He finds there are three adventitious personal rights and one adventitious governmental right: the right of husband over wife, of father over children, of master over servants, and then of chief or sovereign over tribesmen or citizens. These four rights all rest on authority, to be sure, yet when they are examined comparatively and historically some drastic differences appear. For example, Roman law, the source of much European legal and moral thinking, allows the head of the household to treat wife, children and servants as his property to the point even of exposing infants at birth. Such an exercise of authority is completely at odds with anything thought appropriate in a progressive society of the eighteenth century. So things have changed, if without affecting the basic principle that rank rests on authority.

Millar points out how things are still changing, for example, in the labour market. To a great extent it depends on structures of authority too. In the past the structures mirrored relations of dependency in the household, but now they are starting to respond in novel ways to economic forces. Though, as so often in the works of the Scottish Enlightenment, there is in the *Observations* no more than passing reference to local matters, Millar does at this point get specific about the condition of Scots miners, who were serfs. What he stresses, though, is the disadvantage of serfdom to the coalmasters rather than to the miners:

> The detriment ... which arises from thence to the proprietors of those works is manifest. No man would chuse to be a slave if he could earn nearly the same wages by living in a state of freedom. Each coalier therefore must have an additional premium for his labour, upon account of the bondage into which he is reduced: otherwise he will endeavour to procure a livelihood by some other kind of employment.[61]

This information is up to date: the miners had indeed found they could fleece the coalmasters by threatening to strike. Millar observes that in consequence Scots colliers earn on average 12 shillings a week, while free colliers round Newcastle in England earn only 9 shillings. He urges Scots coalmasters to emancipate their serfs, even if 'with a timidity natural to those who have a great pecuniary interest at stake, they are averse from altering the former practice, until such alteration shall be rendered universal by an act of parliament'. He encourages at least one, then, to break with the consensus because he 'would be in the same circumstances with a manufacturer who produces a commodity at less expence than his neighbours, and who is thereby enabled to undersell them in the market'.[62] He would also launch the long delayed modernisation of the mining industry.

In the context of the Scottish Enlightenment, Millar enjoys the reputation of being progressive rather than conservative; certainly the rulers of the country came to view him with suspicion. Yet in fact he sided with the bourgeoisie rather than the workers. While he had sympathy for the lower social ranks, by no stretch of the imagination can he count as an egalitarian. His vision was of technological advance under secure rights of property that would make for stable progress and let the possessing class concede the humanitarian claims of the labouring poor. He was far-sighted: this is just what did happen in Victorian Scotland.[63]

5

Faith: 'Warmth and animosity'

On 13 May 1729, the Revd John Simson, professor of divinity at the University of Glasgow, was suspended from teaching for the rest of his life, which would last another 11 years. During all that time he held on to his stipend and his residence inside the university's beautiful buildings by the High Street, with the Molendinar Burn babbling along behind. Now and again he probably still taught students, among whom he had always been popular, but this needed to be strictly private rather than public instruction. In fact, his university had supported him and sought to insist on his academic freedom right through the process leading to his suspension. The Church of Scotland was the party to the dispute that asserted its control over this ordained minister and its right to judge whether he was a proper person to train up the clergymen of the future. Now the Kirk had not exactly condemned Simson, but rather decided it could never be sure of him. So, instead of being cast into outer darkness, he would merely be silenced for as long as he should yet live.[1]

Simson was quite a venerable figure. His forefathers had served the Church of Scotland since the Reformation. Himself a son of the manse from Renfrew, he was educated at the Universities of Edinburgh and of Leiden in Holland. After his return home he received a call to the parish of Troqueer near Dumfries, but only a couple of years later he moved on to his chair at Glasgow. This should have been the launch of a successful and distinguished academic career. What went wrong?[2]

It seems Simson had breathed in a little too much of the heady atmosphere of freedom in the Dutch universities, at the time the best in Europe. They stood at the forefront of advances in knowledge in everything from medicine to law to philosophy to theology. Theirs was like Scotland a Calvinist country, so Scottish students should have been able to go there to complete their education without risking any taint to their orthodoxy. Yet Holland, which tolerated its religious minorities while also remaining open to the secular world as a great trading nation, was not a place to stand still in its thinking. On the contrary, it enjoyed continuous and widespread intellectual progress.[3]

On returning to the rather different atmosphere of his native land, Simson carried this liberating experience with him. He soon made his mark as an excellent teacher. He got his students to write essays and criticise the efforts of their fellows. He encouraged them to meet for prayer or discussion outside his formal classes and gave them topics to debate. He wanted them not to parrot him but to think for themselves and reach intellectual positions they could set forth and defend. His matter matched his manner. He no longer adhered to the Calvinist belief that the whole human race was predestined to damnation except for a tiny minority that God would gratuitously save regardless of any actions by them. When students asked Simson how they could be sure of their own salvation, he answered with the biblical injunction, 'Seek and ye shall find'. He wished them to become men of enquiring mind, not prigs who happened to have been born into the right Church in the right nation. He believed reason to be the foundation of theology and he aimed to make orthodoxy intelligible.[4]

In his own discipline Simson's outlook kept him in touch with the most audacious thinking of his time, with the deists, who believed the universe must be guided by some divine force perhaps not fully explicable in terms of the Christian revelation, and with the natural theologians, who saw God's expression of himself in nature as a complement to the revelation. Simson did not necessarily accept these novel positions, but he held a command of them by his students to be useful for any future defence they might need to mount of the Church and its teachings. During 20 years they went on to swell the ranks of the Presbyterian clergy in the west of Scotland and the north of Ireland.[5]

But not all ministers possessed Simson's experience or assurance. The Kirk as a whole still feared a little for its established status in the new United Kingdom. Guaranteed though it supposedly was by the Treaty of Union, a lot of the English MPs at Westminster still viewed it with open hostility.[6] Many Presbyterians felt all the more determined never to compromise on their tradition, and least of all in response to any modern spirit of scientific enquiry. In 1710 Simson, while enjoying a break at the spa of Moffat in Dumfriesshire, encountered one of these diehards, the Revd James Webster, minister of the Tolbooth kirk in Edinburgh. In between taking the waters they seem to have passed the time in friendly enough conversation, but it left Webster in no doubt that he did not like what his colleague had to say. Later Simson entered into correspondence on thorny points with the Revd Robert Rowan of Penningham in Wigtownshire and the Revd James Hog of Carnock in Fife. These orthodox enquirers objected to one view they had heard attributed to Simson, that human beings might effect their own salvation, and to a second, that Jesus Christ had died for everybody, not just for the elect. Simson's replies to their queries evidently failed to satisfy them, for they at length complained about him to the Presbytery of Glasgow. Though his university defended him, the complaint went up to the General Assembly of the Church of Scotland in 1714.

The gravamen of this complaint was that Simson attributed too much human capacity to the 'light of nature', so demoting revelation as the sole source of certainty. The General Assembly dealt with this as it was accustomed to deal with all controversies, and referred it to a committee. There, during three years of deliberation, no consensus emerged because a judicious majority wished to absolve Simson from the charges against him while a stubborn minority wanted to hound him out of the ministry. Deadlocked, the committee was by the spring of 1717 having difficulty in summoning up a quorum for its proceedings and voted to call a halt to them. In the event, it cleared Simson of most charges against him.[7] The following General Assembly concurred: he had 'vented some opinions not necessary to be taught in divinity' and had employed expressions 'used by adversaries in a bad and unsound sense'. He was forbidden to do so for the future, but without suffering further censure. He had, in other words, no need to change his mind. His critics thought he had got off lightly.[8]

These critics nursed their wrath to keep it warm, yet it was a dozen years before they could strike at Simson again. Meanwhile the Enlightenment dawned at the University of Glasgow. In 1727 it underwent a thorough reorganisation that did away with the old system of instruction by regents, that is to say, teachers who took a whole class of students right through the entire curriculum. It was replaced with the modern system of specialised professors who taught their own subject to different classes. At this point Glasgow's greatest scholar, Gerschom Carmichael, a theorist of natural law, became its professor of moral philosophy.[9] His death two years later made way for the election of Francis Hutcheson, a Presbyterian clergyman from Ulster, today generally reckoned the first philosopher of the Scottish Enlightenment. He later said his motive in coming to Glasgow had been 'to promote the more moderate and charitable sentiments in religious matters in this country, where yet there remains too much warmth and animosity about matters of no great consequence to real religion'.[10]

But this came a bit too late to help Simson. In 1726 the Presbytery of Glasgow had again picked on him, this time over his position on the doctrine of the Trinity. It sent him a list of questions concerning it. He spiritedly refused to answer any of them, not till the members of the committee answered a list of questions he wanted to send them back. The matter again went up to the General Assembly, with the inevitable result that another committee was asked to investigate. It called as witnesses a succession of Simson's past and present students, but most claimed they could not recall the exact words he had used in his lectures. Even so, the General Assembly decided to suspend Simson from his duties as professor. Only now, perhaps, did it come home to him that his job really was at stake. Supported by his university, he went public with the whole business and unleashed a frenzied battle of pamphlets for and against him. He complained that he had been smeared by 'gross falsehoods and calumny artfully mixed with great pretences to piety'. The strict Presbyterians continued their efforts to get him deposed from his chair, but the next General Assembly merely allowed his suspension to stand. After receiving Simson's clarifications, it found his sentiments to be 'sound and orthodox' even if his teaching was 'subversive' and his explanations tardy. There was now to be a poll of presbyteries. The majority favoured Simson's deposition. Yet that still seemed, to the General Assembly of 1729 at least, to go a little too far. It merely confirmed the offender's suspension yet again; while it would be open to future assemblies to reconsider the matter, in fact none ever did so. Simson retained the emoluments of his chair, though it was officially 'not fit or safe' for him to teach divinity.[11]

As so often in the Church of Scotland this was a political kind of resolution, and it is no surprise to find politicians behind it. Taking an interest in the case were two of the most powerful men in the country, and especially powerful in Glasgow, John Campbell, Duke of Argyll, together with his brother, Archibald Campbell, Earl of Ilay. They came of a family revered by Presbyterians: their grandfather and great-grandfather were martyrs for the

Covenants under Catholic kings of the House of Stewart. These two younger scions had long ago arrived at the view, however, that one basic principle of the Union should be an end to religious persecution – something not actually stated in the treaty though implicit in its provision for two established churches in the United Kingdom, the Church of Scotland and the Church of England, founded though they were on different principles. With this Argyll and Ilay wanted to see also the development of an enlightened theology less concerned with dogmas of salvation than with reason and nature.[12]

It was Ilay especially that interested himself in these matters, out of a genuine desire to promote the well-being of Scotland. One way to do it was through the powers of patronage that people in his position could exercise. Despite his antecedents, he was no friend to the sternest Calvinists. On the contrary, he sought out in his ecclesiastical and academic preferment men who would counter their influence, and Simson filled the bill. Even so, this case went to show how carefully Ilay yet needed to tread. No doubt he agreed with a memorandum sent to him by his chief political adviser, the judge Andrew Fletcher, Lord Milton: 'It is the opinion of all the king's servants here [in Edinburgh] that nothing more should be done against Prof. Simson than the leaving the affair in the state it now is till another assembly, by which time some expedient may be fallen.'[13] And so, still indecisively, the case did at length peter out.

But the strict Presbyterians were not to be put off. They continued to attack professorial candidates they disapproved of. These included Archibald Campbell, a student of Simson's who took the chair of ecclesiastical history at the University of St Andrews, William Wishart junior, who held the same chair at Edinburgh before succeeding as principal of the university, and William Leechman, who at length was to become principal of the University of Glasgow. Suspected of error by Calvinists leery of their liberal theology, these men relied on political support to win their way through. In each case the political support, especially from Ilay, was forthcoming. To be sure, he could not make it work every time. The philosopher David Hume appreciated Ilay's imperviousness to unenlightened pressures, especially after he succeeded his brother as duke in 1743: 'I have not incumbered his levees, but have left him the free disposal of all his favours to voters, cabbalers, and disclaimers, and spies, and other such useful people. I have a regard for his Grace, and desire this trifle [*An Inquiry concerning Human Understanding* (1748)] may be considered as a present, not to the Duke of Argyll, but to Archibald Campbell, who is undoubtedly a man of sense and learning.'[14] Hume would have done better not to be quite so fastidious, because when he applied for and failed to get academic jobs in 1744–45 and 1751–52 his lack of political backing was probably more to blame than his lack of religious faith.

The encounter of presbytery and politics continued for most of the eighteenth century, as it had continued for most of the seventeenth. Then, Presbyterianism became at a crucial juncture also an expression of nationalism, indeed the saviour of the nation against the tyranny of King Charles I. The same spirit carried through right up to 1707 and, but for some statesmanlike accommodation, might well have scuppered the Union. With the resulting compromise Presbyterianism would need to live for the rest of this new and enlightened age.

After the restoration of Presbyterianism as the established religion of the country in 1690, the Kirk had faced the future with confidence. In the next decade it set energetically about various practical projects for the erection of a godly commonwealth in Scotland, from the policing of personal morality to the creation of a national system of parochial schools. That personal morality should be policed was the big idea of the devout David Home, Lord Crossrig, one of the first judges appointed to the Court of Session after the Revolution. He had been a bit of a tearaway as a student at the University of Edinburgh, from which he was expelled for defying a ban on football and for swearing on the park. Perhaps that prompted him to reform himself, for he got back into his course at Edinburgh and then took a further degree in law at the University of Poitiers in France. Yet he had no hope of a normal legal career because he supported the Covenanters, and let them hold conventicles on his land in Berwickshire. With this record, however, he reaped his reward once the oppressive regime of the Stewarts was overthrown in 1688.[15]

The first decade after the Revolution disappointed Crossrig, all the same. He hoped the Scots would now become a nation dedicated to true religion. The General Assembly did indeed take a hard line against profanity and blasphemy, backed up at the outset by Parliament. But Crossrig and his like worried that such victories for a just and godly cause did not banish moral degradation or impiety from the land. On the contrary, there was a 'growth of profanity' amid 'the lukewarmness of many who in the days of suffering had shown some zeal'. The campaign against sin seemed to be failing, or at any rate needed more strenuous effort for 'the restraining and punishing of vice'.[16] The strict Presbyterians' hour of triumph and their brief ascendancy had been followed far too soon by a loss of influence to more temporising churchmen and by backsliding in the nation at large.

Crossrig's plan now was that committed Presbyterians should combine, on a personal and private level, to remind the Scottish state of its obligation to stamp out sin. Their vehicle would be the Societies for the Reformation of Manners that he set about organising from 1699.[17] His efforts may have created a dozen or more of them across the Lowlands, and a few kept going for decades. Yet the project did not get a warm welcome from the government of Scotland, which preferred laws to be enforced by its own agents rather than by self-appointed vigilantes. So it specified that, while members of the societies might go out on nightly patrols in search of drunks and prostitutes, they should only do so in the company of a legally warranted officer and could not themselves arrest or detain the delinquents. In practice, they witnessed offences or alerted the officers to them, and if necessary testified later in court.

While the government felt wary of all this Presbyterian self-righteousness, Scots at large might be positively hostile. The societies were warned it would be a bad idea to snoop round the hostelries where, when Parliament was sitting, the members liked to meet 'for their refreshment or business'. The vigilantes also had the unpleasant habit, when they caught men and women *in flagrante delicto*, of letting the man go and delivering the woman up to jail. When one member brought such a trollop to the captain of the town guard, he released her and clapped the killjoy in the stocks for having impersonated a warranted officer.[18]

But the puritanism also had a more charitable side. The societies took a close interest in Highland education. Among the poor population scattered over the difficult terrain of the north, schooling was woefully deficient. In 1701, the societies contributed to the support of a school at Abertarff, near the present Fort Augustus. While it closed down within a couple of years, it had done well enough to prompt efforts at a more ambitious scheme. The result was the establishment in 1708 of another society, the Society in Scotland for Propagating Christian Knowledge. Its aim would be 'the further promoting of Christian Knowledge and the increase of piety and virtue within Scotland, especially in the Highlands, Islands and remote corners thereof, where error, idolatry, superstition and ignorance do mostly abound, by reason of the largeness of parishes and scarcity of schools'.[19] The foundation of charitable schools became the society's main activity. It did well: by 1758 it was running 176 of them. But most lay near the Highland line, and what they did in effect was prepare their pupils to migrate to the Lowlands for the rest of their lives. The plight of the far greater numbers in the wild country beyond remained largely untouched. They, and usually their parents too, had no language but Gaelic, yet Presbyterians generally reckoned Gaelic to be a mark of Jacobite rebellion and papist superstition. The society refused to use it as a language of instruction – indeed forbade its teachers to speak a word of it, even to little children who knew nothing else. The eighteenth century was not to see this linguistic difficulty solved.

Still, Scotland had meanwhile been busily building a national and public system of education, an achievement on which the relative failure in the Highlands was the only real blot. Provided for by an Act of Parliament of 1696, it aimed to make of the Scots a literate people imbued with the word of God because they had read it in the Bible for themselves. In a country of limited resources the fulfilment of this great educational ideal was an ambitious task, yet despite all difficulties it would in the event be largely accomplished.[20]

The bigger burghs already had high schools that fitted into a national system with ease, the only problem in these places being that soon they would undergo growth outrunning the facilities that a single institution could offer. For smaller towns and villages, and indeed generally over the rural Lowlands, the national system also worked well. Where new schools had to be founded it was the responsibility of the heritors or landowners in every parish, which meant access to the system remained free or cheap for the people. Indeed it became cheaper in real terms, because the schoolmasters had to wait till 1804 for their first pay rise. Their penury encouraged them, however, to widen the curriculum beyond the basics with new subjects for which they could charge.[21]

The overall result was to give the Kirk an educational presence almost everywhere, but no monopoly. The creation of a literate populace in turn set off enough charitable and commercial impetus for the national system to be augmented by private schools, often founded for a special purpose such as education of orphans or training in mercantile skills. After 1750 a rapid rise in the number of such private schools showed the sector as a whole to be providing a great deal more than simple reading literacy.[22]

This was by contemporary European standards an excellent system of education – which has not stopped controversy down to the present day about precisely what, in addition to general literacy, it achieved. There is a big question mark over the degree of selection in the system, and who or what it selected. Of those with a proprietary interest in it, the Kirk's aim would have been to identify and encourage academic ability among boys, regardless of their social background, whom it could recruit to the ministry and to the teaching profession. What on the other hand the heritors probably looked for was universal elementary education, including some access for girls, which would shape a workforce with basic skills in literacy and numeracy, therefore more adaptable than previous generations and less likely to resist social and economic change. In other words, there was bound to be a certain tension between elitism and generalism, between selection and equality: this wrote the saga of Scottish education during the next three centuries.[23]

For the time being, it was enough that education became available over most of the country at low cost, that the majority of the populace achieved literacy and that the channels from school to university opened wide. The consequences for Scottish society proved profound. A century later one of the rulers of the country was to claim that 'the people of Scotland are a sedate, religious people, not easily moved'.[24] Indeed, despite the desperate search by certain historians for every hint of a revolutionary impulse, the overall character of the nation lay in its social peace, conformity and discipline.

This meant above all that, as economic improvement proceeded, there was room for most people to take part in it and to benefit from it. Their general instruction at school, including the Calvinist catechism, equipped them to apprehend and interpret the world about them. They could argue about it in line with the democratic intellectualism that Scots had espoused ever since the Reformation. Now indeed, in the modern nation, the shaping of critical intelligence was possible in every rank of society. 'Even the Scotch peasantry and working classes possess the habit of making observations and reasoning thereon with great acuteness,' the Welsh industrial reformer Robert Owen would find on crossing the border in 1801.[25] The social importance of this was that ordinary, literate folk could readily cast off the trammels of tradition because they found authority in the printed page rather than in the wisdom of their ancestors. The nation learned about progress from books, periodicals and newspapers then went out and reproduced the progress in the real world. This needed no political revolution.

The law of 1696 not only gave basic instruction to as many children as possible but also prepared the brightest to go on to university. Scotland housed five universities, three dating from the Middle Ages, St Andrews (1410), Glasgow

(1451) and King's College, Aberdeen (1495), the others from the era of the Reformation, Edinburgh (1583) and Marischal College, Aberdeen (1596). The Treaty of Union guaranteed their status too, one purpose of the relevant provision being to assure a supply of men qualified for the Presbyterian ministry. In fact, the study of divinity had become rather dangerous in the preceding age of religious strife, as likely to lead to banishment and destitution, even to the scaffold, as to a comfortable living in a pleasant parish. Other disciplines flourished instead: science, mathematics, medicine, with law soon to be added. Even then, after 1688 and 1715 the Scottish universities suffered purges of Episcopalians and Jacobites. They sometimes lost scholars of the highest ability, while the resulting suspicion and injustice generally disrupted academic life. Here was another reason why the Scottish universities trailed intellectually behind the prestigious Dutch institutions. Scots who could afford it had long been sending their sons to Europe to complete their education, and there seemed nothing to dissuade them from doing so in future too.[26]

Yet the upheavals turned out to be the prelude to deeper and more beneficial changes in the Scottish universities. Their curriculum had not changed much since they were founded. It continued the intellectual legacy of the Middle Ages, which was scholastic; in other words, it required the mastery of set texts and of techniques for detailed criticism that had been perfected in defence of religious orthodoxy. The actual cultural function was to secure and perpetuate clerical control of the universities, if since the Reformation by a Calvinist clerisy rather than by a Catholic one. With its academic monopoly and impenetrable learning, this caste overawed the lay population.[27] It was not just a Scottish but also a European problem, and every country had to escape the educational cul-de-sac in its own way.

For Scotland, the necessary transformation came ahead of most nations – and it could hardly have been a consequence of the Union with England, where academic life remained moribund. The links, of intellectual exchange and of personal contact, ran rather to Holland and France. But most changes were home-grown. The Scottish universities grew and flourished under teachers of high quality drawn from among the best clergymen and lawyers, and in the sciences eventually from among the world's leaders in their disciplines. There was a tripling in the number of students through the eighteenth century, for the instruction came cheap and entry was free of any social restrictions.[28] The courses focused not on old texts but on the minds of those young students, developing in them intellectual powers and then professional expertise that could fit everybody, not just the sons of privilege, for a useful and prosperous life. While in other systems of higher education a minute mastery of Greek and Latin often still formed the groundwork for the rest of the instruction, in Scotland the stress lay on moral philosophy and then on natural philosophy (or physical science) with a special interest in the Newtonian combination of experiment with mathematics.[29] It was not under any outside pressure but through the teachers themselves that all these alterations took place, and chiefly at the hands of the Presbyterian ministers who filled most academic posts. We should not therefore be too impressed by the zealots who sought to reform manners or propagate Christian knowledge; the Kirk, with the nation's main concentration of trained minds, had many ministers of a broader outlook.

Already by the time of the Union such ministers were taking over the leadership of the Kirk, to the relief of the politicians who had to deal with it. These ministers, unlike many of the strict Presbyterians, tended to favour the treaty of 1707. That held true, for example, of every Moderator of the General Assembly in the preceding years, each of whom happened to be from Edinburgh: in 1702, the Revd David Cuthbertson of St Cuthbert's, once in his dim and distant past a Covenanter; in 1703, the Revd George Meldrum of the Tron, also professor of divinity at the university; in 1704, the Revd Thomas Wilkie of the Canongate; in 1705, the Revd William Carstares of Greyfriars and principal of the university; in 1706, the Revd William Wishart of South Leith. Venerable figures, some the victims of persecution long ago, they did command genuine personal authority. In running the Kirk, they saw the need to placate the strict Presbyterians. But, in contrast to the wild men on that side, these Moderators, though far from impious, took this world as seriously as the next. Their overriding aim was to maintain the existing religious establishment, if necessary or feasible by reasonable accommodation to the civil power. A *curiosum* of Presbyterianism is that, so long as not established it erupts in revolt and rage, but once established it turns as douce and docile as can be.[30]

Among the clique in charge of the Kirk, Carstares acquired or assumed special eminence. It would have been easy for him to take his appointment in 1703 as principal of the University of Edinburgh to be a sort of lap of honour after his years close to the heart of royal government under William of Orange, with whom he had started working in Holland before the Revolution of 1688. But Carstares set with no less energy and creativity about his academic duties. He also led the way in the delicate adjustment of the Church of Scotland to the Union – and, more important, vice versa. He could rely on his clique in Edinburgh ('the most grave and judicious ministers here'), among whom those with reservations were on his account prepared to swallow them. He pulled secular strings as well. His reward came in the fact that the continued establishment of a Presbyterian Kirk was finally taken as read, by the English government too, and that the assurance in the treaty of the Hanoverian succession would keep the biggest threat to it at bay. It then fell to Carstares to head off a clash between the principles of the treaty as it had been written and the conflicting claims of Presbyterian nationalism, made flesh in young hotheads preaching against the betrayal of Scotland to English apostates.[31]

These militants did find some place among the clergy of Edinburgh too, in the persons of the Revds James Hart at Greyfriars and James Webster at the Tolbooth. Unabashed when the Union went through, they sought within it fresh causes to champion. A particular cavil was with the chance the British Parliament might legislate toleration in Scotland – meaning of Episcopalians. It did do that, though even then it was not finished. It actually went one worse to attack the very foundation of the Presbyterian system that lay in the popular election of the minister by each congregation. And all this happened within five years of the Union. The prophets of doom had been right: or had they?[32]

Webster had indeed warned in 1707: 'A legal toleration in Scotland will be very prejudicial to this Church and nation. Every thinking man knows that such a toleration will certainly follow on the Union, and 'tis as certain that it will bring along with it very mischievous effects, and have a malign influence on all the branches of our Reformation.' In this view the militants and some of the clique in charge of the Kirk actually agreed. Meldrum in particular ranted and raved at any hint of toleration, blaming Episcopalians for his own deposition as rector of Marischal College, Aberdeen, back in 1681. In aims and outlook different from Carstares, he was yet a definite Scottish type, not a discreet backroom boy but a diligent manufacturer of grievances: he had published a manifesto for sneaks and spies on 'the lawfulness of informing against vicious and profane behaviour before the courts of immorality'. Yet Carstares, free of such defensive intransigence, knew no English guarantee could be won anyway. Presbyterians would have to take the matter on trust.

In fact, their fears came true in 1712 when, in a piece of deliberate Tory provocation, Westminster passed a Toleration Act for Scotland. Carstares had gone to London to lobby against it, and his reputation suffered when he was obliged to come back and admit he had achieved nothing.[33]

Yet Presbyterian fears of toleration turned out to be exaggerated. In fact, it proved almost the downfall of the Episcopalians by bringing them out into the open and tempting them to worldly commitments they would have been better off without. At least they were not stalking horses for anglicisation, as Presbyterians might claim. While some Episcopalians used the English Prayer Book, most did not: they depended instead like any Covenanter on the Bible and on extempore prayer, while their priests wore no surplice but a black gown. They had survived the Revolution of 1688 because many Scots still saw in an episcopal Kirk one that, being Protestant, yet linked them with their national history and maintained its continuity. Episcopalians were more in touch with Scotland's heroic medieval past than any iconoclastic Protestants in the Covenanting tradition could ever be. They bore no blame for the destruction of religious painting and sculpture or the suppression of popular literature and festivity. It was Episcopalian households that kept up the older, strongly patriotic traditions of music and poetry, satisfying some instincts that the sterner, indeed often philistine, Presbyterian tradition suppressed. Again, the Kirk now wanted to stamp out Gaelic but there was no such hostility among Episcopalians.[34]

The Episcopalians had, as they have to this day, a stronghold in the north-east of Scotland. After the Revolution it remained so strong that no Presbyterian communion could be offered in the city of Aberdeen before 1704. While, in some areas of the Lowlands, Episcopalian priests were still being roughed up by vengeful mobs, at Fraserburgh attempts to induct a Presbyterian minister led to hostile rioting in 1707. The members of the presbytery of Deer got chased away by 'a rabble of people who threw stones and dub or mire upon them'. Some parishes lacked a Presbyterian minister till 30 or 40 years after the Revolution: Gamrie and Forglen till 1717, Fyvie and Alvah till 1718, Monquhitter till 1727.[35]

On the relations of Church and state, the Episcopalian tradition preached submission to a secular authority that would not have been there unless God had ordained it, sometimes for inscrutable purposes of his own. After 1688 this line of thinking faced the problem that God had, more inscrutably than usual, ordained the deposition of one secular authority that favoured episcopacy by another that did not. In the circumstances, Episcopalians affected indifference to worldly politics. A leading figure, Dr James Keith, wrote in 1715: 'In a time of general perplexity and distress the sober, pious and the good one way or the other must suffer also. Their principle is to submit to all powers and governments, as Christ and his disciples did, and to disturb none.'[36]

In reality, of course, Episcopalians could just as well join in active politics, and indeed they became the main source of support for Jacobite rebellion. When the British state pursued those who took up arms in 1715, Presbyterians helpfully pointed out what encouragement the insurgents had received from Episcopalian clergymen. The scandal of their still clinging on to remote rustic charges was afterwards brought to wider attention by the circulation of a pamphlet not tolerant in tone, *An Apology for the Aberdeen Evictions* (the actions to depose treasonable incumbent ministers). With glee it dredged up 'The Address of the Episcopal Clergy in the Diocese of Aberdeen to the Pretender', a document they had handed to their King James VIII at Fetteresso in December 1715 when presented to him by his host at the castle, the Earl Marischal, and his commander-in-chief, the Earl of Mar. Even according to the normal standards of sycophancy on such occasions the address went somewhat over the top, telling the dull and diffident young prince how like he appeared to Moses, Joseph and David. It was the Jacobite commitment that, despite the Toleration Act, steadily robbed Scottish Episcopalians of all the sneaking sympathy and support they had enjoyed from English MPs at Westminster.[37]

But what turned out to be by far the greater problem for Scotland was the second piece of English-inspired legislation, the Patronage Act. Presbyterianism held that congregations should elect their own ministers. Still, early on in the seventeenth century the religious enthusiasm this had unleashed inside the Kirk proved too much for the secular authorities, which sought ways to tame it. One way was to have the ministers not elected by their parishioners but presented to the parish by its heritors. A second way was to bring back bishops and set them in authority over the rest of the clergy. All this ended with the Revolution of 1688 and the Presbyterian constitution that it restored to the Kirk. Yet after 1707, despite the treaty's guarantees, Presbyterians still did not feel quite secure. A risk remained that the reimposition of patronage on Scotland might prove too tempting to the inbuilt Anglican majority at Westminster. True to form, English Tories were the ones that again did the dirty work and carried the Patronage Act in 1712.[38]

The Church of Scotland naturally opposed the legislation. The General Assembly drew up a formal protest against it, now and in every year till 1784. But Westminster ignored this, and the Kirk had little choice but to knuckle under. It could do no more than require more stringent educational, moral and practical qualifications of candidates for the ministry. A few of the presentations to parishes were still contested through the courts of the Church, though to little avail. The assembly knew that, if it decided against a patron, he could seek civil damages from it. This was why, in cases where the parishioners persisted in their opposition, the presbytery also had the power to call in the army and get the chosen minister into his kirk by force if need be, a proceeding known as intrusion. It did happen from time to time, but the victories usually proved pyrrhic. When, in the parish of St Ninian by Stirling in 1734, the Revd James Meek was inducted against the will of the congregation, about half of it walked out on him for good. In 1773 the same parish had to accept the Revd David Thomson after spending eight years in appeals against him to the General Assembly. Now the rest of the congregation voted with its feet. Still, its members stuck together and set about collecting enough money to buy out the interest of the patrons after Thomson died. Once he was gone in 1787 they did then purchase the legal right to choose their future ministers for themselves.[39] This was hardly something that could be done everywhere, however. Some patrons made a point of consulting the congregation before presenting a minister to it but others, especially if disaffected from the Hanoverian regime, made a point of not doing so.

The Patronage Act was a second measure with results going far beyond any originally intended, some of which might have been welcomed by its framers and some not. The spread of the Enlightenment through the Church of Scotland could well be portrayed as a benign result of the patronage exercised, in many cases, by educated and progressive lairds. Over time it just naturally came about that a large number of the ministers sitting in the General Assembly were there due to the working of patronage in their own favour. In practice, they turned unwilling to challenge the system even if they did still vote their formal protest against it every year. This group, the Moderate party, in due course formed the dominant group in the Kirk. Meanwhile, others continued to object to patronage on principle, as compromising the spiritual independence of the Church of Scotland vindicated by the blood of martyrs. They were called the Popular party.[40]

While the Popular party lost most of its battles in the General Assembly, by and large it could indeed count on the support of the people outside. Things worked both ways. Inside the Kirk, the strict Presbyterians did set out to control the moral conduct of the faithful as the foundation for a godly commonwealth of the future, and refused to compromise on this despite other setbacks. Practising members of the Church of Scotland after all belonged, or so it had to be assumed, to the elect of God. In the end God and the Scots were on the same side, then, and earthly powers should hold no fear for them. Just as they demanded the purest conduct of themselves, so they were justified in punishing their errant fellows. A nation that shrank from the struggle against sin would suffer divine punishment in natural disasters and similar misfortunes, of which indeed the Scots had suffered their full measure; they could then only abase themselves in days of fasting and humiliation that the Kirk would proclaim for them.[41]

Yet even by 1688 this grim Presbyterianism had lightened up a little, compared to the face like flint it had shown during its high noon earlier in the century. The Scottish state was no longer willing to reinforce religious censure with civil sanctions, as had once been the case. Now in the last resort a hardened offender could laugh at the session and get away with it. 'What care I?' said a man threatened with excommunication at Fetteresso in Kincardine in 1748, 'the Pope of Rome excommunicates you every year, and what the waur are ye o' that?'[42] Presbyterians themselves stopped trying to sniff out such sins as pride and avarice that lay all in the heads of the faithful, and concentrated instead on offences leaving outward traces capable of being investigated by the elders, who would then have the pleasant duty of interrogating the culprits before the kirk sessions. Even people found guilty were less likely nowadays to be forced to repent in sackcloth and ashes before the whole congregation. Instead it became acceptable for them to pay a fine, which could be slipped in the poor's box.[43]

But the transfer of scrutiny from inward to outward conduct should not be confused with any softer line against the sins the Kirk did still hold within its purview. It stuck to its conviction that it had the right and duty to impose its standards on all Scots, in small matters as in great. In 1719 the clergy of Edinburgh singled out swimming on Sunday, though the smelly citizens of the capital, a place ill supplied with fresh water, might find neither means nor time for a good wash otherwise. For the local presbytery, dirtiness was preferable to desecration of the Sabbath. It called on the Lord Provost for 'a competent number of soldiers in the city guard to attend upon the elders and deacons every Lord's day that they go to Bonnington Water for suppressing effectually these horrid outrages on the Lord's day' – that is, people splashing about in the Water of Leith. But the presbytery was biting off more than it could chew when it also sought to stop people 'standing in companies in the streets, misspending the time in idle discourse, vain and useless communication', or 'withdrawing from the city to take their recreations in walking through fields, parks, links and meadows', even 'entering into taverns, ale houses, mills, houses, gardens or other places to drink, tipple or otherwise misspend any part thereof', or just 'idly gazing out of windows, beholding vanities abroad'.[44]

Still, it was on sex that the strict Presbyterians cracked down. The kirk sessions had ever since the Reformation shown a deep interest in fornication, adultery, illegitimacy and clandestine marriage (marriage contracted outside the regular rites of the Church). These were misdemeanours often with visible consequences and of a kind that placed burdens on others innocent of them, on the offenders' families or communities. There seems little doubt that most people, at least in the Lowlands, accepted Presbyterian discipline: this was above all why the offenders in their midst felt compelled to submit to it as well. The Kirk's bark was often worse than its bite, however. The sanctions it could impose were limited. Though the fathers of the bastard bairns usually denied paternity at first, most soon admitted it and performed their public penance: 3 times for 'simple fornication', 6 times for a second offence or relapse, 26 times for adultery and 52 times for incest. There was a further price to pay in money for support of the child. In the end, all could feel satisfied that the culprit really was sorry enough. The poet Robert Burns would be a victim of the process more than once, yet he got his revenge by teaching brother Scots to see the sessions as nests of spite, prurience and hypocrisy. The discipline did in fact finally weaken, though not because Scotland became less religious. On the contrary, Christianity remained popular in every sense: it was the depth of the Scots' commitment to the Presbyterian faith that caused the Kirk trouble.[45]

As in the case of Episcopalianism, the Presbyterian commitment had a certain regional bias. Its stronghold lay in the west of Scotland. Not only did this region boast a courageous Covenanting history but it was also still capable of nurturing fresh forms of religious enthusiasm. The most striking came in the Cambuslang Wark of 1742, when tens of thousands of ordinary folk gathered in this village just south of Glasgow for open-air communion and sermons from leading evangelical clergymen, the Revds Thomas Gillespie of Carnock, John Maclaurin of Glasgow, William McCulloch of Cambuslang, James Robe of Kilsyth and Alexander Webster from Edinburgh. 'God was with both ministers and people in a more remarkable way then ever I was witness to before,' wrote another visitor from the capital, the Revd John Erskine.[46] Revival would become a permanent part of Presbyterian witness. If the Moderate ministers of Edinburgh were often politic in their pronouncements, the ministers of the Popular party in Glasgow left the city in no doubt what they expected of it and how far it fell short. It 'seems to be fast ripening for a stroak', proclaimed one preacher in 1757, citing the transformation of a once pious town into a place where irreligion – swearing, public drunkenness, violation of the Sabbath – had become commonplace. This seemed to him far more significant than the superficial prosperity it enjoyed from its flourishing trade in tobacco (which would be the chief sin from today's politically correct point of view). When the philosopher Thomas Reid came down here from Aberdeen in 1764, he disliked the 'gloomy, enthusiastical cast' of the devout in Glasgow.[47]

Over most of Scotland, however, the Church suffered in practice not so much from its own self-righteousness as from the exercise of patronage that the British state imposed on it. Patronage had this effect in the direct, basic sense of alienating those members who refused to accept its legitimacy, price though it might be of a secure religious establishment. For this reason a still defensive General Assembly acted from time to time to tighten the legislation regarding it, and did so again in 1732. One minister, the Revd Ebenezer Erskine of Stirling, asked for his dissent to be recorded, but he was turned down. His supporters saw here an immediate move to silence them and in the background the betrayal of a fundamental element in the Presbyterian system. Later in the year Erskine, as moderator of the synod of Stirling, preached a sermon denouncing this as unscriptural and unconstitutional. Members of the synod objected, and he was censured. On appeal, the General Assembly affirmed the censure. Still Erskine refused to recant, and the Revds William Wilson of Perth, Alexander Moncrieff of Abernethy and James Fisher of Kinclaven joined him in his dissent. The assembly of 1733 ruled them all to be in contempt of it. After six months of contumacy they were suspended.

The four then formed a presbytery of their own, so in effect seceding from the Church of Scotland. In 1736 they began to organise congregations round the country that could join their presbytery. Within a few years they had 45 of them. This became known as the Original Secession.[48]

Once a seceder, always a seceder – and in 1747 the Original Secession itself split. The occasion was parliamentary legislation for the 'burgher oath' requiring all holders of public office to affirm their adherence to established religion. The move had come in reaction to the widespread Episcopalian support for the Jacobite rebellion of 1745, which at last made English MPs think better of the Church of Scotland. Yet it was the strict Presbyterians that took offence at this introduction of civil compulsion into religious affairs. A split followed between those who would take the oath and those who would not, between Burghers and Anti-Burghers. Each sect was to split once again by the end of the century. The Original Secession then had four successors: Auld Licht Burghers and New Licht Burghers, Auld Licht Anti-burghers and New Licht Anti-burghers. The difference between Auld Licht and New Licht was that the one regarded the Covenants as forever binding on Scots, while the other thought they might be adapted to changing needs. Meanwhile, those faithful to the Covenants had anyway to live in an uncovenanted state, and the difference between Burghers and Anti-Burghers still lay in willingness, or not, to swear the oaths it exacted. The four sects' names suggest their permutations of dogma on these matters.[49]

Nor should we forget at this juncture that schism was nothing new in Presbyterianism. Much earlier on the Cameronians or Reformed Presbyterians, warriors in the fiercest religious struggles after 1660, had refused to accept even the settlement of 1690 on the grounds that it did not provide for a covenanted king. They continued to advocate armed resistance to the British state, though nobody seems to have taken this too seriously. All the same, a group of Reformed Presbyterians on those grounds suffered expulsion from a congregation in Edinburgh as late as 1792. Their revolutionary potential was somewhat compromised by the fact that they afterwards split among themselves into Lifters and Anti-Lifters (of the bread being blessed for communion). All such sects would once have brought savage persecution down on themselves, but since 1707 there could be no question of that. What we may conclude is that the Scottish tradition of dogmatic hair-splitting and determined nonconformity remained vigorous. Sir Walter Scott now found it charming in the way it transformed the nation's intellectual vices of pedantry and obtuseness into virtues of honesty and constancy.[50]

An unrelated secession in 1752 produced yet another sect, the Relief Church, which rather became a refuge for those dissatisfied with hard-line Calvinism. Its interest lay more in individual conversion and commitment than in the rule of the saints. But it too was a product of the saga of patronage. A further dispute had come up at Inverkeithing in Fife. Here, when the parishioners objected to the presentee, the presbytery felt reluctant to overrule them. It was the General Assembly that stepped in and ordered the presbytery to induct the new minister regardless of what his parishioners thought. A member of the presbytery, the Revd Thomas Gillespie of Carnock, refused to have any part in this. He was in his turn deposed. Two colleagues, the Revds Thomas Boston of Jedburgh and Thomas Colier of Colinsburgh spoke out in his favour. They got together at the manse of Colinsburgh in the East Neuk and constituted themselves as a 'presbytery of relief', meaning relief from patronage. It too grew rapidly and would be able to form a synod in 1773. A reason for its popularity was that it did not ask after the doctrinal correctness of those who wished to take communion from its ministers. By the early nineteenth century this and the other schisms had attracted wide support. The dissenting congregations were estimated to have won, for example, 40 per cent of the faithful in Edinburgh, mostly artisans – though this would without doubt have been a high figure compared to the rest of Scotland.[51]

The secession of the Relief Church also left a legacy inside the Kirk. There, among those in the General Assembly most insistent that the presbytery of Fife must submit to superior authority was a group of younger ministers. They had met in a tavern to co-ordinate their action: not the sort of behaviour the strict Presbyterians would have permitted themselves. The point the youngsters pressed the next morning in the assembly's proceedings was that the dispute at Inverkeithing should not become another test of the rights and wrongs of the Patronage Act and, by implication, of the iniquity of the British state. Instead it ought to be regarded as a matter of discipline inside the Kirk. Since the assembly was in practice powerless against the Act, it should not let this lead to decay in the hierarchical structure on which Presbyterian order depended. These ministers were just embarking on careers in a spirit enlightened as well as devout that they would carry forward to the end of the century. They were the ones that first took for themselves the winsome name of Moderates.[52]

The Moderates sought to do several things in the course of their coming ascendancy, one of which was to adapt the Church of Scotland to contemporary realities that often proved unpalatable. With secession so common, it had become all the harder to impose discipline inside the Kirk. The faithful anyway began to show more interest in individual salvation than in communal conformity, so they just cared less about public penance. Some of the difficulties indeed arose out of legislation inspired by the perfidious English, but perhaps as many might be ascribed to the enlightened Scottish policies of the House of Argyll.

Among that house's innumerable clients was the architect William Adam, who rebuilt both its Lowland residence at Caroline Park by the Firth of Forth and its splendid feudal castle in the midst of Clan Campbell's territory at Inveraray in Argyll. Adam, at his own townhouse in the Cowgate of Edinburgh, ran a little intellectual salon where he liked to invite the bright young candidates for the ministry of the Kirk who would go on to form the Moderate party. One was his nephew, William Robertson, future principal of the University of Edinburgh. Another was Hugh Blair who at the height of his career would be minister of the Canongate, then of St Giles, a charge he held concurrently with the chair of rhetoric and belles-lettres at the university (that is, as the first professor of English literature in the British Isles). A third was Adam Ferguson, born in a Highland manse, who came south to qualify as a minister but then had problems finding a parish and would get a better bargain as professor of moral philosophy at the university. Then there was John Home, son of the town clerk of Leith and minister of Athelstaneford, who would shock the strict Presbyterians by writing and staging a play, *Douglas*; later he left for London to become private secretary to the Prime Minister, Lord Bute. Finally, Alexander 'Jupiter' Carlyle, minister of Inveresk, renowned for his good looks, verve and wit, would leave us his reminiscences of the rest. They were a good-humoured bunch and long recalled these student years as the best of their lives. Among the excitements was the approach in 1745 of the Jacobite army led by a Prince Charles Edward Stewart the same age as themselves. They joined the volunteers raised to defend the capital. As the clans occupied it, this force was disbanded without a fight. The clerical rookies might otherwise have been ordered out to the Battle of Prestonpans, to die alongside the redcoats: the history of the Church of Scotland would then have been different.[53]

Instead this younger generation could at length set out to take over the Kirk. It had to confront an older generation still championing orthodoxy and intransigence as the best defences of Presbyterianism. But the spirit of the age grew more secular, inclusive and elegant, while the new British state turned more venal, cynical and imperious. So the ground for battles in the cause of innovation sometimes looked rough.

For example, the rising ministerial stars rallied round the philosopher David Hume and the judge Henry Home, Lord Kames, as these came under attacks threatening to ruin their careers. Hume's atheism had already ruled him out for the chair of moral philosophy at the University of Edinburgh – though that did not sate his vengeful clerical enemies. Kames had said or done nothing so offensive, only expounded in his writings a standard theory of the Scottish Enlightenment that the human race had gone through successive stages of development, from hunting and gathering to commercial society, each marked by improved manners and advancing morality. It was an account leaving out the appearance, once and for all in human history, of a Saviour. It could therefore be deemed heretical and deserving of censure.[54]

The strict Presbyterians determined to do for Hume and Kames in 1755. The Revd John Bonar of Cockpen in Midlothian published a pamphlet attacking them for heresies that he called on the forthcoming General Assembly to condemn. If he had got his way, it would have stopped Hume ever finding any public preferment in Scotland, while Kames's position on the bench would have been compromised too. This was an extreme and provocative move. But by now most of the young Moderate ministers had parishes and so sat in the assembly. They did not like Hume's atheism or Kames's history with God left out. But they did see that fanatical attacks on Scots thinkers would show up the Church as an enemy of free enquiry and hold the whole country back. An older ally, the Revd Robert Wallace of Greyfriars in Edinburgh, asked if the assembly proposed to persecute 'calm contemplative wrongheaded writers' because it had got nowhere with 'drunkards, revellers, whore-mongers, adulterers': a good question.[55]

At that General Assembly, thanks to the youngsters' taking a hand, the charges of heresy were watered down almost to nothing. A hostile resolution, as at length amended and passed, did no more than point out the risks of impiety and immorality. 'My damnation is postponed for a twelvemonth,' Hume told the poet Allan Ramsay, 'but next Assembly will surely be upon me.' Yet the renewed attack in 1756 was repelled still more easily. It did not even get to the floor of the assembly, being instead sidelined in committee:

this had all over it the fingerprints of Robertson, already a manipulator of genius. As for Kames, he had consulted his lawyers, who combined offence with defence. They set out his claims to 'freedom of inquiry and reasoning'. Then they published a pamphlet showing that, while he might never have mentioned Jesus Christ, the two of them did not disagree. The move against Kames equally failed to find a place on the agenda of the assembly. He was judged, despite questionable ideas and 'unguarded expressions', to have meant no harm to religion.[56]

Such was the bland, bureaucratic way presbytery was by now learning to go about its business while it secured its hold on Scotland, with anything sensitive kept behind closed doors. But there were still times that did not work. One came in 1756 after Home undertook to give his drama *Douglas* a public performance. The Kirk continued to denounce the theatre for promoting vice, onstage and off. Confrontation looked inevitable.[57]

There is no reason to doubt Home's claim of a moral purpose for his play, to show noble virtue triumphing over base treachery. In that it was no worse and no better than other productions of its time, equating the pathos onstage with the sympathy supposed to be excited in the audience. Most are forgotten, and a revival of *Douglas* at the Edinburgh Festival of 1986 showed it merited the same fate, at least as an aesthetic phenomenon. Perhaps Home had some sense of that, to judge from a hammy patriotic appeal in the prologue:

Often has this audience soft compassion shown
To woes of heroes, heroes not their own.
This night our scenes no common tear demand
He comes, the hero of your native land.[58]

For the first night he need not have worried: there arose in the pit 'an uproar of exultation that a Scotchman had written a tragedy of the first rate'. Out of it came the cry, 'Whaur's yer Wullie Shakespeare noo?' Perhaps contemporary audiences just had a different taste.

The Kirk fumbled its response. Even clergymen had to admit Shakespeare might not be wholly bad. It was then awkward to explain why a modern playwright more decorous (to put it mildly) ought to be denied all tolerance, one of their own brethren though he might be. The Presbytery of Edinburgh pressed on regardless and ordered an 'admonition and exhortation' to be read from every pulpit in the city, condemning plays as illegal and 'prejudicial to the interests of religion and morality'. But again, an attempt to win the backing of the General Assembly was foiled. Home still thought it as well to resign his charge at Athelstaneford. He soon had bigger fish to fry in London.[59]

A pattern emerged from these disparate episodes and lesser ones. The Kirk was conceding secular autonomy in areas of life over which it had since 1690 – indeed since 1560 – claimed jurisdiction. This happened not only with the acquiescence but even with the connivance of the Moderates. They thought the world would improve not through ranting sermons and righteous wrath, rather through general social and intellectual advance to which they could and should be parties. In their outlook Christianity and Enlightenment converged.[60]

The moving spirit of this enlightened Kirk was Robertson, especially after he became principal of the University of Edinburgh in 1762. A crafty auto-crat, his vindication came in results: out of an era of mediocrity he led the town's college to greatness. This was still a poor institution (compared, say, to Oxford or Cambridge), and his genius lay in getting the best out of what he had. When he could he saw to the endowment of new chairs and filled them with brilliant professors (not drawing much pay, but living off fees they collected for lectures). He revised the curriculum – for example, so as to make moral philosophy compulsory for all taking arts, something that marked the Scottish intellect almost down to the present. His pot of gold was the medical school. It burgeoned till it accounted for 400 of the university's 1,000 students, drawing bright youngsters from as far away as America or Russia; here, given a successful professoriate, he was inclined to leave well alone and confine himself to financing new facilities. He did otherwise all he could for any project enhancing the intellectual life of college and town, from the Speculative Society for undergraduate debate (1764) to the Royal Society of Edinburgh for formal scholarly enquiry (1783).[61] And Robertson left us the superb physical memorial of a new home for his university. Today perversely known as Old College, it was the greatest public architectural achievement of Robert Adam. Begun in 1789 though not finished till 1820, the composition is of elegant symmetry, a little ponderous in a Roman sort of way. But its monumental façade makes it the most magnificent building in the city.

The Moderate alliance Robertson personified at Edinburgh between Church and university was a prime feature of the Scottish Enlightenment. It made this Enlightenment different from others in Europe. Those in Paris and Berlin were in religion sceptical and in politics progressive (if in a despotic fashion).[62] The enlightened men of Edinburgh espoused polite religion but still orthodox religion, and in politics remained conservative – the French Revolution, itself a product of Enlightenment, would horrify them. In a small nation with no power over its own fate, public aims had to be modestly confined to the general virtue and happiness of a society intent on rational progress. Scottish thinkers were reasonable without falling for elaborate constructions of rationality, like the Jacobins in France or the idealists in Prussia. The Scots put humane values first. They took a rounded view of the past and the present. They might have been almost too cosmopolitan when they wanted to emulate in many respects the example of England even while, as patriots, they strove for the equality of Scotland. But, whatever its incidental faults, the Scottish Enlightenment was much the nicest one of all – at its most agreeable in its social life, with good drink and good talk. Given the puritanical reputation of Presbyterians, it is odd to reflect how much of this was owed to them.

But Presbyterians, too, go the way of all flesh, and along that way their rumbustious radicals at last declined into crusty conservatives. Such was the fate of the Moderate party after Robertson passed from the scene in 1793. He had managed to ensure that the Church, through the General Assembly and a wide influence on the universities, would remain in harmony with at least a large part of enlightened Scotland. Yet he never succeeded so far as to silence another voice still waiting to be heard after the Moderate one turned into the mere echo of a spineless establishment. The Kirk kept splitting from within because it could not adequately sustain the national role it sought to preserve inside the Union. The Popular party might by the early nineteenth century have turned narrow in all sorts of ways, but it showed there was still one field left for the assertion of Scottish identity.[63] The Church of Scotland, or at least an important part of it, came through the high Enlightenment seeking a fresh role for itself and a new spirit in the nation.

6

Order: 'Dispersing the mob'

On the evening of 7 September 1736, more than 4,000 people assembled in Portsburgh, the suburb extending beyond the West Port of Edinburgh through which the road to Glasgow ran. While this was a poor part of town, the crowd appears to have been mixed in its social composition – something all the same hard to be sure of, then and now, because so many wore disguise. The word would later go round that James Maxwell, a journeyman carpenter, had instigated and organised the gathering, but nothing could ever be proved against him.[1]

Sir Walter Scott, after studying the judicial records 80 years later, would describe what happened next as 'a strong and powerful display of the cool, stern and resolved manner in which the Scottish, even of the lower classes, can concert and execute a vindictive purpose'.[2] The 4,000 passed in good order through the port, which they secured behind them. They hurried along the Grassmarket and Cowgate, taking care to avoid any commotion that might alert the garrison in the Castle looming above. They made their way up the wynds and closes leading to the High Street before converging on the Tolbooth, the venerable but grim and decrepit pile that served as, among other things, the city's jail. They set fire to the wooden door, burst in and overpowered the warders, then liberated all the prisoners except one, John Porteous, who till recently had been the captain of the town guard.

The mob dragged Porteous out, marched him up the Lawnmarket, down the West Bow and so back to the Grassmarket. They broke open a shop and brought out a rope, leaving behind a guinea in payment. They fashioned a noose and put it round Porteous's neck. Over a dyer's pole, they hauled him aloft. For a while they insulted and mocked him as he dangled there. Then

131

they let him down, stripped him of his clothing and hauled him up again with his shirt wrapped round his head. They had not tied his hands, so he continued to struggle. The most brutal of his tormentors at length broke his arm and shoulder, while others hacked at him with axes or applied a flaming torch to his feet. He was let down once more and cruelly beaten. Up he went for the last time and stayed there till he died, just before midnight. It was a horrible way to go, but nobody in Edinburgh felt sorry for Porteous. Even while he had been employed by the city most people regarded him as arrogant and overbearing. Now they just said he deserved his fate.[3]

Earlier in the year, Porteous had led the town guard to perform its official duty of keeping order at the execution of a smuggler from Fife, Andrew Wilson, condemned for robbing the customs house at Pittenweem. Smugglers were, however, popular heroes in Scotland, what with their running rings round the hated regime of British taxes and duties imposed since the Union of 1707. Wilson faced death alone, but he had originally been caught with two accomplices. One escaped and the other had meanwhile been reprieved, so people felt the doom of the third man was unjust and Wilson's hanging in the Grassmarket sparked off a riot. Porteous was then the one that ordered the town guard to open fire on the hostile, jeering crowd; the volley killed six and wounded thirty. He was arrested and charged with murder. When he went on trial himself, most witnesses testified that he had personally fired into the crowd, though others said they had not seen him do so. Feelings anyway ran high in Edinburgh and the jury unanimously found him guilty. He was locked up in the Tolbooth to await his own rendezvous with the executioner.[4]

But the case also aroused attention in London, where politicians still did not trust the Scots. Why, these had risen up in armed rebellion only 20 years before and had not exactly earned the confidence of His Majesty's government since. The Prime Minister, Sir Robert Walpole, wanted them to feel welcome inside the Union but he might have spared himself the trouble. Queen Caroline, who at the relevant time was acting as regent while her husband King George II paid a visit to his native Hanover, shared the Prime Minister's sentiments, and so did the senior Secretary of State, the Duke of Newcastle. On the strength of the reports they had from Edinburgh, all three convinced themselves that Porteous was the victim of a miscarriage of justice, a sacrifice to the mob by cowardly, maybe complicit, magistrates. Walpole decided on a royal pardon, and waited only for things to calm down before announcing it. He waited too long, and so gave the people of Edinburgh the chance to take matters into their own hands.[5]

The English felt outraged. The House of Lords summoned the Lord Provost of Edinburgh, the military commander of the city and then all the judges of the High Court of Justiciary, who got treated at Westminster as if they had been miscreants just hauled off the streets of London. The Lord Justice Clerk, Andrew Fletcher, Lord Milton, was singled out for censure because he had not ordered troops to suppress the riot; in fact he lacked any power to do this. Over the votes of the Scots peers, the House passed a bill of pains and penalties against Edinburgh and sent it to the Commons. The bill denounced the murder of Porteous and offered rewards for information on his killers, meanwhile ordering the burgh to be fined, its Lord Provost to be disqualified, its town guard to be disbanded and its Netherbow Port to be demolished (this the gate securing the main, eastern entrance to the High Street). Walpole, warned that he risked turning an admittedly serious incident into yet another burning Scottish grievance, decided after all to tone the bill down. But the ministers of the Church of Scotland were still ordered to read it from their pulpits every Sunday for a whole year ahead. Many refused: did politicians at Westminster think the Church of Scotland was, like the Church of England, a mere creature of Parliament?[6]

While in London the Scots' behaviour appeared uniquely insolent, it would have been familiar in any other European capital. Popular disturbances had over the centuries acquired almost a ceremonial aspect, of which the Porteous Riot offered a good example with its deployment of disguises and its patterns of reprisal in a conscious, communal act of justice. Behind it, the English suspected, lurked respectable citizens as well as wild young men. Even the passivity of the magistrates, though here probably motivated by fright, might have been recognised as part of old populist rituals that in Edinburgh, as elsewhere, rested ultimately on a broad consensus between rulers and ruled. The consensus possessed its own sense of right and wrong, not always exactly congruent with the law. That sense was what in 1736 moved the people of Edinburgh, goaded besides by economic failure and oppressive government, into taking their revenge. Anyway, it all added up to a great deal more than lawless anarchy.[7]

Like other modes of traditional social behaviour, the rituals of dissent had symbols. In Edinburgh there was the Blue Blanket, the banner of the city's trades originally granted them by King James III when, in 1482, they had rescued him from a plot hatched by his factious nobility. The banner was kept in the High Kirk of St Giles. The trades brought it out and paraded it in the streets whenever they considered themselves to be set on serious business with the state. This typically medieval behaviour was secularised by the Reformation. King James VI wrote in his *Basilikon Doron* (1599), a book of advice to his son and heir apparent, Henry, Duke of Rothesay: 'The craftsmen think we should be content with their work, how bad soever it be; and if in any thing they be controlled, up goes the Blue Blanket.'[8] The tradition continued into the eighteenth century, not only in Edinburgh but also in Dumfries and Dunfermline,[9] possibly in other burghs too. The mind of the masses was a concern to the political manager of Scotland, Lord Islay, who wrote in 1725 of how the Blue Blanket 'in cases of insurrection is held in veneration among them to a degree that is incredible'.[10] Such vivid local customs would not die away before the social upheavals of the next age and the consequent, often deliberate, overthrow of what was ancient and quirky.

If a crowd with a structure seems a contradiction in terms, that is just what historians have been discovering since the work half a century ago of the Marxist pioneer in this field, George Rudé.[11] He has had an influence in Scotland too. The Scottish crowd might have looked like a rabble, but historians on the lookout for structure have succeeded, at least to their own satisfaction, in finding it. For example, after the Porteous Riot the next trouble in Edinburgh came only four years later during the autumn of 1740, after a harvest so disastrous that it seemed to threaten the sort of famine Scotland had suffered before the Union. The riot in question centred on Bell's Mill in the suburb of the Dean village, where grain allegedly destined for export was being stored. The mob broke open and looted the store, as a result of which one man would be at length prosecuted and banished. The modern scholar of this incident discovered here a change in the nature of Scottish large-scale protest, away from that pan-European medieval model of ritualised popular disturbance. Here, at Bell's Mill, was something new, with the well-fed middle class for the first time dissociating itself from the hungry mob. So this became in effect a sectional, proletarian protest with an 'unmitigated ugliness' absent from earlier examples yet setting a pattern that would be revealed more clearly as it repeated itself over time. The mob, from having been broadly based and involved in both urban and national politics, turned narrower in composition and outlook (into a vanguard of the proletariat, perhaps?).[12]

Be that as it may, it seems clear that the more traditional type of riot, with a social as much as a material motivation, did also continue. Later on in the century, Joseph Smith, a cobbler in the Cowgate, acted as leader of Edinburgh's rabble: 'His person was low, almost without legs, and with the sole good property of great muscular strength in the arms,' said the Victorian chronicler, Robert Chambers. Beyond discontent at shortages and high prices, Smith articulated deeper values. 'With all his absolute power over the affections of the mob,' Chambers went on, 'he never employed it in a bad cause, or could be said ... to outrage the principles of what we may call natural justice.' When a poor man was evicted and then hanged himself, Smith had the landlord's house ransacked. Deformed and disreputable as he was, the magistrates needed to deal with him: 'They frequently sent for him in emergencies, in order to consult with him regarding the best means of appeasing and dispersing the mob.' A hogshead of beer was the going rate. Smith died after a fall from a stagecoach while returning drunk from the races at Leith Sands in 1780.[13] George Penny, the Victorian chronicler of Perth, preserved the memory of similar figures in that burgh: James Wilson, a barber and a 'gaunt looking personage, with a spare cadaverous visage'; Blair Flight, an 'odd-looking' watchmaker; and Ned Keillor, 'a little hero with a great soul, a weaver to trade'.[14] No doubt there were others of the type elsewhere.

Scottish historians remain coy, however, about discussing further examples where the mob, apart from not being exclusively proletarian, was in the causes it espoused far removed from anything that would count as politically correct today. Rioters in the streets could be explicitly sectarian, for example. While surviving evidence is scant, the Catholic minority in Scotland might have been victims of rowdy, popular persecution ever since the Reformation. Chambers also mentioned in passing that 'the mob of Edinburgh was wont to amuse itself with an annual burning of the pope'.[15] One particular episode, taking place in the capital and elsewhere, could be read as something more – as a conservative but bigoted restatement and reinforcement of local values against liberal efforts from on high to reform them.

Glasgow was usually a more sober and peaceful city than Edinburgh, probably because of its pronounced Presbyterian character. Following the Union there had been a serious disturbance only in 1724, after Daniel Campbell of Shawfield, the local MP, voted for the imposition of the malt tax in Scotland, something reckoned by most people to be a breach of the Treaty of Union. A mob took over the streets for several days. Among other deeds, the rioters broke into and wrecked Campbell's opulent townhouse at what is now the eastern end of Argyle Street. In Glasgow, too, the provost and magistrates were punished for insufficient vigour in the face of such popular impudence. The city was obliged to pay Campbell £9,000 in compensation. He used the money to buy the island of Islay and usher in its golden age, in which the islanders prospered amid the elegant architecture and the agricultural improvement that their new laird brought with him.[16]

But it was Glasgow's Presbyterianism that made the city a brand for the burning when in 1778 the Lord Advocate, Henry Dundas, proposed to relieve Scottish Catholics of the penal laws that oppressed them, probably to help him in recruiting more men from the remote Highlands for military service against the rebellious Americans. The idea did not go down well in the Lowlands, however. At first there were mere murmurs of dissent. In Glasgow one enterprising fellow sought to exploit them by posting a notice in the streets: 'Any person willing to encourage an original genius may have an opportunity of hearing an oratorical declaration against popery, this evening at six o'clock in the Weighhouse Hall. Admittance 2d each. N.B. If any gentlemen or ladies think the performance worthwhile, their further contributions will be gratefully received by the persons appointed to keep the door.' The murmurs soon turned into the more menacing rant of the Revd Daniel McArthur of the Blackfriars Kirk preaching fiery sermons against any concession to Catholics.[17] This was the spur that brought the mob on to the streets. As it looked for targets to attack, it got out of hand. While at that period only two or three dozen Catholics lived in the city, these unfortunate people became the victims of popular wrath as the rabble ransacked their homes.[18]

The disorder in Glasgow was still on a small scale, but things grew worse when the trouble spread to Edinburgh. A group calling itself the Committee for the Protestant Interest had already been formed to protest against Dundas's proposal. Its agitation was again clearly conservative in spirit, especially in the matter of upholding the established Presbyterian religion. And this concern did not remain confined to one social class. The members of the committee were a solicitor, a solicitor's apprentice, a schoolmaster, three clerks, a goldsmith, a merchant, a grocer, a hosier, an ironmonger, a dyer and 'an intaker for several bleachfields': a fair cross-section of the urban mass. Many others marched behind them as they bore the Blue Blanket along the

High Street. Here again, things got out of hand. The mob sacked a discreet Catholic chapel in Blackfriars Wynd and assaulted peaceable papists living nearby. They wanted to press on to the principal's house at the university and let the Revd William Robertson know what they thought of him too, for they did not like liberal intellectuals either. Dundas had to deploy troops from the Castle round the town. But the trouble was already formidable and embarrassing enough to force him to abandon his proposal for Catholic emancipation. Even then the fiasco almost brought his political career to a premature end when he had to explain himself to Parliament in London. It would be pleasant to record that the men on Edinburgh's streets had been the sturdy, freedom-loving radicals beloved of national mythology. So some of them might have been – yet they were bigots too.[19]

Without Dundas's climbdown the agitation might have spread further, and in one case it did. A few miles up the River Tay from Perth, with its working class of radical weavers, stood the settlement of Stobhall, a tiny Catholic enclave under the protection of the noble family of Drummond, whose Jacobite head, the Earl of Perth, was in exile. The mere proximity of papists proved enough to goad the turbulent townsfolk who set out to march on Stobhall, presumably with the intention of wrecking the place. There, however, the last of the Jacobites still had fight in them. On finding the assault was going to be resisted, the people from Perth thought better of it. The general crisis had by then passed, but this was the only time in contemporary Scotland that popular pressure forced a government to change its mind.[20]

It was not, however, the last time the mob rose up against Dundas as he continued otherwise to tighten his political grip. The people got the chance to take to the streets every year on the king's birthday. This had been for over a century, since the Restoration of King Charles II in 1660, a day of rejoicing for Scots, marked in the alcoholic way Scots usually mark such occasions. In time, indeed, it passed over from a mere expression of loyalty to His Majesty into a general excuse to hit the bottle – and Scotsmen on the skite were, as they still are, apt to misbehave themselves.[21]

The king's birthday was also a movable feast because each king had a different one. During the lifetime of the Old Pretender, the Jacobite claimant to the throne, James VIII to his followers, some Scots demonstrated on his birthday too. Especially in the period just after the Union, the crowds grew bigger every year. In 1712 bands played rebel songs in the streets of

Edinburgh, where toasts were openly drunk to restoration of the legitimate line of Stewarts. Along the Shore at Leith ships put out flags bearing the old royal arms, while at night bonfires lit up the High Street and Arthur's Seat. In 1713 a symbolic coronation of James was staged and a spoof House of Hanover was burned down. From 1714 all this was officially banned.[22]

Yet towards the end of the century the same sort of high jinks still went on. The birthday of King George III fell on 4 June, and in 1784 the Lord Provost of Edinburgh, John Grieve, casually remarked to its MP, James Hunter Blair, that 'as it was the king's birthday, I was not without my fears and apprehensions of rioting as is usual on that day'. He went on to describe how the mob had been joined by the town guard itself, all blind drunk, in an attack against Haig's distillery at Leith, on the pretext, inherently convoluted but perhaps with a certain logic to fuddled brains, that the use of too much grain for whisky was raising the price of bread. The workers there, alarmed for their livelihoods, defended the place with firearms and killed one assailant. The sheriff of Midlothian arrived on the scene just in time to save a corn-merchant from being drowned by the rabble in the Water of Leith. The lucky man was Thomas, grandfather of William Gladstone.[23]

More serious than usual, the trouble in 1784 yet hardly compared to what would happen in 1792, in an outburst that the Lord Advocate, Robert Dundas, called 'very unexpected'.[24] His own family's townhouse in George Square, Edinburgh, was this time the target. Henry Dundas happened to be absent in London, hard at work to counter any spread of sedition from a revolutionary France now going to war with its European neighbours. In Scotland everything had up to this point remained tranquil. Dundas's mother and other relations wanted to celebrate the king's birthday with a dinner at home for their extended family. As a crowd menacingly gathered in the square outside, two nephews, Francis Dundas and Adam Duncan, were foolish enough to provoke the unwelcome visitors by rushing out and attacking them with a golf club and Lady Arniston's crutch. Forced to retreat, they presented their backsides for kissing before disappearing indoors. Luckily, the sheriff soon arrived and troops were called down from the Castle.

The crowd dispersed for a while, if only to go and beset the Lord Provost's house in St Andrew's Square. Later on, doubtless inflamed by more drink, it reassembled outside the Dundases' house and goaded the guards with cries of 'Johnny Cope!' (not 'Liberty, Equality, Fraternity'), in reference to the defeat of the British army at the Battle of Prestonpans in 1745: are we to conclude this was a Jacobite crowd? Soon the hooligans began to hurl cobblestones, to a more frenetic chorus of 'Buggars, fire!' At length the soldiers obliged – they killed one man and wounded six others. Henry Cockburn observed years later that 'no windows could be smashed at that time without the inmates thinking of the bloody streets of Paris.'[25]

It would still be hard to conclude we are observing here, compared to 1784, a new and higher stage of Scottish political consciousness. Meanwhile an effort at Banff to get the people to burn an effigy of Henry Dundas brought only a few boys on to the streets, though disturbances of some kind were recorded across a dozen or so Lowland towns. Glasgow saw another example of 'daring outrage ... too conspicuous for some time past' with 'a loose disorderly rabble throwing brick bats, dead dogs and cats, by which several of the military were severely cut'. Yet this demonstration could hardly be regarded as revolutionary. On the contrary, effigies of two men lauded in progressive tradition, John Wilkes and Thomas Paine, were 'burned by the rabble amid shouts and execrations'. During these years, when the seeds of later Scottish radicalism were sown, not the merest shoot of them appeared in the industrial crucible of Glasgow.[26]

At the Union the Scots had still been in some ways a lawless and ungovernable people but, unlike others in Europe, they did possess a functioning judiciary. Justice in such a turbulent country had been more about keeping the peace on as broad a scale as possible than about establishing guilt and punishing offenders in individual prosecutions. It therefore became a matter rather of negotiation than of trial, so that laws needed to be founded not so much on theory and principle as on custom and convention. Still, a more modern system had emerged, as yet complex, somewhat incoherent, not free of corruption, but reasonably workable and in the Lowlands within reach of all. It was far from establishing itself in remoter regions, however, where kith and kin remained as important as right and wrong, and where judicial power could be inherited or even bought. Only after the loss of independence in 1707 did the greater national jurisdiction gain the upper hand over the lesser heritable jurisdictions, guaranteed though these were by the Treaty of Union. What was tolerated in the prickly, ramshackle Scotland of old would no longer do now. Scots were starting to calm down and take disputes to court rather than fight them out with cold steel. And by the middle of the eighteenth century the problem of securing central control had been solved. Then the law could be reshaped over the entire territory on rational, indeed enlightened, principles.[27]

By and large, Scotland became in the course of the century a peaceable and law-abiding country. Two crushed rebellions doubtless went some way to explain the change. Subsequent urban disorders were, at most, no worse than those among other nations. Scotland's rustic life turned positively tranquil in relation to what might be found going on in the western, southern or eastern peripheries of Europe.[28] Comparison at a later stage draws the contrast still more sharply. In the centre of the Continent the revolutionary era from 1789 to 1848 saw many thousands of deaths, not only of soldiers in the resulting wars but also of civilians during insurrections in France, Poland and other countries. Even in England there must have been some hundreds, and in Ireland again thousands. In Scotland there were no more than a couple of dozen. Contemporary reformers put it about that Scots law had grown uniquely reactionary and oppressive, compared to an English system defending Englishmen's liberties as the Scottish judiciary never deigned to do for Scots: strange that the reformers should have said this after three decades of radical turmoil when England had executed 1,400 people, many merely petty offenders, while Scotland had executed 18.[29]

The centralising and rationalising trend in justice apparent after 1707 was not new, though. In Edinburgh the Court of Session, for civil cases, dated back to 1532, while the High Court of Justiciary, for criminal cases, proceeded in its modern shape out of a reform in 1672. These were the courts guaranteed under the Treaty of Union. They then were supplemented lower down by a system of circuit courts extending over the whole country and manned by sheriffs sitting twice a year in the main burghs, if still sending serious offenders to the High Court. It was hinted at certain points of political crisis that Scotland's judicial independence might be overthrown by an assertion of absolute sovereignty from the Parliament at Westminster. In the event, that Parliament only interfered for the most part when it felt it really had to, as after the Jacobite rebellions. Otherwise it left the Scots to their own devices. The first half of the eighteenth century therefore saw continuity in Scottish legal traditions.[30]

Scotland meanwhile became a peaceable, law-abiding country not by pressure from the top down, in the sense of English authoritarianism, but because of developments from the bottom up (or at least, midway up), in other words, at intermediate levels of its own society. Here the bodies assuring law and order were referred to collectively as 'police', a term borrowed from the France of

King Louis XIV, which had found occasion in the seventeenth century for development of the same sort of structures to fit the widely variant *coutumes* of its provinces; Voltaire said that in France a traveller changed laws as often as he changed horses.[31] In Great Britain, only Scotland needed to follow the French example because the English system had always been centralised anyway. Again this meant that Scots, in order to avoid anglicisation, had to look out for themselves, while often lacking efficient means to do so. In 1723 Duncan Forbes of Culloden, soon to be Lord Advocate, explained the country's doldrums like this: 'What national calamity we have met with, that could have brought us so low, other than that total neglect of our police, which left no distinction between industry and idleness.'[32] Patrick Lindsay, Lord Provost of Edinburgh, published *The Interest of Scotland Considered, with regard to its police in employing of the poor* (1732). Adam Smith defined the term in his *Lectures in Jurisprudence*, delivered in 1762–63, 'as the second general division of jurisprudence ... which properly signified the policy of civil government, but now means the regulation of inferior parts of government, viz: cleanliness, security, and cheapness or plenty'.[33]

In this secondary sphere of police, the Union at first made little difference to Scots. For the great majority of them who lived on the land, justice was still often enforced through the old feudal courts – the courts of regality and barony – in the hereditary jurisdictions covering nearly half the country. They dated from times when it had been in practice impossible for the king's writ to run across the entire territory, so he needed to delegate his judicial power in inaccessible regions to the people who owned the land there, and see to continuity in that power by letting their sons take over from them. In terms of dispensing justice, it was perhaps the best that could be done. In wider social and political terms, in the scope it left for oppressing the lieges or fostering rebellion, it was far from ideal.[34]

The regality was the higher form of hereditary jurisdiction, covering a territory where the feudal superior had the judicial powers of a king, or almost. One power was that of 'pit and gallows', of imprisoning and executing criminals for the more serious crimes, that is, the four pleas of the crown (arson, murder, rape, robbery); only treason, which had to go to the High Court in Edinburgh, was excluded from cognisance. In practice, such cases seldom came up anyway. It was partly a matter of the problem besetting all prosecutions at this level, as explained in court by a victim of robbery in the regality of Argyll in 1741: 'The pursuer begs leave to observe to your lordship that in our Highland countries few or no thieves are taken in the fang [with stolen goods in their possession] or committing the theft, and the only discoveries we have of that crime is by the subsequent confession of the thieves and receivers, or when the cattle, perhaps by chance or accident, are found in their custody or they disposing of them.' Without fingerprints, photographs or forensic scientists, guilt was almost impossible to prove. Hence the justiciary court of Argyll heard only 87 cases between 1705 and 1742 – this in the biggest hereditary jurisdiction under the most powerful political figures in Scotland, figuring among the greatest men in London too.[35]

Business in the hereditary jurisdiction of Atholl appeared to be of much the same kind though conducted at a more personal level because the duke was usually in residence, if only to keep the Jacobite claimants to his title out. So when one struggling tenant found himself pursued for arrears of rent by the estate, he wrote begging the duke 'to restore the poind . . . of my whole working tools with some of the bed cloathes where my sick children should lay them'.[36] This 'high and mighty prince', as his people addressed him, exercised his regality not at Blair, his huge castle in the mountains, but at the traditional site of Logierait, a humble hamlet that yet housed a courthouse, a jail and, on the nearby knoll of the gallows, *Tom na croiche*, a dool tree where criminals were hanged and their cadavers left dangling for the crows to eat. The philosopher, Adam Ferguson, grew up at this spot, and he often brought insights from a more primitive world into the Enlightenment.[37]

A vivid picture of the system at work in its still lower reaches comes from the papers of the great improver, Sir Archibald Grant of Monymusk in Aberdeenshire. He held the court of barony for his lands in his own house, sometimes with himself in the chair, though often he turned it over to a bailie. This court had quite wide powers, but the main practical one was to enforce the payment of rent in cash and kind, or of other charges such as those for maintenance of the kirk and its school. Much time was taken up with servitudes, that is, of obligations on individuals arising from the feudal system of tenure. The court exerted itself to protect dykes, plantations and growing crops. It cracked down on poaching and on the unauthorised kindling of fires. It regulated access to peat-mosses and mills. In punishment it usually fined offenders, but sometimes it put them in the stocks.[38]

As a hereditary jurisdiction the court of barony had earlier on controlled economic relations as well. In the eighteenth century this function was being taken over by the justices of the peace, whose office had been introduced by

King James VI in the hope it would make Scotland more like England. They dealt with beggars and vagabonds, regulated the hiring of servants and their wages, often fined both employers and employees who had paid or been paid too much, penalised people also for being unemployed and directed them into work or into service in the army.[39] But who was the justice of the peace for Monymusk? Sir Archibald Grant. He took a special interest in the payment of the legal wages by his tenants to their sub-tenants or cottars. The problem was that during a period of agricultural specialisation the pressure came rather for wages to rise in order to attract certain types of skilled labour, the farmers being ready to pay what the market would bear. Even if on that point they thwarted Sir Archibald, he still remained in the strongest position to dictate the conditions of labour among the people of the parish. 'There was no hint of benevolence in the tone of the minutes of the justice of the peace court,' says the editor of these papers.[40]

Still, the feudal courts were by now losing their grip. Not only did their volume of business fall, but the central courts also became much more willing to interfere. The courts of regality might just, almost as a reminder of their presence, pick the odd big case to deal with. Otherwise they seemed content to spend their time on the recovery of debts, on the preservation of public order and on the regulation of local markets. Even so, this was enough to maintain the landowners' dominance in local affairs.[41]

Then, at the level of the county, landowners might act together as commissioners of supply, an office established in 1667 to collect the land tax.[42] In time it took responsibility for other taxes, and the commissioners had to spend some of the proceeds on maintaining roads, bridges and ferries (important tasks in Scotland's rugged terrain). They evolved into bodies that expressed the views of the county's landowners. Most were entitled to attend the meetings and vote, the principle being that all who paid taxes should have some say on how the taxes were levied. They entered into correspondence with the authorities in Edinburgh and even in London. Official dealings with the county were directed through the convener of the commissioners, whom his fellows elected.

The landowners' ubiquity in rural life was what let the disaffected among them call out their people in times of mutiny against the British state. For that reason in particular, the Heritable Jurisdictions Act of 1747 abolished this peculiar Scottish institution.[43] The measure met opposition even from some of the loyalist landowning class: on the one hand it breached the Treaty of Union, on the other it did away with courts genuinely useful at a local level. But in the circumstances there was no gainsaying the will of the British government. At least it paid off the holders of the jurisdictions, or anyway those who had remained true to the House of Hanover.

While this reform was prompted by the events of 1745, the time had anyway grown ripe for a centralised system of justice in Scotland – something well appreciated by its author, the Lord Advocate, Robert Dundas, who till the rebellion had been trying in vain to arouse interest in the project in London.[44] The powers of the heritable jurisdictions were now passed instead to the central courts and the circuits. The crown would nominate sheriffs depute in the counties of Scotland; they needed to be advocates of three years' standing, they had to reside for at least four months in their sheriffdoms and they could appoint substitutes.[45] At a still lower level the courts of barony were in the end retained because of a need for cheap justice dispensed by men of authority, not necessarily professional lawyers, who knew their districts and the people living there. Of course they lost their jurisdiction over any serious crimes. Still left to them were minor offences and civil suits, as well as dealings between landlord and tenant; the government had been told in no uncertain terms that a better channel for collecting unpaid rents did not exist.

This legal reform of 1747 was the most significant of the century. After it the sheriff became the chief local official as the judicial and administrative representative of central government. His office had existed since medieval times, often in competition with other jurisdictions. Now it was to supersede all rivals. Sheriffs sat as judges for their counties, called jurors to service, organised elections, ensured payment of taxes and took charge at times of disturbance or threatened disturbance. Their appointment came from the Lord Advocate, principal officer of government in Scotland. But usually he followed the recommendations of local notables. What he did not do was take orders from London. In fact, the existing structures of power would remain important in the work of the sheriffs too. The abolition of heritable jurisdictions by no means ended the landowners' sway in the regions affected or round the country in general. Even with the sheriffs' much stronger official position after 1747 it yet counted for more that they came almost invariably from landowning families with the good sense to train up a son for the law and for membership of the Faculty of Advocates from which the sheriffs were selected. The state attained a new power in Scotland, then, but still worked with the grain of the inherited social order.[46]

Thanks to the Patronage Act of 1712, the Church of Scotland fitted snugly into the pattern as well. Landowners oversaw the parishes, maintained the kirks and chose their ministers who themselves would join with their sessions in imposing discipline on the populace. This discipline was strong, but usually rested on consent: the labouring poor after all had an equal interest in maintaining public peace and containing petty crime.[47] The communal bonds of traditional communities were what above all ensured the quiescence of the Lowland countryside. They remained powerful enough to hold communities together even when landowners embarked on radical schemes of improvement. After the uproar in Galloway over enclosures in the 1720s, little more of rural unrest was heard in Scotland for the rest of the century. But then, the lairds seldom had the purpose of oppressing their tenants, rather of persuading them there was a common interest in progress. While not everybody lived on under this regime in bucolic contentment, for the recalcitrant and reluctant there was always the safety valve of silent migration to the towns or abroad. Altogether the reformed system of law strengthened the fabric of Scottish rural society: precisely the intention of those who gave and practised the law.

Such a system covered most of Scotland, the main exception to it being the royal burghs. They were in theory self-governing, though the aristocracy of the surrounding county really ruled the roost in many of them. But in principle and practice the town councils did exercise the powers of police. Alas, they could not always be relied on to act responsibly. Being self-elected, often run by mercenary cliques, they became notorious for misusing and depleting the 'common good', the collective property of the burgesses. It was nearly impossible for these to mount any effective surveillance. More of a modern civic spirit did develop in Glasgow, where the city fathers grew too wealthy to bother with petty corruption. But in Edinburgh, even while it turned into the Athens of the North, protest at municipal malpractice from the tradesmen's incorporations or from the general kirk session representing all the parishes was little more than water on sand.[48] As we will see below, so long as no general political reform took place at a national level there could be none at a municipal level either.

The need, short of that, for better regulation of the royal burghs was all the same plain, and they did not totally neglect this duty. They had their own courts to try offenders, manned by magistrates from the town council. Urban offences then were much like urban offences now: thefts, assaults, anti-social behaviour. In co-operation with kirk sessions a certain amount of moral policing took place, directed against prostitution and drunkenness, even against violation of the Sabbath, though zeal for such righteousness started to flag. In Edinburgh in 1730 the council overrode the objections of the Presbyterian ministers and ordered the street-lamps to be lit on Sundays as on every other evening.[49]

After all, the law still had to be enforced in the streets on Sunday nights too. The term police might conjure up to the modern mind an image of uniformed bobbies walking their beats (at least before the patrol-car took over). A good number of burghs financed a town guard or at a minimum appointed a couple of constables or watchmen, sometimes clad in a uniform of sorts. Many were old soldiers, and for some a quiet life came first. In Edinburgh these grey-beards, snug round the brazier in a guardhouse of their own in the middle of the High Street, rather won a reputation for keeping well away from any real trouble outside. Instead of stalking the streets, they waited for victims of crime to come to them, to denounce a thief or request a search for stolen goods.[50]

Still, here and elsewhere the arrangements worked well enough in normal times for the average cosy Scots burgh. From the records of Perth, for example, it seems most criminals ended up in court after complaints and tip-offs rather than being caught red-handed. This was to be expected of tight-knit pre-industrial communities where victims knew or recognised offenders, and where sufficient trust and confidence existed between the people and their public guardians. These were less effective in overawing the youngsters who caused much of the trouble otherwise, and the tradesmen's incorporations often felt it incumbent on them to keep rowdy apprentices in order. Their articles might require them to attend church and abstain from fornication or other forms of devilment; if they did get caught they might well be expelled from the craft.[51] Anyway, for Scotland's two biggest cities all this was by the end of the eighteenth century no longer enough. In 1797, the Old and New Towns of Edinburgh were divided into 40 districts, each with a constable.[52] In 1800 Glasgow established a regular police force on something like modern lines, and in 1805 Edinburgh followed suit. But there was as yet no arrangement adequate to the needs of fast-growing conurbations.[53]

With social peace established, Scots law could unfold its potential as a system in its own right, a character that it bears to this day and that represents its greatest debt to the eighteenth century. It was and is a hybrid system composed of several elements: customary law, canon law, feudal law and Roman law. Customary law was ultimately the inheritance from the old Scots and Picts, from the Britons and the Angles, and from the times when the nation began to be formed and secured in the Middle Ages. As Scotland joined the European comity of nations and absorbed influences from abroad, canon law and feudal law were added to the blend. By the same token, it also began to receive Roman law in the shape of a European *ius commune* developed out of the rediscovery of ancient civilisation in the Renaissance. All this went into the common law of Scotland, which was then refined by the decisions of the Scottish courts and after 1707 by certain rulings of the House of Lords (though the criminal law remained outside its jurisdiction). The common law of Scotland should never be confused with the common law of England, which had different historical roots.[54]

Altogether the common law of Scotland was not a closed system but amenable to modernisation, which continued on either side of 1707. For example, feudal law had by this point already fallen into disrepute, though the mere fact of that was not enough to kill it off. As the nation beat its swords into ploughshares, economic improvers found in feudalism an enormous hindrance to progress. The Patriot, Andrew Fletcher of Saltoun, spent much time and effort denouncing its rigidities together with the waste of resources they brought about. They made the superiors reactionary and tyrannical while keeping the vassals poor and backward. Fletcher claimed even slavery might be a better option for his country, at least for the 200,000 vagrants he reckoned to be infesting it, driven on to the road because unable to live off the land. The landowners were not flourishing either, having neither the time nor the incentive to improve their estates while embroiled in feudal lawsuits that got in the way of all rational planning. There was nothing for it but to abolish the system and make Scots a nation of free owner-occupiers.[55] Convinced though many had become that feudalism needed to go, it proved hard to kill off. The peers made sure to get guarantees for their feudal privileges written into the Treaty of Union. It took an upheaval on the scale of the Jacobite rebellion in 1745 to create a consensus in favour of ending them, but even then the system staggered on in Scotland in both its rural and its urban settings, and in the latter even enjoyed a renewal.

As for canon law, in modern times it has in general applied only in the Church's internal affairs, but up to the Reformation it had covered wide areas of civil life. In fact, most law any litigant Scot might encounter, say the law of family and property, fell at that time within the purview of the Church. This was the kind of law dealt with by a promising young notary apostolic, John Knox. He had trained in canon law and his first job in his native East Lothian was to handle local legal affairs of the Church together with secular matters it governed, marriages, wills and so on. Students wanting, like Knox, to practise law for a career often did better to become priests first. Priests, if worldly (as many were), did better to learn law than theology. Yet lesser sins might still lead to greater ones, or to complications not merely personal but legal. Above a certain level, the Scottish state stepped in. It might do so through the agency of the Commissary Court, covering the type of domestic case in which Knox once specialised. There had been an equivalent before the Reformation but one subject to episcopal authority. After the Reformation, in a new court set up in 1564–66, the laity manned the bench and handed down the judgments. This court continued in operation till 1830. Here was an example of how the clergy had got displaced from civil jurisdiction. Canon law was then bound to go into decline.[56]

In the eighteenth century Scots law embarked on a more complete and more strictly national evolution, if still under cosmopolitan influences. This was a general development in the family of nations using the *ius commune*, prompted domestically by a greater volume of legislation, by the elaboration of legal systems and by the emergence of the academic study of civil law. In all these nations the systematic treatises written in consequence went under the name, borrowed from the Roman Emperor Justinian, of institutes (or something of the sort). The Scottish version was the *Institutions of the Laws of Scotland* published in 1681 by James Dalrymple, Lord Stair.[57]

Stair was not himself a legislator. He took the law as he found it and sought to put it on a self-consistent basis, among other things reconciling the various sources it had grown out of. Those he most often cited were the decisions of the Court of Session that he had been collecting since he began to practise there himself in the 1650s. Short of Scottish authority he drew mainly on Roman law. His references to canon law were by contrast sparse. He also used European sources, especially the Dutch authorities on natural law which had reinvented this concept: they changed it from one generally held to be of theological derivation to one that sought its origin in the social nature and the reasoning faculties of human beings. Still, the *Institutions* remain 'an exposition of Scots law based predominantly on native sources',[58] not of some other law with Scottish reference thrown in.

All the same, Stair did share much of his outlook with his Continental counterparts. He felt reluctant to relinquish the religious sources of natural law, yet it was for him a 'dictate of reason' and, once systematically expounded, would become 'a rational discipline, having principles from whence its conclusions may be deduced'.[59] He did not let himself be troubled by the current exertions in Europe to liberate natural law from Holy Writ: to him the divine law and the law of nature were the same thing, known without reasoning or experience because written in the hearts of men. So men might deduce from their experience of humanity and their knowledge of the world a degree of guidance for public and private life. That could then be designated as the law of nature.

Working in parallel, though in a different spirit, was Sir George Mackenzie of Rosehaugh, 'the brightest man in the nation'. He had a chequered public career in and out of office while finding time to establish the Advocates' Library in 1689, defend monarchical absolutism, persecute witches and write the first Scottish novel. As he said, 'being bred to the law . . . requires a whole man and his whole age'.[60] In 1684 he published his own *Institutions of the Law of Scotland* intended for students; at that time they could not take legal degrees in Scotland but only in Europe, learning otherwise on the job as apprentices to an advocate. So this was a practical guide with few pretensions to philosophy.

Mackenzie's work might have been slighter than Stair's but, elementary and systematic, it was much easier to follow. It sought above all transparency in the law, something of benefit to both the rulers and the ruled. Mackenzie therefore preferred to locate his authorities within Scots law, giving a priority to statutes – 'the chief Pillars of our Law'.[61] He wanted the statutes themselves to be more accessible as well, and made them so with his Observations on the Acts of Parliament (1686). The same concern had produced his Laws and Customs of Scotland in Matters Criminal (1678), the first detailed exposition of this branch of the law. Here again, he set out an aim 'that nothing were a crime which is not declared to be so by a statute', since that would render 'subjects inexcuseable, and prevent the arbitrariness of judges'.[62]

Still, it would be fair to say Stair's great work was what above all saved Scots law at the Union. Unless the negotiators had been able to point to it as a system mature and complete in itself, it would have been harder for them to resist pressures for conformity from England. In the text of the treaty, article 18 stated on the contrary that though the laws on trade, customs and excise were to follow the English example, 'all other laws in use within the kingdom of Scotland do after the union and notwithstanding thereof remain in the same force as before . . . but alterable by the Parliament of Great Britain'.[63]

That did not settle the question whether future alterations were to come on Scottish initiative or at English behest. Scots generally held the treaty to be some sort of fundamental law, but it soon grew clear that the English entertained no such view and that for them this solemn compact between two sovereign states was just another Act of Parliament: indeed, to this day they usually refer to the Act of Union. Logically, the Parliament of the United Kingdom could, on the English doctrine of its own absolute sovereignty, claim power to pass statutes on any subject for Scotland, including amendments to the Treaty. Yet it seldom did so. Scots law proved in practice too alien to tamper with unless on the invariably cautious advice of the Lord Advocates. In the ordered state left by Stair it had in effect become irreconcilable with the mish-mash of English common law, and the wiser course lay in accepting the fact. Anyway for a century ahead Westminster did not pass many public Acts at all, relying on private legislation to promote economic and social progress. So the Union never led to wholesale renewal, let alone replacement, of Scots law, and some legislation passed by the Parliament in Edinburgh before 1707 still has legal effect in Scotland today.[64]

In these conditions, indeed, the private law of Scotland became a matter of national pride, one of the prime elements keeping Scotland distinctive within Great Britain.[65] It also turned out crucial to the enlightened culture enabling and encouraging the formation of a more civilised and sophisticated society. In turn, the Enlightenment promoted a better understanding of the Scottish tradition of law and of its place in the legal history of Europe.[66] Once again, this beneficial outcome did not flow of itself from the Union: it had to be sought out and worked at by positive effort. In fact, before long Scots law began, as a result of all the other changes in the nation, to change quite fast. Without a legislature to define the changes, there had to be different means of doing so. The so-called institutional writers provided it. With Stair as the first in a distinguished succession, they have been regarded as formal sources of law in Scotland since at least the nineteenth century.

Andrew MacDouall, Lord Bankton, published his own *Institute of the Laws of Scotland* in 1751–53, specifically intended to bring Stair up to date but also, for the sake of students and practitioners, to be more detailed than Mackenzie. To a society in rapid evolution the law was growing more important. As the numbers and the standards of the legal profession rose, aspirants to it were increasingly taught in Scottish universities rather than foreign ones, and with that came a need for relevant authorities. Still, some students continued to go to Europe to finish their education, and through them the influence of Roman law persisted. From Europe also came renewal through natural law, itself undergoing vigorous development thanks above all to influence of the legal philosopher Samuel Pufendorf, who had roamed the universities of Germany, Holland and Sweden. Stair was possibly already acquainted with his work, but certainly it must have been known in Scotland by the time the University of Edinburgh erected a chair of the law of nature and of nations in 1707, choosing for its title the exact words that Pufendorf used to describe his own studies.[67]

The following half-century of change in Scots law then found a reflection in Bankton's *Institute*: 'Our law has undergone many alterations, and received great improvements . . . and therefore another system thereof seems to be much wanted.'[68] It may appear a significant innovation also that his full title included the words, *'with observations upon the agreement and diversity between them* [the laws of Scotland] *and the laws of England'*. Indeed he was the first Scot to address this novel topic. But it was not his intention to assimilate the two; on the contrary, he sought to maintain the integrity of Scots law. And generally his treatment of it remained inspired from Rome rather than London. Stair cast a long shadow.[69]

To this scene of sober and careful development some colour was added by the tireless intellectual energy of Henry Home, Lord Kames, a judge from 1752. A philosopher as much as a lawyer, he reflected a basic urge in the enlightened Scottish mind to organise and systematise knowledge. His first published book was a collection of past judicial decisions. They had given him invaluable insight into the interplay between politics and the law, and how issues arising from the one impinged on and shaped the judgments made in the other. He came to see this as a normal and not a novel state of affairs under the Union of Parliaments, because it was rather a natural result of human desires and needs. He would write later of the law as a living thing, 'being founded on experience and common life . . . Our law comes thus to be enriched with new thoughts, new discoveries, new arguments, struck out by the invention of our lawyers.' Yet somewhere a few basic principles needed to be set down if the law was not to be abused. One basis for such principles could be found in reason, another in nature – and neither meant the law should be fixed or immutable: 'The law of nature, which is the law of *our* nature, cannot be stationary. It must vary with the nature of man, and consequently refine gradually as human nature refines.'[70]

This was scarcely legal reasoning, but in Kames's *Principles of Equity* (1760) he sought to point out cases where abstract principles and the earthy rigour of the common law could work on each other. Hard though a desirable relationship might be to pin down, he brought out from his philosophical logic some legally feasible and, more to the point, practically persuasive conclusions, of which the virtue lay in the mechanism employed rather than in the adherence to any fixed principle. The aim was to find creative solutions for some of the many unaccustomed legal problems arising in a progressive Scotland needing to rely more on reason than on authority. Here was a compromise between the philosopher who is creative but not too meticulous, and the lawyer who is meticulous but not too imaginative: the foundation for an art of justice rather than for mechanical application of rules and precedents. Yet the *Principles* never really caught on among Kames's contemporaries, who continued to search for parallels to contemporary Scottish problems in the texts of Roman law. He proved a bit too clever for his colleagues on the bench, and equity never developed into a distinct branch of Scots law.[71]

More focused in his approach was John Erskine of Carnock, from 1737 to 1765 the second professor of Scots law at the University of Edinburgh. He initially used Mackenzie's *Institutions* as his textbook, but in 1754 he published his own *Principles of the Law of Scotland* because, he said, his forerunner's work was too concise, marred by omissions and out of date; Erskine meant 'to supply these defects'.[72] His work would introduce generations of Scots lawyers to their legal system and its conceptual approach: the book has never been out of print, though often revised. Mixing Justinian's Institutes with natural law derived from Pufendorf, it fixed in students' minds a powerful map of the law.

After Erskine retired he devoted himself to finishing his *Institutes of the Law of Scotland* (1773), a work on a much larger scale giving a more detailed account of his views. As a work of systematisation, it was well aware of the hybrid nature of Scots law. This rested first of all on custom – 'that which, without any express enactment by the supreme power, derives force from its tacit consent; which consent is presumed from the inveterate or immemorial usage of the community'. But custom was being displaced by statute so that in another sense 'law may be defined [as] the command of a sovereign'. As for natural law, not all civil law had been 'plainly founded' on it: 'That is barely civil, which derives its whole force from the arbitrary will of the lawgiver, without any obvious foundation in nature', for example, the laws 'which have been calculated for the forming and perfecting of the feudal system'. When in doubt, Erskine turned to Roman law: 'Among all the systems of human law which now exist, the Roman so well deserves the first place, on account of the equity of its precepts, and the justness of its reasonings, that wherever the civil law is mentioned, without the addition of any other particular state, the Roman law is always understood by way of excellency.'[73]

The last of the classic succession of institutional writers was George Joseph Bell. His work, especially the *Commentaries on the Law of Scotland and on the Principles of Mercantile Jurisprudence* (1804), showed the influence of emerging capitalism in Scotland. Legal attention was becoming necessary not just to fixed assets such as land and buildings but also to the more abstract aspects of corporate structure. Bell's way into this complex of problems went through the concept of bankruptcy. Though the status of 'notour bankrupt' had been defined by an Act of the Scots Parliament of 1696, it cannot be said the law was ready for the tidal wave of commercial progress that swept over Scotland in the eighteenth century. The earliest financial crisis came with the failure of the Ayr Bank in 1772. It was soon followed by the Bankruptcy (Scotland) Act, for the first time regulating the respective positions of corporate debtors and creditors. Under this law Scotland's prodigious economic expansion proceeded in the nineteenth century, and it could hardly have done so without Bell's elaboration of the topic, enriching from England and Europe the rather meagre Scottish sources.[74]

Altogether, Scots law developed in the eighteenth century out of its own native vigour, even as external influences continued to work on it. The obvious source of that vigour was the autonomy of Scottish civil society, which the Union scarcely touched.[75] After 1707 the anglicisation of Scots law could have been expected, yet in fact never took place. Scots law did change and evolve a good deal, but by being lifted out of one indigenous course into another. Till the middle of the century, it might have been seen as a quaint local curiosity, of little interest beyond the borders of the country and hardly worth the trouble of control by any outsiders (for instance, by English politicians). During that period the Union, so far from being a force for legal development, formed the framework for maintaining this relic.

But then a new dynamism entered into Scots law. It searched its own sources for the right response to deep social and economic changes. It became one of the native structures now giving the Scots' gathering energies their head. So it modernised in the best way any system of law could do faced with a rapidly evolving society, from a depth of legal reasoning and from an understanding of its own history. This great endeavour succeeded: it made justice a living force in the lives of the people yet let them feel it was dispensed in their interests. At the Union it had still been complex and disjointed. Now it was simplified, equitable and efficient, sustained from high professional standards and from an intellectual, not merely judicatory, structure capable of indefinite extension as fresh problems of development arose.

It might be argued that this modern society was a product of the Union, yet it could hardly be argued that the legal response was. At most, the Union offered a framework removing risks of disruption or destruction in the polity so that the law could progress unimpeded by civil breakdown. Within that framework, however, the development came at Scottish hands primarily inspired from Scottish sources. If anything, the task moved Scots law further away from English law, despite the Union. It was a work of the nation itself, and one of its great achievements.

PART III
MARGINS

7

Poverty: 'Neither means nor master'

On 27 January 1744, the Court of Session gave judgment in a dispute between two landowners by the River Irvine in Ayrshire. The case pitched William Fairlie of Fairlie, from one of the county's oldest but most enterprising families,[1] against Alexander Montgomerie, tenth Earl of Eglinton, an imperious fellow who was eventually to be murdered by a poacher he tried to arrest on his land.[2] He should have learned better from his experience in court that he could not browbeat the locals. Both he and the Fairlies owned fields along the banks of the river, his being lower down than theirs. They had a mill there, but Eglinton built another with a dam across the watercourse to regulate its flow for his own purposes. In this way he caused the river to back up and so brought the wheel in the Fairlies' mill to a standstill. While the earl offered to compensate them, they wanted none of that. Instead they went to law.

Such cases were commonplace in the improving Scotland of the time. The reason this verdict went down in the history books was rather because of the *obiter dicta* by one of the judges sitting that day. Probably he was Henry Home, Lord Kames (the record is not quite clear), otherwise an enlightened philosopher – at least the text of the judgment does have a ring of him about it. Be that as it may, this is how the judge summed up Eglinton's position:

> It is the great privilege of property, that the proprietor can be put under no restraint: a man's mind is his kingdom, and the law cherishes freedom and independency, making every man arbiter of his own actions and property, without any other limitation than that of abstaining from doing harm to others. If this rule be once established that a man has power over his neighbour's property to

work upon the same, or to alter it for his own benefit, provided the neighbour suffer not, there is no possibility to stop short: the power over his neighbour's property must take place even where the neighbour suffers by the alteration provided the loss be made up . . . and so the doctrine lands here, that for my neighbour's benefit the law will oblige me to abandon my property, provided he be willing to give an adequate price for the same.

Having set out the case for Eglinton as distinctly as possible, the judge immediately rejected it, or at least any extreme deduction from the initial premiss: 'Was this once an established doctrine, a thousand claims would be made, and a thousand consequences follow, which hitherto have not been thought to have any support from law.'[3]

Every student of philosophy will recognise here the classic arguments for 'freedom from' as opposed to 'freedom to', of how far the liberty we ascribe to individual human beings can be allowed to encroach on the liberty of others. It is in a sense impressive to find such basic theoretical considerations being applied with rigour to a situation in everyday Scottish life by the bank of a river in Ayrshire. Could Socrates have done better in the shade of the trees by the Ilissos on the plain of Attica?[4] Does this not show enlightened Scotland to have been a truly philosophical society? Before we draw such an awestruck conclusion, we might take a look at some of the wider implications of the doctrine set forth by Kames (if that is who it was), that 'the proprietor can be put under no restraint'.

The Court of Session was in practice often the real legislator for Scotland in the eighteenth century, given how seldom Westminster used the power to pass laws for the Scots that it had taken with the Treaty of Union. At any rate, the judgments handed down at Parliament House in Edinburgh more often shaped the law than the legislation voted in the Houses of Parliament in London. One thread running through those judgments was the enhancement of landowners' rights. This need not surprise us when we recall that most of the advocates and all of the judges were landowners themselves. It was primarily Scots of their rank that had benefited from the Union. While much of Scotland's old feudal aristocracy decamped to London to seek preferment and favours it did not always find, the lesser landowners tended to stay at home and set about expanding their economic, political and social base in the vacuum left behind.[5]

The strengthening of a regular system of justice, as seen in the last chapter, was both cause and consequence of this wider development. The men in charge of the system, coming from the part of the landed class still loyal to its native country, also initiated economic development, conducted local or national politics and at a lower level regulated, among other things, the treatment of the poor. On the last matter, the Scotland of the eighteenth century was still a Scotland of the past rather than of the future. In the Lowlands the industrial revolution had already started up, but nobody related the problems of poverty to that. Poverty was instead taken to be not a social but an individual, above all a moral problem, a matter of personal behaviour and of failings in it.[6] It seemed unlikely that the law of Scotland would give such people any real claims over the people who actually owned the country's property. And so, in the course of the eighteenth century, it proved.

Poor relief also counted among the spheres of Scottish life that the Union did not touch. Scotland had its own system based on statutes of the old Scots Parliament as interpreted by the Court of Session, and before 1845 Westminster never added to this legislation. The Poor Law in force during the eighteenth century dated back to 1574. It was an outcome of the Reformation. Before 1560 the poor had been a charge on the monasteries, but now the monasteries no longer existed. The Reformer John Knox himself pinpointed the need for a novel system to be run by the Church of Scotland, though even in his own parish of St Giles in Edinburgh this was easier said than done – and a tall order if he expected the capital's canny burgesses to pay for something of no direct benefit to themselves. Here lay a conundrum of Calvinism: those imbued with its godly sense of personal responsibility could take an unforgiving view of those without. Proper objects of charity they might be, but charity would be wasted on them if their poverty were their own fault – better for them to get off their backsides and fend for themselves. Knox himself endorsed this view: 'We are not patrons for stubborn and idle beggars who, running from place to place, make a craft of their begging . . . but for the widow and fatherless, the aged, impotent and lamed . . . that they may feel some benefit of Christ Jesus now preached to them.'[7]

The Scottish system of poor relief from now on built up slowly, by trial and error. In the burghs, under the law of 1574, the provost and bailies became responsible for it, with the power to raise a tax or assessment on the burgesses if the town council agreed. In the countryside the authority from 1597 was the kirk session in each parish. Another Act in 1672 brought in the heritors or landowners who besides possessed the legal power to raise assessments, half to come from them and half from their tenants. Many Lowland parishes had already made some provision for the poor, and by the early eighteenth century most were doing so. Relief seems at this stage to have been readily given not only to the disabled but also – for example, if the harvest failed – to those sound of body and mind provided they could show the session they were both deserving of the aid and godly in their deportment. Still this relief should not be the sole means of livelihood, and family or friends would be expected to chip in as well.[8]

Though the system had undergone severe tests during famines, in normal times the resources it raised did seem enough for its purposes. Each case would be examined on its merits, but parishes regularly awarded pensions to the old and sickly, supported orphans and foundlings by boarding them out, paid for the schooling of these children and of others whose parents could not afford the fees, arranged for the care of the insane, contributed towards the cost of surgery or wet-nursing, joined with other parishes in supporting poor students at the university, and buried paupers with a ration of beer and tobacco for the mourners, while claiming whatever personal property the deceased had left.[9] The sole estimate we have of the numbers supported is that they amounted to 2 or 3 per cent of population in a typical parish.[10]

The Presbyterian attitude defined poor relief as in essence a matter of charity. Logically then, if it meant help for the helpless, nothing should be done for those who could help themselves. In other words, the whole formed a moral system rather than an economic system. In 1560 the Church had restored itself in Scotland, and the nation with it, but the economy went on as before. It allowed the Scots subsistence, little more, and all needed to exert themselves just to gain that subsistence. In the fermtouns where the great majority of the population lived there was forever work to be done. The royal burghs had been founded on the principle that labour required strict regulation. Over a couple of centuries the stern attitudes induced by the Presbyterian outlook on life were to start bearing more heavily on the poor than had perhaps been envisaged by the Reformers.[11]

For example, where relief was given it had also by law to be restricted to natives of the parish, and got only grudgingly extended to those whose sole qualification was to have been resident for a term of years (usually three). A healthy community had to look out for itself: so ran the basic assumption. This was in fact a unifying rather than a divisive principle. The standard of living among many peasant families only just rose above the level of subsistence, and all hands had to be put to the task of keeping it there. Even the children would be set to work at home in helping to produce textiles and be taken out of school as soon as they could read to start looking after animals in the fields. Such families might live from an unreliable mixture of resources, so it is not useful to think in terms of a level of income. In fact, those receiving parochial relief were little worse off than the humblest working peasants, and a basic social unity existed at this level of society.[12]

Some people still fell outside the rural structures, or their urban counterparts, and were disadvantaged by them. The Poor Law could anyway scarcely be enforced in the north of Scotland. The presbyteries and sheriffs made some effort but in general the region lacked the sort of economic surplus, even for its landlords, that could easily be transferred to the poor.[13] From the Highlands as from other regions these people might emigrate, something Scots had long done. Within the country they might become vagrants, picking up jobs where they could, to form a category often condemned by brother Scots yet in some ways indispensable as the only flexible element in a rigid economy. In all this, however, there was next to no room for what today we call unemployment, except among those who suffered some actual incapacity. With that exception, the social structures of Scotland therefore made no allowance for it. The whole fostered the feeling that each community should fend for itself, with help, support and persuasion for the poor to join in the common endeavour, though also with disincentives to their staying out of it.

The conclusion easily followed that to seek charity without unavoidable cause was a badge of disgrace because it let the community down. Hardening in the course of the eighteenth century, this attitude came out in two ways: among the poor themselves by reducing the number of people who asked for help, and among the people who might have given the help by persuading them it would be bad for the morality of the poor. Ministers of the Kirk and others in charge of the system therefore came to equate low doles with a high moral standard in their communities. They were particularly pleased if nobody at all applied for help, as we often see in the parochial reports of the *Old Statistical Account* written by ministers of the Kirk in the 1790s. Few complained of any oppressive poverty. While they detailed how the parishes made provision for the poor in the ways open to them, there was little suggestion of its being inadequate or of great numbers suffering in consequence. Some progressive modern historians affect to be shocked this. The Scottish system of poor relief appears to one 'incredibly mean', while another concludes that 'social inequality was seen as divinely programmed'.[14]

We must enter the proviso that it is often hard to draw firm general conclusions because of the wholly decentralised nature of poor relief in Scotland, which made any kind of national policy impossible. Each parish relied on its own means. From one place to another the flow of funds could vary unpredictably. Unless a compulsory assessment was raised, the money came from voluntary collections at the door of the kirk every Sunday, then from fines on moral offenders, from dues for use of the communal mortcloth (the covering of the coffin), from fees for the proclamation of marriages and from donations or legacies from local landowners. Any large sum was usually invested, only the yield being available for the poor.[15]

Distribution of the funds varied too. Ministers and kirk sessions were the ones that handed the money out, under the eye of heritors taking this as another of the communal duties they accepted and expected to perform (they were often elders themselves). In each parish all discharged their responsibility as seemed right to them, with no need to note what was happening elsewhere. The elders and more popular or evangelical ministers perhaps formed the compassionate element in the system, willing to provide enough relief for everybody to reach a basic standard of living. Tensions certainly arose between such people and the heritors. The two sides might well get into tussles over property, for example: it could be far from easy for a parish to extract a legacy from the heirs of a deceased laird, and complaints on that head quite often went up to the General Assembly of the Church of Scotland.[16]

Still, there were also ministers taking a stricter line, notably those beneficiaries of lay patronage reluctant to bite the hands that fed them. As a hostile dissenter remarked, 'they cultivated connection with the upper classes of society in their parish, declining intercourse with those of low degree to whom the gospel is preached, and set themselves earnestly to arrange matters connected with the poor so as to save expense to the heritors'.[17] In such cases there could be a consensus to keep outlays on the poor down as far as possible, and in particular to raise no assessment. The parish would every so often examine the available level of funds and allot pensions to the neediest cases they knew about. If prospective expenditure exceeded income the list of beneficiaries would simply be trimmed, so that supply determined the provision of aid and the number accepted as poor was cut to fit the money available. In any extremity the heritors might adopt the alternative of arranging relief privately among themselves. During years of dearth, they often made individual or collective gifts of meal, money and coal for the poor not only in their own parishes but also in adjacent ones, and in a few cases set up schemes on the same lines for whole counties. This meant they were paying out for the poor when they felt ready to do so, rather than when told to by the law. Or to put matters another way, the poor should not get it into their heads that they were actually entitled to anything.

While some assessed parishes tried to work to a fixed level of expenditure, more of them took things the other way round. The poor went on a list and an estimate was made of the likely flow of voluntary contributions. From the prospective shortfall the level of assessment for the parish as a whole could be judged. This procedure seldom bore heavily on a landowner either, but a regular charge on his estate did affect its value and might lead on to a higher burden. By the end of the eighteenth century compulsory assessments were becoming more common in the richer parts of the Lowlands, perhaps because the extra financial commitment had a positive side too. It could be regarded as reducing the possibility of social unrest with a safety net for those threatened with penury. And the rural Lowlands did remain remarkably free of serious strife right through the agricultural revolution. The landowners might reckon that an adequate Poor Law reinforced their social control. In that sense, its development was all of a piece with the rest of Scots law in fostering the peaceful advance of Scottish society under firm native leadership. Within this greater scheme of things, the poor accepted their lot.[18]

The rich did not always accept theirs, however, and in assessed parishes might still seek to limit the obligations laid on them. Tensions sharpened if landlords happened to be absentees, a growing trend as traditional social structures in Scotland began to change. Some did resent it when a kirk session consisting of mere tenants appropriated money for the poor. But these landlords, too, found they had a case they could make at law. In 1751 a dispute reached the Court of Session from Humbie in East Lothian, where the proprietors were in dispute with the minister and kirk session. The judges ruled that no advantage could be taken of absentees: 'The heritors have a joint right and power with the kirk session in the administration, management and distribution of all and every of the funds belonging to the poor of the parish ... and have right to be present and joined with the session in their administration, distributing and employment of such sums.'[19] In future, meetings of the kirk session with the poor rate on the agenda had to be announced from the pulpit ten days in advance, so giving the heritors a chance to attend. By this pronouncement the court in effect relieved absentees of any obligation to contribute to relief in parishes where they merely owned some land.[20] Some parishes suffered in consequence a shortage of funds, but the ruling was amplified in 1752. The court then decided that any heritor would be entitled to call the kirk session to account for its management of the poor's fund. In 1772, a further judgment forbade sheriffs to alter the amount paid to any pauper, which therefore became a matter entirely for the heritors and kirk sessions. Sheriffs might now only intervene by ordering a tardy session to meet and decide, but had no power to alter or review what it did decide. Only in 1824 did a further judgment bring the whole system back under the control of the Court of Session.[21]

The result of these defining legal cases was to hand to landowners all effective control over money for the poor. The General Assembly of the Church of Scotland acquiesced: the elders who were landlords or judges, together with the Moderate clergy, combined to ensure there would be no further argument. By the early nineteenth century the rural operations of the old Poor Law had been restricted so far as they could be, consistent with its remaining in force at all.[22]

In the matter of poverty the urban problems already differed from the rural ones, heralding the huge gap that would open up in Victorian times. The same Poor Law of 1574 remained in force everywhere, but it did start to take on a fresh shape in response to the emergence of industrial society. During the early eighteenth century most Scots burghs were still so small that they could follow rural practice and delegate responsibility for the poor to the Church. Yet in the cities it was becoming impossible for any minister to know everybody in his parish or then to distinguish between good and bad claims. A further difficulty lay in the fact that churchgoing failed to increase in line with population, so that the relative size of collections fell too. This trend would continue: another century on and all Scots burghs had had to impose legal assessment on their citizens. In the new capitalist economy the poverty was unlike anything known before, a matter not of permanent disability but of cyclical deficiency of demand. The burgeoning burghs of Scotland sought novel means of relief, hampered though they were by past practice.[23]

The biggest step came in the development of poorhouses and of what was termed indoor relief, that is, the provision of full board for the paupers of one town in a single public institution. It was supposed to be given in return for work, which would keep them off the streets. But any hope that poorhouses might be viable as productive units soon proved vain, so there was in reality no chance they might pay for themselves. It could hardly have been otherwise when most inmates were the impotent old, the orphaned young or again the disabled. The managers of the poorhouses probably thought they were following the principles of 1574, or at most only adapting them to some inescapable facts of urban life: rootlessness and homelessness, as well as a lack of collective tasks to underpin mutual support among the townspeople. This view of things did not get them far.[24]

As the burghs continued to grow, the number of paupers anyway exceeded the capacity of the poorhouses. Outdoor relief, or a dole to people living in their own homes, then also remained necessary – and had the advantage of being cheaper. It was still insisted that the allowances should never be enough to provide the sole means of support. Those taking them had to sign a disposition giving the poorhouse a claim, if they died, on the value of their possessions in the amount of the relief granted – just as those entering the poorhouse had to turn over all their goods to it. No Scot was going to get something for nothing.[25]

Glasgow took the lead. It was a city of *nouveaux riches* open to social experiment, to an extent not obvious among the more conservative professional class of Edinburgh. For example, Glasgow had no counterpart to the College of Justice and the community of lawyers round it in the capital; the college airily refused to waive its exemption from the poor rate on the grounds of its being a national, not a mere municipal institution. Nor was Glasgow ruled, like Edinburgh, by a corruptible, heavily indebted town council indifferent to the problems its bad management caused for poor relief among many other matters. Glasgow made medical provision for the poor by dividing the city into districts and assigning a surgeon to each, while in Edinburgh it was possible for paupers to get treatment only if surgeons offered it of their own free will. Glasgow was altogether the more charitable city. Still, it looked first after itself and made no attempt to enter into arrangements beyond its bounds with the nearby parishes of the Barony, Gorbals and Govan, where there were people just as much in need as any in the royalty. These peripheral parishes continued to follow the rural system of relief.[26]

Poor relief had been the responsibility of four groups in Glasgow: the general kirk session with ministers and elders from each of its churches, the town council, the incorporated trades and the Merchants' House (the latter two giving help only to their members). But in 1731, amid public complaints about a rise in destitution and begging, the four groups decided to start working together and pool their resources for the poor. They delegated their powers to a board of management chaired by the Lord Provost and operating a new set of rules. The direct result was the construction of the Town's Hospital on a pleasant site by the River Clyde. It would house, clothe, feed and provide work for those unable to look after themselves.[27]

This was the first poorhouse in Scotland, an experiment bold and progressive but in the end no answer to urban poverty as the local economy continued to expand. Industrialisation attracted hordes of immigrants from the surrounding countryside and from further off, the Highlands and later Ireland, whence many of the new arrivals arrived already destitute. By 1774 the Town's Hospital was full. Something needed to be done for those who could find no room there. The answer was outdoor relief delivered in kind, that is, as a monthly allowance of oatmeal financed from an assessment on the citizens; those paupers who wanted cash instead had to apply to one of the kirk sessions.[28]

The proceeds of the poor rate would prove inadequate too. But Glaswegians did not remain indifferent to the growing poverty on their streets. If Presbyterian prudence and civic scruple kept down the money passing through the municipal channels of relief, that still left scope for private charities. The amount collected in the poor rate reached a peak amid the economic crisis near the end of the Napoleonic War, and from 1815 was actually falling as an even deeper depression followed the peace.[29] Relief now had to be spread more and more thinly over the rising numbers out of work, till it amounted to no more than a pittance. By the ethos of the system, this should have been a chance and a spur for jobless Glaswegians to show they could fend for themselves. Still, when some looked as if they were failing the test, their richer fellow citizens did not as a matter of fact leave them in the lurch but concentrated their help in the private charities; the money so dispensed ran at seven times the amounts doled out from the poor rate.[30] Given such circumstances, it is easier to see than some modern scholars have allowed why Thomas Chalmers from 1819 tried his celebrated experiment in the East End of Glasgow of running a system of welfare on an entirely voluntary basis.[31]

Edinburgh also faced the social consequences of booms and busts with an outdated system of poor relief. The local economy remained dominated by the merchants' and tradesmen's guilds, which looked after their own members if they fell on hard times (or after their widows and children if they died). To fulfilment of these obligations the city owed the existence of the merchants' hospital founded in 1694, the trades' hospital founded in 1707, the older Heriot's hospital and then George Watson's hospital founded in 1739.[32] The private charitable institutions were more extensive than Glasgow's. And Edinburgh's huge projects of public works through the second half of the century went along with a steady surge of private building too: together they assured a more constant flow of income in the labouring class and helped families to look after their own older members, otherwise the main recipients of relief.

The inherited regime of the Poor Law provided for administration by the general kirk session in the capital, a body of ministers and elders drawn from all eight of its parishes. The parishes were in their turn divided into 'portions', with an elder responsible for the poor assigned to each. Paupers applied for help to their local elder, who gave them some temporary aid while investigating their claims. If he was satisfied he would place them on the parish's roll and then they got a monthly dole. The session distributed its funds to the parishes in line with the number of poor on the roll of each.[33]

As in Glasgow, the old system faltered with economic expansion. In Edinburgh too, the town council and the general kirk session decided to delegate their direct responsibility for the poor to a board of managers in charge of a centralised system that would deal with all applications for help. Again, the aim was to erect a poorhouse and provide indoor relief financed from the pooled resources. The building arose in 1740 at Bristo Port, and a wing of the original building survives today in a cul-de-sac. The basic purpose was to put all the inmates to work. The managers made arrangements for in-house products to be sold in the town, and in some cases those who had fashioned them earned a proportion of the selling price. In 1743 the managers laid down a rate of twopence in every shilling of sales to be repaid to the workers, but were appalled to find the clerk of the poorhouse had instead taken to handing out drams to them.[34]

The poorhouse held 700 inmates, with strict criteria for admission. First came 'the begging poor entitled to the town's charity', as of old. Then there was always room for those bringing their own blankets or furniture – items in short supply – so the city could save the cost of providing them. Orphans followed; the managers were keen on them too because they could be hired out for external employment. Next came burgesses and their families who had fallen on hard times. Finally, anybody else might get in if room could be found. In the basement lay a bedlam for the insane. Least welcome were the patients discharged as incurable from the Royal Infirmary who tended to end up here as well, having nowhere else to go. A large ward was allocated to people baldly labelled as 'depraved'. Some inmates indeed had criminal tendencies, and in 1791 they got segregated in a house of correction or Bridewell on Calton Hill; it was designed by the great architect Robert Adam but had nothing else nice about it.[35]

The reception at Bristo Port was never warm. Even by local standards of filth the place appeared 'extremely nauseous'. Inmates had to wear drab blue uniforms. They were fed on porridge, broth and bread. It soon became little more than a dump for undesirables. Sir Walter Scott in *The Heart of Midlothian* hints at routine brutality towards them: his character Madge Wildfire often tells the truth in her madness, and sings of her time in the poorhouse:

> I had hempen bracelets strong
> And merry whips ding-dong
> And prayer and fasting plenty.[36]

The poorhouse was besides dogged by financial problems, with an overhang from the capital cost of construction and a never adequate stream of income for current expenditure. Once beggars were cleared off the streets the burgesses found less incentive to give alms. Collections from the churches consistently fell short of expectations. By 1765 the poorhouse was in debt, and the managers appealed to the town council for a grant that in the event failed to solve the problem. Faced with another appeal in 1775 the council told the managers to go to the banks, and it was by a rolling series of loans that they kept going for the future. They still could not keep pace with the increase in the numbers of the poor. The assessment on the capital's citizens remained fixed at 2 per cent of rental value till 1812, when it went up to 3 per cent. It eventually reached 7 per cent. But the problems of poverty grew worse.[37]

The managers of the poorhouse also provided outdoor relief, especially for old people who could be cared for better in their own homes with the help of family and neighbours. By 1800 about 1,000 individuals claimed it. They needed to be natives of the city or to have been resident for three years. The rule therefore excluded the incoming population from the countryside for the crucial period after they first arrived. Those seeking a better life would not find it if they ended up, as many did, in the overcrowded Old Town, soon emptied of all but an underclass, people with no choice where to live. Its conditions would steadily deteriorate in the course of the nineteenth century, and the Poor Law never solved this problem either.[38]

Glasgow ignored its suburbs, but in Edinburgh this was not so easy. Connections between the old royalty and the contiguous parishes of the Canongate and St Cuthbert's grew so intimate that they could be regarded as one conurbation. The problem was to fit this concept to the inherited parochial structures of the Poor Law. While the capital and its suburbs administered the same statute they made little attempt to co-ordinate their operations. Creative paupers took advantage of this to put themselves on three rolls rather than one.[39]

Policy in each area differed. Canongate's liberal poorhouse opened in 1761 and denied relief only to those of bad character. But the kirk session of St Cuthbert's was tough and turned away many applicants. It also wanted rid of the burdens it did have. In 1790 David Dale asked the managers to send him children for New Lanark. He would clothe, feed, educate and finally employ them in adult life too: he got 31 boys and 11 girls. It was in the parish of St Cuthbert's that the New Town arose, but well before that its kirk session had proposed to Edinburgh a scheme for joint management of the poor. It would hand over to the city the entire proceeds of its assessment if it could send its paupers to Bristo Port. The town council responded favourably, and in 1749 petitioned the Parliament at Westminster for an Act to combine not only Edinburgh and St Cuthbert's but also the Canongate and North and South Leith for purposes of poor relief, with joint assessment and management. All the kirk sessions agreed. As the conurbation formed one economic unit, with many workers coming in from the suburbs to jobs in the royalty, it made no sense to discriminate against the poor by place of residence. Yet nothing came of the scheme. For the purposes of the Poor Law, there was a half-hearted extension of Edinburgh's boundaries in 1809 to take in the built-up parts of St Cuthbert's. Here the kirk session was offered compensation by the town council for its loss of taxpayers, but the money would come out of the poor fund! The managers of the poorhouse forecast financial ruin and the council decided not to press for payment. So the system staggered on till the reform of 1845, with the city fathers here doing no better than any parish of absentee landlords in the country.[40]

Poorhouses were a product of the middle decades of the eighteenth century, when urban poverty grew worse but not yet dire. As it later became so, disillusion with this particular solution set in. Though smaller places then closed their poorhouses, the cities shrank from any such step because of the flood of destitution that would have been released onto the streets. The problem of the poor in the modern economy therefore remained baffling. They had found some sort of place in the old agricultural order of things, but this was not so easy amid the volatility of capitalism. Crises came anyway, yet at least in the countryside the poor had been maintained by resilient structures while in the city the lower classes led lives too unstable to form communities capable of supporting their less fortunate members.[41]

The Poor Law of 1574 was not adapted, and never could be adapted, to the enormous economic changes Scotland had undergone in a couple of centuries. It rested on a basic assumption that people belonged in the communities where they were born and that their movement away would be inherently undesirable. Yet, of all peoples, the Scots had become a mobile people, in their own country, in the United Kingdom, in Europe and in the world.[42]

Within Scotland there was constant movement in search of work. Though unemployment fluctuated through economic or climatic conditions (as when the harvest failed), parochial support had become geared to the needs of the regular or deserving poor, whose numbers remained fairly constant or at least predictable. Others who could show only marginal qualifications for relief or merely fell victim to sudden misfortune had little choice but to take to the road and look for a new life. This was anyway enticing to youngsters who sought a way out of endless toil on the land to find their fortunes in the towns, where casual jobs could always be picked up. For such physical labour the poor but mobile provided an invaluably cheap and flexible workforce: something to the advantage of Scotland, though Scotland did not seem to see it.[43]

Permanent employment was seldom on offer at this level of society anyway, so that opportunities in faraway places would always be attractive when a large part of both the urban and rural population lived on, or close to, the breadline. It only took a bit of bad luck to send them off as vagrants.[44]

Such movement, which in most cases would be described today as economic migration, was generally condemned in the older Scotland. It was a country that sought to deal with its problems of poverty by institutionalising the poor, and vagrants were almost by definition people who would or could not be institutionalised. This found a reflection in the wide application of the term 'vagrant' in Scots law. It could be stuck on anybody who exposed obscene images in a public place. Similarly, it covered palmists, and people gaming or betting on the street. Those asking alms under false pretence also counted as vagrants. So did men who ran away and left wife and children chargeable to the parish. Sometimes criminals against whom nothing else could be proved were slammed up as vagrants too: those found carrying a picklock or a gun or a bludgeon, or unable to explain why they were hanging about a barn, tent, cart or wagon, or discovered in any house, stable or outhouse, or in any enclosed yard, garden or area for any unlawful purpose, or loitering round a river, canal, dock or basin, or any quay, wharf or warehouse, or in any street with an intent to commit felony.[45] Vagrants were not hard to find.

In the years of famine and depression before 1707 the Patriot, Andrew Fletcher of Saltoun, had had no patience with any mollycoddling of these wretches: 'Provisions by hospitals, almshouses, and the contributions of churches and parishes have by experience been found to increase the numbers of those that live by them. And the liberty every idle and lazy person has of burdening the society in which he lives, with his maintenance, has increased their numbers to the weakening and impoverishing of it: for he needs only to say that he cannot get work, and then he must be maintained by charity.' Scotland should heed the experience of other countries: 'Though the Hollanders by reason of the steadiness of their temper, as well as of their government (being a commonwealth), may be constant to their methods of providing for the poor; yet in a nation, and under a government like that of France, though vast public workhouses may be for a while kept in order, 'twill not be long before they fall into confusion and ruin.'[46]

Fletcher urged stern measures especially against Highlanders. He seems to have hated them: 'Nor indeed can there be any thorough reformation in this affair, so long as the one-half of our country, in extent of ground, is possessed by a people who are all gentlemen only because they will not work, and who in everything are more contemptible than the vilest slaves, except that they always carry arms, because for the most part they live upon robbery.' He proposed hospitals for the old and feeble beggars among them, with the rest divided in two classes. The harmless ones would be enslaved. The dangerous ruffians should be sent to Venice, to 'serve in the galleys against the common enemy of Christendom'.[47]

Scotland needed rid of such people not least because of their numbers: 'In all times there have been about a hundred thousand of those vagabonds who have lived without any regard or subjection to the laws of the land, or even those of God and nature.' Fletcher's figure has often been taken as a pardonable exaggeration, typical of the time. But there were perhaps a million people in his Scotland, and unemployment amounting to 10 per cent of the population, or 20 per cent of the workforce, is not hard to believe in a country that has suffered higher levels since, as we see from the more accurate statistics available since the twentieth century. Anyway it was the behaviour rather than the volume of vagrants that specially irked Fletcher: 'Many murders have been discovered among them . . . they rob many poor people who live in houses distant from any neighbourhood. At country weddings, markets, burials, and other the like occasions, they are to be seen – both men and women – perpetually drunk, cursing, blaspheming, and fighting together.' But Scotland has weddings like that today.[48]

Though hard to document, one consequence of such a terrible era might have been a more general instability in the pattern of population, in that greater numbers abandoned old abodes of their own where the limits of livelihood had been so starkly revealed. In other words, there were more vagrants on the move and looking for a bare subsistence wherever they could find it. The surviving evidence from the Lowlands shows that, long after the Union, local authorities were still worrying about this inheritance of vagrancy.[49]

Vagrants were officially banned from entering the capital.[50] In times of cold weather and bad harvests the town council of Edinburgh would post a guard at the gates to keep them out. If they found a way in all the same, they would be subject to a periodic round-up. Those caught were held in custody, fed only on bread and water, till returned to the parishes of their birth.[51] But not all the citizens treated vagrants unkindly. When the Highland waif John MacDonald and his siblings arrived in Edinburgh in 1745, 'we strayed down towards the bottom of the Canongate, staring at signs, coaches and fine horses'. A woman encountered them and took pity, 'seeing us strangers, and in Highland dress . . . She was a widow, and let lodgings; her husband, before he died, was a master-chairman, of the name of MacDonald, born near the place where we were born.' The woman came to the rescue again when young John returned the next year by offering him a corner to sleep in. After he and his brother were arrested for vagrancy, another Highlander who ran an inn and stables helped them out and gave them work.[52] By the end of the eighteenth century, when the city had knocked down most of its walls and gates, it appointed a full-time constable for 'clearing the streets of vagrants'. In 1800 it obtained a private Act of Parliament to raise £10,000 in a special fund for them, which was used to set up a school of industry and canteens where they could get food. Despite this streak of benevolence, the council remained determined to have 'some general and efficient mode of abolishing the practice of vagrant begging'. It was one of the reasons for the establishment of a regular force of police in 1805.[53]

The problems of the capital had had their effects on its hinterland, to which the vagrants would be turned out if caught. In 1711 the justices of the peace in East Lothian issued advice on what the ministers and kirk sessions of the county should do about these unfortunates. The authorities in Berwickshire, Roxburghshire and Selkirkshire wanted to follow suit, but it looks as if they could not get enough heritors interested. Lanarkshire issued regulations to deal with vagabonds too: all were to be arrested so that the sheriff could put the idle to work while imprisoning any who refused to comply with his directions. Local measures continued as, round the Lowlands, the process of agricultural enclosure intensified while shortages of food remained common.[54]

The Church of Scotland then took an interest. In 1724 the presbyteries of Edinburgh and Dalkeith decided to follow up a recent act of the General Assembly 'anent the vagrant poor' and demand moves 'to apply the laws about vagrants and to provide for the needful poor'. The General Assembly responded with a fresh appeal to 'use all means' for support of paupers while urging the civil authorities to give effect to the laws against vagrants. Landowners appeared none too happy with this clarion call. They preferred the Church to do what they wanted it to do and not start taking independent initiatives, especially on such a locally sensitive issue as vagrancy. They countered with a scheme of their own. In Midlothian the justices set up a committee on the Poor Law. They sent out a letter to ministers asking for information on the number of poor in their parishes and on the funds available to help them. The answers showed every parish in the county ready to maintain its own poor. Orders were then issued to refrain from helping vagrants from elsewhere, in another example of reluctance to countenance the mobility of labour.[55]

It was the same story over again when in 1731 the justices of Midlothian published their views on vagrancy. Vagrants were 'a great burden' and 'a reproach to the kingdom: for the most part live without all law nor rule sacred or civill'. And things had got worse: 'A numerous brood of such persons are daylie increasing who, if they were set to work and bred to trade and calling, the countrie might not only be disburdened of them but they might in a short time and upon far less expence become usefull and profitable to the whole kingdom.' The justices reaffirmed the legal obligation on vagabonds 'to return to their own parishes of their birth or where they have resided for three years'. Constables were to search them out and bring them to the justices, who would have them confined on bread and water in Edinburgh for 30 days. The expense was to be met by a parochial rate. The order included in the definition of beggars the 'actors of unlawful plays, Egyptians and others who pretend to power of charming . . . all persons having neither means nor master nor using any lawful merchandize . . . all common labourers being able in body living idle'.[56]

In the summer of 1745 the justices of Selkirkshire arrested a group of vagrants, one of whom claimed to be Prince Charles Edward Stewart. An agitated correspondence ensued with Robert Dundas, Lord President of the Court of Session. The judges, backed by the Lord Advocate, did not want this man sent to Edinburgh for trial, since the resulting publicity might be politically embarrassing. They suggested he should be dealt with locally as an idle vagrant, or conscripted for the army, or after threat of a whipping he might 'voluntarily enact himself to banishment'. It would still be a good idea, before that, to have him looked at by somebody who claimed to know the real prince by sight.[57]

This was not the only unexpected problem in dealing with vagrancy in East Lothian. In 1767 the justices used money gathered for the suppression of vagrants to pay for supporting a 'furious madman'. It was a move perhaps only just about legal, and when the next year a woman came up in court who during occasional fits of madness walked round smashing windows (which could only have been in rich men's houses) the justices merely sought somebody to take over the duty of restraining her. In vain: finally they had to put her in jail at Haddington. But later they complained that the practice of imprisoning lunatics was 'turning the county gaol into a madhouse'.[58]

Quickening economic advance did not eliminate vagrancy. It was still a problem in many areas when the *Old Statistical Account* came to be written during the last decade of the century. In the south-west of Scotland the parishes noted an influx of Irish beggars, sometimes moving as families.[59] All over the Lowlands there were reports that, while none of the local people begged from door to door, vagrants from elsewhere still infested the streets of the towns and villages.[60] In the Highlands, on the other hand, begging from door to door was both widespread and acceptable within a tradition of hospitality that made the locals, while poor themselves, reluctant to deny alms or a night's lodging to those who asked. In this region the rising population, the limited opportunities for employment and the lack of money to build up poor funds were bound to put many people on the road in any event.[61] They drifted to the Lowlands where they could supplement their meagre incomes from seasonal labour on the farms or menial jobs in the burghs. Along the way they counted as vagrants.[62]

George Robertson, in his *Rural Recollections* (1829), looked back on changes in the condition of the poor he had witnessed over several decades. In the old days, he recalled,

> no visitors were so frequent as the common beggars. Hardly a single day passed, without some of them making their peculiar chap at the door; nor a single week, without some of them getting a night's lodging in the barn. They were surely more numerous in those times than they have been for many years past; neither were they so ill bestead as their successors in the present day. They had a more honest-like look, and were better happed up. Their clothing indeed was old, but it was seldom ragged being always well clouted, though of many colours (which showed them to be of a thrifty disposition) and far better fitted to face the storm than the scanty garments of the present ragged race. Of all the ranks in society the beggars of modern times have fallen the lowest; or rather, they are the only class whose circumstances have not improved. Happily for the country, there are now fewer of them in number.[63]

A final feature of poverty in the Scotland of the eighteenth century was that it mainly afflicted women. On the surviving lists of poor from the parishes, the women invariably outnumbered the men, often by as much as two to one. The fact was seldom any cause of comment among contemporaries, and perhaps most regarded it as something natural. It was the men who administered the Poor Law, after all. We would be going too far to say it was also administered for the men but, except in terms of the numbers assisted, the women often drew the short straw.[64]

Seldom, anyway, did women take charge of anything in the system. There was a contrary example at the small poorhouse of Haddington in East Lothian. It sheltered orphans and a few adults under the charge of a capable lady who bought large quantities of cloth and used the juvenile labour to make clothes both for the inmates and for paying customers in the town. A destitute schoolmaster was admitted in 1756 in the expectation that he would teach the children to read. But the use for the general benefit of such female efficiency and resource was the exception rather than the rule.[65]

While the Poor Law did not of itself discriminate against women, in practice their treatment under it turned out unequal. Doles to them were often miserly. Again, this did not seem to worry anybody, a common attitude being that women could count themselves lucky for what they got. Sometimes the parish would couple relief with a form of discipline. In 1721 the kirk session at Rothesay on Bute allotted a pound Scots 'to buy shoes for Elspeth NcTaylour' and 'if she pawns them for drink she'll get no more'. In cases where help could only be given either to a man or to a woman, the woman would likely come off worse. At Tranent in East Lothian the parish raised an assessment and from the proceeds built a spinning house where the poor could live and work. In 1750 John Lamb, 'aged near 90' and his wife 'past 71' applied for relief; they were given sixpence and told that to get any more they would need to find something to do at the spinning house. Yet, as Lamb was to point out, the house had no materials and could offer no employment. While the parish then put him on its list of pensioners, to make room for him it knocked off Euphan Waters, who was over 50 but 'not so needful'.[66]

Women were certainly more likely to descend into poverty than men. Married or not, they had to have some special skill in order to achieve any comparable subsistence, and to sustain it through pregnancy, childcare, housework and all the other burdens a woman had to bear. Also, then as now, women lived longer than men. For a working population in which many got by on the narrowest of margins, there did not even exist any means of saving for old age except through hoarding coins that might be stolen. When women outlived their relations, or lost contact with them for one reason or another, destitution beckoned. For that very reason, about 1790, a unique printed 'petition of the women servants within the city of Edinburgh' sought leave to establish a fund for relief because 'we daily see when any of us are rendered incapable to serve either through old age, sickness, infirmity or other accidents, we are presently exposed in an ignominious manner to seek our bread from the charity of others. Which we cannot conceive as it is a melancholy prospect of our future fortune and cannot but be very discouraging any, in often reflecting thereupon, renders us more useless in our service.' A mutual fund 'will prevent the inhuman ejecting of us from families where we serve, in our sickness etc, by which many have been unchristianly exposed to bad houses and company in great want and misery'.[67]

And then, in several though not all of the regions of Scotland there was a high number of women who remained unmarried (the picture is, however, somewhat obscured by the variety of Scottish matrimonial customs).[68] It seems anyway probable that many mature women had difficulty in providing for themselves, especially as the range of occupations open to them was so limited. Spinsters might help the rest of their families in the fermtouns (where part of the income often came, as a matter of fact, from spinning). While women's smaller frames rendered them less useful than men for some physical tasks, there were others not needing so much muscle; for these the less hearty appetites of women made them economical workers. Even so, they were not considered as possible tenants for any except the tiniest agricultural holdings of their own. In the burghs, rules and regulations barred the way into commerce. Women had less expectation of inheriting property than men. They were usually unqualified for work requiring the ability to write, and barred from taking up a craft except under their fathers. A shop selling second-hand clothes and furniture seemed about the best option. Or else women could go into domestic service. Between 1785 and 1792 there was a tax on female servants deemed by the government to be non-essential, and the rolls compiled for this purpose reveal Scotland had more than 10,000 of them (compared with 5,000 men).[69]

Last resort of all was prostitution. It had long been common in Edinburgh, and was well known to the poet of the capital, Robert Fergusson:

> Near some lamp-post, wi' dowy face,
> Wi' heavy een, and sour grimace,
> Stands she that beauty lang had kend,
> Whoredom her trade, and vice her end.[70]

In 1793 William Creech the publisher reported there were now hundreds like her, in unfavourable contrast to 1763 when, he claimed, only five or six brothels had existed in the whole town: 'A person might have gone from the Castle to Holyroodhouse . . . at any hour of the night, without being accosted by a single street-walker.' He is hard to believe. Prostitution had been rife in the capital since at least the sixteenth century, on account of the limited urban opportunities for poor girls and of the numbers of men on having to spend time alone in the capital while there on business.

In 1776, halfway through Creech's period of comparison, the biographer James Boswell had no trouble stilling his lust whenever he felt like it. He would get drunk, wander the wynds and closes and take his pick. From 25 November that year he did so, or meant to, three nights running. The first time, 'as I was coming home at five, I met a young slender slut with a red cloak in the street and went with her to Barefoots Parks [next to the building site of the New Town] and madly ventured coition. It was a short and almost insensible gratification of lewdness.' In the High Street, the second time, he met 'a plump hussy who called herself Peggy Grant. It was one of the coldest nights I ever remember. I went with her to a field behind the Register Office, and boldly lay with her. This was desperate risking.' The third time, 'the girl with whom I was last night had told me she lodged in Stevenlaw's Close, and at my desire engaged to be at the head of it generally at eight in the evening, in case I should be coming past. I thought I could not be in more danger of disease by one more enjoyment the very next evening, so went tonight; but she was not there.' The names do not quite tally but she might have been a girl in the *Impartial List of the Ladies of Pleasure in Edinburgh* circulated in 1775: 'This lady is little, black hair, round-faced, tolerable good teeth, and about 24 years of age. She is extremely shy and artful in her devotions at the shrine of love.' Be that as it may, Boswell had to go home crestfallen to his wife and baby son. The New Town would prove a boon to him because he no longer needed to copulate in the open during Edinburgh's winters. The gardens had room for sheds and the houses fewer windows, so it was not so easy as in the Old Town to spot goings-on in dark corners.[71]

Contraception was primitive, provided by lengths of dried cow-gut that needed softening in water before use: a lengthy process surely often overtaken by passion. A result was that prostitutes tended to have many children. One way for them to deal with their offspring was infanticide, the crime for which females were most commonly sentenced to death.[72] But the great majority preferred to keep their kids. In 1771 the kirk session of Ayr, 'considering that the poor's funds of the place are overburdened' with 'the spurious issue of strumpets', set up a committee to discuss the matter with the town council and the house of correction. It was decided these should be the institutions that in future dealt with women of 'bad character' and their brats.[73] In the same spirit, Edinburgh founded in 1797 a refuge for prostitutes, the Magdalene Institute, to take them off the streets and make honest women of them, as laundresses. Most then ran away from employers they found unbearably condescending; they already knew easier ways to make a living.[74]

Such was the miserable condition of women at the bottom of the social heap, yet perhaps for others the eighteenth century brought a chance of a better life. The pattern varied round the country, but most women worked and made some contribution to the fortunes of their families. So long as their occupational choice did not threaten male hegemony, and remained confined to types of employment seen as right for their sex, it might even be encouraged.[75]

Marriage clearly made a difference. Up and down the social scale, the Scottish marriage was by and large an economic arrangement. In other words, people did not usually marry for love, a possibly dangerous distraction from paternal plans. That went without saying on the upper levels of society. In this era at least the bigger tenant farmers did grow more prosperous, and in the next generation they might remove their daughters from the workforce so as to make them a better match for some upwardly mobile young man. In the burghs, the households of the merchants and tradesmen were often large, including not only the married couple and their children but also their servants and apprentices. It was possible for a division of labour to develop on both the commercial and domestic sides, with the husband providing the wherewithal and making the big decisions while the wife saw to it that his intentions were carried out. Urban social life remained largely segregated. Generally the men went out and enjoyed themselves while the women at best visited one another at home: in this respect, Scotland was not to change for a long time. Indeed, the charge of effeminacy might be levelled at men who spent too much time mixing socially with women, unless in private for the purpose of seduction.[76]

The urban pattern of behaviour was repeated in the landed class, where each estate might be a small economic operation of its own. There would usually be a home farm, but most of the income came from tenanting the rest of the land. Here the people grew their own food and fuel, while using the equipment in mills, breweries and mills to transform crops into consumables. In all these activities the wives played a part but could only look up in awe at the mistress of the estate whose clothes, furniture and luxuries were bought out of its surplus. Still, not every landowner waxed wealthy, and some lairds had also to work in the law or in public office to supplement their income. And then the wife, remaining at home, might assume a more practical role in running the affairs of the household.[77]

At all levels, however, there might in the course of the eighteenth century also have been some movement by women out of economic activity altogether. In previous generations it had been quite common for a woman from the middle and upper ranks of society to own a share in a merchant house, or to be the proprietrix of an urban enterprise or to act for an incapacitated male in the management of an estate. But now a new feminine ideal was emerging with an ideal of domesticity and a stress on softness and sensibility in social life. In the next chapter we will go on to look at a few examples of how, at least among the dominant landowners' class, leisure allowed women to break into a new world of freedom. The promise inherent in this state of affairs was only slowly to be fulfilled, however, and meanwhile it served as another measure of the social power of that class in Scottish society.[78] It was indeed a country where 'the proprietor can be put under no restraint', as the judge had told the litigants from the banks of the River Irvine.[79]

Nothing in the Scotland of the eighteenth century much affected that social power. The conceptions of poverty, too, were steadily forced from the top on to the bottom level of society, and shaped the practice of relief on the ground: the poor were defined as either disabled or idle, deserving either of charity or of discipline. Presbyterianism might have been the chief motivation here, its values imposed with rigour but little regard for individual nuance. Still, as in other spheres, on balance the effect on the self-reliance of the nation and its people would turn out to be positive: in the end, the best way out of poverty was indeed to work.

8

Womanhood: 'Flora will keep watch'

On the night of 28 June 1746, Prince Charles Edward Stewart and Flora MacDonald set sail from Benbecula to Skye in a small boat, with him disguised as her Irish servant, Betty Burke. The exploit gave rise to a song allegedly traditional but in fact first published in 1884:

> Speed, bonnie boat, like a bird on the wing,
> Onward! the sailors' cry.
> Carry the lad that is born to be king
> Over the sea to Skye . . .
>
> Though the waves leap, soft shall ye sleep,
> Ocean's a royal bed.
> Rocked in the deep, Flora will keep
> Watch by your weary head.[1]

In the creation of such myths, historical accuracy soon suffers. Many other tales were told of the prince's escape from the Outer Hebrides, where he had narrowly evaded capture by the redcoats of the British army. Some might have been owed to Flora's own rather saucy sense of humour: her personal favourite was the story of how she told Charles not to carry pistols under the petticoat of his dress because the weapons would give him away should he be frisked. 'If we shall happen to meet with any that will go so narrowly to work in searching as what you mean, they will certainly discover me at any rate,' the prince retorted.[2]

It was ten weeks since Prince Charles had suffered final defeat at the Battle of Culloden. With the Jacobite cause lost, he took to the heather and fled through the Highland wilderness, at length making his way to the Western Isles where he hoped a French ship would pick him up. But none came. Though nobody betrayed the prince, the government somehow got wind of his whereabouts and ordered a systematic search for him over mountain, machair and moor. The danger of being cornered was just too great and he decided to slip back to the mainland. Flora MacDonald, a resident of Skye at that moment on a visit to her brother in South Uist, was selected to provide the prince's cover. According to another romantic tale, he met her by moonlight at a shieling on Seabhal hill, where she was keeping watch over some cattle. Though he came with two companions, he himself was the one that asked if he might accompany her when she left for her home. Despite deep misgivings, she agreed. But why on earth, when she and her family had had no direct Jacobite involvement before? She gave the answer to the puzzle on being later questioned in London by Frederick, Prince of Wales. She said she would have done as much for him if she had found him in the same straits.[3]

Charles and Flora reached Trotternish at the northern end of Skye. She took him to the home of Lord Macdonald of Sleat, whence he was passed on to a factor's house on the estate at Kingsburgh. Unfortunately the boatmen who had sailed them across the Minch were meanwhile sent back to South Uist, where they were arrested and then confessed to what they had done. Redcoats came for Flora and the factor, but the prince had already fled onwards to Raasay. After making his way to the mainland, he remained in hiding till he was at last taken off by a French ship on 19 September from Loch nan Uamh in the Sound of Arisaig, at almost the exact same spot where he had landed more than a year before.[4]

Flora was meanwhile interrogated by the general in charge of the government's mopping-up operations in the Hebrides, John Campbell of Mamore, actually a kindly kinsman of the Duke of Argyll who, unlike English officers, preferred to handle his Jacobite captives with some degree of humanity. While she answered him bravely, she contrived to hide as much as she revealed. Campbell ordered her to be sent with other prominent prisoners to London and to be treated well. For most of her detention she lived in a private house, till released under a general amnesty in 1747. Apparently she could not face returning to the islands and she stayed much of the time in Edinburgh. There she met the Revd Robert Forbes, who was collecting first-hand accounts of the rising that had to wait to be published till 1895–96, as *The Lyon in Mourning*. They tell us most of what we know about the last days of Jacobitism.[5]

In 1750 Flora married a kinsman, Allan MacDonald of Kingsburgh, a good-looking, amiable young fellow with advanced agricultural ideas but a poor head for business. They had seven children while they farmed at Flodigarry in the north-east of Skye, till Allan succeeded his father as factor of Sleat. Samuel

Johnson and James Boswell, during their Highland tour in 1773, visited the couple. Boswell described Flora, now aged 51, as 'a little woman of genteel appearance, and uncommonly mild and well-bred', while Allan was 'completely the figure of a gallant Highlander'. Flora felt much taken with Johnson, and confided more of her story to him than she ever did to others. As their friendship grew, she made so bold as to titillate him a little: she joked of how she had heard in advance that Boswell was on his way to Skye, and 'a young English buck with him'. The MacDonalds did Johnson the honour of inviting him to occupy the bed where Prince Charles had slept the night he stayed at Kingsburgh.[6]

Yet otherwise things had not gone well for the MacDonalds, and they began to despair of ever prospering on Skye. The next spring they emigrated to North Carolina, where many other Highlanders were settled along the Cape Fear River. They had barely arrived when the American War of Independence broke out. By now both Flora and Allan were wholly loyal to King George III. She encouraged the settlers to join the regiment that her husband helped to raise in defence of the colony's royal government. With other Scottish units, it suffered defeat at the hands of the American rebels in the Battle of Moore's Creek Bridge in February 1776. Allan was taken prisoner and interned. He would not be reunited with his wife till 1778, and then in New York. From there he rejoined his regiment but she, ill, lonely and homesick, decided to return to Scotland. She lost two sons in the American war and did not see her husband again till 1785. While they thought of settling in Nova Scotia, they lacked the means to do so. They ended their days still at Kingsburgh, if at the last comfortably off because another son had made a fortune in India. Flora died in 1790 and Allan in 1792.[7]

The rising of 1745 was altogether remarkable for the fearless heroines it brought out of Highland obscurity, attracted not least by the charms of Prince Charles himself. A second of them was Anne Mackintosh of Mackintosh, whose house of Moy lay near Inverness. Born into a stalwart Jacobite family, the Farquharsons of Invercauld, she married into another, to Angus, chief of Clan Chattan. But he had quite unawares complicated his position by previously, before he ever dreamed a Stewart prince would land again in Scotland, having thrown in his lot with the House of Hanover in the sense of recruiting troops for them. What was he to do when Charles did turn up? Perhaps one way to deal with an awkward situation would be to send his wife out on the other side, since split loyalties in a single family were by no means unusual and indeed a good insurance against their all falling foul of whichever party came out on top in the end. It was, though, just as possible that she acted on her own initiative. Without a doubt, in any event, she personally raised 600 men for the Stewarts' cause. Of these 300 guarded Moy, while the rest joined the prince's army on its invasion of England.[8]

By the spring of 1746 that army, having the previous December reached Derby, was falling back on Inverness. On 16 February, Lady Mackintosh received Prince Charles and an escort of 30 Highlanders at Moy. Somehow word of the meeting reached the local Hanoverian commander, the Earl of Loudoun, who after nightfall dispatched a force of 1,500 men to take them all by surprise. Lady Mackintosh yet got warning of their approach and sent a few of her own recruits out to create a diversion while the prince escaped. Firing in the air and calling loudly to one another, they convinced the assailants that a large hostile force lay waiting in ambush. A stray bullet killed Loudoun's piper: at that point the rest of his soldiers fled so fast that this became known as the Rout of Moy. Afterwards Lady Mackintosh was nicknamed Colonel Anne, but we need not take seriously the idea of her as a military commander. Though her regiment fought at Culloden, it did so under Alexander McGillivray of Dunmaglass. She was afterwards imprisoned at Inverness, then sent to London where, like Flora MacDonald, she enjoyed a warm welcome. She even contrived, as a curiosity to the English, to lead an active social life.[9]

While Flora MacDonald had emerged from the rebellion with a positive image, Colonel Anne's was more mixed. In her own time Hanoverian propaganda demonised her as a 'woman of monstrous size', an Amazon armed to the teeth. Yet a surviving portrait by Allan Ramsay, dated 1748, bears out the contemporary observation of her as 'a very thin girl'. According to her own husband, she 'never saw the men [of her regiment] but once, and was at her own house' while they went off to fight. Her correspondence suggests she spent the time sewing Jacobite white cockades for them.[10] All the same, she was in later romantic accounts metamorphosed once again, into a 'Highland Joan of Arc'[11] who had indeed led her 300 men on to the field of Culloden.

Still, there were Jacobite women with an amply justified reputation for toughness, among them the widowed Charlotte Robertson, Lady Lude. She was the daughter of Lord Nairne who had been out (with his wife) in the rebellion of 1715, and a cousin of the Dukes of Atholl, another family split down the middle by Jacobitism with claimants to the noble title on each side of the divide. When Prince Charles stayed at Blair Atholl, it was Duke William that acted as host, and he asked Charlotte to wait personally on the royal guest. She organised entertainments in the castle, as well as a grand ball at her own house of Lude a few miles away. The factor of the Hanoverian Duke James was there, and he described her as behaving 'like a light Giglet'. But she had another side to her character, as a fearsome superior to her feudal tenants. She bullied them into joining the Jacobite army with a threat to burn them out if they refused, and in some cases she actually did this. She was reputed to have raised 1,000 men by such means. After Culloden, royal troops took her prisoner. The people she had threatened and intimidated now gave evidence against her but, like other Jacobite women, she got off lightly.[12]

In Perthshire, Lady Lude was one member of a wide landowning connection faithful to the Stewarts, of which Carolina, Lady Nairne, would be another. She was to figure among the last of the Jacobites, being born at Gask in Strathearn two decades after the rebellion but baptised in honour of the Young Pretender, now in Rome drinking himself to death. In other circumstances, Hanoverian justice would have seen in her only 'corruption of the blood': all three families from which she descended – Oliphants, Robertsons and Nairnes – were attainted for high treason and had forfeited their estates. Still her father, Laurence Oliphant, remained active in the lost cause right till he died in 1792. He reared his children to 'keep them loyal',[13] arranging every possible detail of their lives so as to remind them that the Stewarts, and not a lot of upstart Germans, were their lawful sovereigns. Yet the girls had a governess who trained them to speak English, for they would need at length to find genteel husbands too; it was felt that their 'very broad Scots . . . will not be graceful in a young lady'.[14] In the event Carolina married her cousin William Nairne, whose title was restored at the time of King George IV's visit to Scotland in 1822; so she became best known as Lady Nairne.

Quite apart from politics, Lady Nairne had from early on in life taken a patriotic interest in Scots song, which came in two kinds. There was the incredibly fecund fund of it to be found in the hearts, minds and mouths of the people, still a vital tradition stretching far back into Scottish history. And then there was art-song, consciously composed by modern poets after the older style. Robert Burns, the most famous of these poets, demonstrates in his oeuvre the rich relationship such work enjoyed with the existing oral culture.

The national tradition of song appealed across all levels of Scottish society from the humble cottage to the nobleman's castle. No doubt it was the art-song that got more often performed at the upper end of the social scale, for the simple reason that the songs of the popular tradition had no inhibitions about sex. Of course, this was true of a good many of Burns's art-songs too. But while the work he published in his lifetime often dealt with love, even passionate love, it never got into physical detail. We know all the same, from the posthumous publication of *The Merry Muses* and the like, that Burns was bawdy with the best of them in the poems he did not care to publish, and could not have got published anyway.[15]

Lady Nairne took a deep interest in Burns's work, especially his gift for setting new words to old tunes. In straitlaced imitation she started editing inherited material that might be thought morally dubious and worked with the publisher Robert Purdie on 'a collection of the national airs, with words suited for refined circles'.[16] It appeared as *The Scottish Minstrel* in six volumes (1821–24). Since such work was still considered incompatible with Lady Nairne's status as a gentlewoman, she took elaborate steps to conceal her authorship: she sent her contributions through intermediaries and when she really needed to visit the publisher she went in disguise. Over time she devoted more of her energies to devout or charitable pursuits, which enhanced her status as poetess laureate to the aspiring and respectable in Victorian Scotland. But it all turned the blithe and musical Carolina Oliphant into the prim and pious Lady Nairne. Luckily nothing came of her project for a bowdlerised edition of Burns.

The feminine interest in Scots song was not confined to Jacobite circles. Jean Elliot, daughter of a Whig judge, Lord Minto, did get caught up in the rising of 1745 to the extent that a unit of Prince Charles's army passed by her house in Roxburghshire on its way into England. But her family was true to King George II, and her father took refuge in the nearby hills while Jean entertained the rebel officers till they moved on. Her later reputation depended on a song celebrating a different era, 'The Flowers of the Forest', the lament for the Battle of Flodden in 1513, which she wrote for a wager with her brother Gilbert. The two of them were travelling in a coach together and discussing the battle when he bet 'a pair of gloves or a set of ribbons' against his sister's ability to write a good ballad on the subject. According to old oral tradition in the Borders, of the 80 'flowers' of Selkirk Forest who had gone to Flodden only one returned, bearing a captured English flag. There may have been an existing art-song on the subject, but Jean transformed it by the powerful use of the Scots language in her own text, with lines that became famous: 'I've heard them lilting at the yowe-milking' and 'The flowers of the forest are a' wede away'.[17]

After Lord Minto died Jean moved to Edinburgh, to offer her social circle 'a prodigious fund of Scottish anecdote'. Some said ungraciously that she 'did not appear to have ever been handsome', while others allowed that she displayed 'a sensible face, and a slender, well-shaped figure'. In character she was 'from her youth . . . remarkable for her discrimination, discretion, and self-control', and in taste 'fond of French literature', though not of the French Revolution. By her old age she had become the only lady in Edinburgh still using a sedan chair.[18] Though her social status made her unwilling to claim the authorship of 'The Flowers of the Forest', the fact of it was well known; she acquired the nickname 'the Flower' in consequence. Walter Scott printed the verses in *Minstrelsy of the Scottish Border* (1802–03).[19]

A further female individualist of blue blood was Susanna, Countess of Eglinton, born a Kennedy of Culzean in Ayrshire. From her childhood her family expected her to become a noblewoman. For a husband they fixed their gaze on a particular candidate. While she was playing in the gardens of their castle a hawk landed on her shoulder, with the name of the owner engraved on the bird's bells: Alexander Montgomery, ninth Earl of Eglinton. He was already a friend of her own family, who took this as a sign she would one day marry him – though he already had a wife and was old enough to be her father.[20]

The time came for the girl's social debut, and she went with her father to Edinburgh. A striking six-foot beauty, she at once attracted suitors. Among them figured the dashing and handsome Sir John Clerk of Penicuik. Knowing she was musical, he gave her a flute. When she tried to play it no sound came out, and she discovered inside a scroll of paper with a poem he had composed:

Go, happy pipe and ever mindful be
To court bewitching Sylvia for me . . .[21]

She was falling in love with him, but of course the marriages of well-born girls could not be decided by personal attraction. While Sir John was wealthy, to Susanna's father only noble rank counted. He met his old friend Eglinton, whose advice was brief but to the point: 'Bide a wee, Sir Archie', he said, with a twinkle in his eye, 'My wife's very sickly'. To Susanna's chagrin, her father rejected Sir John's proposal and, sure enough, the Countess of Eglinton died soon afterwards. In 1709, Susanna married the earl.[22]

Eglinton already had six daughters and needed a male heir. He was angry and disappointed when his first four children with Susanna turned out to be girls too, and he threatened to divorce her unless she bore him a son. She replied calmly, 'By all means, but first of all, give me back all that I brought you.' He blustered that he would restore every penny of her dowry. She smiled. 'Na, na, my lord,' she answered, 'that winna do. Return me my youth, my beauty and my virginity and then dismiss me whenever you please.'[23] He had nothing to say. The next year their first son James was born. They divided their time between Eglinton Castle in Ayrshire and a townhouse in Edinburgh. Susanna entertained magnificently and became patron to a circle of literary friends. Allan Ramsay dedicated *The Gentle Shepherd* to her, praising her 'superior wit and sound judgement',[24] while the Jacobite poet, William Hamilton of Bangour, described her as:

> Pure in thy thought, and spotless in thy deed
> In virtues rich, in goodness unconfin'd.[25]

The eldest son of the marriage, James, was the tenth Earl of Eglinton destined to be killed by a poacher he sought to catch on his lands in Ayrshire.[26] Susanna never really recovered from his death, but even in old age she kept her handsome appearance and her independent spirit. Lonely with many of her family gone, she made pets of the rats that lived in the walls of her house. After a meal she would summon them for scraps with a rap of her knuckles on the panelling, then sent them away again with another rap. When friends shuddered at her peculiar pets, she would claim the rats were better than many of her human guests because they knew when it was time to leave. A visitor whose departure she did regret was Dr Johnson. He came to see her during his visit to Edinburgh in 1773, and they took to each other at once. She bantered with him that, as she had wed a year before he was born, she could have been his mother. 'My dear son, farewell!' she cried, embracing him when he went. He later told his friend Mrs Hester Thrale, 'I was sorry to leave her.' Susanna died in 1780, at the age of 90. Johnson said that she 'for many years gave the laws of elegance to Scotland'.[27]

These aristocratic women were bearers of culture not only in a literary but also in a linguistic sense. It seems the Countess of Eglinton and others habitually spoke Scots inside the house and English only outside it, so preserving the use of the native tongue to a greater extent than the men at this social level did. The men had more opportunity to travel to London, often leaving their wives at home, and within Scotland also followed professions – in law,

Church and university – where mastery of English was, if not quite indispensable, at least highly desirable. Women remained excluded from these spheres, spending more time in the circles of tradesmen and servants where everybody felt more comfortable speaking Scots.[28]

A crucial point was that the ladies spoke Scots with one another as well. Scott gave the example of Anne Murray Keith, whom he would disguise as Mrs Bethune Baliol in his *Chronicles of the Canongate* (1827–28). Her recent death, he wrote then, 'had saddened a wide circle, much attached to her, as well for her genuine virtue and amiable qualities of disposition, as for the extent of information which she possessed, and the delightful manner in which she was used to communicate it. In truth, the author had, on many occasions, been indebted to her vivid memory for his Scottish fictions.' Her 'peculiar vivacity of look and manner' together with 'the pointed and appropriate action which accompanied her words' had been, Scott went on, 'of real old-fashioned Scottish growth, and such as might have graced the tea-table of Susanna, Countess of Eglinton, patroness of Allan Ramsay'. To listen to Anne was to turn back the pages of history: 'It seemed to be the Scottish as spoken by the ancient court of Scotland, to which no idea of vulgarity could be attached.'[29]

There did indeed just about survive one prestigious form of the language, Court Scots, not in the least owed to any anglicisation. Probably it had last been used in public when the future James VII was resident at Holyrood in 1679–81. Henry Cockburn recalled how during his childhood in the 1780s he had heard ancient ladies speaking it. One might have been Mrs Baird of Newbyth, mother of David Baird, member of a group of young officers captured in India and chained together in pairs: 'Lord pity the chiel that's chained tae oor Davie,' she exclaimed when she heard. Another might have been Miss Johnstone of Westerhall, who had a cousin forced by penury to sell her furniture: 'But before the sale cam on, in God's gude providence, she just clinkit aff hersell.'[30] Perhaps the very last of these venerable dames was one who in 1879 died at Rothesay Place in Edinburgh, aged 85 – just such 'a genuine Scottish matron of the old school', Dame Margaret Sinclair of Dunbeath. She had been born in the Canongate in 1794 into a class even then vanishing, 'the clear-headed, stout-hearted yet reverent and gentle old Scottish ladies whom Lord Cockburn loved to portray'.[31]

We might also sadly speculate, for this nation of male chauvinism, that in their well-born husbands' eyes the linguistic usage also marked the ladies out as inferior. Some coped with the prejudice better than others, or even turned the tables. James Primrose, second Earl of Rosebery, was a difficult character who wasted most of what talents he had on strife within his family, including violence towards his wife Mary, a redoubtable scion of the Campbells of Mamore, and their children. In such circumstances there was little a spouse could do to help herself under Scots law: it had developed in such a disadvantageous fashion to married women that a friend of the family needed to apply to the courts for the protection of the countess and her offspring. In this case it was granted on the grounds that Rosebery himself had gone insane and so should be confined inside his home of Barnbougle Castle by the shore of the Firth of Forth. Once Mary had him where she wanted him, she took control of the household. He wrote to protest to his friend Sir John Clerk of Penicuik about the treatment he received at the hands of his minders:

> She made them use me so ill and caused abuse so much that the soldiers were like to sink down with grief to see such barbarities used to me, to name but one things, one night at ten o'clock, for I was denied liberty to my servants, paper, pen and ink or to provide my own victuals, I was refused one chapin of oil coals or candle; did I with my ears hear my lady Rosebery in next room doting upon her cully [sweetheart] Archibald Campbell of Burbank; who was in his bed and feeding him with venison collaps telling him was sure he loved them.[32]

Perhaps the most formidable of all the Scottish ladies of the eighteenth century was Jean Maxwell of Monreith, later Duchess of Gordon. On a colourful career she started young: born and brought up in Edinburgh, as a child she used to ride through the streets on a pig. Her marriage to a great nobleman of the north turned out unhappy, but did not quell her quick wit, animated conversation or mischievous behaviour. As duchess, her local involvements ranged wide. When her husband raised the Gordon Highlanders, she and her daughters played recruiting sergeants, and stood in the marketplaces with guineas between their lips. She built a house of her own on the River Spey, where she entertained lavishly. Lady Elizabeth Grant of Rothiemurchus recalled: 'Half the London world of fashion, all the clever people that could be hunted out from all parts, all the north country, all the neighbourhood from far and near, without regard to wealth or station, and all the kith and kin of both Gordons and Maxwells, flocked to this encampment in the wilderness during the fine autumns to enjoy the free life, the pure air, and the wit and fun the duchess brought with her to the mountains.'[33] It was not all just pastoral play-acting: the duchess helped besides to manage her husband's estates in Badenoch and Strathspey. She encouraged the cultivation of flax and manufacture of linen, for which she set up a market at Kingussie.

The Duchess of Gordon endeared herself in Scotland, but by the same token startled the polite society of London. One rhyme about her ran:

> The duchess triumphs in a manly mien,
> Loud is her accent and her phrase obscene.

As a political hostess she organised extravagant soirées. She found admirers among the leaders of the United Kingdom, including the Prime Minister, William Pitt the Younger, and his right-hand man, Henry Dundas. It was with her compatriot Dundas that she struck up the warmest relationship, one of bantering intimacy. She went drinking with him and perhaps further – she often appeared, scantily clad, in scurrilous cartoons. She even inspired Dundas's one literary effort, of four lines:

> She was the mucklest of them aw,
> Like Saul she stood the tribes aboon;
> Her gown was whiter than the snaw,
> Her face was redder than the mune.[34]

Towards the end of the century Elizabeth Mure of Caldwell looked back on all the changes that had come over the existence of gentlewomen in an era of progress. At the outset, she recalled, their lives had not been at all interesting: 'Domestic affairs and amusing her husband was the business of a good wife . . . No attention was given to what we call accomplishments.' As daughters grew up, 'they were allowed to run about and amuse themselves in the way they choiced even to the age of women, at which time they were generally sent to Edinburgh for a winter or two, to learn to dress themselves and to dance and see a little of the world.' Then, after marriage, it was back to rural idiocy: 'If they read any it was either books of devotion or long romances, and sometimes both. They never ate a full meal at table; this was thought very undelicate, but they took care to have something before dinner, that they might behave with propriety in company.'[35]

But more refined manners did at length spread round the country. As Elizabeth Mure noted, it was at the tea tables that the women 'pulled to pieces the manners of those that differed from them; everything was a matter of conversation; religion, morals, love, friendship, good manners, dress'. It is interesting that she associates this in a social sense with the easing of Presbyterian rigour that we have also observed at an intellectual level. About 1730, she reckons, 'those terrors began to wear off and religion appeared in a more amiable light. We were bid draw our knowledge of God from his works, the chief of which is the soul of a good man; then judge if we have cause to fear. The Christian religion was taught as the purest rule of morals; the belief of a particular providence and of a future state as a supporting every situation.' And then 'the old minister was ridiculed who preached up hell and damnation; the mind was to be influenced by gentle and generous motives alone'.[36]

All these were well-born women of character who, without any academic training, became ornaments of enlightened society through their intelligence, vivacity or indeed eccentricity. In turn, they helped to give the Scottish philosophers a lively interest in the social standing of women, not only in practice but also in theory – it was something taken to reveal deeper truths about the level of civilisation in any given time or place. Exceptional women might have presented a somewhat skewed vision of the norm for their sex. But they did bring out one important aspect of enlightened Scotland with the role they played in its sociability. A concept of womanhood informed by politeness was bound to change the lives at least of those belonging to the social elite. As they enjoyed the experiences opening up to them they could flatter themselves that their developing feminine culture formed part of a broader programme of improvement. In an age with such hopes of progress and of the potential for the new to better the old, these social changes deserved to be viewed alongside advances in industry, agriculture or commerce, all as active agents of progress.[37]

Not that Scotland was likely to be unanimous on such matters. Presbyterians had always sought to tame sexuality, and this was not a part of the national heritage that most enlightened thinkers wished to reject out of hand. They were never libertines: they continued to praise marital fidelity and to link sexual excess to a low stage of human development. They even thought a new Scotland, one that had cast off bigotry and persecution, might wish to improve its self-discipline as well, in contrast, say, to the practices among the sort of dissolute aristocracy that supported the Jacobites.

Yet even in the second half of the eighteenth century Presbyterian misogyny remained a force to be reckoned with. The minister of Brechin and then of Alloa, the Revd James Fordyce, published *Sermons to Young Women* (1766) in which he snapped at them: 'Have modern manners so warped your minds that the simplicity of ancient virtue, instead of appearing to you as an object of veneration, looks romantic and ridiculous?' Morality was being lost amid the flighty fashions of the day, with women to the fore in 'numberless pleasing services and amiable attentions'. Perhaps this might prove of some small moral use in that women had a greater 'fund of what may be termed sentiment, or a pathetic manner of thinking, which I have not so frequently met with in men'. We expected some males to be rough and harsh, but in 'female furies' such qualities always shocked us. When sensible men sought a partner, they looked for a woman with soft features, a flowing voice, a 'form not robust' and a 'demeanour delicate and gentle'. The best were those with that 'wonderful dexterity for disarming fierceness and appeasing wrath'. Fordyce wondered how this role could possibly be regarded as servile. Women who fulfilled it would occupy the most 'honourable station'. They were 'the formers of a rational and immortal offspring', who refined a family's pleasures and soothed its pains with their 'nameless delightful sympathies and endearments'. It was in the domestic sphere that women could use their sympathetic skills to best effect, tempering the necessary parental authority with affection as they helped to construct a loving and harmonious household. The trouble was how so few women nowadays appreciated that.[38]

But most Scots who wrote on the subject of women took a wider view. One of the great accretions to knowledge in the early modern period had come from the European voyages of discovery to distant parts of the globe and the resulting awareness of the great diversity among its peoples, sprung though they might be from common ancestors. Clearly they must meanwhile have progressed at variable rates, and the attempt to account for this differentiation helped to shape the most important Scottish input to the European Enlightenment.[39] It transformed the study of history, shifting attention from a traditional emphasis on chronology to the observation of society, and from conquering kings to the story of everyman or indeed everywoman. By comparative method, it could be shown how development edged forward all over the world, not simultaneously but still in a consistent manner. The general pattern remained unmistakable: it had taken humanity from scarcity and simplicity to riches and refinement.[40]

The Enlightenment set itself the great intellectual task of understanding this world not by reference to traditional religious teachings, rather by seeking a naturalistic basis for its analysis through scrutiny of the present in the light of known facts about the past, or at least with the aid of reasonable inferences ('conjectural history') where such evidence was deficient or lacking.[41] A basic theory emerged that the human race had passed through four stages of development marked by successive forms of economic activity: hunting and gathering, pasturage, agriculture, commerce. Even with the limited empirical evidence available at the time, it was easy to see how women, half of humanity, surely could and should form part of this narrative. Without aspiring to any of the power wielded by men in history, women had yet played a vital part. They fostered the communal contacts and constructive communications through which full humanity would at last unfold. Here was a complementary model of progress, in the social route that women had themselves followed from an initial condition almost in slavery to men up to a status of companionship with them. It led from weariness and woe to closeness and co-operation, while also civilising the rude and savage males. In that sense women could be seen as motors of history in their own right.[42]

These questions were profound but one thing enlightened Scotland could readily do was create forums in which they might be tackled, as had scarcely been possible in an older Scotland (except in an orthodox fashion from the pulpit). The new Scotland never had anything like the fashionable French salons, where men and women mixed, yet it was still a convivial place. It did have clubs, all for men – though, as ever in such clubs, the talk often turned to women. The most celebrated club was the Select Society, which contained all Edinburgh's intellectual stars. Among the questions it debated was 'Whether ought we to prefer ancient or modern manners, with regard to the condition and treatment of women?' and 'Whether it would be of advantage that the women held places of trust and profit in the state?'[43] Alas, no record remains of what was actually said on such occasions, but we do get one hint from a passing remark by Jupiter Carlyle, who recorded that a member of another club, the Poker, was 'laughed at and run down' for 'enlarging on his favourite topic, the superiority of the female sex'.[44] What could have been going on here?

We can make a guess because we know the name of the speaker, John Gregory, a medical professor at the University of Edinburgh. Originally from Aberdeen, he had been a member there of the local philosophical society and read to it papers that he eventually published as a collection under the title, *A Comparative View of the State and Faculties of Man, with those of the Animal World* (1765). There were two sides to human nature, he wrote, and 'the task of improving our nature, of improving man's estate, involves the proper development and exercise of the social principle and the other principle of instinct, with reason subordinate to instinct and serving as a corrective on it'. But in order to become morally educated individuals we needed to cultivate both these sides of ourselves – 'a good taste and a good heart commonly go together'.[45] Here was a role for women to play. Clearly isolation from female company caused in men 'great ignorance of life and manners' and deprived them 'of all those little accomplishments and graces which are essential to polished and elegant society, and which can nobly be acquired by mixing with the world'. The stages of history imposed their own limits, however. Gregory gave the example of the hardiness of savage mothers who 'recover easily and speedily after bringing forth their young', in contrast to 'the feebleness of mothers in civil society, whose pregnancies are attended by diseases unknown in savage life'.[46] Here he spoke from the heart: he had lost his own wife in such circumstances. Afterwards he wrote a little book, *A Father's Legacy to his Daughters*, to relieve his loneliness and preserve the dead woman's views on the education of their children. He told his daughters, for the sake of their reputations in the world, to be cautious and prudent – and never to let on how clever and witty they were.[47] So it was not exactly women's liberation he envisaged.

There was probably a similar sort of discussion at the Mirror Club, so called after the purpose it chose for itself: to reflect reality. It came together at different hostelries in Edinburgh and counted in its ranks a literary lion, Henry Mackenzie, a rising lawyer who wrote a successful novel, *The Man of Feeling* (1771); little to modern taste, it yet won high praise from Robert Burns among others. A second member was another lawyer, Henry Dundas, who before his 30th birthday had become Solicitor General for Scotland, so launching a long and eminent public career.[48] The other members of the club were young blades of variable standing in life.

The club's proceedings are again lost, but there is reason to think Mackenzie drew on them in editing two magazines, *The Mirror* (1779–80) and then *The Lounger* (1785–87), largely written by himself. Here he took what he deemed to be the ideal attitude of the most progressive class in Scotland, the landed gentlemen middling in rank, to the sort of economic and social change going on all round them. This was moral journalism, praising virtue, damning vice, if with some effort to tackle real problems rather than preach in the abstract. Mackenzie therefore also aimed many of his articles at an educated and cultivated female readership. In reaching out especially to the younger ones, he wanted to warn them against the male-dominated world they would need to deal with once married. A sign of the times, he suggested, was that the women of Scotland had begun to lose their former 'purity of conduct and delicacy of manners'. A smart set among them might even have trouble in finding husbands. There was altogether need of a new kind of woman who could 'tread the slippery path of youth with care and, uninfected, breathe the tainted air' of an adult society exposed to all kinds of corruptions.[49]

The proceedings of these clubs are of some significance because of their links to other enlightened activities in Scotland. The Scots enjoyed by far the nicest of all the European Enlightenments – at its most agreeable in its social life, with good drink and good talk (even if no women). We can see its influence when the philosophers got up in the morning and, assuming they had escaped a hangover, picked up their pens – often to sketch a lively picture of the society they moved in. From the range of what they found to write about women, it may be interesting to select two topics apparently unrelated and show how Scotland's philosophers could yet relate them. One topic was the condition of women among the Indian tribes of North America; the other topic was the role women played in the fashionable salons (in other countries) of the eighteenth century.

Adam Ferguson, a member of the Select Society, always felt fascinated by the 'rude nations', as we see at once on looking into his *Essay on the History of Civil Society* (1767). He noted the condition of women in tribal societies was one of 'real servitude' and 'continual toil'. A reason for this interest of his was that Scots had more first-hand information about tribal societies than about any others in the earlier stages of conjectural history, and he was always assiduous in gathering the widest range of evidence for his writings. It might have come from the Highlands, especially for Ferguson, a Gael born on the edge of the region at Logierait in Perthshire. But the history and culture of the clans, only a couple of decades after the last Jacobite rebellion, remained perhaps too sensitive a subject.[50] Ferguson preferred the example of America: it now had many Scots settlers, some of the most prosperous engaged in trade with the Indians. Sifting the information from this and other sources, Ferguson concluded the tribes in the wilderness had reached a middle stage of conjectural history, 'where savage nations ... mix with the practice of hunting some species of rude agriculture'.

The Indian warriors enjoyed the excitement of the chase and left the squaws to the drudgery of growing food, while notions of property (a litmus test of social advance) had not yet entered the minds of any of them: 'After they have shared the toils of the seed-time, they enjoy the fruits of the harvest in common. The field in which they have planted, like the district over which they are accustomed to hunt, is claimed as a property by the nation, but is not parcelled in lots to its members.'[51] In Ferguson's view it was the women that held such a society together: 'As the fur and the bow pertain to the individual, the cabbin and its utensils are appropriated to the family; and as the domestic cares are committed to the women, so the property of the household seems likewise to be vested in them. The children are considered as pertaining to the mother, with little regard to descent on the father's side.' Indeed the succession to the chieftaincy of most tribes was matrilinear: 'The males, before they are married, remain in the cabbin in which they are born; but after they have formed a new connection with the other sex, they change their habitation, and become an accession to the family in which they have found their wives.'[52] Yet, Ferguson insisted, no observer should delude himself over the respective status of the sexes: 'While one sex continue to value themselves chiefly on their courage, their talent for policy, and their warlike achievements, this species of property which is bestowed on the other, is, in reality, a mark of subjection; not, as some writers allege, of their having acquired an ascendant. It is the care and trouble of a subject with which the warrior does not chuse to be embarrassed.' The general result was the brutal subordination of women.[53]

In his turn William Robertson, principal of the University of Edinburgh, published a *History of America* (1777) enlivened in its detail by information sent him from the McGillivrays of Dunmaglass, now of Savannah. They were exiled Jacobite fur-traders who had intermarried with the chiefly families of the Creek nation and so themselves risen into the ruling caste of this confederacy of tribes occupying what is today Georgia and Alabama: Highland warriors found themselves at home in such a setting. Like Ferguson, Robertson saw in the savage woman only a drudge, labourer, slave and servant: 'To despise and degrade the female sex is the characteristic of the savage state in every part of the globe.' In particular, 'the savage of America views his female with disdain, as an animal of a less noble species. He is at no pains to win her favour by the assiduity of courtship, and still less solicitous to preserve it by indulgence and gentleness.' There was a 'dispassionate coldness of the American young men in their intercourse with the other sex'.[54] Robertson concluded that 'to despise and degrade the female sex is the characteristic of the savage state in every part of the globe', while a society in which women won respect for their virtues was a truly civilised one.[55]

This was seldom a problem affecting Scots, some of whom attributed the lack of interest in sex among full-blooded Indian males to the small size of their generative organs. Looking at the problem from afar, Robertson felt not so sure:

> We may well suppose, that amidst the hardships, the dangers, and the simplicity of savage life, where subsistence is always precarious, and often scanty, where men are almost continually engaged in the pursuit of their enemies, or in guarding against their attacks, and where neither dress nor reserve are employed as arts of female allurement, that the attention of the Americans would be extremely feeble, without imputing this solely to any physical defect or degradation in their frame.[56]

Still Robertson had no doubt of his overall conclusion: 'Man, proud of excelling in strength and courage, the chief marks of pre-eminence among rude people, treats woman, as an inferior, with disdain.' This was a common trait in primitive societies but worst among the Indians who, 'from that coolness and insensibility which has been considered as peculiar to their constitution, add neglect and harshness to contempt . . . Marriage itself, instead of being an union of affection and interest between equals, becomes, among them, the unnatural conjunction of a master with his slave.' Not only that, 'a wife, among most tribes, is no better than a beast of burden, destined to every office of labour and fatigue. While the men loiter out the day in sloth, or spend it in amusement, the women are condemned to incessant toil. Tasks are imposed on them without pity, and services are received without complacence or gratitude.' Altogether, 'social life is perverted. That state of domestic union towards which nature leads the human species, in order to soften the heart to gentleness and humanity, is rendered so unequal, as to establish a cruel distinction between the sexes, which forms the one to be harsh and unfeeling, and humbles the other to servility and subjection.'[57]

David Hume was also a member of the Select Society, but one who at length found it easy to adapt himself as *le bon David* to the Parisian salons and take with grace and charm to a libertine life far away from stern Scotland.[58] He had prepared for it intellectually before he left. An early essay, 'Of the Rise and Progress of the Arts and Sciences' (1741), was an exercise in conjectural history that again included a sober contrast of the modern relationship of the sexes with that in savage and barbarous societies. Here male superiority over woman in body and mind was displayed 'by reducing . . . females to the most abject slavery, by confining them, by beating them, by selling them, by killing them'. But things had been not that much better in the classical civilisations of Greece and Rome: 'Among the ancients, the character of the fair sex was considered altogether domestic; nor were they regarded as part of the polite world or of good company. This, perhaps, is why the ancients have left us not one piece of pleasantry that is excellent.' Among the polite peoples of today, by contrast, men expressed their authority more generously, 'by civility, by respect, by complaisance and in a word by gallantry', to receive then an education in virtue as the sexes engaged in a mutual endeavour to please. This relationship was not just compatible with commercial prosperity but a necessary component of it.[59] The effects stretched from the modern economic order into the detail of everyday life: 'Both sexes meet in an easy and sociable manner; and the tempers of men, as well as their behaviour, refine apace.' Women were now not considered to be 'altogether domestic' but on the contrary had been accepted as integral to polite society, where their company helped to improve the manners of the men they met. But there was a vital qualification in that the women in question were of good character, modest and virtuous. Only the right sort of woman, imbued by rank and breeding with cultivated manners and an understanding of polite society, could generate this social good.[60]

In a later essay, 'Of Refinement in the Arts' (1752), Hume again picked out gallantry as the signal mark of social refinement. It was the 'natural produce of courts and monarchs', though also rooted in human nature, given that 'nature has implanted in all living creatures an affection between the sexes'. In an aristocratic setting sexual intrigue flourished along with artistic excellence, both being motivated by agreeable behaviour towards women. While, as between the two sexes, nature had given men the superiority, gallantry mitigated this: 'What better school for manners than the company of virtuous women; where the mutual endeavour to please must insensibly polish the mind, where the example of the female softness and modesty must communicate itself to their admirers, and where the delicacy of that sex puts every one on his guard, lest he give offence by any breach of decency?'[61] In such social skills France strode far ahead of less urbane European nations (England, and the republics of Holland and Switzerland). That was because, through the cultural institution of the Parisian salon where intellectuals mixed with politicians under discerning female eyes, France gave a prominent, if informal, part to women in public life. The importance they had acquired in French society formed part of its historical progress.[62] We may wonder if Hume really thought this could be reproduced in Scotland, but there was no harm in hoping so. Despite the somewhat patronising tone he often adopted when referring to the fair sex, he would write in his memoir 'On My Own Life' (composed not long before his death in 1776) that he 'took a particular pleasure in the company of modest women'.[63]

Hume's friend Adam Smith never said a word on women in either of his major works, *The Theory of Moral Sentiments* (1759) or *The Wealth of Nations* (1776); presumably living at home with his mum in Kirkcaldy either satisfied or killed his curiosity. For the subject to be raised to a new level we need to rely on the *Observations concerning the Distinctions of Ranks in Society* (1771) by John Millar, professor of civil law at the University of Glasgow. During this classic exercise in conjectural history he devoted an entire section of the book to 'The Rank and Condition of Women in the Different Ages'. Here his treatment of sexuality and love showed the Scottish Enlightenment, taken as a whole, to be a matter of anything but bloodless abstraction. On the contrary, it often analysed social ideas in terms of human emotions. For Millar, too, sex lay at the source, since 'sensual pleasures may be connected in many cases with the exercise of social dispositions'. In later essays he sought to explore this intricate relationship of civil society and domestic affection. Sexual passion, once sublimated in the love of a married couple, cemented the family and gave a basis for morality to the whole community, so that it 'laid the foundation of political society'. This was a cause of culture too, for development of taste and appreciation of beauty marked it out, not least in the 'delicacy of sentiment' revealed in modern conventions of politeness.[64]

Women, Millar agreed, had had to wait for the emergence of commercial civilisation to 'become neither the slaves, nor the idols of the other sex, but the friends and companions, in the modern and domesticated family'. This was an institution united by 'esteem and affection' even as it remained divided by labour. The later stages of material development, especially the acquisition of immovable property, had brought greater inequality to society yet also a higher status for certain female beneficiaries of the process. The resulting leisure and tranquillity for this lucky minority then started to evoke from men 'a great respect and veneration for the female sex'. The effect on European manners had been lasting.[65]

On the same lines, but rather more raffishly, Henry Home, Lord Kames, wrote his *Sketches of the History of Man* (1774). It was deliberately a popular collection of aperçus rather than any kind of formal treatise, but beneath it lay the same sort of arguments as Hume's. The author was a great ladies' man himself: he figured among the most ardent admirers of the Duchess of Gordon, for example. He also liked young women, whose minds he sought to form. He took time out from a busy life to write them letters and suggest reading, or to indulge in courtly banter with them.[66]

In his capacity as a scholar, Kames pointed to the bad historical example of ancient Greek or Roman society in excluding women from power or influence. It had slowed down the advance of civilisation: 'Without a mixture of the two sexes, society can never arrive at any degree of refinement, not to talk of perfection.' By contrast, 'in a society of men and women, every one endeavours to shine: every latent talent and every variety of character, are brought to light'. Not that men and women, as the two halves of humanity, enjoyed or could enjoy equality in all spheres. Instead nature, 'intending them for mates, has given them dispositions different but concordant, so as to produce together delicious harmony. The man, more robust, is fitted for severe labour and for field-exercises: the woman, more delicate, is fitted for sedentary occupations; and particularly for nursing children. That difference is remarkable in the mind, no less than in the body.' It could all be observed even from childhood, when boys played rough games while girls cuddled dolls. This was why, in later life, 'the man, bold and vigorous, is qualified for being a protector: the woman, delicate and timid, requires protection. The man, as a protector, is directed by nature to govern: the woman, conscious of inferiority, is disposed to obey. Their intellectual powers correspond to the destination of nature: men have penetration and solid judgement to fit them for governing: women have sufficient understanding to make a decent figure under good government.' The difference extends from the outer to the inner life: 'Women have more imagination and more sensibility than men; and yet none of them have made an eminent figure in any of the fine arts. We hear of no sculptor nor statuary among them; and none of them have risen above a mediocrity in poetry or painting.' All the same, women might be superior in their own ways: 'The gentle and insinuating manners of the female sex . . .

tend to soften the roughness of the other sex; and wherever women are indulged with any freedom, they polish sooner than men.'[67]

So much about womanhood was being observed, thought and written in enlightened Scotland as to generate the first attempt at a systematic survey in William Alexander's *History of Women* (1779). Alexander was a medical doctor in Edinburgh, not a prominent member of the city's intellectual circles but a writer clearly with access to the ideas circulating among them, and a man with a liberalising mission. His book was a pioneering study of changing relations between the sexes down the centuries, where necessary in conjectural form. It was not a story of relentless progress: Alexander felt dismayed at the misogyny in much literature of his own time. The supposed shortcomings it showed up in women might, he suggested, be due to men's failure to give them 'more judicious instructions'.[68]

For himself, Alexander provided the clearest summary of the theory that women were a civilising influence:

> As strength and courage are in savage life the only means of attaining to power and distinction, so weakness and timidity are the certain paths to slavery and oppression: on this account, we shall almost constantly find women among savages condemned to every species of servile, or rather, slavish drudgery; and shall as constantly find them emerging from this state, in the same proportion as we find the men emerging from ignorance and brutality, and approaching to knowledge and refinement; the rank, therefore, and condition, in which we find women in any country, mark out to us with the greatest precision, the exact point in the scale of civil society to which the people of such a country are arrived; and were their history entirely silent on every other subject, and only mentioned the manner in which they treated their women, we should, from thence, be enabled to form a tolerable judgement of the barbarity, or culture of their manners.[69]

Perhaps Alexander had in mind a second aspect of Scottish thinking on women which, rather than integrating them into conjectural history, drew an unfavourable contrast of their present with their past. The Enlightenment committed itself to progress, both as explanation of human history and as programme for future development. Scotland's philosophers knew the course of progress did not always run smooth, however, but remained vulnerable to checks, setbacks and reversals. Still, the idea of decline and decay in the long run of history was alien to the optimism of the age – except, for some, in the history of women.[70]

Outside strict Calvinist circles it was in Scotland rare to find the enlightened assumptions of progress coming under question, as in France they so powerfully did at the hands of Jean-Jacques Rousseau. Perhaps this basic philosophical difference lay at the bottom of his famous falling out with Hume, though to all appearance it had only superficial causes.[71] Yet we can observe in Scotland as well the beginnings of a more pessimistic sensibility, taking account of darker aspects of humanity than the Enlightenment was usually prepared to acknowledge. Here, too, there were reflections on women.

The most notable figure in Scotland who implicitly took Rousseau's intellectual part was a man from beyond the normal pale of enlightened society. James MacPherson arrived in Edinburgh from Strathspey, which as a boy he had seen ravaged in the aftermath of the Battle of Culloden: not something likely to induce optimism. In adulthood he achieved global fame with his claims for the Gaelic poetry of Ossian, sparking off a stupendous controversy that even today has not fully died down. This work attracted critical comparisons with Homer, Virgil and Milton – heady stuff for any literary novice. It crystallised an emerging taste for the purity and simplicity of primitive virtues as opposed to the corruptions of civilisation (exemplified by Rousseau's concept of the 'natural man'), and prepared the way for the Romantic movement of the nineteenth century.[72]

Literary adventurers from remote regions often need at some stage to live off hackwork, something that held true for MacPherson too. One product of this phase of his career was his *Introduction to the History of Great Britain and Ireland* (1771). Hackwork though it was, it took a different line on the feminine aspect of this history from other contemporary works. Drawing heavily on evidence from the *Germania* of Tacitus, MacPherson wrote in particular about the northern European peoples, the 'Goths' – a category including both Celts and Germans. He disputed the view that women in such early European tribal societies could be compared to the drudges and slaves still found among the American Indians. In olden days, the women did not yield to the men in stature, and almost equalled them in strength of body and in vigour of mind. MacPherson conceded that 'the picture we have drawn will not probably please the refined ideas of the present times. But the high spirit of the Celtic women gave them more influence over our ancestors than our modern beauties derive from all their elegant timidity and delicacy of manners.' Those fierce females on the periphery of Europe might even have exceeded in rude virtue their German sisters that Tacitus so admired: 'To such a pitch had some branches of the Celtae carried their veneration for the fair sex, that, even in their lifetime, a kind of divine honours was paid to some distinguished women. The ancient Britons were peculiarly fond of the government of women', as seen in Boadicea's rebellion against the Romans. It was fairly easy to tell from all this what type appealed to MacPherson, himself a notorious womaniser. In other ways, too, he prefigured the self-image of the modern Scottish male, something for which he pointed up an ancient lineage: 'Some late writers have ascribed the enormous size and corpulence of the Barbarians of ancient Europe to their use of beer.' Beneath this train of thought there might even have been a certain idea of rough equality between the sexes, rather than a rationale for male superiority.[73]

Times were indeed changing, if slowly, for women and for the conceptions of womanhood. An early sign of emergent modern nationalism was that European peoples began to personify themselves, usually in female form: Britannia in Britain, Marianne in France. The personification could be depicted as rejoicing or suffering just like a real human being, and women were held more likely than men to show their feelings. Here surely lay scope for an image of Scotland too, even though this nation was now absorbed into a larger entity. The scope had already been perceived in the last Scottish Parliament by John Hamilton, Lord Belhaven, a leader of the opposition to the Union, when in a celebrated speech he evoked his rhetorical picture of 'our ancient Mother Caledonia, like Caesar, sitting in the midst of our senate, ruefully looking round about her, covering herself with her royal garment, attending the fatal blow, and breathing out her last with an *Et tu quoque mi fili* [the final words of Julius Caesar when struck down by Brutus]'.[74] Caledonia also figures in Burns's work, in a poem of the same name, where now she appears as 'bold, independent, unconquer'd and free',[75] a warrior doing battle with allegorical enemies, the Anglian lion or the Scandinavian boar. For more tender emotions, as in 'The Cottar's Saturday Night', he prefers a sister called Scotia:

> O Scotia! My dear, my native soil!
> Long may thy hardy sons of rustic toil
> Be blessed with health and peace and sweet content.[76]

Finally Sir Walter Scott combined two sides of the feminine character, the fierce but fond with the firm and fertile, in the image of his *Lay of the Last Minstrel* (1805), 'O Caledonia! stern and wild, meet nurse for a poetic child'.[77] After Scott the feminisation of Scotland failed to take any tighter hold. In the industrial era this again became a nation feeling itself much more masculine, no longer a victim-nation but a hero-nation. Women found it hard to extend even their limited social progress of the eighteenth century.

9

Gaeldom:
'Under the foot of strangers'

On 27 August 1746, Major-General Humphrey Bland sat down in his quarters at Stirling Castle to write a report to the Commander-in-Chief, Scotland, George Keppel, Earl of Albemarle. Bland wanted to get something off his chest, his military martinet's obsession with the continuing problems of security here right in the middle of a recently rebellious nation. The bloody defeat of the Jacobites had not solved these problems, even though a chain of permanently manned outposts now dissected the country in order 'to catch the rebel or thieving Highlanders' who might try to escape the retribution of the redcoats in the areas under their occupation. Bland and other bluff British general officers rather hoped that, behind this cordon, they might be able to starve the entire Highland population to death.

Yet, as Bland pointed out, still some Scots loyal to King George II were foolish enough to impede such a useful aim of public policy: 'If the officers commanding the several posts now forming the chain now follow their instructions, the rebels in the Highlands can't be supplied with victual, as they call meal, from this country, unless the justices of the peace and the ministers are accessory to it by granting certificates for that purpose; nor will I answer for their not doing it from a mistaken notion of Christian charity, now they think the rebellion, in a manner, over.'[1] Believe it or not, Bland spluttered, men armed to the teeth were crossing the cordon under his very nose. Why, only in the last few days, two huge droves of black cattle had passed Stirling on their way from the territory of the MacLeods on Skye to the great tryst at Falkirk. They came escorted by men with official passes exempting them from the ban on bearing arms. Something must be done, Bland fumed.

In fact, nothing could be done. If trade was to continue (a surer means of civilising the Highlands than repression could ever be), then the drovers, like any travellers through the region, had to furnish themselves with some protection from the colourful customs of its natives. Otherwise these would just steal cattle whenever they could, as they always had done regardless of the political situation. This reality was acknowledged even by the Parliament at Westminster when it got round to its programme of legislation for a new order in the north of Scotland: the Disarming Act of 1748, like the Disarming Act of 1716, exempted drovers of cattle from its provisions.[2]

Yet the picturesque practice of raiding cattle had over the past century never actually stopped a vast expansion of business in the beasts. The background to it was that during this period most of the Highlands had enjoyed, except for erratic interventions by central governments, a reasonable degree of stability, probably greater than at any time since the destruction of Clan Donald's Lordship of the Isles in 1493. Even within the surviving Celtic social system, with its own language and culture, the region proved able to play its part in the general economic development of Scotland. There was still mayhem enough, but only on a scale that the clans – by now rather settled and complex institutions – could deal with and keep from descending into anarchy. This was not in its inner nature a peaceable society like the Lowlands or other progressive areas of Europe. But it had learned to hold its tensions within bounds. These then remained calculable by chiefs seeking to strike a balance of power.[3]

The events of 1745–46 overturned this tried and trusted state of affairs, to the extent that the supposed reimposition of law and order turned out to be no such thing. In the Highlands it had always been hard to catch and condemn thieves or persuade witnesses to testify. It now became harder than ever because of the collapse of much of the native authority in the region, with chiefs on the run and the people in fear and loathing of the Hanoverian forces that ravaged and terrorised the glens. For the purpose of pacification these methods were quite as useless here as they have ever been in any time or place.

William, Duke of Cumberland, was the one who after his victory at the Battle of Culloden embarked on the campaign of terror in the Highlands, but soon he handed it over to the Earl of Albemarle. In his hands, within a few weeks more, there were reports indicating how the spirits of the men of

Morvern, for example, had survived undaunted the burning of their town-ships by raiding parties landed from ships of the Royal Navy.[4] The clansmen hid their cattle in the hills while keeping by them plenty of weapons together with some foreign gold. Now they were nursing their wrath, rebuilding their homes and talking of help from France once spring came. Their neighbours in Moidart showed the same defiance. Short of food and fuel though they were, they had enough firearms to defend themselves against attack and enough whisky to pass away the time otherwise. Albemarle heard 'there are great thefts committed all over Moidart, Morvern and Sunart and about Strontian'. He felt obliged to repeat to his political master in London, the Duke of Newcastle, a version of the same advice as Bland had passed on: the way to restore peace and tranquillity in Scotland was to devastate its northern counties and deport their natives.[5]

It was a solution for simple military minds only. These years indeed witnessed an upheaval in Highland history, appearing all the greater from our coign of vantage because we can look back and observe as much. This chapter will try to see things more as contemporaries might have seen them. Then some continuities may appear – or at least the fact that in the real world things can move much more slowly than politicians, let alone soldiers, want them to.

The sudden eruption of Jacobite revolt in 1745 did not of itself change as much as has often been assumed. Many of Prince Charles's nominal support-ers told him, after his sudden and daring descent on them, to turn round and go straight back to France. His personal magnetism often did the trick of persuading them all the same to follow him, though he turned out to be not much of a military leader in the field. What then really sustained his enterprise was the steadfastness of the Gaels. For eight months during 1745–46, though poorly commanded and pitifully equipped, they held at bay the armed might of Great Britain in a tragic yet inspiring and heroic struggle. They risked all and lost all. At Culloden, Cumberland finally crushed the Highland army because Prince Charles insisted on tactics ill suited to its traditions of warfare. But, in the dark days that followed, the clansmen showed their mettle by refusing to accept their defeat as final. Weary and worn out by long, fruitless marches, often while half-starved, they waited to avenge Culloden, despite the disheartening observation from Lord George Murray, their ablest com-mander, that 'there was neither money nor provisions to give: so no hopes were left'. Charles fled, leaving those who had stood beside him with nowhere to turn for direction or support, and so to their miserable fate. The steadfastness of the Gaels still shone through.[6]

To appreciate it we need to look not at the reports sent back to London by Hanoverian generals but at what the Gaels were saying about themselves – something that has remained inaccessible because cast in a language that academic historians cannot understand. The Gaels expressed themselves first and foremost in their poetry. In 1933 the great ethnologist, John Lorne Campbell of Canna, was to publish a volume of it, *Orain Ghàidhealach mu Bhliadhna Theàrlaich* [Highland Songs of the '45]. His introduction pointed out that, in the century that had started with the military exploits of the Marquis of Montrose and ended with those of Prince Charles, the Highlands attained the greatest political importance they ever enjoyed. It arose out of the Gaels' readiness to fight for what they believed in, above all the cause of their legitimate monarchs. The character of these warriors had often been misrepresented and Campbell sought in his anthology to show their true thoughts and feelings, so far as revealed in the vernacular poetry.[7]

It was not destructive and predatory barbarism or Celtic mental depression that Campbell found there, but an aspirational public sentiment: a passionate attachment to the legitimate royal house, coupled with a bitter hatred for the usurping Hanoverian dynasty, and a pride in the spirit of clans ready to fight and die for the one against the other.[8] Perhaps its most fervent expression came in the poems of Alasdair mac Mhaighstir Alasdair, who left his day job as a schoolmaster in Ardnamurchan to join Prince Charles and teach him Gaelic. Alasdair had anticipated the sequence of events, several months before, in his 'Oran do'n Phrionnsa' [Song to the Prince]:

> O, hì-ri-rì, tha e tighinn,
> O, hì-ri-rì, 'n Righ tha uainn,
> Gheibheamaid ar an-airm 's ar n-èideadh,
> 'S breacan-an-fhèlidh an cuaich.
>
> 'S eibhinn liom fhìn, tha e tighinn,
> Mac an Righ dhlighich tha uainn,
> Slios mòr rìoghail d'an tig armachd,
> Claidheamh us targaid nan dual.

Oh, hi ri ri, he is coming,
Oh, hi ri ri our exiled king,
Let us take out arms and clothing,
And the flowing tartan plaid.

Joyful I am, he is coming,
Son of our rightful exiled king,
A mighty form that becomes armour,
The broadsword and the bossed shield . . .[9]

But the high hopes of 1745 were to end by the next spring in catastrophic defeat and humiliation at the hands of people whose lack of physical and military prowess the Highlanders had always despised. John Roy Stewart, an officer in the Jacobite army as well as a poet, then wrote bitterly of *Latha Chuil-lodair* ['Day of Culloden']:

Fhuair na Goill sinn fo 'n casan,
Is mòr an nàire 's am masladh sud leinn.

We are under the foot of strangers,
Great the shame and disgrace that we feel.[10]

After the rebellion was all over it became something too dangerous to mention, even in Gaelic. During the late 1760s one of the next generation of poets, Duncan Bàn MacIntyre, left his home in Glen Orchy to take a dead-end job in Edinburgh as a member of the town guard; many in its ranks were Gaels and freely used their language in the High Street, to the annoyance of the locals, when they did not want to give away what they were talking about. MacIntyre was illiterate and composed his poetry in his head for others to write down. He could in his happy-go-lucky fashion cast from his obscurity a cool eye on the gentlemen he was supposed to be protecting:

'S iomadh fleasgach uasal ann e,
A bha gu suairce grinn,
Fùdar air an gruagan
A suas gu bàrr an cinn.

Many noble beaux are there,
Urbane and elegant,
Having powder on their wigs
Right up to their crowns.

Or indeed on their ladies:

> *'S mor a tha de bhaintighearnan*
> *A null 's a null an t-sràid*
> *Gùntaichean de 'n t-sìoda orr,*
> *'Gan sliogadh ris a 'bhlàr.*

> Many patrician ladies
> Go up and down the street
> All wearing gowns of silk
> That brush against the ground.

Only in two lines of over 300 in this poem does MacIntyre allow himself a hint, here in the high temple of Hanoverianism, of an older allegiance. He says there are in town

> *Na taighean mòra riomhach*
> *Am bu choir an rìgh bhigh stad.*

> Large and splendid houses
> Wherein the king should stay.[11]

It was an era of disasters not only for the chiefs but above all for the ordinary Gaels, yet from the whole corpus of their poetry the reader carries away an impression of liberation – and in their culture, if not in their politics and society, this also reflects what was actually happening to them. Till now Gaelic culture had been a culture of the chiefs, who employed bards to sing their praises to the music of the clàrsach in traditional poetic forms going back to the Middle Ages. Great prestige attached to these bards, who were not only the masters of a labyrinthine prosody but also, by extension, the keepers of ancient lore, which could be turned into political advice to the chief. If he did not take it, and suffered as a result, they could still give the world an indignant rant on his unwisdom.[12]

But then Gaelic poetry seemed to lose its old obsession with status and hierarchy, and the constant compulsion to burst out in praise of chieftains. The Gaels, released from their past not only socially but also poetically, experienced a great literary awakening – quite as powerful as the one which, for example, had come over the Scots language in the sixteenth century. Its aesthetic achievements will be dealt with in their proper place below. For the moment suffice it to say that, while after Culloden the Gael was marked down by the dominant anglophone culture as an inferior, and one destined to be extinguished from history, at the literary level he was far from inferior. In fact, he was in some ways superior.[13]

After Culloden, the basic political change from the past was that the British government took ultimate responsibility for the Highlands, if seldom knowing what to do with it. Till now, the region had lived for itself. In the western parts the various fragments of the historic MacDonalds' lordship survived in the septs of Clanranald, Glengarry, Keppoch, Sleat and so on, but in its place new powers had arisen. The greatest, at least at the southern end, was Clan Campbell, which had seized much territory from the MacDonalds in the sixteenth century, more from the MacLeans in the seventeenth century, and in the eighteenth century started to provoke and harass the Camerons – these, however, showed they could not be pushed around. The Campbells usually achieved their purposes by allying themselves with the Scottish monarchy, unreliable beacon as it was for them to steer by. But after the Union of 1707 came also the stodgily consistent House of Hanover, and with this the chiefs of Clan Campbell, now Dukes of Argyll, felt quite comfortable.[14]

If Clan Campbell had turned into a byword for selfish rapacity, it was in practice little worse than Clan Mackenzie at the northern end of the region. Originating in Kintail, this race of warrior herdsmen pushed out both eastwards and westwards over land and sea, to engross Lewis at one extremity of their territory and the Black Isle at the other. The Mackenzies, too, enjoyed a fraught relationship with the Scottish crown, after first finding high favour under King James VI who had ennobled their chieftain as Earl of Seaforth. They ended up a century later on the Jacobite side, though they split in 1745 and afterwards made their peace with the British state. Still further north they had been attacking the Mackays and Sutherlands, good Presbyterian clans. The Mackenzies also debouched into the Great Glen, which brought them into conflict with the Frasers – led from 1699 by Simon Fraser, Lord Lovat, the most devious player on the Highland scene, indeed on the Scottish one, as he proceeded along his circuitous route to a rendezvous with the public executioner in 1747. In a vain effort to outmanoeuvre him, the Mackenzies entered into strategic alliances with the Mackintoshes and MacPhersons, members of the confederal Clan Chattan scattered over Lochaber, Strathnairn and Badenoch. As if all this were not complicated enough, the Scottish and then the British state had its own presence in the Great Glen, at Fort William founded (or refounded) in 1692, at Fort George founded in 1715 (at that time right next to the burgh of Inverness) and in between at Fort Augustus founded in 1729. In the neighbourhood of these strongholds there was a rough balance between the clans and the British army.[15]

Otherwise it all looked like a version on a small scale of the concert of Europe, with different players pursuing long-term interests by the most variable, not to say treacherous, means. The clans were physically remote and spoke a language nobody else understood. Still it could not really be said they were uncivilised when they had preserved their ancient and intricate Gaelic culture. Nor were they utterly anarchic, for the people had as much government as they wanted or needed, and they remained freer from the tyranny of kings or statesmen than less fortunate folk. Certainly their ruling class had risen above anything that could reasonably be called barbarism: its cosmopolitan members felt quite at home in Paris or London, addressing aristocrats and even monarchs with a sense of the purity and nobility of their own blood. The basic handicap of the Highlands was just poverty, an inescapable result of geology and climate, yet nothing unusual on the peripheries of Europe.[16]

After the Union of 1707 Lowland Scotland turned peaceful, and that might have become true of the Highlands too. There was instead the Jacobite rebellion of 1715, though in the end it made little difference to anything. Besides, it turned out to be only to a limited degree a Highland rebellion; rather, it was a national Scottish rebellion with its epicentre north of the central belt. In fact, it was those loyal to Hanover that found a leader in one of the great clan chieftains, the Duke of Argyll, whose military success, if by a narrow margin, represented a stepping stone towards his later political dominance in the whole country. Aggrandiser though he remained on behalf of the Campbells, he also saw the value of the polycentric balance among the most powerful clans. In the rebellion Lord Lovat had contrived to zigzag to the Hanoverian side and into an alliance with Argyll, on whose behalf he recaptured Inverness from the rebels. He went on to expel the Mackenzies from the upper end of the Great Glen, so ensuring there would be no general Jacobite outbreak in the far north.[17]

With these minor adjustments, the Highlands attained greater stability than for a long time. There was still a problem of inconstant political loyalties and of the related instinct that kinship should always trump justice. But no clan lost much of its territory, because the Jacobites' forfeited property was often wangled into the hands of close relations or agents of those who suffered attainder. Even if land went on the market, few customers from outside a warlike region wanted to buy it. As for government, in day-to-day terms the clans remained perfectly capable of ruling themselves. The leading Highland Jacobite, the Earl of Seaforth, made his peace with the British authorities by 1726. Westminster, actually often a source of mischief hereabouts, reverted to its only legitimate task, of ensuring the clans did not interfere by force in Lowland politics. One fresh role for the Highlands did appear, as a reservoir of fighting men for the new United Kingdom in its European and colonial wars. From the 1750s Britain could, with the growth of empire and the demand for regiments to serve abroad, tap into the military culture in the north that needed an outlet after the end of open armed conflict among the clans.[18]

As for the economy, the trade in cattle continued to flourish and there were now efforts to develop other Highland natural resources or even manufactures. The clans had a complex relationship with commerce. By the turn of the eighteenth century war was no longer their priority: they could now resolve their feuds by means other than fighting, and they left banditry to outlawed gangs of caterans. For most Highlanders the new priority in their precarious natural environment was for the peaceful and productive settlement of the land. In this first turn away from a militaristic society, it remained at the outset an open question whether improvement and commerce would or could disrupt the existing structure of the clans. Each had its chief, but in many respects the tacksmen, the clan's gentlemen or *daoine uaisle*, were the people that held it together. Often related to the chief, they helped to maintain a myth that the whole clan shared bonds of blood. They had two main practical roles. They served as military officers in time of war and in periods of peace as the middle management for the system of communal agriculture; this, with minute divisions of good and bad ground for the tenants of each township, demanded organisational skills even while it preserved indigence and inefficiency. In supervising either role the chief often found it prudent, for the sake of his own authority, to act on a consensus of the tacksmen.[19]

This social structure was to be battered and in many places broken during the course of the eighteenth century, if only to a limited extent by the adventurism of Prince Charles. We should look rather at the steady progress of Clan Campbell, which remained loyal to the House of Hanover and so suffered none of the retribution visited on fellow Gaels. The chiefs of the clan had been closely allied with the Scottish crown ever since the time of King Robert Bruce, but they finally parted from the House of Stewart over religion, as they were almost always strong Presbyterians, indeed martyrs for the Covenants, while the monarchs backslid. In their ancestral territory these chiefs were meanwhile left pretty much to their own devices.[20]

The ancient core of the Campbells' estate, the tract under the management of the chamberlain of Argyll, was actually less valuable than the lands they had conquered from the MacDonalds and the MacLeans of Duart. The fall of Clan Donald brought Knapdale to the House of Argyll in 1476 and Kintyre in 1607, both fertile tracts by Highland standards. The annexation of the lands of Duart then added vast territories in Mull, Morvern and the islands of Tiree and Coll in 1674. To reward friends, to ensure a military following and to preserve order in the annexed lands, the chiefs settled on them their own kinsmen and allies. These lorded it over or pushed aside the native MacLeans, now mostly reduced to the status of lowly vassals and landless cottars.[21]

In these northern districts newly subject to the House of Argyll, it was the tacksmen that led the colonies of followers and dependants onto the conquered terrain. The tacksmen were for the most part themselves Campbells, but some might be men of other names possessing territories in their own right. The incoming population, with its sub-tacksmen and sub-tenants, lived as loyal, privileged and envied colonists amid the dispossessed clans. At their best, the tacksmen were also entrepreneurs in initiatives to realise the commercial value of the acquired territory. They earned their place by giving proof not of traditional valour in war but of novel acumen in business: to the duke at Inveraray, their punctuality in paying rents was what counted above all. The main reason they could pay their rents was that they brought the northern districts into Scotland's pastoral production and trade, devoting large parts of their farms to grazing the cattle they then sold to Lowland or English markets.[22]

The northern districts remained less valuable, however, as a source of military strength. It could come there only from the immigrant Campbells and their friends who, if controlling the greater share of the land, formed a mere minority of the population. In the majority bearing other names the bonds of kinship endured, perhaps even strengthened in resentment of the Campbells. Often the whole population of a township, or much of it, shared the same name, like the 45 Camerons at Inniemore in Morvern, or the 12 families called MacLean on Coll or the 17 of them round Cornaigmore on Tiree. They clung on to their ancestral homes and, though only small tenants, they preserved the ancient Celtic practice of sharing the holding among all their children and near relations. As the violence of the old feuds died down and rendered defensive measures less necessary, these communities still sustained themselves in a kind of strong local patriotism. Since the northern districts were therefore not to be completely relied on by the House of Argyll, they might in any crisis be more of a handicap than an asset to the dukes.[23]

John Campbell, second Duke of Argyll, who succeeded to his title in 1703 and died in 1743, became the most powerful politician in Scotland but pursued aims in that greater station which, if arguably good for the country as a whole, went down less well on his own lands. For him his local policies had in the first instance a financial motivation, since he was always deep in debt and wanted to divert more of his estate's resources and opportunities directly to himself. Increases of rent had already been imposed in the seventeenth century, but failed to bring a decisive improvement in chiefly finances. The second duke concluded that progress on this front could only come through a far more drastic step, the removal of the tacksmen.[24]

In the old system, Argyll portioned out his territory to his kith and kin who, as tacksmen, rented it to tenants. In the new system, the tenants would lease their farms directly from the duke's factors, that is to say, from the managers and lawyers who provided him with administrative or other services but had no further personal interest in the land themselves. With the tacksmen gone, rents could be raised all over the estate, right down to the smallest croft. The service of the duke's debts cost him more than the entire rental of Argyll, and now more of the revenue it generated would come straight to him.[25]

In this way, from 1710 in Kintyre and then from 1737 elsewhere in his territory, the duke tried to sidestep and cut out the tacksmen from their occupation of the land in order to release its monetary value for his own purposes. Acting on his instructions, no less a personage than the Lord Advocate, Duncan Forbes of Culloden, visited the region, relieved the great tacksmen of their tacks and auctioned leases to the sub-tacksmen and sub-tenants, now answerable not indirectly to more senior members of the clan but to the duke himself or to his employed underlings. A whole tier of the Highland hierarchy was to vanish.[26]

But problems arose even as the policy took shape. In particular, it seemed by no means clear that, in the new system, the land would actually remain under the occupation of Campbells and their friends. In the open bidding of 1737, some of these were ousted by old indigenous tenants whom they had themselves earlier displaced. Even for a Campbell there was suddenly no more automatic favour from the duke. A tenant needed not ties to his chieftain of blood and soil but the money to win at auction. As a means of raising the rental this radical measure appeared at first successful, yet it soon became clear that the higher rents were unrealistic. No greater total could be actually collected than under the tacksmen. Worse, a burden of arrears accumulated. There was widespread insolvency among tenants, and in some areas most new leases were surrendered, forfeited or never taken up. The rents had risen too high for poor peasants to pay, and the profit fell short of the duke's hopes.[27]

Commercial business as this was in the first instance, it brought inexorable military and political effects in its wake. Argyll was a soldier himself, victor of the Battle of Sheriffmuir and a commander in the new Britain's European wars. All the odder, then, that he should have believed he could transform the Highlands by tearing down the military structure dependent on the tacksmen. What he did do in the event was ruin the Campbells as the martial mainstay of Scots Whiggery, at a time when few other chiefs found it necessary or desirable to follow his lead and many remained Jacobites. The military outcome was calamitous: the Campbells had saved Calvinist Scotland in every conflict since the Reformation, yet in 1745 they did next to nothing because their structure of command had been eliminated while other clans preserved theirs. It was left to the Duke of Cumberland to reconquer Scotland on behalf of his father King George II.[28]

The second Duke of Argyll was by then dead. The third duke, Archibald Campbell, previously Lord Ilay, had understood his brother's huge mistake and set about trying to reverse it. On succeeding to the title and estate, he told his factors to select tenants according to their loyalties rather than their pockets. Tacksmen made a comeback, if too late to rescue the House of Argyll's military might. The experience of 1745 confirmed that Campbells after all made the best tenants, since for a start they were unlikely to go running off after a Jacobite Pretender: perhaps a sound political outlook should remain a normal part of being a useful, hard-working farmer. That was the conclusion reached anyway by the third duke – but again he had difficulty in realising the concept, even though on occasion he reverted to the tyrannous chieftainship of old. His factors sought to break up some of the clusters of disaffected clansmen, especially in Morvern where Campbells were brought in to displace earlier inhabitants by the names of MacDonald or MacInnes or Cameron. That did not stop dispossessed Camerons plundering and terrorising the tacksmen here. Donald Campbell of Airds, one who needed to collect his own rents, never ventured forth on that errand without an armed escort.[29]

The third Duke of Argyll lived till 1761, otherwise pushing improvement forward with renewed vigour and exhorting his people to adopt habits of thrift, sobriety and industry (to help them along, he shut down their distilleries and drinking dens). Inveraray, till now a Highland clachan adorned by nothing better than the chief's battered tower-house, blossomed into magnificence. The castle was rebuilt as a piece of Gothic make-believe while the surrounding policies were developed as gardens, farms and woodlands. The inhabitants, previously clustering under the walls in wretched huts with smelly middens, found themselves shifted into a new town erected at a suitable distance. In some years these building works absorbed the whole of the duke's revenues from his lands, offices and prerogatives. He had to augment his income by expanding his personal domain round Inveraray and Rosneath, then exploit it to the full by grazing cattle for the market, by selling agricultural produce and by growing timber for sale to a new iron foundry beside Loch Fyne. Wherever minerals, fishings and timber were to be found on the estate, he asserted his rights to them too. His economic success still did not go far enough to restore the Campbells' martial power. But by now that no longer mattered because the military capacity of every other clan had been destroyed too.[30]

After Culloden, Argyll set himself the further aim of providing an example for the whole Highlands to follow. For him and his right-hand man, Andrew Fletcher, Lord Milton, military and political measures could by themselves never be enough to pacify the region. That would only happen once commerce and manufactures were introduced, to woo the natives from any disaffection by the manifest benefits of a new economic order. Milton framed a plan to change Gaeldom for ever by radical social engineering. He meant to get rid not just of tacksmen but of chiefs too (Argyll himself now counted as something greater). In addition to dismantling the entire feudal hierarchy, Milton wanted most of the central Highlands to be taken into public ownership and administered by an official commission in Edinburgh (which he, of course, would run). The nationalised territory would comprise not only forfeited lands but also any others in the rebellious region that the crown might care to purchase.[31]

Such an extension of public power at the expense of private property was startling to the mind of the eighteenth century even at its most autocratic. But Milton worked hard on Newcastle, who stood at the centre of the web of British government and owed him a debt of gratitude for clearing up the mess after 1745. The metropolitan politician proved not impervious to the lurid message from the periphery. It was to the effect that the clan chieftains, whose prosperity and security depended on the number of fighting men at their disposal, still maintained control of the Gaels by keeping them in ignorance and poverty. This discouraged 'all attempts to introduce the knowledge of the Protestant religion and our happy constitution, and the true notions of husbandry, trade and manufacture'. Tacksmen had 'been successful instruments to keep the common people in slavery', though themselves 'of too high blood to stoop to trade and manufacture'. The only freedom for the clansmen was, with the connivance of their chiefs, to indulge 'in thefts, rapines and all other villanies they can commit'. Not till the structure of Highland power had been wholly recast could further measures, such as the encouragement of industry, succeed. The key was the chiefs: 'so far as we can get rid of them, we ought.' Their lands 'should be purchased at the public expense, so far as they are not already forfeited, and vested in the crown'. And if that seemed a little bold, Milton assured Newcastle, most proprietors would be not unwilling to sell them at a reasonable price, 'and the purchase money of these lands would be but a trifle in comparison of the sums that have, and probably must still be laid out to keep these parts of the Highlands in subjection'.[32]

In the stunned aftermath of 1745 this argument carried some weight, though in the conditions of the age it could not ultimately prevail. Milton himself grew old, and the long wrangle between Edinburgh and London about what to do next in Gaeldom told against a simple but thoroughgoing solution. The eventual legislation for the forfeited estates, the Annexing Act of 1752, turned out a pale shadow of what he had wanted. But even their rejected policy brought out how far Argyll and Milton, two well-informed gentlemen charged with the practical conduct of affairs, thought clans and chieftains were still vital forces in the Highlands, which had to be deliberately done away with if the future was to turn out better than the past. The Annexing Act applied to only 13 of the original 41 forfeited estates; most had meanwhile found purchasers on the free market by whom their debts could be paid off. The remainder stretched from Stirling to Inverness, with outliers in the west and north. For more than three decades they were managed as a public enterprise, with a half-hearted purpose of making a profit but a keener intention of instilling Hanoverian loyalty in their people. The unpaid commissioners who ran them were instructed to apply the rents to promoting 'the Protestant religion, good government, industry and manufactures, and the principles of duty and loyalty to His Majesty'.[33] Little of this in the end came to anything. We must look to the Duke of Argyll's own estate to see how much further his conceptions might go – though still not as far as he wanted.

On the death of the third duke without legitimate offspring there followed the brief rule of John Campbell of Mamore, the cousin who had directed the mopping-up operations against the Jacobites along the western seaboard and, in the course of them, received Flora MacDonald with exemplary chivalry. His son John, the fifth duke, an English-born professional soldier (and veteran of Culloden) inherited in 1768 a realm about to reach the height of its splendour. At the limit of its long expansion, it now extended from the Mull of Kintyre in the south to cover a large portion of Inverness-shire in the north, and from Cowal and Inveraray in the east to Coll and Tiree in the west. The properties paying rent to the duke probably ran to 500 square miles, but in the feudal system he was the superior of a huge tract of 3,000 square miles including, beyond the county of Argyll, all or part of the estates of chieftains such as Clanranald and Glengarry.[34]

Ducal improvements went on, but in some areas amid populations that even yet remained hostile to them. In 1745 Morvern had been openly Jacobite, while the people of Coll and Tiree also resisted Hanoverian recruitment of their sons. Their old allegiances could not be conjured away. The rivalries of the clans, once fought out on the battlefield or redressed in plunder, continued now on a commercial level in furious contests for the occupation of land. On Coll, James Boswell found during his Highland tour of 1773 that Donald MacLean of Cornaig, who farmed much of the duke's estate on the island, had paid 'a very advanced rent rather than let the Campbells get a footing'.[35] Tiree was a priority for improvement, which turned it into an island prosperous from potatoes, cattle and kelp. But its natives could not be mollified, and the leaders of the earlier Jacobite resistance still stirred up trouble. Incomers had created a dozen modern farms: the resulting dispossession was now answered with conspiracy and refusal of all co-operation, led by the old MacLean tacksmen. A report drawn up for the duke in 1771 left the matter in no doubt: 'The small tenants of Tiree are disaffected to the family of Argyll. In this disposition it is thought that long leases might render them too much independent of them, and encourage the people to that sort of insolence and outrage to which they are naturally prone, and much incited by their chieftains of the MacLean gentry.'[36]

The same report was even more specific on the duke's estate in Mull, which extended to about half of this big island: 'The hail of the common tenants on this estate are natives of the country and followers of the MacLeans.' After reciting examples of their misbehaviour, the report continued: 'The observer begs leave to remark that the present disaffection and independence of most of the duke's small tenants in Mull would render it a matter of difficulty to his grace to obtain from them that sort of obedience that has been formerly often found necessary for great men in circumstances where the command of well-attached tenants and followers has been employed to support dignity and respect.' Power at the grassroots lay in the hands of men like Sir Allan MacLean of Broloss, of a family who had once been leaders of the clan in the west of the island, a wild and formidable place to this day. Sir Allan had nine sub-tacksmen renting from him. Not a single one bore the name of Campbell. All except a MacDonald from Tiree were MacLeans, and no doubt figured among those who stirred up the peasants' old passions. The Duke of Argyll had to abandon a claim to Broloss in 1783 after a lengthy lawsuit against Sir Allan, but perhaps this was not without advantages for the smooth running of his estate.[37]

The gulf separating off the northern districts was almost impossible to bridge for a distant landlord with background and tastes like those of the fifth duke. Compared even to Inveraray this represented a different world, physically and mentally. In 1768–69, using the fastest transport available, a surveyor, James Turnbull, took five weeks to get from Edinburgh to Tiree and back. Gales cut the islands off in winter, and even in summer the lack of harbour and shelter discouraged shipping. There were no roads, so that wheeled transport remained more or less unknown. Few travelled unless they really needed to, and little English was spoken. Towns, or indeed villages, hardly existed. The people lived in hovels clustered on the infield of the farms. Isolation intensified self-sufficiency, and while the trade in cattle stretched from the isles and glens to the markets of the Lowlands and of England, much Highland commerce was internal, the shortages of one district being relieved by the plenty of another.[38]

The duke had therefore to formulate overall plans for his estate against a dauntingly disparate background: some parts run by efficient tacksmen keen to join in profitable new ventures, others populated by natives living a traditional life bound by close ties of kinship in a spirit of opposition to all change, and especially to the old enemies they blamed for their deprivations. This problem was never to be overcome by any scheme of improvement. Yet it grew more pressing because of the inexorable rise in population, as the fragmentation of holdings impoverished the peasants and mocked the estate's hopes of revenue.[39]

What could be done? Highland emigration to America had already started up, but this was not something the fifth Duke of Argyll (unlike the second) wanted to encourage. Some of the people yet tried to leave in defiance of their landlord's wishes, though for most the ties of home and kinship still overcame any economic motive. The duke never sought to change this mentality.[40] He was not to be put off even in the years of failed crops and depressed markets, when fresh surges of emigration took place. He still believed the best solution was more benevolent rule by himself in introducing new economic activities. Surely the spread of improvement from the Lowlands to the Highlands, in agriculture and even in industry, would be bound to make a difference in the end. Perhaps, however, only ducal intervention could bring it about. Argyll ordered the people off their wretched farms as these were reorganised and into planned villages where they could learn to weave and fish.[41]

In truth, the ancient feudal order of things in the Highlands was dissolving into the modern commercial order of things, and nowhere more clearly than on the estate of the Duke of Argyll. Not only here but also right across the region, the tacksmen and tenants would at length succumb to forces originating far beyond and outside their control – outside the control, for that matter, of the landowners too. These increasingly sought to manage their estates on the principles of the free market, and the more fortunate among them survived or even made a bit of money. While the fifth Duke of Argyll, like some others, still felt a benevolent sense of responsibility towards his people, he could not turn a blind eye to his own needs or the swelling rentals of his neighbours. Never were his finances easy, rather the whole time in a state of acute embarrassment. But improvement took much longer than anybody imagined in the optimistic eighteenth century. In the county of Argyll at least, the changes proceeded in reasonably good order and on the whole with positive results for those concerned. This could not and would not be true everywhere.[42]

Such was the complex result on the richest Highland domain to escape the destructive power of Jacobitism. On others its effect turned out more equivocal still. For example, a big estate lay along the banks of the River Garry tumbling down into the Great Glen out of western Inverness-shire, one of the watercourses dissecting the huge massif in that part of the Highlands. It was home to a Catholic sept of Clan Donald that had sent a regiment of 600 men to join Prince Charles's army. Their chief, John MacDonell of Glengarry, could not lead them in person because the government managed to detain him. After Culloden, Glengarry became a prime target for the redcoats: they burned all its houses and destroyed or carried away its goods, including the papers and charters of the chief's family. Yet all was not lost. MacDonell's son, Alasdair Ruadh, had been serving in the French army when the rebellion broke out, and was captured at sea while trying to make his way back to Scotland to join it. Imprisoned for a couple of years, he probably obtained his release by offering to return to France and provide the British government with information about the plots still going on there among Jacobites. His codename was Pickle, and his activities remained unsuspected for over a century till Andrew Lang dug them up out of the archives and pieced them together into a coherent narrative. Alasdair Ruadh got what he wanted: he was spared the forfeiture of his estate. On the death in 1754 of his father, he returned to the Glengarry he had left as an eager youngster to become a soldier of fortune in Europe.[43]

Despite the military reprisals, life in Glengarry had continued much as ever and the years after 1745 possibly saw some renewal of its prosperity. A drove-road passed the whole length of the glen and the estate itself was considered without peer for the raising of cattle, so it could only benefit once trade to the south picked up again. Perhaps there seemed little objective reason to disturb the people in their traditional way of life, on a string of farms along the dozen miles of the river where they cultivated the limited area of arable land and shared the common grazings on the hills behind. While it might not have seemed all that civilised to any outsider, the MacDonells showed no desire for anything else.[44]

The way of life had allowed the clansmen to hold all government in contempt, except that of their own chiefs. Unlike in other parts of the Highlands, there were to be no new masters in Glengarry after 1745. Even so, law and order would be imposed, and then the way lay open for commerce to exert its modernising effects. In Glengarry it was not, however, the landowner that took the initiative. Right through the middle decades of the century the clansmen here in effect lacked a chieftain, who for most of the time was an absentee, a prisoner or a minor. This handed the real leadership of the clan to the tacksmen. None sought to usurp the chieftain's position, but they took advantage of the situation for their own purposes while sparing little thought for the livelihood of their rack-rented sub-tenants. Since there could be no question here of any planned improvement, it was a haphazard, though not unsuccessful, business. Alasdair Ruadh, once he got back, just let things carry on, now under a regime of his own no less harsh than that of the tacksmen. Still, it lasted only seven years till he died in 1761. He left a young son, Duncan, who came of age in 1768, and now control of the estate did shift into the hands of a man with a clear idea of the changes he wanted. Shortly after his marriage in 1772, he relet his lands on commercial principles, giving notice to the remaining tacksmen and offering them their tenancies once again but on more stringent terms. Glengarry had turned from the home of a clan into a commercial unit, though that did not in the end secure its people a place in the new Highland economy either. By the turn of the nineteenth century they were emigrating en masse to Canada.[45]

Travellers intrepid enough to ascend Glengarry would at length come to Loch Quoich, behind which ranged *na Garbh-Chrìochan*, the Rough Bounds – country as inaccessible as any in Scotland, even today crossed by no road. But it was possible to follow the track used by the drovers back across the watershed to Kinlochhourn, at the head of a sea-loch that here brings the Atlantic Ocean into the heart of the mountains. By a still lesser and wilder path the traveller could then make his way along the southern shore of Loch Hourn to the territory of the MacDonells of Barrisdale. This was actually easier to get to from the western side by walking 10 miles, again always across wilderness, from Inverie in Knoydart, which itself could only be reached by sea.[46]

Before 1745 this was, unsurprisingly, another district that existed quite outside the reach of any external authority. Only the chieftain gave law to the people, whose lives were otherwise regulated by their own customs and practices, transmitted orally through the Gaelic language; they could not write it because there was nobody to teach them, and only five people on the estate spoke English. A dense network of kinship set the pattern of existence for this traditional Highland community where even second and third cousins counted as close family. Its values were its own. A lawyer in Edinburgh would have called illegal what the clansmen saw as justice. They never stole from each other, since people who lived close to subsistence could not tolerate pilfering among themselves, but raiding cattle was another matter – and no outsider would ever get a cow back from Barrisdale.[47]

In 1745 the chief here was Archibald MacDonell of Barrisdale, who came out in the rebellion and after Culloden spent seven years hiding in his native mountains. That did not immediately change the local way of life, as noted by the surveyor, David Bruce, who was sent in by the Commission for Forfeited Estates: 'They have the insolence, ever since the year 1746, to pay their rents to the attainted Barrisdale . . . who since that time absolutely rules them, and ranges up and down that country and the neighbourhood with a band of armed men dressed, as well as himself, in the Highland habit.' Bruce evidently feared it would reflect on him if no rent was collected from the tenants, but he could do nothing about it.[48] The Welsh traveller, Thomas Pennant, managed to get this far and recorded that MacDonell 'carried the art of plunder to the highest pitch of perfection . . . he raised an income of five hundred a year by blackmail and behaved with genuine honour in restoring on proper consideration the stolen cattle of his friends'.[49]

MacDonell was finally captured in 1753 and imprisoned till he obtained a pardon from King George III that would allow him to serve as a British officer in the Seven Years' War. The peace in 1763 brought him reduction to half-pay and forced him to look for another source of income. He then applied to the Commission for Forfeited Estates to get a lease of several farms on his former property. In his application, he appealed directly to their ambition to modernise Highland agriculture. His request was granted. The old Jacobite outlaw then transformed himself into an improving landlord, to introduce even on the estate of Barrisdale some of the same transformations that were now taking place elsewhere in the Highlands. The commission intended to break one support of traditional society, the power and authority of the chief, and at least to erode another, the notion that it was the clan that owned its lands. The example of Barrisdale showed how difficult, in practical terms, the programme would be. Here there was nobody other than the chief to give a lead, while the people scarcely even understood the concept of individual ownership.[50]

Naturally, then, the clansmen responded less eagerly than their chief to the new social order. He had been brought up in the Highland tradition of personal rule on the estate with a profitable collective sideline in rustling cattle, but in middle age he accepted the ultimate external supervision of his property and fell in with its official aims. Now complaining of his clansmen as ignorant and lazy, he brought in sheep, started the harvesting of kelp and contributed to making Inverie into a village (or at least a line of stone-built cottages along the shore of Loch Nevis). He appointed a schoolmaster and at length put everybody on new leases. These were all standard measures, but again they did not here cause the old world of clanship to collapse altogether. The chief at least recognised the automatic right of kin to succeed to

Highland Cattle with a Collie, by Joseph Adam and Joseph Denovan Adam. Scotland's most successful exports at the time of the Union were the cattle driven from their Highland pastures to be fattened in fertile England for roast beef. (© The Drambuie Collection, Edinburgh/ Bridgeman Images)

The water wheel at Preston Mill. The main source of energy for the early development of Scotland was water, powering hundreds of mills like this one at Preston, East Lothian. (© National Trust for Scotland. Licensor www.scran.ac.uk)

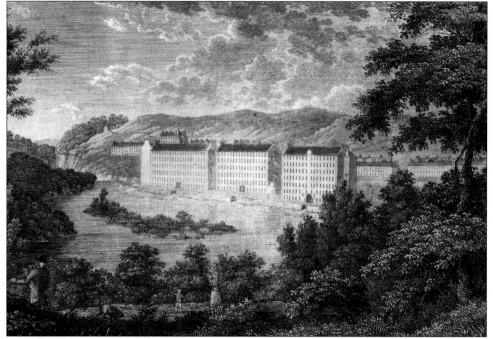

New Lanark. Water power allowed the construction even of major industrial complexes, the biggest being New Lanark on an upper reach of the River Clyde. (© Royal Burgh of Lanark Museum. Licensor www.scran.ac.uk)

The Shore at Leith with the Martello Tower of 1807. Growing exports of industrial products required redevelopment of Scotland's ports, as here on the Shore at Leith with the Martello Tower of 1807 as protection against French attacks. (© RCAHMS. Licensor www.scran.ac.uk)

Dr Webster's sermon, by John Kay. The nation's hardworking ethos was reinforced by
Calvinist sermons, but here Dr Alexander Webster strives to hold his congregation's attention
in the Tolbooth Kirk, Edinburgh.

Cromarty east kirk, 'unquestionably one of the finest eighteenth-century parish churches in
Scotland'. The traditional Presbyterian preaching box acquired more elegant dimensions as the
Church of Scotland developed enlightened religion. (© Cromarty Court House Museum.
Licensor www.scran.ac.uk)

Duncan Forbes of Culloden, after Jeremiah Davidson. As Lord Advocate, this humane Highland landlord guided the nation through the perils of Jacobite rebellion. (© National Portrait Gallery, London)

Robert McQueen, Lord Braxfield. Scottish justice showed its sterner face in this judge who told one condemned man he would be 'nane the waur o' a hangin'. (Scottish National Portrait Gallery)

ABOVE. Engraving in Thomas Pennant, *A Tour of Scotland*, 1772: a weaver's cottage. Travellers to Scotland, like the Welshman Pennant, were often shocked by the primitive living conditions.

RIGHT. Flora MacDonald, by Allan Ramsay. The woman who saved Prince Charles from his pursuers was arrested and then detained in London, where fashionable society feted her. (Ashmolean Museum, University of Oxford/Bridgeman Images)

LEFT. Lady Nairne with her son. A great cultural legacy of the Jacobite movement is a huge fund of traditional song, which Lady Nairne helped to preserve. (Scottish National Portrait Gallery)

BELOW. A Highland Wedding at Blair Atholl, by David Allan. Once the Jacobite danger was past, the picturesque customs of Highland society became the subject of romantic celebration. (On loan from a Private Collection to the Scottish National Gallery)

The Old Pretender, by Louis Gabriel Blanchet. James VIII, King of Scots *de jure*, was the dull bearer of the House of Stewart's claims to three thrones on the British Isles. (© National Portrait Gallery, London)

The Young Pretender, by Louis Gabriel Blanchet. Prince Charles Edward Stewart led the spectacular Jacobite rebellion of 1745 yet failed to make good his family's claim to the crown. (© National Portrait Gallery, London)

An Incident in the Rebellion of 1745, British School, eighteenth century. For this vivid reconstruction of the height of the bloody Battle of Culloden, Highland prisoners captured there were used as models. (Royal Collection Trust © Her Majesty Queen Elizabeth II, 2014/Bridgeman Images)

John Campbell, 2nd Duke of Argyll, by William Aikman. The duke narrowly defeated the Jacobites at the Battle of Sheriffmuir in 1715, then rose to political ascendancy in Scotland. (© National Portrait Gallery, London)

LEFT. Inveraray Castle. The Campbells of Argyll built themselves this symbol of their national power in the middle of their traditional Highland domain.

BELOW. Henry Dundas, Viscount Melville, by Sir Thomas Lawrence. In the second half of the eighteenth century, the Lowland clan of Dundas, lawyers and politicians, took over the leadership of Scotland. (© National Portrait Gallery, London)

The Dunmore Pineapple. The most exquisite architectural work of the age was this folly built, probably by William Chambers, for the Earl of Dunmore. (© Falkirk Museums. Licensor www.scran.ac.uk)

Old College, Edinburgh. The grandest architectural work of the age was Robert Adam's new University of Edinburgh, worthy of imperial Rome. (© British Geological Survey/NERC. Licensor www.scran.ac.uk)

LEFT. Statue of Allan Ramsay, senior, Princes Street Gardens. The Union brought a cultural reaction in which Ramsay took a lead by preserving and developing the poetic tradition of the Scots language.

BELOW LEFT. Statue of Robert Fergusson, Canongate Kirk. The native poetic tradition gained new life from Fergusson's vivid depictions of ordinary life in his native Edinburgh.

BELOW RIGHT. Robert Burns, by James Hutcheson. The native poetic tradition finally achieved universality with Burns's satires and songs of love, these often adapted from vernacular originals. (Reproduced by permission of James Hutcheson)

ABOVE. David Hume, by Allan Ramsay. Scottish culture achieved universality in a different sense with Hume's revolutionary revision of the western philosophical inheritance. (Scottish National Portrait Gallery, Edinburgh)

RIGHT. Adam Smith (centre), by John Kay. The universality of the Scottish Enlightenment remains a living presence even in the modern world in Smith's influence on its economics and politics.

holdings of land, so to that extent allayed the problems of adjustment to the new order. But he only put off a far more harrowing fate for his people.[51]

The estate of Cameron of Lochiel was one of the biggest in the West Highlands. It had long been divided into extensive farms for the raising of cattle and supported a large population of peasants on its 100,000 acres. While some afforestation had started, cattle remained the main business. Compared to Barrisdale this was civilised country, open to the outside world by reason of lying near the crossroads of trade and communication where the Great Glen runs into Loch Linnhe and the Road to the Isles turns off to the west. The social structure was typical of the region with, in 1745, a chieftain and his immediate family at the top, 13 tacksmen on the estate, supervising 50 super-ior tenants of their own, the other three-quarters of the population being sub-tenants, cottars and servants. As at Barrisdale the traditional organisation of the farms did not much change during the period of forfeiture, and small communities continued to occupy each of them.[52]

John Cameron of Fassifern, a member of the chiefly family otherwise now in exile, had kept his nose clean and stuck around to keep an eye on things. He seems to have co-operated closely with the factors appointed by the Commission of Forfeited Estates, and perhaps this was another reason why no radical schemes of improvement went forward. There was an imme-diate job on hand after Culloden, to get burned-out farms into production again and to impose a new framework of law and order on an estate where previously the chief had been an autocrat, if a benevolent one.[53] Now the clan ceased to be self-governing in that sense, while steady economic progress turned warriors once famous for their ferocity into honest, well-behaved ten-ants. As the last traces of Jacobitism died a bloodless death, they started to send a steady stream of men to serve in the British army.[54]

The only jarring element in the life of the estate was the attempt by a cadet of the chiefly family, Allan Cameron of Erracht, to usurp the position of the absent Camerons of Lochiel and to be recognised in their stead as head of the clan. He went to the trouble of raising a regiment, the Cameron Highlanders, in the hope of persuading the British government to back him. But the people of the estate spurned his blandishments and waited for the return of the chief from over the water. By 1784 this was 15-year-old Donald Cameron, whose affairs lay in the hands of tutors. These told the clansmen that, if they wanted the young man back, they would need to pay the estate's outstanding debts of £3,000. It was a hefty sum for the time, but the tutors could raise it by increasing the rents. The tenants agreed to pay one-third more: short of removing their claymores again from the thatch, they could scarcely have given better proof of their fidelity to the legitimate chieftain. Still, willing as they were to pay, they could not all afford it. Those who failed to pay got thrown off their holdings, and many were forced to emigrate – this long before any sheep had appeared in the area.[55]

By now it was hard to argue there had been any outstanding success for the grand strategy since Culloden, that is, a reliance on intervention by agents of the British government to bring civilisation to benighted Gaeldom and to set up models for its development. We have looked here at some typical examples, none of which offered an ideal for the future of the whole region.[56] In part this was a result of particular policies pursued by the Commission of Forfeited Estates. At the outset in 1746, a freeze on rents to foster loyalty had removed one incentive for the natives to emulate hard-working, law-abiding, Lowland Presbyterians. After the Seven Years' War places such as Callander and Kinlochrannoch were seeded with settlements of old soldiers thought more promising than the natives, but they only took on the local habits, lolling about and tippling whisky; they also introduced venereal disease. The original idea had been for accumulated profits from forfeited estates to be used in continuous development so that disaffection could be tackled at root. But their revenue never even covered the expenses of administration. The commission itself seemed affected by Highland indolence. Its sluggish bureaucracy performed no better than any other absentee landlords who let their lands run down and lose money. The commissioner Lord Kames felt obliged to admit that the money spent in the Highlands was 'no better than water spilt on the ground'.[57]

In fact, by now the mark of the forfeited estates was their lack of improvement, compared to what, say, the Dukes of Argyll had achieved. It seemed time to turn back to the private sector. The Lord Advocate, Henry Dundas, lobbied for the general restoration of the estates to their original Jacobite owners. He won agreement to that in principle from the governments he served in and he himself became a commissioner for the estates in 1783, effectively with a brief to wind the old policy up.[58] In 1784 he introduced at Westminster a bill to disannex the estates from the crown. Forfeited families had been atoning for the crimes of their ancestors, he told the House of

Commons, 'and there is not one of those families in which some person has not since spilt his blood in his country's cause'. He stipulated that if the estates were to be restored, so too should their debts as they had stood when the government took over. Otherwise the heirs would be getting them back in better condition, and a premium would have been placed on rebellion. The return to the exchequer (£90,000 in the event) could be used for a variety of public works. By contrast, the estates, though valued at £9,000 a year, were producing £6,700 gross and, after deducting for management and repairs, £4,000 net. This 'is no extravagant boon that I ask for,' Dundas justly remarked, but he promised it would please the inhabitants of the estates and discourage emigration.[59]

It was the first time the Parliament at Westminster had adopted a reform in the Highlands, as opposed to suppressing rebellion or raising revenue. By it, according to the most eminent Gael, Adam Ferguson, 'the affection of all Highlanders [was] gained to the state and the king'.[60] Actually the state retreated, or rather gave up any pretence to a control it could not exert. Of course, this would never have happened had there been any risk of a return to rebellion. Instead Dundas relied, after the state had achieved so little, on private landowners to rebuild a sound fabric for the region. This would not destroy but reinforce the social order. The landowners agreed. Conservatives, they favoured – in contrast to their Liberal successors – keeping and increasing the population on the land, in a hierarchy that would be a social and economic good for the nation.

Some agency that could pay heed to the needs of the region as a whole was still desirable, but now it would have to be a private or voluntary body with public, philanthropic purposes. Filling the bill was the Highland Society, founded in London in 1778 to promote development and also to preserve the best of Gaelic culture.[61] The Duke of Argyll became its president, with a membership consisting of landowners and literary men. It had economic aims: it published essays on improvement and enclosure, management of livestock, new crops and so on, with gold medals for their authors. It also had cultural aims: it investigated the authenticity of Ossian and in the process collected many Gaelic manuscripts, afterwards deposited in the Advocates' Library in Edinburgh. It brought out a vocabulary of Gaelic in 1794, an Old Testament in 1803 (the New Testament had already been published in 1767) and a full dictionary in 1828. With these the society set off quite a flood of Gaelic publishing. Leaving aside some short-lived periodicals, the market wanted sacred literature, Bibles and catechisms. The Highland Society also encouraged non-literary activities such as piping: all a stark contrast to, not to say complete reversal of, the previous official suppression of Gaelic culture. The rulers of Scotland now viewed linguistic renewal with goodwill.[62]

The linguistic renewal showed how economic and cultural improvement might interact to benefit the people, so long as the Highlands preserved the peace and good order attained only within living memory. As political boss of Scotland, Dundas was not so naïve as to think peace and good order came of themselves; they had to be fostered, even imposed on a region still in the throes of profound long-term transformation. Yet this should not turn into counterproductive tyranny. On a crucial point at issue in 1792 the Lord Advocate voiced the dilemmas. In reporting unrest to Dundas, he begged leave to point out how the spread of sheep-farming was 'a measure very unpopular in those Highland districts where sheep are not yet introduced, as it tends to remove the inhabitants on those estates from their small possessions and dwelling houses'. This was, surely, an expression of sympathy for the peasants who became victims of improvement – if not, of course, for any illegality in resisting it on their part.[63]

Gaeldom was not inevitably doomed. But its social structures did need to change for it to survive and flourish, just as Lowland social structures were changing. An essential impetus to that had emerged in the undermining of the traditional subsistence economy by markets. In parts of the Highlands, people already made a living from the cattle they sold outside the region, rather than attempting to remain self-sufficient on patches of poor soil. This was a new system of extensive pastoral agriculture, where capitalist farmers employed landless labourers – and it survives yet, in reasonable condition, to the east of the Great Glen. Yet to the west and north, that was not how things worked out. Instead the traditional subsistence economy survived, little affected by markets. There was no extensive pastoral agriculture, but a system of individual smallholdings which grew smaller and smaller still as the tenants subdivided their plots to accommodate their ever increasing population. Rather it was the big farmers, the tacksmen, that vanished from this scene, to leave a society of peasants barely able to support themselves from their distressingly meagre resources. And so the groundwork was laid for the harrowing Highland crises of the nineteenth century.

PART IV

POLITICS

10

Stewart: 'Hazardous game'

On 7 June 1753, Dr Archibald Cameron was hanged, drawn and quartered at Tyburn, the traditional place of execution at the spot where the Marble Arch now stands in London. He was the last man to die in the cause of restoring the House of Stewart to its thrones. A younger son of the eighteenth chief of his clan, Cameron had been brought up at its fastness of Achnacarry on Lord Arkaig in the wilds of western Inverness-shire. He was a brother of the 'Gentle Lochiel', Donald Cameron, the nineteenth chief, a man renowned for his gallant, magnanimous character in both war and peace. The normal course in life for Archibald would have been to serve as a soldier while running some part of the Camerons' 100,000 acres, but he preferred to study medicine in Edinburgh, Paris and Leiden. This unusual trajectory for the career of a Highland gentleman did not save him from the same grisly fate as others had suffered in the revenge taken by the British state on the Jacobite rebels.[1]

When Prince Charles had landed on the Scottish mainland at Loch nan Uamh in August 1745, the first man he asked for was the Gentle Lochiel. Before the prince and the chief actually met, Archibald Cameron was their go-between. The chief from the start believed the whole adventure to be a terrible mistake, yet he would faithfully follow the prince to the end. Without his initial support, made flesh in the 400 Camerons who came as the biggest contingent of fighting men when the Jacobite army first mustered at Glenfinnan, the rebellion would never have got off the ground. Lochiel and his brother were afterwards companions-in-arms on the long road into England and back, though Archibald only ever acted as a medical officer. Lochiel was wounded at the Battle of Culloden but Archibald escaped unscathed, afterwards helping Prince Charles to keep one step ahead of his pursuers. While the prince hid with MacPherson of Cluny at the 'cage' on Ben Alder, a camouflaged shelter in the rocks, it was Cameron that brought news of the arrival of two French warships, once again in Loch nan Uamh, to rescue him at last.[2]

The Cameron brothers escaped to France as well. Donald died there in 1748 while Archibald got mixed up in impractical schemes for a Jacobite comeback. One plot, concocted by Alexander Murray of Elibank, would have co-ordinated a fresh rising in Scotland with a *coup d'état* in London and the seizure of the Tower and St James's Palace. Meanwhile King Frederick the Great of Prussia would be sending 15,000 men to invade England. It was all pure fantasy: though Frederick did not at this point enjoy friendly relations with Britain, he was far too calculating to place any reliance on losers like the Jacobites. In any case, the British government had an agent in their inner counsels, in the person of Alasdair Ruadh MacDonell of Glengarry, who worked under the codename of Pickle the Spy. After Archibald Cameron landed in Scotland to join the plot, information supplied to the redcoats allowed them to pick him up easily as he made his way north.[3]

Cameron was sent a prisoner to London. Evidence enough existed to convict him of treason, but the government never even bothered with a trial. He was already among the Jacobites listed by name in an Act of Attainder of 1746 and, once captured, he could be put to death without further ado. On the scaffold, he bore himself with great courage. The Revd James Falconar offered him the consolations of religion and then, according to Horace Walpole, was 'not content with seeing the Doctor hanged, [but] let down the top of the landau for the better convenience of seeing him disembowelled!'[4] The scene led Dr Samuel Johnson to vilify the king 'as one who, upon all occasions, is unrelenting and barbarous'.[5] Cameron had claimed the plot of 1752 was just an invention by the government, 'to cover the cruelty of murdering me at [such a] distance of time from the passing of [the Act]'.[6]

Was there anything in this allegation? Sir Walter Scott took an interest in the question and wrote in a new introduction to *Redgauntlet* (1832): 'There were circumstances in his case, so far as was made known to the public, which attracted much compassion, and gave to the judicial proceedings against him an appearance of cold-blooded revenge on the part of government ... his death remains in popular estimation a dark blot upon the memory of George II, being almost publicly imputed to a mean and personal hatred of Donald Cameron of Lochiel, the sufferer's heroic brother.' All the same,

Scott thought the British state was better than merely arbitrary in its actions: 'The unfortunate sufferer had not come to the Highlands solely upon his private affairs, as was the general belief; but it was not judged prudent by the English ministry to let it be generally known that he came to inquire about a considerable sum of money which had been remitted from France to the friends of the exiled family.' He was meant to meet MacPherson of Cluny, too, still in hiding though in touch with Prince Charles. Scott concluded: 'That Dr. Cameron should have held a commission to assist this chief in raking together the dispersed embers of disaffection, is in itself sufficiently natural . . . But neither ought it to be imputed to George II that he suffered the laws to be enforced against a person taken in the act of breaking them. When he lost his hazardous game, Dr Cameron only paid the forfeit which he must have calculated upon.' At the same time, Scott believed the government preferred to draw a veil over these matters in order to avert suspicion from Pickle the Spy, 'lest they had indicated the channel of communication which, it is now well known, they possessed to all the plots of Charles Edward'. According to different reports, the government was anxious not to upset London's financial markets during an initiative to convert the national debt into securities with a lower long-term rate of interest, and there might have been panic in the City on any rumours of a further rebellion. From what we have learned of relations between British finance and British government in the twenty-first century, this version of events does not seem so far-fetched.[7]

By now not only was Archibald Cameron dead but so in effect was the whole Jacobite movement – so much so that, according to the philosopher David Hume, Prince Charles could visit London incognito in that same year of 1753. In particular, Hume had heard of a call he paid on Anne, Lady Primrose:

> The Pretender came to her house in the evening, without giving her any preparatory information; and entered the room, when she had a pretty large company with her, and was herself playing at cards. He was announced by the servant under another name. She thought the cards would have dropped from her hands on seeing him. But she had enough presence of mind, to call him by the name he assumed; to ask him when he came to England, and how long he intended to stay there. After he and all the company went away, the servants

remarked how wonderfully like the strange gentleman was to the prince's picture, which hung on the chimney-piece, in the very room in which he entered.[8]

Hume adds that Prince Charles was again in London in 1760, at the time of the coronation of King George III: though these are all matters of hearsay, there is no particular reason to doubt the truth of them. 'It was curiosity that led me', the prince is reputed to have told an inquirer, 'but I assure you that the person who is the object of all this pomp and magnificence is the man I envy the least.' If those were indeed his sentiments, then not even his most devoted follower needed to bother himself any further with the lost Jacobite cause.

The Jacobite cause had seemed far from lost in 1707. Across the narrow seas from the new United Kingdom a long European conflict continued. The War of the Spanish Succession had started in 1701 with the English and the French ranged against each other, but during several years of combat neither side decisively gained the upper hand. King Louis XIV of France awaited his moment to sponsor a diversionary expedition by the exiled Old Pretender, King James VIII of Scotland and III of England to his followers. It sailed in March 1708 for the northern kingdom, at a time when there seemed a good chance of winning support from wounded Scottish patriotism and, more to the point, of stretching overextended British resources to the limit.[9]

Thirty vessels carried 6,000 French troops across the North Sea from Dunkirk to the Firth of Forth. The 20-year-old James boarded his own ship full of youthful ardour, ready to fulfil his destiny. Alas, the admiral and general in charge of the expedition did not share his enthusiasm. Battered by storms, the fleet reached its goal and cast anchor off Crail and Pittenweem. James had been wretchedly seasick, but the sight of Fife's sandstone cliffs and knobbly hills lifted his heart. The proclamation he carried with him appealed to the fidelity of his ancient realm: if it would just break the Union with England, all other political arrangements could be left to a free Parliament in Edinburgh. This was a shrewd programme for a deeply disgruntled nation.[10]

It still went for nothing in the end. While locals rowed out to the ships to see if they could get free brandy, there was no response from anybody else on land to the signals the French fleet sent aloft. With a superior squadron of the Royal Navy, Admiral George Byng came up in pursuit. A tearful James begged to be put ashore, even with just a few followers, but the French commanders would not listen and weighed anchor to hasten away northwards. They toyed with the idea of a descent on Inverness though finally, as stormy weather blew up again, they swung on a course right round Scotland and Ireland to head for home. If the outward voyage had been bad, the return was appalling, and completed only with great loss in ships and lives. The Jacobite rising of 1708 had turned out a fiasco.[11]

This did not stop the British government exacting retribution in Scotland. It gave orders to its military commander there, the Earl of Leven, to carry out a swift and indiscriminate round-up of disaffected local leaders. He then sent them down to London, a move that outraged Scottish opinion because those under arrest included not only Jacobites but also men who had been prominent critics of the Union on quite different grounds: Lord Belhaven, impeccable Presbyterian Whig, and the Duke of Hamilton, calamitous leader of the opposition in the defunct Scots Parliament. Still, he and the rest (though not Belhaven) found no trouble in negotiating their release because the British government offered a deal – freedom in exchange for their votes in favour of the official slate of Scottish representative peers at the forthcoming general election. The situation in Scotland now counted for nothing, the situation at Westminster for all. A pattern had been set for the next 300 years.[12]

It took just five of those years for Scots to understand what was happening to them. Then they made their one serious effort to break the Union by constitutional means. In 1713 the Scottish representative peers at Westminster lost a motion in favour of that by a mere four votes, the majority being made up of English proxies. The next year Queen Anne died. There still appeared to be some chance of recalling the Stewarts and averting the Hanoverian succession. When King George I succeeded anyway, Scotland seethed with discontent. Trouble could have broken out anywhere, but actually came first of all from a man who had been one of the authors of the Union, who had indeed till recently served in the British government as Scottish Secretary of State.[13]

John Erskine, Earl of Mar, had loved his job in the Cabinet, revelled in its status and, apart from anything else, needed the salary. Political principle was never his forte. One of the moderate Tories in the last government of Queen Anne, he did his official duty in completing arrangements for a smooth transfer of the crown to King George I under the Act of Settlement (1701). Though Mar possessed the sense to see he could not afterwards hope to remain in office, he seemed to cherish delusions about the Tories' ability to bide their time as a loyal opposition before coming in again at some point – something that was in fact just not going to happen under the Whig hegemony that the Hanoverian monarchs would enforce. Mar wrote obsequious pledges of eternal allegiance to the new sovereign who, however, had already made up his mind about the earl on the strength of Whig whispers that he harboured secret Jacobite sympathies. When he appeared at court, the boorish German snubbed him. A man merely worried at his prospects turned into one desperate to salvage them.[14]

How the Earl of Mar set about it is revealing. He did not bother to consult the Pretender. The exiled court was forever engaged in futile intrigues, but its real standing and influence could be measured against the fact that it was taken by surprise at what the earl did next. He left London for the north, passed by his lands in central Scotland and reached Aberdeenshire, where he also owned an estate. Here he set up rounds of meetings with restless Highland and Lowland lairds. Some camouflage for their transactions was provided by advertising them as a traditional great hunt to trap herds of deer, *timchioll* in Gaelic, a sport that involved hundreds of beaters over several days driving the beasts past the gentry who waited for the kill. This time the gentry had another kind of kill in mind. It was on the Braes of Mar on 6 September 1715 that they raised the Jacobite standard to bear before them as they advanced to the expulsion of the House of Hanover and to the restoration of the House of Stewart.[15]

Yet the Earl of Mar's own rebellion was at bottom on behalf of himself – and all because he had been deprived of patronage, life's blood of politics though that was in the eighteenth century. He knew well, of course, that the only cause other men would fight for was the cause of the Stewarts. He then proceeded to confound the two causes, and in the end to ruin the greater one. The British political system in 1715, rotten and repellent, was ripe for a fall, yet would be saved by the fact that one of its own led the challenge to it. Many brave men went to their doom behind this egocentric bungler: Mar deserves all the scorn and contumely that history has showered on him. At least from his behaviour we learn some useful things about the condition of Scotland at the time. It was a nation split between nationalists and unionists, clearly, but why did people opt for one side rather than the other?[16]

A prime point to note is that the rebellion of 1715 was not in the first instance a Highland affair, as the rebellion of 1745 would largely turn out to be. We should specify this because, in popular myth, both rebellions have been equated with outbreaks among the clansmen, or even depicted as an elemental clash of Celt and Anglo-Saxon. But Celtic society and culture, like most societies and cultures, were complex, and never monolithic enough to be encapsulated in a single political cause. In respect of Jacobitism, too, a cleft existed in Highland society, just as a cleft existed in Lowland society. It ran deepest in the one quarter that really mattered, among the chieftains and landowners, who would carry their clansmen or vassals with them.[17]

And then the Highland gentlemen that did come out for the Pretender in 1715 were not grisly old Celts but quite cosmopolitan figures. However colourful their past and however strong their patriotism, their families now fitted into an aristocratic culture embracing the entire ruling elites of the three kingdoms under the British crown – and recognisably the variant of a European phenomenon dominated by the values and achievements of the French Bourbons. Even if we descend one level to the lairds or tacksmen, we still meet a rank of men with many connections beyond the Highlands, notably in a tradition of mercenary service for the armies of foreign powers. Nor is there any reason to believe that the clergy, the lowest echelon of the Highland elite, were much different from their betters. Thinner on the ground than their opposite numbers in the Lowlands, they did not need to come to terms with the Gaelic culture of their flocks, which many of them anyway shared. But the Scottish universities that had shaped their mental world were European institutions, where the strongest influence derived from the humanism of the Renaissance. A broader neoclassical culture was what Scots students gained access to when they went and studied abroad, as many did after suitable preparation at their own colleges. Altogether, none of the Highland elites by now owed much to the Celtic past. On the contrary, they shared their Lowland counterparts' concerns about the Scottish future.[18]

In any case, when Mar rode for the north it was not to the Highlands he went. He made rather for that outlying part of the Lowlands known in modern times (on and off) as the Grampian region, rather richer than the Highlands and, apart from anything else, more loyal to the Stewarts. It was true that here landowners existed who still acted like chieftains. Mar himself wrote to one of his own tacksmen, Black Jock Forbes of Skellater in upper Strathdon, telling him to burn out his vassals in Kildrummy if there was no other way to make them join the Jacobite army.[19] Yet for the most part the earl did address himself here to a society Lowland in character. It was, to be sure, a conservative Lowland society, so far without the urban refinements or the colonial opportunities starting to transform its counterparts to the south. Its trade had been damaged by the Union, which put up barriers to its traditional commerce across the North Sea for which fresh opportunities in distant England probably did not compensate. And while the region had started to try out agricultural improvements, they could not in themselves create content with the current political situation. Whether in burgh or county, it would have been hard for the locals to see a worse future outside the United Kingdom than in it.

The conservatism of the north-east of Scotland was complex, but most marked in religion. Here lay the stronghold of the Episcopalians, from whom the Presbyterians had wrenched control of the Kirk in 1690. After 1707 it was unlikely the tables would ever be turned again because the existing religious establishment was guaranteed by the terms of the Union. At the outset, the balance of numbers between the Episcopalians and the Presbyterians had been much more even than it later became. The Episcopalians counted 14 bishops and 1,000 priests, numbers that over the coming century would be whittled down to 4 bishops and 42 priests. The Presbyterians persecuted them and their flocks and, despite a modest degree of toleration insisted on from Westminster after 1712, the two main branches of Scottish Christianity remained far from equal before the law. Episcopalians did now have freedom to worship but only in so-called chapels, that is to say, not inside buildings belonging to the established Church. Inside that established Church, in other words, Presbyterian ministers had completely displaced Episcopalian priests, and coexistence had become impossible. The exclusion extended beyond religious offices: those ministers had the sole right to register births and baptisms, or to collect tithes and other dues, while before the priests could perform any sacred functions at all they needed to swear allegiance to the Hanoverian monarch and to abjure the Jacobite Pretender.[20]

A smaller minority of Catholics also survived in defiance of even more severe penal legislation, though only in remote parts the Reformation had never reached. The situation after 1714 threatened to eject both them and the Episcopalians permanently into an outer darkness of Scottish society where honest individuals might suffer serious economic penalties and perhaps lose their liberty. Fraught with danger and difficulty as any repudiation of the Union was bound to be, Episcopalians and Catholics had, this side of the grave, little to lose.[21]

As in other places and times, religious persecution became in crucial respects a source of strength to its victims. The Episcopalians still had a hierarchy and a second focus of loyalty in the liturgical forms once favoured by the Stewart kings for the whole Church of Scotland. Behind these outward signs lay also a sustaining culture. At its heart was an elegiac view of the world as a vale of tears: it could scarcely have been more different from the enlightened optimism emerging elsewhere in Scotland. William Hamilton of Bangour, who was to fight at the Battle of Culloden and afterwards flee to Gothenburg in Sweden, wrote on his arrival there a paraphrase of Psalm 137, 'By the rivers of Babylon'. It began:

> On Gallia's shore we sat and wept,
> When Scotland we thought on,
> Robb'd of her bravest sons, and all
> Her ancient spirit gone.[22]

According to this gloomy outlook on life, the individual could only submit with stoic resignation to the fate God had ordained for him and endure it without flinching in his faith or in his fidelity to established secular authority. Such had been the teaching of three occupants of the chair of divinity at King's College, Aberdeen, since the middle of the seventeenth century: John Forbes of Corse, Henry Scougall and George Garden. They believed that God intervened directly in human affairs, and that the part of the good Christian was to submit passively to his fate in contemplation of the power and majesty ordaining it. This had meant submission to the Stewarts, however outrageously they acted. We might suppose it also implied submission to the Hanoverians, yet here was an implication often rejected in the north-east of Scotland.[23]

While no complete identity existed between Episcopalians and Jacobites, the religious sensibility of the one did nurture a powerful account of recent Scottish history that fed the political commitment of the other. It came out, for example, in a sermon preached in 1715 by Professor Garden. He depicted the Union of 1707 as one of the calamities God had visited on Scotland in punishment for what happened at the Revolution of 1688 – abolition of the ancient apostolic form of government in the Church, usurpation of its rights by schismatic preachers and disobedience to the monarch. For these 'heinous sins and abominations of rebellion, injustice, oppression, schism and perjury,' declaimed Garden, 'God in his just wrath hath visited and plagued us with a long, a bloody and expensive war, several years of famine and extraordinary dearth, accompanied with epidemical diseases and a great mortality . . .

with the loss of the liberty, privileges and independence of this our ancient kingdom.' Presbyterians had betrayed the nation, in other words, and only Episcopalians could save it.[24]

Still, whatever it did for their political loyalties, this religious sensibility did not necessarily make social conservatives of those who shared it. In economic matters, for example, no consistent link can be found between Jacobite conviction and resistance to improvement. In Inverness-shire, William Mackintosh of Borlum made a name with bold agricultural schemes, for example in reafforestation. Later imprisoned for years in Edinburgh Castle, he passed the time writing two books, respectively published in 1729 and 1732, that urged a modernising programme on the Scots gentry: long leases, systematic enclosure, fallowing and new crops of roots and grass – things it would take much of the south of Scotland several decades to catch on to.[25] But here the Earl of Mar had himself become a progressive landlord full of bright ideas, with a special interest in industrial development ranging from his extensive workings of coal, where he harnessed water-powered machinery on a large scale, to the manufacture of glass which he helped to stimulate from exile after 1715.[26] We have already seen, too, how George Lockhart of Carnwath, principal Jacobite agent in Scotland, placed himself as a landowner at the forefront of early industrial development, investing in the revolutionary steam engine devised by Thomas Newcomen to open up and work coal-mines in Midlothian.

There being so little social difference between Jacobites and Hanoverians, they appeared side by side almost everywhere in Scotland. Of course their respective strengths varied from region to region. The Jacobites did have the upper hand north of the River Tay, but in the burghs as much as in the hills and the countryside generally. In fact, the Highlands presented the patchiest picture of support, with the Campbells in Argyll and the Presbyterian clans of Munro and Mackay at opposite extremities of the region to balance the greater Jacobite strength round the central massifs. The Hanoverians had the upper hand in the south of Scotland, but again in patchy fashion. They could not even count fully on Edinburgh and the Lothians, despite the influence here of such Scottish government as still existed. The capital's Episcopalian chapels were thronged. The Faculty of Advocates went in for some Jacobite posturing. The Royal Company of Archers, the king's bodyguard in Scotland, was deemed most unsound from a Hanoverian point of view.[27] Enough Jacobites lived in this region for them to make an impudent attempt at seizing

Edinburgh Castle for the Pretender in 1715, an attempt that failed not because of an implausible plan but because of its botched execution. Only by the skin of his teeth did Sir George Warrender of Lochend, zealous Whig merchant and Lord Provost of the capital, manage to keep it in Hanoverian hands.

Taking one thing with another, Mar was in a highly favourable position in Scotland in the autumn of 1715. Beyond the general desperation of a Tory interest faced with political and social oblivion at Whig hands, he could make a much broader appeal simply by dint of his promise to repeal the Union. To this many of his countrymen remained sullenly unreconciled. There had so far seemed nothing for it but to bottle up their resentment. Now something clicked and prompted them, as patriotic Scots and disgruntled Britons, to resort to force as the only way out of the complex of political dilemmas that beset them. The rising of 1715 was the last great national rising in Scottish history. It drew support from all ranks of men because, apart from a small element of Cameronian nationalism, the Stewarts remained the only available vehicle for anti-unionist feeling. Some Jacobites were actually Presbyterians – for example, the family of the later heroine, Flora MacDonald, whose father farmed as a tacksman on South Uist and whose mother was the daughter of a minister of the Kirk.[28] They and others would have seen the Stewarts as offering the only chance to preserve Scottish cultural and political identity in the face of growing pressure for conformity from England. The range of different expectations, idealistic or pragmatic, being frustrated by the Union could, for any real chance of fulfilment, only be vested in the Stewarts.

As the revolt got under way the two sides converged towards Stirling, right in the middle of the country astride the main route between Highlands and Lowlands. A commander who held this spot could call on support from most directions while blocking any advance from the south. At Perth, the Earl of Mar gathered a sizable rebel army, perhaps 12,000 men, then advanced against the government's forces. These, under the Duke of Argyll, numbered no more than 4,000. Even this Highland warlord quailed at the prospect before him. All Mar needed to do was attack. Though his assaults might have been repulsed, sheer attrition was bound to reduce Argyll's strength to the point where he could no longer resist because he lacked the wherewithal to replace his losses. As the Battle of Sheriffmuir was actually being fought on 13 November amid autumnal murk, a southern Jacobite army surrendered in Lancashire while the northern Whigs stormed Inverness. Yet if Mar had shoved Argyll aside it would have amounted to a more decisive turning point, surely with profound consequences. There could have been nothing to stop the Jacobites taking over Scotland, and making it the base for advance into England. In the event, Sheriffmuir turned out a blundering, chaotic affair. At the end of the short day, before the light failed, Argyll, with a mere 1,000 soldiers, was left making a stand behind some turf walls in the expectation that Mar and the roughly 4,000 men still under his control would launch a final, irresistible attack to wipe out the remnant of the Hanoverian army. The attack never came.[29]

Six weeks later the tardy arrival of James, the Old Pretender, did little to cheer the army fighting for him, especially as he brought no serious French aid in troops or supplies. When Argyll moved north after New Year in arctic weather, the Pretender's army just fell back. In a cruel but futile attempt to slow the advance, Jacobite troops torched the villages lying in its path – Auchterarder, Blackford, Crieff, Dunning and Muthill. The Pretender was mortified at this, and it certainly did his cause no good. Far worse for him, though, was how he, Mar and other Jacobite leaders just abandoned their army by slipping away in a sloop from Montrose on the night of 3 February 1716. Here was no stuff of heroic legend. The revolt had at one stage been a grave threat to the Whigs, in fitting reward for their own misdemeanours. Once it failed so miserably it became a gift to them.[30]

The Pretender returned disconsolate to France, but could not stay there under the terms of the Treaty of Utrecht (1713) now being enforced by Philippe, Duc d'Orléans, regent since the death of King Louis XIV a year before. Most unusually for a Frenchman, Philippe was an anglophile, at least in foreign policy, because he could foresee circumstances in which he might need British aid. The infant King of France, Louis XV, was sickly and seemed unlikely to survive – in which case Philippe stood next in line to the throne, provided he could repel any bid for it from the grandson of Louis XIV who was now King Felipe V of Spain, the final beneficiary of a decade of war.[31] For Orléans's own personal project of alliance with Great Britain, he therefore needed rid of the Stewarts from Versailles. James was obliged to move to Avignon, a papal enclave, then to Rome itself where, in the Palazzo Muti on the Piazza dei Santi Apostoli, he lived out the rest of his days.

In Rome the Pretender had little to do and not much money to do it with, yet time enough to fish in troubled waters wherever in Europe he spotted a chance to revive his cause. For the time being, the Anglo–French rapprochement continued, despite deep misgivings in the political elites of both nations.

Yet it was easy to see the benefits of resolving their differences by diplomacy rather than war. If they could go on to identify common interests, they would wield, as the only two great powers in Western Europe, enough of a joint military and naval power to impose their will on any neighbour nation whatsoever. Previous rivals, Holland or Sweden, had now ceased to be great powers and even the Austrian empire needed subsidies from wealthy allies to keep fighting for any length of time.[32]

Anyway, what real interest had France in the House of Stewart? It was never an especially reliable friend. The last king regnant, James VII and II, had been a British blimp of almost comic dimensions. By comparison the Hanoverians were convenient for France because their Continental territory remained vulnerable to its military power. It could always use Hanover as a bargaining counter at international conferences, typically with a view to recovering colonies and trading rights lost to the superior strength of the Royal Navy. In 1717 France publicly abandoned the Jacobite cause and entered into formal alliance with Britain. Philippe d'Orléans needed it so badly that he let his opposite number largely dictate the terms. The crushing of the Jacobite rebellion had anyway strengthened the hand of King George I, who was able to insist that the exiled Stewarts should leave French soil.[33]

If no foreign government would now make the Pretender's restoration a prime aim of policy, his cause could still be exploited should conflict with Britain threaten. Spain, for example, was attempting a revival from the mayhem of the disputed succession to its throne, in part through a forward foreign policy under the direction of Cardinal Giuliano Alberoni. He had made his way up from Italian obscurity by means eternally useful in politics. The commander of the French army in Italy, the Duc de Vendôme, liked to greet visitors while on his portable privy; Alberoni, received in this way, knelt and kissed his excellency's buttocks, exclaiming 'O culo d'angelo!' Following Vendôme to Spain, Alberoni passed into Spanish service and at length insinuated himself into high ministerial office. As a result he was in charge of the War of the Quadruple Alliance (1718–20), by which Spain sought to win back the territories it had lost in Italy under the Treaty of Utrecht. Britain was one of the countries determined to stop this. In Madrid, Alberoni welcomed an Irish Jacobite envoy, the Duke of Ormonde, who recommended a big expedition to invade England and a small diversion to invade Scotland, this to be led by the Earl Marischal.[34]

For the big expedition, Spain assembled an armada. It sailed from Cadiz in

March 1719 but, like its forerunner in 1588, was broken up by storms.[35] It was then just a tiny force of 300 Spanish soldiers that set off with the Earl Marischal and managed to reach Scotland. The sole plan for this force had been to tie up regular Hanoverian troops while the main invasion got under way, but since there was not now going to be a main invasion the lesser enterprise rather lost its point. All the same, the Jacobites established a base in the old fortress of the Mackenzies at Eilean Donan Castle at the head of Lochalsh, the long sea-loch opposite Skye. Support from the clans had been expected, but little came. Among the senior officers present, William Murray, Marquess of Tullibardine, wanted to return to Spain. The Keiths – the Earl Marischal and his brother James – were made of sterner stuff and answered Tullibardine's argument by sending the Spanish frigates away home empty of the soldiers they had brought here. This happened just in time for a squadron of the Royal Navy to enter Lochalsh. A mere 45 Spaniards defended the castle with its supplies and stocks of munitions. A bombardment and a storming party soon overwhelmed them. It captured all the arms, burned the stores and blew the castle up.[36]

But most of the Spanish troops had already gone on to the mainland with a Scottish contingent containing some famous Jacobite names, the Earl of Seaforth, Lord George Murray, Sir William Mackintosh of Borlum and Rob Roy MacGregor. They advanced up Glenshiel to be met by a British force coming from Inverness under the command of General Joseph Wightman. The site of the ensuing battle is still an awesome place, especially beneath the sort of swirling mist that lowered over the actual encounter on 5 June. On both sides of the glen huge mountains soar up from the narrow track along the River Shiel in steep slopes of rock and heather, where much of the action took place. The fighting was fierce, with the Spaniards proving themselves especially valiant, but in the end the Jacobites broke and fled. As they ran back down the glen they saved their lives because they were then too scattered a target to be mown down by the Hanoverian ordnance.[37]

This further fiasco deflated the cocky insistence of Scottish Jacobites that they were at the first chance spoiling for another round of their fight. They still had many supporters, yet it was odd how powerless these proved to shake a Hanoverian regime far from totally secure, at least to judge from its regular overreaction to internal unrest. There were two relevant examples in Scotland, the riots caused by the malt tax in Glasgow in 1725 and the Porteous Riot of 1736 in Edinburgh.

From Glasgow the government's informants were telling it, as informants often do when trouble brews, what it wanted to hear. It had, for example, this report to hand: 'Those who are enemys to the government and some who perhaps may be exasperated by what they call ill usage have I fear laid hold on the present uneasiness of the people which has been some time a fomenting, to inflame them against the English.'[38] In fact, Glaswegians were less inflamed against the English than against their own MP, the bloated Daniel Campbell of Shawfield, no romantic rebel but rather the sort of cold-blooded capitalist becoming typical of the place, and harshly Hanoverian besides. Its maddened mob made a target of this Whig wheeler-dealer as the supposed author of a detested malt tax and cause of a rise in the price of beer. When they burned down his magnificent mansion on the edge of the city they were showing also what they thought about the regime of the Prime Minister, Sir Robert Walpole. Campbell sought to shift the blame onto those mendacious merchants of Glasgow, all up to their necks in illegal trafficking of tobacco, who he claimed were seeking means to discredit good government and its steady supporters like himself as these tried to suppress corruption in the customs on the River Clyde. He linked this also to Jacobitism: 'The common cry at Glasgow nowadays is down with Walpole, down with Mr Campbell, down with the malt tax and up with Seaforth, a strange alteration in that place.'[39] The Seaforth prayed in aid here is the earl who, six years before, led his clan against the government's forces in Glenshiel (in fact now intent on making his peace, though he had not yet actually done so). The alteration that Campbell professes to find so strange in Glasgow arises from the fact of its having long been a Presbyterian stronghold unlikely to support any Jacobite – yet here it is apparently doing so. General William Wade, the Englishman commanding the troops sent to suppress the unrest, concurred. But what would he have known?

In the Edinburgh of 1736 there were those who argued it was Jacobites that incited the mob to lynch Captain John Porteous, though others, searching for an explanation at the opposite end of the political spectrum, blamed extreme Presbyterian clergymen. Probably the true explanation was the most obvious one – that this had been the ordinary people of the city with enough drink in them to give vent to feelings it was normally better to suppress. The Parliament at Westminster still felt provoked enough to indulge a proposal from blimpish English backbenchers for a bill of pains and penalties on the Scottish capital. The Duke of Argyll publicly defended it and spoke out against the punishments. The government, however, was more interested in cringing to critics than in satisfying supporters. It agreed to take over the bill and introduced its own version in the House of Lords. When pushed to take a vote on it, enough Scots peers limply followed the official line. The normal manager of Scottish affairs, the Earl of Ilay, refused to do the same yet could not bring himself to oppose his ministerial colleagues and abstained. Argyll stood firm, and so broke with the government.[40] Mischief-makers whispered that his motivation was Jacobite.

Far away in Rome, meanwhile, the Old Pretender had been steadily miscalculating the implications for himself of these British events. In 1727, as soon as he heard of the death of King George I, he set off on a year of frenzied travel and intrigue aimed at generating another Jacobite rebellion. He wrote excitedly from Nancy in Lorraine to George Lockhart of Carnwath, saying he felt it his duty 'to put myself in a condition of profiting of what might be the consequence of so great ane event, which was sensible I could never do at so great a distance as Italy'. Lockhart entertained no such illusions, knowing that in Scotland the accession of King George II had been greeted 'with the favour of the populace'. Soon the Pretender was back empty-handed in Rome, while Lockhart lost all heart for the struggle. He died in 1731, though well before then he had given up writing the account of events known to us as the Lockhart Papers. He laid down his pen in deep dejection because he now saw no way forward for the Jacobite cause: the generation ready to fight and suffer for it was dying out and giving way to one that regarded it at best with cool indifference. It must 'consequently daylie languish and in process of time be totally forgot. In which melancholy situation of the king's affairs, I leave them in the year 1728.'[41]

Scottish Jacobitism in between the two great rebellions was a paradoxical movement. It failed to exploit the widespread, often violent demonstrations of popular hostility to the government in London. Yet it survived as an ideology. Episcopalian or Catholic clergymen preached it, and plenty of landed gentlemen still listened. Scottish connections with Europe found a fresh channel through Jacobite intrigue. And in odd corners of the country, the people themselves stayed true to their old allegiance. Religion sat lightly on Prince Charles but, when he did finally appear on Scottish soil in 1745, it was in safe havens that had remained Catholic. While the social forces for another national outburst like that of 1715 were no longer to hand, just enough survived to let a new and different uprising take shape.[42]

Without Prince Charles, of course, there would have been no such thing. That still did not make him an ideal leader. He neither gave nor won trust: he never even told his father what he was up to, let alone sought parental blessing. Irresponsibility towards others, masked by exquisite manners and outward charm, remained basic to the character of this supreme egotist. He did have his virtues, those of a soldier, skill with gun or horse and endurance in adversity. In politics (as in love) he was hopeless. For every other kind of expertise in 1745 he relied on two disreputable groups of men, those governing France and those, some of them exiled Jacobites, who directed privateering business from northern French ports, partly to spite their Hanoverian enemies but more just to make money. A revolt in Scotland would force the British government to withdraw naval squadrons from convoy and patrol in the Western Approaches in order to guard the northern coastline. Piracy would then prosper, as would the nefarious designs of the French government.[43]

Britain and France were at each other's throats yet again, this time in the War of the Austrian Succession. As always their combat proved an expensive business. Feudal France, unlike booming Britain, was becoming little by little less capable of fighting such wars. In the 1740s the same arguments began to crop up at Versailles as had prevailed in the 1710s: could not some way be found for the hostility of these hereditary enemies to be replaced by an alliance that could then dictate its own terms to any conceivable rival and, even better, open up commerce between the two? The project arose from the problem that the amity, such as it was, under the regency of the Duc d'Orléans had steadily dissolved. Britain was already in the first place a maritime power and did not have means for major military campaigns in Europe. But it did meddle endlessly, often in matters to do with Hanover, and this meddling usually brought it into confrontation with France. The only solution appeared to be a change of dynasty in the United Kingdom, preferably to one that had attained its sovereignty with French help. Who else could that be but the Stewarts? Beyond this one admittedly challenging goal, there was no serious plot in Paris to seize British territory or even British colonies. The French would merely meet meddling with meddling.[44]

So the high aspirations of the young Prince Charles came in handy. He informed King Louis XV in advance of his plans, but in a way implying France itself had no part in the adventure. In fact, the reverse was true. The prince entered Scottish waters on board a frigate, the *du Teillay*, privately owned by an Irish Jacobite, Antony Walsh, but carrying a cargo of arms and ammunition collected under the express authority of the Ministry of Marine in Paris. More to the point, it came escorted by a regular French ship of the line, *L'Élisabeth*, which fought off an interception by HMS *Lyon* and allowed the prince to land on Eriskay in the Outer Hebrides on 2 August. Later, when the first encouraging reports of his success reached Versailles, the official story continued to ascribe the whole business to his personal initiative, so that French involvement could still be denied. Yet before long France openly allied itself with him and sent aid in troops, equipment and money.[45]

The French goodwill required to carry Charles to the Hebrides could not, however, raise an army for him: this he needed to do for himself. The British authorities at first kidded themselves that the rebellion could hardly be serious. They thought a mere show of force would be enough to crush it, for example, by mobilising Whig clans eager to cleave Jacobite skulls with their claymores. But, makeshift as the prince's following might be, locals with no protection were not going to stand in its way. Then the authorities in Edinburgh and London saw they had to send out General Sir John Cope, Commander-in-Chief, Scotland, to march into the Highlands and meet the Jacobites head on, just as General Joseph Wightman had done in 1719. Cope did not feel at all confident about the mission: he knew how raw and undisciplined his own troops were; otherwise they would not have been sitting in Scottish garrisons while a European war went on. So he also made them carry 1,500 spare stand of arms to hand out to loyal Highlanders. In the event there were no takers. To a muster at Crieff only the Duke of Atholl and Lord Glenorchy, heir to the Marquess of Breadalbane, turned up. They came to say they could not raise a single man.[46]

Sir John Cope's orders were then to march to Fort Augustus, the central military base in the Great Glen. On the route north, he got as far as Dalwhinnie before his nerve failed him. There at the summit of that route, a bleak spot indeed, he had to steel himself to strike west and force the dreaded 17 zigzags of the military road over the Pass of Corrieyairack, where the prince's army, eager for the fight, stood ready to meet him. Cope decided he was unlikely to manage this part of the assignment, yet he could hardly stand still and wait for the enemy to come to him. He would need for a start to be supplied in a place where there were no supplies except too much water and the diminishing herd of cattle he had brought with him. And back he could not go either because areas supposedly loyal had turned out sullenly indifferent, not even yielding enough recruits to furnish him with scouts knowing the country and able to protect him from ambush. He had to proceed to Inverness, then, and as fast as possible. He would be obliged to march still further to Aberdeen before he could ship his army south again to land at Dunbar.[47]

Meanwhile, the incredible fact was that Prince Charles and his army conquered most of Scotland by dint of walking from Glenfinnan to Edinburgh. The military roads built by General Wade across the Highlands in the last couple of decades, all at the expense of the British government, rendered the advance easier and quicker than it otherwise would have been.[48] When the Jacobite army reached Perth it gathered a second wave of recruits and doubled its strength. Once it crossed the Fords of Frew on the upper reaches of the River Forth, nothing stood between it and the capital.

With Sir John Cope wandering round the north, Edinburgh could offer at best a token resistance. Alexander Carlyle, in 1745 a student of divinity and eager amateur soldier in a volunteer company, found the Lord Provost, Archibald Stewart, so slow to arm the people 'that there was not a Whig in town who did not suspect he favoured the Pretender's cause' (he had the right name, after all). Stewart was prosecuted for this after the rebellion, but surely a proper solicitude for his citizens was his true motive. Even the venerable Dr William Wishart, principal of the university, regarded fighting as 'this rash enterprise ... exposing the flower of the youth of Edinburgh, and the hope of the next generation, to the danger of being cut off, or made prisoners and maltreated, without any just or adequate object'.[49] It was still an age when armies that suffered heavy casualties in storming a marginally defensible city might revenge themselves in rape and pillage, even massacre. For douce Edinburgh, the game was not worth the candle. Once arrived before the walls, all the Highlanders needed to do was force a gate, which they did on the evening of 16 September. In a bloodless coup, the capital of Scotland fell.[50] Cheered by an enormous crowd, Prince Charles entered the Palace of Holyroodhouse, where he would hold court for the next two months. He at once revoked the Treaty of Union.[51]

When Sir John Cope finally landed at Dunbar and Prince Charles marched out to meet him at Prestonpans, both armies were tiny, 2,500 men apiece. The battle, as distinct from the pursuit of the routed Hanoverian regiments, lasted no more than a quarter of an hour. One reason for such a swift, clean victory was the local knowledge the Jacobites managed to enlist from a sympathiser who led them across a bog and allowed them to send in their charge against Cope over dry ground. The second, and decisive, factor was the way the general's untried troops panicked and ran away. But it was a fluke. The Highland line wavered at the single discharge of Cope's artillery before his gunners abandoned it and fled, so fine was the balance of morale between the two forces.[52]

While Prestonpans decided some Scots so far sitting on the fence, it still failed to persuade any of those greater noblemen who had to be the key to eventual success. The Earl of Seaforth – out with his Mackenzies in both 1715 and 1719 – refused to move this time. The reigning Duke of Atholl was hostile, though Lord George Murray and the exiled Jacobite Duke William mobilised many of his tenants. In the same sort of way, Lord Lewis Gordon, younger son of Alexander, second Duke of Gordon, was used to rally their clan to the Jacobite side, but the duke himself lined up with the minority of Hanoverians in his county of Banff. In the Highlands and islands the passage of time had cost the prince vital support, though it had done the same for the king too. On the Hanoverian side, the Campbells were now reduced by their own chief to military impotence while, right in the north, the Mackays and the Sutherlands remained too far away to make much difference before the very end of the rebellion. Only the Munros joined Sir John Cope on his march round the region. On Skye, formerly Jacobite chiefs such as MacLeod of MacLeod and MacDonald of Sleat stayed at home; Mackinnon of Mackinnon alone came out.[53]

It was the Jacobites that needed men more, however, and they remained even weaker elsewhere, notably in the burghs. In 1715 they had been able to hold municipal elections in order to tighten their grip on some towns, but in 1745 Prince Charles could do nothing better than appoint local governors. In Edinburgh he failed to raise a regiment, as he hoped to do. Once he moved out of the capital to march south, the Whigs moved back in and stayed in charge. He only occupied Glasgow at the turn of the year after his retreat from England, and even he admitted the citizens wanted nothing to do with him. Jacobites were more or less in charge of Aberdeen in between Sir John Cope's departure for Prestonpans in September 1745 and the Duke of Cumberland's arrival on his way to Culloden in February 1746, but nobody would fight to hold the place for the prince. Inverness stayed in Hanoverian hands almost to the end of the rebellion under a motley force of independent companies formed by the Lord Advocate, Duncan Forbes of Culloden, and latterly commanded by Lord Loudoun. They retreated at the approach of Prince Charles, who then had to send part of his own force to chase them round the far north, eventually to Skye. In the same final, desperate attempt to construct a Highland bastion that could be defended till French aid came, Fort Augustus was captured, though not Fort William.[54]

Everywhere the backing Prince Charles got was marginal. This is also the right description for his whole enterprise, which never raised an army better than barely adequate for its operations. He came with little money and never raised much of that either, even though along his way he threatened to ravage the estates of lairds who would not pay him a cess, or local tax. He used the same tactic to encourage them to provide him with a quota of fighting men. But from the start, even with the boost he got from the Battle of Prestonpans, he always found it hard to hold the rebellion together. The first thought for many clansmen after such a victory was to bear their booty home, and their chieftains might need to return with them simply to recruit them all over again. On Scottish territory the prince's army was constantly vulnerable to these comings and goings, and while still in the capital he at one point found himself unable to scrape together 1,500 soldiers for a march on Berwick that he had in mind in order to seize the fortress there (Edinburgh Castle still held out against him).[55]

More support did dribble in, yet a lot of it was ambivalent. Some landed families sent their sons while the fathers stayed at home. For the few rebels of sense and substance such as Donald Cameron of Lochiel or Lord George Murray, the decision to join up with the Jacobites had clearly been difficult. This army was officered by men usually marginal to the landed elite by reason of their poverty or recklessness, while a high proportion of the foot-soldiers had been forced out – as the legal evidence later collected against them clearly confirmed, even taking account of their anxiety now to stress their unwill-ingness.[56] Altogether, Prince Charles needed to strain every nerve to bring together the 5,500 men he led into England on his foray of six weeks at the end of 1745.

It was a force pitifully small for the conquest of a European great power, and with hindsight the hopelessness of the whole enterprise can scarcely be denied. At the time, indeed, most of Prince Charles's advisers had never wanted to leave Scotland. He managed to overrule them on two grounds. The first was that massive support awaited him across the border. There was a trickle of recruits through the north-western counties of England, which housed a Catholic minority, and it even proved possible to raise a regiment in Manchester. But as the Jacobites trudged into the Midlands nobody else joined their ranks. The prince still wanted to press on to London in the bland assumption that any troops sent against him would run away without fighting, he being the representative of their lawful sovereign. This second proposition was never tested because, at the crucial council of war in Derby on 5 December, the other leaders of his army prevailed in their contrary view that, without any greater response from the English people, it would be folly to proceed. The energy of Lord George Murray's generalship and the fighting qualities of his men had got them this far, aided by the sclerotic reactions of such aged Hanoverian commanders as General George Wade. But even now the regime of King George II showed no sign of collapse. He, an experienced military commander himself, kept his head, for he could see the Jacobites' weaknesses – their shaky hold on Scotland and (here in agreement with Murray) their terminal lack of support in England. By standing firm, the king in effect forced the long retreat that ended at Culloden. The Jacobite advance had anyway been a hand-to-mouth affair, and on the road back the prince's fatal shortfalls of manpower and money would be pitilessly exposed.[57]

At Culloden on 16 April 1746, the final confrontation of Stewarts and Hanoverians took place. Prince Charles's army consisted largely of Highlanders, with small contingents of Lowlanders and then the Manchester Regiment from England, supported also by units, some Irish, of the French army. The force commanded by the Duke of Cumberland, younger son of King George II, was mostly English, but with a good number of Lowland and Highland Scots, a battalion of Ulstermen and some German mercenaries. The clash on the moor turned out quick and bloody, finishing within an hour. Following an unsuccessful Highland charge against the government's lines, the Jacobites were routed and driven from the field. Between 1,500 and 2,000 died or were wounded, while losses on the government's side amounted to 50 dead and 259 wounded. In the last pitched battle fought on British soil, the Hanoverians crushed the Stewarts.[58]

The remnants of the Jacobite army, probably no more than 2,000 men, rallied the following day to Lord George Murray at Ruthven in Badenoch. The regiments of MacPhersons and Ogilvies remained virtually intact, but the rest were the leaderless wreckage of shattered units, and nearly all the Highland chiefs had gone missing. From this force there could be no serious resistance against the British regiments about to ravage the Highlands. The region had so far escaped subjugation because its own armed strength always exceeded whatever garrisons and patrols could be spared for the far north by a basically indifferent government at Westminster. Now, perforce, a powerful

Hanoverian army had been drawn in, and almost at the first blow broke the power of the Jacobite clans. For once, Prince Charles saw things clearly. He told his remaining followers to disperse, and himself fled west towards the ocean.[59]

Along with the clansmen, the Jacobite concept and cause died at Culloden, yet these had an extraordinary afterlife in sublimated forms that survive down to our own day – and still contribute to ideas of Scotland.[60] One reason is, of course, the tragic drama of an enterprise that has never failed to appeal to posterity. It was not without an effect at the time even on the majority of Scots who had acquired an allegiance to the Hanoverian crown, who therefore deplored the arrival of Prince Charles and who would never have dreamed of following him. But many, even after Jacobitism was over and done with, still thought about Scotland. They did not wish to be members of a subjugated nation reshaped at English whim. They wanted it to retain its semi-independent status inside the United Kingdom. Despite the sacrifice of sovereignty, it preserved to them for the future much that had shaped their history while opening up new possibilities. In Scotland's black past, the winners had often hunted down and destroyed the losers. Yet now the Scots unionists shielded their anti-unionist compatriots from English witch-hunts, and did so in good conscience without in any way questioning the treaty of 1707. Jacobites in Scotland had been Scots first and Jacobites second, but now all Scots were in it – that is to say, in a new state of the nation – together. It could and did evolve to the point where nobody wanted to be a Jacobite any more.

11

Campbell: 'The whole power of Scotland'

On 15 April 1761, Archibald Campbell, third Duke of Argyll, passed away at his English country house of Whitton, 11 miles west of London. It was an easy death. In the morning, Argyll had been to see his banker, James Coutts, a brother Scot. He came home and sat down to lunch with his natural son, John Maule, and his doctor, Charles Stewart. The duke did not feel hungry, however, and said he would take nothing but a 'camomile puke'. While his companions tucked in he dozed off. Suddenly he suffered 'a convulsive motion over his body, and died in a minute'. Bleeding was the usual treatment for such conditions in the eighteenth century, yet the heart had already stopped and no blood would flow: Argyll was gone.[1]

Though the duke had been approaching 80 years of age, he remained right to the end active politically, if no longer so much physically. A general election was approaching and, as the man who ran Scottish politics, he had been busy with all sorts of local electoral deals. Now this activity came to an abrupt halt, for the successor to the dukedom, the kindly old soldier John Campbell of Mamore, had no public ambitions at all.[2] What Scotland could at least do was pay fitting tribute to the last of the great territorial noblemen who had helped to keep the nation going through its turbulent history, the turbulence being owed not least to the frequent regal minorities and, since the Union of Crowns in 1603, to the absence of the monarch in London. From there Argyll, for his final journey, retraced his steps to his ancestral home.

The duke's embalmed body lay in state at his townhouse (on the site of the London Palladium) till 1 May. Then a funeral procession formed to bear him up the long road north. Carried 'in a superb hearse richly ornamented with escutcheons', he did not reach Edinburgh till 15 May. A delegation of gentlemen waited for him at the bounds of the burgh. They led the way to the Palace of Holyroodhouse, of which he had been the hereditary keeper. He again lay in state over a weekend, and on the Monday 'the funeral procession, which was very grand, passed through the city, the great bells tolling all the while'. Crowds lined the streets. The procession took an hour to pass the West Port, and that night it stopped at Falkirk.[3]

The next day the cortège continued to Glasgow, a city the Campbells had long controlled. The Lord Provost, Andrew Cochrane, an old friend and ally of the duke, received him for the last time. Here again he lay in state. The following morning his hearse proceeded through streets lined by the militia of Argyll. It arrived at Greenock where the coffin was placed on the ducal barge, which bore it across the Firth of Clyde to the northern shore of Holy Loch, to Kilmun, the traditional resting place for the chiefs of Clan Campbell. The vault of the church of St Munn housed most of the third Duke of Argyll's ancestors, right back to Sir Duncan Campbell who had died in 1453, and here he too was buried.[4]

Campbells had been running Scotland for most of the time since the Union of 1707. During that period its politics did not really change much in some ways, even from the era of national independence before. Then the Scots had possessed a Parliament, which made them exceptions among the nations of Europe. Yet this never altered the fact that, as in most of those nations, the substance of public life in the seventeenth and the eighteenth centuries consisted in the rivalry of aristocratic factions. Ideology might enter just a little into it. Scottish Presbyterianism had political implications because it posited the co-equality of Church and state. But politicians took a different view of the matter from clerics and, while the General Assembly of the Church of Scotland made some attempt to dictate national policy in matters of interest to it, secular men of affairs seldom showed any great eagerness to accept its views. This was why the strictest Presbyterians remained dubious of an uncovenanted state. Most did not actually reject it, or at least never went so far as to fight it, but they still represented a force that the uncovenanted state did better not to provoke. A second ideology was Jacobitism, in other words, allegiance to the royal House of Stewart with its claim to indefeasible right and its tradition of absolutist government. Still, perhaps the deeper appeal to

Scots lay at an emotional level, in the conviction that they had lived from their remotest origins under the same line of kings, who always defended them and defined them as a nation separate from every other.[5]

Given how these two ideologies were diametrically opposed and how probably neither commanded a majority in the nation, the way still lay open for rule by aristocratic faction. A faction might draw strength from one or other of the ideologies, as the Campbells did from Presbyterianism or the Mackenzies did from Jacobitism. But both, like others, drew greater strength from more contingent matters, from the weight of the groups ranged behind them or from the successful careers by the great men that led them. Collective or individual fortunes rose and fell, however, and the Scottish political system remained after the Union of 1707 not much more stable than it had been before, merely diminished in stature.[6]

The reason for the diminution in stature was that the Scottish system had now been attached to the greater and somewhat different English system. For Scots, the adjustment to the ways of Westminster proved difficult and confusing. While faction is about the best term we can apply to the groups that had formed and reformed in Edinburgh, party is about the best term we can apply to the English Whigs and Tories, distant as their resemblance was to a modern party. In any event, neither gave an especially warm welcome to their new northern colleagues, and the problem was to fit faction to party. Perhaps the Jacobites, hoping to restore the legitimate line of Stewarts on the death of Queen Anne, most easily found English soulmates. Even for them, though more particularly for their rivals, it would all turn out a messy business.[7]

Up to the Union there had been four main aristocratic factions in Scotland, with little in common except each was led by a duke: Argyll, Atholl, Hamilton and Queensberry. Queensberry headed the biggest group in the old Scots Parliament, a Court party ready to support anything that the crown, represented by him as Lord High Commissioner in Edinburgh, wanted it to do. It was in many ways a random assemblage of people, some with genuine commitments (as to the Union), others with none apart from royal favour for themselves. Queensberry himself set the tone. His father had been the trusty taxman to King James VII, extracting cash from every conceivable source and, by the way, siphoning off enough to build a splendid baroque palace at Drumlanrig in Dumfriesshire as well as a townhouse in Edinburgh in the elegant style of a Parisian *hôtel particulier,* today a portal to the new

Scottish Parliament. The son won his spurs in royal service by going out in company with Bluidy Claverhouse to kill Covenanters. At the Revolution of 1688, however, he immediately reversed his position. According to George Lockhart of Carnwath, he was 'the first Scotsman that deserted over to the Prince of Orange, and from thence acquired the epithet (among honest men) of Proto-rebel. Indeed, he has ever since been so faithful to the revolution party ... that he laid hold on all occasions to oppress the royal party and interest.'[8] He continued to do signal service, notably by controlling the parliamentary protests against betrayal of the Scottish colony at Darien from 1699 to 1701. When Queen Anne came to the throne in 1702, he retained her confidence. And he was the one that at length carried the Union through the Scots Parliament. After 1707, he had a place at Westminster and remained active in the House of Lords. He served as Scottish Secretary of State from 1709 till his death in 1711. But during this couple of years his power and influence at last waned. Since some genuine competition went on between the English parties, the old Scottish Court party rather lost at Westminster its purpose and its cohesion as a rallying point for anybody and everybody wishing to support the government.

In Edinburgh, crucial support for the Court in passing the Treaty of Union had come from the faction dubbed Squadrone Volante. It won its exotic epithet for its opportunism, and got its reward in continued representation at Westminster. Its members were dissident Whigs, some of them strong Presbyterians intent above all on defending and preserving the political and religious settlement of 1688–90. They had needed to decide if the Union was the best means of achieving their aims, personal and public. In the end they did so decide, even if they could only at the last minute be sure of getting the Presbyterian establishment of the Kirk written into the treaty. Once they reached Westminster they busied themselves in different affairs, usually with a view to pleasing the English: they made friends of important leaders in the Whig party at Westminster, the so-called Junto, and in this way assured themselves of further influence in politics that their small numbers alone would hardly have merited.[9]

A further part of the winning coalition in 1707 had been the supporters of the Campbells, Dukes of Argyll after 1701, the most potent lords of the Gàidhealtachd; they were called Argathelians from the Latin name for the dukes' native county. It was typical of the winning coalition (and of Scottish politics generally) that they all the same remained at daggers drawn with the Squadrone Volante, because the latter had obstructed Argyll while he served a session as Lord High Commissioner. Their bitter rivalry extended well beyond the walls of Parliament House in Edinburgh. One leader of the Squadrone was the Duke of Montrose, who competed with Argyll for political, economic and social hegemony in the southern Highlands. This was why Argyll gave protection to Rob Roy MacGregor, who largely lived from preying on Montrose's lands. These feuds in their turn continued beyond the Union. Because in London the Squadrone had linked up with the Junto, it was all the harder for the Argathelians to form the alliances among English Whigs that their strength and their convictions should have brought them. Even inside Scotland, the Duke of Argyll managed to muddle his natural alliance with the Presbyterians. Unlike his forefathers he was in religion indifferent, which made him practical rather than dogmatic in policy on the matter, tolerant of others' convictions and favourable to a close connection of Church and state. But he was always much more interested in the army than in the Church, a matter he preferred to leave to his clever brother Archibald, Earl of Ilay (and later third duke).[10]

In the Scots Parliament, the two other main factions had usually been in opposition. One led by the Duke of Atholl was unpredictable in all but its greed. On the great question of succession to the thrones of the British Isles, Murrays of Atholl stood on either side up to the last Jacobite rising of 1745 and beyond. After a show of favour to them from Queen Anne, who created the dukedom in 1703, their fickleness merely helped their rivals, Argyll and Queensberry. The leadership of those most truculent against the Hanoverian succession was left to the House of Hamilton. The third Duke of Hamilton, 'the person of first quality and most interest in the nation', had been a gentleman of the bedchamber to King James VII and refused to desert him: 'I cannot violate my duty to my master. I must distinguish between his Popery and his Person.' The fourth duke succeeded in 1698 and found himself, for such a great lord, rather a poor man. His mother, strong-willed Dowager Duchess Anne, lived on and grudged him his allowance from their lands in Lanarkshire.[11] Still, her son would soon make his parliamentary name as leader of the Country party, to use the contemporary term for the main body of opposition in the Scots Parliament.

Even as the factions still squabbled away after the Union, there were novel and serious questions they really needed to address. First came the matter of how Scotland should actually be governed inside the United Kingdom, on which the treaty had little to say. A high degree of autonomy might be possible, with the Scots left to their own devices unless the English saw reason to intervene. Closer integration into the new realm of Great Britain was not unattractive either, though the treaty's preservation of national institutions set limits to this. The new order would see a number of variations on the possible themes played out.

The political alliance that first mastered the novel relationship of the two capitals was the one between the Squadrone Volante and the Junto. In Scotland, the Squadrone went on the offensive and sought to undermine the old Court party. The first feint came in abolishing the Scottish Privy Council. The Treaty of Union left its future open, and for the time being it still sat in Edinburgh. It was a body largely made up from the Court party just because Queensberry, as Lord High Commissioner, had for so long appointed its members. Now it seemed available as a springboard for his British ambitions, of which an initial test would come at the general election due in 1708. Neither the Junto in London nor the other factions in Scotland – Tories, Squadrone or Argathelians – were willing to leave Queensberry a clear run.[12]

In a clumsy blow at the Court party, these factions joined in legislating the Privy Council away. That had two results, one in the short term and one in the long term, one conscious and one unconscious. In the short term, the move threw the general election wide open, if in the event without much helping either the Squadrone Volante or the Argathelians. In the long term, it created a gaping void in the executive government of Scotland. For temporary, partisan reasons, an agency of evident utility just vanished: not a hopeful precedent. Some of its minor powers passed formally to the justices of the peace, some of the major ones informally to the most senior Scottish official remaining, the Lord Advocate, but this did not fully address the practical problems now so casually created. As he had been primarily a legal rather than political figure and was himself often away in London, no obvious locus existed where, above a local level, Scottish affairs could be handled in Scotland.[13]

At the general election of 1708 the Court party yet retained a majority of Scottish seats, which Queensberry would use in support of Whig government in London. The next year he became Secretary of State, though by now past his political peak. He had a Tory rival in the Earl of Mar, but less to worry about from the local Whigs so long as they stayed split between Squadrone Volante and Argathelians. The Squadrone also held fast to the Whigs in London, though over time Argyll and Ilay did manage to enhance their own connection there. Through Ilay's painstaking efforts in recruitment of new clients, the brothers' influence silently grew – 'like a pike in a tank of goldfish', as one historian put it.[14] They still aroused suspicion in England, mainly on account of the duke's imperious but erratic character, which made him enemies more powerful than he was. Anyway, in his contempt for the Squadrone he could hardly get closer to the Junto.[15]

Then at Westminster a snap general election in 1710 put the Whigs out and the Tories in. Of all the extraordinary things the Duke of Argyll now sought alliance with the latter, evidently in the hope of taking political control in Scotland. He got something else. He was offered command of an army meant to bring the War of the Spanish Succession, so far fought out in central Europe, into the heart of Spain itself. A keen soldier ever ready to put himself in the line of fire, he could not resist the offer. In 1711 he sailed for Barcelona, only to preside over a debacle that saw the extinction of Catalan autonomy: the second time he had performed that sort of service for a small nation. He retired to Minorca, ruling it as governor for a year or two.[16] Meanwhile in Scotland, the incumbent Secretary of State, Queensberry, was kept on so as not to alienate the old Court party but he got rather ignored and was soon to die anyway. The Earl of Mar moved into the political void, only to demonstrate that a Tory trying to govern Scotland faced even greater problems than any Whig.

Of course all this political manoeuvring proceeded with no reference to the Scots people, yet 1713 saw one of the few occasions when they did impinge on it slightly. As the Spanish war drew to a close, the government still sought to raise the money for it. The resort now was to a malt tax, something unexceptionable in England – but the Treaty of Union promised no such tax would be imposed on Scotland while the war lasted. It was not enough that the war had reached its endgame. The war had yet actually to stop, something that enraged Scotland so furiously as to prompt the Earl of Seafield, another architect of the Union, to move its repeal in the House of Lords. Even Ilay was reported as having 'insisted very violently upon the necessity of prosecuting the desolutione, be the consequences what will'.[17] This was the division lost only by four votes that marked the sole effort by Scotland, before 2014, to end the Union peacefully.

Perhaps for many the point lay not so much in ending the Union as in thwarting the government, so fickle and febrile was the political mood of the age. Anyway, everybody now awaited the death of Queen Anne. When she did die in August

1714 and the Elector of Hanover succeeded, the game changed. King George I ushered in the epoch of Whig hegemony for both Scotland and England.

The Argathelians should have found a big opportunity in the Hanoverian succession, yet it was the Squadrone Volante that again seized the advantage. One of its leaders, the Duke of Roxburghe, had somewhere along his path through life learned German, an accomplishment almost unheard of at the time. So he could converse easily with King George (others had to stumble along in Latin). While Argyll did hold on to his minor offices, it was the Squadrone that got the plum jobs, the Duke of Roxburghe as keeper of the great seal (who controlled patronage) and the Duke of Montrose as Scottish Secretary of State.[18]

The Hanoverian succession dissolved Parliament. For the following general election, George I wanted to impress unity on all who had rallied in his support, so as to be able to form a government of king's friends free from faction and formidable to the remaining opposition. Among the Scots, therefore, the Squadrone Volante and the Argathelians had to grit their teeth and work together. They won their reward in reducing the Tory opposition to a mere 7 out of Scotland's 45 seats. Otherwise, in the division of the spoils, the Squadrone came out a little ahead of the Argathelians. Between the two the competition for favours left little over for anybody else, and in their melee the concept of a Court party vanished. The haughty Duke of Argyll led an exclusive group bound to him by ties of family and clientage, while the Squadrone was more open only in its structure, under a cabal of leaders, not in its aims.[19]

The Jacobite rising soon exposed a further political norm of the completed Union, that the parliamentary representation by no means reflected opinion in the country. On the Whig side, the Campbells did well out of the affair, even though a cadet branch of the family, headed by John, Earl of Breadalbane, actually joined the rebels; he died before official inquiries into his behaviour had been concluded, and he left his title to a loyal son. As for the chief of the clan, the Duke of Argyll did contain the rebellion. Yet King George I took a dim view of all the indulgence to Jacobites in the aftermath. He thought they should have been hotly pursued from the field of Sheriffmuir – yet Argyll, instead of cornering and slaughtering them, had let them get away, perhaps on purpose. Leaving aside the small fact that the duke did not command the troops to do anything else, there might have been some truth in the jaundiced royal reading of events. Argyll, as a member of the Scottish elite, knew that for the sake of the nation it needed in the end to reconcile the vanquished. All agreed that impatient English pressure should not be allowed to damage the fabric of society in Scotland, at least not its landowning class. If in that cause the conduct of some had to be forgiven and forgotten, rather than held up to grisly example, then so be it: the duke's behaviour was testimony to an underlying good sense and humanity he seldom displayed in public.[20]

The main Whig casualty of 1715 was rather the Secretary of State, the Duke of Montrose, who resigned. This leader of the Squadrone Volante would accept no other office, and after the rebellion was over he, too, sought pardons for some of the miscreants. He wrote to a kinsman that punishment was being 'extended much further than either you or I would wish, the consequence of which . . . can never be pleasing to us as Scots men and will not do the K[ing] service'.[21] This was as close as Montrose ever came to a principle, his exertions being otherwise devoted to a quest after the money he needed for purchases of land and for the subsequent repayment of debts incurred through his unerringly bad investments. His difficulties were not eased by his ill-advised quarrel with Rob Roy MacGregor. The two of them had once been on quite friendly terms, probably motivated from Montrose's side by the hope Rob Roy might supply evidence of secret correspondence between the Duke of Argyll and the Pretender. Montrose and Rob Roy engaged together in profitable trade in cattle, till one of Rob's drovers ran off with £1,000 of the duke's money. He demanded redress and threatened legal proceedings, which must have caused loud laughter among the unruly MacGregors. What the duke got instead was open war, with Rob Roy raiding him and his tenants from a safe haven in the neighbouring territory of the Campbells. This war the outlaw won. Rob Roy's 'insolences are insupportable', the duke fumed as he had troops called in to collect rents in the Highland parts of his estate. None of this said much for his political nous.

The Duke of Roxburghe was meanwhile serving as Secretary of State. Every Scottish politician of any standing in the new era had to keep abreast of developments in London. Roxburghe, though not lacking ability, never seemed to realise this. He made little effort to build up his puny faction. For all existing political interests a crux came with the Septennial Act of 1716, extending the life of a Parliament from three years to seven. Its main purpose was to curb the Tory opposition, but it had the wider and more durable effect of isolating British politicians even further from anything that might be called public opinion. In Scotland it allowed the leaders of the various factions all the time they needed to consolidate a hold on the parliamentary seats they had already won, amid greater stability and with less cost now that they so seldom needed to bother about the voters.[22] Roxburghe neglected the opportunities; not so Ilay.

The other British political development every astute parliamentarian needed to watch out for was the rise of Sir Robert Walpole, the first man to whom history accords the title of Prime Minister. By the general election of 1722 he had secured this position. The Duke of Roxburghe failed to read the signs but the brothers Campbell were quick to move in where the Squadrone Volante feared to tread. A member of it, George Baillie, MP for Berwickshire, observed that the Duke of Argyll, 'by the favour of the ministry, in the controverted elections for Scotland has at least two-thirds of the Scots members in the House of Commons and for what I know R[oxburghe] has none who depend on him except the Advocat and one or two more.'[23] Such successes persuaded Walpole to harness Argyll's Scottish strength, however rebarbative his personality. Thanks especially to hard graft by the Earl of Ilay, the favourable position won in 1722 steadily turned into a complete ascendancy supported by a well-oiled electoral machine. The next time the voters went to the polls in 1728, the machine carried all before it.

The Duke of Roxburghe, last of the king's friends of 1714, had still managed to cling on as Secretary of State for a while and even retained disposal of some patronage. But the writing was on the wall for him and the Squadrone Volante. Sir Robert Walpole moved swiftly when the duke not only opposed the malt tax of 1725 but also condoned or even encouraged the unrest and civil disobedience that followed its imposition. The Prime Minister sent the Earl of Ilay to Scotland to restore order, which he promptly did. Roxburghe was dismissed but not replaced – or rather, Ilay now moved up to become the first of the great Scottish managers, in other words, a man not needing any high post in government for political control of the country but resting content with the informal manipulation of offices and elections, all in an environment practically free of ideology. Duncan Forbes of Culloden, the new Lord Advocate, rejoiced at the effects: 'For some time at least, we shall not be troubled by that nuisance, which we have so long complained of, a Scots Secretary, either at full length or in miniature; if any one Scotsman had absolute power, we are in the same slavery as ever, whether that person be a fair man or a black man, a peer or a commoner, 6 foot or 5 foot high, and the dependence of the country will be on that man, and not on those that made him.'[24]

For this fresh start the Earl of Ilay could build on a strong base in the

Argathelian faction that his brother, not himself caring to get involved in any managerial detail, delivered over to him. The two had worked together so far but, now they were accepting some serious political responsibility, it was perhaps better for them to part company to some extent. As their kinswoman Lady Louisa Stuart remarked, 'the duke thought Lord Ilay undignified and time-serving; Lord Ilay thought the duke wrongheaded and romantic.'[25] Ilay worked instead with Duncan Forbes and the judge, Andrew Fletcher, Lord Milton. The trio dispensed patronage, rigged elections and supervised administration. For Sir Robert Walpole their value lay in keeping the Scots quiet. The English establishment had realised it could not forget Scotland, as it would doubtless have preferred to do. Yet it could not leave Scotland in the hands of some local bigwig who might enlist his countrymen to form an independent interest, possibly defiant, even capable of blackmailing the government in London. The bottom line was that, then as now, English Ministers found Scotland hard to understand. What they needed was a local agent or agents to guide their hands or act for them without claiming any independent authority. The Scottish system of political management gave them just that.

The Earl of Ilay perfected the methods, dangling preferments and favours before his MPs or, even in advance, working in the constituencies to get complaisant candidates elected. He then made a handsome contribution to Sir Robert Walpole's dominance in the House of Commons, where he could rely on a bloc of trusty Scots, and in the House of Lords too, where a biddable group of representative peers got chosen from the 'king's list'.[26] However dubious the methods, the Scottish political nation now had, thanks to Ilay, something it had not had before, and something it soon decided it liked: politicians sitting squarely at the centre of a British system in slavish adherence to the dominant figure of the day, in this case Walpole. Few Scots needed to feel left out – on the contrary, once they learned to cultivate the habits of dependence they found it easy to surmount any mere differences of political opinion.

Walpole himself remarked in 1725 at the generosity of Ilay in not aiming 'to ingross the whole power of Scotland into his own hands'. The Squadrone Volante offered a fine example: crushed in real terms, it still claimed a small share of patronage, with the Duke of Montrose, for example, retaining some minor offices. Official promotion turned into the main mechanism of a political system where the formal apparatus of government had been largely dismantled. Even Jacobites might return to the fold now that nobody really reckoned with a comeback for the House of Stewart, so long as they took an oath of allegiance, acted circumspectly and kept their inner thoughts to themselves. There were areas of the country where, without such compromise, the government's writ could hardly run. When General George Wade was building roads in the north, he got approaches from people with no other means of contacting the government. One arrived in 1731 from the still suspect Alexander Robertson of Struan, who was told he could work his way back into favour if he passed on information about papists in his part of Highland Perthshire. For the government it surely made sense to treat wayward local leaders with kid gloves rather than chastise them with scorpions. That could only make open enemies of them, whereas a lenient approach might lead them from grudging initial compliance towards long-term effective submission even to a dynasty they detested.[27]

Kings were still potent politicians in their own right, and in 1727 a new one, George II, made a difference in Scotland. He saw in the Duke of Argyll an over-mighty subject, and disliked the Earl of Ilay. Though, for the sake of his close links to Sir Robert Walpole, the earl was tolerated, he had no chance of getting into the Cabinet. Yet in practice this scarcely affected the part he played as Scottish manager. In London a mere aide, in Scotland he ruled the roost – and continued to enjoy Walpole's confidence in either case. Not least, Ilay helped to keep his own obstreperous elder brother quiet. He had shown his commitment to law and order, dealing with disturbances and restoring repose, occasionally sitting himself in the High Court of Justiciary as Lord Justice General, one of his honorary offices, which he sometimes turned into a real one. He again did sterling electoral service at the first parliamentary polls of the new reign.[28] As for positive policies, he lent a guiding hand to the foundation of both the Royal Bank of Scotland and the board of trustees for manufactures. Over time he extended his influence in the Church of Scotland and in the universities. In both spheres he was a benign force, damping Calvinist recalcitrance, promoting enlightened talent: among other beneficiaries, the architect William Adam, the poet Allan Ramsay and the playwright John Home all enjoyed his patronage. Scotland lived on largely through its institutions, and these institutions became Argathelian strongholds.[29]

In the Earl of Ilay's hands, then, management stretched far beyond conventional politics. On behalf of the crown, he chose the judges and the lawyers needed for other offices. He himself regularly attended the House of Lords, where a growing number of civil appeals from the Court of Session in

Edinburgh gave him a useful role in London and many legal contacts at home. As for the Church, the crown presented about one-third of the ministers, and co-operation with the rest of the lay patrons began to build up a tame majority in the General Assembly. The crown also named most professors in the universities; under Ilay, himself a high intellectual, this was a progressive and creative influence. Over Scotland at large, his system developed in particular a strong urban base. Campbells ruled Glasgow anyway. In Edinburgh, a perennial struggle between the two interests represented on the council – the merchants and the tradesmen – produced a string of legal disputes concerning the burgh's sett. In 1729, the parties asked Ilay in his capacity as Lord Justice General to act as their arbiter. He had no political interest to advance here, or so he said: 'My chief business is to reconcile or determine some disputes and mutual claims that have lately arisen between the merchants and the trade people of this town.' He personally heard the evidence right through and issued his decree in 1730. With it he gave wider power to the Lord Provost and the merchants but set out more clearly how the electoral rights of the trades might be safeguarded or even extended. This redefined the sett, which from now on continued almost unchanged till it was reformed away in 1833. In practically all that time the town council of Edinburgh remained a loyal, not to say subservient, supporter of government, as Ilay had meant it to be.[30]

But the Scottish manager's life before long grew more complicated. This was partly because of fresh challenges to Sir Robert Walpole in London, where the parliamentary opposition (including the remnants of the Squadrone Volante) had passed its nadir and begun to revive a little. Its members now called themselves Patriots, vaunting themselves as defenders in the last ditch of national interests and liberties against the overweening Prime Minister. Still, their first big effort, at the general election of 1734, came to little. In Scotland the Squadrone cried corruption, but the contrast between them and Ilay was simply the contrast between unsuccessful corruption and successful corruption. A rising star of the opposition, Andrew Mitchell, complained to the former Lord Advocate, Robert Dundas of Arniston, about the appointment of sheriffs, that 'the whole nomination seems to be little more than a list of the sons, sons-in-law, and alliance of those gentlemen whom the D[uke] of A[rgyll] has thought fit to place upon the bench.' Dundas in turn evinced contempt for the representative peers, saying that if God 'hath destined us for destruction, to be sure we must fall into it. For the other house, nothing can be expected of them, such a sixteen as we have. God pity them.'[31]

It took the fortuitous Porteous Riot of 1736 to make a real difference. The riot was over in a single night, but big trouble for Scotland followed from the subsequent investigation by the House of Lords. It reached conclusions humiliating to the nation and its capital, therefore offensive to both the Duke of Argyll and the Earl of Ilay. Lord Carteret, an old enemy of Sir Robert Walpole's, had pressed for this. He sought to show the Scots that 'by taking the Campbells to govern them, they had chosen governors that could not protect them'. As Lord Hervey observed, Walpole resisted the move because 'he feared it might hurt Lord Ilay, for he had no more mind to be thought incapable of protecting Lord Ilay than Lord Ilay had a mind to be thought incapable of protecting the Scotch'. The inquiry went ahead all the same and afterwards Ilay, or more ruefully his brother, proved powerless to prevent the retribution meted out on Edinburgh. Even the cautious Ilay ventured to abstain on the government's bill of pains and penalties, while Argyll could scarcely contain his fury. Once the legislation was in force, Ilay set about limiting the damage, but Argyll awaited his chance to strike back.[32]

The chance came in 1739. Sir Robert Walpole was trying to resist a chauvinist clamour in London for war against Spain over trading rights in the Caribbean Sea, and the Duke of Argyll swung his weight behind the popular demand. In a speech to the House of Lords, he declared Britain had been dishonoured yet caught out unprepared for a naval conflict. This proved too much for Walpole, who sacked the duke from his remaining offices.[33] It did not affect the more reliable Earl of Ilay, who also preferred peace if at all possible. What finally decided the matter was the Prime Minister's inability to silence the combative chorus in the House of Commons. By the end of the year Britain was again fighting Spain.

This sequence of events split the Argathelians, between the followers of Ilay and the 'Duke of Argyll's gang'. The duke's defection from the government was a huge coup for the Patriots. Through the parliamentary sessions of 1740 and 1741, he lashed Sir Robert Walpole over corruption, runaway public expenditure and conduct of the war with Spain, in speeches making him the idol of the opposition. Ilay went to Scotland in an effort to limit the damage to the government there. With little love now lost between the two brothers, they needed for long periods to communicate through go-betweens, usually William Steuart, MP for the Elgin Burghs. He was, according to Lord Hervey, 'an adroit fellow and a common friend to them both' and through him 'they acted as much in concert as if they both had been the most intimate and most cordial friends'.[34] This was a rosy view of their relations, which in fact threatened to reduce Scottish politics to a state of factional confusion not seen since the first years of the Union.

At the next general election in 1741 the brothers Campbell openly fought each other, at least by proxy. In the Aberdeen Burghs, for example, the Earl of Ilay secured the return of John Maule, his own private secretary (and illegitimate son). In Ayrshire it was the Duke of Argyll's candidate, Patrick Craufurd, that triumphed by turning out the incumbent James Campbell: really, what had things come to if the duke could do this to a man of his own name?[35] He gave a vituperative explanation to his nephew, James Stuart Mackenzie:

> Ilay wants to make all his friends tools to Walpole because he finds his ends in so doing. Your brother [the Earl of] Bute and I would have all our friends independent and of all other Ministers whatsoever. My brother Ilay prefers his places to all other considerations, friendship, honour, relation, gratitude and service to his country seem at present to have no weight with him. Your brother Bute and I think our honour that these considerations should weigh with us.[36]

After the election Walpole remained Prime Minister, just about, now without the support of a majority of Scots MPs. Neither for him nor for them was it a stable situation. Failing to control the new House of Commons, he stepped down within a year. Ilay went with him, and told Lord Milton that 'the political game is over'.[37]

The government next formed in London was intended as a broad bottom, strengthening the thinned following of the retired Sir Robert Walpole with the addition of some Patriots. In Scotland, it owed most to the Duke of Argyll. Though solicitous for the public positions of his clients, and even urging an overture to the cowed Tories, he remained uninterested in any high political office for himself. What he wanted was to be commander-in-chief of the British army, and this prize he now won. As for the humdrum business of running Scotland, there was nothing for it but to turn back to the remnant of the Squadrone Volante. The leader it offered was the Marquess of Tweeddale, just re-elected as a representative peer and 'a man of truth and honour' according to the judge, Lord Tinwald. To mark the difference from the previous regime, the government revived for Tweeddale the post of Scottish Secretary of State, dormant since 1725. He brought his own men in with him, Robert Dundas of Arniston as Solicitor General and Thomas

Hay of Huntington who became his correspondent and political representative in Edinburgh. They hardly compensated for the manifold failings that Tweeddale's conduct of affairs soon revealed, typified by the fact that he only bothered to visit Scotland once during his four years in post. But he did have at his right hand the tireless Lord Milton, still serving as Lord Justice Clerk, who drew no distinction between law and politics but went ahead and tackled any problem he saw.[38]

Lord Milton also continued to hobnob, however, with the Earl of Ilay. That helped the earl, though out of power, to preserve a prominence built up over two decades and difficult to dismantle. The Squadrone Volante, while yearning to exclude him, found this easier said than done. Unlike his brother, he did not throw tantrums at being thwarted, but merely made in his turn a mild request for clients holding office to be left in place. To Tweeddale it seemed a small price for neutralising a potential enemy. John Drummond, MP for Perthshire, commented: 'Lord Ilay keeps still all he had and makes his court well but some of his old friends have been unkind in their characters of him and he was a harsher minister and slower and indolent in the last elections, but he could make bricks without straw.' Herein lay his superiority over his rivals. Meanwhile it was the Duke of Argyll's career that hastened to an end. Once in command of the army he found himself, needless to say, at odds with the government in the conduct of the War of the Austrian Succession now under way. He soon resigned and rushed off again into the political wilderness. In October 1743 he died. His stormy character had damaged Ilay who remained, however, able to give this cool assessment: 'The great error in my brother's conduct was that he was too apt to quarrel and knew whom he fought against, but never considered whom he fought for.'[39] Since the dead man had left no legitimate issue, Ilay came into his kingdom as third Duke of Argyll.

The new duke was different from the old in many ways: calmer, wiser, deeper in his thinking and finer in his tastes – in that respect, as a ruler, almost worthy of the Italian Renaissance. At the least, he did establish a generous tradition of noble patronage for the awakening Scottish Enlightenment. Horace Walpole said he 'had a great thirst for books; a head admirably turned to mechanics; was a patron of ingenious men, a promoter of discoveries, and one of the first great encouragers of planting [of trees]'. Sir John Clerk of Penicuik called on him in London to view the large room in which he kept his books, a vast collection of them together with all sorts of curiosities, especially mathematical instruments, lying 'in a very careless philosophic manner'. When the duke built himself a new library it was 90 feet long, 27 feet broad and 21 feet high, with galleries at either end: he considered it one of the finest rooms in London and it gave him 'great joy'. His real home was here, rather than in the Highlands, but that did not make the British political establishment any less suspicious of him after 1745.[40]

As the Jacobite rebellion unfolded, Lord Milton reported loyally and dutifully to the Marquess of Tweeddale, though there was nothing the Secretary of State knew that the Duke of Argyll did not know too. The reason Milton could straddle both camps was his incredible industry, which made him not just a judge but also the linchpin of the entire civil administration. It allowed him besides to befriend and advise the English military commanders in Scotland, Sir John Cope and Joshua Guest, though he wondered why they took so little notice of his reports on the first, ominous Jacobite stirrings in the north; they regretted it once Prince Charles landed. All these connections led Milton straight, after the Duke of Cumberland arrived in Scotland, into his inner counsels. Two months before the Battle of Culloden, the duke wrote: 'The Justice Clerk is as able and willing a man as there exists, but too much an Argyle man to be trusted with all that will be necessary in this affair ... he is of vast use to me and does all I want with the greatest readiness imaginable.'[41] The immediate aftermath of the rising even widened the range of Milton's authority. He corresponded with London, directed intelligence, prepared evidence for trials, smoothed relations between the military and civil powers, enforced new laws against Episcopalians and organised the transport of Jacobite prisoners to England.[42] This was all to the good because the incompetent Tweeddale had resigned as Scottish Secretary in January 1746 while the rebellion was still in full swing. The office lapsed till 1885.

The problem of how Scotland should be managed therefore dragged on well beyond the Battle of Culloden. Lord Milton would have been the obvious person to take over the task, except that in the immense labour of clearing up after the Jacobite rebellion he drove himself to the point where his health suffered. He resigned as Lord Justice Clerk and became keeper of the signet, a job that involved virtually no work, paid him more and gave him some patronage.[43] Could this be the basis for a new, more relaxed form of management? The problem was that Milton probably liked all the detail he had had to deal with, and that in any event he would always regard himself as subordinate to the Duke of Argyll. The duke was the only man really capable of filling the political void, but stood under suspicion of closet Jacobitism, if groundlessly so; while Clan Campbell had failed to mobilise effectively during the rebellion, the blame lay rather at the door of the old duke and his tampering with the social and military structures on his lands. But the new duke's critics were right to think that once again he wanted to treat the rebels leniently, just as after the rebellion of 1715.

Jacobitism had spent itself, but there were still prominent Englishmen blind to the fact. An anti-Scottish backlash was whipped up by, among others, the Duke of Cumberland who, not being a bright man, had come to the conclusion that most Scots were at least passive Jacobites. The notion inspired a rare burst of Scottish legislation at Westminster. Undoubtedly beneficial was the Act abolishing heritable jurisdictions and ending the power of the Highland chiefs or others to oppress their people. The measure gave further satisfaction to those distrustful of the Duke of Argyll, who held the biggest heritable jurisdiction of all.[44] Much less beneficial was the Disarming Act, including a ban on Highland dress that Lord Milton correctly feared would cause hardship to poor, innocent peasants who had never worn breeks.

While the Duke of Argyll's survival as a politician seemed for the time being doubtful, he still could not be ignored. With his nominees entrenched in so many institutions, little went on in Scotland that he was not somehow party to, while rising men even yet sought patronage from him before they sought it elsewhere. And new leaders in London, the Duke of Newcastle or his brother Henry Pelham, saw Argyll as somebody they could and should work with, especially for the valuable votes he commanded in the House of Commons. At the same time, they tried to bypass him and build a Scottish parliamentary interest of their own, making clear that jobs could be had through channels other than the Argathelian ones. The more local notabilities that got involved in the management of Scotland, they reckoned, the more that English politicians like themselves would need to act as arbiters.[45] But their efforts to breathe life into the Squadrone Volante came to nothing. They contacted one of its survivors, the Earl of Marchmont: 'He said he knew no heads of it, but the tails of it made a great bustle and were very violent.'[46] At any rate, all this was something Argyll could live with, as a man who in various wary working relationships had been balancing interests for two decades. In 1748 he even consented to the appointment of a sworn enemy, Robert Dundas of Arniston from the Squadrone, as Lord President of the Court of Session – something that could scarcely have happened at any earlier point.

By the general election of 1747 the Duke of Argyll and Henry Pelham were co-operating on a list of favoured candidates, and 35 of the 45 men on it got in. To Westminster this was an impressive demonstration of the duke's power, and his stock with the Pelham brothers rose higher. Altogether, he was getting through the bad patch he had struck at the fall of Sir Robert Walpole, and taking up again his accustomed role of managing Scotland for the government in London. After Pelham's death in 1754 the Duke of Newcastle became Prime Minister. He followed the same tactic of working with Argyll while trying to subvert him with favours for his rivals, notably Robert Dundas younger of Armiston who became Lord Advocate. But again, English interference in Scottish politics amounted to little otherwise. After the general election of 1754, Newcastle found he controlled 3 MPs out of the 45. It was time to come to terms with Argyll.[47]

So far from being dislodged, the Duke of Argyll had continued to accumulate political capital that he vested with both old friends and former enemies. Alexander Carlyle recorded that the duke, now aided once more by Lord Milton, 'wisely gained the heart of the Jacobites, who were still very numerous, by adopting the most lenient measures and taking the distressed families under their protection, while the Squadrone party continued as violent against them as ever. This made them almost universally successful in the parliamentary election that followed the rebellion, and established their power till the death of the duke in 1761.'[48] Unfriendly manoeuvres in any other quarter scarcely troubled him. By 1749 or 1750 he had in effect already resumed his position as manager of Scotland and he then made so bold as to hold lavish court at the Palace of Holyroodhouse just four years after Prince Charles had trodden the same hallowed halls. The signal came over loud and clear: legitimate authority was in charge once again, and in this abode of kings Scots could do business with it.

For the next decade Argyll kept a working majority in the various public bodies essential to the running of Scotland – the Courts of Session and Justiciary, the exchequer, the board of trustees and, after 1755, the commission for the forfeited estates. In the General Assembly of the Church of Scotland, he supported the young men of the Moderate party who would offer leadership not in a doctrinal but in a political sense, as genteel, learned, tolerant and respectable clerics promoting sound learning and good morals.[49] The duke showed special favour to the city of Edinburgh, supervising at Westminster the complex of legislation that authorised improvement of the Old Town, including the City Chambers and the North Bridge, and that laid the foundations for building the New Town.[50] He did not forget Glasgow in various regulations favourable to the commodities it traded. From commissions for Scots officers in the British army to bounties for Scots skippers in their fishing fleet, Argyll's magnanimity spread far and wide. He did not take office as Secretary of State: he did not need to and doubtless preferred not to while he had Lord Milton to perform all the official drudgery.[51] King George II himself called Argyll 'the viceroy of Scotland'.[52]

The surprising thing would have been if the influence of this stable and benign regime had not spread beyond Scotland to reinforce its place in the Union. What clinched the matter was that the Scots and the English began to fight willingly side by side, instead of against each other. For the Scottish majority of non-Jacobites, French aid for the Stewarts fixed the idea of France as a political enemy, lively though old cultural contacts remained. When the Seven Years' War broke out in 1756, it offered Scotland a great and popular British cause. Even the English began to notice, even indeed the English political oligarchy, especially William Pitt the Elder, who managed the war. Scotland's vital contribution to victory included the raising of 26 regiments. Pitt later recalled that these, 'the very rebels', were employed 'in the service and defence of their country . . . They were reclaimed by this means; they fought our battles, they cheerfully bled in defence of those liberties which they had attempted to overthrow but a few years before.' The Duke of Argyll, 'the old governor of Scotland' as colleagues in London dubbed him, got great credit for his part in raising the troops.[53] In the last few years before his death in 1761, his political reputation stood higher than ever before. And with justice: it was a matter not just of the Highland regiments he raised, but also of the example he set in the development of his own estates with, for the rest of Scotland, the encouragement of industry and banking – indeed, a general extension of prosperity and contentment. Argyll's life had been quite a stormy one but it drew to a close in tranquillity, with the duke equally at home and secure in two capitals, and altogether a pillar of the British state.

The only problem was that this third Duke of Argyll, too, died without a legitimate heir of his body. The title passed to his cousin John Campbell of Mamore, a veteran soldier – too elderly to participate in politics and uninterested in doing so. But the brothers Campbell had had a sister, Lady Anne, married to James Stuart, second Earl of Bute. He died young, and the Campbells became guardians to his two sons, John, the third earl, and

James Stuart Mackenzie (who assumed the additional surname to secure an inheritance). The boys possessed their own seat of Mountstuart on the Isle of Bute, but they spent a lot of time at Inveraray. The intellectual influence of Argyll on his nephews could be discerned in their enthusiasm respectively for botany and astronomy, and later in the elder one's generous cultural patronage of Robert Adam (who built him an English residence at Luton Hoo), of Tobias Smollett and of William Robertson. Yet in politics Bute evinced independence. From the middle of the 1750s he built up a small group of friends in Scotland who acted outside the Argathelian interest. The two noble houses had been closely related, by marriage and politics, for many years. They quarrelled in 1758, but soon a new king in London and a new duke at Inveraray called for a patching up.[54]

The Earl of Bute had by then also made his own mark in London. He moved there in haste at the outbreak of rebellion in 1745. With introductions at the highest level, he soon became, despite his surname, a close friend of the Hanoverian royal family, first of Frederick, Prince of Wales (who died in 1751), then of others. So trusted was Bute as then to be appointed tutor to the teenager who in 1760 would ascend the throne as King George III. The fatherless young prince came to hero-worship the earl. The latter's political instruction was evidently idealistic, a little too idealistic for the age: it exalted patriotism, while deploring faction and corruption. On his succession, George wished to end the jaded Whig hegemony and declared he would rule free of partisan pressures – in token of which, he appointed his tutor as his Prime Minister. While he aimed to be a patriot king, all he really did was destabilise, for a period, the evolving parliamentary system.[55] Bute himself had never been a permanent resident of Scotland since 1745 and, whatever his countrymen's hopes, did not now intend to deal personally with their affairs: he was far too busy being a bad Prime Minister. It might have counted as a great success for the nation that a Scot achieved the highest political office just half a century or so after the Union, but things did not work out like that.

As Prime Minister, the Earl of Bute did on the odd occasion intervene in Scotland when a matter specially interested him: for example, it was at his hands that the decisive appointment of William Robertson as principal of the University of Edinburgh came, along with a few other academic promotions. But in general Bute found jobbery in his homeland as distasteful as jobbery in London. Alas, by now Scottish politics consisted of little else, and perhaps what most Scots feared was alien control of it through somebody like the busybody Duke of Newcastle.[56] Aware of this, Bute first entrusted patronage to one of his acolytes, Gilbert Elliot of Minto, MP for Selkirkshire. Elliot wrote to Lord Milton in Edinburgh: 'I protest I do my part in it from a mere sense of duty, for this detail is to me no amusement, and hardly comes within the pale of what is called ambition.'[57] Milton's skills and knowledge remained indispensable, but for advice – as opposed to proficiency – the new order relied on two younger men, William Mure of Caldwell, a baron of exchequer, and the Revd John Home, minister and tragedian, who between them knew all the rising stars in the universities and the Church. Finally the whole operation was drawn together when Bute recalled his brother from a budding diplomatic career, made him MP for Ross and set him to work on all the Scots drudgery. Caustic and cocky but careless, James Stuart Mackenzie by no means liked being dragged home from an agreeable posting in Turin. Bute told him this was necessary to protect their late uncle's friends. From 1761 to 1763 Stuart Mackenzie in London shared the patronage with Milton in Edinburgh, still active till he lapsed into senile dementia in 1764. Mackenzie learned a lot, though that made the chores of management no more palatable to him. Still, overall this regime did have an air of rejuvenation about it, with its preference for new blood and fresh hopes rather than old lags pestering for preferment.

But, from his outset as Prime Minister, Lord Bute ran into the barrage of abuse and obstruction that within a year drove him from office. London's political old lags found no trouble whipping up English public opinion against a Scot whom they cruelly pilloried as a crawler to the king and a leech on their liberties. He lacked the political skills to counter this, in fact even the spirit to fight back. After he resigned in 1763 he went straight back to his private pursuits and devoted himself to them for the rest of his life. Just to make sure he was gone for good, the head of the next government, George Grenville, extracted from the king a promise that his predecessor 'should never directly or indirectly . . . have anything to do with his business, nor give advice on anything whatsoever'.[58] Bute had been the first Scottish Prime Minister of the United Kingdom, and perhaps the worst. For a century no Scot would seek to emulate him in the highest office. Stuart Mackenzie soon followed his brother out, dismissed as lord privy seal for Scotland, banished from court and cut off from all patronage.

Renewal of Scottish politics had run into the sands. With the entire Argathelian connection now out of power and not coming back, it remained unclear what would happen next in Scotland. That really depended on what would happen next in London, which was equally unclear. Even if it had been clear, or clearer, there remained the problem that English understanding of Scottish politics remained minimal. The Lord Chancellor of England, Lord Hardwicke, wrote at this juncture to the Duke of Newcastle: 'My apprehension is, to keep down the Highland influence, which has always been either Jacobite in itself, or has supported the Jacobites in order to avail itself of their strength. The remains of the Squadrone are the true Whig interest in Scotland, but they have few capable men amongst them.'[59]

The question of how to manage Scotland was not going to disappear, however. On the formation of Lord Rockingham's government in 1765, the Duke of Newcastle asked the Lord President of the Court of Session, Robert Dundas, Lord Arniston, to act for it. Arniston declined because he thought that incompatible with his judicial duties – a significant decision since it established from now on the political impartiality of the Scots bench, if not of the bar. Anyway, Rockingham himself did not really want to put any one man in charge of Scotland. The Duke of Grafton, who followed him as Prime Minister in 1768–70, apparently relied again on James Stuart Mackenzie to carry out some of his former functions. James Boswell called Sir Alexander Gilmour, MP for Midlothian, the real power in Scotland: hardly a serious idea when he owed his seat to the Dundases. The Lord Chief Justice of England was a Scot, born William Murray at Scone, and now Earl of Mansfield. He lacked the time to deal with Scottish affairs in person, but he had the means to queer the pitch for anybody else through his membership of the Cabinet and his standing in the Upper House; he might have worked in Scotland through his own heir and nephew, Viscount Stormont, who, however, happened to be out of the country as British ambassador to Vienna. The Dukes of Buccleuch, Gordon and Hamilton were minors, the Dukes of Atholl and Montrose, as well as the Marquess of Tweeddale, were in their dotage.[60] It did not help matters in Scotland that in London there followed meanwhile a succession of brief governments, none of them trusted by King George III. With the old differences between Whigs and Tories fading, political parties were not organised or powerful enough to impose themselves on the monarch.

After 1707 the Scottish governmental apparatus had been largely dismantled without any care being taken for adequate substitutes. In these circumstances the country's political management could be quite informal and often turned out erratic. That followed from the terms of the new British politics as set from London, which aimed at adequate control of Scotland in return for minimal attention to it; from the Scottish point of view the trick was to get the rewards without arousing English suspicions. Sixty years after the Union, this no longer seemed to be working. The scope for Scottish management had indeed shrunk because it depended in good part on parliamentary stability at a higher level – and that dissolved with the accession of King George III. Aspirant Scots, having nobody to speak for them in London who was not himself prey to the conflict of faction, needed to fend for themselves even in routine patronage. For their part, governments neither knew nor cared who were likely to prove their more able or faithful Scottish servants. Scotland hardly ever came up in Cabinet, for example, and further down the administrative chain nothing at all was known of it. Of course, this did allow Scotland to carry on developing as a sort of semi-independent nation, at least in purely domestic affairs. But as a structure for the Union it just would not do.

12

Dundas: 'Never completely subdued'

On 15 November 1773, the justices of the peace of Perthshire gathered at Ballindean House, Sir James Wedderburn's mansion near the village of Inchture overlooking the Carse of Gowrie. They came to hear the case of Joseph Knight, a black man about 20 years old who had been Sir James's slave in Jamaica. The landowner bought him as a small boy just off a ship from Africa, but he was a kind master who treated his pathetic piece of human cargo well, taught the lad to read and write and at length had him baptised as a Christian. When Wedderburn returned home with a fortune earned from his plantation, he took Joseph with him. Now he acquired the house and estate of Ballindean with the purpose of becoming a Scottish country gentleman, common practice among those who had gone out to the colonies in pursuit of ambitions that would have been much harder to fulfil at home. Joseph continued to attend him as a personal servant.

At the big house there was also a chambermaid, a local lass called Anne Thomson. Joseph Knight fell in love with her, and they conceived a child. Sir James Wedderburn sacked the offending girl, but still gave Knight money to support the expenses of the pregnancy, including the rent of a room for mother and baby in nearby Dundee. The newborn infant died, however, and Wedderburn stopped the allowance. Nothing daunted, Joseph went ahead and married Anne. He then wanted to leave his position in Sir James's household and move in with his wife. His master would not agree and sought a warrant from the justices of the county to have Knight detained as his slave, whom he was now intent on sending back to Jamaica: hence the hearing of the case at Ballindean.

The justices questioned Joseph Knight and at the end of their inquiry found against him. But he still managed to get his case brought before the sheriff of Perth, John Swinton of Swinton, who reversed the decision, ruling that 'that the state of slavery is not recognised by the laws of this kingdom and is inconsistent with the principles thereof'. In any event, 'the regulations in Jamaica concerning slaves do not extend to this kingdom'. Swinton therefore 'repelled the defender's claim to perpetual service'. Sir James Wedderburn appealed in his turn. The resulting litigation in the Court of Session went on till 1778, for the case aroused great attention and in it the foremost counsel of the day took part. The printed pleadings were comprehensive and learned. Those for Knight stressed the iniquities of the slave trade and challenged traditional legal and economic arguments in favour of slavery. The final opinions of the 12 judges varied. All denied Wedderburn could send somebody back to Jamaica against his will, but three accepted he had the right to Knight's services for life without wages. Only Alexander Boswell, Lord Auchinleck, asserted that slavery was unchristian and that Knight was 'our brother; and he is a man, although not our colour'.[1] Overall the court confirmed Swinton's judgment. By this decision, slavery was in effect declared illegal in Scotland: from now on any slave setting foot in the country would become by that fact free.[2]

Pleading for Joseph Knight, the Lord Advocate, Henry Dundas, had put up a brilliant defence of him. Lord Auchinleck's son, James Boswell, a former classmate of Dundas's at the University of Edinburgh, wrote: 'I cannot too highly praise the speech which Mr Dundas generously contributed to the cause of the sooty stranger.' The performance typified the man during this early liberal stage of his career, a career that in general was already well advanced. In 1766 he had been appointed Solicitor General for Scotland at the age of 24. The job doubtless came to him as a member of the most distinguished legal dynasty in the land, whose ancestors had graced the bench in the Court of Session for more than a century. In this first official position the young lawyer handled a number of big cases, and handled them well. The job was besides a good springboard into politics, and at the general election of 1774 Dundas got himself elected MP for his native Midlothian. A few months later the post of Lord Advocate became vacant, so he had almost at once risen to be the chief officer of government for the whole of Scotland. Boswell turned from goodwill to scarcely controllable jealousy: 'Harry Dundas is going to be made King's Advocate – Lord Advocate at 33!' he howled. 'I cannot help being angry and somewhat fretful at this. He has, to be sure, strong parts. But he is a coarse, unlettered, unfanciful dog. Why is he so lucky?'[3]

The answer to the anguished question came in Dundas's own behaviour. He treated the Lord Advocate's job as not only a legal but also a political one, by contrast with others who regarded it as a mere stepping stone to the bench. Indeed, bred as a lawyer though Dundas was, he always saw himself as first and foremost a politician, and never hesitated to spurn at once the chances of further legal preferment that came his way. This was good for Scotland, because Scotland needed effective politicians more than clever lawyers, having a dearth of the first and a glut of the second.[4]

And Dundas did all this as an urbane child of the Scottish Enlightenment. He might not have been a thinker profound enough to make an original contribution to its evolution, but he knew a good mind when he met one, and he took practical advice from both Adam Smith and Adam Ferguson, among many others. If it had been true, as some have claimed, that Dundas lacked all interest in ideas, then it was strange that the favourite pastime of his youth, which he could have spent just boozing and whoring, should have been to move in Edinburgh's literary circles, where endless ideas were discussed; strange, too, that he should have won and kept the friendship and respect of leading intellectuals of his day.[5]

As for his political career, Dundas started that at the right time too, stepping into the void of leadership and management left in Scotland by the decay of the Argathelian regime. This regime had been an aristocratic one, but none of the other great Scots noblemen found himself in a position to take it over. Many had since 1707 been absentees, no longer ruling their estates in person. In politics they might command the odd parliamentary seat, perhaps two, but most Scottish constituencies were nowadays fought and won by shifting coalitions among the lesser landed gentry. While still according the nobility a distant deference, these men were the ones that occupied the local seats of power. In other words, they emerged as a political class, if at first lacking organisation and direction. As they often also had a legal and administrative background lacking in the superior ranks, a national governing interest formed that was more or less free of party. The change from a Scotland ruled by the high aristocracy to a Scotland ruled by the landed gentry may seem in today's terms a minor one. All the same, it marked a decisive step away from the nation's past and towards modernity.

It remained for this new national governing interest to be bound together in connection with London. Here was the part taken by Dundas, himself typical of it. In Midlothian his family had supported the Whig faction, the Squadrone Volante, since its formation in the final Scots Parliament. He enjoyed a legacy to draw on, then, and at first it prompted him to liberal measures. They give a clue to his underlying motives later obscured by the demands of a darkening era in British and imperial politics. At heart he was a cautious reformer.[6]

Dundas's reforms arose in the main from personal, practical experience of politics and government, and of defects he discovered there. Standing at the top of his agenda when he got to Westminster in 1774 was the electoral system of the Scottish counties. It was a hot topic among the Scots who had just been to the polls, in Midlothian and elsewhere. The system needed reform merely to preserve it in the condition envisaged back in 1707, which was to keep things going as they had been before. Voters qualified themselves not by possession or occupancy of land but by feudal superiority over it; owners and feudal superiors were usually the same people but not always, and they did not need to be. At the outset any such distinction was rare, with the result that the same sort of MPs sat in the House of Commons as had sat in the Scots Parliament – men from old families, at one with and attentive to the fellows they represented. Given a narrow franchise, some constituencies did soon turn moribund. But in others the member had to work hard, to an extent unnecessary in English seats, to court, sweeten or cajole the electors. These did not hesitate to issue instructions to him on how to cast his vote in Parliament, something thought outrageous in England. He could, after all, lose the next poll by the defection of just a few supporters when the electorates ranged in size from few more than 200 in the most populous countries down to a handful in the smallest.[7]

The antique Scottish system did have some small virtues of its own, then, but since the Union it had been corrupted. Scots law allowed a technical separation of superiority and ownership of the land. As time went on this separation became more frequent. The purpose was to create individual feudal holdings that carried with them a vote. In this way a superior could multiply the votes he controlled and so expand his electoral influence. He did it by dividing up his superiority into portions qualifying for the franchise and selling them or even giving them away, to friends and supporters, perhaps to an obliging lawyer from Edinburgh, a rich merchant from Glasgow, an influential resident of London. Such exploitation of the superiority in no way affected the ownership of the land, but it meant that in the constituency the actual proprietors might come to be outnumbered at the polls by various species of carpetbagger. The system lent itself to abuse, and by the later eighteenth century the abuse had sometimes grown gross in the pursuit of local political feuds among the superiors.[8]

The system was perhaps not beyond saving. Hope of saving it was strong in many electorates, including Midlothian's. The county contained big estates but many of the landowners were public-spirited lawyers of wealth, culture and independence, resident here because they could ride into Edinburgh in an hour or two. It was easy for Dundas to appeal to them, as at one public meeting: 'The abuse which has crept in of late years, of allowing gentlemen of large estates as many proxies in the election of a member of Parliament as they have qualifications on their estates, is a most shameful practice, utterly repugnant to the spirit and intention of the election laws, and totally subversive of the constitution.' Instead a big landowner should 'seek to gain influence not by a preponderating number of votes, but by the way he does his duty to his neighbours, and thus deserves popularity'.[9]

Dundas was speaking in support of a bill to redefine the voting qualifications, which he introduced in 1775. It would have repealed the Act of the Scots Parliament allowing the feudal superiority of land, and the vote with it, to be separated from the ownership. Now, even if the superiority should be transferred, the vote would have remained with the original feuar, rendering impossible the creation of further fictitious votes. The bill dealt with the existing ones by stipulating that for purposes of qualification the superiority had to be genuine, not in temporary conveyance or subject to conditions. And finally Dundas wanted to impose an oath on each freeholder that he fulfilled the terms of all the relevant statutes. Had the bill passed, noblemen could no longer have manipulated the polls from a distance. But it got lost in the maze of parliamentary procedure, and Dundas in the end was forced to abandon it. Already formidable obstacles existed to an active programme of legislation for Scotland, as no special arrangements for it existed in a Parliament at Westminster dominated by Englishmen.[10]

A second piece of liberal legislation from Dundas was the bill for relief of Scottish Catholics that he intended to introduce in the parliamentary session of 1778–79. Most of its potential beneficiaries lived in the Highlands, and he hoped to recruit among them for regiments to fight in the War of American Independence now reaching a critical stage. These communities had suffered disabilities ever since the Reformation of 1560, intensified after the Revolution of 1688. Various laws forbade, under draconian penalties, the saying of Mass and any form of Romish instruction or proselytisation, as well as the inheritance of land by a Catholic if the nearest Protestant heir objected.[11]

Persecution under the penal laws had ceased, however, and the current practical effect was a gradual shrinking of the Catholic population. It included now just one resident noble family, Traquair, and no more than a handful of other landowners. The rest were poor, illiterate peasants, numbering 30,000 at the outside; even so, whenever they had got the chance – as in the Jacobite rebellions – they showed they could produce a useful fighting force.[12] Now there seemed little reason to maintain on the statute book laws that had fallen into disuse. Dundas proposed a basic change: Catholics, so long as they took an oath renouncing the Stewarts' claim to the throne and the civil jurisdiction of the Pope, should be able to own property, inherit land and join the army just like any other Scot. In stating his intentions, he said that 'the object is only to repeal a penal law, which from the beginning has been considered so cruel as to have been seldom executed'.[13]

This time the resistance arose not at Westminster, where some relief of English Catholics had already been legislated, but at home in Scotland. In fact, Dundas's measure met with such ferocious popular opposition – culminating in riots, burning and looting in Edinburgh and Glasgow – that an astonished and appalled government had to drop it. The failure of Catholic relief was a trauma not just for the country's leading politician but also for the entire community of enlightened minds; Principal William Robertson of the University of Edinburgh, for example, had been a leading advocate of it, and for his pains was threatened in person by the furious mob. All the political weight he and the other leaders of society could muster had been thrown on the side of a liberal reform, yet the people of Scotland showed they could not always be led from the top. When it came to Catholicism, they saw their bigotry as part of their liberty.[14]

In an enlightened age, more liberal attitudes had at least started to trickle down, however, fast enough for Dundas at length to bring about with little trouble a general emancipation of religious minorities. Under his legislation for Episcopalians in 1792 (perhaps a trial run) and then again for Catholics in 1793, they were to enjoy the same freedom of worship and rights to property as everybody else. By now war had broken out between Britain and revolutionary France, a war destined to last two decades. It tested the social resilience of both countries and, against this background, everybody did better to forget older domestic enmities.[15]

The Episcopalians were a second denomination against which the worst of the penal laws had not been enforced in recent times. They remained ineligible for civil or military service in the state, and neither noblemen nor commoners could vote for parliamentary representatives. But a sect so long in decline was incapable of posing any real threat, even if minded to. It was hard put just to maintain a clergy, which numbered about 50, compared to 800 at the turn of the century. They continued to pray for the king, unspecified, and not for the Hanoverians by name right till the death in 1788 of Prince Charles, to them King Charles III *de jure*. The Revd Abernethy Drummond, Bishop of Edinburgh, was a Jacobite yet also a realist. He knew most of his flock would balk at recognising the succession of the prince's brother, Henry Cardinal of York. A meeting of the eight bishops resolved, with just two dissentients, that Henry had commitments to the Pope disqualifying him as head of a sovereign state. The Episcopalians then started to pray for King George III. Drummond brought this to the attention of Dundas, who at once agreed to repeal the penal laws.[16]

In the light of experience, Catholic relief appeared a more delicate matter. That the climate of opinion had changed so much in a couple of decades might be hard to credit. But the enlightened elite was all along in favour of toleration: Abbé Paul MacPherson said 'it was perfectly ashamed of the barbarity and wild enthusiasm which had pervaded and blinded the inferior ranks of our countrymen.' And the intolerance of Scots at large seemed by now allayed. Economic growth began to attract Catholics into the central belt from the Highlands and from Ireland; if not popular, they were no longer alien. War with France made a difference in reminding people of the military prowess of the Catholic clans. Revolutionary excesses awakened sympathy for the persecuted French church – and the Scots College in Paris was closed down. The Comte d'Artois, one day to ascend the throne as King Charles X of France, fled to Edinburgh and set up court in the Palace of Holyroodhouse. Mass was celebrated there for the first time since the residence of the Duke of Albany, later King James VII, more than a century before. It became quite a social attraction. In the Lowlands, priests had not been seen out and about for a quarter of a millennium. Now clerical refugees could be spotted on their way to give French lessons to the natives or, in time, to minister to prisoners of war.[17] Altogether, there was no longer any great opposition in Scotland to Catholic emancipation, and the legislation passed with little trouble.

Dundas found it necessary not just to repeal outdated Scottish laws but also to deal with some signs of institutional wear and tear, most obvious in the judicial system. Social and economic change overloaded it. Proceedings in the courts grew slower and more uncertain, vitiating the virtues of Scottish jurisprudence. One problem lay in the quality of the bench. Because of the rewards, then as now, in private practice, it could be hard to persuade the best advocates to become judges. Mediocrities had to be promoted instead, sometimes on partisan grounds. Here too, Dundas sought to impose higher standards.[18]

Yet little improvement could be effected without greater financial resources for a system always run on a shoestring. Dundas had suggested raising the judges' salaries in 1779, and again in 1781, but was told in Whitehall the money could not be found. In 1785 he tried a different tack, suggesting the number of gowns in the Court of Session should be reduced, by natural wastage, from 15 to 10, while the salary left over would be divided among the rest. He embodied these proposals in his Diminishing Bill.[19]

It was in the circumstances a sensible measure, yet again Dundas found it impossible to win enough support. Instead he provoked a typical Scottish political row, of a type to become wearily familiar over the next two centuries, with much hot air expended on the systematic misrepresentation of motives while serious debate never got off the ground. Resistance at Westminster was fanned by uproar in Scotland. Dundas soon found he was touching a raw nerve burning with anxieties, less about the merits of the case than about the nation's status in the Union. And he was doubtless surprised, as we might be, to find in its natural leaders such perturbation on that score so long after 1707.[20] As soon as the bill was introduced in the House of Commons, its critics claimed it needed the prior consent of the king for a measure that would alter article 19 of the Treaty of Union, the one guaranteeing for ever the form and status of the Court of Session. The consent, once obtained, still failed to satisfy the opposition, which with petitions and protests and personal pressures on the MPs proved strong enough to force the withdrawal of the measure. The Solicitor General, Henry Dundas's nephew Robert, remarked: 'We did everything in our power to carry it through. But though the interest and influence of administration was at that time most intensive, and though every exertion was needed to persuade people of the necessity of some such change, our most steady and zealous personal friends even deserted us.'[21]

Abandonment of the Diminishing Bill still failed to calm ruffled feelings in the country at large. Henry Dundas at length conceded that 'so great a prejudice went forth in Scotland against the proposition that the design was necessarily abandoned'.[22] This was in the course of his announcement that the judges' salaries were to be raised anyway, having fallen so far behind the English equivalents. The increase would be financed by a charge against the revenue from the customs and by a new stamp duty on Scottish legal proceedings. These constitutional sensibilities also carried a cost, then. It had turned out that at any given time there were in fact two obstacles to be reckoned with against an active programme of Scottish legislation, not just indifference and congestion at Westminster, but also prickliness and fault-finding at home: the arrogance of the English and the obstinacy of the Scots.

Beyond the technicalities of ruling Scotland, Dundas saw some social problems looming large, especially in the Highlands now that the Jacobite dust had at last settled. The legislation for the region after 1745 succeeded in dismantling the traditional structure of clanship. Relations among the different ranks of Highland society turned from feudal to commercial. But this meant that in remote and inhospitable regions there might be little to hold communities together and to keep the people where they were when they had become free to leave as they wished. Emigration to America was rife. It disturbed the conservative landowners of the eighteenth century who – in contrast to their utilitarian successors of the nineteenth century – favoured retaining and increasing the population on the land as a social and economic asset for themselves and the nation. In this particular, the old hierarchical view of society lived on.[23]

Dundas studied and understood the problems. In a paper of 1775, he gave due weight to one conventional explanation: 'The severity of some great proprietors by a precipitous and injudicious rise of rents was the immediate cause of emigration in some part of the country.' But this could not be the whole story. Dundas went on to note that the old Highland chiefs had wanted as many men as possible on their lands in order to manifest their power. Stripped of that after 1745, they were left with little choice but to regard themselves as commercial landlords and their dependants as mere tenants. There had always been emigration from the overpopulated north of Scotland, attested not least by the many Highlanders in the Lowlands: 'more than half of our day labourers, of our menial servants, our chairmen, porters, of our workmen of every kind'. But it was by the collapse of a whole social system that they were 'induced to look for protection on the other side of the Atlantic, or, to speak more properly, are induced to wander there for want of that cherishment and protection that their fathers had felt in their old habitation'.[24]

The answer would be to find some substitute for the traditional social order. Striking was Dundas's conclusion that the state ought to see to this, though it followed from his view of how legislation had helped to cause the problem. He dismissed any objection that the state should not be expected to pamper a rebellious race: 'It is to talk like children to talk of any danger from disaffection in the north. There is no such thing and it ought to be the object of every wise ruler in this country to cherish and make proper use of the Highlands of Scotland.' What was more, he doubted the value, not to say legality, of banning emigration: 'in a small country, where there are daily opportunities of getting away, such an idea is impracticable.' Policy should instead be concentrated on inducements for people to stay. As a first step, the estates forfeited by Jacobite families might be handed back to them, to symbolise a new policy of repairing the social fabric.[25] This policy Dundas would implement as soon as he could – though in the event that meant not till 1784.

Meanwhile the outbreak of war in America in 1776 demanded more immediate action, since every able-bodied emigrant might add to the rebels' strength and reduce Britain's. Highland proprietors, led by Sir James Grant of Grant, clamoured for the government to do something. Only administrative measures could be taken quickly enough. So Dundas did forbid the Scottish board of customs to clear from its ports, while hostilities lasted, any more ships carrying emigrants, while sheriffs instructed ministers of the Kirk to pass news of the prohibition on to their flocks. But he still insisted this could not be, once normal conditions returned, a permanent solution: 'If there were no such pretence as that of rebellion in America, it would be wild to think of keeping your subjects at home by force.' He had seen the true reason for the rising tide of emigration: the social and economic revolution in the Highlands since 1745. He was the first politician to put his finger on that and to draw the consequences: the region could not be left to itself, but would need much more systematic thought about its problems as well as concentrated effort to solve them.[26]

As he rose higher in politics, Dundas had to spend more and more time in London, but he was fortunate in the dependable lieutenant he could rely on at home in Scotland – his nephew, Robert Dundas of Arniston, whom he made first Solicitor General and then Lord Advocate. A diligent factotum, Robert proved his worth. For example, he it was that brought to his uncle's attention how Highland policy showed no sign of working the benign effects expected, so that more radical remedies were starting to be imposed by the independent actions of landowners. In 1792 he already deplored the spread of sheep-farming, 'a measure very unpopular in those Highland districts where sheep are not yet introduced, as it tends to remove the inhabitants of these estates from their small possessions and dwelling houses'.[27] What became known in Gaelic oral tradition as *Bliadhna nan Caorach*, 'the year of the sheep', indeed saw in Easter Ross the first popular protest against the sort of agricultural improvement that expelled poor Highlanders from their old homes.

The problem was not going to go away, and there was still some hope that new laws might be able to deal with it. A further burst of legislation followed after 1801, at a time when Henry Dundas himself was out of office but continued to control Scotland through another nephew, William Dundas, MP for Sutherland, and his cousin by marriage, Charles Hope of Granton, the new Lord Advocate. Their emphasis at first lay still on curing the symptoms of emigration rather than on tackling deeper causes. Hope passed in 1803 an Act with the declared purpose of ending hardship on voyages across the Atlantic Ocean by setting minimum standards of equipment and victualling for the ships. Yet, in his words, the actual intention was 'to prevent the effects of that pernicious spirit of discontent, which had been raised among the people . . . aided, no doubt, in some few cases, by the impolitic conduct of the landholders, in attempting changes and improvements too rapidly'. The law pushed up the cost of a passage and by that alone emigration was stanched.[28]

Yet this could be but a temporary measure, and it did not answer the long-term needs. A new century made new solutions possible. There was, for example, a question whether capital investment in the Highlands would be useful. To answer it the rulers of Scotland turned to Thomas Telford, born in Dumfriesshire, apprenticed as a stonemason in Edinburgh and now, after half a lifetime of big projects in England, the outstanding civil engineer of his age. The first task handed him was to think up fresh ideas for economic development. He wrote two reports. One concerned what was to become the Caledonian Canal, to open the West Highlands to European commerce by linking the region up the Great Glen with the North Sea and avoiding hazardous voyages round Cape Wrath. Completed in 1822, it was as a piece of construction a work of genius – but still an economic failure. The second report detailed the region's need for roads and bridges, and became the blueprint for its modern network of communications on which work started up from about 1810.[29]

The big question remained why emigration still continued, and on to this the Dundases put an old friend, Henry Mackenzie, best remembered today as a sentimental novelist though he also, being a qualified lawyer, had an official career as collector of taxes for Scotland. His report indicated how distant sentiment in the Scottish elite lay from the brutal commercialism now commencing its Highland reign. He recalled that the earlier phase of emigration had followed from destruction of the clans. An impersonal cash nexus filled their place. Worse, the population had risen beyond the region's capacity to feed it. Now underlying discontent was aggravated by war, emigration and the introduction of sheep. This, Mackenzie reported, 'tends evidently to dissolve all connection between the great landed proprietors and the body of the people, it turns the domains of the latter [*sic*] into a mere chattel, productive only of so much money to the proprietor without influence or attachment even from the few inhabitants who occupy them. It may thus be considered as tending to increase the propensity to a mere trading and manufacturing community.'[30]

The double aspect of this interventionist policy, what we might call the Tory approach to Highland improvement, was still being recommended in official papers two decades later. Yet it did not work. In expecting the same spectacular success from application to the Highlands of means used earlier for improvement of the Lowlands, it hopelessly underestimated the problems of soil, terrain and climate. Nor, since the application was not coercive, did it overcome reluctance among Highlanders to co-operate. Above all, it was just unable to cope with their soaring population. There had always been a demographic safety valve to ease similar strains in the Lowlands because it was easy for displaced agricultural workers to move to the towns. That would be much more difficult in the Highlands. At the time of Dr Alexander Webster's unofficial census of Scotland in 1755, the population of what were to become the seven crofting counties had stood at about 250,000. When it reached its peak in the 1840s, it would be over 400,000. Such congestion made it impossible to deter emigrants when North America offered them unlimited freehold land. A fundamental aim of the Tories' approach proved, if benevolent, impracticable. With their own policy faltering, they could not stop much more drastic changes being imposed on a helpless people by what can be called the Liberal approach to Highland development – that is, the clearances.[31]

Altogether, we must conclude, the legislative achievements of the Dundas despotism were rather meagre. It is true the men governing Scotland were far from obsessive legislators, but only passed laws when they had to. Otherwise administrative instruments and discretionary powers were thought quite adequate for domestic purposes. At the same time, it must be admitted that, even in cases of recourse to legislation, neither Dundas nor his closest associates were good at getting it through. They tended to balk at the first opposition, which just encouraged their critics. But it would turn out they were not alone: complaints about the many hindrances to Scottish legislation at Westminster, mainly because of English ignorance and indifference, sounded right up till the re-establishment of the Scottish Parliament in 1999.

Yet the regime of the Dundases cannot be regarded as an ineffective one. On the contrary, they were without doubt the most successful governors of Scotland till we come to the twentieth century. It was just that the great virtue of their rule lay in what we might call their pre-modern politics. To their covetous countrymen, the best things they did were to obtain and distribute the largesse of the British state, for particular projects of expenditure and then for official appointments or for pensions awarded to public servants, their wives and children. All this went on not in response to democratic pressures, as in a later Scotland, but mainly through applications and solicitations by well-connected persons. In this sense, Henry Dundas revived the role of Scottish political manager, and he played it more successfully than his predecessors. It outlived him and remained of prime importance in Scottish public life right till the Reform Act of 1832, indeed beyond.[32]

Dundas acquired his skills in patronage early on as he set about constructing at Westminster a Scottish faction of his own that he could add to the majority of whichever governments he served in. Through all the ups and downs in his career, he made sure this stock of political capital remained profitably invested. For the British state there were obvious rewards in accommodating Dundas and his requirements. Before 1782, he was already providing the government of Lord North with a phalanx of Scottish support in the House of Commons, much appreciated as the going got tough in America. With that war lost, he steered an astute course through the consequent crisis at Westminster. He came out on the other side with a firm attachment to the Prime Minister who cured the crisis, William Pitt the Younger. The first big test of their alliance came in 1784, when they fought and won a general election against both the recently dislodged Lord North and the leader of the Whig opposition, Charles James Fox. Robert Burns, no less, celebrated the achievement with an honourable mention for the 'slee Dundas [who] aroused the class, benorth the Roman wa', man'. It should be noted that the Scots 'slee' is of wider reference than the English 'sly', meaning skilled, clever, expert or wise rather than just crafty or cunning. In the final stanza of his poem on the election, recounting what Scotland had done for Willie (Pitt), Burns fairly swaggered:

> But, word an' blow, North, Fox and Co.,
> Gowffed Willie like a ba', man,
> Till Southron raise, an' coost their claise
> Behind him in a raw, man:
> An' Caledon threw by the drone,
> An' did her whittle draw, man,
> An' swoor fu' rude, thro' dirt and blood
> To mak it guid in law, man.[33]

For the next two decades, the most important personal bond in British politics was that between the English Prime Minister, austere and distant, and his Scottish right-hand man, bluff and hearty. It was their difficult path to power that forged their bond, which grew ever stronger as they then worked in unison on complex administrative problems and fought a war together. Amid the vagaries of political life, it loosened somewhat afterwards, but never broke. Right at the end of Pitt's days, in 1805 and 1806, it was restored to being as close as it had ever been. Nathaniel Wraxall described the initial stage: 'If Pitt attained the first place in the state, Dundas may with truth be said to have gained the second; for though he was not a Cabinet Minister, yet in essential functions of official authority and influence, he far outweighed either of the Secretaries of State, or even the Chancellor [who were all in the House of Lords]. Dundas, by his presence on the Treasury bench, came into daily contact with Pitt during many months of the year.' Wraxall, an English MP, was a ludicrous pest, but his judgments could be shrewd. Here he saw to the bottom of a situation that escaped many observers. They regarded Dundas as a politician of the second rank, diligent and useful to be sure, but now at his limits – this might have been Pitt's opinion too. He himself made the difference by overshadowing his Cabinet and reducing it to a nullity. The way was then clear for Dundas, a man from outside the magic ruling circle and by no stretch of the imagination a rival, to reach an unusually powerful informal position. His surviving correspondence with Pitt is small, and they seldom even had official meetings. They would discuss and settle everything when they went for a ride or walk at the beginning and end of the day, in summer often staying out till 10 or 11 o'clock.[34]

Secure in London and with his finger in every political pie in Scotland, from this point on in charge of India too, Dundas could steadily build his edifice of patronage, picking out able Scots to sponsor as the best candidates for particular posts or tasks. The clincher in the process might take place at the mansion he bought on the western side of Wimbledon Common outside London. Called Cannizaro after an Italian duke who had lived there, it proved perfect as a social venue for politicians, with 'burgundy and blasphemy' always on offer. Pitt often came to stay overnight, as did many others. In March 1787, Dundas wrote to the father of economics, Adam Smith, who was visiting from Scotland: 'I am glad you have got vacation. Mr Pitt, Mr [William] Grenville and your humble servant are clearly of opinion that you cannot spend it so well as here. The weather is fine, my villa at Wimbledon a most comfortable healthy place. You shall have a comfortable room and as the business is much relaxed we shall have time to discuss all your books with you every evening.' This was the occasion when, on Pitt's insistence, the company stood till Smith was seated, because they were all his pupils.[35]

If that was Dundas in London, there could be no end to what he might do in Scotland. According to Thomas Somerville, he 'was incessantly and disinterestedly active in meliorating the condition of all orders of men to the utmost extent of the influence which he derived from his official station . . . The augmentation of the salaries of the judges and officers of the Court of Session, of the stipends of the clergy, and of all the servants of the public in Scotland are chiefly to be ascribed to his influence and advice.'[36] Of course it was of advantage to him to increase the size and wealth of the official establishment. But it is easy to forget, in times when the state does so much, the importance that patronage assumed in times when the state did little. It represented far and away the biggest item of business for Scottish government, and nobody conducting this government could avoid engaging in it. A comment of Dundas's own confirmed how painstaking he was: 'I never made a promise in my life to any man. When I intended to serve a man, I waited till I could do it. I can also say that I never allowed a second day to pass without answering every letter addressed to me requiring one.'[37]

Dundas's papers overflow with applications for patronage. Some of the material was summarised for him in 1801, when he started clearing his cupboards on what he assumed to be his retiral. A bundle of 600 solici-tations was weeded out for destruction. In fact, it escaped and found its way at length to the National Library of Scotland. How much of the business it contains is impossible to say; it includes only unsuccessful and not any successful requests, (for which the papers must have been forwarded else-where) nor any appointments that might have been made without written application, nor anything in India. The volume of cases here, at 100 a year, two a week, at least shows the minimum of what Dundas had to deal with, and there is no reason to think the sample unrepresentative. The most appli-cations, 27 per cent of the total, were for the armed forces, about evenly divided between the navy and the army. The next biggest group, of 19 per cent, was for posts in the civil service. Then, at 14 per cent, came appeals for pensions, often from dependants of dead officials. About 9 per cent were for patronage in the Church and 6 per cent for appointments in the universities or patronage of literary works. Legal posts accounted for 2 per cent, as did requests for jobs in the colonies. Applications for peerages, or elevations within the peerage, were the subject of 1 per cent. The rest was miscellaneous.[38]

Scotland's share of patronage did rise. After the turn of the nineteenth century, when it had a population one-sixth of England's, it was getting, in value, more than one-quarter of official pensions and one-third of sinecures. Even then demand outran supply – 'at present I stand debarred from granting any more pensions on the Scotch establishment by a representation from the Chief Baron [of Exchequer],' Dundas once reported. The English thought the Scots got too much, and Parliament would at length limit the amount available to them. The manager defended his system, however: 'I believe for a number of years back the small funds at the king's disposal in Scotland have been distributed with great purity and impartiality. They are given either to people of rank, with inadequate fortunes, to literary characters, or to females in urgent and needy circumstances.' If this was corruption, contemporar-ies found it hard to see.[39] Without doubt, however, the main purpose from Dundas's point of view was to build up the Scottish faction he controlled in the House of Commons. It was a successful endeavour, crowned at the general election of 1796 when, of the 45 Scots MPs, he got 43 returned in his own interest.[40]

A secondary effect of Dundas's system was much more important: it reconciled Scots to the British state, about which many had had mixed feelings ever since 1707. Once a source of ills, it was now a source of benefits, not just in any general political or social sense but also often in a personal sense. A tertiary effect was that Scots came to feel more British, and to be accepted by the English as British. Their domestic affairs were then no longer merely cosy and couthy and of interest only to themselves. These affairs often took on a British dimension, and became also an object of attention to the British authorities. This might be an advantage, but could also have less welcome consequences.[41]

So much started to become clear during the existential crisis the United Kingdom faced about the turn of the nineteenth century in its titanic confrontation with revolutionary France. Sometimes it stood alone in resisting that transformed nation's aggression and the worldwide consequences. Britain feared not just the loss of imperial territories vital to trade and prosperity but even an invasion of the home islands. Comradeship between the Scots and the English in this great struggle in its turn strengthened their mutual bonds, for victory in battle often needed the bold bravado of the one nation's sons to consummate the tough tenacity of the other's.[42]

Dundas now emerged, in addition to everything else, as a global strategist. He insisted the United Kingdom's priorities must lie across the seven seas rather than on the European Continent, so as to safeguard its oceanic trading routes. At the same time, he took a lead in enforcing the internal disciplines imperative for a state engaged in total war. He served as Home Secretary from 1791 to 1794, and in England his campaign to contain outbursts of radicalism potentially helpful to the enemy is little remembered – if at all, then as the standard precaution any leader in his position would have taken against rumblings of popular discontent. An interesting sidelight on where he stood inside the ruling circle was cast by a comment from one of his many lady admirers, Georgiana, Duchess of Devonshire, the sister of a colleague and adept at winkling out what went on in Cabinet: 'You are the only person I have met for a long time who has power, and yet seems to feel the necessity of not staking everything on coercion.'[43]

Britain exalted its heroes but persecuted its anti-heroes, those who for one reason and another resisted recruitment to the common patriotic cause. It fell to Dundas to act against them. In Scotland this formed the prelude to a period often depicted as one of deep, bitter conflict between the just claims of the people and the tyrannies of an oppressive regime. The actual course of events scarcely bears that view out.

The first Scottish disorder Dundas had to deal with at this time was the riot in Edinburgh on the king's birthday, 4 June 1792, followed by commotions in some other places. It brought an attack by the mob on his family's own town-house in George Square – he himself was away in London. The scuffles in the capital, bloody though they turned out, followed an old tradition of popular riot, as recounted in a previous chapter. We would do better to distinguish them from any revolutionary tumults aimed at a transformation of society (though Scottish historians do not always do this).[44]

Certainly, in Britain as a whole, frustrated ideas for reform did now begin to generate a more radical programme, mainly focused on the electoral franchise and other parliamentary matters. Even then, by the standards of the following century, the demands were not extreme – least of all in Scotland, where those wider issues got bound up with the problem of preserving the national institutions guaranteed in 1707. In the Scottish counties, reformers were often conservative in motivation: they aimed to save the shaky position of the old landed elite. Nor did their brethren in the burghs much want to bring in democracy, rather to prevent abuse. And in Scotland such agitations came not from outside but from within the political nation, even if sometimes from aspirant rather than actual members of it. The agitations had started before the era of the French Revolution and carried on under their own momentum into it. This does not mean they were linked with it, still less caused by it, or that they had much in common with demands for universal suffrage from some English radicals. Scots rather assumed, at the outset anyway, that France was passing from royal absolutism to constitutional government just as Scotland had done a century before.[45]

The more radical agendas were first and foremost British ones. For purposes of practical organisation, the plan was to form in each part of the country a local Society of Friends of the People, autonomous but in touch with others. The first was established in London in April 1792, and Edinburgh had its equivalent by July, with a membership of 'shopkeepers and artisans'. The authorities took alarm and blamed some popular demonstrations on 'an almost universal spirit of reform and opposition to the established government and legal administrators which has wonderfully diffused through the manufacturing towns'. While most of the discontent was economic, it might take on a political complexion. Radical weavers in Perth and Dundee put up 'trees of liberty' and capered round them. Yet the Friends of the People officially condemned this sort of thing and threatened to expel from membership anybody disturbing public order.[46]

The Friends of the People held three conventions in Scotland, the last being also open to English delegates. They seemed to have the effect of progressively frightening wider public opinion. Dundas thought he would make himself most useful by returning from London to deal in person with them. Politicians' movements were in those days not usually reported, and he told the Lord Advocate: 'it would appear that they either wished to murder myself or to burn my house, for I was not two days arrived before a notification of it was given in a very suspicious mode.'[47] In watchful mood, then, he set about gathering intelligence of his own. To penetrate the radical ranks he sent spies who, encouraged by the payment of piece-rates, produced a stream of long and lurid reports. Then, at official prompting, supporters of the British constitution formed their own societies while Henry Mackenzie led a band of hacks churning out suitable propaganda. All public bodies of any standing were urged to send in loyal addresses to King George III. More than 400 at once did so, and many continued to at every excuse. By 1796 the king felt sick of the sight of them and ordered them to be sent straight to Dundas without bothering him.

To the first Scottish convention of the Friends of the People in December 1792 about 80 radical societies sent 160 delegates, representing 35 different places in the central belt, though more than half came from Edinburgh. The majority affirmed their attachment to the constitution and actually rejected calls for manhood suffrage and annual Parliaments. The delegates resolved to go on and hold public meetings or organise petitions round the country, before meeting again to see what headway they had made. They made none, for France's declaration of war in February 1793 extinguished most remaining public or parliamentary sympathy for its Revolution. This was the inauspicious background to the Friends' second convention in April. It attracted 116 delegates from 29 places, most new to the agitation. They were also more extreme than the last lot. After some preliminary shilly-shallying they espoused democracy. They opposed the war too: considering that Britain had not started it, they perhaps wanted submission to any demands the French might make. The most radical fringe of the Friends, undeterred by growing public antipathy, decided on a final push at a third and all-British convention. They chose Edinburgh as the venue. There it met at the end of 1793, indeed with representation from all over these islands. Robert Dundas had a close watch kept on the proceedings, 'and I hope they do not break up without doing something which will enable us to interfere'.[48] One Irishman obliged by challenging the Lord Advocate to a duel. The law officers anyway moved in after a few days and dispersed the convention. That was about the sum of Scottish protest directly related to the events in France. The authorities continued vigilant, cracking down on suspect individuals or groups. But it cannot be said Scotland was seething with barely repressed revolutionary fervour. On the contrary, the nation worked and fought for Britain as never before.

The sole subsequent outburst of wider unrest was connected to the war in the sense of being sparked off by an official initiative to conscript a militia for defence of the homeland. But there is no evidence of any political motivation beyond the anger of those young men about to be marched off to a military life they did not want. Apart from furnishing labour for a still growing economy, Britain had to be garrisoned. Its stretched military resources contrasted with those available to France from the *levée en masse* on a population three times greater. At the outbreak of hostilities Britain had had 9,000 men in the army and 15,000 in the navy. These figures had meanwhile tripled or quadrupled – but then there were more than 850,000 Frenchmen under arms. Could a war be sustained against such hordes? At any rate, the need for more men was clamant.[49]

An endless flow of ideas for finding them, above all in his homeland, came from Dundas. He asked the Highland chiefs to revive the custom of calling out their clans. He circularised the nobility with the idea that gamekeepers might be given specialised training in the use of fowling pieces so they could serve as sharpshooters in case of invasion. Out of 60 regiments of fencible foot and 46 of horse raised in Great Britain, Scotland produced respectively 37 and 14. During the wars, 50,000 Scots served in the non-regular defensive forces.[50]

But there was a limit to what could be done without compulsion. In 1797 the government passed a Militia Act for Scotland, though doing so contrary to the advice it had received. According to Adam Ferguson, the resort to 'compulsory statute' left 'an impression of servitude' which might provoke popular riot. An official committee consisting of the Lord Advocate, the Duke of Buccleuch and Lord Adam Gordon, Commander-in-Chief, Scotland, cautioned that 'a militia law would now be felt by the country as if the government took advantage of the laudable spirit which has shown itself to introduce an oppressive measure, that of forcing men to be soldiers, to which the lower ranks of the people have the most rooted dislike'. Officers would be hard to find and great expense would be incurred; it was rather too much trouble for a modest force.[51]

Dundas would not listen. He refused to believe there existed any reservoir of willing recruits so far untapped. His legislation authorised the raising, by a quota on each county, of 6,000 men to serve for the duration, though not outside Scotland. A list of those eligible was to be compiled by the schoolmaster in each parish. He would have to inscribe all fit men aged between 18 and 23 except if they were married with two children; also exempt were sailors, apprentices, articled clerks, parish constables, ministers, schoolmasters, professors and men serving otherwise in the forces. But anybody chosen could get out of his service by finding a substitute or paying £10 to hire a volunteer. In practice, then, the burden was to fall on fit young fellows of the labouring class, perhaps the least inclined to accept it meekly.[52]

When the Act came into force in August 1797, 'Scotland went stark mad', according to Sir Gilbert Elliot. Those in the targeted group felt aggrieved at the high probability of being picked. Since no limit of time was placed on their service, they also feared it amounted to conscription, perhaps with a view to sending them out of Scotland. Riots began in Berwickshire in the middle of the month and spread as far as Aberdeenshire. They bore hard on the hapless schoolmasters, who were often beaten up for their pains by gangs of youths. When the time came for the ballot at Tranent, a wretched mining village in East Lothian, the situation was so tense that a military detachment of English dragoons arrived to parade itself and daunt the locals. These muttered over their drinks in the alehouses then, sufficiently fortified, sallied forth to shout, swear and throw stones at the soldiers who, after enduring it for an hour, ran amok. Twelve people were killed including two women and a boy.[53] But even this brutality failed to open up any hidden depths of opposition to the government. The fact was that the vast majority of Scots remained united in favour of the war with France: united among themselves and united with the English too.

In what was by now a global conflict, the real danger to the domestic security of the British Isles came from Ireland. The danger turned real in 1798, when a French force landed in County Mayo and sparked off a native uprising. The sequel was bloody, but Dundas also saw in it an opportunity: 'If the rebellion can be speedily got under ... the thing in Ireland may be of the happiest consequences to that country.' The answer he had long proposed to its state of endemic revolt was union with Great Britain, accompanied by Catholic emancipation.[54] Though these ideas, shared with William Pitt, were far from popular, it was Dundas's conviction that their time had now come. They animated a speech of his to the House of Commons in February 1799, which was much admired and which he himself reckoned his finest parliamentary performance. Its message was that a union would benefit both Great Britain and Ireland, in the current circumstances more than ever. He conveyed it through an extensive survey of Scotland and the course of its affairs since 1707, with the implication that the Irish could in their turn expect the same advantages.[55]

The speech started by admitting relations among the three kingdoms had sometimes been unhappy. That offered temptations to their enemies, and at present only British intervention on the sister island was foiling them. Any civilised nation needed the mutual confidence of governors and governed, yet the 'melancholy truth' was that Ireland did not enjoy it. The right remedy was for the Parliament at Westminster to restore such confidence. It would do so by assuring equal privileges and freedoms to the peoples of both islands in an 'incorporating union', like that of Scotland and England. The Irish Protestants, secure as part of a majority in the whole United Kingdom, could then lay aside their suspicions, while Catholics could aspire to the same rights as others, knowing that one government for all three nations would be free of narrow Irish animosities. 'I have no hesitation in maintaining that an incorporated Parliament, partly English, partly Scotch and partly Irish is much better calculated for the management of the affairs of the British Empire than separate Parliaments in England, Scotland and Ireland.' For proof, Dundas turned to his own country:

> I, as one of the 45 Scotch members, can, in the face of the 513 English members, freely discuss and watch the interests of Scotland. The Parliament, thus constituted by the Union, has not deprived Scotland of any of the privileges enjoyed previously to its incorporation with England. The Union has increased the privilege of the Scotch members: for, instead of confining their deliberations to the affairs of Scotland, they are empowered to take part in discussions respecting the affairs ... of the whole British Empire ...

When gentlemen pretend to think lightly of the sacrifices of Scotland compared with those of Ireland, let them recollect that Ireland has not for many centuries been free or independent of England, but that Scotland was never completely subdued or under the control of England; that Scotland gave up, what Ireland cannot give up, an independent Parliament of King, Lords and Commons; and that Scotland gave up, what Ireland cannot give up, an independent and separate crown. The Scots undoubtedly surrendered those honours at the time with reluctance, and evinced the greatest hostility to the Union, until experience made them acquainted with its blessings.

This was important as Dundas's sole lengthy treatment of Anglo-Scottish relations. The unionist who claims a pride in Scotland, in its historical traditions as in its present progress, has become a character of unconvincing cliché in the intervening two centuries, and often a figure for the anglicising toady. But we would be rash to see anything of the sort in Dundas. At the turn of the nineteenth century, the amalgam of Scottish and British patriotism was still an innovation not yet compromised or jaded. True, the depth of Dundas's personal commitment, to the one or to the other, was never put to the test, for there existed in his time no real conflict between Scottishness and the Union. That was in large measure because all the national institutions safeguarded in the Treaty of 1707 remained intact and under indigenous control. Dundas meant to keep things like this. One side of his Union was a United Kingdom and an Empire opened up to his countrymen – and the other side a Scotland for the Scots.[56]

In June 1804, Charles Hope was called on in the House of Commons to defend controls he had placed on the mails between Scotland and Ireland in order, he said, to foil radical plots. In passing, he gave a succinct exposition of the office of Lord Advocate as it had developed since 1707. Before then, the Lord High Chancellor, Lord Justice General, Lord Privy Seal and Lord Advocate had formed the Scottish administration, but the first three offices had disappeared or lost their powers, which in effect devolved on the last. All lower grades of the public service in Scotland now looked to him, so that 'it may be said he possesses the whole of the executive government under his particular care'. Such claims might have sounded extravagant to English ears but despite the Union, Hope went on, 'Scotland is to all intents and purposes a separate kingdom. Its law, its customs and its manners have undergone no change.'[57] These were not assertions that would fully stand up to historical scrutiny, but they give the essence of the semi-independence Scotland continued to enjoy after the Union right up to the Reform Act of 1832.

As soon as the Parliament of the new United Kingdom of Great Britain and Ireland met at the beginning of 1801, William Pitt got the leading members of his Cabinet to confirm an earlier agreement among themselves, reached without King George III's knowledge, that they should proceed straight to a measure for Catholic emancipation. Dundas was a party to this. All through their career together, he and his leader had taken care to buttress the consensus in favour of their many innovations by elaborate deference to the sensibilities of the ruling elite. For once, they now miscalculated. Everybody might appreciate their desire to win Irish Catholics for the Union and so for continuation of the war against France. But that still did not outweigh the general conviction that a prime function of any government, however enlightened, was to defend political and religious establishments – and not to sacrifice them to a creed which opened Ireland to alien and subversive influences, and might do the same in the whole United Kingdom. It became clear that the number so minded among Pitt's usual supporters in the House of Commons was large, and in the House of Lords preponderant. The decisive resistance came, however, from a disquieted monarch. Egged on by intriguers, he declared himself bound to refuse the royal assent to any Catholic emancipation by the oath he had taken at his coronation to maintain the Protestant religion.[58]

Things already looked black when Dundas went to a royal levee at St James's Palace and found his sovereign in testy mood. King George III at once launched into a diatribe against Catholic emancipation: 'I shall consider every man who supports that measure as my personal enemy.' Dundas, yet more committed to it than his chief, would not cave in. He tried to blind the king with science, arguing that the passage of the bill in both Houses of Parliament could in effect set aside the royal oath, for it bound him only in his executive rather than also in his legislative capacity. George would have none of it, retorting that he was prohibited from allowing Catholics in Parliament or in any high office of state, and from endangering the Protestant establishment in any other way. Finally he exploded: 'None of your damned Scotch metaphysics, Mr Dundas!' Afraid his spluttering sovereign might go mad if further pressed, he allowed the interview to come to a rapid end. The monarch remained implacable, leaving William Pitt no choice but to resign. Dundas followed him. It was the end of an era in Scotland and in Britain.[59]

In the United Kingdom the state never strove towards the kind of absolutist authority it attained in the other multinational monarchies of Europe. It resorted in achieving unity neither to force nor to the sweeping rationalist reform of institutions. Unity instead came in peace, without upheaval, through evolution of a shared culture, in distribution of proceeds from bourgeoning commerce and in political management. This set common purposes for the national elites, from which they were diffused downwards through the chains of dependence that bound civil society together. The development was not altogether symmetrical, for the identity of the Scottish junior partner needed special consideration to avoid submersion by the English senior one. And the methods were somewhat contradictory. On the one hand, the power of the central state was circumscribed, by keeping it at arm's length. On the other hand, the central state became colonised and its opportunities were exploited with as much gusto as those in any distant imperial outpost.[60]

Dundas made partners of Scotland and England, to an extent never matched before or since. There was joint responsibility in all undertakings, if not in mutual affection, then at least in mutual respect. Perhaps this could only be possible with a small British state and with Scotland ruled by an elite. In future the central state would expand and swamp the local elite, as part of the struggle in the United Kingdom by which reform overcame reaction, a struggle that to contemporaries cast England in a progressive role and Scotland in a reactionary one. With the passions spent, however, this does not today seem a useful distinction, since Scottish contributions to the general development went far beyond the narrow political sphere. If conventional views are cast aside, it should be possible to see Dundas's regime in a kinder light, for what it did in Scotland and for what it did with the Union.

Part V
CULTURE

13

Things: 'Refinement of every kind'

The Dunmore Pineapple, probably built in 1776, is 'the most bizarre building in Scotland'.[1] It stands in what used to be southern Stirlingshire, in the grounds of the now ruined Dunmore House, near the village of Airth.[2] The pineapple was constructed to the commission of John Murray, fourth Earl of Dunmore. He came from one of the Jacobite families that had hedged its bets in 1745. His uncle, the second earl, stayed at home while his father and young John himself, aged 15, marched away with Prince Charles Edward Stewart. The two of them fell into the government's hands as the uprising collapsed and were placed under house arrest. The son gained his freedom when, in 1750, he volunteered for the British army. Now his career could prosper, so much so that a quarter-century later he was appointed Governor of Virginia. It proved, however, to be a bad time to arrive in America. He got into disputes with the restive colonists, one of whom, the Patriot, Patrick Henry, denounced him in their assembly with the immortal words, 'Give me liberty or give me death!' As armed revolt broke out, Dunmore had to abandon his palatial residence at Williamsburg and take refuge on a British warship. From there he issued a proclamation to emancipate all black slaves who would volunteer for a loyal force he was organising as the Ethiopian Regiment; he attracted 2,000 recruits. But neither this nor any other among his desperate measures regained him control of the colony and by the middle of 1776 he sailed for home.

Lord Dunmore continued to draw his governor's salary till Britain finally recognised American independence in 1783, so he was probably well off. Doubtless it is to this that we owe the Dunmore Pineapple, which he must have had built as soon as he got back to Scotland. It took advantage of the fact that the policies of his house contained two large walled gardens sloping down over ground sheltered from wind and frost. They created a microclimate enjoying a temperature several degrees higher than in the surrounding landscape, enough to allow the growth of tropical fruits, vegetables and ornamental plants that could not otherwise have survived so far north. The gentle forcing of such flora was an agreeable sideline of the Scottish Enlightenment. Its interest in all things scientific encouraged landowners of a horticultural bent to spend money on grand tours to faraway places whence they could bear back botanical booty and, in constant battle with the elements of their native country, create an exotic setting for their own homes. To achieve all this, they had to rely on Scottish gardeners, for it was unlikely anybody else could command the necessary patience and perseverance. It might be hard for the landowners to hang on to their gardeners, however: they became an exportable workforce, bringing to the rest of Britain, to Europe and to the world the techniques learned at the extreme limits of cultivation in Scotland.[3] These green-fingered fellows would be found applying their skills anywhere from the royal botanical gardens at Kew to equivalents in South Africa, India and Australia – even at Mount Vernon in Virginia where George Washington employed a Scottish gardener, David Cowan.

After Lord Dunmore arrived home from America, he divided his chosen piece of ground by a retaining wall that allowed the formation on each side of flat and level spaces, upper and lower, so there was no longer a slope but an abrupt drop between the one and the other. In the course of the work, a great deal of earth had to be shifted about and banked up. The required retaining wall attained formidable dimensions, 60 feet long, 16 feet high and 3 feet thick. To intensify the microclimatic effect, the wall had space for a furnace. Chimneys drew the smoke upwards, but the heat escaped into the immediate area. Then, facing south, it was possible to place a hothouse behind framed windowpanes for growing tropical fruit. How better for Dunmore to celebrate his achievement than to crown the entire structure with a folly in the shape of a pineapple? In the two centuries since Christopher Columbus first brought this fruit back from America, it had become to Europeans a symbol of power, wealth and hospitality, as such a frequent architectural motif. The Dunmore Pineapple is the finest example.[4]

From its base in the lower garden to the top of the cupola rising above the upper garden, the Dunmore Pineapple stands 30 feet high. Its architecture shows a mixture of styles. On either side are simple bothies for the gardeners. The chimneys coming up from the furnace take the shape of Grecian urns.

At the lower level a Palladian arch faces out on the garden, with behind it a vestibule under the pineapple flanked by pairs of carved and painted Ionic columns. At the higher level an octagonal pavilion, with sash windows surmounted by Gothic ogee arches, has a door on the north side leading into the upper garden. In the pavilion, the interior walls of the octagon gently curve to make a circular room. The door and panes of glass in the seven windows are curved too, so as to match the walls. Similarly, a round table with chairs is placed in the middle. Above everything soars the pineapple. From the outside it comes across as a remarkably accurate representation of the fruit, altogether a stunning example of the stonemason's craft. Each of the leaves is separately drained to prevent damage by frost. The stiff serrated edges are all cunningly graded so that water will not gather anywhere, ensuring no freeze can spoil the delicate stonework. A pretty little tufted crown of the plant surmounts the whole. Despite the unconventional design and stylistic mix, the effect is harmonious because of the consistent width between pineapple and portico, which are of the same stone and colour all over. This width also matches the height of the south façade. The height of the whole building, from lower floor to tufted crown, amounts to exactly half the width of the retaining wall. Despite its exotic aspect, it represents altogether an exercise in classical proportion.[5]

The Dunmore Pineapple is a masterpiece, yet we do not even know for certain who its architect was. The best guess is William Chambers, the designer of similar fanciful structures at Kew Gardens near London, and a man who in all his works never failed to show the same meticulous attention to detail. The exoticism also fits him as a good example of a new breed of global Scot, often of Jacobite origins. Born at Gothenburg in Sweden, the city of refuge and exile for his family, he was apprenticed to the Swedish East India Company, set up mainly to smuggle tea into Britain. He voyaged to China as a teenage trader to finance his real ambition, a grand tour of the classical monuments of Italy and France. Then he went back to his ancestral homeland to become one of its great architects.[6]

But William Chambers never did that much work in Scotland. He had many more buildings to his credit in London, Somerset House being his finest achievement. He probably stayed just a year or two in Edinburgh, where his domicile in St Andrew's Square is recorded. He was there as architect for his most notable structure in the city, the luxurious mansion that Sir Lawrence Dundas had built for himself on one side of the square; it used to dominate the eastward vista along George Street till the hideous

St James Centre was erected behind it in the 1970s. In the original scheme of things, the site had been designated for a church to match one at the opposite end of the first New Town. Sir Lawrence, rich and greedy, appropriated the plot of ground for himself. His house is at least justified by its classical elegance.[7]

Classicism is the outstanding feature of Scottish architecture in the eighteenth century. We can point to two main sources for it. Its basic geometry is simple, so fitted easily onto Scotland's own plain native tradition of building. In a poor country, most houses were put up, with little or no embellishment, by the communal effort of the occupants, their neighbours and friends. In outlying regions such dwellings were primitive, with single rooms, slit windows and earthen floors, shared by a large family and its animals too. But in richer parts of the Lowlands the structures grew more elaborate, with distinct rooms and chambers, clad in plaster and paint, sometimes even lit by glazed windows. In the burghs also, many buildings were of timber and thatch, but here they stood in more direct contrast to the larger townhouses of merchants with stone walls and slated roofs. Because of the urban risk of fire, construction in stone came to be preferred even for the homes of poorer people.[8]

The architecture of vernacular buildings depended on local materials and styles,[9] that is to say, on the stone available or on the traditions of particular burghs. In Edinburgh the main material was the yellow sandstone readily quarried round about, which weathered to a silver grey in turn often blackened by Auld Reekie's domestic and industrial burning of coal from Midlothian. Though from Glasgow rugged mountains were visible, most of its distinctive red sandstone came from huge deposits at Locharbriggs in Dumfriesshire, easily transported by sea. After a destructive fire in the largely wooden Aberdeen of 1748, the town council decided its big buildings should for the future be of the local granite. That civic ordinance prompted mining on a large scale and led to the construction of the Granite City, which also exported to the rest of Scotland and to England this most durable of stones, useful for pavements, pillars and – because it glitters in sunshine after rain – façades.

As Scottish development proceeded, the abundant building materials made it easy for the older and bigger burghs to extend themselves in new towns. The suburbs of Edinburgh and Glasgow had been humble places, overcrowded and insanitary sprawls where poor people lived in exclusion from the privileges of the burghs, often with problems of crime on top of everything else because here no authority had responsibility for public order. Altogether different were the new towns built, by both private and public interests, on the wave of growing prosperity from the middle of the eighteenth century. Edinburgh offered the great example, with Glasgow and Aberdeen not far behind, followed by others round the country from Kelso to Ayr to Inveraray to Perth to Elgin to Wick. These new towns were usually symmetrical, built as a gridiron of long, wide streets with spacious squares, later varied by handsome circuses or elegant crescents, and offering sites for monumental public buildings.[10]

The interiors of the houses might show a corresponding spaciousness, even splendour. One in Princes Street, Edinburgh, was advertised as comprising a dining room, drawing room, seven bedrooms, kitchen, scullery, servants' apartments, cellars, laundry, stable, coach-house and pigeon-house, together with a wonderful new amenity, 'a lead cistern with a pipe within the house' (in contrast to the gardy-loo of the Old Town). Doubtless the owners entertained, but the design of the house was above all meant to assure them a private life away from the intrusion or even gaze of neighbours and employees. Nobody in scruffy and penniless yet intimate and demonstrative Scotland had ever lived this way. It was the cool, clean, coherent statement of a rank of people with the will to break from a chaotic past and impose their own values inside this machine for a rational existence.[11]

Some of the approach carried over even into the countryside. Scotland became dotted with planned villages, a product of the agricultural revolution built by improving landlords to absorb the labouring population displaced from the earlier communal farms.[12] The new order was transferred to the emerging proletariat as well when, from 1800, Robert Owen erected New Lanark as a self-contained community combining industrial production and social order. Round the country benign entrepreneurs used domestic design, utilitarian but graceful, to bring life into harmony with its environment. Nothing realised enlightened values so visibly.[13]

Yet amid this progress Scottish tradition persisted in both rural and urban settings. The centres of agricultural enterprise were now the farmhouses, often of some architectural merit, and their steadings, which also might disguise in a certain style their workaday purpose. In the burghs most homes, even along the classical terraces, were again built as flats inside tenements.

The tenants shared a common stair and the smallest flat might have only one room while the largest boasted several parlours and bedrooms.[14] This in some sort continued the way of life in the crowded old burghs in a form that has proved its worth right down to the present day.[15]

The second great influence on contemporary Scottish architecture came from ancient Greece and Rome. Europeans generally were casting off the Gothic inheritance of the Middle Ages to acknowledge in stone what a debt modern civilisation owed to the classical world for its example of peace, order, regular government and intellectual achievement. Architects gave physical expression to this gratitude. In Scotland too, though it had never belonged to the Roman Empire, classical styles came to dominate new construction.[16] Perhaps here they had more special meanings: of growing intellectual self-confidence, of national redefinition in the wake of the Union, of mutual reinforcement between commercial society and polite culture.

Across Europe the classical styles followed a discernible spatial and temporal evolution, starting from Italy where architects had the example of Roman ruins all round them, passing through France and the pretensions of its imperial monarchy, going on to the Low Countries with their republican simplicity and then at last arriving in faraway Scotland. Individual Scots followed different stretches of this path. Sir William Bruce of Kinross, after beginning his career as a merchant in Rotterdam, returned home at the Restoration of 1660. He found favour in various respects with the new royalist regime, not least as an architect – though, so far as we know, he had had no form of professional training. That never deterred him from the ambitious scheme of remodelling the still largely medieval Palace of Holyroodhouse into more or less its modern shape. He then rebuilt Thirlestane Castle for the regime's boss, the Duke of Lauderdale, Prestonfield House for a Lord Provost of Edinburgh and finally a mansion of his own, at Kinross on Loch Leven, Scotland's most important early classical work. Beyond construction, he developed a new relationship not only between the house and its grounds but also with the wider landscape to be seen beyond it – with Loch Leven at Kinross House, with the Bass Rock at Balcaskie in Fife and with the River Forth at Hopetoun House.[17]

One assistant employed by Sir William Bruce was young James Smith. He had lived in Rome while studying for the Catholic priesthood, but did not stay the course and returned home to take up his family's trade (they were masons at Forres in Moray). In 1683 he succeeded Bruce in charge of the works at Holyrood. He was responsible for maintaining the palace, but went further and restored the ruined medieval abbey next door as a chapel royal for King James VII; this work did not survive long, because it was sacked by a Protestant mob as the first act of the Revolution of 1688. Nothing daunted, Smith built Caroline Park for the Duke of Argyll, Drumlanrig for the Duke of Queensberry and, to accommodate the Presbyterian congregation displaced from Holyrood, the Canongate kirk on an Italianate plan of basilica with baroque façade (if much more austere than anything in Italy). Smith's most exquisite work was also the smallest: the mausoleum of Sir George Mackenzie of Rosehaugh in the kirkyard of Greyfriars. He had besides a hand in Hamilton Palace, Dalkeith Palace and Yester House, though these were all altered later. Such was the formidable record of Scotland's first truly professional architect.[18]

Details are sketchy, but it seems Smith might in person have passed on his classical precepts to the next generation of architects, notably Colen Campbell. Given his surname, he was unlikely to share Smith's political or religious convictions. Campbell became an architectural nationalist but a British nationalist, with a programme of purging from new buildings on these islands any corrupt Catholic character. He preferred the Palladian style, an Italian one indebted to Andrea Palladio in the Republic of Venice, which sought to combine dignified order with natural simplicity, its effects achieved by perspective, proportion and symmetry rather than by devout detail. Again, Colen Campbell did little of his work in Scotland, the notable exception being the mansion that Daniel Campbell of Shawfield put up for himself on the edge of Glasgow; unfortunately it was burned by the mob during the riots over the malt tax in 1725. Colen Campbell made a deeper mark rather with his three volumes of example and instruction, *Vitruvius Britannicus, or the British Architect*, published from 1715 to 1725 and dedicated to King George I. They became bibles for the architectural profession. And they probably did more than anything else to form the classical taste of the Whig oligarchy, which, in building mansions to match their mastery of Britain, followed the book's patterns for the rest of the century.[19]

Colen Campbell found a rival in the Aberdonian, James Gibbs, who also went to Rome to study for the Catholic priesthood. In turn he, too, abandoned this vocation and devoted himself to mastering the principles of the city's architecture instead. Once back in Britain, he settled in London. Unlike Campbell, Gibbs was tolerant of baroque detail within the classical forms, which he developed in novel ways: the Parthenon with spire of St Martin-in-the-Fields in London and the remarkable circular library, the Radcliffe Camera in Oxford.[20] These were only the best known of many buildings he constructed in England, often under the patronage of the Duke of Argyll. Dedicated to him, Gibbs published *A Book of Architecture, containing designs of buildings and ornaments* (1728). It offered a portfolio of 380 building types, some executed and some not, with many ornamental details as well; he was the first British architect to bring out a volume of his own designs. In Scotland he executed just one of them, at the west kirk of St Nicholas in his native Aberdeen, for which he replaced the ruined nave.

For architects, the Union of 1707 worked. They could not do without the patronage, from great men or the state, always more available in London than in Scotland. So nearly all leading Scottish architects spent part of their careers in England, where they did much to shape its Georgian architecture out of the variety of classical influences they introduced.[21] That proved true of Chambers and his Somerset House, even truer of his great rivals, the family of Adam of Blair Adam. Their careers were about equally divided between Scotland and England, though they left their mark much more on Scottish townscapes, especially on Edinburgh.

The family had started off as masons at Kirkcaldy. William Adam, the man who led them to fame and fortune, remained all his adult life a member of the masons' guild in his native burgh.[22] In the words of John Clerk of Eldin, Adam was Scotland's 'universal architect'.[23] While he built great houses he never spurned the workaday world of urban renewal and industrial investment, of brickworks, coal-mines, saltpans, quarries and mills. He moved across the Firth of Forth to put his money into the lofts, granaries and warehouses of Leith, to develop underground workings at Cockenzie, to dig a canal at Pinkie. He became a burgess of Edinburgh and erected for himself a big house in the Cowgate, while at home in Fife he had already bought and started to develop his estate of Blair Adam.

All the same, it is as a builder of country houses in classical style that William Adam has won enduring renown, though the precision and regularity of that style seldom stopped him doing whatever he wanted. Externally and internally his decoration was amazingly inventive, making it hard for scholars to trace its exact source. Several of his houses seem to be owed to Smith's *Vitruvius Britannicus* or to Gibbs's *Book of Architecture,* others to French or Italian pattern books. In fact, Adam borrowed freely all over the place with little regard for consistency. Yet a rich harmony remained the keynote to his work.[24]

In a career of four decades, William Adam designed, extended or remodelled more than 40 country houses.[25] He started with large additions to Sir William Bruce's Hopetoun House. Adam's development of the original building turned an already big place into a palace, with curved sections at the end of the main range, colonnades, pavilions and new wings, not to mention the formal gardens all around. Nothing so ambitious or imaginative had ever been tried in Scotland.[26] By contrast, Mavisbank House in Midlothian, built between 1723 and 1727, was an exercise in discipline. Its owner, Sir John Clerk of Penicuik, wrote a long didactic poem, *The Country Seat,* on the principles he meant to apply in having it built. It turned out to be Scotland's first Palladian villa, the result of close collaboration between Clerk and Adam. The house fell into ruin in the twentieth century, but efforts are today under way to save and restore it.[27] In the same county and started about the same time, the most ambitious early work for which Adam took full responsibility was the Arniston House of the Dundas family. It specially featured a spectacular entrance hall, what would nowadays be called an atrium, decorated with marvellous plasterwork. Adam also laid out the grounds with a parterre and cascade, and an avenue centred on a distant view of Arthur's Seat to the north. Duff House at Banff was his greatest achievement of the following decade. It showed how in his full maturity local and foreign influences crowded in on his style, to produce here 'a medieval castle in baroque dress'.[28] The Scottish feature is the height of the house, recalling times when lairds needed for safety to build vertical fortresses, and Duff has towers at the corners rising over an already lofty façade. Drumlanrig and Heriot's Hospital in Edinburgh offer precedents, though neither ever became a canvas for the baroque decoration with which Adam perfected Duff.

William Adam died in 1748 leaving his business to three sons, Robert the most distinguished. He took the lead in a further stage of the classical revival in Scotland (and England).[29] He rejected the Palladian style as 'ponderous' and 'disgustful', and went himself to renew acquaintance with authentic antiquity during a stay of four years in Rome, Spalato (Split) and elsewhere.[30] As much an interior designer as an architect, he wanted his houses to work not only on the outside world but also from the inside on their owners. He set in stone the politeness and sociability of the Scottish Enlightenment with increasingly imaginative designs for great and small rooms, for passages and stairs. Even today some of these works remain unsurpassed: the blue drawing room and pewter corridor at Dumfries House, the entrance hall and staircase at Paxton House, the delicate and colourful plasterwork all over Mellerstain House (the only remaining complete building that Adam designed), the breathtaking drum tower and circular saloon at Culzean Castle overlooking the Firth of Clyde.

And these are only Adam's greatest works in Scotland. South of the border his remaining structures (the English have a stupid habit of demolishing them) include the Pulteney Bridge at Bath, Fitzroy Square in the centre of London and Kenwood House at Hampstead. His influence spread far beyond Britain. His brother Scot, Charles Cameron, took his patterns to Russia, where for the Empress Catherine the Great he built her palaces of Tsarskoye Selo and Pavlovsk near St Petersburg. His own great-nephew, Frederick Adam, reintroduced classical styles to Corfu, of which he was governor, and built the palace of Mon Repos (birthplace of Philip, Duke of Edinburgh) together with other public buildings in the city.[31]

Robert Adam's country houses usually stood in splendid isolation, or at least in a sculpted landscape, but he could transform an existing townscape too. Edinburgh would be the best example. Here it was as if, after 1745, the city made a resolution to put the past behind it and enter on a fresh phase of its history, not now in the guise of anything so banal as a national capital. Instead it set out to reinvent itself as a republic of letters, a universal realm of progress free from the constraints of mere borders. Its physical shape would be adapted to this enlightened vision.[32]

During the seventeenth century some improvements had already been in train in the squeezed, swarming, stinking capital, to clean it up, clear away its worst slums and adorn it with new public buildings. In his own time George Drummond, six times Lord Provost between 1725 and 1764, pushed this agenda forward. Early on, in 1729, he commissioned William Adam to build the Royal Infirmary in a style of Palladian pomp (only a fragment survives).[33]

A much greater opportunity arrived in 1751 when a tenement collapsed and opened up a gap-site in the middle of the High Street, almost opposite St Giles. The town council resolved to turn it to profitable account: 'So lucky an opportunity for a well situate exchange ought not to be lost,' it minuted.[34] On the gap-site arose Robert Adam's Royal Exchange, meant as a meeting place for the merchants still wont to hang, as they had always had done, round the Cross on the other side of the road. In fact, they would spurn this new abode, which in 1811 was transformed into, and today remains, the City Chambers, seat of the council. It was the first example of Adam not just putting up a building but creating an urban composition too: despite the cramped site, he set the block back from the Royal Mile with a quadrangle screened off from the thoroughfare by an open arcade, while the rear of the building turns a steep slope into a precipice.

Greater works were soon afoot. The most ambitious part of Drummond's plans began with the draining of the Nor' Loch in 1759, something essential for a healthier Edinburgh. It exposed a chasm to be crossed by the North Bridge: Drummond laid its foundation stone in 1763, during his final term as Lord Provost. He would not live to see the New Town, but the way to it now stood open.[35] The bridge was also the key to a reordering of the Old Town. The thoroughfare it created could be extended back to make a new axis at right angles to the historic one of the Royal Mile. The main part of the capital would cease to be long and skinny and become cross-shaped instead. The South Bridge created a square in the middle of the High Street, traversed the gorge of the Cowgate, reached out to the university in its crumbling old monastic buildings on the edge of the built-up area and beyond that formed a new gateway to the open countryside (as things stood the burgh could only be exited on this side by the narrow Horse Wynd – today Guthrie Street – leading into Potterrow).

Here was an opportunity worthy of Robert Adam. His ideas proved visionary, with plans for towering colonnaded buildings right along the South Bridge. Henry Dundas felt impressed and delighted, but in 1786 noted 'a good deal of conversation circulating abroad as if the town of Edinburgh was going to do the shabby thing in departing from the monumental part of Adam's plan'.[36] Yet it turned out just too expensive, and in the end the thoroughfare was lined with ordinary tenements and shops. Even so, it created a vista along the Bridges, terminated at either end by two of Adam's masterpieces: to the south a new university, today confusingly called Old College, with its massive walls, grand gateway and ponderous dome, and to the north his exquisite Register House, with its graceful, even playful exploitation of simple rectangular form.

Meanwhile the construction of the New Town got under way. The town council provided the infrastructure, the roads, pavements and sewerage, and enforced architectural uniformity. But it was left to the private developers, the aspiring occupants or the enterprising builders, to erect the private properties along the thoroughfares. Edinburgh now decisively breached the bounds that had since its foundation confined it to the tail of the Castle Rock. The New Town would first cover the terrain, a mile by half-a-mile in extent, on what had been the further shore of the Nor' Loch, along a shallow ridge falling on one side gently into its former bed and on the other more steeply down towards the Firth of Forth. This was still farmland that six centuries of the burgh's existence had barely touched – open fields corrugated by runrig. Now it would yield to an experiment in living by the light of reason, a triumph of the will over nature and history. The will was first to regularity and symmetry. Formal townscape would sweep over the whole site, ironing out valleys, filling lochs and spanning rivers. It outdid by far any scheme of improvement ever contemplated in Scotland before. A backward economy with a peasant population would here find fresh focus in an ideal urban community with hundreds of houses on dozens of streets.[37]

The revolutionary nature of the New Town took shape not just in stone but also in flesh and blood, because it changed lives. A prime feature of the Old Town had been how different social classes lived cheek by jowl. There was room for all, only on different levels of the high tenements: lower class at the bottom or top, middle class in the middle (together with such of the upper class as kept a pied-à-terre in the capital). But before long anybody who could afford it moved to the New Town. The philosopher David Hume was one who led the pack: not quite a wealthy man, though of independent means, he flitted in 1769 from James's Court in the High Street to a house in what became St David's Street – facetiously so named after him. The rich did not rush: it took half a century for them all to go. But the last gentleman in the Royal Mile, James Ferguson of Pitfour, left for good in 1817. Those then occupying the New Town embraced the idea of an ordered society because they would sit at its summit.[38]

The amplitude of the project can be traced back to a pamphlet of 1752,

'Proposals for Carrying on certain Public Works in the City of Edinburgh', from the hand of a rising political star, Gilbert Elliot of Minto. He argued that the whole of Scotland would benefit by his bright ideas:

> The national advantages which a populous capital must necessarily produce are obvious. A great concourse of people brought within a small compass occasions a much greater consumption than the same number would do dispersed over a wider country. As the consumption is greater so it is quicker and more discernible. Hence follows a more rapid circulation of money and other commodities, the great spring which gives motion to general industry and improvement. The example set by the capital, the nation will soon follow. The certain consequence is general wealth and prosperity, the number of useful people will increase, the rents of the land rise, the public revenue improve and in the room of sloth and poverty will succeed industry and opulence.

It was odd to claim cities caused riches, rather than the other way round. But Elliot filled the holes in his argument with explicit proposals 'to enlarge and beautify the town, by opening new streets to the north and south', while the Nor' Loch would become a canal with promenades along each bank. He assured readers that there were previous examples of provincial capitals – Berlin or Turin – which had been transformed into centres 'of trade and commerce, of learning and the arts, of . . . refinement of every kind'. Edinburgh, in other words, need not mourn its old status as grim citadel of an embattled kingdom.[39]

An architectural contest was at length chosen as the way forward. Announced in 1766, it called for 'plans of a New Town marking out streets of a proper breadth, and by-lanes, and the best situation for a reservoir, and any other public buildings, which may be thought necessary'. A year later the adjudicators named the winner: James Craig, a young man already working on St James's Square at the head of Leith Walk. He got a gold medal and freedom of the city. The basic plan of rectangular blocks with open squares at each end was 'entirely sensible, and almost painfully orthodox', says A.J. Youngson, historian of classical Edinburgh. It seems to have followed the example of a project at Nancy in Lorraine. The houses were, with rare exceptions, uniform. They had three storeys, three windows on each and a basement beneath. Some offered scope for the semiotics of status in the style of doorways and rustication of ground floors, later in giant pilasters and bow windows. But there was rather a risk of monotony, which only a little vernacular eccentricity at the gables of cross-streets relieved. It cannot be said the domestic architecture (as opposed to the setting and layout) of the first New Town was of any great interest.[40]

Robert Adam made the difference. The construction of the first New Town proceeded east to west, starting in 1767 and not finishing for a quarter-century, with no noticeable change in the character of the place. Princes Street was already becoming more of a commercial than residential thoroughfare, while at Queen Street the city just halted and looked out over open countryside. Any concept of urbanity therefore really depended on George Street in between. So far it had been monotonous, but its monotony became at last sublimated in higher unity once Adam built his Charlotte Square (1791). In this composition, regularity blended into subtle variation held together by a refined classical vocabulary. Adam gave the four terraces unified frontages reaching a climax at the central pediments of the northern and southern sides. All the parts fitted into a greater whole, which came to more than the sum of its parts.[41] The square still followed Craig's ground-plan, suiting the site while setting a pattern that could transcend it: the best of examples for the extension of classical Edinburgh.

We can often read the evolution of the Scottish Enlightenment in stone. Order and harmony at the eastern end of the first New Town are also plain and modest, in architectural metaphor Doric rather than Corinthian. But by the time we arrive at the western end we have made a transition not only geographical and temporal but also aesthetic, from severity to vivacity. That mirrored the intellectual development of the nation – above all, of the city, soon dubbed the Athens of the North. A more relaxed creativity then admitted early revivals of Gothic, which would become much more important in the next century. There was little of it inside the capital but much more outside, the first examples in the toytown castles of Henry Dundas at Melville and the Duke of Argyll at Inveraray. They articulated a renewed yearning for distinctive national cultural identity, rooted in history. In architecture, Scotland was finding itself again after the century since 1707.

Before the Union, Scottish painters painted houses rather than people. There was a modest school of portraiture, composed in good part of foreigners who had come to earn money, presumably against feeble local competition, out of practising their art in Scotland. Most native Scottish painters were first and foremost decorators, craftsmen making their way in life just as the members of other trades did, first training as apprentices and then following a laborious career. Painters of lasting reputation – Alexander Runciman, Jacob More, Alexander Nasmyth, even Henry Raeburn – all began as apprentices, though Raeburn was apprenticed to a goldsmith, not a painter. Only slowly did such craftsmen start to think of themselves as artists and look for more ambitious ways to deploy their skills, prompted in part by the foreign rivals among them and in part by the growing sophistication of rich patrons who had perhaps gone on the grand tour in Europe. There was the odd exception to the pattern, such as William Aikman, a landowner who came into painting just because he liked it, but this was rare.[42]

The Union made a big difference here too. It took away from the capital of Scotland the political class bound to be a prime source of artistic patronage. The bearers of the nation's culture needed to find new means of livelihood; still, the Ramsay family, for example, with the father the leading Scots poet and the son the greatest painter of the eighteenth century, showed it could be done. But a couple of dead decades had to follow the Union before cultural life stirred once again. In the case of painting it was in part nurtured by renewed contact with Rome where the Jacobite court had finally settled. Rome housed its Accademia di San Luca, an artists' association dating from 1578, and in 1729 Edinburgh got its Academy of St Luke (the patron saint of painters); the elder Ramsay promoted it for the sake of his promising son. Its charter is preserved in the Royal Scottish Academy, its eventual heir. The aims are described as the 'encouragement of these excellent arts of painting, sculpture and architecture, etc, and the improvement of the students'. The charter also contains an agreement 'to erect a public academy, whereinto everyone that inclines, on application to our director and council, shall be admitted on paying a small sum for defraying charges of figure, lights, etc. For further encourage-ment some of our members who have a fine collection of models in plaister from the best antique statues are to lend the use of them to the academy.'[43]

An official agency of the British state, the board of manufactures, was meanwhile promoting higher standards in the crafts as an aid to economic development, and painters offered it an obvious clientele. At length, in 1760, the board in effect took over as the main artistic institution for the country, when it established its own trustees' academy for education in the relevant skills.[44] The Academy of St Luke had by this time faded away, but it found a sort of successor in the Foulis Academy set up in Glasgow in 1755 by the two brothers Foulis, Andrew and Robert. They ran a publishers' business in the city and had become printers to its university, specialising in editions of classical works that won renown for their accuracy and elegance; the first, in 1743, was the περι Ἑρμηνειας of Demetrios Phalereos. The brothers spared no pains in perfecting their products: Robert went to France to procure manuscripts and to engage skilled craftsmen. Beyond their commercial operations they wanted to establish an institution for the encouragement of the fine arts generally. They spent their money on collecting pictures and statues, endowed a travelling scholarship for young artists and had masterpieces of foreign painting copied for exhibition in Glasgow. In fact, they spent far too much money on all these things and in the end went bust. But at least enlightened Scotland had managed to find some means, however precarious and modest, for the philanthropic, rather than aristocratic, patronage of artists.[45]

Otherwise, Scottish painting remained associated with the decoration of houses, as landed gentlemen wishing to mark up status built themselves grander residences: then they wanted the interiors, too, to reflect well on themselves and on their nation. A didactic poem by Sir John Clerk of Penicuik, *The Country Seat*, devoted special attention to this latter aspect, giving over more than 100 lines to an exact iconographic programme for the walls of public rooms. Clerk thought the history of Britain furnished the best subject matter, especially how King James VI had united the Crowns, and Queen Anne the Parliaments, while King George I now reigned benevolently over the whole.[46]

It was, of course, possible to take a different view. The second Duke of Gordon, a Jacobite and a Catholic, celebrated his release from captivity after the rebellion of 1715 by doing up Gordon Castle in Moray. He employed John Alexander, who shared his political and religious loyalties, to paint a magnificent ceiling with the legend of *Pluto and Proserpine*. Sadly, it has long vanished, though Alexander's small sketch of it survives in the National Gallery of Scotland.[47] He had been in Italy from 1710 to 1720, enjoying the patronage both of the Medici in Florence and of the Pretender in Rome, where he may have received the commission for the ceiling. On it, a fictive architectural border with the Four Seasons in the corners opened in an oculus at the centre to show Pluto clutching the frantic Proserpine as his chariot plunged over the edge of a fiery abyss. Was this meant to be something to do with Scotland? At any rate, it would turn out to be the only major Scottish work directly inspired by Italian baroque painting.

Landed gentlemen wanted their Scottish homes to keep up with European fashion and were prepared to pay for the craftsmen they employed to go and gain the right experience. Scots artists gathered in Rome especially, where penniless painters mixed with jaded Jacobites. The doyen of this community was Gavin Hamilton, a distant connection of the eponymous ducal family, who stayed in the Eternal City for 40 years and furnished the church of his Catholic compatriots, San Andrea degli Scozzesi, with an altarpiece depicting the martyrdom of St Andrew. Inspired also by excavations of the Emperor Hadrian's villa at Tivoli, Hamilton turned to depicting classical subjects on a huge scale, notably a cycle of six scenes from Homer's *Iliad*. Another of his pictures was *The Oath of Brutus*, which prompted a series of 'oath paintings' by European painters, notably Jacques-Louis David's *Oath of the Horatii* (1784), itself an inspiration for the real Oath of the Tennis Court taken by the Third Estate early in the French Revolution. And this in turn was to be the model for David Octavius Hill's painting of the first General Assembly of the Free Church of Scotland in 1843.[48]

Scots passed through Rome all the time, and one who joined Hamilton's circle was Alexander Runciman. He came from Edinburgh, where he had built up a decorative painting business successful and prestigious enough to be engaged by Sir John Clerk for Penicuik House. Clerk planned a classical interior, and the deal was that he would pay for Runciman to go to Rome and acquire the necessary skills. The artist stayed nearly five years and came back with ideas of his own. On his return he completed, apparently with incredible speed, one of the iconic works of the age, the Hall of Ossian at Penicuik (1772). It was a room 36 feet by 24 feet with a coved ceiling. Its central part formed an oval where Ossian could be seen singing to an audience on the seashore. The four corners of the rectangle left by the oval were filled with gods of the Scottish rivers, the Spey, the Tay, the Tweed and the Clyde, gigantic figures set in dramatic landscapes. The cove (the curved surface between the flat of the wall and the flat of the ceiling) contained 12 further compositions, mostly illustrating Ossian. Runciman also completed four paintings with the story of St Margaret of Scotland on one of the adjacent stairs. He continued to work as fast as possible so as to emulate Ossian's 'vehemence and fire'. While we know from sketches and photographs how all this extraordinary achievement looked, the originals went up in smoke when Penicuik House was gutted by a blaze in 1899.[49]

That was one direction Scottish painting took; the other lay in portraiture.

From the portraits we have of the people in the circle round Allan Ramsay the Elder, we gain a vivid impression of who it was that brought about the artistic recovery from the Union. He himself might have been an unlikely cultural guru, a native of the wretched mining village of Leadhills in Lanarkshire who had initially established himself in Edinburgh as a wigmaker. But then he opened its first bookshop at the Luckenbooths in the High Street, and all its intellectuals came to browse there. Some would have been lawyers from nearby Parliament House, Sir John Clerk and Sir Hew Dalrymple, even the Lord Advocate, Duncan Forbes of Culloden, if ever he could find the time. William Aikman, the artist–landowner from Angus and cousin of Sir John, doubtless also felt at home in this company. Ramsay would have made his fellow poet James Thomson welcome, and Aikman would have done the same for the painter John Smibert, while the architects William Adam or Colen Campbell might drop by if they happened to be in town. Sometimes, perhaps, a sudden silence fell on Ramsay's shop when the bookish Archibald Campbell, Earl of Ilay, the most powerful politician in Scotland, walked in.[50]

In their portraits, Aikman and Smibert recorded for posterity at least the lesser lights in this galaxy. Both had spent time in Rome and developed a style mixing formal classicism with a naturalism that could only have come out of painting from life. In Aikman's case it attained a high dignity, clarity and order, as in his images of Clerk and Dalrymple, of the Revd William Carstares, of George Watson (founder of the college) and of Allan Ramsay himself. Aikman prospered from these commissions and at length went to London to paint two Prime Ministers, Sir Robert Walpole and the Earl of Bute. Smibert also left us portraits of Ramsay but his finest achievement in this genre was the double portrait of *Sir Archibald Grant of Monymusk and his Wife*, painted in 1727. Smibert in his turn at length left Scotland to join Bishop George Berkeley in an expedition to set up a Christian college in the Bermudas, and his depiction of the group is his best-known work. They got across the Atlantic Ocean but the project for the college failed. Smibert settled in Boston, to found the tradition of American painting.[51]

These were the friends of his father that Allan Ramsay the Younger grew up with, but he would exceed them all. He was sent to Italy in 1735 and returned ready to embark on a glittering career of his own. With him, Scottish art in general came of age and reached a level of intellectual and imaginative achievement as impressive as anything else in the culture of the age. He started by depicting the people in his father's circle, most triumphantly in the portrait of *Sir Hew Dalrymple, Lord Drummore* (1754). It is of three-quarter length, beautifully observed and illuminated by natural daylight. Drummore sits directly facing us so we that make immediate contact with him. Yet the social distance is just right. We feel this is an exceptional character, a man of humanity and intelligence.[52]

Ramsay meanwhile moved onwards and upwards. His father's friendship with the Earl of Ilay paid off when in 1744 the son was asked to paint him soon after his succession as third Duke of Argyll. He would produce three portraits of the great man, all formal but still varied. For the first, the duke chose to sit in the robes of Lord Justice General (it is the head of this study that figures today on the banknotes of the Royal Bank of Scotland). The second portrait, of 1749, gives us the most majestic image. Ramsay does not strain for effect, though Argyll has garbed himself in ducal robes of state, scarlet and ermine. But he is doing things any man would do if he had to sit still for a long time, flipping the pages of a book while looking quizzically outwards at us. The ultimate model of such a portrait is Titian's painting of the Emperor Charles V seated, but Ramsay puts his own subject much further back in the space than most painters following the example – so that the most remarkable thing about the picture is the light. The last portrait of 1759, a couple of years before the duke's death, shows him old but still strong, with a rheumy coldness in the eyes, the product of old age and long experience of politics.[53]

The ascent of Ramsay was not over yet. His tact and integrity in dealing with the state portrait, the abstract and formal depiction of office and status, brought him even to the attention of the royal house. His work at this level began in 1758 with a commission from the Earl of Bute to paint a full-length portrait of his pupil, the youth who was then Prince of Wales; Ramsay also did a full-length portrait of Bute himself. After King George III came to the throne in 1760, Ramsay was appointed his official painter. Portraiture at this level required delicate political as well as aesthetic judgment, but Ramsay worked his way through the problems to produce a convincing image of a real person, perhaps idealising though not prettifying the slightly odd facial features of the king (and later of his even odder-looking consort, Charlotte of Mecklenburg-Strelitz).[54]

Master as Ramsay became of all this, his finest work lay in more intimate portraits of women. His style had already matured by the time he came to paint the first of two beautiful pictures of his first wife, *Anne Bayne* (1740).

He describes her without flattery, but in a truthful, simple way more loving than any embellishment could make it. He again uses the vehicle of light, not dramatically but as the means to bring out a living sense of the subject. Light is so subtly described, reflected on to Anne's cheek from the edge of her white bonnet, for example, that the reality dispels all notion of portraiture as an abstraction. We need to go back to the Dutch painting of the golden age to find such precise observation so gently qualified by a feeling for human life.[55]

One of the most lastingly popular of all Scottish pictures is Ramsay's portrait of his second wife, *Margaret Lindsay* (1757). The two had eloped in 1752 because her parents objected to her marrying a mere painter, most successful in the country though he might be. The lovers went to Italy and stayed till 1757. While there he painted her twice. Both are beautiful pictures, but it is the second, later portrait that has captured the imagination of generations of Scots. It shows Margaret in a lovely pink dress with a lace fichu and sleeves, and a blue ribbon in her hair. She is arranging flowers and has a rose in her hand. Her action is suspended as she turns at the entry of the artist. We know it is her husband because of the way she looks at him, frank but trusting. A measure of Ramsay's strength as a portraitist is that, within the polite conventions of contemporary art, he can yet convey such a complex account of the relationship between two people.[56]

After 1769, Ramsay's practice diminished. Royal portraits took up his time. They also left him comfortably off. But in his last years he produced a particular pair of paintings especially remarkable for fragile delicacy, in his second portrait of *David Hume* and its companion, the portrait of *Jean-Jacques Rousseau*, both of 1766 and both painted for Hume. In these the painter meets as an equal the two most influential thinkers of his time and provides penetrating commentary on them. In both pictures the sitter is caught in a fleeting shaft of light. Hume sits facing us, a bright figure in lace and brocade, even foppish, but the light leaves his face partly in shadow and his eyes meet us with a level gaze. By contrast, Rousseau appears fugitive, turning away as if about to vanish in the shadow and, though caught at this moment in visible form, he remains an elusive figure. The central preoccupation of Scottish philosophy, the relationship between seeing and knowing, is here made flesh. We cannot doubt that, in its clarity and humanity, the art of Scotland has become a high expression of European civilisation.[57]

The maturity of Scottish art was confirmed and strengthened by the fact that Scots also thought and wrote about it with increasing sophistication. To put the matter another way, the intellectual interests of the Enlightenment extended into aesthetics too. This launched itself as a peripheral movement, first in the sense that it started out in Aberdeen rather than in the usual enlightened circles of Edinburgh, and then in the sense that it originally grew from literary rather than artistic criticism. Thomas Blackwell, professor of Greek at Marischal College, wrote an *Inquiry into the Life, Times and Writings of Homer* (1735) denying its subject had belonged to a polite culture, to use the contemporary term. On the contrary, Homer lived in a primitive world, in any event preliterate (the transmission of his epics being oral). The power of his poetry lay in its imagination and spontaneity, not in obedience to anything like the rules governing the neoclassical literature of the eighteenth century. That was what made Homer gripping: 'So unaffected and simple were the manners of those times that the folds and windings of the human breast lay open to the eye.'[58] And we had to take into account the huge difference not only in the people who recited but also in the people who listened to the poetry: while for these 'the marvellous and wonderful are the nerve of the epic strain', their equivalents today 'can think nothing great or beautiful but what is the product of wealth. They exclude themselves from the pleasantest and most natural images that adorn the old poetry, wealth and luxury disguise nature.'[59]

One of Blackwell's pupils was George Turnbull, another man of letters who enjoyed the ample capacity for friendship of the younger Allan Ramsay; he also became the teacher at Marischal College of the philosopher Thomas Reid. For the particular matter of aesthetics Turnbull carried the argument, in his *Treatise on Ancient Painting* (1740), on from the literary to the artistic. He too started with Homer, and asserted that the superiority of Greek painting lay in its being able to choose its subjects out of a literature 'founded on fact and observation', less in the foreground of heroes and gods than in the background with its often exact, intricate description of human actions and their material props. This also linked onto Greek philosophy, because Plato especially spent a good deal of time, for instance in the *Symposium,* trying to decide exactly what beauty was. The idea appealed to the Greeks that the promptings of our moral sense operated in a manner analogous to our intuitive identification of beauty. This psychological intertwining of ethics and aesthetics was just the sort of thing that in turn intrigued Scottish philosophers. Turnbull furthered the discussion by claiming that – in the modern as in the ancient world – the appreciation of art, like the study of history and literature, made for politeness and refinement.[60]

The younger Ramsay joined in these aesthetic debates, in effect commenting on his own career as he went along. He did so especially after he befriended Hume; both were much of an age and both sons of Edinburgh. While Hume's philosophical works notoriously fell dead from the press, in Ramsay they found a fan. They said, after all, that we cannot understand the world around us except through what we actually perceive and, as Hume said, 'everything in nature is individual'.[61] Generalisation therefore becomes impossible in the eye as in the mind. It is imagination that allows us to reach out beyond the limits of our immediate impressions. In dealing with other people, the vehicle for our imagination is sympathy. So though Hume's analysis ruthlessly dismantles intellectual structures that we have created for ourselves, he leaves intact our sense of our humanity. In just the same way Ramsay paints. He analyses what he sees with the same clarity as Hume, but the image, held together by sympathy and imagination, becomes more than the sum of the observations.[62]

Ramsay contributed aesthetic essays of his own. His 'On Ridicule' (1753) asserted a need for realism: 'The agreeable cannot be separated from the exact, and a posture in painting must be a just resemblance of what is graceful in nature, before it can hope to be esteemed graceful.'[63] Nature is not to be improved by art, then. Our classical models, whether from antiquity or the Renaissance, had been the result of a process of discovery, not of invention. But while embarking on a process of discovery, we should not slavishly copy the results. Then in 1755 Ramsay published 'A Dialogue on Taste'. The dialogue takes place between Colonel Freeman, who speaks for the author, and Lord Modish who, as his name implies, speaks for the world of unreflecting fashion. From it we learn that Ramsay believed art must mirror experience directly and therefore not require a high degree of sophistication to be understood. It should be just as simple to apprehend as the world about us is to perceive. There is no place in art or in reality for abstract ideas: 'No analysis can be made of abstract beauty, nor of any abstraction whatever.'[64] This anti-idealism even led Ramsay to condemn the notion of a classical canon of human beauty. He said it was an uneasy compromise because any such generalisation was incompatible with the fact that the human race consisted of individuals, none of whom were identical.[65]

Scottish aesthetics were empirical: they proceeded not from any desire to define universal principles and derive practice from them, but from the actual problems that past or present artists faced in trying to turn life into art. Minute attention to everyday reality was an essential starting point, but did not need to be photographic: the artist intervened, and was entitled to intervene, with his own interests and interpretations. Scottish art, if driven by technical, social and indeed by international ambition, in the end felt confident enough of itself to pursue concerns of its own – not least the subject matter of its native country embarking on the most profound changes ever to be experienced.[66]

As in other forms of cultural expression, Scottish painting at length turned round from high art to look once more at the people, not abandoning its aspirations to compare with the best in Europe but returning to Scotland enriched by those aspirations. The perfect vehicle was what has come to be known as genre painting, an academic term for pictures of humble folk rich in the details of still life with pots, pans, nails in cracked walls and so on. It transferred to Scotland a style previously best practised by the Dutch masters of the seventeenth century. It satisfies as composition yet makes a social statement, comic or moving.[67]

The man who took the lead in the development of Scottish genre painting was David Allan.[68] He was a student at the Foulis Academy in Glasgow before he went to Rome in 1767. Over his career, his art fell broadly into three categories. One was the classical studies he did in Italy or soon after his return, of which *The Continence of Scipio* is the best example. A second was, once he got home again, formal portraits of Scottish notables, but with excursions in a lighter vein, such as his picture of *The Connoisseurs*. And finally there were the images of ordinary life in Scotland, from the uncompromisingly realistic in his sketches of mining operations at Leadhills to the gently ironical in his genre paintings. The latter include his most celebrated commission for the illustrations to an edition of Allan Ramsay the Elder's *The Gentle Shepherd* published in 1788, where the artist's fidelity to nature encounters the poet's pastoral charm. From 1792 Allan produced illustrations to the songs Robert Burns was either composing or amending for the collection George Thomson published as *Select Scottish Airs*. The affinity with Burns then turned still more explicit in Allan's *The Penny Wedding* (1795), an exemplary scene of Scottish peasant life in all its human worth and homely detail. Allan became perhaps the first modern painter to claim it was the very lack of sophistication, the naivety of his art that made it so lucid and so authentic.

In no other creative fields had Scotland come further since 1707 than in the achievements of its architecture and its painting. At the outset there was imitation of superior foreign models, but by the end of a century these had grown into patriotic arts. While this fact is underplayed in most accounts of the Enlightenment, it is scarcely possible to understand either of those arts except as the products of a nation on a course of rapid cultural advance. If something beyond visual proof is necessary, we can find it in the contemporary writings on aesthetics that are also largely forgotten by modern academic scholarship. This scholarship concentrates on the printed page and tends to forget that ideas and theories had a life beyond it. Certainly Scots of the time were coming to believe that the primitive and unspoiled possessed a special quality as aspects of the imagination not yet staled by custom or corrupted by worldliness. Perhaps they might offer a way towards a new, imaginative purity of vision. There was no better place to explore the concept than in the realities of Scotland.

14

Words: 'The kilt aërian'

On 31 July 1786, John Wilson, printer and publisher at Kilmarnock, brought out a slim volume of verse, *Poems, chiefly in the Scottish dialect*, by an unknown young farmer also from Ayrshire, Robert Burns. The books cost 3 shillings a copy, and 612 of them were printed. They sold out in a month. From them the author earned £20 – hardly a fortune, but still three times what he got from working his farm every year. The sum saved him from imminent destitution, out of which emigration to the West Indies had seemed to him the only escape. Better than that, the poems won him immortality.[1]

Wilson was also a young fellow, at 28 just a year senior to Burns, and he had run his printer's shop in his home town, selling books and stationery besides, since 1780. He started with reprints of older Scottish titles, Allan Ramsay's *Tea Table Miscellany*, Blind Harry's *William Wallace* and King James I's *Kingis Quair*, which found a market among booksellers in other towns too. As Wilson became established he also started producing original works, either at the author's own expense or (in the case of the penniless Burns) after collecting subscriptions from friends and well-wishers. The mix of business was typical of the many small but enterprising printing houses that sprang up in Scottish towns. They could even be agents of the Enlightenment, not always of the high Enlightenment and the profound works it produced but rather of a popular Enlightenment that diffused the great ideas in society at large.[2]

Still, most of Wilson's books were religious, geared to the theologically orthodox yet often dissenting Presbyterianism of the west of Scotland. With the Kilmarnock edition of Burns, Wilson published his first original work of secular literature: small wonder the author chose carefully which of his verses to include, and left out his sharpest satires on the Kirk. Still, critical views at once waxed warm. As soon as copies reached Edinburgh, the city's literary arbiter, Henry Mackenzie, wrote of the author in his magazine, *The Lounger*.

> I think I may safely pronounce him a genius of no ordinary rank. The person to whom I allude is Robert Burns, an Ayrshire ploughman, whose poems were some time ago published in a country town in the west of Scotland, with no other ambition, it would seem, than to circulate among the inhabitants of the country where he was born, to obtain a little fame from those who have heard of his talents. I hope I shall not be thought to assume too much if I endeavour to place him in a higher point of view, to call for a verdict of his country on the merit of his works, and to claim for him those honours which their excellence appears to deserve.
>
> In mentioning the circumstances of his humble station, I mean not to rest his pretensions solely on that title or to urge the merits of his poetry when considered in relation to the lowness of his birth, and the little opportunity of improvement which his education could afford. These particulars, indeed, might excite our wonder at his productions; but his poetry, considered abstractedly, and without the apologies arising from his situation, seems to me fully entitled to command our feelings and to obtain our applause.
>
> One bar, indeed, his birth and education have opposed to his fame – the language in which most of his poems are written. Even in Scotland the provincial dialect which Ramsay and he have used is now read with a difficulty which greatly damps the pleasure of the reader; in England it cannot be read at all, without such a constant reference to a glossary as nearly to destroy the pleasure.
>
> Some of his productions, however, especially those of the grave style, are almost English.[3]

This was a favourable review, indeed, yet it could not avoid the patronising attitudes that the prevailing taste of the time might call forth even from a sympathetic critic.

Burns rose above all this. It was enough for him that the Kilmarnock edition saved him having to emigrate. His passage to Jamaica was already paid, and a job as bookkeeper on a plantation awaited him. One reason he felt he had to leave Scotland was the impossibility of earning a decent living from the farm he worked with his brother Gilbert at Mossgiel, near Mauchline. Doubtless an extra incentive lay in Rabbie's chaotic love life, now proving expensive too. In 1785 he had already fathered one child, Bess, on his family's servant, Elizabeth Paton. In 1786 he found that his new sweetheart and fiancée, Jean Armour, was also pregnant. Her father took the news badly, turned against their marriage and started legal proceedings for maintenance of the prospective bastard. Burns sought solace in the only way he knew – in the arms of yet another woman, Mary Campbell or Highland Mary, from Dunoon. His new plan was for her to go to Jamaica with him. He needed £20 to buy tickets for the two of them. It was to raise this money that he published his poems.[4]

Just a week before Burns was due to sail, quite prepared never to see his homeland again, two things happened to change his mind. Jean Armour gave birth to twins, called after their parents Robert and Jean – and their father was always soppy about his bairns. Then he learned that the Kilmarnock edition had been a success and that his little volume was selling like hotcakes, not least because of Mackenzie's favourable review. When Mary Campbell died of a fever in October, Burns finally gave up all idea of leaving Scotland. With a little money and a rapidly rising reputation, he headed instead to Edinburgh, to be feted for the next couple of years by its intellectuals and especially by their wives and daughters. It is there we will pick up his progress later in this chapter.[5]

Burns was not only a poet of the first literary importance to his nation but also had a big effect on its linguistic history. He played a prime part in rescuing Scots from decline and perhaps from speedy extinction. After the Union, and already in his own time, standard southern English had been generally adopted as the literary medium in Scotland even while Scots remained the spoken vernacular. This is still the position now, broadly speaking, except that the Scots of the eighteenth century was a good deal richer and racier than the Scots of today, and a long time could be spent arguing whether the latter is still really a language or has become in effect just a dialect of modern English more non-standard than most. A big difference is that in the twenty-first century attitudes towards the Scots language are on the whole benign, allowing some hope it might yet revive as a living, or more living, tongue. If it ever does, nobody would have done more than Burns to bring that about.[6]

In the eighteenth century the prevailing attitude was often the reverse: polite society, at least, had come to consider Scots as limited and coarse. While many then did their best to rid their speech of its taint, others balked. With their interest and support a new literary Scots came into being, based on

contemporary colloquial speech. It was written down in some form of historical Scottish orthography while still uneasily acknowledging a superior status
for English in the nervous swarms of apostrophes used to mark deviations
from that standard. Here was the language of Ramsay and Burns. It combined, again often somewhat awkwardly, reasonable authenticity with their
need to sell to readers unfamiliar with it. When in 1808 John Jamieson published his *Etymological Dictionary of the Scots Language*, it could be regarded as the
thesaurus of the new literary medium. It provided access to this medium also
for Scots who in everyday life no longer used many of the words included.
It was not really a record of the actual speech of the people, which went on
developing and in some ways diverging even from such a sympathetic attempt
at its preservation: Jamieson would not be of much use with the Weegie of
the twenty-first century, for example.[7]

Jamieson's was all the same an enlightened project, even while it rejected
the usual enlightened ambition of anglicising Scots towards a single linguistic norm valid for the whole United Kingdom. This would have proscribed
regional or socially unacceptable grammar and pronunciation, and would
have prescribed a model based on the English of London – not so much
Cockney as the speech of the royal court or at least of the professional
classes. The example could then be turned back on the Scots language, to
stigmatise it as vulgar and if possible to eradicate it. In truth, this was clearly
a less enlightened project than Jamieson's, being formulated not out of
any empirical observation but simply as a matter of dogma. Its advocates,
most with a classical education, laboured under the delusion that, once a
language had been purified and standardised, it could in that perfect state
be frozen and made immune to innovation or change, on the model of
Latin. In the real ancient world, however, it had been the despised rustic
vernaculars that took over from the language of caesars and consuls and
developed into the modern Romance tongues. The Scottish Enlightenment,
ever respectful of historical fact, fell short of its habitual standards in
this case.[8]

The anglicising movement yet remained powerful. The principal of
Marischal College, Aberdeen, the Revd George Campbell, set out its ideal
in *The Philosophy of Rhetoric* (1776): 'reputable use' of the language resided in
the 'conversation of men of rank and eminence', already a universal standard
'found current, especially in the upper and the middle ranks, over the whole
British empire'.[9] Though not an academic and presumably in touch with his
own Scots-speaking peasantry, the agricultural improver, Sir John Sinclair

of Ulbster, also relegated their language to a subsidiary status.[10] 'The Scotch dialect' was merely 'a dialect of the Saxon or Old English, with some trifling variations'. While there might be value in its 'quaintness', it could hardly be compared with the political and economic advantage of a 'national language'. James Buchanan described 'Scotch' as 'that rough and uncouth brogue which is so harsh and unpleasant to an English ear', and in the United Kingdom threatened to make aliens of those who used it: 'The people of North Britain seem, in general, to be almost at as great a loss for proper accent and just pronunciation as foreigners.' Their 'errors ... barbarisms and vulgarities' did a disservice to their cultural achievements. If only they could be taught standard English, 'their acquiring a proper accent and graceful pronunciation ... would embellish and set off to far greater advantage the many excellent and rhetorical speeches delivered by the learned both from the pulpit and at the bar'.[11]

Many enlightened Scots found these arguments persuasive, but some did not. An appeal for tolerance of the Scots language came from a second Aberdonian professor, James Beattie, for 'every nation and province has a particular accent'. Yet even he still recommended as 'the standard of the English tongue' what he characterised as 'the language ... of the most learned and polite persons in London, and the neighbouring universities of Oxford and Cambridge'.[12] All this ignored the fact that Scots itself had once had, and to an extent still had, a refined and prestigious version not owed to any effort at anglicisation: the Court Scots probably last heard in public during the residence at Holyrood by the future King James VII in 1679–81. According to Henry Cockburn, it was still used during his youth by old ladies, who in that era did not often leave Scotland and get their accent diluted. There is no particular reason why, without the Union of 1707, this could not have developed a standard of its own, drawing on the speech and writings of the legal, clerical and academic professions in Edinburgh or other Scottish cities. It might in the end have differed from standard English just as American English and British English differ today, without any imputation of inferiority on one or the other. In general, we should not underestimate the extent of resistance to or even resentment of these contemporary efforts to purify Scots from its perceived vulgarities. Learned men still knew it had a long and respectable pedigree together with an outstanding literary history.[13]

The situation was different for Gaelic, the other national language. Perhaps a quarter of the population spoke it, heirs to a rich oral and literary tradition. History would soon pass a harsh verdict on them, but meanwhile their language and literature enjoyed a final blaze of glory, in a cultural development more vigorous than anything in Scots. One big reason for it lay in the fact that the practitioners of the prime literary genre, the poetry, abandoned the use of classical Gaelic, the ancient bardic tongue shared by Scotland with Ireland, in favour of modern Gaelic. After the destruction of the chiefs' power in the Jacobite rebellions, they no longer headed households with room for a bard. Poets still sang, but now they had to make their own way in the world. It was a world where most Gaels scarcely understood classical Gaelic anyway, competence in it being confined to those with some specialised training. For the people to express themselves, they needed a different medium.[14]

The medium was to be the Scottish Gaelic vernacular, a group of closely related dialects by now all a long way from the classical standard. Its self-expression found a locus in the popular institution of the ceilidh rather than, at first anyway, in manuscripts and books. The ceilidh is a social gathering that survives today, of which the history was traced by Alexander Carmichael in his introduction to the *Carmina Gadelica* (1900).[15] In its modern form it has become a sort of sit-down party, with song or instrumental music performed to an audience that can join in and, as the evening wears on, is often moved to do so by the amount of drink taken. In the old days, more or less anything could prompt a ceilidh, for there was no other entertainment in the scattered Highland townships. They found a frequent excuse in the coming of a stranger, and one who told his tale till dawn would be sure of a warm welcome.

The ceilidh offered these isolated communities a window on their cultural past too. Across the central Highlands the stranger was asked as soon as he appeared, *A bheil dad agad air an Fhèinn?* 'Do you know anything of the Fianna?' In medieval lays, the Fianna had been the semi-regular militia of Finn MacCool, performing fearless feats in athletic defence of the underdog when not too busy with erotic entanglements or with discussions in elegant but complex poetry on the relative merits of the active and the contemplative life. If the stranger to the township could add any good stories or verse about the Fianna to those already known there, he was invited to do so that night at a ceilidh. James MacPherson, visiting Uist in 1760 in search of the poems of Ossian, reaped little reward when he reversed the roles and asked the question of the poet John MacCodrum, since it can also mean, 'Do the Fianna owe you anything?' No, said MacCodrum, *Chan eil, 's ged a bhitheachd, cha ruiginn a leas iarraidh a'nis,* 'And if they did there would no point in looking for it now.'[16] Here, however, was a living tradition of orally transmitted poetry, just like the old Greek or Germanic epics.

It is true that the dawn of modernity also saw an increase in the use of Gaelic prose, arising first and foremost from the practice of Protestant religion. This was strongly influenced by translation from the Irish and English versions of the Bible, with the constructions, imagery and vocabulary these had developed to meet the challenge of representing the Hebrew or Greek originals. And then, in English, a huge volume of sermons and religious writings was published from the Reformation onwards, to bring theology for the first time to the people – though usually to the more learned of the people, if we may judge from the somewhat abstract rhetorical style of such literature. This again was an example the Gaels sought to follow, but their written language did gradually evolve towards their spoken vernacular. The earliest devotional works, John Carswell's *Foirm na n-Urrnuidheadh* (1567) and Neill MacEwen's *Adtimchiol an Chreidimh* (1631), are in classical Gaelic. From the Shorter Catechism of 1659 modern Gaelic starts to enter in, till we reach the pretty solidly vernacular Scottish Gaelic of the Bible – the translation of the New Testament by James Stuart of Killin and Dugald Buchanan of Rannoch published in 1767, and the translation of the Old Testament published in 1803 by John Stuart (son of James).[17]

In the dominant poetic tradition there was already a wide divergence between the ornate panegyrics that the bards composed for their chiefs, often not obviously of much interest to anybody else, and the Fenian lays, popular epics with roots deep in the Middle Ages; John Francis Campbell of Islay found them still being recited to pass the dark winter's nights in the Outer Hebrides of the late nineteenth century.[18] Given all this, literary transition in Gaelic, from classical to modern, from one genre to another, was bound to be gradual and untidy. But the early eighteenth century saw it clearly going on in the work of two men who wrote poetry and prose in both forms of the language, indeed were masters of the whole literary and linguistic gamut: Niall Mac Mhuirich, bard and historian to MacDonald of Clanranald, and Alasdair mac Mhaighstir Alasdair who, among other things in a varied and colourful career, would be Prince Charles Edward Stewart's interpreter and Gaelic teacher in 1745.

Niall, a tacksman on South Uist, was also a scholar as happy among men of letters in both Scotland and Ireland as among the Highland aristocracy. He died about 1719 in his eighties, having lived through the waning of the old world and the dawning of modern times in the Gàidhealtachd. He brought the bardic and the vernacular language together in both his poems and the prose he deployed in his Clanranald Histories. For the latter he used an intermediate dialect, which might actually have been already established as a normal mode of expression at this higher level of Highland society, enabling it to preserve its cultural heritage, to cherish its links with the rest of the Celtic world and yet to maintain contact with the ordinary life of the clan. The theory of an intermediate socio-linguistic form of Gaelic has been advanced by William Gillies and surely offers a more plausible picture of the real situation than the older notion of an abrupt change from classical to modern Gaelic.[19]

Alasdair mac Mhaighstir Alasdair's linguistic exuberance represented still more decisive progress. He was the greatest poet in Gaelic of the eighteenth century and arguably of all time, for only Sorley MacLean in the twentieth century can be counted in the same league. Whereas Sorley, for all his undoubted modernity, consciously linked himself to the Gaelic past, Alastair leaped forward from it and innovated in practically all he did – except only, perhaps, after being recruited as principal Jacobite propagandist in 1745, when he had to sing in praise of his chief and pupil, Prince Charles. Otherwise Alasdair, a broad-minded and generous man, always had originality to spare as much in his matter, manfully martial or lyrically libidinous, as in his manner, pushing Gaelic verse out from its exhausted conventions. Experiment offers the key to his whole oeuvre, blending the human and the animal, the living and the dead, the prosaic and the musical, the traditional and the innovatory.[20] His greatest work is, as it were, a recollection of epic, *Birlinn Chlann Raghnaill*, 'The Ship of Clanranald', the ship being a metaphor for a world where man needs to struggle with nature:

> *Éireadh seisear ealamh ghleusta,*
> *Làmhach, bheòtha,*
> *Shiùbhlas 's a dh'fhalbhas 's a leumas*
> *Feadh gach bòrd dhith*
> *Mar gheàrr-fhiadh am mullach slèibhe*
> *'S coin da còpadh,*
>
> *Streapas ri cruaidh-bhallaibh rèidhe*
> *Den chaol chòrcaich*

Cho grad ri feòragan cèitein
  Ri crann rò-choill,

Bhios ullamh, ealamh, treubhach,
  Falbhach, eòlach
Gu toirt dhi 's gu toirt an abhsadh
  As clabhsail òrdan –
Chaitheas gun airtneal gun èislean,
  Long MhicDhòmhnaill.

Let six men rise who're quick and lively
  Handy, active,
Who'll move about and shift and leap
  Round all her planks
Like a hare on mountain-top
  With hounds pursuing her,

Who'll struggle with hard slippery ropes
  Of slender hemp
As nimbly as the maytime squirrels
  Up forest tree,

Who're ready, nimble, valiant,
  Swift and expert
In spreading sails and taking in a reef
  In systematic order –
Who'll sail, untiring and unflagging,
  MacDonald's ship.[21]

While capable of poetic achievement at the highest level, Alasdair also amused himself with versified pornography. Indeed he was dismissed from one of his jobs, as schoolmaster in Ardnamurchan, for the offence he gave to 'all sober and well-inclined persons, as he wanders through the country composing songs stuffed with obscene language'. But he never found it hard to keep himself busy. Bored though he grew with the project, he persisted in the compilation of a Gaelic–English vocabulary, which was the earliest Highland schoolbook, providing lists of words for the children to learn. He became the first to collect and publish an anthology of original Gaelic verse, *Ais-eiridh na Sean Chanain Albanaich*, 'The Resurrection of the Old Highland Language'. He developed an orthographic system to replace the old Irish script and, switching languages, also wrote English prose that was racy, elegant and witty. In effect he constructed a rare vision of a Scottish culture with room for all traditions.[22]

With the linguistic liberation, poetic voices arose not just among learned Gaels but also among the people. Duncan Ban MacIntyre was actually illiterate and never held more than a menial position in his society, first as a gamekeeper for the Duke of Argyll, finally as a member of the town guard in Edinburgh (which was full of Highlanders). He is the best-loved figure in all of Gaelic literature, for he takes the view of the common man and articulates it with dazzling fluency. Most of his work is descriptive, and much of it shows the influence of Alasdair mac Mhaighstir Alasdair. It is in the poetry of nature that Duncan excels: his best-known poem is *Moladh Beinn Dòbhrain*, 'Praise of Ben Doran', a bare mountain near Bridge of Orchy visible from the modern railway to Fort William. This was not an especially promising subject but a refined talent and a mature imagination transformed it.[23]

From an equally humble station in life came Rob Donn, the poet of Sutherland. Also illiterate, he got what education he had from the ceilidhs. He never lived permanently outside the parish of Durness, where he worked for a tacksman first as herd-boy, then as cattleman, finally as drover. He used his dialect quite self-consciously, imitating its natural rhythms in his verse, in a way that struck Gaels further south as outlandish. In the intervening quarter of a millennium, the dialect has largely vanished, and might have been forgotten altogether but for Rob's preservation of it. To that extent, he represents the relatively settled nature of the community of Reay during his lifetime, which comes across as a sort of golden age that we know – as he did not – was before long to be ended by economic upheaval. His work represents finally a powerful blend of the rhetorical strengths and moral values of traditional Gaelic verse with the newer linguistic sobriety and social realism of Presbyterian culture.[24]

Despite incomparable cultural achievement, the Gaelic tongue would before long suffer a more devastating fate than the Scots tongue, and this already loomed on the horizon. Not even the Scottish state had looked kindly on Gaelic, and from 1745 the British state adopted an official policy of extirpating the language, together with all the visible aspects of its culture, the pipes, the tartan and so on. The period of total proscription did not, it is true, last too long. Ironically, Gaelic culture would afterwards become more closely bound into a wider Scottish identity, if as a legacy of the past, and as a matter more of images than of words.[25]

One root of this development lay in the greatest literary controversy of the age, in Scotland, in Britain and indeed in the whole of Europe. It blew up over James MacPherson's publication of several volumes purporting to be translations into English of poems originally written in Gaelic by the ancient bard Ossian. It caused such a sensation because it burst on a world of letters used to mannered fiction, decorous poetry and high-minded history, all with heavy admixtures of moral philosophy. Beneath this polished literary surface there suddenly stood revealed abysses of raw instinct and emotion, of lust and bloodlust, and the reading public loved it. From Lisbon to Riga young men (young women less often) went into fits of gloom, contemplated love-lorn suicide and so on. It marked the start of the Romantic movement. Yet the question remained whether Ossian was authentic.[26]

MacPherson hailed from Badenoch. As a child he had witnessed the after-math of the Battle of Culloden: since his clan was Jacobite, its territory suffered the ravages of the redcoats. He still grew up in a Gaelic culture, though as a tacksman's son he was schooled in English and went on to the University of Aberdeen. His professor was Thomas Blackwell, whose literary theory exalted the sublime as found in the epics of Homer. MacPherson could link this with his own tradition, which sometimes constructed new epics out of classical ones, just as the Iliad had been put together by the recension of Pisistratus in ancient Athens. MacPherson was to imitate Alastair mac Mhaighstir Alastair's method of collecting, copying, collating and concocting. So the affair of Ossian was not quite, as received wisdom has it, the tall story of a louche loner and his literary hoax.[27]

Certainly the young MacPherson's main ambition was to make a name for himself. In 1760 he brought out his *Fragments of Ancient Poetry Collected in the Highlands of Scotland*.[28] The slim volume contained a dozen or so poems, said to be by Ossian but translated by MacPherson, and it got rave reviews. This encouraged MacPherson to follow up the next year with an epic in six books, *Fingal,* which he said had been lost and now rediscovered by him. In its published form it came across as a sort of wistful prose-poem, bearing not much resemblance to any extant Gaelic verse. Yet it pleased the contemporary taste for formal but lyrical descriptions of nature (to modern taste they seem merely hackneyed). Was this a valid adaptation of a genuine tradition?

341

There can be no definitive answer to the question. The translations might have misrepresented the originals, but they did more or less work in their own terms. At any rate, they achieved a huge readership, and perhaps transmitted some essence of Gaelic poetic tradition to readers otherwise knowing nothing of it.[29]

Since few of MacPherson's critics had a word of Gaelic either, and because he treated with contempt any questioning of his sources, a definite conclusion on their authenticity proved for the time being impossible. The poems were no mere forgeries, as his fiercest foes claimed. But if he could not exactly produce his originals, this was because they did not exactly exist. He was by training a student of Latin and Greek, not Gaelic, literature and had no special philological skills. He had found some manuscripts in Old Irish (hard to read even for trained scholars today) and some bards declaiming a classical Gaelic different from his vernacular of Strathspey. A youth ambitious to get into print could make little of all this. What he could do was concoct an epic out of the materials and ideas he had gathered, if couched in another language, so as to tickle current literary taste. And why not? In Gaeldom plagiarism had no meaning. Bards never claimed copyright or troubled themselves whether others thought them original. Their aim was to give the best possible performance of material familiar to everybody for the audience right in front of them. Modern poets had already used Ossianic material and, since Gaels were the ones that produced the epic, they surely had some right to fix its character. MacPherson did imitate, as best he could, a genuine tradition, if overlain by a polite veneer for the intended audience. Yet it remains true that no poem like *Fingal*, or the less authentic sequel of 1763, *Temora*, has ever existed in Gaeldom.[30]

The cavils about MacPherson's techniques are anyway secondary to the main historical point, the extraordinary contemporary reactions to Ossian. It was a bitter irony how a society obsessed with pale imitations of antique Celtic poetry should have been so blissfully unaware that it also had on its doorstep the very finest exponents of the living art. If Dr Samuel Johnson had known this, even he might have been tempted to exercise his literary judgment rather than find a pretext for yet another stream of his boring anti-Scottish invective. Edinburgh's intellectuals sprang to the defence of Ossian, but it was an embarrassment that they then had nothing useful to say because of their own ignorance of Gaelic. The trail laid by MacPherson might have looked to some brother Scots like a way forward for a national literature otherwise at an impasse. It was to prove a false trail, though: Gaelic literature, however great, would never become common to both Scotland's linguistic communities. At any rate, the general conclusion had to be that at this stage there was no possibility of a new Scottish identity drawing on, and reflected in, the whole nation's cultures.[31]

The Scots language, the language of the majority, lay at the heart of the dilemmas. If the Gaelic language, or at best translation out of it, would not do as the vehicle for a national literature, the only available alternative lay in Scots. Yet was it an adequate vehicle either? The idea of the language as itself a problem cannot be traced back much beyond 1707, even if before then the Scottish people were already reading an English Bible and one or two poets, notably William Drummond of Hawthornden, adopted English as their normal means of expression. But after 1707 writers grappled continually with the problem of how far, inside the Union, a people using a tongue similar to English could be said to possess, or should seek to retain, a distinct cultural identity. One big reason for its attenuation lay in the fact that, amid the religious and political upheavals of the seventeenth century, Scots literature had declined in quality and especially in quantity. Its older tradition was not destroyed, but now lay back before most Scots could remember. Some special effort would be needed to bring it to life for them again.[32]

An obvious thing to do in reinvigorating the Scots language was demonstrate that it did have a literature worth reading. Luckily there were still men of letters willing to rise to this challenge. They took it on themselves to publish celebratory editions of earlier Scottish poetry. A leading printer in Edinburgh, James Watson – also a member of the Jacobite underground – advertised in the newspapers asking people to dig up examples of Scots poetry they knew about that were still in manuscript or unknown otherwise. He produced three volumes of it in his *Choice Collection of Comic and Serious Scots Poems* (1706–11). This, the first printed anthology of verse 'in our own native *Scots* dialect', set forth what was known at the time of the nation's older literature. Watson took up a pen himself to record his respect for the standards of early Scottish printing: its decline, he said, had gone hand in hand with disloyalty to the Stewarts.[33]

Crucial to the literary revival was Allan Ramsay the Elder. Scots culture meanwhile withdrew behind closed doors, to private clubs and convivial dinners where the state of the nation could be bemoaned all the more gloomily and patriotism fired all the more brightly with each glass downed. Serious drinking might also go along with serious thinking, though. The clubs would become vehicles of Enlightenment too, especially in Edinburgh. Among the first of them was the Easy Club, so called 'because none of ane empty conceited quarrelling temper can have the privilege of being a member'. It was run for young men of literary leanings to read aloud and discuss their work. In going on to subsidise publication by Ramsay, among others, the club helped to turn him into Edinburgh's leading man of letters.[34]

In that capacity Ramsay had a long career. After he had set up his book-shop in the Luckenbooths and established the artistic Academy of St Luke, he undertook a further, and expensive, cultural venture by opening a theatre in Carrubber's Close in 1736. It had only a short life before being forced to close under pressure from the Presbytery of Edinburgh. He protested at 'the impoverishing and stupefying the good town by getting everything that tends towards politeness and good humour banished'. He suspected the dirty work was being orchestrated from the 'sad shadow of a university'. In 1740 he retired from business and on Castlehill built himself an octagonal house, still standing, known as the Goose-Pie: not the only pie in which he had put a finger.[35]

Just as Allan Ramsay the Younger would theorise his painting, so Allan Ramsay the Elder had theorised his literary activity. In the preface to *The Evergreen* (1724), his own anthology of neglected Scots poetry, he proposed that the art of the past, the art of the 'good old bards', could provide a model of 'natural strength of thought and simplicity of style' that stood in contrast to effete modern taste. This was a view held also by his friend, Sir John Clerk of Penicuik, who pointed to the ancient Caledonians as rep-resentative of just such virtues.[36] Clerk himself was a unionist, but shared with Ramsay an anxiety about the effect of the Union on Scottish identity. As they looked to the past, the Caledonian resistance to Rome seemed to offer an example of the advantage of primitive simplicity over deca-dent civilisation. It was a model that went through many variations as the century advanced.

As for Ramsay's own writing, it is versatility that endows him with cultural consequence rather than the quality of his poetry as such. He builds a bridge between the classic corpus of the medieval Makars and the later Romantic revival of Scots verse, though his work is not as good as the best of either. His linguistic persona remains a bit uncertain. His range of themes or moods is limited, at their best when comic. One popular poem was the elegy for Maggy Johnston, who had run a tavern at Bruntsfield:

> *Auld Reeky! Mourn in sable hue,*
> *Let fouth of tears dreep like May dew.*
> *To braw Tippony* [beer] *bid adieu,*
> *Which we with greed*
> *Bended as fast as she could brew,*
> *But ah! she's dead.*

Even in mock-elegiac mode, Ramsay shows the forthrightness about physical function that gave and gives the national muse a distinct savour:

> *Fou closs we used to drink and rant,*
> *Until we did baith glowre and gaunt,*
> *And pish and spew, and yesk and maunt*
> *Right swash I true;*
> *Then of auld stories we did cant*
> *Whan we were fou.*

> Tanked up we used to drink and rant,
> Until we did both stare and yawn,
> And piss and spew, and belch and burble
> Well oiled indeed;
> Then we would tell merry old tales
> When we were drunk.[37]

Ramsay's achievement was to renew Scots literary language out of the mouths of the people, rather than in the various learned ways that others had embarked on for the task. It helped that the nation possessed a huge fund of folk song, which for the future would inspire not just natives, Robert Fergusson or Robert Burns, but also foreigners, Joseph Haydn or Ludwig van Beethoven. Ramsay was the first to set out in conscious effort to preserve that fund. He began to record or imitate it, if not always as faithfully as his successors did. But he deserves credit for showing how its language, its genres and its metres could still bear fruit.[38]

Was modern Scotland going to listen? In Edinburgh, the Old Town and all the venerable scenes of national history would soon be abandoned by fashionable citizens for a regime of rational living in the New Town. It often included cultivation of the English language, for example through the elocution lessons offered by the Irish impresario, Richard Brinsley Sheridan, who came here to exploit the snobbery of gullible provincials. At this stage the New Town also found, perhaps surprisingly, a poet, James Thomson, who happened to be the uncle of James Brown, winner of the architectural competition for this development. Of course, Thomson wrote in English:

> August, around, what public works I see!
> Lo! stately streets, lo! squares that court the breeze!
> See long canals and deepened rivers join
> Each part with each, and with the circling main,
> The whole enlivened isle.[39]

Thomson had established his reputation with a poetic cycle called *The Seasons*, but posterity remembers him above all as the author of 'Rule, Britannia!' This was about the highest point that Anglo-Scottish poetry attained. Its linguistic medium sprang from the head, not from the heart, and was more suited for prose than poetry. The prose would also be better cultivated from an English rather than Scottish domicile, if the author wanted to immunise himself against Scotticisms. Such, at any rate, was the strategy of the most accomplished Scottish novelist of the time, Tobias Smollett. In fact, he put 400 miles between himself and his birthplace in Dunbartonshire, though his picaresque novel, *The Adventures of Roderick Random* (1748), at least featured an émigré Scots hero. In the next generation Henry Mackenzie achieved even greater commercial success, though he never left home. He won his literary fame from a single novel, *The Man of Feeling* (1771), a distillation of rarefied emotions that attained a popularity truly remarkable (even Burns liked it) considering how deadly dull it is. But it was an era of frequent disjunction between prescriptive literary programme and practical literary product. At one extreme, Thomson took the high road to London and fleeting English celebrity, while at the other extreme Robert Fergusson and Robert Burns trod the bumpy, meandering low road through vernacular Scots expression with no assurance of any reward: not, happily, that this ever put them off.[40]

If Thomson was the poet of the New Town, Fergusson was the poet of the Old Town. He had been born in a close swept away for construction of the North Bridge. He was educated at the High School of Edinburgh. He went on to the University of St Andrews, and in travelling backwards and forwards he must often have surveyed one of the great prospects of his hometown, where the road out of the Howe of Fife comes over a saddle down to the northern shore of the Firth of Forth; the traveller can never be sure if he will be soothed by the serenity of the scene, will be scowled at under a storm or will sense his mood turn as sunny as the light dancing on the waters before him. Fergusson could have captured any of these sights but, in addressing the panorama, preferred the last:

> *Aft frae the Fifan coast I've seen*
> *Thee tow'ring on thy summit green;*
> *So glowr the saints when first is given,*
> *A fav'rite keek o' glore and heaven;*
> *On earth nae mair they bend their ein,*
> *But quick assume angelic mein;*
> *So I on Fife wad glower no more,*
> *But gallop'd to Edina's shore.*[41]

Fergusson had not yet finished his studies when his father died and left the family destitute. He needed to return to Edinburgh and take any job he could get. He found one in the commissary office dealing with wills and matrimonial cases. It was ill-paid drudgery, unworthy of him but not too onerous on a young fellow eager to write. What he did write shows he spent his free time in taverns, or else at the club he joined, the Knights of the Cape, towards the bohemian end of the range available. Any visitor to Edinburgh's best pubs today will recognise what Fergusson found irresistible in them:

> *Auld Reekie! thou'rt the canty hole,*
> *A bield for mony caldrife soul,*
> *Wha snugly at thine ingle loll,*
> *   Baith warm and couth'*
> *While round they gar the bicker roll*
> *   To weet their mouth.*

Edinburgh! you are the cheerful hole,
A shelter for many a spiritless soul,
Who snugly at your fireside loll,
    Both warm and cosy;
While round they make the glasses roll
    To wet their mouth.[42]

Fergusson is often the poet of such humdrum scenes – also, for example, of girls cleaning the stairs in the Old Town:

> *On stair wi' tub, or pat in hand*
> *The barefoot housemaids looe to stand,*
> *That antrin fock may ken how snell*
> *Auld Reekie will at morning smell:*
> *Then, with an inundation big as*
> *The burn that 'neath the Nor' Loch Brig is,*
> *They kindly shower Edina's roses,*
> *To quicken and regale our noses.*

> On stair with tub, or pot in hand
> The barefoot housemaids love to stand,
> That strangers may know how keen
> Edinburgh will smell in the morning:
> Then, with an inundation big as
> The stream that runs beneath North Bridge,
> They kindly shower excrement,
> To quicken and regale our noses.[43]

Fergusson could be outrageous at the expense of people towards the upper end of the social scale too. When Boswell brought Dr Samuel Johnson to Edinburgh in 1773 Fergusson asked, in merciless derision of his sesquipedalian Latinity, what might ensue if the 'Great Pedagogue' tried porridge or whisky, perhaps while wearing a kilt:

> Have you as yet the way explorified
> To let lignarian chalice, swelled with oats,
> Thy orifice approach? . . .
> . . . Or can you swill
> The usquebalian flames of whisky blue,
> In fermentation strong? Have you applied
> The kilt aërian to your Anglian thighs,
> And with renunciation assignized
> Your breeches in Londona to be worn?[44]

Still, it was low life Fergusson preferred to write about – because he knew it. Syphilis would kill him in 1774. His last months were wretched, and terminated by an accident. He fell down a stair, banged his head and was carried home delirious to his mother. She could not look after him so he had to be removed as a 'pauper lunatic' to Edinburgh's bedlam, where conditions were frightful. He died there.[45]

Yet in his short span Fergusson did make an impression on brother Scots as one that gave the vernacular muse a further lease of life after her revival by the elder Ramsay. Burns would address Fergusson, for some reason in English, at his grave in the kirkyard of the Canongate:

> O thou my elder brother in misfortune,
> By far my elder brother in the muse,
> With tears I pity thy unhappy fate.
> Why is the bard unfitted for the world,
> Yet has so keen a relish for its pleasures?[46]

This is doubly circumspect: both Burns and Fergusson knew well enough they belonged to the Devil's party. But Burns, unlike Fergusson, was a country bumpkin, a bit awestruck at coming to the capital even though its men of letters received him as an equal. He was a guest at aristocratic gatherings, where he bore himself with unaffected dignity. He encountered, and made a lasting impression on, the 16-year-old Walter Scott, who recalled:

> His person was strong and robust; his manners rustic, not clownish, a sort of dignified plainness and simplicity which received part of its effect perhaps from knowledge of his extraordinary talents. His features are presented in Mr [Alexander] Nasmyth's picture but to me it conveys the idea that they are diminished, as if seen in perspective. I think his countenance was more massive than it looks in any of the portraits ... there was a strong expression of shrewdness in all his lineaments; the eye alone, I think, indicated the poetical character and temperament. It was large, and of a dark cast, and literally glowed when he spoke with feeling or interest. I never saw such another eye in a human head, though I have seen the most distinguished men of my time.[47]

Still, none of this actually seemed to be all that good for Burns, if we can fairly judge him by the lifeless Augustan style he now felt moved to adopt for some of his poetry – as in a contrived paean to the capital, 'Edina! Scotia's darling seat!', or an elegy on the death of the second Lord President

Arniston, 'O heavy loss, thy country ill could bear!', which the Dundases understandably did not bother to acknowledge. Burns, feted in the salons as the 'heaven-taught ploughman', was doubtless giving a genteel audience what he thought it wanted: a style 'correct' in the sense of being written in English and conforming to classical canons (similar to the correctness of the New Town's architecture). We might wonder if this classicism was not starting to turn into a façade for sterility.[48]

Burns sensed as much himself. The best thing he wrote in Edinburgh was the 'Address to a Haggis', still popular today for its innocent irony couched in earthy Scots, and most familiar in the ritual of the Burns Supper. In real life, too, he felt a need now and again to burst out, get drunk and seduce servant girls, his May Cameron or his Jenny Clow. His hosts knew all about this: it gave them, or especially their wives and daughters, a frisson. When Burns met Agnes McLehose, niece of the judge, Lord Craig, and deserted wife of an erring husband, the pair entered into an intense relationship. But they conducted it largely by letter, he signing himself Sylvander and she Clarinda. We do not know if this stylised courtly romance led them to bed: Burns, however dapper in the drawing room, probably remained barred from the boudoir. Anyway Clarinda broke off the affair, such as it was, once she came to understand how unstoppable Sylvander's sex-drive might be. All that remained was one of his greatest songs, 'Ae Fond Kiss'.[49]

Beneath the polite fictions Burns's power of expression remained intact, then, as we see from the poems more truly representing himself that at length went into *The Merry Muses*:

> *Put butter in my Donald's brose,*
> *For weel dis Donald fa' that;*
> *I loe my Donald's tartans weel*
> *His naked erse an a' that.*
>
> *For a' that, an a' that,*
> *An twice as meikle's a' that,*
> *The lassie gat a skelpit doup,*
> *But wan the day for a' that.*
>
> *For Donald swore a solemn aith,*
> *By his first hairy gravat!*
> *That he wad fecht the battle there,*
> *An stick the lass, an a' that.*

His hairy ballocks, side and wide,
Hang like a beggar's wallet;
A pentle like a roarin-pin,
She nichered when she saw that!

Then she turned up her hairy cunt,
An she bade Donald claw that;
The Deevil's dizzen Donald drew,
An Donald gied her a' that.[50]

Pieces like this also remind us that since at least the sixteenth century, and Sir David Lindsay's *Satyre of the Thrie Estaits*, Scots poetry had been unembarrassed by sex, or in general by the various discharges from the human body, or yet by frank terms to refer to them. In the late eighteenth century, Alasdair mac Mhaighstir Alasdair as well as Burns showed the bawdy tradition to be still alive and kicking. It was in fact an integral part of the canon: the poem above has exactly the same metre and rhyme-scheme as 'A Man's a Man for A' That', carrying its emotional charge, in the end a stronger one, from the earthy and hedonistic over to the elevated and idealistic. Burns's poetic genius readily crossed boundaries. But it could also run up against limits.[51]

Much of Burn's poetry does remain limitless in its appeal, coming to us from 'probably the most powerful lyric poet the world has ever seen', according to his distant successor, Hugh MacDiarmid.[52] The way Burns deals with love is proof enough. 'My Love is Like a Red, Red Rose': what could be more simple and more touching? Burns was able to portray the whole range of love, from the innocence (or the burning lust) of youth to the tenderness of a maturing relationship to the faithful familiarity of a long partnership:

John Anderson, my jo, John,
When we were first acquent;
Your locks were like the raven,
Your bonnie brow was brent;
But now your brow is beld, John,
Your locks are like the snaw;
But blessings on your frosty pow,
John Anderson, my jo.[53]

A second genre in which Burns excels is satire, the supplementary outlet for a robust and imaginative youngster who, before his escape, had seemed likely to remain confined in a narrow provincial society of which the prevailing tone was a grim and often hypocritical puritanism. On grounds of propriety, he had felt it better not to put 'Holy Willie's Prayer' into the Kilmarnock edition. The time at length came when he could publish it, but perhaps there was meanwhile pleasure enough merely in having written this devastating satire on Willie Fisher, an elder at the kirk of Mauchline, who made it his business to denounce backsliding members of the congregation:

O Lord! yestreen, Thou kens, wi' Meg
Thy pardon I sincerely beg;
O may't ne'er be a livin' plague
   To my dishonour,
An' I'll ne'er lift a lawless leg
   Again upon her.

Besides, I farther maun avow,
Wi' Leezie's lass, three times I trow –
But Lord, that Friday I was fou,
   When I cam near her;
Or else, Thou kens, Thy servant true
   Wad never steer her.

Maybe Thou lets this fleshly thorn
Buffet Thy servant e'en and morn,
Lest he owre proud and high shou'd turn,
   That he's sae gifted:
If sae, Thy han' maun e'en be borne,
   Until Thou lift it.[54]

And then the third type of poetry in which Burns excelled, though less appreciated by posterity, was the folk song, or perhaps we should use the term art-song for the original poems that he wrote in imitation of it. In any case, like the elder Ramsay before him, Burns never preened himself as a purist in this genre, as later scientific folklorists would feel the need to do. He simply treated the raw material as it pleased him: another point of contact he (and Ramsay) had with the Highland bards. He himself described how he dealt with it:

My way is: I consider the poetic sentiment, correspondent to my idea of the musical expression, then chuse my theme, begin one stanza, when that is composed – which is generally the most difficult part of the business – I walk out, sit down now and then, look out for objects in nature around me that are in unison or harmony with the cogitations of my fancy and workings of my bosom, humming every now and then the air with the verses I have framed. When I feel my Muse beginning to jade, I retire to the solitary fireside of my study, and there commit my effusions to paper, swinging, at intervals, on the hind-legs of my elbow chair, by way of calling forth my own critical strictures, as my pen goes.[55]

The legacy of song we have from Burns is, then, the product of a variety of processes: he collected and preserved the originals, sometimes revising, expanding and adapting them, as well as turning his hand to fresh compositions of his own. The genuine and the invented songs are all but impossible to distinguish. 'Auld Lang Syne' is known as his the world over, yet what he had to say about it when he first put it together was this: 'The following song, an old song, of the olden times, and which has never been in print, nor even in manuscript until I took it down from an old man.'[56] A piece like 'Killiecrankie' was Burns's setting of his own words to a traditional tune, recalling the horrors of a battle as if he had fought there himself. And finally he was sometimes content just to collect. As he once reported, 'I have still several MS. Scots airs which I picked up mostly from the singing of country girls.'[57] In every one of its forms, he felt altogether enthralled at this huge legacy of songs, delightful in their tunes and moving in their words, that Scotland had inherited from the dark drama of its past: and he transmits it all to us. Once he started collecting, he went much further than Ramsay and conceived the ambition of gathering a storehouse of song as complete as he could make it; this would leave to coming times at least some memories of the older Scotland already vanishing in Burns's own day.

For Burns, folk song became far and away his main literary preoccupation during the last decade of his life; it was in truth a heavy burden on a man whose health steadily broke down, though he did not work alone. While in Edinburgh in 1787 he had met James Johnson, who made a living from engraving and selling musical scores and who shared his love of old Scots folk song. Johnson was already at work on *The Scots Musical Museum* (1787–1803), and to this Burns became a prime contributor. The first volume included only three songs by him, but the second had 40 and he ended up being responsible for about a third of the 600 items in the whole lot, as well as editing much of the rest. Once involved, he could not let the project go.[58]

Later Burns heard from George Thomson, an official at the board of manufactures (for the promotion of every kind of improvement) who again shared the interest in folk song. Thomson asked if Burns would apply his literary skills to a further project of collection: 'We are desirous to have the poetry improved wherever it seems unworthy of the music ... Some charming melodies are united to mere nonsense and doggerel, while others are accommodated with rhymes so loose and indelicate as cannot be sung in decent company.' It is unlikely Burns thought the last feature a defect, but at all events he responded eagerly while spurning any offer of payment: 'In the honest enthusiasm with which I embark in your undertaking, to talk of money, wages, fee, hire, and etc. could be downright Sodomy of Soul! A proof of each of the songs that I compose or amend, I shall receive as a favour' – and this from a poor man. In the end he contributed more than 100 items to Thomson's *Select Collection of Original Scottish Airs for the Voice*, which came out in five volumes (1799–1818).[59]

Thomson harboured wider ambitious for the poetry and song of his nation, believing it to be worthy not just of preservation in Scotland but also of diffusion abroad. This vast fund of traditional material was one of the richest in Europe – and elsewhere the classical composers had often turned to its local counterparts to enrich their art, at least from the time of Johann Sebastian Bach. The practice would go from strength to strength during the nineteenth century, especially in the small nations, at the hands of Antonín Dvořák in Bohemia or Edvard Grieg in Norway, or indeed into the twentieth century, at the hands of Jan Sibelius in Finland or Béla Bartók in Hungary. Still, not every nation could count on a composer with the necessary genius to raise the popular tradition to a classical standard. Spain was one long in this quandary, though French composers largely filled the gap. Scotland was another. In the traditions of the fiddle or the clàrsach, or even in the metrical psalms, it had a rich musical heritage. But the Kirk frowned on the secular part of it, and at any more elevated level Scottish composition tended to be derivative, as in the cantatas of Sir John Clerk of Penicuik, who during his grand tour had studied in Rome under Arcangelo Corelli, or the symphonies, overtures and sonatas that the Earl of Kellie cast in the avant-garde style of the Mannheim School. In the twentieth century, Hugh MacDiarmid would think at last to have found the right composer for the national repertoire in

Francis George Scott, but this judgment has not been borne out. Even less can any Scot of the nineteenth century be said to have played the part, though a few neglected virtuosi have been identified. Rather, Scotland stood in the same position as Spain, of needing to call on composers of other nationalities to clothe its unadorned tradition of folk song in the finest classical dress.[60]

As a cultural capital, Edinburgh did not lack an audience for such music. It housed a society for concerts at a venue still in use, St Cecilia's Hall in the Cowgate. Audiences were used to hearing arrangements of Scots songs performed there, for example, by an Italian castrato, Ferdinando Tenducci. Thomson hit on a new idea after Burns's death in 1796. He proposed to continue the poet's labours through having Scottish songs set by leading composers of the day – Haydn, Beethoven and others. With Europe at war it was not easy. Thomson persevered and by hook or by crook managed to send his commissions to Vienna, financing the whole business himself. He was to do this over 40 years.[61]

Haydn composed about 200 Scottish settings, most veering on the side of hackwork. Beethoven composed about 100, but took more seriously the task of turning the melodious ballads and laments, by turns rousing and haunting, into modern music. Alas, he was too avant-garde for Thomson who, though bowled over by the quality of the results, had to write back and ask for something simpler; he after all hoped to recoup his investment with settings he could sell to ladies and gentlemen for performance in their drawing rooms. Beethoven was not amused, and his contacts with Thomson descended into acrimony.[62]

None of this affected Burns's reputation, which had burgeoned in the years after his premature death. Great poet as he was, we would falsify his story if we left it without remarking that he also had his failures, not only material but also literary, and trying to define the significance of them. While his poems have probably done more than anything else to keep the Scots language alive, his achievement here stood in marked contrast to the frequent lifelessness of his verse when he sought to write in English. He told Thomson: 'I have not that command of the language that I have of my native tongue. In fact, I think my ideas are more barren in English than in Scottish.'6[3] Yet he did try: it was not as if his English poetry formed a negligible part of his output. And sometimes it worked. Even amid the vernacular vigour of 'Tam O' Shanter', Burns pauses for a moment to linger on the border of the real and the imagined, almost as if he had just returned from a break in his composition and a dip into a volume of David Hume. Before Tam steps out from his couthy, drouthy reality to be chased home by bogles, Burns reminds us that the nature of time is often a puzzle of things disappearing:

> But pleasures are like poppies spread,
> You seize the flower, its bloom is shed;
> Or like the snow falls in the river,
> A moment white – then melts for ever;
> Or like the borealis race,
> That flit ere you can point their place;
> Or like the rainbow's lovely form
> Evanishing amid the storm –
> Nae man can tether time or tide;
> The hour approaches Tam maun ride.[64]

With beautiful economy, and merely by the change from Augustan English (what other form of the language would say 'evanishing'?) to the Scots of Kirk Alloway, Burns brings us back, not from the imaginary to the real world, for that is not what Tam rides into, but to a place where the real and the imagined alike show us the transitory nature of existence. The linguistic contrast of Scots and English is what does all the work here.

In other poems, such as 'The Jolly Beggars', Burns draws out that contrast at greater length. But a vital spark goes missing when he tries to use English on its own as contemporary taste expected a poet to use it. MacDiarmid found his depictions of landscape particularly abstract and feeble, and it is striking that a man who, from his plough, could gaze across the Firth of Clyde to the jagged mountains of Arran seems to have been left cold by Highland scenery, even when at length he had the means to go on tours through it: he was more interested in the crops than in the crags. One or two of his love poems in English, 'Clarinda, mistress of my soul!' or 'Flow gently, sweet Afton' are not bad. But Burns cannot rise with these efforts to a higher poetic level where intellect deepens emotion, as MacDiarmid would have liked him to do. Scots poetry, in the whole course of its history, has shown no lack of capacity to transcend itself in this way, in everything from metre to content. This was as true of the medieval Makars as it became true of MacDiarmid himself in the twentieth century: it is no doubt a characteristic of what he called the 'Caledonian antisyzygy',[65] the Scottish urge to link opposites. Yet Burns does not stand in this tradition. In relation to his nation he is the man of the people rather than the lonely poetic pioneer – and of course, happier and more fulfilled to be so, because this status satisfies in him his natural instinct for generosity and inclusion. On the other hand, his attitude excluded paradox and any need to reconcile paradox: plain speaking took its place. We love Burns not for his incoherently contradictory opinions, ranging from the Jacobite to the Jacobin, but as a poor farmer's son from Ayrshire who had an uncanny connection with people's cares and wishes for a better life.

> It's coming yet for a' that,
> That man to man the world o'er
> Shall brothers be for a' that.[66]

This is a poem that MacDiarmid labelled 'unspeakable'.[67]

Burns does find it hard to bring his poetic sensibility together with other qualities of mind. This need be no great matter from an aesthetic point of view if the poetry is good enough, as it usually is, yet it may point us towards a wider cultural disjunction. Linguistic capacities limiting a poet to love, satire and folklore are not inflicting on him a fatal flaw, not if his poetry within the given limits attains a universal level. In fact, Burns raised those capacities to an unexampled height, in the process saving the Scots language and finding durable expression for values that the Scots people thought and think of as their own. Clearly, however, there is still much about the human condition he leaves unsaid. It is a reflection on the general state of Scottish culture that there were certain things now only to be expressed in English. Not all hope was lost: the next generation nurtured a Scot who successfully negotiated the conflicting pressures of cultural assimilation and literary difference. He became in his turn the dominant force in Scottish, almost so in British and to a large extent so in European and even American culture. His name was Walter Scott.

15

Ideas: 'The very frame of our nature'

On 20 May 1795, the philosopher Adam Ferguson wrote to his old friend Sir John MacPherson to say he was contemplating a 'scheme of country life' that might be fulfilled if he could take up residence at Neidpath Castle on the River Tweed near Peebles, now standing empty. This pile, dating from the fourteenth century, belonged to the Duke of Queensberry, and 'has been lately dismantled or stript of its furniture and so far destined to become the habitation of bats and owls or what is little better such a tenant as I am. The servant who showed the place told me that His Grace has been asked to let it: but declined, which makes my prospect somewhat desperate.' Ferguson had no regular access to dukes but MacPherson did, being a retired Governor General of India who, like quite a few Scottish veterans of the Orient, had come home with an enormous fortune. In fact, it was even more enormous than most – to the extent of getting him into a bit of trouble and requiring him to defend himself against public criticism while he sued the British government for recalling him early. This mattered not one whit to Ferguson in his own straits, but anyway the two of them, both sons of Highland manses, had known each other for years.[1]

MacPherson acted promptly: by 1 June, Ferguson had a letter from Queensberry agreeing to lease Neidpath to him. Still his friend wished to know why on earth the philosopher should want to abandon enlightened Edinburgh, where he had been living for the better part of four decades in circumstances at once convivial and productive of infinite intellectual stimulation. Perhaps one reason was that Ferguson had stopped drinking alcohol, and so cramped his own social style. But more generally, 'I have nothing to do in this town and wish to avoid the expense of living in it.'[2] The sole condition the duke imposed was that, before Ferguson arrived at Neidpath, the whole stretch of woods round the castle on its picturesque bend of the river should be chopped down and sold for timber. For this act of vandalism Queensberry was to be severely criticised by later visitors, Robert Burns and William Wordsworth, but his new tenant seemed not to mind in the least. Ferguson must all the same have come shortly to repent somewhat of his flitting, because his letters to friends urging them to visit him struck an ever more frantic note. Certainly the number of callers seems to have been small. The problem found a different solution when, five years later, part of the castle collapsed. Then Ferguson had to move out to the even greater solitude of Hallyards in the Manor Valley, where he stayed for most of the rest of his life.

At Neidpath, Ferguson found plenty of time to sit and think even as he sought to get his new home shipshape. Both activities were congenial to him, and indeed struck him as similar. He wrote again to MacPherson on 4 September 1795: 'The best that can be said even of the universe itself or any created thing is that it is coming into order. And so are my chairs, tables and books, etc, etc,' – then followed the inevitable invitation – 'but if you were here we should not give ourselves any trouble about them.' Order, and more especially the conditions under which things come into order, or afterwards fall again into disorder, is a recurring theme in Ferguson's writings.[3] Like his friends David Hume and Adam Smith as well as other Scottish philosophers, Ferguson stressed the importance of spontaneous order, that is to say, of coherent and even effective outcomes resulting from the uncoordinated actions of many individuals who, while usually acting out of self-interest, could sustain economic and social structures that nobody ever planned or deliberately created.

It was an idea basic to the Enlightenment in Scotland, but Ferguson came at it from an angle of his own. In later times he would win the epithet of the 'father of sociology', and his writings do reflect a wide range of social interest, not only in structures but also in ethics and politics. Like the rest of the Scottish philosophers, he always stressed the need for any seeker after truth to put himself in another's shoes. But it never led him into any bland consensus. He remained suspicious of the argument, for instance from Adam Smith, that a modern commercial society functioned best through individual liberty. On the contrary, Ferguson insisted, society should be looked at not as a collection of competing individuals but as an organic whole, for it was by playing a part in achievement of the common good that individuals might best realise their own potential.[4]

This aspect of Ferguson is hard to divorce from the fact that he was a Highlander, born the son of the minister of Logierait in the Gaelic-speaking uplands of Perthshire. While Lowlanders still suspected Highlanders of being barbarians at heart, and looked forward to the eradication of their society and culture, Ferguson knew better. As a boy he too had bantered in Gaelic with the other lads of his village, and his first published work was the Gaelic sermon he preached as chaplain to the Black Watch in 1745, urging the troops to remain faithful to the House of Hanover even though they had friends and relations on the Jacobite side.[5] His men might have been rough and tough, but he also knew they were brave, loyal and generous. From his classical education at Perth Grammar School and the University of Edinburgh, he decided Highland soldiers were not unlike the Greek warriors celebrated by Homer. The destruction of their way of life would be the destruction of something precious, and leave Scotland the poorer. Here was the argument he expanded, for his country and for the world, in his masterpiece, the *Essay on the History of Civil Society* (1767).[6]

It is in this book that Ferguson shows himself sceptical about the theories of progress advanced by his enlightened fellows and their attempts to subject human history to a single intellectual scheme: 'Like the winds that we come we know not whence and blow whither soever they list, the forces of society are derived from an obscure and distant origin. They arise before the date of philosophy, from the instincts, not the speculations of men.'[7] He proceeds to compare modern Western society both with its contemporaries in other continents and with its forerunners in classical antiquity – this all in great detail, ranging from Greece and Rome to the tribesmen of South America to the great civilisations of India and China, not forgetting some acute observations on modern Scotland and England. He is besides the first to hazard guesses at the obscure origins of phenomena scarcely amenable to scientific research: marriage, poetry, property, the arts. Overall, he constructs a rich comparative framework for a naturalistic explanation of human beings and their social environment.

The comparisons turn out little to the advantage of Western civilisation. Ferguson fears that the onset of capitalism and its human consequences are causing a loss of civic and communal virtues, in contrast to the ancients with 'their ardent attachment to their country, their contempt of suffering, and of death, in its cause; their manly apprehensions of personal independence, which rendered every individual, even under tottering circumstances, and imperfect laws, the guardian of freedom to his fellow citizens'. Here is, in other words, a huge difference from the current situation, when 'the individual considers his community only so far as it can be rendered subservient to his personal advancement and profit'. Ferguson might agree with his fellows that humanity is moving forwards, but he has a different idea of where they are all heading:

> The boasted refinements, then, of the polished age are not divested of danger. They open a door, perhaps, to disaster, as wide and accessible as any they have shut. If they build walls and ramparts, they enervate the minds of those who are placed to defend them; if they form disciplined armies, they reduce the military spirit of entire nations; and by placing the sword where they have given a distaste to civil establishments, they prepare mankind for the government of force.[8]

Certainly not everybody agreed with Ferguson: Hume, though conceding he had 'more genius than the rest', disliked the *Essay* and regarded it as superficial.[9]

Yet Ferguson's pessimism was far from total. He did believe that, given human moral capacities, progress might be made towards ordered liberty and free government. Still, as an ordained Presbyterian minister (though not a practising one), he also saw the fallen nature of man and the imperfections of human society. History could in fact move in two modes: in the natural history that followed God's laws, or in the social history where human beings sometimes used the faculties they were endowed with to improve themselves and their communities – or sometimes failed to use them properly and suffered setbacks. God, in a plan encompassing both progress and human free will, had provided for both. But it was then easy to see why movement towards them might turn out erratic.[10]

On the same arguments, human behaviour was driven not only by the peaceful pursuit of pleasure, but also, indeed perhaps primarily, by a will to power, by aggression, by animosity, by confrontation and at a less admirable level by corruption. 'To overawe, or intimidate, or, when we cannot persuade with reason, to resist with fortitude, are the occupations which give its most animating exercise, and its greatest triumphs, to a vigorous mind; and he who has never struggled with his fellow-creatures, is a stranger to half the sentiments of mankind.'[11] Though human beings possessed common attributes and instincts, they interacted in ways that might bring out not so much uniformity and harmony as diversity and conflict. Amid all this, social institutions still emerged, and in their turn evolved in a variety of ways: 'Every step and every movement of the multitude, even in what are termed enlightened ages, are made with equal blindness to the future; and nations stumble upon establishments, which are indeed the result of human action, but not the execution of any human design.'[12]

Ferguson in some respects set a seal on the Scottish Enlightenment, or rather marked a divergence from a century of development that was reasonably coherent even though it had arisen from many sources – from the classical antiquity in which Scots were schooled, from neo-Latin writers they could all read, from the English they were now politically united to, from the French they maintained lively intellectual links with, from a range of other European nations, Dutch, Germans, Italians and so on.[13]

Yet for the reception of enlightened ideas in Scotland on a scale likely to make a difference to the life of the nation, there also needed to be receptors – meaning something more than isolated individuals capable of intellectual profit from access to European culture. It was here that the existence in this small, poor, remote nation of five universities, always remarkable enough, came into its own. Till now their prime function had been to train ministers for the Church of Scotland, so as to fulfil the Reformation's aim of a literate clergy. Liberal learning was not always the result, though the universities did teach subjects other than theology. In recent times, indeed, theology had come to look almost a risky option for any student: in the seventeenth century, the Kirk had switched back and forth from Presbyterian to Episcopalian, sometimes a bit of both, and further switches were by no means inconceivable. Divinity could be dangerous in an age of such furious religious strife, as likely to lead to banishment and destitution, even to the scaffold, as to a comfortable living in a pleasant parish. The natural and human sciences looked by comparison safe. In Europe, academic reform had brought their widespread introduction into the curriculum. Scotland followed: the Enlightenment would be hard to imagine under any other condition.[14]

If we look to the native roots of the Scottish Enlightenment we do encounter science, broadly defined as stretching from mathematics to medicine. In the universities, the first chair in mathematics was erected at St Andrews in 1668, then at Edinburgh in 1674. James Gregory went from the one to the other. He had previously spent nine years at Padua, where he talked to people once pupils of Galileo Galilei. In a fundamental branch of his discipline, the differential calculus, Gregory was one of three Europeans working at its furthest frontier – the others being Gottfried von Leibniz in Hanover and Sir Isaac Newton at Cambridge. No academic journals or conferences yet existed to publicise the results of research. The three kept abreast by personal correspondence, which had drawbacks: they could choose to be frank with one another or not, out of uncertainty or for some different reason. Gregory let Leibniz and Newton know when he was the first to solve Kepler's Puzzle, of how to determine at any given time the location of a planet in its orbit. But he did not care to divulge further results in which he suspected Newton had anticipated him, even if Newton himself would publish nothing short of the epochal *Principia Mathematica* (1687). Scholarly scruples of the age could never, all the same, hold up its scientific revolution, of which the culmination came in Newton's discovery of gravity. It proved that the universe obeyed natural laws. Edinburgh was one place this scientific revolution reached early.[15]

James Gregory soon died but, when his no less brilliant nephew David succeeded him in the chair at the age of 22, Edinburgh became the first university in the world to hear lectures on Newton's teachings. Not content with exposition, David Gregory and others would apply the latest discoveries to various branches of science, in the process extending the scope of theoretical advance so as to start changing human conceptions of reality. The younger Gregory did that for astronomy and remodelled the discipline. He cast off its theological past – its mumbo-jumbo of empyrean spheres and the like – to make it consistent with Newtonian physics. Vital to this was his interest in Greek geometry, manifested in his edition of Euclid in 1703. In the changing conceptions of reality, this geometry no longer served as just a formal exercise, a part it had played in Western learning since antiquity. With Newton's revelation that mathematical law related physical bodies to one another, Greek geometry became a key to reality. Newton had done much to revive it on his own account, and Gregory made it central to Scottish intellectual tradition.[16]

The University of Glasgow joined Scotland's Newtonian network in 1711 when it elected Robert Simson to a chair of mathematics, where he spent much of his time in the study and editing of classic Greek texts.[17] He was a devoted teacher too, numbering among his students one destined to become the greatest Scottish mathematician and natural philosopher of the age, Colin MacLaurin. In the elegant thesis MacLaurin defended in 1713, he expounded Newton's theory of gravitation and sketched out a programme of research using its concept of an attractive force in operation on particles of matter to explain a wide range of natural phenomena.[18] MacLaurin's reputation for brilliance spread fast, and he was called as professor of mathematics to Marischal College, Aberdeen, in 1717, at the age of 19; he held the record for the youngest professor of anything ever till 2008. The college was at this point just reopening after the Jacobite rebellion had ended here with all but one of the staff being expelled by a royal commission sent out to purge the universities of disloyalty. As a faithful Presbyterian and Hanoverian, MacLaurin was just the sort of man now being looked for.

MacLaurin shifted to the University of Edinburgh in 1724 and there his career took wing. Each year he had a heavy teaching load, but he remained an active scientist publishing papers, textbooks and his *Treatise on Fluxions* (1742).[19] In 1737 he was a founder of the Edinburgh Philosophical Society, which in 1783 would become the Royal Society of Edinburgh. Also a member of the Society of Improvers in 1723, he could offer its landowning members advice on schemes of theirs that might require some mathematical expertise. He and his students gave public lectures on useful subjects to the capital's ladies and gentlemen.[20] In this an associate of MacLaurin's was James Stirling of Keir, who after a colourful but risky Jacobite career at last found a secure niche as manager of the Scots Mining Company at Leadhills in Lanarkshire, one of the country's earliest successful commercial enterprises; he also devised the first scheme for deepening the River Clyde at Glasgow by regulating the flow of water. MacLaurin's own career was to be cut tragically short in 1746. Having organised the unsuccessful defences of Edinburgh against the Jacobite army, he died of an infection he caught while in flight from it. It was left to his family to publish his masterly *Account of Sir Isaac Newton's Philosophical Discoveries* (1748), a model for popular exposition of a challenging subject. Altogether, the vigorous and accomplished MacLaurin had led a most useful life, helping both to consolidate Newton's hold on the Scottish universities and to create public interest in enlightened science, including its application to economic improvement. Here was something for everybody, not just for professors but for landowners, merchants and manufacturers too.

A further perhaps unexpected feature of this broad enlightened advance in Scotland lay in its religious orthodoxy, even in the teaching of science.

MacLaurin was again typical. He denied that Newton had cast any doubt on Christianity, for 'natural philosophy is subservient to purposes of a higher kind, and is chiefly to be valued as it lays a sure foundation for natural religion and moral philosophy'. In a letter of 1714, MacLaurin said he had in his own thesis wanted to establish the universality of the law of gravitation 'because it is of the greatest importance and use seeing it furnishes us with a most clear and mathematical proof of the existence of a God and his providence'. He added it was 'a sort of impiety to have no regard to the course and frame of nature as indeed it is a piece of real worship to contemplate the beautiful drama of nature, the admirable law by which the world's great Lord rules this his workmanship'.[21] The religious orthodoxy helped the natural philosophy to secure its place in Scotland's academic and public culture. David Hume, Thomas Reid and others agreed that Newtonian methodology could be adopted for moral philosophy. Tensions would at length appear, but not yet; there is, for example, little sign that Hume owed his infidelity to Newton.[22]

Given that no coherent critique of the Book of Genesis yet existed, natural history could also give birth to geology as a distinct science. The man who acted as midwife, James Hutton, had already started his own original geological enquiries before he returned from his higher education in Paris and Leiden, but it was systematic study right through the second half of the century of his native Edinburgh's dramatic landscape that allowed him to perfect a revolutionary theory of the earth. These labours yielded a vision of its physical development in which we find 'no vestige of a beginning, no prospect of an end'.[23] When questioned by Presbyterian critics, Hutton said he simply did not know how God fitted into all this. He was himself certainly no atheist. He held firm to a deistic belief in a benevolent Creator who had allotted the human race a privileged moral status in the natural order of things. Yet the hostile orthodox reaction to Hutton's system showed that the friendly Scottish relations between natural science and Christianity were now being clouded. Still they would not break down before the middle of the nineteenth century.

From natural history, it was an easy step to human science. Medicine had long been taught privately among the surgeons who in the big royal burghs formed an incorporated trade, but for a century or more some had set out to raise their status above that of other artisans, the mere butchers and bakers and candlestick-makers. The physicians and surgeons of Glasgow received a charter in 1599. In Edinburgh, the charter for a Royal College of Surgeons came in 1697; the college then built the Surgeons' Hall in the Old Town, still standing. This housed a library stocked with medical literature from Europe and a theatre for dissection, another key to advancing knowledge. For it, a supply of bodies was needed, but only the town council could authorise that. In 1705 the surgeons sought to move matters along by naming one of their number, Robert Eliot, as public dissector charged with regular teaching from cadavers on a slab. To a request for the council's support in this delicate venture, it responded by appointing him professor of anatomy. An unintended consequence was owed to enterprising citizens: in 1711 the council had to make it an offence to dig up fresh corpses from their graves and flog them, at 40 shillings each, to the surgeons. For customers still alive there was a massage parlour by Surgeons' Hall. In 1723 John Valentine and his daughter would be named public 'rubber and rubberess'.[24]

In the quest for higher status, the surgeons of Edinburgh needed also to fend off rivalry from the Royal College of Physicians, already chartered in 1681. This institution was the brainchild of Robert Sibbald, Scotland's leading scientific boffin, who counted King Charles II among those consulting him for medical advice. Sibbald had been one of the students who in his choice of career sought an antidote to the tumults of the age: 'I saw none could enter to the ministry without engaging in factions. I preferred a quiet life, where I might not be engaged in factions of Church or state. I fixed upon the study of medicine, wherein I thought I might be of no faction and might be useful to my generation.'[25]

The surgeon's craft, with its violent, bloody, often inadvertently lethal interventions in the human body, perhaps grew rather out of urban conditions, while the physician's skills could be bucolic in their emphasis on external treatment with mainly herbal drugs and medicines. To a superstitious age, this was hard to tell from witchcraft, and Sibbald saw the need to place it on a less fishy footing. All over Scotland grew plants held locally to have curative properties, and one of his aims was to find a place to cultivate and test them: 'I had from my settlement here in Edinburgh a design to inform myself of the natural history this country could afford, for I had learned at Paris that the simplest method of physic was the best, and these [plants] that the country afforded came nearest to our temper, and agreed best with us.'[26] On part of the grounds of Holyrood, he founded in 1677 what would become the Royal

Botanic Garden of Edinburgh. From there it moved to a site later covered by platform 11 at Waverley Station, where a plaque commemorates it, and finally down to Inverleith.

Sibbald's third project was to start instruction in medicine at the University of Edinburgh. He envisaged the university as the teaching institution for physicians and his Royal College as their licensing authority. This was a good idea, not least in eventually helping to relaunch the university after its first century of catering just for local students of arts and divinity. In 1685 Sibbald won appointment as one of three inaugural professors of medicine, along with James Halket and Archibald Pitcairne. Halket had been trained as an obstetric surgeon at the University of Leiden in Holland. That was where Pitcairne had gone too, and he had written a thesis on the circulation of the blood so distinguished that in 1692 he was offered a chair there. But he preferred Edinburgh. Beside his contributions to learning, he was an active and charitable general practitioner. He held a surgery in the Lawnmarket in a cellar so dark it was known as the 'grope shop' (in Scots the words rhyme); Pitcairne also tickled his patients with anti-Presbyterian jokes. By agreement with the town council, he treated paupers free and got their corpses when they died. In the event, however, the three first chairs of medicine at Edinburgh remained titular. Sibbald did not succeed in establishing regular medical instruction – Dutch universities remained just too famous for any Scottish one to compete. At least that was now an aspiration.[27]

In fact, from these modest beginnings it did not take Scottish medicine long to grow. Modern medical schools were founded at Edinburgh in 1726, Glasgow in 1751 and Aberdeen in 1787; St Andrews offered degrees in medicine but did not teach it. Edinburgh went into the lead. By the first quarter of the nineteenth century it was producing more surgeons and doctors than anywhere else in Britain, with 2,000 degrees awarded during this period.[28] But some of its old Scots habits died hard. The inaugural holder of the chair of anatomy, erected in 1721, was Alexander Monro *primus*, so called because he sired a dynasty. He stayed in harness up to his death in 1767, when his son Alexander Monro *secundus* succeeded him in the chair, he being followed on his own death in 1817 by his son Alexander Monro *tertius*, who expired only in 1859. Half a dozen more medical chairs had been created by the end of the eighteenth century. Diverse courses could then be offered leading to a comprehensive medical degree and a range of careers from scientific research to general practice. The professors ruled the whole roost. They all seemed especially long-lived too, which must have said something for their talents. Most clung to their chairs till the Grim Reaper prised them loose: they wished in clannish Scotland to make sure who would take over from them, for preference one of their own kin. The Monros were just the best example of this nepotism.[29]

Glasgow came second only to Edinburgh in medical development, though it assumed here a different form. William Cullen was in private practice in the city; he used this everyday experience as the basis for a wide range of intellectual speculation, in botany or in chemistry as well as in physiology.[30] When he launched a series of public lectures, enlivened by practical demonstrations and by his own enthusiasm at the lectern, he drew large audiences. In 1747 he was chosen president of the Faculty of Physicians and Surgeons of Glasgow and awarded Britain's first independent lectureship in chemistry. In 1751 he got a medical chair at the university, though he continued to lecture on chemistry too. But then in 1755 he was enticed by Lord Kames to be professor of chemistry and medicine at the University of Edinburgh.

This struck a blow at chemical science in Glasgow, but the discipline could not be allowed to languish – it had grown too valuable for the city's early industries and for the skilled workers needed by them. Cullen's successor in 1756 was his pupil, Joseph Black, already renowned for the thesis he had written at Edinburgh on magnesia alba, a substance with a wide range of industrial applications. In 1762 he announced from Glasgow his doctrine of latent heat. One interested hearer was the young James Watt, maker of instruments to the university, who first measured there the latent heat of steam and used this knowledge to perfect a steam engine. Chemistry at Glasgow went on to play a prime role in its industrial revolution; the chemical works established at St Rollox just to the north of the city in 1798 became the biggest in Europe. The era produced what a thinker of the twentieth century, George Davie, called 'the accepted Scottish approach to the sciences'.[31] He meant by this that in Scotland pure science always had an experimental and technological bent, and one strong enough to continue right through the nineteenth century. From James Watt to William Thomson, Lord Kelvin, the connections were preserved rather than lost or dropped amid a growing division between pure and applied science.

In Glasgow beyond the university, clubs and societies promoted discussion of the natural sciences, as did the courses offered by itinerant lecturers, while scientific subject matter filled newspapers, periodicals and books.[32]

John Anderson, professor of natural philosophy, held extramural classes where artisans and other townspeople could improve their knowledge and skills; they were open to women too. This activity was formalised in 1796 as Anderson's Institute, the ancestor of Strathclyde University.[33] Popular science spread to Edinburgh as well, where Joseph Black lectured to 200 students at a time in his course of chemistry at the university, while the successor to his chair, Tommy Hope, sometimes addressed more than 500. Handsome and debonair, Hope attracted listeners with 'amusing and brilliant experiments', according to Henry Cockburn. He hit the jackpot when he let his students bring their girlfriends: 'the ladies declare there was never anything so delightful as these chemical flirtations. The Doctor is in absolute ecstasy with his audience of veils and feathers . . . I wish some of his experiments would blow him up. Each female student would get a bit of him.'[34]

Today the eighteenth century is often remembered as an age of reason. But from what we have seen here so far of the diffusion of its high culture outwards from the most brilliant and original minds to wide circles of a literate population, it would be more accurate to call it an age of nature. It was nature that appealed to everybody from the professor at the university to the weaver at his loom (or indeed his wife) – nature as the key to understanding the world about them in a way never available from the old, classical learning. In this way, the Scots were people who also enlightened themselves. Enlightenments in other nations had different characteristics: they might be more academic, or more aristocratic, or more political. But in poor and stateless yet ambitious and aspiring Scotland this was how Enlightenment turned out. It is something we see confirmed when we turn to the central activities of the Scottish Enlightenment, the traditional discipline of philosophy together with the new social sciences now being derived from it. Nature figures everywhere.[35]

One of the sources of the Scottish Enlightenment relatively neglected in the existing literature is the European tradition of natural law. It arose in the seventeenth century with Hugo Grotius in the United Netherlands and Samuel Pufendorf, an itinerant scholar born a subject of the Elector of Saxony. Natural law exerted a big influence on Scottish legal thinking, as we saw above. Since Scots lawyers were also often enlightened intellectuals, it exerted a wider influence as well.[36]

Grotius, the greatest jurist of the Dutch Republic, had been the man who shaped natural law in its modern form, different from the previous conception of it as part of God's creation and so grounded in religion and theology. Grotius sought its origins rather in the social nature and the reasoning faculties of human beings: it would still be there *etiamsi daremus non esse Deum*, even if God did not exist.[37] Because so many Scots went to study at the Dutch universities, Grotius became familiar in Scotland too. Adam Smith, in his lectures delivered in 1762 at the University of Glasgow, said: 'Jurisprudence is that science which inquires into the general principles which ought to be the foundation of laws of all nations. Grotius seems to have been the first who attempted to give the world anything like a regular system of natural jurisprudence, and his treatise, *On the Laws of War and Peace*, with all its imperfections, is perhaps at this day the most complete work on this subject.'[38]

Pufendorf carried natural law still further away from theology, and for good reasons of his own. In his youth German Christians had still been fighting and killing one another, all for a Peace of Westphalia (1648) that at the end of the devastating Thirty Years' War left things little changed from how they had stood before the Defenestration of Prague (1618). Never again, said reasonable men like Pufendorf. But they needed to show, in the face of orthodox rebuff, how religion and politics might be separated. Pufendorf did not argue with the reformer Martin Luther that in reason or morality a huge gulf divided God from man. Yet that could be no bar, for instance in the scientific revolution of the seventeenth century, to man's use of his reason to push out the bounds of knowledge – and without (so far) casting doubt on divine revelation. The same with morality: given the narrow scope of the law of Moses, written on tablets of stone for ancient nomads, modern society might validly decide for itself, in all due fear of the Lord, how to deal with cases not covered by it. The theory went further. At a political level, Pufendorf found no reason to believe states had been founded for the purpose of religion, *propter religionem civitates non esse institutas*.[39] It followed that religion might be freed of control by any sovereign. Conversely, it also followed that a polity might seek for its law a secular or natural basis. If the divine dispensation, however defined, had proved itself wanting for modern times (as in Germany), a solution would be to rediscover natural law in the original pre-Christian or non-Christian sense.

Scots followed these controversies. In 1724 Gershom Carmichael, about to become the first professor of moral philosophy at the University of Glasgow

– indeed in all Scotland – published with supplements and observations his own edition of some of Pufendorf's work, intended expressly for the use of his classes. He had employed Pufendorf for his teaching since at least 1702, as we know from notes for his lectures he left behind. At that stage, this rather demanding academic, speaking always Latin to his students, covered the whole of the philosophical curriculum (including even natural philosophy or physics). But it seems clear from the later course of his career that his main interest lay in moral philosophy, in line with the European preoccupations he was introducing. His own work concentrated on the concept of natural rights. If these were to be acknowledged in any moral system, they had to be grounded not in the scrutiny of scripture but rather in the facts of nature.[40]

Carmichael died in 1729, to be succeeded in his chair by one of his own pupils, Francis Hutcheson. He was an Ulsterman of Scottish descent, sprung from at least two generations of Presbyterian ministers. After he completed his studies at the University of Glasgow, he was in his turn licensed to preach by the Church of Scotland in 1716. But then he took himself off to Dublin to teach in Presbyterian academies, catering for students who, being in law dissenters, were not allowed into Trinity College. For the language of instruction in these relatively informal circles he used English, which made it easier for him soon to get into print, with his *Enquiry into the Original of our Ideas of Beauty and Virtue* (1725) and *An Essay on the Nature and Conduct of the Passions and Affections* (1728). The electors to the chair at Glasgow must have been delighted to find a candidate so young and so well qualified, as well as already intimately acquainted with their own institution.[41]

At Glasgow, Hutcheson again lectured in English, breaking the college's tradition of Latin. He prepared for his students *A Short Introduction to Moral Philosophy* in which he generously acknowledged his debt to Carmichael. The philosophical battle against the supreme authority of divine revelation was being won, and Hutcheson moved on to enquire in more detail into the nature and extent of the understanding about the external world we might gather instead from our own observation and experience. He accepted the human mind had no direct contact with that external world itself but only with mental phenomena, that is, with perceptions and sensations of it. The ultimate results of this line of enquiry could be astounding, as Hume would show.[42]

But Hutcheson remained more interested in the moral implications. For him they were, contrary to the tenor of orthodox Presbyterianism, sunnily optimistic. He raised the basic question how humans could become moral beings co-operating in kindness and consideration rather than fighting a brutal and savage war of all against all. For Presbyterians the answer to this question, as to all others, lay in the Bible. But, under the influence of Pufendorf and Carmichael, Hutcheson came to a different conclusion. The human race, rather than being in its fallen state necessarily dependent on divine decrees, possessed an innate moral sense because God, by creating men in his own image, had given them a basic understanding of right and wrong.[43]

As Hutcheson put it: 'From the very frame of our nature we are determined to perceive pleasure in the practice of virtue, and to approve of it when practised by ourselves or others.' Just as we are born able to see or hear or taste, so we are born to make moral judgments. This natural human faculty differs from others in coming from the heart rather than from the head, from our feelings and emotions rather than from our judgment and calculation. But the most important part of morality is love. If human beings can love others as well as themselves (which they obviously can), it becomes hard to dismiss them as incorrigibly selfish by nature: 'There is no mortal without some love towards others, and desire to the happiness of some other persons as well as his own.' This benevolence underpins our sense of right and wrong. What pleases and helps the people we love is good, because it also gives us pleasure; what distresses and hurts them is bad, because it upsets us to see them suffer. We come to understand that the happiness of others is also our own happiness.[44]

Hutcheson concluded that everybody's ultimate goal in life is happiness. 'He is in a sure state of happiness who has sure prospect that in all parts of his existence he shall have all the things he desires.' The happy here might have threatened to become a bit clappy, but the basic idea left a huge legacy to the development of Scottish moral philosophy in its conviction that human beings possessed social and communal instincts prompting them through an inner moral sense to act benevolently. Hutcheson summed it up so: 'The moral virtues have their foundation in the nature of things.'[45]

Such optimism is a typical trait of the eighteenth century, but we move smartly into sceptical modernity with the philosophy of David Hume. This is not to say that he was pessimistic, rather that he showed himself serene in the face of a human condition we cannot alter but only learn to live with: his fortitude in the months of physical pain up to his own death was, for all who knew him, a testimony to this. A sad loss to his many friends, he had happily pursued the agreeable sociable life of enlightened Edinburgh and enjoyed it to the full while also leaving himself the time to think and write. His tubby jollity still had an edge, for he found special delight in devastating attacks on the bland assumptions held especially in the capital's religious and academic establishments. So he played the outsider too, though the butts of his wit returned the compliment by making sure he never won a professorial chair: Scottish academic habits do not change much. Still, in other places and times freed of such petty rancour, Hume would come into his own.[46]

Much of his youth Hume spent in solitary philosophical contemplation. Seeing what he had been missing, he felt especially disappointed that his first book, *Treatise of Human Nature* (1739–40), fell 'deadborn from the press'.[47] Yet it contained the kernel of all he would write on philosophy for the rest of his life, indeed the kernel of a new philosophic outlook for the Western world. In an effort to achieve greater public impact, he reworked his material for the *Inquiry concerning Human Understanding* (1748) and the *Inquiry concerning the Principles of Morals* (1752). He also stuck some stuff he really wanted to say away into the more pointed and provocative *Dialogues concerning Natural Religion* (1779), while specifying this work should not be published till after his death. Still he could never earn a living from his philosophy, which if anything hindered a regular career. Only when he turned to writing history did things look up. It was as a historian that Hume made his contemporary reputation.[48]

Hume in his *History of England* (1754–61) set a new standard in his creative scholarship, conjectural methods, expansive thinking and polemical impudence. It made for an attractive product, sharp, witty, fluent, provocative. The urbane packaging did not fool perceptive readers, though, and both Whig and Tory critics felt outraged. But if people could decipher Hume, they should also be able to decipher in the present the sort of behaviour he depicted among politicians of the past. Things had not changed much: a current example at Westminster was the peddling, by 'the barbarians who inhabit the banks of the Thames', of absurd English myths festooning not just the politics but also the history of the country, like the one about the ancient Anglo-Saxon constitution being miraculously preserved against all attacks whether from the usurping Norman conquerors or from the Stewarts importing their Scottish absolutism. If the intelligent reader could cultivate a moderate frame of mind, however, he would see through all this and come to understand history as often the product of accident rather than design, of miscarriage rather than of conspiracy.[49]

Hume's only equal among historians was William Robertson, principal of the University of Edinburgh. He wrote a series of works as original in conception as they were assured in execution, and covering novel topics such as the histories of the Americas and of India. But he kicked off with a *History of Scotland* (1759).[50] Here he showed himself less partisan than Hume, for instance in the treatment of the controversial Mary Queen of Scots; Hume took her side, while Robertson offered an assessment that could still stand today as a model of even-handedness. About these matters their countrymen continued to feel strongly enough not just to give a rousing send-off to Robertson's own literary career but also to salvage that of Hume the flagging philosopher, who had previously set the pace in Marian studies with a sympathetic account of the doomed queen. It is an open question if he wrote that out of scholarly conviction or out of mischief, to annoy the Whigs. Our suspicion of him is fed by a story the novelist Henry Mackenzie told. Hume once wanted to borrow a book from the Advocates' Library, then under the care of Walter Goodall, an antiquarian who had published vindications of Mary. Goodall was a drunkard to boot. Hume came along with a friend to find him fast asleep in his chair. They could do nothing to wake him till Hume leaned over and bellowed in his ear, 'Queen Mary was a strumpet and a murtherer.'

'It's a damned lie,' grunted Goodall, starting out of his slumber – and Hume soon had the book he was looking for.[51]

Such was the literary scene on which Robertson launched his own account of Mary, Queen of Scots. It posed a test of his political as well as his authorial skills that he was by temperament well fitted to face. To one side of him stood the Whigs, who had won most of the political victories in the last couple of centuries and crowned them by bringing Scotland into the Union of 1707. They thought Mary an evil creature for trying to restore popery and for ordering her husband's murder. To the other side stood the Tories, history's recent losers, finally at the Battle of Culloden in 1745. For them, Mary had been the innocent victim of Protestant bigotry and of jealousy from her ruthless English rival, Queen Elizabeth I. How did Robertson deal with all this? He split the difference. A plague on both Whigs and Tories, he cried: Mary 'neither merited the exaggerated praises of the one, nor the undistinguished censure of the other'. She might have made mistakes, as in her choice of husbands and her means of disposing of them. But at heart she had not been a bad woman.[52]

It was a studied exercise in impartiality, appealing beyond raucous partisans to the people Robertson really wanted to reach, the thousands of general readers who might buy his book and make his fortune, both monetary and professional – as they soon did. His impartiality approached the level of genius when he applied it also to the queen's diametric opposite, John Knox. Robertson was a Presbyterian too, and entertained no doubt that the Reformers of the sixteenth century had been right to cast down 'Romish superstition'. Still, he himself was tolerant, an advocate in his own time of Catholic emancipation. And here he went out of his way to stress, if somewhat improbably, the 'moderation of those who favoured the Reformation'. Even when obliged to describe how severe Knox had been at times, Robertson let him off on the grounds that 'those very qualities, which now render his character less amiable, fitted him to be the instrument of Providence for advancing the Reformation among a fierce people'. Providence was always useful to Robertson when he wanted to glide from one awkward position to another by a route not on the face of it obvious.[53]

Robertson did have his prejudices, though: against Catholic idolatry but also against Protestant enthusiasm. And, like Hume, he strongly believed in the Union of 1707. This commitment led both men to view with scarcely disguised disdain the history of the old Scotland. They drew the stark contrast of its wretched material poverty and violent feudal politics with the blessings poured on their own generation by partnership with the richer and steadier neighbour nation.[54]

History might bestow temporal fame and fortune on Scottish thinkers, but it was philosophy that won them immortality. Of none was this truer than of Hume, though he stood in no tradition and struck off on a different path from that of Hutcheson or anybody else in the Scottish Enlightenment. While Hume's enemies accused him of atheism, his sceptical approach did not really have God at its main target: he just left deity out of account rather than directly attacking it. This was because he could see no reliable basis either in logic or experience for any kind of religious knowledge. It might be found neither in the stern doctrines of Presbyterian orthodoxy nor yet in the more comforting deism or natural religion espoused by others who, if they could not accept the Christian revelation, still thought to perceive some divine force at work in the cosmos. Among these deists, a common defence of the existence of God was the argument from design, asserting how only some such divine force could have created the cosmos in its vastness and complexity.[55]

Hume demolished this line of thinking. He pointed out that, since none of us has ever manufactured a universe, we have no idea from the single example available to us of how well or badly it has been done. In reason, we can then infer nothing at all about who constructed it and how or why he did so, much less offer judgments on the relative skill (or, Hume mischievously hinted, even the basic competence) of the supposed Creator. Here again already provocative enough, Hume once more preferred to put off publishing some still dicier details on points of Christian dogma. So it was only posthumously that he let an essay of his on suicide appear ('prudence and courage should engage us to rid ourselves at once of existence when it becomes a burden') or another on the immortality of the soul ('what a daring theory is that! How lightly, not to say how rashly, entertained!'). Disputatious, rebellious but always creative, Hume could yet appreciate how unready Presbyterian Scotland was for much of what he had to say.[56]

Content to leave God aside, then, Hume felt far more concerned with the fact that, ever since the rise of Western philosophy in ancient Greece, its practitioners had praised reason as the guide to all human action and virtue. The main purpose of his *Treatise* was to overthrow this tradition and define a fresh starting point: 'Reason is, and ought to be, the slave of the passions.'[57] Hume went on to argue that human beings are not, and never have been, governed by their reason. Its role is purely auxiliary: it helps people to get what they want. Just what they want is determined by their emotions, their passions: anger, envy, fear, grief, lust on the bad side; courage, hope, joy, love, peace of mind on the good side. A desire to live by rational principles can itself be counted among these passions, because it prompts us to recognise necessity and act on it.

Still the most basic human passion, the one thing we all have in common, is self-interest. By the same token, this sets the necessary basis for any system of morality and for any system of government. It is our hunger to gratify ourselves with love and approval that determines our moral conduct. Any virtue in this is not something foreordained but only that which 'fixes to the spectator the pleasing sentiment of approbation'[58] – therefore a socially conditioned construct rather than a divinely ordained constant. If we do some good, it is not because we are by nature benign and reasonable but because we have appetites and passions that make us so. After that, there was not much room left for Hutcheson's moral sense. He himself felt appalled when he first read the *Treatise*, and joined in the efforts to stop Hume getting an academic chair on the strength of it: what price innate benevolence?

There were other thinkers who had recognised and did recognise the importance of self-interest in human affairs: *amour-propre* was the talk of the salons Hume frequented during his long stay in Paris. But he carried this concept to unprecedented lengths. For him self-interest is all that exists. Not reason is the guide to human actions, nor a feeling of obligation towards others, nor an innate moral sense: these are mere products of experience and habit. We each undergo different experiences in our lives, but habit is a frame of mind that associates for us certain effects with certain causes or actions. We are creatures of habit, the habit being set by the physical and social environment in which our emotions and passions operate. We learn to avoid harmful passions and to cultivate useful passions. Everything we know comes from this subjective experience: our own psychology is therefore what frames our knowledge of the outside world and how we deal with it.[59]

Hume's telling combination of experience and habit sent Western philosophy off on a new tangent. The association of ideas, the practice by which our minds integrated separate mental phenomena into a seamless web, now stood revealed as the foundation of what knowledge was available to us. A string of uncomfortable conclusions followed. The mind was forever denied direct contact with the outside world and, being only a receiver of what Hume dubbed 'impressions and ideas',[60] it could have no independent knowledge of things beyond its own limits. Then any relationships that arose among those perceptions, especially the ways they built up complex ideas, were not determined by the actual structure of the external world: again, habits of mind formed them, in the mere operations or sorting processes of our mental apparatus that revealed nothing about the reality of the world outside. Finally, certain crucial and apparently intuitive forms of knowledge, such as the connection between cause and effect, were in the same manner no more than products of the mind's habit of associating specific ideas, otherwise 'entirely loose and separate', in particular ways. As Hume reasoned, 'the falling of a pebble may, for aught we know, extinguish the Sun, or the wish of man control the planets in their orbits.'[61] The overall result was a complete upending of almost all claims to certain knowledge about the world round us, even of apparently the simplest kind. Brilliantly innovative and powerfully compelling, Hume the sceptic has never really been refuted in his basic arguments by anybody from his horrified contemporaries down to their successors today.[62]

It was for this reason that over contemporary Europe, and much of the modern world, Hume's work laid the foundation of modern philosophy – yet not in Scotland. Scotland, like a few other countries, developed a sort of national school of philosophy that remained during a whole century strong and thriving, though today it is of no more than academic interest. In essence, it came together among the adversaries of Hume, shocked at the implications of his thought for Christianity in particular. They retorted with the philosophy of Common Sense.[63] The label of Common Sense arose from the fact that its pioneers, Thomas Reid, Dugald Stewart and Sir William Hamilton, wanted to philosophise out of the ordinary thoughts of human beings – which after all even the greatest philosopher of paradox and scepticism had to make use of when not engaged in abstract speculation. In the process Reid, Stewart and Hamilton arrived at basic positions opposed to Hume's – that all human beings are intuitively sure they exist, that all see and feel objects external to themselves, and that they may then apprehend some first principles on which morality and religious beliefs can be founded.

Reid, the initiator of the school, fixed Hume firmly in his sights and set out to deconstruct what he considered the wilfulness of his rival. There was, for once in Scotland, no malice in this: when Reid went into a second edition of his seminal book, *Inquiry into the Human Mind on the Principles of Common Sense* (1765), he even out of courtesy sent the proofs for correction by Hume. Reid's meticulous care served him well. By the time he burst into print he had already moved from the University of Aberdeen to fill the chair of moral philosophy at Glasgow vacated by Adam Smith. Reid remained productive, with his *Essays on the Intellectual Powers of Man* (1785) and *Essays on the Active Powers of the Human Mind* (1788), all of them destined for wide readership in Britain, Europe and America. His reputation, once made, remained secure so long as universities conceived it their duty to inculcate moral propriety and religious belief into young students – and so keep them away from Hume.

As Reid said, 'If there are certain principles, as I think there are, which the constitution of our nature leads us to believe, and which we are under a necessity to take for granted in the common concerns of life, without being able to give a reason for them – these are what we call the principles of common sense; and what is manifestly contrary to them, is what we call absurd.'[64] This was obviously quite different from Hume's position, which Reid could all the same see was a strong one. He had for himself come to understand, however, that the 'sceptical system ... leans with its whole weight upon a hypothesis, which is ancient indeed, and hath been very generally received by philosophers, but of which I could find no solid proof.' He preferred to hold that the mind did indeed have direct contact with external reality, in accordance with our ordinary presumptions. It was then false to argue that 'we do not really perceive things that are external, but only certain images and pictures of them imprinted upon the mind, which are called impressions and ideas.' All the same, Reid never proceeded much further with this frontal attack on Humean scepticism, but rather feinted with a mixture of terminological hair-splitting and loaded appeals to everyday occurrences. Still, Common Sense then came across as something accessible and agreeable, unlike the difficult and disturbing philosophy of Hume.

In the process Common Sense also established itself as the central Scottish philosophical tradition, expounded in the universities most famously by Dugald Stewart, Reid's brightest pupil, whom students came from as far away as America or Russia to hear. He confidently began his course of lectures at Edinburgh with 'some elegant general illustrations of the excellencies of science and the superiority acquired by the philosopher by means of its study'. The young Cockburn was among the throngs that sat at his feet, later according him as fulsome a tribute as any ever paid to a professor: 'To me his lectures were like the opening of the heavens. I felt I had a soul. His noble views, unfolded in glorious sentences, elevated me in into a higher world . . . they changed my whole nature.'[65] Learning how to think and discourse philosophically became the main intellectual preoccupation of educated Scots. They were proud to reflect that their philosophy could produce such transformation in an obscure corner of Europe and such illumination in places far beyond.

Only as the sunny optimism of the Enlightenment turned complacent, then began to decay into the dim depths of Romanticism, did the intellectual vitality and the international reputation of the Scottish universities wane somewhat. 'The young vacant mind was furnished with much talk about the Progress of the Species, Dark Ages, Prejudice and the like,'[66] wrote Thomas Carlyle, who in 1808, at the age of 13, walked from Ecclefechan in Dumfriesshire to Edinburgh to start his studies: soon disillusioned, he would turn elsewhere for intellectual and spiritual sustenance. He was not alone. Most of the philosophers being themselves Christians, it had been convenient for them to define scepticism as absurd, or so far contrary to ordinary experience that it needed to be rejected. Alas, later generations did not agree, and for that reason among others ceased to find the philosophy of Common Sense of any further interest. Still, for much of the nineteenth century it dominated Scottish thought, as well as winning adherents in Europe and America.

The one great philosopher we have not dealt with so far is Adam Smith, though he has finally had the deepest effect of all on today's world – and not because he espoused Common Sense. Like his colleagues, he did start off from moral philosophy: it was for him, as for them, the introduction to new, apparently unrelated fields which he found himself drawn to not by theory, or not only by theory, but by experience of the common business of life. While he liked most to live at home with his mother at Kirkcaldy, in between he made long excursions into the wider world. As an undergraduate at the University of Glasgow, he fell under Hutcheson's spell. He went on to the University of Oxford, which he hated. He returned to teach at Glasgow, where he hobnobbed with local merchants to learn at first hand of their trading ventures and commercial practice. Then he took the chance to escort the young Duke of Buccleuch to Paris, where he made contact with the French school of economists, the physiocrats, though remaining unimpressed by their theories. After that, he came back to Kirkcaldy (his mother died only in 1784) and ended his days in Edinburgh. The real inspiration for his work was his brother Scots and the development of their civil society, as 'commerce and manufactures gradually introduced order and good government, and with them, the liberty and security of individuals'.[67]

Today we regard Smith's *Inquiry into the Nature and Causes of the Wealth of Nations* (1776) as the culmination of his life's work, yet he meant it only as part of a much greater project that he never completed. This would have expounded in several volumes an all-embracing survey of human society, and we can only guess how the whole might finally have turned out (he ordered his executors to destroy his unpublished manuscripts). The best clue we get is that the series would have established, in his words, 'the science of a legislator'[68] – presumably one disseminating the knowledge and techniques necessary for governing a commercial society. It would also have been a work of natural law, 'the most important and the least cultivated science of all'.[69]

So much for the usual Scottish polymathy – yet otherwise, in the general scheme of the philosophical Enlightenment that has been developed here, with Hume opposed by Common Sense, Smith presents a bit of a puzzle. He could be little less forthright than Hume, though he was never deliberately provocative. He avoided polemics and called forth no Christian critique of his work. But he revealed one of his own underlying impulses in a remark he made on Hume's death in 1776. Smith said this best of his friends had approached in life 'as nearly to the idea of a perfectly wise and virtuous man, as perhaps the nature of human frailty will permit'. In other words, Smith, too, denied a necessary connection between Christianity and morality. In private he had been blunter, writing how Hume on his deathbed was departing 'with great cheerfulness and good humour and with more real resignation to the necessary course of things than any whining Christian ever died with pretended resignation to the will of God'.[70]

Yet, despite this devotion to Hume, it is striking that Smith's first book, *The Theory of Moral Sentiments* (1759), shows him to be in the first place a disciple of Hutcheson. It is a work based again not on theological but on material or rational assumptions, notably the natural sympathy among human beings. Though Smith might be caricatured in the twenty-first century as a shameless proponent of capitalist egotism, here he does largely share Hutcheson's theory of benevolence as the mainspring of morality and of an impartial observer as its judge. Smith never argues that we possess a moral sense implanted in us by God (of whom he seldom has much to say anyway). But he does depict human beings in society as being guided by sympathy and turning to the impartial spectator for approval of their natural desires. Self-interest is thereby transformed from obsessive selfishness into something more nuanced and useful. And so morality is formed.[71]

How is that different from Hutcheson? Part of the answer surely lies in the fact that Hume has meanwhile intervened, with his cool, sceptical distrust of human moods and motives. For Hutcheson, morality is inborn, a gift of God and nature, while for Hume it comes from outside through experience of success and failure in real life. Smith brought in besides the 'awful virtues': discipline, self-restraint, moral rectitude and righteous anger at wrongdoers, the qualities lauded by the ancient Stoics (and indeed preached by the Calvinist Kirk). They were as socially necessary as civility and compassion, to rectify errors and deviations from virtue in our dealings with others. It seems ironic that the Presbyterian clergyman Hutcheson should overlook the utility of correction, while the sceptic Hume should see the need for our impulses to be curbed. Smith was at the same time casting about for some instinct that corresponded to this inborn moral sense, but of a kind more recognisable in real life than Hutcheson's abstract and rather too sweeping conception. Perhaps Smith never quite succeeded in his quest, which was why in the end he came to rely more on the self-regulating behaviour of the market. In fact, the concept of the invisible hand had already appeared in *The Theory of Moral Sentiments*: 'The rich . . . are led by an invisible hand to make nearly the same distribution of the necessaries of life, which would have been made, had the earth been divided into equal portions among all its inhabitants, and thus without intending it, without knowing it, advance the interest of the society.'[72]

The Theory of Moral Sentiments is nowadays eclipsed by *The Wealth of Nations*, but it would be wrong to judge the later book in splendid isolation. It was in large part a practical work, written up from actual observation of contemporary conditions. It starts with the famous description of the pin factory, as a good example of the division of labour that formed the basis of Smith's whole system (and from this the basis for the entire analytical framework of modern economics). But he was not merely a cheerleader for it; the reader is often hard put to distinguish what he favoured from what he was just trying to explain. While the division of labour let workers produce more, that came at the cost of dehumanisation in their boring and repetitive labour. Here Smith already offered a moral critique of emerging industrialism, and long before Britain's factories had actually set up production lines. From it stemmed also his insistence that to the state and to the state alone fell certain public responsibilities – including adequate education for the general populace, essential if society was to counteract the bad side of economic development. Yet in the end, against Hutcheson, Smith was happy to rely for the most part on individual purposes: 'It is not from the benevolence of the butcher, the brewer, or the baker that we expect our dinner, but from their regard to their own interest.'[73]

The book also seeks to shed historical light on the motivational and material processes by which Britons (especially Scots) enriched themselves, so as the better to identify for active statesmen, like Smith's admirer and correspondent Henry Dundas, the specific roles these too might play. But Smith knows active statesmen are not philosopher kings. For all its reputation as a handbook of capitalism, *The Wealth of Nations* abounds with disparaging examples of collusion between politicians and businessmen, in what today we call rip-offs. Smith writes: 'People of the same trade seldom meet together, even for merriment and diversion, but the conversation ends in a conspiracy against the public, or in some contrivance to raise prices.'[74] He did not live into the age of the lobbyist, but he had already got the general idea. When businessmen put to government some wonderful new scheme of overwhelming benefit to the public, we should always remember that 'it comes from an order of men, whose interest is never exactly the same with that of the public, who have generally an interest to deceive and even oppress the public, and who accordingly have, upon many occasions, both deceived and oppressed it.'[75] That also seems a perfect description of their role in the Scottish referendum of 2014.

At a more intellectual level, it is easy to see within *The Wealth of Nations* the promise of the yet greater study of the operations of natural law that Smith had in mind. Economics as he conceived it would work because it could follow the inborn desires and inclinations of human beings – at least in the right conditions of 'perfect liberty'[76] without heavy-handed intervention from governments handing out sops to special pleading in the shape of protectionist privilege. On the other hand, if left in the course of nature, self-interest would make the world go round – and make it prosper to boot. All the detailed observation, even just in the particular case of what the Scots called political economy, does point us to the fact that *The Wealth of Nations*, like *The Theory of Moral Sentiments*, was going to contribute to the construction of a grand general treatise of human society, alas never to be completed.

We can reasonably speculate what it might have taught the future generations that profited so much even from the fragments (admittedly quite large fragments) of the unfinished masterwork. Smith was a psychologist as much as an economist, and the uncanniest part of his genius lay in telling us, in every case, what actually went on. He remained a cautious fellow, but his very caution allowed him to read the reality of motives. And once he had read them, he was always on the side of the small man likely to suffer from the presumption of the rich and powerful. When he called for liberty, as he constantly did, it was to secure the rights of the small man against the rich and powerful.[77]

Of course the rich and powerful retain a greater freedom of action, and the scope to abuse it. How did Smith propose to deal with this, a problem in any polity? To answer the question we need to turn back from *The Wealth of Nations* to *The Theory of Moral Sentiments*, and there we learn that morality is never secured by the multiplication of laws, nor yet by the interventions of government, which are both inevitably corruptible. It is secured not at a public level but at a private level, in each person through the cultivation of his or her own moral sensibilities. We have no need to be consciously and constantly selfless, which is probably an impossible demand of human beings. We can in fact develop our morality just by being normal, moderate, sensible members of society. The very first sentence of Smith's earlier book says this: 'How selfish soever man may be supposed, there are evidently some principles in his nature, which interest him in the fortunes of others, and render their happiness necessary to him, though he derives nothing from it, except the pleasure of seeing it.'[78] At the end, as at the beginning, Smith remains a very Scottish figure.

Studies of the Enlightenment have proliferated in the last half-century, and of nothing is this truer than of the Scottish Enlightenment in particular, even though it had been an expression scarcely known or used at the outset of the period. Now it may be overused, to the extent that calls have come for us to be rather more precise in our deployment of it – otherwise a term commonly applied to so much in the Scotland of the eighteenth century could come in the end to mean little.[79] But perhaps we should not worry excessively, because Enlightenment was anyway a term unknown to that Scotland. For all the many things going on in their country Scots had no single name: perhaps 'improvement' came nearest, but this did not really refer to anything intellectual.

In the present book we have seen the vast range of activities in Scotland over which improvement did take place, so that by the turn of the nineteenth century hardly anything remained untouched. Scots opened up their minds in every way, and to this process it is not unreasonable to apply also the term Enlightenment: other countries might have had more specific Enlightenments, intellectual or religious or political, but the Scottish case was a general one. It succeeded to such an extent that the effect and the impact spread not only to every corner of the land but also far beyond its narrow limits. Setting an example in many fields, it gave this small nation its one era of truly global significance. Never again was it to be so exemplary: unless, perhaps, in the twenty-first century.

Epilogue: 'Whom fate made brothers'

The centenary of the Union of Parliaments, 1 May 1807, found Walter Scott somewhere on the Great North Road between London and Edinburgh. He had gone south six weeks earlier for a bout of intensive parliamentary lobbying. A reform of the Court of Session was in prospect under a bill introduced at Westminster by the Whig government of Lord Grenville. Among other things, it threatened at a personal and practical level to rob Scott of a large part of the fees making up his income as a clerk to the court, and he wanted to secure himself on that score – but also to put across in high places some general arguments against a piece of legislation he deeply disapproved of. In his view, it would add up to an anglicising reform of the Scottish courts, in particular through creating a right to trial by jury in civil causes, in place of the hallowed native practice of having them heard only by a judge or judges. A patriot in the law as in everything else, Scott regarded the new proposal with intense distaste.[1]

Still, the Whig government had already run into big problems and, during Scott's stay in London, it fell. Its biggest problem of all was the war to contain the incessant aggressions of Napoleon Bonaparte. The Whigs, or at least a large part of them, had long been critics of this war and their spell in office allowed them to test their criticism; it did not pass the test. Ever since the outbreak of hostilities with revolutionary France in 1793, Britain's strategy had been to let other European powers do all the fighting on land, with support from the Royal Navy at sea and from the City of London in finance. The Whigs changed tack. First, Charles James Fox as Foreign Secretary sought to negotiate a peace with Napoleon, but this turned out a complete waste of time. When Fox suddenly died, the Cabinet decided to concentrate on operations demonstrably beneficial to Britain and leave to one side any consideration of

387

its allies' interests. None of the independent operations worked out, however, and those in the Dardanelles and at Alexandria in Egypt did no more than annoy the Russians, the sole allies the British really wanted to keep. In any case, a foreign policy concentrated on imperial concerns, which was what this fresh outlook meant in practice, could not answer the basic question of how to defeat Napoleon in Europe. The government actually made things worse by driving the Russians into the arms of the French and prompting them to sign the Treaty of Tilsit in 1807, under which they proposed to carve up the Continent between them.[2]

Scott had been penning poetry inspired by war, but war of the sixteenth century. He was about to publish his *Marmion*, which reaches a climax in the Battle of Flodden (1513). It had been the greatest military disaster Scotland ever suffered, when King James IV fell on the field along with the flower of his nobility and thousands of his soldiers. It inflicted such a deep wound on the nation that three centuries later it still lived on in popular memory, as poetry and as song. We might have expected Scott, in adding to this legacy, to look at the doleful event from a patriotic point of view, in grief and mourning for all that had been lost and in painful recollection of what this meant for the future – since Flodden was certainly one of the events that paved the way for the two Unions, of Crowns in 1603 and of Parliaments in 1707.[3]

Yet, for the central character of *Marmion* the author chose an Englishman. In fact, it was remarkable how often he reflected Scottishness through an English prism in this way: the precedent for a non-Scottish hero was to be carried forward into some of his Waverley novels of the following decade. In the poem's rather improbable plot, Marmion dots back and forth across the border as war breaks out between Scotland and England. But that gives him the chance to get to know and to appreciate the points of view on both sides, even to share in them: so an Englishman comes to understand the deepest Scottish emotions. At one stage, Marmion and a companion look down on Edinburgh from Blackford Hill, a view a good deal more picturesque in the author's day than it is now. They are moved by the same feelings as Scotsmen might experience:

> Fitz-Eustace' heart felt closely pent;
> As if to give his rapture vent,
> The spur he to his charger lent,
> And raised his bridle hand

And, making demi-volte in air,
Cried, 'Where's the coward that would not dare
To fight for such a land!'[4]

Similarly, in the novel *Waverley* (1814), Scott will organise the action round the adventures of young Edward Waverley, almost an anti-hero in his bland English contrast to the fierce Jacobite clansmen he encounters. The eponymous hero of *Guy Mannering* (1815) will be another Englishman, by chance drawn into the fiendish legal intricacies abundant in a Scotland opening by the mid eighteenth century to the big wide world. And in *Rob Roy* (1817) we will meet the representative of an English merchant house arriving in Scotland to collect a debt, Frank Osbaldistone, but then led astray into the barbaric Highlands. 'To see ourselves as others see us' is a famous line of Robert Burns (it might have been used by David Hume too): no less is it a favourite posture of Scott's, as he holds a mirror up to his fellow countrymen.[5]

In the same mirror Scott urges them to look for other English reflections. Though *Marmion* is a historical poem, he manages to include an elegy for three recently dead Englishmen still mourned by Scots too, Admiral Horatio Nelson, William Pitt the Younger and Charles James Fox:

Deep graved in every British heart,
O never let these names depart.

Pitt and Fox had for more than 30 years, in all domestic affairs as well as in matters of foreign war and peace, been political enemies. Yet

Here let their discord with them die,
Speak not for those a separate doom,
Whom fate made brothers in the tomb.[6]

Readers might then reflect on a broader brotherhood – that between the Scotsmen and the Englishmen fighting for Britain in the great existential test of the Napoleonic Wars still going on as the backcloth to domestic events. Perhaps Scott thought this the best he could do to keep up his compatriots' fighting spirit. He would yet remain, like many men of letters, fascinated by the figure of Napoleon, and one day write a biography of him remarkable for its objectivity – but only after all the passion of war had been spent.

The country's perils could yet affect the personal and professional relationships

even of this most sociable and amiable of men. Scott remained on reasonably friendly terms with the group of young Whigs, led by Francis Jeffrey, who in 1802 had launched the *Edinburgh Review*. It was a revolution in itself, a journalistic one, with its long, weighty articles on the great issues of the day, and its short, sharp critiques of books just out. Before it appeared, no British newspaper or magazine wrote candidly about politics or culture; the press was shackled by regulation or bought by official subsidies or full of puffs for people the editors knew. In contrast, the *Review* set out to mould opinion by force of argument. It was the ancestor of modern serious journalism – clever, probing, irreverent. It succeeded because it identified a gap in the market among a rising bourgeoisie wanting to learn about and judge of events for itself. According to Henry Cockburn, Jeffrey's sidekick and biographer, it was 'an entire and instant change of everything that the public had been accustomed to in that sort of composition. The learning of the new journal, its writing, its independence, were all new; and the surprise was increased by a work so full of public life springing up, suddenly, in a remote part of the kingdom' (meaning Edinburgh). Scott bought and read it too, without going overboard for it like Cockburn (who was a leading contributor himself). On the contrary, Scott once observed in some scorn how the authors 'have a great belief in the influence of fine writing and think that a nation can be governed by pamphlets and reviews'.[7]

But from the appearance of *Marmion* onwards there was a more decisive parting of the ways. Jeffrey wrote a scathing criticism: 'a broken narrative – a redundancy of minute description – bursts of unequal and energetic poetry – and a general tone of spirit and animation, unchecked by timidity or affectation, and unchastised by any great delicacy of taste, or elegance of fancy'. It says a great deal about his literary standards that he evidently thought spirit and animation were bad things in poetry, delicacy and elegance good things. Astoundingly, this pundit who in his later years became a toadying anglophile also had the cheek to find Scott deficient in patriotism: 'There is scarcely one trait of true Scottish nationality or patriotism introduced into the whole poem; and Mr. Scott's only expression of admiration or love for the beautiful country to which he belongs, is put . . . into the mouth of one of his Southern favourites.'[8]

Even now the target of these strictures did not lose his temper. It was a measure of the man that in the end a public rather than a private matter actually produced the breach that was no doubt coming anyway. Out of the blue in 1808 the *Edinburgh Review* published an article apologising for the outrageous treatment by France of its ally Spain. In Madrid, King Ferdinand VII had just ascended the throne and he wanted to call a halt to plans previously drawn up with the Emperor Napoleon for a joint invasion of Portugal, on account of its deficient subservience to them and its alliance with Britain. When Ferdinand crossed the French frontier to make his case at a summit with Napoleon, he found himself placed under arrest, indeed deposed in favour of the despot's brother, Joseph Bonaparte. Yet the *Review* defended the French action on the grounds of the utter corruption of Spanish government (accurate though this description was). Scott felt so furious that he cancelled his subscription, cut off all contact with the editors and soon set up his own *Quarterly Review* in rivalry to them. After that he never had much time for Whigs.[9]

Anyhow it had been no surprise that in 1807 Scott welcomed the political change at Westminster, the fall of a weak government and the return to straightforward confrontation with the French, even though final victory over them would take another eight years. With Grenville stepping down as Prime Minister, a broad coalition was formed under the Duke of Portland. It brought together again most of the factions that had once supported William Pitt the Younger but drifted apart after his resignation over Catholic emancipation in 1801. Portland wasted little time in asking King George III to dissolve Parliament, and on 27 April a general election was called. Given the disarray of the outgoing ministry, the duke's first task lay in keeping his somewhat ramshackle alliance together under his own leadership. At least he could look to thoroughly reliable support from the Scottish following of Henry Dundas, now Viscount Melville.[10]

Melville had in the last few years seen more ups and downs in his career than most of his colleagues. In 1805 he should have been the object of universal public acclaim for his recent work, while First Lord of the Admiralty, in finding for Nelson all he needed in men and material to win his smashing victory over the French and Spanish fleets at the Battle of Trafalgar on 21 October. Alas, Melville was on that date facing impeachment for various fiddles that had arisen in the Admiralty even as it prepared the Royal Navy for this triumph: it was a time when new ships needed to be built at almost any cost, and many corners were cut. Still, as the impeachment proceeded it seemed churlish to lay all the blame at the door of a man who had done, whatever else, signal service for his country. He was finally acquitted and, at least in his own mind, vindicated – though not so far as to tempt any future government to offer him a job. Early in 1807 that remained as yet unclear, however, and he would on Portland's behalf mount a vigorous electoral campaign in Scotland.[11]

Scott had been a Tory since driven to that position by the Scottish radical disturbances of the 1790s – but not least because of his friendship with the Dundases, especially with Melville's son Robert, an exact contemporary at school and university in Edinburgh. Scott wrote: 'I was not only very early disposed to what have been called Tory principles by the opinions of those whom I respected and was bound to respect but the favours I received and the intimacy in which I lived with many of Lord Melville's family, his nephew and son in particular, was founded as much upon attachment to their measures in 1792–3 as to gratitude for favours received at a time when they were truly valuable.'[12] Still, Scott might not have then been quite the terrible Tory he later appeared to be: 'I am candid enough to esteem the principles and cherish the [friendship] of many whose political opinions are different from my own, because I know they are adopted by those who hold them from an internal conviction of their rectitude.'[13] Perhaps indeed at some point in the past he himself had been less certain in his political allegiance than he was now, and perhaps some people in Edinburgh knew this: 'More than one distinguished individual of the party who were last in power paid me much attention till they saw I would not be coaxed to leave Lord Melville's standard in Scotland by any prospect which could be held out to me.'[14]

In any event, with the legal reform at Westminster dead in the water Scott had no reason to linger in London and he set off for home. He took his time about it, and in the English counties he passed through he found the electoral campaign already in full swing, in the inimitable fashion of unreformed Britain:

> I had a most stormy passage to Scotland for the tempest of disputed election was raging in every town almost through which I past. Post horses were generally speaking out of the question and the public coaches on the outside and in the inside of which I performed the greater part of my journey were crowded with drunken voters whom the candidates were transporting in that manner through the country and who drank brandy at every furlong for the good of their

country . . . The cry of King and Constitution was the favourite through every part of the country I passed.[15]

Once across the border, Scott discovered the Tories' prospects to be no less rosy. Melville's troubles had still left his formidable political machine more or less intact. A fresh challenge renewed it, as he set about wheeling and dealing in his practised way. Scott wrote: 'Here Lord Melville is at work with election business from morning till night and I think will give a very good account of the returns. I hardly think that opposition will be able to make ten out of the forty-five although they supposed they would have double that number.'[16]

Melville was not in fact to do quite so well this time as in some previous elections. In the end he returned 29 out of Scotland's 45 MPs, while the Whigs had 13 and independents made up the rest. He blithely apologised that 'from the constitution of our burghs and sheer habits on occasion of elections, the popular voice does not operate with equal effect as in England.'[17] In fact, a disorganised opposition needed to rely for the most part on a handful of aristocrats, like the Duke of Argyll, from a family Whig since the revolutions of the seventeenth century, and the Countess of Sutherland, who was about to apply liberal economic doctrines on her vast Highland estates in the clearance of their superfluous population. Melville could still supply the Tory government with a useful component in the overwhelming majority of 200 that it won. A range of political forces had been reassembled by Portland, covering Scotland and Ireland as well as England, and this new coalition would under him and his successors dominate British politics right down till it finally broke apart during the prelude to the Reform Act of 1832.

Perhaps all the political excitement had stopped Scott marking the passage of the days as he made his way back to Edinburgh. At any rate, there is nothing in his correspondence to tell us just where he was on 1 May, or what exactly, if anything, he did to mark the centenary of the Union. Perhaps neither he nor anybody else felt it necessary. The picture that emerges from scenes like those he had witnessed on his way home is of a Scotland integrated into the United Kingdom as never before, committed to its causes, brave in its battles.

Yet, beneath the tranquil surface, tensions did lurk ready to bubble up now and again, even if only in such minor matters as a literary tiff. The falling out of Scott and Jeffrey, for example, had a meaning beyond itself in the attitudes to the nation it exposed. It is true that all the straight struggles of nationalist and unionist were by now overcome, the choices facing Scots being no longer so stark. The crude efforts to anglicise Scotland had been abandoned, and the people felt able to reassert their Scottishness once again, not now in the old truculent, defiant way but in a gentler, romantic way that satisfied national sentiment without posing any kind of threat. Yet the entire activity of Jeffrey and his Whig friends reminds us how anglicisation did remain on the agenda in some quarters, as a serious option that continued to find support in the nineteenth century too: it also encountered mounting resistance, from Scott and many others. And then in the twentieth century the cycle took yet another turn, this time with anglicisation from the centralising policies of the British state. Right through the 300 years from 1707, in any event, Scotland survived, if often battered and bruised, to preserve a nationhood with a great deal more life in it yet.

Chronology

(SS = Secretary of State for Scotland; LA = Lord Advocate)

1707 Union of Scotland and England. SS Earl of Mar.

1708 First British general election. Abortive Jacobite invasion. Foundation of Society in Scotland for Propagating Christian Knowledge.

1709 SS Duke of Queensberry.

1710 In Nova Scotia, Samuel Vetch is first Scot appointed a British colonial governor.

1711 James Watson completes *Choice Collection of Comic and Serious Scots Poems*. Edinburgh town council makes it an offence to dig up fresh corpses.

1712 Patronage Act. Toleration Act.

1713 SS Earl of Mar. Vote to dissolve Union narrowly lost in House of Lords. Treaty of Utrecht ends War of Spanish Succession.

1714 Death of Queen Anne; accession of King George I. SS Duke of Montrose.

1715 Jacobite rebellion under Old Pretender, James VIII *de jure*. SS Duke of Roxburghe. Colen Campbell, *Vitruvius Britannicus, or the British Architect* (to 1725).

1716 Jacobite rebellion collapses; first Disarming Act. Septennial Act.

1717 Colin MacLaurin professor of mathematics at Marischal College, Aberdeen.

1718 War of Quadruple Alliance (to 1720) sets Spain against Britain.

1719 Spanish invasion and Jacobite rising defeated at Battle of Glenshiel.

1720 LA Robert Dundas I.

1721 Clan Mackenzie defeats British army at Battle of Glen Affric.

1722 Wooden wagon-way starts operating Tranent to Cockenzie.

1723 Levellers in Galloway. Society of Improvers in the Knowledge of Agriculture formed.

1724 Allan Ramsay the Elder, *The Evergreen*. MacLaurin professor of mathematics at University of Edinburgh. Daniel Defoe, *Tour through the Whole Island of Great Britain*.

1725 Riots over malt tax in Glasgow. Duke of Roxburghe resigns as SS; office lapses. LA Duncan Forbes of Culloden. George Drummond Lord Provost of Edinburgh for first time. Francis Hutcheson, *Enquiry into the Original of our Ideas of Beauty and Virtue*.

1726 Medical school founded, Edinburgh.

1727 Death of King George I; accession of King George II. Board of Commissioners and Trustees for Improving Fisheries and Manufactures formed. Royal Bank of Scotland founded. Gershom Carmichael professor of moral philosophy at University of Glasgow. John Smibert, *Sir Archibald Grant of Monymusk and his Wife*.

1728 James Gibbs, *A Book of Architecture, containing designs of buildings and ornaments*. Hutcheson, *An Essay on the Nature and Conduct of the Passions and Affections*.

1729 William Adam builds Royal Infirmary, Edinburgh. Academy of St Luke, Edinburgh. At University of Glasgow, Frances Hutcheson appointed professor of moral philosophy, John Simson suspended from teaching.

1730 Rent rises force first systematic Highland emigration to America. Right of recorded dissent removed in General Assembly of Kirk.

1731 Poorhouse established in Glasgow.

1732 Right of Kirk's congregations to elect ministers removed even in cases where patron has failed to nominate.

1733 Patrick Lindsay, *The Interest of Scotland*. Original Secession from Church of Scotland.

1734 At general election the Earl of Ilay, political manager, achieves maximum degree of control over Scottish constituencies.

1735 Thomas Blackwell, *Inquiry into the Life, Times and Writings of Homer*.

1736 Porteous Riot. Ramsay the Elder opens theatre in Edinburgh, soon forced to close.

1737 Edinburgh Philosophical Society founded. Duke of Argyll tries to remove tacksmen from his territory.

1738 Failed harvest and threat of famine (repeated in each year till 1741).

1739 David Hume, *Treatise of Human Nature*.

1740 Poorhouse established in Edinburgh. Allan Ramsay the Younger, *Anne Bayne*. George Turnbull, *Treatise on Ancient Painting*.

1741 Hume, *Essays, Moral and Political*.

1742 SS Marquess of Tweedsdale. Cambuslang Wark. MacLaurin, *Treatise on Fluxions*.

1743 Death of second Duke of Argyll.

1744 Allan Ramsay the Younger, first portrait of *Archibald Campbell, third Duke of Argyll* (others in 1749 and 1759). Hume rejected for chair at University of Edinburgh.

1745 Jacobite rebellion of Young Pretender, Prince Charles Edward Stewart. British Linen Bank founded.

1746 Battle of Culloden; collapse of Jacobite rebellion. Tweeddale resigns as SS; office lapses.

1747 Abolition of heritable jurisdictions, and further legal reforms. Original Secession splits into Burghers and Anti-Burghers.

1748 Second Disarming Act. Tobias Smollett, *The Adventures of Roderick Random*. MacLaurin, *Account of Sir Isaac Newton's Philosophical Discoveries*. Hume, *Inquiry concerning Human Understanding*.

1749 Factory opens at Prestonpans for manufacture of vitriol.

1750 Adam Smith applies for chair of logic at University of Glasgow; will stay there till 1764.

1751 Andrew MacDouall, Lord Bankton, *Institute of the Laws of Scotland*. Court of Session rules absentee landlords not liable for parochial poor relief. Hume rejected for chair at University of Glasgow. Medical school founded, Glasgow.

1752 Annexing Act confiscates estates of leading Jacobites. Relief Church founded. Gilbert Elliot of Minto, 'Proposals for Carrying on Certain Works in the City of Edinburgh' (New Town). Hume, *Inquiry concerning the Principles of Morals*.

1753 Blast furnace opens at Bonawe, Loch Etive. Dr Archibald Cameron, last Jacobite victim, executed.

1754 LA Robert Dundas II. John Erskine of Carnock, *Principles of the Law of Scotland*. Hume, *History of England* (to 1761). Ramsay the Younger, *Sir Hew Dalrymple, Lord Drummore*.

1755 Dr Alexander Webster's census shows Scottish population at 1,265,000. Commission for forfeited estates starts work. Foulis Academy, Glasgow.

1756 Outbreak of Seven Years' War. John Home, *Douglas*.

1757 Ramsay the Younger, *Margaret Lindsay*.

1758 Ramsay the Younger, first portrait of *George, Prince of Wales* (later George III).

1759 Adam Smith, *Theory of Moral Sentiments*. William Robertson, *History of Scotland*. Carron ironworks opens. Highland regiments distinguish themselves at capture of Quebec.

1760 Death of King George II; accession of King George III. William Adam completes Royal Exchange (later City Chambers), Edinburgh. Trustees' Academy, Edinburgh, founded. Henry Home, Lord Kames, *Principles* *of Equity.* James MacPherson, *Fragments of Ancient Poetry Collected in the Highlands of Scotland.*

1761 Death of third Duke of Argyll. Earl of Bute Prime Minister (to 1763).

1762 William Robertson principal of University of Edinburgh. Adam Smith delivers lectures on jurisprudence in University of Glasgow. Joseph Black states doctrine of latent heat.

1763 Treaty of Paris ends Seven Years' War. Construction of North Bridge started, Edinburgh.

1764 Speculative Society founded, Edinburgh.

1765 Thomas Reid, *Inquiry into the Human Mind on the Principles of Common Sense.* John Gregory, *A Comparative View of the State and Faculties of Man, with those of the Animal World.*

1766 Ramsay the Younger, *David Hume* and *Jean-Jacques Rousseau.* James Fordyce, *Sermons to Young Women.*

1767 Edinburgh New Town started. Sir James Steuart, *Principles of Political Economy.* Adam Ferguson, *Essay on the History of Civil Society.* Old Testament published in Gaelic.

1768 *Encyclopaedia Britannica* published in Edinburgh.

1769 James Watt patents the steam engine.

1770 Monkland Canal opened.

1771 Henry Mackenzie, *The Man of Feeling.* James MacPherson, *Introduction to the History of Great Britain and Ireland.*

1772 Failure of Ayr Bank. Court of Session excludes sheriffs from intervention in parochial poor relief. Alexander Runciman paints Hall of Ossian, Penicuik.

1773 John Millar, *Observations concerning the Distinctions of Ranks in Society.* Erskine, *Institute of the Law of Scotland.* Highland tour of Dr Samuel Johnson and James Boswell.

1774 Kames, *Sketches of the History of Man.*

1775 LA Henry Dundas. First emancipation of Scottish serfs. *Impartial List of the Ladies of Pleasure in Edinburgh* (anonymous).

1776 Smith, *Inquiry into the Nature and Causes of the Wealth of Nations.* George Campbell, *The Philosophy of Rhetoric.* Outbreak of American War of Independence. Emigration from Scotland banned. Dunmore Pineapple built.

1777 Robertson, *History of America.*

1778 Highland Society founded to promote private enterprise.

1779 Dundas abandons Catholic relief after widespread riots. Hume, *Dialogues concerning Natural Religion.* William Alexander, *History of Women. The Mirror* magazine starts up.

1780 Society of Antiquaries of Scotland founded.

1781 Lord Dundonald extracts tar from coal.

1782 Dundas becomes Treasurer of the Navy.

1783 Treaty of Versailles, end of American war. In Scotland, threat of famine. William Pitt the Younger becomes Prime Minister, supported by Dundas. Royal Society of Edinburgh founded.

1784 Forfeited estates restored to original Jacobite owners. Kirk abandons annual protest against Patronage Act.

1785 Dundas's Diminishing Bill fails. David Dale opens cotton mill at New Lanark; with George Macintosh, opens dyeworks at Barrowfield, Glasgow. Reid, *Essays on the Intellectual Powers of Man. The Lounger* magazine starts up.

1786 Robert Burns, Kilmarnock edition of *Poems, chiefly in the Scottish dialect.*

1787 First mechanically powered flax mill, Brigton, Angus. Weavers' riot suppressed in Glasgow. James Johnson, *The Scots Musical Museum* (to 1803). Medical school founded, Aberdeen.

1788 Death of Prince Charles Edward Stewart. Reid, *Essays on the Active Powers of the Human Mind.*

1789 French Revolution. LA Robert Dundas III.

1790 Forth–Clyde Canal opened.

1791 Henry Dundas becomes Home Secretary. Sir John Sinclair, *Old Statistical Account* (to 1799). Robert Adam builds Charlotte Square, Edinburgh.

1792 *Bliadhna nan Caorach,* the Year of the Sheep. Riot on king's birthday in George Square, Edinburgh.

1793 Britain declares war on France. Scottish sedition trials. Henry Dundas becomes President of the Board of Control for India. Glasgow chamber of commerce founded, first in Britain.

1794 Henry Dundas becomes Secretary of State for War. Highland Society publishes vocabulary of Gaelic.

1795 David Allan, *The Penny Wedding.*

1796 General election: Henry Dundas's greatest victory. Anderson's Institute founded, Glasgow.

1797 Militia Act. Magdalene Institute (refuge for prostitutes) founded in Edinburgh.

1798 Charles Tennant founds St Rollox chemical works at Springburn, Glasgow. Irish rebellion.

1799 Tennant patents dry bleaching powder. Final emancipation of Scottish serfs. George Thomson, *Select Collection of Original Scottish Airs for the Voice* (to 1818).

1800 Glasgow establishes police force.

1801 Union of Great Britain and Ireland. Government of William Pitt, including Henry Dundas, falls over Catholic emancipation. LA Charles Hope. First official census shows Scottish population at 1,608,000.

1802 Peace of Amiens. Henry Dundas created Viscount Melville. *Edinburgh Review* launched. Walter Scott, *Minstrelsy of the Scottish Border.*

1803 War with France renewed. New Testament published in Gaelic.

1804 Melville becomes First Lord of Admiralty. George Joseph Bell,

Commentaries on the Law of Scotland and on the Principles of Mercantile Jurisprudence.

1805 Melville impeached and resigns. Battle of Trafalgar. Edinburgh establishes police force. Scott, *Lay of the Last Minstrel.*

1806 Melville acquitted.

1807 Emperor Napoleon imposes Continental System.

1808 Peninsular War starts. Court of Session reformed. John Jamieson, *Etymological Dictionary of the Scots Language.*

1809 Tally Toor (Martello Tower) erected to protect harbour of Leith.

1810 Acts to limit Scottish patronage and set minimum stipend in the Kirk.

1811 Death of Melville.

1812 Strikes and disturbances in West of Scotland. Robert Dundas, second Viscount Melville, becomes First Lord of Admiralty. War with United States (to 1814).

1813 East India Company's monopoly abolished; Glaswegian merchants set up in Calcutta.

1814 Scott, *Waverley.* Emperor Napoleon abdicates.

1815 Battle of Waterloo, end of French wars.

Notes

Abbreviations

BL   British Library
ECA   Edinburgh City Archives
EUL   Edinburgh University Library
HMC   Historical Manuscripts Commission
NAS   National Archives of Scotland
NGS   National Gallery of Scotland
NLS   National Library of Scotland
NRS   National Records of Scotland
OSA   *Old Statistical Account*, ed. I.R. Grant & D.J. Withrington, 20 vols (Wakefield, 1991; first published 1791–9)
PP   Parliamentary Papers
SNPG   Scottish National Portrait Gallery

Prologue: 'My wedding day'

1. J. Clerk, *Memoirs,* ed. J.M. Gray (Edinburgh, 1892), 65.
2. HMC, *Portland MSS* (London, 1899), IV, 398.
3. HMC, *Mar and Kellie MSS* (London, 1904), I, 389.
4. *Òrain Iain Luim*, ed. A.A. Mackenzie (Edinburgh, 1942), 225–9.
5. Clerk, *Memoirs,* 66.
6. Glasgow University Library, Letters to Principal Stirling, MS Murray 652/5, III, 32.
7. Clerk, *Memoirs,* 67–8; *The Marlborough–Godolphin Correspondence,* ed. H.L. Snyder, 3 vols (Oxford, 1975), II, 765.

1 Agriculture: 'To do useful things'

1. D. Stevenson, *The Hunt for Rob Roy* (Edinburgh, 2004), 23.
2. NAS, Montrose MSS, GD 200/6/795–8.
3. NAS, Buchanan of Leny Muniments, GD 161/2, Bardowie writs, no. 70.
4. NAS, Breadalbane MSS, GD 112/78/1.
5. B. Lenman, *An Economic History of Modern Scotland* (London, 1977), 31.
6. Stevenson, *Rob Roy,* 28–30.
7. C. O'Rahilly, *The Táin Bó Cuailgne from the Book of Leinster* (Dublin, 1967).
8. T.M. Devine, 'The Union of 1707 and Scottish Development', *Scottish Economic and Social History*, V (1985), 23–40.
9. A.R.B. Haldane, *The Drove Roads of Scotland* (London, 1952), 343.
10. W. Mackintosh, *A Short Scheme, whereby is proposed, by the help of the military road . . . now extended . . . effectually to stop depredations and theft, so frequently committed in, and so destructive to the northern counties of Scotland* (Edinburgh, 1742), 8.
11. A. Murray, 'The Scottish Mint after the Recoinage 1709–1836', *Proceedings of the Royal Society of Antiquaries in Scotland,* CXXIX (1999), 861–86.
12. W.A.J. Prevost, 'A journie to Galloway in 1721 by Sir John Clerk of Penicuik', *Transactions of the Dumfries and Galloway Natural History and Antiquarian Society,* XLI (1962–3), 194; A. Symson, *A Large Description of Galloway* (Edinburgh,1896), 61–2; P.H. M'Kerlie, *History of the Lands and their Owners in Galloway* (Edinburgh, 1878), III, 98.
13. D. Defoe, *Tour through the Whole Island of Great Britain* (London & New Haven CT, 1991; first published, 1724), 216.
14. A. Livingston, 'The Galloway Levellers, a study of the origins, events and consequences of their actions', M. Phil thesis, University of Glasgow, 2009.
15. D. Turnock, *The Historical Geography of Scotland* (Cambridge, 1982), 57.
16. Compare, for example, J.E. Handley, *Scottish Farming in the Eighteenth Century* (London, 1953), with I. Carter, *Farm Life in North-East Scotland* (Edinburgh, 1979), T.M. Devine (ed.), *Lairds and Improvement in the Scotland of the Enlightenment* (Dundee, 1979), M.I. Parry & T.R. Slater, *The Making of the Scottish Countryside* (London, 1980).
17. A. Fenton & T.C. Smout, 'Scottish Agriculture before the Improvers, an exploration', *Agricultural History Review,* XIII (1965), 73–93.
18. A. Wight, *Present State of Husbandry in Scotland* (Edinburgh, 1778), I, 24–9.
19. B. Bonnyman, 'Agrarian Patriotism and the Landed Interest, the Scottish Society of Improvers in the Knowledge of Agriculture 1723–1746', in J. Marjanen & K. Stapelbroek (eds), *The Rise of Economic Societies in the Eighteenth Century* (Basingstoke, 2012), 26 *et seq.*

20. R. Mitchison, 'Patriotism and National Identity in Eighteenth-century Scotland', in T.W. Moody (ed.), *Nationality and the Pursuit of National Independence* (Belfast, 1978), 76–7.

21. R. Maxwell (ed.), *Select Transactions of the Society of Improvers in the Knowledge of Agriculture in Scotland* (Edinburgh, 1743), iv.

22. *A Treatise concerning the manner of fallowing of ground, raising of grass seeds and training of lint and hemp for the increased and improvement of the linen manufactories in Scotland* (Edinburgh, 1724), 4–5. This anonymous work is usually attributed to Thomas Hope of Rankeillour.

23. Maxwell, *Select Transactions,* 5–8, 235.

24. *A Treatise concerning the manner of fallowing of ground . . .* (Edinburgh, 1724); *An Essay on Ways and Means for Inclosing, Fallowing, Planting, etc.* (Edinburgh, 1729); P. Lindsay, *The Interest of Scotland Considered, with regard to its police in imploying of the poor, its agriculture, its trade, its manufactures and fisheries* (Edinburgh, 1733).

25. *Letters of John Cockburn of Ormiston to his Gardener,* ed. J. Colville (Edinburgh, 1904), passim.

26. J. Clerk, *Memoirs,* ed. J.M. Gray (Edinburgh, 1892), 155–6, 225, 243–4.

27. I.D. Whyte, 'George Dundas of Dundas, the context of an early eighteenth-century improving landowner', *Scottish Historical Review,* LX (1981), 1–13.

28. G.M. Fraser (ed.), 'Alexander Jaffray's Recollections of Kingswells 1755–1800', *Miscellany I of the Third Spalding Club* (Aberdeen, 1935), 139–42.

29. Sir A. Grant, *The Farmer's New-Year's Gift* (Aberdeen, 1757), *The Practical Farmer's Pocket Companion* (Aberdeen, 1766).

30. G. Turnock, 'Stages of Agricultural Improvement in the Uplands of Scotland's Grampian Region', *Journal of Historical Geography,* III (1977), 327–47.

31. See P. Aitchison & A. Cassell, *The Lowland Clearances: Scotland's Silent Revolution* (East Linton, 2003).

32. Revd James Goldie, *OSA,* X, 497.

33. M. Flinn (ed.), *Scottish Population History* (Cambridge, 1977), 219–23.

34. T.C. Smout, 'Where had the Scottish economy got to by the third quarter of the eighteenth century?' in I. Hont & M. Ignatieff, *Wealth and Virtue: The Shaping of Political Economy in the Scottish Enlightenment* (Cambridge, 1983), 45–72.

35. E. Burt, *Letters from a Gentleman in the Highlands of Scotland,* ed. R. Jamieson, (London, 1818), I, 216.

36. V.I. Lenin, 'Capitalism in Agriculture', *Collected Works* (Moscow, 1972), IV, 105–59.

37. I.S. Macdonald, 'Alexander Macdonald Esq of Glencoe, insights into early Highland sheep-farming', *Review of Scottish Culture,* X (1996–7).

38. E.R. Cregeen (ed.), *Argyll Estate Instructions 1771–1805* (Edinburgh, 1964), xxiv.

39. M.R.G. Fry, *Wild Scots: Four Hundred Years of Highland History* (London, 2005), ch. 10.

40. Revd George Tarbat, *OSA,* XVII, 634, 649.

41. *Edinburgh Evening Courant,* 18 October 1792, quoted in E. Richards, *The Highland Clearances* (Edinburgh, 2000), 118.

42. D. Stewart, *Sketches of the Character, Manners and Present State of the Highlanders of Scotland* (Edinburgh, 1822), 437.

43. T.M. Devine, *Clanship to Crofters' War: The Transformation of the Scottish Highlands* (Manchester, 1994), ch. 1.

44. M. Gray, *The Highland Economy 1750–1850* (Edinburgh, 1957).

45. Flinn, *Scottish Population History,* 250–60.

46. For example, A.I. Macinnes, 'Scottish Gaeldom, the first phase of clearance', in T.M. Devine & R. Mitchison, *People and Society in Scotland, I, 1760–1830* (Edinburgh, 1988), 70–90.

47. A. McDouall (Lord Bankton), *An Institute of the Laws of Scotland. . .* (Edinburgh, 1752), II, 435.

48. Sir J. Sinclair, *Analysis of the Statistical Account of Scotland* (London, 1826), 102.

49. R.A. Dodgshon, 'The origins of traditional field systems', in M.L. Parry & T.R. Slater (eds), *The Making of the Scottish Countryside* (London, 1981), 69–92.

50. R.A. Dodgshon, 'The Removal of Runrig in Roxburghshire 1680–1766', *Scottish Studies,* XVI (1966), 121–37.

51. Turnock, *Historical Geography,* 67.

52. M. Gray, 'North East Agriculture and the Labour Force 1790–1875', in A.A. MacLaren (ed.), *Social Class in Scotland, past and present* (Edinburgh, 1976), 86–91.

53. R.A. Dodgshon, *Land and Society in Early Scotland* (Oxford, 1981), ch. 7.

54. I.D. Whyte, 'Some Aspects of Rural Society in Seventeenth Century Lowland Scotland', in T.M. Devine & D. Dickson (eds), *Ireland and Scotland 1600–1850* (Edinburgh, 1983), 32–45.

55. M. Gray, 'Farm workers in North East Scotland', in T.M. Devine (ed.), *Farm Servants and Labour in Lowland Scotland 1770–1914* (Edinburgh, 1984), 10–28.

56. T.M, Devine, 'Social Stability in the Eastern Lowlands of Scotland during the Agricultural Revolution 1780–1840', in T.M. Devine (ed.), *Lairds and Improvement in the Scotland of the Enlightenment* (Dundee, 1979), 59–70.

57. T.C. Smout, *A History of the Scottish People 1560–1830* (London, 1969), chs. 5, 13.

58. Compare I.D. Whyte, *Agriculture and Society in Seventeenth Century Scotland* (Edinburgh, 1979), chs. 3, 6.

59. I.D. Whyte, 'Continuity and Change in a Scottish Farming Community', *Agricultural History Review,* XXXII (1984), 160–6.

60. Revd George Home, *OSA,* I, 81.

61. Revd Robert Arnot, *OSA,* V, 383.

62. T.M. Devine, 'Scottish Farm Service in the Agricultural Revolution', in Devine, *Farm Servants,* 1–8.

63. M. Gray, 'The Social Impact of Agrarian Change in the Rural Lowlands', in Devine & Mitchison, *People and Society,* 61.

64. Revd Thomas Birnie, *OSA,* XV, 450.

65. H. Hamilton, *An Economic History of Scotland in the Eighteenth Century* (Oxford, 1963), 46–54.

66. Revd David McClellan, *OSA,* VIII, 315.

67. R.H. Campbell, 'The Landed Classes', in Devine & Mitchison, *People and Society,* 91–108.

68. J.G. Kyd, *Scottish Population Statistics, including Webster's analysis of population, 1755* (Edinburgh, 1952).

69. Under the Highways (Scotland) Act, 1803, commissioners compiled a not quite annual series of reports on the country's roads, bridges and harbours. See also D.G. Lockhart, *Scottish Planned Villages* (Edinburgh, 2012).

2 Industry: 'Very great profits'

1. S. Moreton, *Bonanzas and Jacobites: The Story of the Silver Glen* (Clackmannan, 2007), 31.

2. Master of Sinclair, *Memoirs of the Insurrection in Scotland,* (Edinburgh, 1858), 174–5.

3. NLS, MS 5073, f. 81; MS 5098, f. 6; MS 5116, f. 1–8.

4. R.W. Cochran-Patrick, *Early Records relating to Mining in Scotland* (Edinburgh, 1878).

5. HMC, *Stuart MSS,* I, 476, 486–7.

6. NLS, MS 5073, f. 222; J. Ramsay, *Scotland and Scotsmen in the Eighteenth Century,* (Edinburgh & London, 1888), II, 110–11.

7. A. Smith, *Inquiry into the Nature and Causes of the Wealth of Nations,* ed. A. Skinner (Glasgow edn, 1976; first published, 1776), bk. I, ch. 11, part iii.

8. J.S. Shaw, *The Management of Scottish Society 1707–1764* (Edinburgh, 1983), ch. 7.

9. A.J. Durie, *The Scottish Linen Industry in the Eighteenth Century* (Edinburgh, 1979), 10.

10. *Extracts from the Records of the Burgh of Edinburgh 1701–1718,* ed. H. Armet (Edinburgh, 1967), 186.

11. R.H. Campbell (ed.), *States of the Progress of Linen Manufacture in Scotland 1727–1754* (Edinburgh, 1973).

12. A.J. Durie, 'The Markets for Scottish Linen 1730–1775', *Scottish Historical Review*, LII (1973), 30–49; 'Imitation in Scottish Eighteenth-century Textiles: The Drive to Establish the Manufacture of Osnaburg Linen', *Journal of Design History*, VI (1993), 71–6.

13. *Glasgow Mercury,* 16 January 1783.

14. C. Marchetti, 'A Post Mortem Technology Assessment of the Spinning Wheel: The Last Thousand Years', *Technological Forecasting and Social Change,* XIII (1971), 91–3.

15. H. Coghill, *Discovering the Water of Leith* (Edinburgh, 1988), 115–18.

16. F. Home, *Experiments on Bleaching* (Edinburgh, 1756); *The Principles of Agriculture and Vegetation* (Edinburgh, 1757).

17. A.J. Durie (ed.), *The British Linen Company 1745–1775* (Edinburgh, 1996), 17.

18. Sir J. Steuart, *An Inquiry into the Principles of Political Economy,* ed. A.S. Skinner (Edinburgh, 1966; first published, 1767), I, 306; Smith, *Wealth of Nations,* bk, I, ch. 2.

19. B. Lenman, *An Economic History of Modern Scotland* (London, 1976), 90.

20. NLS, Cowie Collection, MS 15953.

21. Durie, *British Linen Company,* 9–12.

22. A.J. Durie, 'Market Forces or Government Intervention: The Case of the Scottish Linen Industry', *Scotia,* XV (1991), 1–12.

23. R.H. Campbell (ed.), *States of the Progress of Linen Manufacture in Scotland 1727–1754* (Edinburgh, 1973).

24. Durie, *Scottish Linen Industry,* 90.

25. J. Gray, 'The Irish, Scottish and Flemish Linen Industries during the Long Eighteenth Century', in B. Collins & P. Ollerenshaw (eds), *The European Linen Industry in Historical Perspective* (Oxford, 2003), 159–86.

26. A. Cooke, *The Rise and Fall of the Scottish Cotton Industry* (Manchester, 2009), 100 *et seq.*

27. J. Lindsay & Renwick, *History of Glasgow* (Glasgow, 1921), ch. 30.

28. J. Butt, 'The Scottish Cotton Industry during the Industrial Revolution 1780–1840', in L.M. Cullen & T.C. Smout, *Comparative Aspects of Scottish and Irish Economic and Social History 1600–1900* (Edinburgh, 1977), 120–1.

29. PP 1834 X, *Report from the Select Committee on Handloom Weavers' Petitions,* 41–60, 72–84.

30. PP XIII 1835, *Report from the Select Committee on Handloom Weavers' Petitions,* iii–iv, xii.

31. *James Finlay & Co, manufacturers and East India merchants 1750–1950* (Glasgow, 1951).

32. I. Donnachie & G. Hewitt, *Historic New Lanark, the Dale and Owen industrial community since 1785* (Edinburgh, 1993).

33. R. Stenlake, *Catrine Then and Now* (Catrine, 2012), 3.

34. Smith, *Wealth of Nations,* bk. I, ch. 11, part iii.

35. I am grateful for these points to Peter Smaill, who holds the records of the Cowan family.

36. M. Dominiczak, 'William Cullen and Joseph Black: chemistry, medicine and the Scottish Enlightenment', *Clinical Chemistry,* LVII (2011), 1632 *et seq.*

37. A. & N.L. Clow, *The Chemical Revolution: A Contribution to Social Technology* (London, 1952), ch. 9, 'The Scottish Bleaching Industry'.

38. C. Gordon, *Memorial of Mr Cuthbert Gordon, relative to the discovery and use of cudbear* (London, 1785); R.A. Peel, 'Turkey Red Dyeing in Scotland: Its Heyday and Decline', *Journal of the Society of Dyers and Colourists,* LXVIII (1952), 496–505.

39. Smith, *Wealth of Nations*, bk. IV, ch. 6.

40. J. Thomson, *The Man who Lit the World: William Murdoch, Inventor of Gas Lighting* (London, 2003).

41. R. Bald, *A General View of the Coal Trade of Scotland* (Alloa, 1812).

42. M.R.G. Fry, *Edinburgh: A History of the City* (London, 2009), 229.

43. B.F. Duckham, *History of the Scottish Coal Industry* (Newton Abbot, 1970).

44. Smith, *Wealth of Nations,* bk. I, ch. 6.

45. M.J.T. Lewis, *Early Wooden Railways* (London, 1970), 160–5; J. Lindsay, *The Canals of Scotland* (Newton Abbot, 1968), ch. 1.

46. NAS, Clerk of Penicuik Papers, GD 18/1007; Court of Session Papers, 62, 68, petition of Andrew Scott, Feb. 27, 1747; Royal Commission on Children's Employment, PP, XVI (1842), pt. 1, appendix, 450.

47. B.F. Duckham, 'Serfdom in Eighteenth-century Scotland', *History,* LIV (1969), 178–97.

48. [A. Cochrane, 9th Earl of Dundonald], *Description of the Estate of Culross, particularly of the mineral and coal property* (Edinburgh, 1793), 63.

49. *Considerations on the Present Scarcity and High Price of Coals in Scotland* (Edinburgh, 1793), 20.

50. M.R.G. Fry, *The Dundas Despotism* (Edinburgh, 1992), 42–3.

51. W.I. Macadam, 'Notes on the Ancient Iron Industries of Scotland', *Proceedings of the Society of Antiquaries of Scotland,* XXXV (1886), 89 *et seq.*

52. G.D. Hay & G.P. Stell, *Bonawe Iron Furnace* (Edinburgh, 1984).

53. R.H. Campbell, *Carron Company* (Edinburgh, 1961), ch. 1.

54. B. Watters, *Where Iron Runs like Water: A New History of Carron Ironworks 1759–1982* (Edinburgh, 1998).

55. *An Attempt to Improve the Method of Arming Trading Vessels, with a description of the carronade and some hints concerning shot* (Falkirk, 1779).

56. A. Hogg & M. Maciver, *Industry: Coal and Iron 1700–1900* (Edinburgh, 1977).

57. C.K. Hyde, *Technological Change and the British Iron Industry 1700–1870* (Princeton, 1977), 151–5.

3 Trade: 'To supply all their want'

1. T.C. Smout (ed.), 'Journal of Henry Kalmeter's Travels in Scotland 1719–1720', in R.H. Campbell (ed.), *Scottish Industrial History: A Miscellany* (Edinburgh, 1978), 1; Rolf Vallerö, 'Henric Kalmeter', in *Svenskt biografiskt lexikon, XX* (Stockholm, 1973–5), 574.

2. Smout, 'Journal', 48.

3. S.M. Lockhart, *Seven Centuries: A History of the Lockharts of Lee and Carnwath* (Carnwath, 1977), 61–2.

4. Smout. 'Journal', 22.

5. Ibid., 16.

6. Ibid., 17.

7. Ibid., 33.

8. Ibid., 49.

9. Ibid., 50.

10. D. Defoe, *A Tour through the Whole Island of Great Britain*, ed. G.D.H. Cole (London, 1928), 715.

11. Ibid., 643.

12. M. Lynch, 'Introduction: Scottish Towns 1500–1700', in M. Lynch (ed.), *The Early Modern Town in Scotland* (London, 1987), 1–35.

13. Defoe, *Tour,* 693.

14. T.C. Smout, *Scottish Trade on the Eve of the Union* (Edinburgh & London, 1963), 25–9.

15. D. Watt, *The Price of Scotland: From Darien to the Wealth of Nations* (Edinburgh, 2007).

16. T. Keith, *Commercial Relations of England and Scotland 1603–1707* (Cambridge, 1910), 70.

17. M. Buist, *At Spes non Fracta, Hope & Co. 1770–1815* (The Hague, 1974); B. Lenman, 'The English and Dutch East India Companies and the Birth of Consumerism in the Augustan World', *Eighteenth-century Life,* XIV (1990), 100–1; *The Jacobite Clans of the Great Glen* (Aberdeen, 1995), 25; V. Enthoven, 'The Last Straw, Trade Contacts along the North Sea Coast: The Scottish staple at Veere', in L. Heerma van Voss & J. Roding, *The North Sea and Culture* (Hilversum, 1996), 211.

18. S. Talbott, 'Beyond "the Antiseptic Realm of Theoretical Economic Models": New Perspectives on Franco-Scottish Commerce and the Auld Alliance in

the Long Seventeenth Century', *Journal of Scottish Historical Research*, XXXI (2011), 149–68.

19. L.E. Cochran, *Scottish Trade with Ireland in the Eighteenth Century* (Edinburgh, 1985), 116, 122–5.

20. E.J. Graham, *The Shipping Trade of Ayrshire 1689–1791* (Ayr, 1991), 12–17.

21. J.I. Israel, 'England's Mercantilist Reponse to Dutch World Trade Primacy', in *Conflicts of Empire* (London, 1997), 305–18.

22. P.R. Rössner, *Scottish Trade with German Ports 1700–1770* (Stuttgart, 2008), 300–6.

23. Ibid., 68.

24. E.F. Heckscher, *Mercantilism* (London, 1935), II, 419.

25. P.R. Rössner, *Scottish Trade in the Wake of the Union 1700–1760: The Rise of a Warehouse Economy* (Stuttgart, 2008); 'New Avenues of Trade: Structural Changes in the European Economy and Foreign Commerce As Reflected in the Changing Structure of Scotland's Commerce 1660–1760', *Journal of Scottish Historical Studies*, XXXI (2011), 1–25.

26. A.M. Carstairs, 'Some Economic Aspects of the Union of Parliaments', *Scottish Journal of Political Economy*, II (1955), 58; J.H. Soltow, 'Scottish Traders in Virginia', *Economic History Review*, XII (1959–60), 90–6; H. Hamilton, *An Economic History of Scotland in the Eighteenth Century* (Oxford, 1963), 255; R.H. Campbell, *Scotland since 1707, the rise of an industrial society* (Oxford, 1965), 43.

27. Defoe, *Tour*, 743.

28. J.M. Price, 'The Rise of Glasgow in the Chesapeake Tobacco Trade', in P.L. Payne (ed.), *Studies in Scottish Business History* (London, 1967), 299–395; *Capital and Credit in British Overseas Trade, the view from the Chesapeake 1700–1776* (Cambridge MA, 1980), 24–9; 'Glasgow, the Tobacco Trade and the Scottish Customs 1707–1730', *Scottish Historical Review*, LXIII (1984), 27.

29. Rössner, *Trade in the Wake of the Union*, 12–20.

30. B. Lenman, *The Jacobite Cause* (Edinburgh, 1986), 51.

31. W.R. Scott (ed.), *The Records of a Scottish Cloth Manufactory at New Mills, Haddingtonshire 1681–1703* (Edinburgh, 1905); C. Gulvin, *The Tweedmakers* (Newton Abbot, 1973), ch. 1.

32. A.G. Thomson, *The Paper Industry in Scotland 1590–1861* (Edinburgh, 1974), 4.

33. ECA, SL 144/1/10, 177, Dec. 8, 1736.

34. D. Forbes, *Some Considerations on the Present State of Scotland* (Edinburgh, 1744), 4.

35. W. Mackay (ed.), *The Letter-book of Bailie John Steuart of Inverness 1715–1752* (Edinburgh, 1915), xxxiii–xxxiv.

36. Smith, *Wealth of Nations*, bk. 5, ch. 2.

37. C.A. Whatley, *The Scottish Salt Industry 1570–1850* (Aberdeen, 1987), 85.

38. Forbes, *Some Considerations*, 31.

39. C.A. Whatley, 'An Uninflammable People? Lowland Scots from the Union to the Radical War', in I. Donnachie & C.W. Whatley (eds), *The Manufacture of Scottish History* (Edinburgh, 1992), 51–71.

40. NAS, CE.53.1/1, Montrose.

41. Rössner, *Trade with German Ports*, 10, 17, 21, 61, 175.

42. N. Laude, *La Compagnie d'Ostende et son Activité Coloniale au Bengale* (Brussels, 1944), I, 23–31, 110, 217; G.B. Hertz 'England and the Ostend Company', *English Historical Review*, XXII (1907), 255–79.

43. A.A. Cormack, 'Scots in the Swedish East India Company', *Aberdeen University Review*, XLII (1967–8), 38–47; M. Roberts, *The Swedish Imperial Experience* (Cambridge, 1979), 1–2, 21, 39–43, 51–5, 64–71, 101.

44. J.K. Fairbank, *Trade and Diplomacy on the China Coast* (Cambridge MA, 1953) I, 60; M.M. Greenberg, *British Trade and the Opening of China 1800–1842* (Cambridge, 1951), 25; L. Dermigny, *La Chine et l'Occident* (Paris, 1964), II, 642, 659, III, 941. 968, 1242, 1246.

45. W. MacDowall, *History of the Burgh of Dumfries* (Edinburgh, 1856), 305; Cochran, *Scottish Trade with Ireland*, 8–11, 76.

46. R.C. Nash, 'The English and Scottish Tobacco Trades in the Seventeenth and Eighteenth Centuries: Legal and Illegal Trade', *Economic History Review*, XXXV (1982), 364.

47. T.C. Barker, 'Smuggling in the Eighteenth Century: The Evidence of the Scottish Tobacco Trade', *The Virginia Magazine of History and Biography*, LXII (1984), 393–7.

48. J.M. Price, 'The Rise of Glasgow in the Chesapeake Tobacco Trade', in P.L. Payne, *Studies in Scottish Business History* (London, 1967), 304.

49. J.M. Price, *France and the Chesapaake* (Ann Arbor, 1973), I, 604; 'Glasgow, the Tobacco Trade and the Scottish Customs 1707–1730', *Scottish Historical Review*, LXIII (1984), 1–36.

50. R.F. Dell, 'The Operational Record of the Clyde Tobacco Fleet 1747–1775', *Scottish Economic and Social History*, II (1982), 1.

51. Ibid., 12, 19.

52. Rössner, 'New Avenues', 14, 17, 25.

53. J. Gibson, *The History of Glasgow from the Earliest Accounts to the Present Time* (Glasgow, 1777), 106.

54. T.M. Devine, *The Tobacco Lords* (Edinburgh, 1975), 11, 56; 'The Colonial Trades and Industrial Investment in Scotland', *Economic History Review*, XXIX (1976), 3; A. Slaven, *The Development of the West of Scotland 1750–1960* (London, 1975), 20–1; B. Lenman, *An Economic History of Modern Scotland* (London, 1977), 91;

Integration, Enlightenment and Industrialisation, Scotland 1746–1832 (London, 1981), 23–4, 42–7.

55. Library of Congress, George Washington Papers, series 4, general correspondence, no. 926, letter from Robert Donald, June 6, 1793.

56. J. Knox, *View of the British Empire* (Edinburgh, 1784), xliii.

57. T.M. Devine, 'Glasgow Colonial Merchants and Land 1770–1815', in J. Ward & R.G. Wilson, *Land and Industry* (Newton Abbot, 1971), 205–35; 'Glasgow Merchants and the Collapse of the Tobacco Trade', *Scottish Historical Review*, LII (1973), 50 *et seq.;* 'Sources of Capital for the Glasgow Tobacco Trade 1740–1780', *Business History*, XVI (1974), 113–26; *The Tobacco Lords* (Edinburgh, 1975), 18, 130, 157–8, 161, 171–3.

58. Gibson, *History of Glasgow*, 105.

59. T.M. Devine, 'A Glasgow Tobacco Merchant during the American War of Independence: Alexander Spiers of Elderslie 1775–1781', *William and Mary Quarterly*, XXIII (1976), 11; 'Colonial Commerce and the Scottish Economy 1730–1815', in L.M. Cullen & T.C. Smout (eds), *Comparative Aspects of Scottish and Irish Social and Economic History 1600–1900* (Edinburgh, 1977), 177 *et seq.*

60. Slaven, *Development of the West of Scotland*, 163–6; R.H. Campbell, *The Rise and Fall of Scottish Industry* (Edinburgh, 1980), 56–60.

61. C. Booth, *Zachary Macaulay* (London, 1934), 4–11.

62. D. Hancock, *Citizens of the World: London Merchants and the Integration of the British Atlantic Community 1745–1785* (Cambridge, 1995), ch. 5.

63. Ibid., ch. 10.

64. M. Duffill, 'The Africa Trade from the Ports of Scotland', *Slavery and Abolition*, XXIV (2004), 102–22.

65. D.S. Macmillan, 'Scottish Enterprise and Influences in Canada 1620–1900', in R.A. Cage (ed.), *The Scots Abroad* (London, 1985), 57 *et seq.*

66. W.S. Wallace, *Documents relating to the North West Company* (Toronto, 1934), 1–10.

67. M.W. Campbell, *The North West Company* (Toronto, 1957), 19, 52–6, 67, 105; *McGillvray, Lord of the Northwest* (Toronto, 1962), 11, 27–9, 45, 95.

68. G. Woodcock, 'Alexander Mackenzie and the River of Disappointment', *History Today*, XIV (1964), 334–43; D.S. Macmillan, 'The "New Men" in Action: Scottish Mercantile and Shipping Operations in the North American Colonies 1760–1825', in D.S. Macmillan (ed.), *Canadian Business History, selected studies* (Toronto, 1972), 62.

69. Macmillan, 'New Men', 45–6; E.A. Mitchell, 'The Scot in the Fur Trade', in W.S. Reid (ed.), *The Scottish Tradition in Canada* (Toronto, 1976), 41.

70. A.M. Cain, *The Cornchest for Scotland, Scots in India* (Edinburgh, 1986), 12, 16; P.J. Marshall, *East India Fortunes, the British in Bengal in the eighteenth century*

(Oxford, 1976), 12, 214, 231; G.J. Bryant, 'Scots in India in the Eighteenth Century', *Scottish Historical Review*, LXIV (1985), 22–41; J.G. Parker, 'Scottish Enterprise in India 1750–1914', in R.A. Cage, *The Scots Abroad: Labour, Capital and Enterprise 1750–1914* (London, 1985), 40–2; J. Riddy, 'Warren Hastings – Scotland's Benefactor?', in G. Carnall & C. Nicholson (eds), *The Impeachment of Warren Hastings* (Edinburgh, 1989), 40–2.

71. *Extracts from the Records of the Burgh of Glasgow*, ed. J.D. Marwick & R. Renwick (Glasgow, 1894–1900), VIII, 397.

72. J.K. Fairbank, *Trade and Diplomacy on the China Coast* (Cambridge MA, 1953), 70.

73. Ibid., 63–6; M.M. Greenberg, *British Trade and the Opening of China 1800–1842* (Cambridge, 1951), 74, 104–5; W.E. Cheong, *Mandarins and Merchants: Jardine, Matheson & Co, a China agency of the Early Nineteenth Century* (London & Malmö, 1979), 5–6.

4 Rank: 'This most sacred property'

1. R. Chambers (ed.), *Domestic Annals of Scotland* (Edinburgh & London, 1874), III, 281.

2. Ibid., 282.

3. D. Findlay & A. Murdoch, 'Revolution to Reform: Eighteenth-Century Politics 1690–1800', in E.P. Dennison, D. Ditchburn & M. Lynch (eds), *Aberdeen Before 1800: A New History* (East Linton, 2002), 267–76.

4. *OSA,* I, 425; IV, 518.

5. B. Lenman, *The Jacobite Risings in Britain 1689–1746* (London, 1980), ch. 7.

6. E. Gregg, 'The Jacobite Career of John, Earl of Mar', in E. Cruickshanks (ed.), *Ideology and Conspiracy: Aspects of Jacobitism 1689–1759* (Edinburgh, 1982), 179–200.

7. J.J.H. Stewart-Murray, seventh Duke of Atholl, *Chronicles of the Atholl and Tullibardine Families, IV* (Edinburgh, 1908); W.C. Gillies, *In Famed Breadalbane* (Edinburgh, 1938); W.C. MacKenzie, *Simon Fraser, Lord Lovat, his life and times* (London, 1908).

8. Lenman, *Jacobite Risings,* 159.

9. H. Tayler, *Lady Nithsdale and her Family* (London, 1939), 47.

10. J. Sinclair, *Memoirs of the Insurrection in Scotland in 1715,* ed. W. Scott (Edinburgh, 1858).

11. M. Sankey, *Jacobite Prisoners of the 1715 Rebellion* (London, 2005), 138 *et seq.*

12. J. Ramsay, *Scotland and Scotsmen in the Eighteenth Century* (Edinburgh & London, 1888), I, 198.

13. A.M. Smith, 'The Administration of the Forfeited Estates 1751–1784', in

G. Barrow (ed.), *The Scottish Tradition: Essays in Honour Of R.G. Cant* (Edinburgh, 1974), 198 *et seq.;* A. Macinnes, 'Scottish Gaeldom: The First Phase of Clearance', in T.M. Devine & R. Mitchison, *People and Society in Scotland, I, 1760–1830* (Edinburgh, 1988), 82.

14. *Parliamentary History,* XXIV, cols. 1316 *et seq.;* EUL Papers, DC 1. 77, no. 71.

15. T.C. Smout, 'Scottish Landowners and Economic Growth', *Scottish Journal of Political Economy,* XI (1964), 218; D. Kettler, *The Social and Economic Thought of Adam Ferguson* (Columbus OH, 1965), 20 *et seq.;* E.J. Hobsbawm, 'Scottish Reformers and Capitalist Agriculture', in E.J. Hobsbawm (ed.), *Peasants in History* (Oxford, 1980), 7.

16. G. Crawford, *The Peerage of Scotland* (Edinburgh, 1716).

17. A. Bayne, 'A Discourse on the Rise and Progress of the Law in Scotland', in A. Bayne (ed.), *Sir Thomas Hope's Minor Practicks* (Edinburgh, 1726), 186–7.

18. M.W. McCahill, 'Peerage Creations and the Changing Character of the British Nobility 1750–1830', *English Historical Review,* XCVI (1981), 259–84.

19. *Warrender Letters,* ed. W.K. Dickson (Edinburgh, 1935), 27–8.

20. G. Watson (ed.), *Bell's Dictionary and Digest of the Law of Scotland,* 7th edn (Edinburgh, 1890), 138–9.

21. T.B. Smith, 'Master and Servant', in G.C.H. Paton (ed.), *An Introduction to Scottish Legal History,* Stair Society Vol. 20 (Edinburgh, 1958), 134–6.

22. P. Baxter (ed.), *The Shoemaker Incorporation of Perth 1545–1927* (Perth, 1927), 28.

23. Dean of Guild Court Records, Edinburgh, SL 144/1/14, April 20, 1743, SL 144/1/18, August 4, 1755; EUL Papers, La.III.552.

24. A. Heron, *The Rise and Progress of the Company of Merchants of the City of Edinburgh 1681–1902* (Edinburgh, 1903), 18–22.

25. W. Paterson, *Records of the Convention of Royal Burghs of Scotland* (Edinburgh, 1866), 10.

26. P. Lindsay, *The Interest of Scotland Considered, with regard to its police in imploying of the poor, its agriculture, its trade, its manufactures and fisheries* (Edinburgh, 1733), xxviii–xxix.

27. W. Creech, *Letters respecting the mode of living, trade, manners, literature etc. of Edinburgh, in 1763, and the present period* (Edinburgh, 1792), 36.

28. S.R. Epstein, 'Craft Guilds, Apprenticeship and Technological Change in Preindustrial Europe', *Economic History,* LVIII (1998), 684–713.

29. The best study of this social phenomenon (which was a European one) is in French: H. Desroche, *Solidarités ouvrières, I, sociétaires et compagnons dans les associations coopératives* (Paris, 1981).

30. H. Lumsden (ed.), *The Records of the Trades House of Glasgow 1713–1777* (Glasgow, 1934), 354–5.

31. A. Smith, *An Inquiry into the Nature and Causes of the Wealth of Nations* (1776), bk I, ch. 10, pt. c.

32. Strathclyde Regional Archives, minute book of the Merchant House of Glasgow, II, 1711–1754, T-MH/2; T. Donnelly, 'The Economic Activities of the Aberdeen Merchant Guild, 1750–1799', *Scottish Economic and Social History*, I (1981), 27; H. Arnot, *History of Edinburgh* (Edinburgh, 1779), 517.

33. A. Murdoch, 'The Importance of being Edinburgh: Management and Opposition in Edinburgh Politics 1746–1784', *Scottish Historical Review*, LXII (1983), 1–16.

34. N. Phillipson, 'Lawyers, Landowners and the Civic Leadership of Post-Union Scotland', *Juridical Review*, NS XXI (1976), 101–6; 'The Social Structure of the Faculty of Advocates 1661–1840', in A. Harding (ed.), *Law-making and Law-makers in British History* (London, 1980), 155–6.

35. S.G. Checkland, *Scottish Banking: A History 1695–1973* (Glasgow & London, 1975), pt.1.

36. M.R.G. Fry, *The Dundas Despotism* (Edinburgh, 1992), 82.

37. J. McUre, *History of Glasgow* (Glasgow, 1736), 158–60; R. Renwick (ed.), *Extracts from the Records of the Burgh of Glasgow, VI, 1691–1717,* 462–6. J. McGrath, 'The Medieval and Early Modern Burgh', in T.M. Devine & G. Jackson (eds), *Glasgow, I, Beginnings to 1830* (Manchester, 1995), 32.

38. J, Bell & M. Paton, *Glasgow, its municipal organisation and administration* (Glasgow, 1896), 20–1.

39. M. Lynch, 'Continuity and Change in Urban Society 1500–1700', in R.A. Houston & I.D. Whyte (eds), *Scottish Society 1500–1800* (Cambridge, 1989), 105–8.

40. T.M. Devine, 'The Merchant Class of the Larger Scottish Towns in the Later Seventeenth and Early Eighteenth Century', in B. Dicks & G. Gordon (eds), *Scottish Urban History* (Aberdeen, 1983), 95.

41. *Origins, Rules and Constitution of the Chamber of Commerce and Manufactures of the City of Glasgow* (Glasgow, 1833), 5–6.

42. I. Blanchard et al., 'The Economy: Town and Country', in E.P. Dennison, D. Ditchburn & M. Lynch (eds), *Aberdeen Before 1800: A New History* (East Linton, 2002), 159–89.

43. E. Bain, *Merchant and Craft Guilds, a history of the Aberdeen incorporated trades* (Aberdeen, 1887), 256–7.

44. *OSA,* XIII, 174–7.

45. Lindsay, *Interest of Scotland*, xxvii; ECA, Moses Collection, SL 30/4/6.

46. W.H. Fraser, 'Patterns of Protest', in T.M. Devine & R. Mitchison (eds), *People and Society in Scotland, I, 1760–1830* (Edinburgh, 1988), 268–91.

47. J. Ivory, *Notes as to the Rights of the Burgesses of Scotland* (Edinburgh, 1819).

48. J. Butt, 'Labour and Industrial Relations in the Scottish Cotton Industry during the Industrial Revolution', in J. Butt & K. Ponting (eds). *Scottish Textile History* (Aberdeen, 1987), 144–50.

49. C. Whatley, *Scottish Society 1707–1830* (Manchester, 2000), 208.

50. A. Durie, *The Scottish Linen Industry in the Eighteenth Century* (Edinburgh, 1979), 80.

51. W.H. Fraser, *Conflict and Class: Scottish Workers 1700–1838* (Edinburgh, 1988), 39.

52. R.A. Houston, 'Popular Politics in the Reign of George II: The Edinburgh Cordiners', *Scottish Historical Review*, LXXII (1993), 189.

53. N. Murray, *The Scottish Hand Loom Weavers 1790–1850: A Social History* (Edinburgh, 1978), 29.

54. Ibid., 30.

55. Ibid., 31.

56. W. Carlile, 'A Short Sketch of the Improved State of Paisley', *Scots Magazine*, July 1806, 17–18.

57. T.M. Devine, 'The Failure of Radical Reform in Scotland in the Late Eighteenth Century', in T.M. Devine (ed.), *Conflict and Stability in Scottish Society 1700–1850* (Edinburgh, 1990), 51.

58. Compare A. Broadie, *The Scottish Enlightenment: The Historical Age of the Historical Nation* (Edinburgh, 2001), 29.

59. F. Hutcheson, *A System of Moral Philosophy*, 2 vols (Glasgow, 1755), II, bk 3, 'Of Civil Polity'; A. Smith, *Lectures on Jurisprudence, Report of 1762–3*, ed. R.L. Meek, D.D. Raphael & P.G. Stein (Oxford, 1978), III, 1–147; J. Millar, *Observations concerning the Distinction of Ranks in Society* (London, 1771).

60. Millar, *Observations*, iii.

61. Ibid., 307.

62. Ibid., 309.

63. W.C. Lehmann, *John Millar of Glasgow 1735–1801* (Cambridge, 1960), 169.

5 Faith: 'Warmth and animosity'

1. A. Skoczylas, 'The Regulation of Academic Society in Early Eighteenth-century Scotland: The Tribulations of Two Divinity Professors', *Scottish Historical Review*, LXXXVIII (2004), 171–95.

2. J. Cunningham, *Church History of Scotland* (Edinburgh, 1859), 418.

3. Anon., *Scotland and the Netherlands* (Edinburgh, 1987), 1–13.

4. A. Skoczylas, *Mr Simson's Knotty Case: Divinity, Due Process and Politics in Early Eighteenth-Century Scotland* (Montreal & London, 2001), 289–321.

5. P. Gay, *The Enlightenment: An Interpretation* (London, 1967), 278.

6. J. Ramsay, *Scotland and Scotsmen in the Eighteenth Century*, ed. A. Allardyce (Edinburgh & London, 1888), I, 273.

7. R. Wodrow, *The Wodrow Correspondence*, ed. T. McCrie (Edinburgh, 1842–3), II, 691–3.

8. Skoczylas, 'Regulation', 185.

9. J. Moore & M. Silverthorne, 'Gershom Carmichael and the Natural Jurisprudence Tradition in Eighteenth-century Scotland', in I. Hont & M. Ignatieff (eds), *Wealth & Virtue: The Shaping of Political Economy in the Scottish Enlightenment* (Cambridge, 1983), 73–87.

10. W.R. Scott, *Francis Hutcheson: His Life, Teaching and Position in the History of Philosophy* (Cambridge, 1900), 134.

11. Skoczylas, 'Regulation', 195.

12. R.L. Emerson, *An Enlightened Duke: The Life of Archibald Campbell, Earl of Ilay, third Duke of Argyll* (Kilkerran, 2013), 44–7.

13. NLS, Fletcher of Saltoun Papers, MS 16582, f. 30.

14. *Letters of David Hume*, ed. J.Y.T. Greig (Oxford, 1932), I, 113.

15. D. Home, *Domestic Details* (Edinburgh, 1843), 1–16.

16. Ibid., 66–7.

17. NLS, MS 1954, *Journal of the Proposals made to, and the Resolutions taken by, the Society for endeavouring Reformation of Manners* (Edinburgh, 1699), 1.

18. D. Home, 'A Narrative of the Rise, Progress and Success of the Societies of Edinburgh for Reformation of Manners', ed. N. Gray, in *Miscellany of the Scottish History Society XIV* (Woodbridge, 2013), 119–20.

19. NAS, Minutes of the Society in Scotland for Propagating Christian Knowledge, GD 95/1/1/2.

20. D.J. Withrington, *Going to School* (Edinburgh, 1997), 12.

21. J. Scotland, *History of Scottish Education* (London, 1969), I, 174.

22. But compare R.A. Houston, *Scottish Literacy and Scottish Identity* (Cambridge, 1985), especially 1, 8.

23. D.J. Withrington, 'A Half-educated Nation?', *Scottish Economic and Social History*, VII (1987), 74; 'Schooling, Literacy and Society', in *People and Society in Scotland 1760–1830* (Edinburgh, 1988), 185.

24. W. Dundas, *Parliamentary Debates*, XL, col. 186.

25. R. Owen, *Life of Robert Owen by Himself* (London, 1857), 74.

26. G.E. Davie, *The Democratic Intellect* (Edinburgh, 1961), xvii.

27. P. Jones, 'The Polite Academy and the Presbyterians 1720–1780', in J. Dwyer, R.A. Mason & A. Murdoch (eds), *New Perspectives on the Politics and Culture of Early Modern Scotland* (Edinburgh, 1982), 156–8.

28. W.R. Scott, *Adam Smith as Student and Professor* (Glasgow, 1937), 28 *et seq.*

29. Jones, 'Polite Academy', 172–4.

30. J. Stephen, *Scottish Presbyterians and the Act of Union 1707* (Edinburgh, 2007), 99.

31. D.J. Patrick, 'The Kirk, Parliament and the Union 1706–1707', in S.J. Brown & C.A. Whatley (eds), *The Union of 1707: New Dimensions* (Edinburgh, 2008), 94–115.

32. G. Lockhart, *The Lockhart Papers* (London, 1817), I, 417–8.

33. J. Webster, *Lawful Prejudices against an Incorporating Union with England* (Edinburgh, 1707), 11; G. Meldrum, *A Private Letter, asserting the lawfulness of informing, against the vitious and prophane, before the courts of immorality* (Edinburgh, 1701), 4.

34. F. Goldie, *Short History of the Episcopal Church in Scotland* (Edinburgh, 1976), 19 *et seq.*

35. G. Donaldson, 'Scotland's Conservative North in the Sixteenth and Seventeenth Centuries', *Transactions of the Royal Historical Society,* 5th series, XVI (1966), 65–79.

36. Quoted in G.D. Henderson (ed.), *Mystics of the North-east* (Aberdeen, 1934), 102–3.

37. M.K. & C. Ritchie, 'An Apology for the Aberdeen Evictions', *Miscellany of the Third Spalding Club III* (Aberdeen, 1960), 57–95.

38. J. Johnstone, *The Select Anti-Patronage Library, consisting chiefly of reprints of scarce pamphlets connected with lay patronage in the Church of Scotland* (Edinburgh, 1842).

39. *OSA,* XVIII, 401–2.

40. J.R. McIntosh, *Church and Theology in Enlightenment Scotland: The Popular party 1740–1800* (East Linton, 1998), chs. 5 & 7.

41. Ibid., ch. 3.

42. G.D. Henderson, *The Scottish Ruling Elder* (London, 1935), 140.

43. J. Miller, 'Beliefs, Religions, Fears and Neuroses', in E. Foyster & C.A. Whatley (eds), *A History of Everyday Life in Scotland 1600–1800* (Edinburgh, 2010), 234–51.

44. NAS, Edinburgh Presbytery Register, CH2/121/9/14, 12/47

45. L. Leneman & R. Mitchison, 'Scottish Illegitimacy Ratios in the Early Modern Period', *Economic History Review,* 2nd series, XL (1987), 50; this is a brief introduction to their work, for which see also and at greater length *Girls in Trouble* (Edinburgh, 1998) and *Sexuality and Social Control, Scotland 1660–1780* (London, 1989).

46. 'John Erskine's Letterbook 1742–1745', ed. J. Yeager, *Miscellany of the Scottish History Society XIV* (Woodbridge, 2013), 235.

47. H. Innes, *Scotland Alarmed by the Loud Cry of Threatened Judgments* (Glasgow, 1757), 24–5; letters of T. Reid, Nov. 14, 1765 & July 13, 1765, in *Philosophical Works,* ed. Sir W. Hamilton (Edinburgh, 1895), I, 40–1.

48. D. Fraser, *The Life and Diary of the Revd Ebenezer Erskine of Stirling, father of the Secession Church* (Edinburgh, 1831).

49. D. Scott, *Annals and Statistics of the Original Secession Church* (Edinburgh, 1886).

50. J. Goodlet, *A Vindication of the Associate Synod* (Edinburgh, 1764).

51. Royal Commission on Religious Instruction, PP (1837), XXX, 12–13, and (1837–8), XXXII, 13; W. McKelvie, *Annals and Statistics of the United Presbyterian Church* (Edinburgh, 1873), 187 *et seq.*; R. Small, *History of the Congregations of the United Presbyterian Church* (Edinburgh, 1904), 441.

52. *Annals of the General Assembly of the Church of Scotland, from the final secession in 1739 to the origin of the relief in 1752* (Edinburgh, 1838), 265 *et seq.*

53. *The Autobiography of Alexander Carlyle of Inveresk 1722–1805*, ed. J.H. Burton (Edinburgh, 1910), ch. 7.

54. I.S. Ross, *Lord Kames and the Scotland of his Day* (London, 1972), ch. 6; E.C. Mossner, *Life of David Hume* (Oxford, 1980), ch .25.

55. [J. Bonar], *An Analysis of the Moral and Religious Sentiments Contained in the Writings of Sopho [Kames] and David Hume, Esq.* (Edinburgh, 1755), especially 49; R. Wallace, *Various Prospects of Mankind, Nature and Providence* (London, 1761), 238.

56. *Letters of David Hume*, I, 224; *Scots Magazine*, XIX, Feb. 1757, 108–9.

57. *Annals of the General Assembly of the Church of Scotland, from the origin of the relief in 1752 to the rejection of the overture on schism in 1766* (Edinburgh, 1840), 130 *et seq.*

58. J. Home, *Douglas*, ed. G.D. Parker (Edinburgh, 1972), II. 9–10.

59. *Autobiography of Alexander Carlyle*, ch.8.

60. R.B. Sher, *Church and University in the Scottish Enlightenment* (Edinburgh, 1985).

61. S.J. Brown, 'William Robertson (1721–1793) and the Scottish Enlightenment', in S.J. Brown (ed.), *William Robertson and the Expansion of Empire* (Cambridge, 1997), 7–35.

62. R.R. Palmer, *The Age of Democratic Revolutions*, 2 vols (Princeton, 1959–64); E. Hobsbawm, *The Age of Revolutions, Europe 1789–1848* (London, 1962).

63. D. Daiches, *The Paradox of Scottish Culture: The Eighteenth-Century Experience* (London, 1964), 51–2.

6 Order: 'Dispersing the mob'

1. W.F. Gray, 'Edinburgh in Lord Provost Drummond's Time', *Book of the Old Edinburgh Club*, XXVII (1949), 9.

2. Sir W. Scott, *Heart of Midlothian* (Edinburgh, 1818), ch. 7.

3. Edinburgh Central Reference Library, Porteous mob pamphlets, 1–2.

4. NAS, Justiciary MSS, JC26 series.

5. NLS, Saltoun Papers, MS 17509.

6. *The Autobiography of Alexander Carlyle of Inveresk 1722–1805*, ed. J.H. Burton (Edinburgh, 1910), 45–6.

7. H. T. Dickinson and K. Logue, 'The Porteous Riot: A Study of the Breakdown of Law and Order in Edinburgh, 1736–1737', *Scottish Labour History Review*, X (1976), 21–40.

8. James VI, *Basilikon Doron* (Edinburgh, 1599), 164.

9. These are the only other burghs in which I have been able to trace the existence of a Blue Blanket.

10. National Archives, London, Newcastle Papers, SP 54/16.

11. G. Rudé, *The Crowd in History: A Study of Popular Disturbances in France and England 1730–1848* (London, 2005).

12. R.A. Houston, *Social Change in the Age of Enlightenment: Edinburgh 1660–1760* (Oxford, 1994), 322–9.

13. R. Chambers, *Traditions of Edinburgh* (Edinburgh, 1824), II, 141–55.

14. G. Penny, *Traditions of Perth* (Perth, 1836), 47.

15. Chambers, *Traditions,* II, 188.

16. E. Wehrli, *Scottish Politics in the Age of Walpole* (Chicago, 1988), 388.

17. *Glasgow Mercury,* 10 December 1778.

18. 'Senex', *Old Glasgow* (Glasgow, 1844), 255; *Extracts from the Records of the Burgh of Glasgow, IV*, ed. R. Renwick (Glasgow, 1881), Jan. 28, 1778, April 2, 1779; G. Macgregor, *History of Glasgow* (Glasgow, 1881), 364

19. NAS, Home Office Papers; RH 2/4/87/85; Scottish Catholic Archive, Blairs Letters, 3/307/2, 3/309/11; Scottish Mission Papers, 4/16/3, 4/17/2–3, 10; 4/19/1–2; 4/40/6–9; Thomson–Macpherson Papers, sect.13, 1779.

20. Scottish Catholic Archive, Blairs Letters, 3/309/11.

21. C.A. Whatley, 'Royal Day, People's Day: The Monarch's Birthday in Scotland 1660–1860', in R. Mason & N. Macdougall (eds), *People and Power in Scotland* (Edinburgh, 1992), 183.

22. *Extracts from the Records of the Burgh of Edinburgh, ed.* J.D. Marwick et al. (1869–), XIII, 266, 368.

23. Hunter Blair Papers, Blairquhan, June 5, 1784; K. Miller, *Cockburn's Millennium* (London, 1975), 9–11.

24. Though Prof. Christopher Whatley claims, without citing any source, that the events of this day were 'anxiously anticipated' by the authorities in Edinburgh.

25. NAS, GD 235/10/2/4; Home Office Papers, RH 2/4/63/79; H.W. Meikle, 'The King's Birthday Riot in Edinburgh, June 1792', *Scottish Historical Review*, VII (1910), 21 *et seq.*; *Scotland and the French Revolution* (Glasgow, 1912), 83; K. Logue, *Popular Disturbances in Scotland* (Edinburgh, 1979), 134.

26. 'Senex', *Old Glasgow,* 258–9; Logue, *Popular Disturbances,* 147–51; J. Brims,

'The Covenanting Tradition and Scottish Radicalism in the 1790s', in T. Brotherstone (ed.), *Covenant, Charter and Party: Traditions of Revolt and Protest in Modern Scottish History* (Aberdeen, 1989), 50–62; I.G.C. Hutchison, 'Working-class Politics', in R.A. Cage, *The Working Class in Glasgow 1750–1914* (London, 1987), 98–134.

27. D.M. Walker, *The Scottish Legal System* (Edinburgh, 1959), 154.

28. E.J. Hobsbawm, *Bandits* (London, 1985), 25.

29. *Parliamentary History*, new series, VII, col. 1205.

30. G.S. Pryde, *The Treaty of Union of Scotland and England* (London, 1950), viii.

31. N. de la Mare, *Traité de la Police, où l'on trouvera l'histoire sur l'établissement, les fonctions et les prérogatives de ses magistrats, les lois et règlements qui la concernent . . .* 4 vols (Paris, 1707–23).

32. D. Forbes, *Considerations upon the State of the Nation* (Edinburgh, 1723), 4.

33. R.L. Meek, D.D. Raphael & P.G. Stein (eds), *Adam Smith, Glasgow edition of the works and correspondence, V, lectures on jurisprudence* (Oxford, 1976), pt. 2, ch. 1.

34. K. Reid, 'Introduction', in K. Reid & R. Zimmermann (eds), *A History of Private Law in Scotland* (Oxford, 2000), I, 20.

35. B. Lenman & G. Parker, 'Crime and Control in Scotland 1500–1800', *History Today*, XXX (1980), 14.

36. L. Leneman, *Living in Atholl: A Social History of the Estates 1685–1785* (Edinburgh, 1986), 57, 75.

37. M.R.G. Fry, 'Ferguson the Highlander', in E. Heath & V. Merolle (eds), *Adam Ferguson, philosophy, politics and society* (London, 2009), 11.

38. H. Hamilton (ed.), *Selections from the Monymusk Papers 1713–1755* (Edinburgh, 1945), xxxii.

39. F. Bigwood, 'The Courts of Argyll 1664–1825', *Scottish Archives*, X (2004), 26–38.

40. Hamilton, *Monymusk Papers*, xxxix.

41. C.B. Gunn (ed.), *Records of the Baron Court of Stitchill 1655–1807* (Edinburgh, 1905).

42. NAS, PA8/1, ff. 167–73.

43. B. Lenman, *The Jacobite Risings in Britain 1689–1746* (London, 1980), 155–60; C. Kidd, *Subverting Scotland's Past: Scottish Whig Historians and the Creation of an Anglo-British Identity, 1689–1830* (Cambridge, 1993), 170–80.

44. L. Paterson, *The Autonomy of Modern Scotland* (Edinburgh, 1994), 33, 47.

45. L. Farmer, *Criminal Law, Tradition and Legal Order: Crime and the Genius of Scots Law, 1747 to the Present* (Cambridge, 1997), 60–6.

46. C.A. Malcolm, 'The Sheriff Court, the eighteenth century and later', in Stair Society, *An Introduction to Scottish Legal History* (Edinburgh, 1958), 50 *et seq.*

47. I.D.L. Clark, 'From Protest to Reaction: The Moderate Party in the Church

NOTES

of Scotland 1752–1805', in N.T. Phillipson & R. Mitchison (eds), *Scotland in the Age of Improvement* (Edinburgh, 1970), 135 *et seq.*

48. R.B. Sher, 'Moderates, Managers and Popular Politics in Mid-Eighteenth-Century Edinburgh', in J. Dwyer, R.A. Mason & A. Murdoch (eds), *New Perspectives on the Politics and Culture of Early Modern Scotland* (Edinburgh, 1982), 152.

49. D.G. Barrie, *Police in the Age of Improvement: Police Development and Civic Improvement in Scotland 1765–1865* (Cullompton, 2008), 29.

50. J. Grant, *Old and New Edinburgh* (Edinburgh, 1880) I, 137.

51. Barrie, *Police*, 24, 28, 30.

52. J.D. Marwick, *Sketch of the History of the High Constables of Edinburgh* (Edinburgh, 1865), 192.

53. Barrie, *Police,* 31.

54. T.B. Smith, *Short Commentary on the Law of Scotland* (Edinburgh, 1962).

55. A. Fletcher, *Second Discourse concerning the Affairs of Scotland* (1698), in *Works* (London, 1732) 125–41, 154–63, 170–1; J. Donaldson, *Husbandry Anatomised* (Edinburgh, 1697), 124; J. Hamilton, 2nd Lord Belhaven, *The Countrey-Man's Rudiments* (Edinburgh, 1699), 38–45.

56. H. McKechnie (ed.), *An Introductory Survey of the Sources and Literature of Scots Law* (Edinburgh, 1936), 133–53.

57. K. Luig, 'Institutionenlehrbücher des nationalen Rechts im 17. und 18. Jahrhundert', *Ius Commune,* III (1970), 64 *et seq.;* J. Cairns, 'Institutional Writings in Scotland Reconsidered', *Journal of Legal History,* IV (1983), 76 *et seq.*

58. D.M. Walker, introduction to James Dalrymple, Lord Stair, *Institutions of the Laws of Scotland* (Edinburgh, 1981; reprint of edn of 1693), 21.

59. Stair, *Institutions*, bk I, ch 1, §1, §16.

60. G. Mackenzie, *Works* (Edinburgh, 1716–22), II, 574.

61. G. Mackenzie, *Observations on the Acts of Parliament* (Edinburgh, 1686), sig. A2r.

62. G. Mackenzie, *Laws and Customs of Scotland in Matters Criminal* (Edinburgh, 1678), 1.1.3.

63. *Acts of the Parliament of Scotland,* XI, appendix, 203.

64. J.S. Shaw, *The Management of Scottish Society 1707–1764* (Edinburgh, 1983), 262.

65. N.T. Phillipson, 'Lawyers, Landowners and the Civic Leadership of Post-Union Scotland', *Juridical Review,* NS XXI (1976), 92.

66. Barrie, *Police,* 32.

67. T. Richter, 'Did Stair Know Pufendorf?', *Edinburgh Law Review,* VII (2003), 367–78.

68. A. MacDouall, Lord Bankton, *Institute of the Laws of Scotland* (Edinburgh, 1751), I, preface, v.

423

69. Cairns, 'Institutional Writings', 92–3.

70. H. Home, Lord Kames, *Essays on the Principles of Morality and Natural Religion* (Edinburgh, 1751), 192.

71. M. Lobban, 'The Ambition of Lord Kames's Equity', in A. Lewis & M. Lobban (eds), *Law and History* (Oxford, 2004), 97–121.

72. J. Erskine, *Principles of the Law of Scotland* (Edinburgh, 1754), advertisement, 3.

73. G. McLeod, 'Erskine: The Long Afternoon of Roman Law', in K. Reid & R. Zimmermann, *History of Private Law in Scotland* (Oxford, 2000), I, 235–9.

74. EUL, G.J. Bell, notes of lectures on Scots law 1836–7, GB 237, coll-238, Dk.2.4.

75. Paterson, *Autonomy*, chs. 1 & 2.

7 Poverty: 'Neither means nor master'

1. D.O. Fairlie of Myres, *Fairlie of that Ilk: History and Genealogy of the Family* (Auchtermuchty, 1987), 3.

2. W. Fraser, *Memorials of the Montgomeries, Earls of Eglinton* (Edinburgh, 1859), I, 245.

3. H. Home, Lord Kames (ed.), *Remarkable Decisions of the Court of Session* (Edinburgh, 1776), 79–82.

4. Plato, *Phaedrus*, 229.

5. J.D. Ford, 'The Community of the College of Justice, Edinburgh and the Court of Session 1687–1808', *Journal of Legal History*, XXXIV (2013), 234–6.

6. The two standard modern works are R.A. Cage, *The Scottish Poor Law 1745–1845* (Edinburgh, 1981) and R. Mitchison, *The Old Poor Law in Scotland* (Edinburgh, 2000).

7. *Extracts from the Records of the Burgh of Edinburgh*, ed. J.D. Marwick et al. (1869–), IV, 48.

8. Sir G. Nicholls, *A History of the Scotch Poor Law* (London, 1856), chs. 1 & 2.

9. R. Mitchison, 'The Poor Law', in T.M. Devine & R. Mitchison (eds), *People and Society in Scotland, I, 1760–1830* (Edinburgh, 1988), 253–4.

10. C.A. Whatley, 'Women and the Economic Transformation of Scotland 1740–1830', *Scottish Economic and Social History*, XIV (1994), 21.

11. Cage, *Poor Law*, 2–5.

12. Mitchison, *Poor Law*, 22 et seq.

13. Cage, *Poor Law*, 35–8.

14. B. Lenman, *An Economic History of Modern Scotland* (London, 1977), 163; Mitchison, *Poor Law*, 27.

15. Cage, *Poor Law*, 23–4.

16. Mitchison, *Poor Law*, 92 *et seq*.
17. J. Mitchell, 'Memories of Ayrshire', *Miscellany VI of the Scottish History Society* (Edinburgh, 1939), 302–3.
18. Nicholls, *Poor Law*, ch. 3.
19. W.M. Morison, *The Decisions of the Court of Session* (Edinburgh, 1811), 10,555.
20. J. Fergusson, Lord Kilkerran, *Decisions of the Court of Session from the year 1738 to the year 1752* (Edinburgh, 1775), 405.
21. G.J. Bell, *Principles of the Law of Scotland* (Edinburgh, 1829), 281.
22. M.R.G. Fry, *A New Race of Men, Scotland 1815–1914* (Edinburgh, 2013), ch. 7.
23. Cage, *Poor Law*, iii.
24. Mitchison, *Poor Law*, 103–9.
25. Nicholls, *Poor Law*, 32.
26. Cage, *Poor Law*, 50.
27. *Regulations of the Town's Hospital of Glasgow, with an abstract of the first year's expenditure* (Glasgow, 1735).
28. *Report for the Directors of the Town's Hospital of Glasgow on the Management of the City Poor* (Glasgow, 1818).
29. J. Cleland, *Statistical Tables relative to the City of Glasgow* (Glasgow, 1823), 56.
30. J. Cleland, *The Rise and Progress of the City of Glasgow* (Glasgow, 1819), 225.
31. Fry, *New Race*, 175–6.
32. NAS, CH2/212/6, 72.
33. I. Duncan (ed.), *Minutes of the General Kirk Sessions of Edinburgh at their several Sederunts* (Edinburgh, 1763).
34. A. Birnie, 'The Edinburgh Charity Workhouse 1740–1845', *Book of the Old Edinburgh Club*, XXII (1938), 38.
35. ECA, minutes of the Edinburgh charity workhouse, 'Categories for admission', April 14, 1743.
36. Ch. 29; because of the innumerable editions of Scott's novels, exact page references are not normally given in this book.
37. Birnie, 'Charity Workhouse', 55.
38. M.R.G. Fry, *Edinburgh: A History of the City* (London, 2009), 244–5.
39. ECA, SL 11, 146 & 222.
40. Cage, *Poor Law*, 52–5.
41. Ibid., ch. 8; Mitchison, *Poor Law*, ch. 9.
42. T.M. Devine, *To the Ends of the Earth: Scotland's Global Diaspora 1750–1950* (London, 2012).
43. Cage, *Poor Law*, 1–3.
44. I.D. Whyte & K.A. Whyte, 'The Geographical Mobility of Women in Early Modern Scotland', in L. Leneman (ed.), *Perspectives in Scottish Social History* (Aberdeen, 1988), 83–107.

45. G. Watson (ed.), *Bell's Dictionary and Digest of the Law of Scotland*, 7th edn (Edinburgh, 1890), 1105.

46. A. Fletcher, *Political Works*, ed. J. Robertson (Cambridge, 1997), 60.

47. Ibid., 69.

48. Ibid., 70.

49. Mitchison, *Poor Law*, 53–5.

50. R.A. Houston, *Social Change in the Age of Enlightenment: Edinburgh 1660–1760* (Oxford, 1994), 134.

51. J. Marwick et al. (eds), *Extracts from the Records of the Burgh of Edinburgh* (Edinburgh, 1956), XII, 180, 241.

52. J. MacDonald, *Memoirs of an Eighteenth Century Footman 1745–1779* (London, 1927), 10.

53. J. McGowan, *Policing the Metropolis of Scotland* (Musselburgh, 2012), 325.

54. NAS, Papers of the Brooks of Biel, GD 6/117.

55. Cage, *Poor Law*, 132–6.

56. Mitchison, *Poor Law*, 54.

57. NAS, JP 132/1.

58. NAS, JP 2/2/2.

59. *OSA*, I, 175, 198; III, 139, 222, 321.

60. Ibid., III, 229, 232, 475.

61. Ibid., II, 455.

62. Ibid., II, 207.

63. G. Robertson, *Rural Recollections* (Irvine, 1829), 109.

64. Cage, *Poor Law*, 128.

65. Mitchison, *Poor Law*, 105.

66. Ibid., 104.

67. NLS, Advocates' MSS 1.1.109.

68. M. Flinn (ed.), *Scottish Population History* (Edinburgh, 1977), 271–84.

69. NRS, E326/6.

70. *Poems by Allan Ramsay and Robert Fergusson*, ed. A.M. Kinghorn & A. Law (Edinburgh, 1985), 144.

71. *Boswell's Edinburgh Journals 1767–1786*, ed. H.M. Milne (Edinburgh, 2001), 275–6.

72. D.A. Symonds, 'Reconstructing Rural Infanticide in Eighteenth-century Scotland', *Journal of Women's History*, X (1998), 63–84.

73. Mitchison, *Poor Law*, 102.

74. W. Creech, *Letters respecting the Mode of Living, Trade, Manners and Literature . . . of Edinburgh*, (Edinburgh 1792), 18; *Report on the State of the Edinburgh Magdalene Asylum for 1806* (Edinburgh, 1806), 1–5.

75. J. Stark, *Picture of Edinburgh* (Edinburgh, 1806), 407.

76. E. Ewan, 'The Early Modern Family', in T.M. Devine & J. Wormald (eds), *A Companion to Modern Scottish History* (Oxford, 2012), 268–84.

77. H. & K. Kelsall, *Scottish Lifestyle 300 Years Ago* (Edinburgh, 1988), 122.

78. K. Barclay, *Love, Intimacy and Power: Marriage and Patriarchy in Scotland 1650–1850* (Manchester, 2011).

79. See Court of Session judgment quoted on p. 157.

8 Womanhood: 'Flora will keep watch'

1. H. Boulton & A.C. MacLeod, *Songs of the North* (London, 1884), 31.

2. R. Gordon, *The Lyon in Mourning* (Edinburgh, 1895–6), I, 11.

3. A. MacGregor, *The Life of Flora MacDonald* (Stirling, 1901), 134.

4. Gordon, *Lyon in Mourning*, II, 32, 46.

5. H. Douglas, *Flora MacDonald: The Most Loyal Rebel* (London, 1994), 174.

6. F.A. Pottle & C.H. Bennett (eds), *Boswell's Journal of a Tour of the Hebrides with Samuel Johnson* (New York, 1936), 159.

7. NLS, MS 2618, ff. 82–4.

8. M. Craig, *Damn' Rebel Bitches: The Women of the '45* (Edinburgh, 1997), ch. 3.

9. F. MacDonald, *Colonel Anne: Lady Anne Mackintosh* (Edinburgh, 1987), 16.

10. Ibid., 7.

11. W. D. Norie, *The Life and Adventures of Charles Edward Stuart* (London, 1903–4), III, 102.

12. John Stewart-Murray, seventh Duke of Atholl, *Chronicles of the Atholl and Tullibardine Families* (Edinburgh, 1908), 140, 209, 267.

13. C. Rogers, *Life and Songs of the Baroness Nairne* (Edinburgh, 1869), 20.

14. G.F. Graham, *The Songs of Scotland* (London, 1861), 290, 322.

15. R. Burns, *The Merry Muses*, ed. J. Barke & S.G. Smith (Edinburgh, 1959).

16. Rogers, *Baroness Nairne*, 43.

17. G.F.S. Elliot, *The Border Elliots and the Family of Minto* (Edinburgh 1897), 285.

18. G. Eyre-Todd, *Scottish Poetry of the Eighteenth Century* (Glasgow, 1896), I, 204; S. Tytler & J.L. Watson, *The Songstresses of Scotland* (Edinburgh, 1871), I, 201–2.

19. Graham, *Songs*, 337; G. Eyre-Todd (ed.), *Abbotsford Series of the Scottish Poets* (Glasgow, 1891–7), I, 204.

20. W. Fraser, *Memorials of the Montgomeries, Earls of Eglinton* (Edinburgh, 1859), II, 8.

21. H. Graham, *A Group of Scottish Women* (London, 1908), 167.

22. Ibid., 168.

23. Ibid., 169.

24. Fraser, *Memorials of the Montgomeries*, II, 168.

25. Ibid., 111.

26. See Chapter 7 above.

27. Graham, *Group*, 177.

28. H. Cockburn, *Memorials of his Time* (Edinburgh, 1856), 57.

29. W. Scott, *Chronicles of the Canongate,* ch. vi.

30. E.B. Ramsay, *Reminiscences of Scottish Life and Character* (Edinburgh, 1858), 48.

31. J. Grant, *Cassell's Old and New Edinburgh* (London, Paris & New York, 1883), III, 62.

32. NAS, Clerk of Penicuik Papers, GD18/5167/14.

33. Lady E. Grant, *Memoirs of a Highland Lady,* ed. A. Tod (Edinburgh, 1988), 46.

34. R. Chambers, *Life of Robert Burns* (Edinburgh, 1896), III, 243; C. Matheson, *Life of Henry Dundas* (London, 1933), 129.

35. E. Mure, *Some Remarks on the Change of Manners in My Own Time 1700–1790*, in W. Mure, *Caldwell Papers* (Glasgow, 1854), I, 262.

36. Ibid., I, 269–70.

37. K. Glover, *Elite Women and Polite Society in Eighteenth-century Scotland* (Woodbridge, 2011), 167–72.

38. J. Fordyce, *Sermons to Young Women* (London, 1766), I, sermons i & vi; II, sermons xii & xiv.

39. J. Robertson, 'The Scottish Contribution to the Enlightenment', in P. Wood (ed.), *The Scottish Enlightenment: Essays in Reinterpretation (*Woodbridge, 2000), 37–62.

40. S. Sebastiani, 'Race, Women and Progress in the Scottish Enlightenment', in S. Knott & B. Taylor (eds) *Women, Gender and Enlightenment* (Basingstoke, 2005), 75.

41. S. Sebastiani, *The Scottish Enlightenment: Race, Gender and the Limits of Progress* (Basingstoke, 2013), 163–92.

42. H. Home, Lord Kames, 'On the Progress of the Female Sex', *Sketches of the History of Man* (Edinburgh, 1734), sketch vi.

43. NLS, Advocates' MSS, .23.1.1, 'Minutes of the Select Society', 32–3, 79, 81, 157.

44. *The Autobiography of Dr Alexander Carlyle of Inveresk,* ed J.H. Burton (Edinburgh, 1989), 484.

45. L.B. McCullough, *John Gregory and the Invention of Professional Medical Ethics* (Dordrecht & Boston MA, 1998), 150–4; M.C. Moran, 'Between the Savage and the Civil: Dr John Gregory's Natural History of Femininity', in Knott & Taylor, *Women*, 14 *et seq.*

46. J. Gregory, *A Comparative View of the State and Faculties of Man, with those of the Animal World* (1765), 51–2.

47. J. Gregory, *A Father's Legacy to his Daughters* (Edinburgh, 1774).

48. M.R.G. Fry, *The Dundas Despotism* (Edinburgh, 1992), 57.

49. *The Mirror,* 1779, no. 69.

50. M.R.G. Fry, 'Ferguson the Highlander', in E. Heath & V. Morelle (eds), *Adam Ferguson: Philosophy, Politics and Society* (London, 2009), ch. 1.

51. A. Ferguson, *An Essay on the History of Civil Society,* ed. D. Forbes (Edinburgh, 1976), 76–7.

52. Ibid., 79.

53. Ibid., 104.

54. W. Robertson, *Works,* ed. D. Stewart (London, 1817), IX, 103; XII, 281–92.

55. Ibid., XII, 319.

56. Ibid., XII, 295.

57. Ibid., XII, 319–20.

58. E.J. Clery, *The Feminisation Debate in Eighteenth-century Britain* (Basingstoke, 2004), 193.

59. D. Hume, *Essays, Moral, Political and Literary* (Edinburgh, 1741), I, XIV.25 *et seq.*

60. Ibid., II, II.5

61. Ibid., II, II.6.

62. D. Hume, *Essays, Moral and Political* (Edinburgh, 1758), iii.

63. D. Hume, *History of England* (London, 1776), I, 21.

64. J. Millar, *Observations concerning the Distinction of Ranks in Society* (London, 1771), 183–4, 199–204; 'Of Justice and Generosity', in fourth edn of *An Historical View of the English Government* (London, 1803), 565 *et seq.*

65. Millar, *Observations,* 57, 63–5.

66. I.S. Ross, *Lord Kames and the Scotland of his Day* (Oxford, 1972), 72.

67. Ibid., 171.

68. W. Alexander, *History of Women* (London, 1779), I, iv, xiii.

69. Ibid., I, 107.

70. M. Gardiner, *Modern Scottish Culture* (Edinburgh, 2005), 195–6.

71. J.T. Scott & R. Zaretsky, *The Philosophers' Quarrel* (New Haven CT, 2009).

72. F.J. Stafford, *The Sublime Savage: A Study of James Macpherson and the Poems of Ossian* (Edinburgh, 1988), 200.

73. Ibid., 224–33.

74. *The Lord Belhaven's Speech in the Parliament, Saturday, the second of November* (Edinburgh, 2006), 3.

75. R. Burns, *Complete Poetical Works,* ed. J.A. Mackay (Darvel, 1993), 350.

76. Ibid., 151.

77. K. Stirling, *Bella Caledonia: Women, Nation, Text* (Amsterdam, 2008), 22–32.

9 Gaeldom: 'Under the foot of strangers'

1. C.S. Terry (ed.), *The Albemarle Papers, being the correspondence of William Anne,*

second Earl of Albemarle, Commander-in-Chief, Scotland, 1746–1747 (Aberdeen, 1902), II, 181–4.

2. George II 19 c. 39.
3. J. Bannerman, 'The Lordship of the Isles', in J.M. Brown (ed.), *Scottish Society in the Fifteenth Century* (New York, 1977), 137–51.
4. Terry, *Albemarle*, 178–9, 195–6.
5. Ibid., 329–40.
6. J. Black, *Culloden and the '45* (Gloucester, 2000), 202.
7. *Orain Ghàidhealach mu Bhliadhna Theàrlaich, Highland Songs of the '45* (Edinburgh, 1933), xiii.
8. Ibid., xxii.
9. Ibid., 48. In transcribing this and further poems from the published text, I have adopted the modern convention of abandoning the distinction between the grave and the acute accent, and using only the grave.
10. Ibid., 41.
11. *The Songs of Duncan Bàn MacIntyre,* ed. A. MacLeod (Edinburgh, 1952), II, 4929–33, 4937–40, 5015–16.
12. D.S. Thomson, 'Gaelic Learned Orders and Literati in Medieval Scotland', *Scottish Studies,* XII (1968), 65.
13. D.S. Thomson, *An Introduction to Gaelic Poetry* (Edinburgh, 1990), ch. 3.
14. A. Campbell, *A History of Clan Campbell* (Edinburgh, 2004), III.
15. A. Mackenzie, *History of the Mackenzies* (Inverness, 1879), 69–70, 101–2
16. B. Lenman, *The Jacobite Clans of the Great Glen 1650–1784* (London, 1984), 17.
17. D. Szechi, *1715, The Great Jacobite Rebellion* (New Haven CT, 2006).
18. A. Mackillop, *'More Fruitful than the Soil': Army, Empire and the Scottish Highlands 1739–1815* (East Linton, 2000).
19. T.C. Smout, *A History of the Scottish People* (London, 1969), 128–9.
20. Campbell, *History of Clan Campbell,* II.
21. E.R. Cregeen, *Argyll Estate Instructions* (Edinburgh, 1964), xiii.
22. Ibid., xiv–xvi.
23. P. Gaskell, *Morvern Transformed* (Cambridge, 1969), introduction.
24. Cregeen, *Instructions,* xi.
25. Smout, *History of the Scottish People,* 336.
26. *Culloden Papers,* ed. H.R. Duff (Inverness, 1815), 53 *et seq.*
27. Cregeen, *Instructions,* xvi.
28. R. Whitworth, *William Augustus, Duke of Cumberland: A Life* (London, 1992), 133.
29. R. Emerson, *An Enlightened Duke: The Life of Archibald Campbell (1682–1761), Earl of Ilay, third Duke of Argyll* (Kilkerran, 2013), 305–8.
30. Ibid., 309–12.

31. J.S. Shaw, *The Political History of Eighteenth-century Scotland* (Basingstoke, 1999), 103–4).

32. Terry, *Albemarle Papers*, 480–4.

33. Annette Smith, 'The Administration of the Forfeited Annexed Estates 1752–1784', in G. Barrow (ed.), *The Scottish Tradition* (Edinburgh, 1974), 198–210.

34. R. Cohn & J. Russell, *John Campbell, fifth Duke of Argyll* (Key Biscayne FL, n.d.)

35. C.H. Bennet & F.A. Pottle (eds), *Boswell's Journal of a Tour of the Hebrides* (London, 1963), 260.

36. Cregeen, *Instructions,* xviii, xxii.

37. Ibid., iv, xviii, xxiv.

38. Ibid., xx.

39. M. Flinn (ed.), *Scottish Population History* (Cambridge, 1977), 241–50.

40. *OSA,* XIV, 189.

41. Cregeen, *Instructions,* xxi, xxix–xxx.

42. Ibid., xxxiii.

43. M. McLean, *The People of Glengarry* (Montreal, 1991), 63.

44. A. Mackenzie, *A History of the MacDonalds and the Lords of the Isles* (Inverness, 1881), 307–8.

45. N.H. MacDonald, *The Clan Ranald of Knoydart and Glengarry* (Edinburgh, 1979), 100.

46. D. Rixson, *Knoydart: A History* (Edinburgh, 1999), 69.

47. V. Wills (ed.), *Reports on the Annexed Estates from the Records of the Forfeited Estates preserved in the Scottish Record Office* (Edinburgh, 1973), 26.

48. Ibid., 50.

49. T. Pennant, *A Tour in Scotland and Voyage to the Hebrides* (London, 1790), I, 404–5.

50. Wills, *Reports on Annexed Estates,* 24.

51. McLean, *People of Glengarry,* 36–41

52. Ibid., 42–50.

53. The most famous account is in Adam Smith, *Wealth of Nations* (London, 1776), III, ch. 4.

54. McLean, *People of Glengarry,* 51–61.

55. L. MacLean, *Indomitable Colonel* (London, 1986), 89 *et seq.*

56. A.J. Durie, 'Lairds, Improvement, Banking and Industry in Eighteenth-century Scotland: Capital and Development in a Backward Economy, a Case Study', in T.M. Devine (ed.), *Lairds and Improvement in the Scotland of the Enlightenment* (Glasgow, 1979), 30–40.

57. Smith, 'Forfeited Estates', 204.

58. J. Ramsay, *Scotland and Scotsmen in the Eighteenth Century* (Edinburgh & London, 1888), I, 198; A. Macinnes, 'Scottish Gaeldom: The First Phase of Clearance',

in T.M. Devine & R. Mitchison (eds), *People and Society in Scotland 1760–1830* (Edinburgh, 1988), 82.

59. *Parliamentary History* (1782), XXIV, cols. 1316 ff.; EUL Papers, DC I. 77, no. 71.

60. V. Merolle (ed.), *Correspondence of Adam Ferguson* (London, 1995), II. 306–7.

61. Sir J. Sinclair, *An Account of the Highland Society of London from its Establishment* (London, 1813).

62. NLS, Dep. 313, Sutherland Papers, MS 1578.

63. NAS, Home Office Papers, RH 2/4/64/2544.

10 Stewart: 'Hazardous game'

1. F. McLynn, *Charles Edward Stuart: A Tragedy in Many Acts* (London, 1988), 568.

2. R. Forbes, *The Lyon in Mourning* (Edinburgh, 1895), III, 41–2.

3. H. Walpole, *Correspondence,* ed. W.S. Lewis (New Haven CT, 1937–83), XX, 373.

4. Ibid., XX, 384.

5. J. Boswell, *Life of Johnson,* ed. R.W. Johnson (Oxford, 1970), I.147.

6. BL, Add. MS 32732, f. 47.

7. J.L. Beatty, 'Henry Pelham and the Execution of Archibald Cameron', *Scottish Historical Review,* XLI (1962), 44–54.

8. J.Y.T. Greig (ed.), *The Letters of David Hume* (Oxford, 1932), II, 273.

9. J.A. Lynn, *The Wars of Louis XIV 1667–1714* (London, 1999), 210.

10. H.T. Dickinson, 'The Jacobite Challenge', in M. Lynch (ed.), *Jacobitism and the '45* (London, 1995), 7.

11. N. Rouffiac, *Le Grand Exil, les Jacobites en France 1688–1715* (Vincennes, 2007), 351 *et seq.*

12. B.Hill, *The Early Parties and Politics in Britain 1688–1832* (Basingstoke, 1990), 28.

13. R. Hatton, *George I, Elector and King* (London, 1978), 156.

14. E. Gregg, 'The Jacobite Career of John, Earl of Mar', in E. Cruickshanks (ed.), *Ideology and Conspiracy: Aspects of Jacobitism 1689–1759* (Edinburgh, 1982), 180.

15. D. Szechi, *1715, The Great Jacobite Rebellion* (New Haven CT, 2006), 186.

16. C.S. Terry, *The Chevalier de St George and the Jacobite Movements in his Favour* (London, 1901), 305.

17. I.J. Murray, 'Letters of Andrew Fletcher of Saltoun and his Family 1715–1716', *Miscellany X of the Scottish History Society* (Edinburgh, 1965), 143–73.

18. M. Sievers, *The Highland Myth* (Munich, 2007), 22–5.

19. F. McDonnell, *Jacobites of 1715 and 1745: North-East Scotland* (np, 2007), 14.

20. F. Goldie, *Short History of the Episcopal Church in Scotland* (Edinburgh, 1976), 91 *et seq.*

21. W. Forbes-Leith, *Memoirs of Scottish Catholics in the Seventeenth and Eighteenth Centuries* (London, 1909).

22. N.S. Bushnell (ed.), *William Hamilton of Bangour, Poet and Jacobite* (Aberdeen, 1937), 83.

23. G.D. Henderson (ed.), *Mystics of the North-East* (Aberdeen, 1934), 11–14.

24. Ibid., 88.

25. J.A. Symon, *Scottish Farming, Past and Present* (Edinburgh, 1959), 303.

26. J.L. Carvel, *One Hundred Years in Coal* (Edinburgh, 1944), ch. 1.

27. I. Hay, *The Royal Company of Archers 1676–1951* (Edinburgh, 1951), 7–9.

28. A. Macgregor, *Life of Flora Macdonald* (Stirling, 1901), 15.

29. B. Inglis, *The Battle of Sheriffmuir* (Stirling, 2005).

30. Szechi, *1715,* 315–67.

31. D.B. Horn, *Great Britain and Europe in the Eighteenth Century* (Oxford, 1967), ch. 3.

32. J. Black, *Natural and Necessary Enemies: Anglo-French Relations in the Eighteenth Century* (London, 1986), 48.

33. E. Cassavetti, *The Lion and the Lilies: The Stuarts and France* (London, 1976), 156.

34. S. Harcourt-Smith, *Cardinal of Spain: The Life and Strange Career Of Giuliano Alberoni* (London, 1955), 191.

35. W.K. Dickson (ed.), *The Jacobite Attempt of 1719* (Edinburgh, 1895), 222–3.

36. Ibid., 60–1.

37. Ibid., 342–3.

38. NAS, RH 2/4/317, ff. 230–1.

39. Ibid., ff. 266–9.

40. H.T. Dickinson & K. Logue, 'The Porteous Riot, 1736', *History Today,* XXII (1972), 272 *et seq.*

41. G. Lockhart, *The Lockhart Papers* (London, 1817), 336, 404.

42. H. Erskine-Hill, 'Literature and the Jacobite Cause: Was There a Rhetoric of Jacobitism?', in Cruickshanks, *Ideology and Conspiracy,* 55.

43. McLynn, *Charles Edward Stuart,* 628.

44. B. Simms, *Three Victories and a Defeat: The Rise and Fall of the First British Empire 1714–1783* (London, 2007), 51–9.

45. J.S. Gibson, *Ships of the '45* (London, 1967), ch. 1.

46. R. Cadell, *Sir John Cope and the Rebellion of 1745* (Edinburgh, 1898), 2–4.

47. I.F. Burton & A. Newman, 'Sir John Cope', *English Historical Review,* LXXVIII (1964), 655–68.

48. T. Ang & M. Pollard, *Walking the Scottish Highlands: General Wade's Military Roads* (London, 1984), 24.

49. A. Carlyle, *Autobiography* (Edinburgh, 1860), 112–18.

50. R.C. Jarvis, *Collected Papers on the Jacobite Risings* (Manchester, 1971), I, ch. 1.

51. D. Daiches, *Charles Edward Stuart* (London, 1973), 132.

52. M. Margulies, *The Battle of Prestonpans, 1745* (Prestonpans, 2013).

53. A. & H. Tayler, *Jacobites of Aberdeenshire and Banffshire in the 'Forty-Five* (Aberdeen, 1928); W.B. Blaikie, *Origins of the 'Forty-Five* (Edinburgh, 1916), 80.

54. M.G.H. Pittock, *The Myth of the Jacobite Clans* (Edinburgh, 1995), 64.

55. W.B. Blaikie, *Edinburgh at the Time of the Occupation of Prince Charles* (Edinburgh, 1910).

56. NLS, Walter Blaikie Collection, MS 298, ff. 5–15.

57. F. McLynn, *The Jacobite Army in England, 1745* (Edinburgh, 1998).

58. J. Prebble, *Culloden* (London, 1962).

59. S. Reid, *1745, A Military History of the Last Jacobite Rising* (Staplehurst, 1996), 232.

60. J.A. Smith, 'Some Eighteenth-century Ideas on Scotland and the Scots', in N. Phillipson & R. Mitchison, *Scotland in the Age of Improvement* (Edinburgh, 1970), 107 *et seq.*

11 Campbell: 'The whole power of Scotland'

1. M. Cosh & I.G. Lindsay, *Inveraray and the Dukes of Argyll* (Edinburgh, 1973), 77–8.

2. D. Warrand (ed.), *More Culloden Papers,* (Inverness, 1923–30), II, 60; III, 161.

3. NLS, Saltoun Papers, MS 17612, ff. 202–9.

4. F.A. Walker, *The Buildings of Scotland: Argyll and Bute* (London, 2000), 352.

5. M.R.G. Fry, *The Union: England, Scotland and the Treaty of 1707* (Edinburgh, 2006), 297–310.

6. K.M. Brown, 'Party Politics and Parliament: Scotland's Last Election and Its Aftermath', in K.M. Brown and A.J. Mann (eds), *Parliament and Politics in Scotland, 1567–1707* (Edinburgh, 2005), 245–86; P.W.J. Riley, 'The Scottish Parliament of 1703', *Scottish Historical Review*, XXXVII (1968), 129–50.

7. C.J. Whatley & D.J. Patrick, *The Scots and the Union* (Edinburgh, 2007), 91.

8. *'Scotland's Ruine', Lockhart of Carnwath's memoirs of the Union*, ed. D. Szechi (Aberdeen, 1995), 9.

9. P.W.J. Riley, *The Union of Scotland and England: A Study in Anglo-Scottish Politics of the Eighteenth Century* (Manchester, 1978), 143.

10. P. Dickson, *Red John of the Battles* (London, 1973), 136.

11. R.K. Marshall, *The Days of Duchess Anne 1656–1716* (Edinburgh, 1973).

12. P.G.B. McNeill, 'The Jurisdiction of the Scottish Privy Council 1632–1708', unpublished PhD thesis, University of Glasgow, 1960,

13. G.W.T. Omond, *The Lord Advocates of Scotland* (Edinburgh, 1883), I, 300 *et seq.*

14. D. Hayton, 'Constitutional Experiments and Political Expediency 1689–1725', in S.G. Ellis & S. Barber (eds), *Conquest and Union: Fashioning a British State 1485–1725* (Harlow, 1995), 302.

15. P.W.J. Riley, *The English Ministers and Scotland 1707–1727* (London, 1964), 105–13.

16. Dickson, *Red John,* 209.

17. HMC, *Laing MSS,* II (London, 1925), 169.

18. B. Williams, *The Whig Supremacy 1714–1760* (Oxford, 1939), 22.

19. W.A. Speck, 'The General Election of 1715', *English Historical Review,* XC (1975), 507–22.

20. D. Szechi, *1715, The Great Jacobite Rising* (New Haven CT, 2006), 149–51.

21. NAS, Montrose Muniments, GD 220/5/9/1.

22. O.C. Lease, 'The Septennial Act, 1716', *Journal of Modern History,* XXII (1950), 42 *et seq.*

23. HMC, *Polwarth,* III, 329.

24. Warrand, *More Culloden Papers,* II, 322.

25. A. Carlyle, *Autobiography,* ed. J.H. Burton (London, 1910), 400–1.

26. Sir J. Fergusson, *The Sixteen Peers of Scotland* (Oxford, 1960), 13–19.

27. NAS, GD 27 5/10 & 18.

28. R. Scott, 'The Politics and Administration of Scotland 1725–1748', unpublished PhD thesis, University of Edinburgh 1981, 396.

29. R.L. Emerson, *Academic Patronage in the Scottish Enlightenment* (Edinburgh, 2008), 424–5; J.S. Shaw, *The Management of Scottish Society* (Edinburgh, 1983), 91–8.

30. NRS, SP54 19/90 & 114.

31. G.W.T. Omond, *Arniston Memoirs* (Edinburgh, 1888), 81, 89.

32. R. Sedgwick (ed.), *Lord Hervey's Memoirs* (London, 1963), II, 660–1.

33. NLS, Saltoun Papers, MS 16756, f. 86.

34. Sedgwick, *Lord Hervey's Memoirs,* II, 297.

35. Scott, thesis, 442–4.

36. Ibid., 440.

37. NLS MS 16584, f. 55.

38. A. Murdoch, *The People Above, politics and administration in mid-eighteenth-century Scotland* (Edinburgh, 1980), 49.

39. Saltoun Papers, NLS MS 16951, ff. 53–6.

40. Ibid., NLS MS 16552, ff. 53–6.

41. D. Warrand (ed.), *More Culloden Papers* (Inverness 1923–9), V, 36.
42. Scott, 'Politics and Administration of Scotland', 514–15.
43. NRS, SP 54/14/90.
44. R. Browning, *Political and Constitutional Ideas of the Court Whigs* (New Haven CT, 1982), 172.
45. M.S. Bricke, 'The Pelhams vs. Argyll: A Struggle for the Mastery of Scotland 1747–1748', *Scottish Historical Review*, LXI (1982), 161–2.
46. HMC, *Polwarth*, V, 263–4.
47. R.L. Emerson, *An Enlightened Duke: The Life of Archibald Campbell (1682–1761), Earl of Ilay, third Duke of Argyll* (Kilkerran, 2013), 303–16.
48. Carlyle, *Autobiography*, 272–3.
49. R.L. Emerson, *Academic Patronage in the Scottish Enlightenment* (Edinburgh, 2008), 230–63.
50. H. Arnot, *The History of Edinburgh* (Edinburgh, 1779), 574–5.
51. R. Sunter, *Patronage and Politics in Scotland* (Edinburgh, 1986), 2–22; A. Chitnis, 'Agricultural Improvement, Political Management and Civic Virtue in Enlightened Scotland: A Historiographical Critique', *Studies on Voltaire and the Eighteenth Century*, CCLXV (1986), 475 *et seq.*
52. H. Walpole, *Memoirs of King George II* (London, 1984), I, 187.
53. E.M. Lloyd, 'The Raising of the Highland Regiments in 1757', *English Historical Review*, XVII (1902), 466–9.
54. K. Schweizer (ed.), *Lord Bute: Essays in Reinterpretation* (Leicester, 1988), 22.
55. J. Brooke, *King George III* (London, 1972), 612.
56. R.L. Emerson, 'Lord Bute and the Scottish Universities', in Schweizer, *Lord Bute*, 151 *et seq.*; A. Murdoch, 'Literary and Learned Culture', in T.M. Devine & R. Mitchison, *People and Society in Scotland, I, 1760–1830* (Edinburgh, 1988), 117–40.
57. A. Murdoch, 'Lord Bute, James Stuart Mackenzie and the Government of Scotland', in Schweizer, *Lord Bute*, 129.
58. BL, Newcastle Papers, Add. MSS 32970, f. 375.
59. Ibid., Add. MSS 32922, ff. 3–4.
60. W. Mure, *Selections from the Family Papers preserved at Caldwell* (Glasgow, 1854), I, 134; Omond, *Arniston Memoirs*, 177–9; J. Ramsay, *Scotland and Scotsmen in the Eighteenth Century* (Edinburgh & London, 1888), I, 346; F. Brady, *Boswell's Political Career* (New Haven CT & London, 1965), 9.

12 Dundas: 'Never completely subdued'

1. D. Dalrymple, *Decisions of the Lords of Council and Session 1776–1791* (Edinburgh, 1826), II, 777.

2. NAS, CS 235/K/2/2.

3. F. Pottle & C. Ryskamp (eds), *Boswell, the Ominous Years* (London, 1963), 160.

4. M.R.G. Fry, *The Dundas Despotism* (Edinburgh, 1992), ch.3.

5. See especially W. Ferguson, *Scotland, 1689 to the Present* (Edinburgh & London, 1968), 236.

6. G.A. Sinclair, 'Periodical Literature of the Eighteenth Century', *Scottish Historical Review,* II (1905), 140–3; W.J. Couper, *The Edinburgh Periodical Press* (Stirling, 1908), 138; H.A. Cockburn, 'Edinburgh Clubs', *Book of the Old Edinburgh Club*, III, (1910), 142; M.E. Craig, *The Scottish Periodical Press 1750–1789* (Edinburgh & London, 1931), 28–9; J. Dwyer, R.A. Mason & A. Murdoch (eds), *New Perspectives on the Politics and Culture of Early Modern Scotland* (Edinburgh, 1982), 5, 222–3; J. Dwyer, *Virtuous Discourse: Sensibility and Community in Late Eighteenth-Century Scotland* (Edinburgh, 1987), 24–41.

7. W. Ferguson, 'The Electoral System in the Scottish Counties before 1832', in D. Sellar (ed.), *Stair Society Miscellany II* (Edinburgh, 1984), 261–94.

8. J. Dwyer & A. Murdoch, 'Paradigms and Politics: Manners, Morals and the Rise of Henry Dundas', in J. Dwyer et al. (eds), *New Perspectives on the Politics and Culture of Early Modern Scotland* (Edinburgh, 1982), 238–9; Fry, *Dundas Despotism*, 60.

9. *Scots Magazine,* XXXVII (1775), 569; H. Craik, *A Century of Scottish History* (Edinburgh & London, 1901), II, 60; P. Kelly, 'Constituents' Instructions to Members of Parliament in the Eighteenth Century', in C. Jones (ed.), *Party and Management in Parliament* (Leicester, 1984), 178–9.

10. Fry, *Dundas Despotism,* 62.

11. Ibid., 70.

12. J. Darrach (1953), 'The Catholic Population of Scotland since the Year 1680', *Innes Review,* IV (1953), 50; R. Macdonald, 'The Highland District in 1764', *Innes Review,* XV (1964), 140 *et seq.*

13. *Parliamentary History*, XIX, col. 1142.

14. D.B. Horn, *A Short History of the University of Edinburgh* (Edinburgh, 1967), 76.

15. Compare the situation described in R.K. Frace, 'Religious Toleration in the Wake of Revolution, Scotland on the eve of Enlightenment', *History,* XCIII (2008), 355–75.

16. J.P. Lawson, *History of the Scottish Episcopal Church* (Edinburgh, 1843), 336; F.C. Mather, 'Church, Parliament and Penal Laws, some Anglo-Scottish interaction in the eighteenth century, *English Historical Review,* XCII (1977), 540 *et seq.*

17. A.J. Mackenzie-Stuart, *A French King at Holyrood* (Edinburgh, 1995).

18. D. Walker, *Legal History of Scotland* (Edinburgh, 2000), V, 31.

19. NAS, Melville Papers, GD 51/3/396; NAS, Professor Hannay Papers, GD

214/650/4; R. Mitchison & N.T. Phillipson, *Scotland in the Age of Improvement* (Edinburgh, 1970), 127.

20. N.T. Phillipson, *The Scottish Whigs and the Reform of the Court of Sessions* (Edinburgh, 1990), 176.

21. Mitchison & Phillipson, *Age of Improvement,* 129.

22. *Parliamentary History,* XXV, col. 1369.

23. M.R.G. Fry, *Wild Scots: Four Hundred Years of Highland History* (London, 2003), ch. 9.

24. BL, Auckland Papers, Add. MSS 34412, f. 352; R. Campbell & J.B.A. Dow, *Sourcebook of Scottish Economic and Social History* (Oxford, 1968), 2; J.M. Bumsted, 'Sir James Montgomerie and Prince Edward Island', *Acadiensis,* X (1978), 78; B. Bailyn, *Voyagers to the West* (New York, 1986), 9, 26, 41–54, 57–70, 92, 394–9.

25. BL, Auckland Papers, Add. MSS 34412, f. 353; C.R. Fay, *Adam Smith and the Scotland of his Day* (Cambridge, 1956), 11 *et seq.;* J.R. Bumsted, *The People's Clearance: Highland Emigration to British North America* (Edinburgh, 1982), 23.

26. NAS, Seafield Muniments GD 248/52/1/23.

27. NAS, Home Office Papers, RH 2/4/64/2544.

28. Ibid., RH 2/4/89/140.

29. *First Report of the Commissioners for Making and Maintaining the Caledonian Canal,* PP (51), 1803–4a; *First Report of the Commissioners for Roads and Bridges in the Highlands of Scotland,* PP (108), 1803–4b.

30. NAS, Melville Papers, GD 51/5/52/4.

31. Fry, *Wild Scots,* chs. 10 & 11.

32. M.R.G. Fry, *A New Race of Men: Scotland 1815–1914* (Edinburgh, 2013), ch. 12.

33. R. Burns, *Complete Poems and Songs,* ed. J. Kinsley (Oxford, 1968), 37–8.

34. H.B. Wheatley (ed.), *The History and Posthumous Memoirs of Sir Nathaniel Wraxall* (London, 1884), IV, 10; J. Farington, *The Farington Diary* (London, 1923), V, 162; Cumbria Record Office, Lonsdale Papers, I.1/2/9.

35. EUL, Laing Papers, La. II. 295; *The Album of Streatham, or ministerial amusements* (London, 1788), 60; W.R. Scott, *Adam Smith as Student and Professor* (Glasgow, 1937), 302.

36. T. Somerville, *My Own Life and Times* (Edinburgh, 1861), 316.

37. Farington, *Diary,* V, 163; NLS, MS 6524, f. 199.

38. NAS, Melville Papers, GD 51/5/423/2.

39. NLS, Melville Papers, MS 1078, ff. 20 *et seq.*

40. Fry, *Dundas Despotism,* 201–4.

41. Ibid., 308–10.

42. A. Bryant, *Years of Endurance* (London, 1942).

43. National Library of Ireland, Melville Papers, 54A/83.
44. See pp. 137–38.
45. H.W. Meikle, *Scotland and the French Revolution* (Glasgow, 1912), 154.
46. K.J. Logue, *Popular Disturbances in Scotland 1780–1815* (Edinburgh, 1979), 139.
47. NAS, Home Office Papers, RH 2/4/63/79.
48. NLS, Melville Papers, MS 7, f. 17.
49. *Parliamentary History,* XXX, col. 1247.
50. NLS, Melville Papers, MS 3834, f. 27; HMC, *Laing MSS* (London, 1925), II, 646; EUL, Laing Papers, La. II. 500, March 7, 1798.
51. NAS, Home Office Papers, RH 2/4/80/1 & 186.
52. J. Prebble, *Mutiny* (London, 1975), 270.
53. EUL, Laing Papers, La. II. 500. Sept. 3, 1797.
54. J.S. Corbett (ed.), *Private Papers of George, second Earl Spencer 1794–1801* (London, 1914), I, 357; BL, Add. MSS 40100, f. 2114.
55. *Parliamentary History,* XXX, cols. 345–65.
56. P.W.J. Riley, 'The Union of 1707 as an Episode in English Politics', *English Historical Review,* LXXXIV (1969), 523–4.
57. *Parliamentary Debates,* II, cols. 797–803.
58. P.M. Geoghegan, *The Irish Act of Union: A Study in High Politics 1797–1801* (Dublin, 1999), 212.
59. C.J. Fedorak, 'Catholic Emancipation and the Resignation of William Pitt in 1801', *Albion,* XXIV (1992), 49–64.
60. N. Henshall, *The Myth of Absolutism* (London, 1992).

13 Things: 'Refinement of every kind'

1. J. Stevenson, *Exploring Scotland's Heritage: Glasgow, Clydesdale and Stirling* (Edinburgh, 1995), 83.
2. Now part of the district of Falkirk.
3. H.R. Fletcher, 'Explorations of Scottish Flora', *Transactions and Proceedings of the Botanical Society of Edinburgh,* XXXVII (1959), 30–49.
4. J.L. Collins, *The Pineapple: Botany, Utilisation, Cultivation* (London, 1960).
5. Royal Commission on the Ancient and Historical Monuments of Scotland, *Stirlingshire* (Edinburgh, 1963), II, 341.
6. J. Harris & M. Snodin, *Sir William Chambers, Architect to George III* (London & New Haven CT, 1996).
7. M.R.G. Fry, *The Dundas Despotism* (Edinburgh, 1992), 79.
8. M. Glendinning, R. MacInnes & A. MacKechnie, *A History of Scottish Architecture* (Edinburgh, 2002), 70 *et seq.*
9. C. McKean, 'Improvement and Modernisation in Everyday Enlightenment

Scotland', in E.A. Foyster & C.A. Whatley (eds), *A History of Everyday Life in Scotland 1600 to 1800* (Edinburgh, 2010), 55–6.

10. I.H. Adams, *The Making of Urban Scotland* (London, 1976), 90–3.

11. F. C. Mears & J, Russell, 'The New Town of Edinburgh', *Book of the Old Edinburgh Club*, XXII (1938), 106.

12. D. Lockhart, *Scottish Planned Villages* (Edinburgh, 2012).

13. M. Gardiner, *Modern Scottish Culture* (Edinburgh, 2005), 164.

14. R.W. Brunskill, *Houses and Cottages of Britain* (New Haven CT, 2000), 234–5.

15. I. Maxwell, 'A History of Scotland's Masonry Construction', in P. Wilson (ed.), *Building with Scottish Stone* (Edinburgh, 2005), 27.

16. Glendinning, MacInnes & MacKechnie, *History of Scottish Architecture*, 276–85.

17. H. Fenwick, *Architect Royal: The Life and Work of Sir William Bruce* (Kineton, 1970).

18. C. Gonzalez-Longo, 'James Smith and Rome', *Architectural Heritage,* XXIII (2012), 75–96.

19. H.E. Stutchbury, *The Architecture of Colen Campbell* (Manchester, 1967).

20. J. Summerson, *Architecture of Britain 1630–1830* (New Haven CT, 1993), 330–3.

21. Glendinning, MacInnes & MacKechnie, *History of Scottish Architecture*, 73.

22. C. McWilliam, *The Buildings of Scotland: Lothian except Edinburgh* (London, 1978), 57; M. Glendinning, R.G. MacInnes & A. MacKechnie, *Building a Nation: The Story of Scotland's Architecture* (Edinburgh, 1999), 48.

23. D. Gifford, 'William Adam and the Historians', *Architectural Heritage,* I (1990), 33.

24. D. Howard, 'William Adam: Architectural Heritage', *Journal of the Architectural Heritage Society of Scotland,* XVII (1990).

25. D. Gifford, *William Adam 1689–1748* (Edinburgh, 1989), 72, 109–10. 176–8.

26. Ibid., 78–9, 126–7.

27. J. Fleming, *Robert Adam and his Circle* (London, 1944), 44.

28. J. Dunbar, *Architecture of Scotland* (London, 1978), 106.

29. N. Pevsner, *An Outline of European Architecture* (London, 1951), 237.

30. Glendinning, MacInnes & MacKechnie, *History of Scottish Architecture*, 106–7.

31. G, Lukomsky, *Charles Cameron, Architect* (London, 1943); A. von Reumont, *General the Right Honourable Sir Frederick Adam* (London, 1855).

32. M.R.G. Fry, *Edinburgh: A History of the City* (Edinburgh, 2009), ch. 5.

33. *History and Statutes of the Royal Infirmary of Edinburgh* (Edinburgh, 1778).

34. ECA, town council minutes, May 6, 1752, SL 1/1/70, ff.138–9.

35. Fry, *Edinburgh,* 222–4.

36. NLS, Melville Papers, MS 580, f. 330.

37. M. Glendinning & A. MacKechnie, *Scottish Architecture* (London, 2004), 120.

38. F.C. Mears &. J. Russell, 'The New Town of Edinburgh', *Book of the Old Edinburgh Club*, XXII (1938), 106.

39. G. Elliot, *Proposals for carrying out certain works in the city of Edinburgh* (Edinburgh, 1752), 21, 43.

40. A.J. Youngson, *The Making of Classical Edinburgh 1750–1840* (Edinburgh, 1966), 38, 83.

41. D. Gifford, C. McWilliam & D. Walker, *The Buildings of Scotland: Edinburgh* (London, 1975), 293–7.

42. E.K. Waterhouse, *Painting in Britain 1530–1790* (London, 1953), 330.

43. Edinburgh City Archive, Moses bundles, 202/7260.

44. M.R.G. Fry, *A New Race of Men: Scotland 1815–1914* (Edinburgh, 2013), 337.

45. P. Gaskell, *Bibliography of the Foulis Press* (London, 1964).

46. N. Uglow, 'Antiquity, Architecture and the Country House Poet: Sir John Clerk and *The Country Seat*', *St Andrews Journal of Art History and Museum Studies*, XIII (2009), 35–45.

47. NGS, accession no. 1784.

48. R. Rosenblum, *Transformations in Late Eighteenth Century Art* (Princeton, 1969), 62.

49. One sketch is preserved at NGS, accession no. 299.

50. R.L. Emerson, *An Enlightened Duke: The Life of Archibald Campbell (1682–1761), Earl of Ilay, third Duke of Argyll* (Kilkerran, 2013), 209.

51. D. Macmillan, *Scottish Art 1460–2000* (Edinburgh, 1990), 91–2, 99–100.

52. SNPG, accession no. 2800.

53. The portraits are respectively in NGS, accession no. 1293; Glasgow Art Gallery; SNPG, accession no. 908.

54. I.G. Brown, 'Allan Ramsay's Rise and Reputation', *Walpole Society*, L (1984), 209–47.

55. SNPG, accession no. 2603.

56. NGS, accession no. 430.

57. D. Fordham, 'Allan Ramsay's Enlightenment, or Hume and the Patronising Portrait', *Art Bulletin*, LXXXVII (2006), 508–24.

58. T. Blackwell, *An Inquiry into the Life, Times and Writings of Homer* (London, 1735), 34.

59. Ibid., 24–6.

60. V. Bevilacqua, 'Introduction' to G. Turnbull, *A Treatise on Ancient Painting* (new edn, Munich, 1971).

61. D. Hume, *A Treatise of Human Nature*, ed. A. Selby-Bigge (Oxford, 1888), 29.

62. D. Macmillan, *Painting in Scotland: The Golden Age* (Oxford, 1986), 23–30.

63. A. Ramsay, 'On Ridicule', *The Investigator*, CCCXXII (1769), 63.

64. A. Ramsay, 'A Dialogue on Taste', *The Investigator,* CCCXXII (1769), 29.
65. Ibid., 21.
66. J. Friday, *Art and Enlightenment: Scottish Aesthetics in the Eighteenth Century* (Exeter, 2004).
67. M. MacDonald, *Scottish Art* (London, 2000), 81–4.
68. B. Skinner, *The Indefatigable Mr Allan* (Edinburgh, 1973).

14 Words: 'The kilt aërian'

1. F.M. Thomson, 'John Wilson, an Ayrshire Printer, Publisher and Bookseller', *Bibliotheck,* V (1967), 21–41.
2. A. Murdoch & R.B. Sher, 'Literary and Learned Culture', in T.M. Devine & R. Mitchison, *People and Society in Scotland, I, 1760–1830* (Edinburgh, 1988), 127–41.
3. *The Lounger,* XCVII (1786), 385–8.
4. H. Adcock, 'Robert Burns: Rampant Robbie', *The Midgie,* 1 December 2008.
5. Burns wrote a song to Highland Mary in 1792, though it can by no means be certain the same one is meant.
6. D. Murison, 'Robert Burns and the Scots Tongue', *Scotland's Magazine,* VI (1959), 31.
7. S. Rennie, *Jamieson's Dictionary of Scots: The Story of the First Historical Dictionary of the Scots Language* (Oxford, 2012).
8. C. Jones, 'Nationality and Standardisation: The English Language in Scotland in the Age of Improvement', *Sociolinguistics,* XIII (1999), 112–18.
9. G. Campbell, *The Philosophy of Rhetoric* (Edinburgh, 1776), 133.
10. Sir J. Sinclair, *Observations on the Scottish Dialect* (Edinburgh, 1782), 1–4.
11. J. Buchanan, *An Essay towards Establishing a Standard for an Elegant and Uniform Pronunciation of the English Language throughout the British Dominions* (London, 1766), xv.
12. J. Beattie, *Scoticisms Arranged in Alphabetical Order* (Edinburgh, 1787), 88.
13. C. Jones, 'Scottish Standard English in the Late Eighteenth Century', *Transactions of the Philological Society,* IX (1993), 95–131.
14. R. Black, 'The Gaelic Manuscripts of Scotland', in W. Gillies (ed.), *Gaelic and Scotland, Alba agus a' Ghàidhlig* (Edinburgh, 1989), 146–74.
15. A. Carmichael, *Carmina Gadelica* (Edinburgh, 1900), I, xxii–xxiii.
16. R. Black (ed.), *An Lasair* (Edinburgh, 2001), 485–6.
17. See R.L. Thomson (ed.), *Adtimchiol an Chreidimh,* Edinburgh, 1962; (ed.), *Foirm na n-Urrnuidheadh,* Edinburgh, 1970; 'The Language of the Shorter Catechism (1659)', *Scottish Gaelic Studies,* XII (1976), 34–51; 'The language of the *Caogad*', *Scottish Gaelic Studies,* XII (1976), 143–82.

18. J. F. Campbell, *Leabhar na Féinne: Heroic Gaelic Ballads Collected in Scotland* (Edinburgh, 1872).

19. W. Gillies, 'The Gaelic of Niall Mac Mhuirich', *Transactions of the Gaelic Society of Inverness*, LXV (2006–9), 69–96.

20. A. MacDonald & A. MacDonald, *The Poems of Alasdair MacDonald* (Inverness, 1924). Alasdair MacDonald was the standard anglicised form of Alastair mac Mhaighstir Alastair, seldom used nowadays.

21. Black, *An Lasair*, 214–17.

22. C. Dressler & D.U. Stiùbhart (eds), *Alasdair Mac Mhaighstir Alasdair, bard an t-soillearachaidh Ghàildhealaich, bard of the Gaelic Enlightenment, a collection of essays on his life and work* (Kershader, Lewis, 2012).

23. *The Gaelic Songs of Duncan MacIntyre,* ed. G. Calder (Edinburgh, 1912).

24. I. Grimble, *The World of Rob Donn* (Edinburgh, 1999).

25. V.E. Durkacz, *The Decline of the Celtic Languages* (Edinburgh, 1983).

26. J. MacPherson, *The Poems of Ossian and Related Works,* ed. H. Gaskill (Edinburgh, 1996).

27. F. Stafford, *The Sublime Savage: A Study of James MacPherson and the Poems of Ossian* (Edinburgh, 1988).

28. H. Mackenzie (ed.), *Report of the Committee of the Highland Society of Scotland, appointed to inquire into the nature and authenticity of the poems of Ossian* (Edinburgh, 1805), appendix 4; H. Mackenzie, 'Account of the Life of Mr John Home', in *The Works of John Home* (Edinburgh, 1822); D.S. Thomson, '"Ossian" Macpherson and the Gaelic World of the Eighteenth Century', *Aberdeen University Review,* XL (1963), 7–20.

29. D.S. Thomson, 'James MacPherson, the Gaelic Dimension', in H. Gaskill & F. Stafford (eds), *From Gaelic to Romantic: Ossianic Translations* (Amsterdam & Atlanta GA, 1998), 23.

30. H. Gaskill, *Ossian Revisited* (Edinburgh, 1991).

31. T.M. Curley, *Samuel Johnson, the Ossian Fraud and the Celtic Revival in Great Britain and Ireland* (Cambridge, 2009).

32. R.D.S. Jack, 'The Language of Literary Materials', in C. Jones (ed.), *The Edinburgh History of the Scots Language* (Edinburgh, 1997), 213–65.

33. I.S. Ross & S.A.C. Scobie, 'Patriotic Publishing as a Response to the Union', in T.I. Rae (ed.), *The Union of 1707* (Glasgow, 1974), 96–108.

34. EUL, Allan Ramsay MSS, La.II.212, especially f. 3.

35. NLS, Advocates' MSS, 23.3.6, ff.23–5.

36. I.G. Brown, 'Modern Rome and Ancient Caledonia', in C. Craig (ed.), *History of Scottish Literature* (Aberdeen, 1988), II, 33.

37. *Poems by Allan Ramsay and Robert Fergusson,* ed. A.M. Kinghorn & A. Law (Edinburgh, 1985), 3–7.

38. J. Porter, *Defining Strains: The Musical Life of Scots in the Seventeenth Century* (Oxford, 2007), 22 *et seq.*

39. J. Thomson, *Liberty, The Castle of Indolence and other poems,* ed. J. Sambrook (Oxford, 1986), 19.

40. R. Crawford, *Scotland's Books: A History of Scottish Literature* (Oxford, 2009), 313 *et seq.*

41. *Poems by Allan Ramsay and Robert Fergusson,* 150–1.

42. Ibid., 121.

43. Ibid., 142.

44. Ibid., 182.

45. R. Crawford (ed.), *Heaven-taught Fergusson* (East Linton, 2003), 24.

46. *Robert Burns: Complete Poetical Works 1759–1796,* ed. J.A. Mackay (Darvel, 1993), 269.

47. J.G. Lockhart, *The Life of Sir Walter Scott 1771–1832* (Edinburgh, 1837–8), I, 121–2.

48. *Burns: Complete Works,* 262, 300.

49. Ibid., 264, 434.

50. [R. Burns], *The Merry Muses* (np, 1911), 43.

51. S. Douglas, 'Maidenheids and Moudiewarks: Scotland and the Bawdy Song Tradition', *Studies in Scottish Literature,* XXXI (1999), 210–20.

52. H. MacDiarmid, *Contemporary Scottish Studies* (Edinburgh, 1925), 114.

53. *Burns: Complete Works,* 391.

54. Ibid., 94.

55. *Letters of Robert Burns,* ed. G.R. Roy & J.D. Ferguson (Oxford, 1985), I, 79.

56. Ibid., II, 246.

57. Currie, *Works of Robert Burns* (Liverpool, 1800), VI, 247.

58. A modern edition (Aldershot, 1989) is edited by D. Low.

59. J.C. Hadden, *George Thomson, the Friend of Burns: His Life and Correspondence* (London, 1898).

60. H. Myers (ed.), *Ethnomusicology: An Introduction* (London, 1992).

61. J. Rock, 'The Temple of Harmony: New Research on St Cecilia's Hall, Edinburgh', *Architectural Heritage,* XX (2009), 59–74.

62. B. Cooper, *Beethoven's Folksong Settings* (Oxford, 1994).

63. *Letters of Robert Burns,* II, 318.

64. *Burns: Complete Works,* 411.

65. H. MacDiarmid, 'The Caledonian Antisyzygy and the Gaelic Idea', *The Modern Scot,* II (1936), 42–4.

66. *Burns: Complete Works,* 536.

67. MacDiarmid, *Contemporary Scottish Studies,* 113.

NOTES

15 Ideas: 'The very frame of our nature'

NB Several authors cited in this chapter have appeared in so many editions that there seems little point in giving precise page references to their works. In the following notes I have therefore in many cases dispensed with them.

1. *The Correspondence of Adam Ferguson, II, 1781–1816,* ed. V. Merolle (London, 1995), 364.
2. Ibid., 365.
3. *The Unpublished Essays of Adam Ferguson* ed. W.M. Philip (Philadelphia, 1986), no. 1, 'Of Perfection and Happiness'; no. 2 'What may be Affirmed or Apprehended of the Supreme Creative Being'; no. 13, 'Of Cause and Effect, Ends and Means, Order, Combination and Design'.
4. E. Heath, 'Ferguson and the Unintended Emergence of Social Order', in E. Heath & V. Merolle (eds), *Adam Ferguson: Philosophy, Politics and Society* (London, 2009), 155–68.
5. A. Ferguson, *A sermon preached in the Ersh language to His Majesty's First Highland Regiment of Foot . . . at their cantonment at Camberwell on the 18th day of December, 1745* (London, 1746).
6. M.R.G. Fry, 'Ferguson the Highlander', in Heath & Merolle, *Adam Ferguson,* 9–24.
7. A. Ferguson, *Essay on the History of Civil Society* (Edinburgh, 1767), pt. III.2.
8. Ibid., pt. VI.1
9. *Letters of David Hume*, ed. J.Y.T. Greig (Oxford, 1932), II, 306.
10. L. Hill, 'Adam Ferguson and the Paradox of Progress and Decline', *History of Political Thought*, XVIII (1997), 677–706.
11. Ferguson, *Essay,* I.4.
12. Ibid., III.2.
13. R.H. Campbell & A.S. Skinner, *The Origins and Nature of the Scottish Enlightenment* (Edinburgh, 1982), ch.1.
14. R.L. Emerson, 'Science and the Origins and Concerns of the Scottish Enlightenment', *History of Science,* XXVI (1998), 333–66.
15. A. Malet, 'Studies on James Gregorie (1638–1675)', unpublished PhD thesis, Princeton University (1989).
16. J. Friesen, 'Archibald Pitcairne, David Gregory and the Scottish Origins of English Tory Newtonianism', *History of Science*, XLI, 2003, 163–95.
17. *Mathematical Correspondence: Robert Simson, Matthew Stewart, James Stirling,* ed. J.S. Mackay (London, 1903).
18. R. Schlapp, 'Colin MacLaurin, a Biographical Note', *Edinburgh Mathematical Notes,* XXXV (1946), 1–6.

19. C. Tweedie, 'The *Geometria Organica* of Colin MacLaurin', *Proceedings of the Royal Society of Edinburgh,* XXXVI (1915), 87–150.

20. I. Tweddle, 'The Prickly Genius, Colin MacLaurin (1698–1746)', *Mathematical Gazette,* LXXXII (1998), 373–8.

21. S. Mills, *The Collected Letters of Colin MacLaurin* (Nantwich, 1982), 159–61; MacLaurin, *An Account of Sir Isaac Newton's Philosophical Discoveries and Treatise of Algebra* (1748), III, 377–92.

22. M. Barfoot, 'Hume and the Culture of Science in the Early Eighteenth Century', in M.A. Stewart (ed.), *Studies in the Philosophy of the Scottish Enlightenment* (Oxford, 1990), 151–90.

23. J. Hutton, 'The Theory of the Earth', *Transactions of the Royal Society of Edinburgh,* I (1788), 304.

24. H. Dingwall, *Famous and Flourishing Society: A History of the Royal College of Surgeons of Edinburgh* (Edinburgh, 2005), ch.2; W.N.B. Watson, 'Early Baths and Bagnios in Edinburgh', *Book of the Old Edinburgh Club*, XXXIV (1979), 57–60.

25. R. Sibbald, *Autobiography* (Edinburgh, 1833), 15.

26. Ibid., 26.

27. L.J. Jolley, 'Archibald Pitcairne', *Edinburgh Medical Journal,* LX (1953), 65–95.

28. D. Hamilton, 'The Scottish Enlightenment and Clinical Medicine', in A. Dow (ed.) *The Influence of Scottish Medicine* (Carnforth, 1986), 205 *et seq.*

29. R. E. Wright-St Clair, *Doctors Monro: A Medical Saga* (London, 1964).

30. J.P. Wright, 'Materialism and the Life Soul in Eighteenth-century Scottish Physiology', in P. Wood (ed.), *The Scottish Enlightenment: Essays in Reinterpretation* (Woodbridge, 2000)*,* 177–97.

31. G.E. Davie, *The Democratic Intellect: Scotland and Her Universities in the Nineteenth Century* (Edinburgh, 1961), 101.

32. J.A. Cable, 'The Early History of Scottish Popular Science', *Studies in Adult Education,* IV (1972), 34–45.

33. J. Butt, *John Anderson's Legacy: The University of Strathclyde and its antecedents 1796–1996* (East Linton, 1996), 22–9.

34. *Letters of John Cockburn of Ormiston to his Gardener,* ed. J. Colville (Edinburgh, 1904), 137–8.

35. E. Spary, 'The "Nature" of Enlightenment', in W. Clark, J. Golinski & S. Schaffer (eds), *The Sciences in Enlightened Europe* (Chicago, 1999), 281–2.

36. K. Haakonssen, *Natural Law and Moral Philosophy: From Grotius to the Scottish Enlightenment* (Cambridge, 1996).

37. H. Grotius, *De jure belli ac pacis* (Paris, 1625), prolegomena XI.

38. A. Smith, *Lectures on Justice, Police, Revenue and Arms,* ed. E. Cannan (Oxford, 1896), pt. 1, I.2.

39. S. Pufendorf, *De habitu religionis christianae ad vitam civilem* (Bremen, 1687), §5.

40. J. Moore & M. Silverthorne, 'Gershom Carmichael and the Natural Jurisprudence Tradition in Eighteenth-century Scotland', in I. Hont & M. Ignatieff (eds), *Wealth and Virtue: The Shaping of Political Economy in the Scottish Enlightenment* (Cambridge, 1983), 74.

41. W.R. Scott, *Francis Hutcheson: His Life, Teaching and Position in the History of Philosophy* (Cambridge, 1900), chs. 1 & 2.

42. Ibid., 234–5.

43. J.W. Cairns, 'The Origins of the Glasgow Law School: The Professors of the Civil Law 1714–61', in P. Birks (ed.), *The Life of the Law, Proceedings of the Tenth British Legal History Conference, Oxford 1991* (London, 1993), 151–94.

44. F. Hutcheson, *A Short Introduction to Moral Philosophy* (Glasgow, 1753), pt. III, ch, 2.

45. F, Hutcheson, *An Inquiry concerning the Original of our Ideas of Virtue or Moral Good* (Dublin, 1725), I.viii, 83.

46. E.C. Mossner, *The Forgotten Hume, le bon David* (New York, 1943).

47. D. Hume, *The Life of David Hume, written by himself* (London, 1777), §6.

48. See the page of 'Hume texts' at http://www.davidhume.org.

49. L. Okie, 'Ideology and Partiality in Hume's *History of England*', *Hume Studies*, I (1985), 1–32.

50. C. Kidd, 'The Ideological Significance of Robertson's *History of Scotland*', in S.J. Brown (ed.), *William Robertson and the Expansion of Empire* (Cambridge, 1997), 210–40.

51. *Anecdotes and Egotisms of Henry Mackenzie*, ed. H.W. Thompson (Oxford, 1927), 171.

52. W. Robertson, *History of Scotland* (London, 1759), preface.

53. Ibid., 34–5, 133.

54. D.R. Raynor, 'Hume and Robertson's *History of Scotland*', *Journal for Eighteenth-century Studies*, X (1987), 59–63.

55. P. Byrne, *Natural Religion and the Nature of Religion: The Legacy of Deism* (London, 1989).

56. D. Hume, *Two Essays, of Suicide and of the Immortality of the Soul* (London, 1777).

57. D. Hume, *Treatise of Human Nature* (London, 1739), II.3.iii.4.

58. D. Hume, *Enquiry concerning the Principles of Morals* (London, 1751), app. I.10.

59. D. Hume, *Enquiry concerning Human Understanding* (London, 1748), V.

60. Hume, *Treatise*, I.1.i.1.

61. Hume, *Human Understanding*, VII.26, XII.29.

62. D. Allan, *Scotland in the Eighteenth Century* (London, 2002), 138–40.

63. A. Broadie, *A History of Scottish Philosophy* (Edinburgh, 2009), 235–300.

64. T. Reid, *An Inquiry into the Human Mind on the Principles of Common Sense*, ed. D.R. Brookes (Edinburgh, 1997), 255.

65. H. Cockburn, *Memorials of his Time* (Edinburgh, 1852), 175.

66. T. Carlyle, *Sartor Resartus* (London, 1833), ch. 3.

67. A. Smith, *Inquiry into the Nature and Causes of the Wealth of Nations* (London, 1776), III.4.

68. E.S. Cohen, 'Justice and Political Economy in Commercial Society, Adam Smith's science of a legislator', *Journal of Politics,* LI (1989), 2.

69. A. Smith, *The Theory of Moral Sentiments*, 6th edn (London, 1790), pt. VI, ch. 2.

70. *Correspondence of Adam Smith*, ed. E.C. Mossner & I.S. Ross (Oxford, 1982), 203.

71. S. Darwall, 'Sympathetic Liberalism: Recent Work on Adam Smith', *Philosophy and Public Affairs,* XXVIII (1999), 139–64.

72. Smith, *Theory of Moral Sentiments,* IV.1.

73. Smith, *Wealth of Nations,* I.2.

74. Ibid., I.10.

75. Ibid., I.11.

76. Ibid., IV.9.

77. N. Ashraf, C.F. Camerer & G. Loewenstein, 'Adam Smith, Behavioural Economist', *Journal of Economic Perspectives,* XIX (2005), 131–45.

78. Smith, *Theory of Moral Sentiments,* I.1.

79. J. Robertson, *The Case for the Enlightenment: Scotland and Naples 1680–1760* (Cambridge, 2005), introduction.

Epilogue: 'Whom fate made brothers'

1. N.T. Phillipson, *The Scottish Whigs and the Reform of the Court of Session* (Edinburgh, 1990), 87.

2. P. Jupp, *Lord Grenville* (Oxford, 1985).

3. R.C. Paterson, *My Wound is Deep: A History of the Later Anglo-Scottish Wars 1380–1560* (Edinburgh, 1997).

4. *Marmion,* canto V, II. 628–34.

5. S. Kelly, *Scott-Land: The Man Who Invented a Nation* (Edinburgh, 2010).

6. *Marmion,* canto I, introduction.

7. H. Cockburn, *Life of Lord Jeffrey* (Edinburgh, 1852), 131; J.G. Lockhart, *Memoirs of the Life of Sir Walter Scott* (Edinburgh, 1837), 149.

8. *Edinburgh Review,* XII (1808), 1–13.

9. Ibid., XIII (1808), 215–54.

10. M.R.G. Fry, *The Dundas Despotism* (Edinburgh, 2004), 278 *et seq.*

11. Ibid., 242 *et seq.*

12. *Letters of Sir Walter Scott,* ed. H.C. Grierson (London, 1932–7), I, 345.

13. Ibid., 346.

14. Ibid., 368.
15. Ibid., 361.
16. Ibid., 365.
17. NAS, Melville Papers, GD 51/1/119.

Index